Contents

II Travel information

  II European driving: cut through the confusion
  IV Driving regulations
  VII Ski resorts

1 Route planning maps

  1 Key map · Distance table

17 Road maps

  17 Key map

121 City plans and urban area maps

  121 Legends to city plans and urban area maps

Alicante C	121	Madrid U	135
Amsterdam CU	122	Madrid C	136
Antwerpen Antwerp C	121	Málaga C	136
Athina Athens U	122	Marseille Marseilles C	136
Athina Athens C	123	Milano Milan CU	137
Barcelona CU	123	Moskva Moscow CU	138
Basel C	123	München Munich CU	138
Beograd Belgrade C	125	Nápoli Naples CU	139
Berlin CU	124	Oslo U	139
Bordeaux CU	125	Oslo C	140
Bruxelles Brussels U	125	Paris C	140
Bruxelles Brussels C	126	Paris U	141
Budapest CU	126	Praha Prague CU	142
Dublin CU	127	Roma Rome CU	143
Düsseldorf C	127	Rotterdam C	142
Düsseldorf (Ruhrgebiet) U	128	Sankt Peterburg	
Edinburgh C	127	St Petersburg U	142
Firenze Florence C	129	Sevilla Seville C	144
Frankfurt C	129	Stockholm CU	145
Genève Geneva C	129	Strasbourg CU	144
Génova Genoa C	129	Stuttgart C	144
Göteborg Gothenburg C	130	Torino Turin U	146
Granada C	130	Torino Turin C	147
Hamburg CU	130	Venézia Venice C	146
Helsinki CU	131	Warszawa Warsaw CU	147
İstanbul U	131	Wien Vienna U	147
København Copenhagen CU	132	Wien Vienna C	148
Köln Cologne C	132	Zagreb C	148
Lisboa Lisbon CU	133	Zürich C	148
London C	133		
London U	134	C City street plan	
Luxembourg C	135	U Urban area map	
Lyon CU	135		

149 Index to road maps

Legend to route plan...

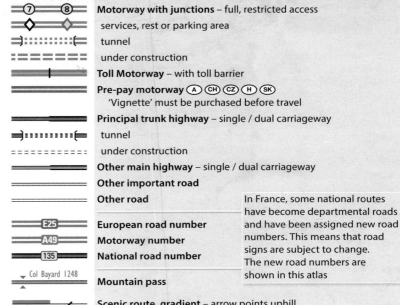

Motorway with selected ju...
tunnel, under constructio...
Toll motorway
Pre-pay motorway
Main through route
Other major road
Other road

25 European road number
56 Motorway number
55 National road number
56 Distances – in kilometres
International boundary
National boundary
LE HAVRE Car ferry and destination
1089 Mountain pass, international airport, height in metres

	Town – population		Town – with Low Emission Zone
MOSKVA	5 million +		5 million +
BERLIN	2–5 million		2–5 million
MINSK	1–2 million		1–2 million
Oslo	500000–1million		500000–1million
Århus	200000–500000		200000–500000
Turku	100000–200000		100000–200000
Gävle	50000–100000		50000–100000
Nybro	20000–50000		20000–50000
Ikast	10000–20000		10000–20000
Skjern	5000–10000		5000–10000
Lillesand	0–5000		0–5000

Scale

1:3 200 000
1cm = 32km 1 in = 50.51 miles

0 20 40 60 80 miles
0 20 40 60 80 100 120 140 km

Legend to road maps pages 18–120

7 8 Motorway with junctions – full, restricted access
services, rest or parking area
tunnel
under construction
Toll Motorway – with toll barrier
Pre-pay motorway A CH CZ H SK
'Vignette' must be purchased before travel
Principal trunk highway – single / dual carriageway
tunnel
under construction
Other main highway – single / dual carriageway
Other important road
Other road

E25 European road number
A49 Motorway number
135 National road number

> In France, some national routes have become departmental roads and have been assigned new road numbers. This means that road signs are subject to change. The new road numbers are shown in this atlas.

Col Bayard 1248 Mountain pass
Scenic route, gradient – arrow points uphill
143 Distances – in kilometres
major
28 minor

Principal railway
tunnel

Ferry route
Short ferry route

International boundary
National boundary

HEATHROW	Airport	SANTA CRUZ	Religious building
KNOSSOS	Ancient monument		Ski resort
	Beach	DISNEYLAND PARIS	Theme park
SCHLOSS LAHNECK	Castle or house	POMPEI	World Heritage site
GROTTE DE HAN-SUR-LESSE	Cave	PARQUE JURASSICO	Other place of interest
GIVERNY	Park or garden	1754	Spot height
	National park	Sevilla	World Heritage town
	Natural park	Verona	Town of tourist interest
			Town with Low Emission Zone

Scales

1:753 800 · Pages 18–110 and 120
1cm = 7.5km 1 inch = 12 miles

1:1 507 600 · Pages 111–119
1cm = 15km, 1 inch = 24...

0 5 10 15 20 miles
0 5 10 15 20 25 30 35 km

0 10 20
0 10 20

www.philips-maps.co.uk
First published in 1998 by Philip's,
a division of Octopus Publishing Group Ltd
www.octopusbooks.co.uk
Carmelite House,
50 Victoria Embankment
London EC4Y 0DZ
An Hachette UK Company
www.hachette.co.uk

Eighteenth edition 2015
First impression 2015

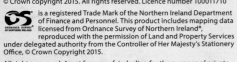 This product includes mapping data licensed from Ordnance Survey*, with the permission of the Controller of Her Majesty's Stationery Office
© Crown copyright 2015. All rights reserved. Licence number 100011710

is a registered Trade Mark of the Northern Ireland Department of Finance and Personnel. This product includes mapping data licensed from Ordnance Survey of Northern Ireland*, reproduced with the permission of Land and Property Services under delegated authority from the Controller of Her Majesty's Stationery Office, © Crown Copyright 2015.

While every reasonable effort has been made to ensure that the information contained in this atlas is accurate, complete and up-to-date at the time of publication, some of this information is subject to change and the Publisher cannot guarantee its correctness or completeness.

The information in this atlas is provided without any representation or warranty, express or implied and the Publisher cannot be held liable for any loss or damage due to any use or reliance on the information in this atlas, nor for any errors, omissions or subsequent changes in such information.

The representation in this atlas of any road, drive or track is not evidence of the existence of a right of way.

The maps of Ireland on pages 18 to 21 and the urban area map and town plan of Dublin are based upon the Crown Copyright and are reproduced with the permission of Land & Property Services under delegated authority from the Controller of Her Majesty's Stationery Office, © Crown Copyright and database right 2015, PMLPA No 100503, and on Ordnance Survey Ireland by permission of the Government © Ordnance Survey Ireland / Government of Ireland Permit number 8982.

Cartography by Philip's
Copyright © Philip's 2015

Printed in China

*Nielsen BookScan Travel Publishing Year Book 2014 data

**Independent research survey, from research carried out by Outlook Research Limited, 2005/06.

Photographic acknowledgements:
Page II, top imageBROKER / Alamy · right mladn61 / iStockphoto ·
bottom Mode Images / Alamy
Page III centre zstock / Shutterstock · right Nathan Wright / Shutterstock

European driving:
cut through the confusion
Stay safe with GEM Motoring Assist

- Do you need advice about equipment requirements and which documents to take?
- Are you confused about European driving laws?
- How will you know what speed limits apply?
- Are you new to driving on the right hand side?
- Who do you call if you have an accident or break down?

Since its foundation in 1932, GEM Motoring Assist has been at the forefront of road safety in the UK. Now one of the largest member-led road safety organisations, GEM provides a wide range of discounts and benefits for its 75,000+ members, including the UK's best-value range of breakdown recovery insurance products for motorists, motorcyclists and caravanners. GEM members also benefit from discounts on European breakdown cover and travel insurance, as well as enjoying free access to GEM's Accident Management Service, which provides free-of-charge legal help following any road traffic collision. Members receive Good Motoring, a free quarterly magazine and access to an excellent line-up of road safety leaflets and web-based advice.

Why not make GEM Motoring Assist your one-stop shop for trouble-free motoring! Visit www.motoringassist.com/philipsmaps today.

Millions of us drive abroad on holiday each year. Perhaps it's a long motorway trip to the Mediterranean, a selection of historic cities and sites or a gentle tour along quiet country lanes. Whatever the purpose, it makes sense to ensure that both we and our vehicles are properly prepared for the journey.

It's not easy getting to grips with the finer points of driving in other countries, however experienced you may be as a motorist. Whether you have notched up thousands of miles of European driving or are preparing to make your first journey, the chances are you will always manage to find some road sign or legal requirement that will cause confusion.

What's more, 'driving in Europe' covers such a huge area. There are 28 countries in the European Union alone, each with its own set of road traffic laws and motoring customs. Driving in Europe can mean a spectacular and sunny coastal road that's within sight of Africa, or a snowy track amid the biting cold of the Arctic Circle, where the only others on the road are reindeer. Add to this some of the world's most congested cities, dense clusters of motorways (many with confusing numbers) and a big variation in safety standards and attitudes to risk. No wonder we often risk getting lost, taking wrong turnings or perhaps stopping where we shouldn't.

Depending on the country we're in, our errors at the wheel or our lack of familiarity with the rules of the road can sometimes bring unwelcome consequences. In any country, foreign drivers are subject to the same traffic rules as residents, enforceable in many situations by hefty on-the-spot fines and other sanctions. The situation across Europe is complex, simply because of the number of different sets of rules. For example, failure to carry a specific piece of breakdown equipment may be an offence in one country, but not in another. It's easy to see why the fun and excitement of a road trip in Europe could be spoilt by a minefield of regulations.

But we want to ensure that doesn't happen. Preparation and planning are key to a great holiday. It certainly pays to do a bit of research before you go, just to ensure you and your vehicle are up to the journey, your documents are in order and you're carrying the correct levels of equipment to keep the law enforcers happy.

Before you go
Some sensible planning will help make sure your European journey is enjoyable and – we hope – stress-free. So take some time before departure to ensure everything is in good shape: and that includes you, your travelling companions and your vehicle.

For you:
Try to become familiar with the driving laws of your holiday destination, including the local speed limits and which side of the road to drive on. You will be subject to these laws when driving abroad and if you are stopped by the police, it is not an excuse to say that you were unaware of them. Police officers in many countries have the power to impose (and collect) substantial on-the-spot fines for motoring offences, whether you are a resident or a visitor.

The European Commission's 'Driving Abroad' website http://ec.europa.eu/transport/road_safety/going_abroad gives detailed information on different road traffic rules in different European countries.

The Foreign and Commonwealth Office also gives country-specific travel advice www.gov.uk/driving-abroad with information on driving.

Passports
Check everyone's passport to make sure they are all valid.

Don't wait for your passport to expire. Unused time, rounded up to whole months (minimum one month, maximum nine months), will usually be added to your new passport.

New passports usually take two weeks to arrive. The Passport Office (0300 222 0000, www.gov.uk/renew-adult-passport) offers a faster service if you need a replacement passport urgently, but you'll have to pay a lot more.

Driving Licence
The new style photocard driving licence is valid in all European Union countries. However, you must ensure you carry both parts: the credit card-size photocard and the paper licence. The previously used pink EU format UK licence is also valid, though it may not be recognized in some areas. So if you haven't already done so, now is the time to update your old licence. For more information, contact the DVLA (0300 790 6802, www.dft.gov.uk/dvla)

Travel Insurance
Travel insurance is vital as it covers you against medical emergencies, accidents, thefts and cancellations, and repatriation. Ask for details before buying any travel insurance policy. Find out what it covers you for, and to what value. More important, check what's not covered. One of the key benefits of GEM membership is the excellent discount you can get on travel insurance. For more details, please visit: www.motoringassist.com/philipsmaps

European Breakdown Cover
Don't risk letting a breakdown ruin your European trip. Ensure you purchase a policy that will cover you for roadside assistance, emergency repair and recovery of your vehicle to the UK, wherever in Europe you may be heading. Once again, GEM members enjoy a specially discounted rate. You'll find the details at www.motoringassist.com/philipsmaps

EHIC
The E111 medical treatment form is no longer valid. Instead, you need an EHIC card for everyone travelling. These are free and cover you for any medical treatment you may need during a trip to another EU country or Switzerland. However, do check at the time of requiring assistance that your EHIC will be accepted. Apply online (www.ehic.org.uk), by telephone (0300 3301350) or complete an application form, available from a Post office. Allow up to 14 days for the cards to arrive.

For your vehicle:

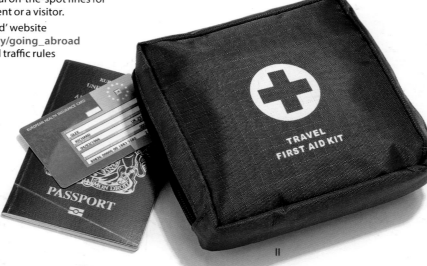

Service
It makes sense to get your car serviced before you travel. As a minimum, ensure the tyres have plenty of tread left and that water and oil levels are checked and topped up if required. Check them regularly during your time away.

Vehicle Registration Document
Police in many countries can demand that you prove you have the right to be driving your car. That means you need to show the registration document, or a suitable letter of authorization if the registration document is not in your name. Remember you should never leave the registration document in the car.

Nationality plate
Your vehicle must display a nationality plate of an approved pattern, design and size.

MOT
If your car is more than three years old, make sure you take its current MOT test certificate with you.

Insurance
If you are planning a trip to Europe, you should find that your car insurance policy provides you with the minimum amount of cover you need. But it's important to contact your insurer before you go, to confirm exactly what level of cover you have and for how many days it will be valid.

Mechanical adjustments
Check the adjustments required for your headlights before you go. Beam deflectors are a legal requirement if you drive in Europe. They are generally sold at the ports, on ferries and in the Folkestone Eurotunnel terminal, but be warned – the instructions can be a little confusing! The alternative is to ask a local garage to do the job for you before you go. If you choose this, then make sure you shop around as prices for undertaking this very simple task vary enormously.

Equipment check-list
This checklist represents GEM's suggestions for what you should take with you in the car. Different countries have different rules about what's compulsory and these rules change from time to time. So it's important to check carefully before you set out. For country-by-country guidance, visit www.motoringassist.com/europe or see page IV of this atlas.

- Fire extinguisher
- First aid kit
- High-visibility jacket – one for each occupant
- Two warning triangles
- Replacement bulbs and fuses
- Spare spectacles (if worn) for each driver
- Snow chains for winter journeys into the mountains
- Camera and notebook. Keep in your glove compartment and record any collisions or damage for insurance purposes (if it is safe).

Contact details
Make sure you have all relevant emergency helpline numbers with you, including emergency services, breakdown assistance, the local British consulate and your insurance company. There are links to embassies and consulates around the world from the Foreign Office website. (www.fco.gov.uk) For information, the European emergency telephone number (our equivalent of 999) is 112.

STOP AND GIVE WAY

Who has priority?

Make sure you keep a watchful eye on signs telling you who has priority on the road. Look for a yellow diamond sign, which tells you that traffic already on the road has priority. If you see the yellow diamond sign crossed out, then you must give way to traffic joining the road.

Priorité a droite

Despite the use of the yellow diamond signs, be aware that on some French roads (especially roundabouts in Paris), the traditional 'priorité a droite' practice is followed, even though it may no longer be legal. In theory these days, the rule no longer applies unless it is clearly signed. In practice, though, it makes sense to anticipate a driver pulling out in front of you, even though the priority may be yours.

Headlight flash

Bear in mind that the practice of flashing headlights at a junction in France does not mean the same thing as it might in the UK. If another motorists flashes his headlights at you, he's telling you that he has priority and will be coming through in front of you.

Stop means stop!

If you come to a solid white line with an octagonal 'STOP' sign, then you must come to a complete stop. In other words your wheels must stop turning. Adherence to the 'STOP' sign is generally much more rigorously enforced in European countries than you may be used to here.

HELP ME, PLEASE!

If you're in a difficult situation and need local help, then the following words and phrases might prove useful if language is a problem:

Do you speak English?	Parlez-vous anglais?	¿Habla usted inglés?	Parla inglese?	Sprechen Sie Englisch?
Thank you (very much)	Merci (beaucoup)	(Muchas) Gracias	Grazie (mille)	Danke (sehr)
Is there a police station near here?	Est-ce qu'il y a un commissariat de police près d'ici?	¿Hay una comisaría cerca?	C'e' un commissariato qui vicino?	Gibt es ein Polizeirevier hier in der Nähe?
I have lost my passport.	J'ai perdu mon passeport.	He perdido mi pasaporte	Ho perso il mio passaporto.	Ich have meinen Reisepass verloren.
I have broken down.	Je suis tombé en panne	Mi coche se ha averiado.	Ho un guasto.	Ich habe eine Panne.
I have run out of fuel.	Je suis tombé en panne d'essence.	Me he quedado sin gasolina.	Ho terminato la benzina.	Ich habe kein Benzin mehr.
I feel ill.	Je me sens malade.	Me siento mal.	Mi sento male.	Mir ist schlecht.

WORTH KNOWING

You will need a separate GB sticker in EU countries if your car doesn't have a registration plate containing the GB euro-symbol.

Fuel is generally most expensive at motorway service areas and cheapest at supermarkets. However, these are usually shut on Sundays and Bank Holidays. So-called '24 hour' regional fuel stations in France seldom accept payment by UK credit card, so don't rely on them if your tank is running low during a night-time journey.

If you see several fuel stations in short succession before a national border, it's likely that fuel on the other side will be more expensive, so take the opportunity to fill up.

Radar speed camera detectors are illegal in most European countries.

The insurance 'green card' is no longer required for journeys in Europe, but it is important to make sure you have contact details for your insurer in case of an accident or claim.

Speed limits in France are enforced rigorously. Radar controls are frequent, and any driver (including non-residents) detected at more than 25km/h above the speed limit can have their licence confiscated on the spot. Furthermore, if you are caught exceeding the speed limit by 50km/h, even on a first offence, you will face a term of imprisonment. • New legislation introduced in France in 2012 required every driver to carry a self-breathalyser test kit. However, the imposition of a €11 fine for failing to produce a breathalyser when required has been postponed indefinitely. So, in theory, you are required to carry a breathalyser kit, but no fine can be imposed if you don't.

In Spain you must carry two warning triangles, plus a spare pair of glasses for every driver who needs to use them.

In Luxembourg, there are specific rules relating to how you fix a satnav device to your windscreen. Get it wrong and you could be fined on the spot.

In Germany it is against the law to run out of fuel on the motorway. If you do run out, then you face an on-the-spot fine.

Norway and Sweden have particularly low limits for drink-driving: just 20mg per 100ml of blood (compared to 80 in the UK). In Slovakia, the limit is zero.

In Hungary, the limit is also zero. If you are found to be drink-driving, your driving licence will be withdrawn by police officers on the spot.

In most countries, maps and signs will have the European road number (shown in white on a green background) alongside the appropriate national road number. However, in Sweden and Belgium only the E-road number will be shown.

Other laws and motoring advice to be aware of across Europe:

Austria Recent rules require the mandatory use of winter tyres between 1 November and 15 April.

Belgium You will have to pay to use most public toilets – including those at motorway service stations • You are not permitted to use cruise control on motorways when traffic is heavy • There are also specific penalties for close-following on motorways • Roadside drug-testing of drivers (using oral fluid testing devices) forms a regular part of any police controls.

Cyprus There have been important changes in how speeding and drink-driving are sanctioned. Cyprus now has a graduated system of speeding fines, ranging from one euro per km/h over the limit in marginal cases through to fines of up to €5,000 and a term of imprisonment for the most severe infringements. There are also graduated fines for drink-driving, ranging from fixed penalties for being slightly over the limit to terms of imprisonment and fines of up to €5,000 for the most severe.

Denmark Cars towing caravans and trailers are prohibited from overtaking on motorways at certain times of day.

Finland Speeding fines are worked out according to your income. Access to a national database allows police at the roadside to establish a Finnish resident's income and number of dependants. Officers then impose a fine based on a specific number of days' income. The minimum speeding fine is 115 euros • If you hit an elk or deer, you must report the collision to the police.

France Any driver must be in possession of a valid breathalyser (displaying an 'BF' number), either electronic or chemical, to be shown to a police officer in case of control • Motorcyclist's helmets must have four reflective stickers fitted, and there is an on-the-spot fine of €135 for non-compliance (by foreign riders as well as French) • Jail terms for drivers caught at more than 50km/h above the speed limit – even first time offenders • Radar detectors, are banned with fines of €1500 for anyone using them • There are stiff penalties for driving while using a mobile phone.

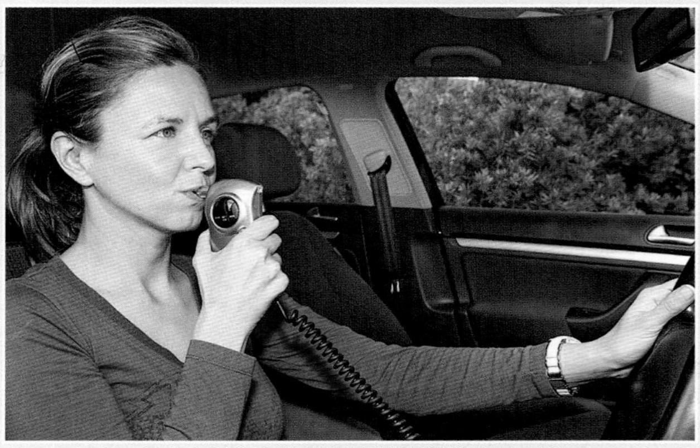

Germany Check your fuel contents regularly as it's an offence to run out of fuel on a German motorway • It's also an offence to make rude signs to other road users.

Greece has Europe's highest accident rate in terms of the number of crashes per vehicle. Pay particular attention at traffic light junctions, as red lights are frequently ignored • All drivers detected with more than 1.10 g/l of alcohol in blood, or more than 0.60mg/l in breath will be prosecuted for the offence • Carrying a petrol can in a vehicle is forbidden.

Ireland The drink-drive limit was reduced in 2011 from 0.8 mg per ml to 0.5. • Beware of rural three-lane roads, where the middle overtaking lane is used by traffic travelling in both directions. On wider rural roads it's the accepted practice for slower vehicles to pull over to let faster traffic through.

Italy Police can impound your vehicle if you cannot present the relevant ownership documents when requested • You will need a red and white warning sign if you plan to use any rear-mounted luggage rack such as a bike rack • Zero alcohol tolerance is now applied for drivers who have held a driving licence for less than three years, as well as to drivers aged 18 to 21, professional drivers, taxi drivers and truckers.

Norway Under new legislation, police officers can perform roadside drug impairment saliva tests. There are specific limits set for the presence of 20 common non-alcohol drugs. • You'll find what amounts to a zero tolerance where drinking and driving is concerned. Only 0.1mg of alcohol per millilitre of blood is permitted (compared to 0.8 in the UK) • Speeding fines are high. For example, a driver caught at 25 km/h over the 80 km/h speed limit on a national road could expect a fine of around £600.

Portugal If you are towing a caravan, you must have a current inventory of the caravan's contents to show a police officer if requested.

Slovakia It is mandatory to use dipped headlights on every road journey, regardless of the time of day, season or weather conditions.

Spain Motorway speed limits in Spain are 120km/h • If you need glasses for driving, then the law requires you to carry a spare pair with you in the car • It's compulsory to carry two spare warning triangles, spare bulbs for your car and reflective jackets.

Turkey Take great caution if you're driving at dusk. Many local drivers put off using their lights until it's properly dark, so you may find oncoming traffic very hard to spot • During the time of Ramadan, many people will not eat or drink between the hours of sunrise and sunset. This can seriously reduce levels of alertness, especially among people driving buses, trucks and taxis.

TOP TIPS FOR STAYING SAFE

Collisions abroad occur not just because of poor driving conditions locally, but also because we do not always take the same safety precautions as we might expect to take at home, for example by not wearing a seatbelt or by drinking and driving.

1. Plan your route before you go. That includes the journey you make to reach your destination (with sufficient breaks built in) and any excursions or local journeys you make while you're there.

2. Remember that, wherever you drive, you will be subject to the same laws as local drivers. Claiming ignorance of these laws will not be accepted as an excuse.

3. Take extra care at junctions when you re driving on the 'right side' of the road. If driving in a family group, involve every member in a quick 'junction safety check' to help reduce the risk of a collision. Having everybody in the car call out a catchphrase such as "DriLL DriLL DriLL" (Driver Look Left) on the approach to junctions and roundabouts is a small but potentially life-saving habit.

4. Take fatigue seriously. The excellent European motorway network means you can cover big distances with ease. But you must also make time for proper breaks (experts recommend a break of at least 15 minutes after every two hours of driving). If possible, share the driving and set strict daily limits to the number of driving hours. Watch a short video that explains the risks of driver fatigue: **www.motoringassist.com/fatigue**

5. Drink-driving limits across Europe are lower than those in the UK. The only exception is Malta, where the limit is the same (0.8mg per ml). Bear this in mind if you're flying to a holiday or business destination and plan to have a drink on the plane, as the combination of unfamiliar roads and alcohol in your bloodstream is not a safe one. It's also worth remembering that drivers who cause collisions because they were drinking are likely to find their insurance policy will not cover them.

6. Expect the unexpected. Styles of driving in your destination country are likely to be very different from those you know in the UK. Drive defensively and certainly don't get involved in any altercations on the road.

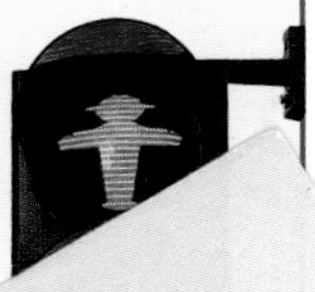

7. Don't overload your car while away, however tempting the local bargains may appear. Make sure you have good all-round visibility by ensuring you don't pile up items on the parcel shelf or boot, and keep your windscreen clean.

8. Always wear a seatbelt and ensure everyone else on board wears one. Check specific regulations regarding the carriage of children: in some countries children under the age of 12 are not permitted to travel in the front of the c

9. Don't use your mobile phone while driving. Even though laws on phone use while driving differ from country, the practice is just as dangerous wherever you are.

10. When you're exploring on foot, be wise to road safety as a pedestrian. You may get into so don't just wander across a road. Use a proper crossing, but remember that drivers may no Don't forget that traffic closest to you approaches from the LEFT.

Driving regulations

Vehicle

A national vehicle identification plate is always required when taking a vehicle abroad.

Fitting headlamp converters or beam deflectors when taking a right-hand drive car to a country where driving is on the right (every country in Europe except the UK and Ireland) is compulsory.

Within the EU, if not driving a locally hired car, it is compulsory to have either Europlates or a country of origin (eg GB) sticker. Outside the EU (and in Andorra) a sticker is compulsory, even with Europlates.

Documentation

All countries require that you carry a valid passport, vehicle registration document, hire certificate or letter of authority for the use of someone else's vehicle, full driving licence/International Driving Permit and insurance documentation/green card. Some non-EU countries also require a visa. Minimum driving ages are often higher for people holding foreign licences. New exit checks at the Eurotunnel and ferry terminals mean that drivers taking vehicles from the UK should allow extra time.

Licence

A photo licence is preferred; with an old-style paper licence, an International Driving Permit (IDP) should also be carried. In some countries, an IDP is compulsory, whatever form of licence is held. Non-EU drivers should always have both a licence and and IDP. UK (except NI) drivers with photo licences should check in advance whether a hire company will wish to check for endorsements and vehicle categories. If so, visit https://www.gov.uk/view-driving-licence to create a digital code (valid for 72 hours) that allows their details to be shared.

Insurance

Third-party cover is compulsory across Europe. Most insurance policies give only basic cover when driving abroad, so you should check that your policy provides at least third-party cover for the countries in which you will be driving and upgrade it to the level that you require. You may be forced to take out extra cover at the frontier if you cannot produce acceptable proof that you have adequate insurance. Even in countries in which a green card is not required, carrying one is recommended for extra proof of insurance.

Motorcycles

It is compulsory for all motorcyclists and passengers to wear crash helmets. In France it may become compulsory for all motorcyclists and passengers to wear a minimum amount of reflective gear.

Other

In countries in which visibility vests are compulsory one for each person should be carried in the passenger compartment, or panniers on a motorbike, where they can be reached easily.

Warning triangles should also be carried in the passenger compartment.

The penalties for infringements of regulations vary considerably from one country to another. In many countries the police have the right to impose on-the-spot fines (ask for a receipt). Penalties can be severe for serious infringements, particularly for exceeding the blood-alcohol limit; in some countries this can result in immediate imprisonment.

In some countries, vignettes for toll roads are being replaced by electronic tags. See country details.

Please note that driving regulations often change, and that it has not been possible to cover all the information for every type of vehicle. The figures given for capitals' populations are for the whole metropolitan area.

The symbols used are:

- 🏛 Motorway
- ⚠ Dual carriageway
- ⚠ Single carriageway
- 🚗 Surfaced road
- 🚙 Unsurfaced / gravel road
- 🏭 Urban area
- ⏱ Speed limit in kilometres per hour (kph). These are the maximum speeds for the types of roads listed. In some places and under certain conditions they may be considerably lower. Always obey local signs.
- Seat belts
- Children
- 🍷 Blood alcohol level
- △ Warning triangle
- First aid kit
- Spare bulb kit
- Fire extinguisher
- ⊖ Minimum driving age
- Additional documents required
- Mobile phones
- **LEZ** Low Emission Zone
- ★ Other information

Andorra Principat d'Andorra (AND)

Area 468 sq km (181 sq miles)
Population 85,000 **Capital** Andorra la Vella (44,000)
Languages Catalan (official), French, Castilian and Portuguese
Currency Euro = 100 cents
Website http://visitandorra.com

🏛	⚠	⚠	🏭
n/a	90	60/90	50

- 🚗 Compulsory
- Under 10 and below 150 cm must travel in an EU-approved restraint system adapted to their size in the rear. Airbag must be deactivated if a child is in the front passenger seat.
- 🍷 0.05% △ Compulsory
- Recommended
- Compulsory
- Recommended
- ⊖ 18
- Not permitted whilst driving
- ★ Dipped headlights compulsory for motorcycles during day and for other vehicles during poor daytime visibility.
- ★ On-the-spot fines imposed
- ★ Visibility vests compulsory
- ★ Winter tyres or snow chains compulsory in poor conditions or when indicated by signs

---

Austria Österreich (A)

Area 83,859 sq km (32,377 sq miles)
Population 8,505,000
Capital Vienna / Wien (2,419,000)
Languages German (official)
Currency Euro = 100 cents
Website www.austria.gv.at

🏛	⚠	⚠	🏭
130	100	100	50

If towing trailer under 750kg / over 750 kg

100	100	100/80	50

- 🚗 Compulsory
- Under 14 and under 150cm cannot travel as a front or rear passenger unless they use a suitable child restraint; under 14 over 150cm must wear adult seat belt
- 🍷 0.049%; 0.01% if licence held less than 2 years
- △ Compulsory
- Compulsory
- Recommended
- Recommended
- ⊖ 18 (16 for motorbikes under 50 cc, 20 for over 50 cc)
- Only allowed with hands-free kit
- **LEZ** LEZ On A12 motorway non-compliant vehicles banned and certain substances banned, night-time speed restrictions; Steiermark province has LEZs affecting lorries
- ★ Dipped headlights must be used during the day by all road users. Headlamp converters compulsory
- ★ On-the-spot fines imposed
- ★ Radar detectors and dashboard cameras prohibited
- ★ Winter tyres compulsory 1 Nov–15 Apr
- ★ To drive on motorways or expressways, a motorway sticker must be purchased at the border or main petrol station. These are available for 10 days, 2 months or 1 year. Vehicles 3.5 tonnes or over must display an electronic tag.
- ★ Visibility vests compulsory

Belarus (BY)

Area 207,600 sq km (80,154 sq miles)
Population 9,609,000
Capital Minsk (2,002,000)
Languages Belarusian, Russian (both official)
Currency Belarusian ruble = 100 kopek
Website www.belarus.by/en/government

🏛	⚠	⚠	🏭
110	90	90	60*

If towing trailer under 750kg

90	70	70	

*In residential areas limit is 20 km/h • Vehicle towing another vehicle 50 kph limit • If full driving licence held for less than two years must not exceed 70 kph

- 🚗 Compulsory in front seats, and rear seats if fitted
- Under 12 not allowed in front seat and must use appropriate child restraint
- 🍷 0.00%
- △ Compulsory
- Compulsory
- Recommended
- Compulsory
- ⊖ 18
- Visa, vehicle technical check stamp, international driving permit, green card, health insurance. Even with a green card, local third-party insurance may be imposed at the border
- Use prohibited
- ★ A temporary vehicle import certificate must be purchased on entry and driver must be registered
- ★ Dipped headlights are compulsory during the day Nov–Mar and at all other times in conditions of poor visibility or when towing or being towed.
- ★ Fees payable for driving on highways
- ★ It is illegal for vehicles to be dirty
- ★ On-the-spot fines imposed
- ★ Radar-detectors prohibited
- ★ Winter tyres compulsory; snow chains recommended
- ★ Vehicles registered outside Eurasian Economic Union or over 3.5 tons are required to use BelToll device for automatic payment of motorway tolls. See www.beltoll.by/index.php/en/faq /

Belgium Belgique (B)

Area 30,528 sq km (11,786 sq miles)
Population 12,000,000
Capital Brussels/Bruxelles (1,830,000)
Languages Dutch, French, German (all official)
Currency Euro = 100 cents
Website www.belgium.be/en

🏛	⚠	⚠	🏭
120*	120*	90	50**

If towing trailer

90	90	60	50

Over 3.5 tonnes

90	90	60	50

*Minimum speed of 70kph may be applied in certain conditions on motorways and some dual carriageways
**Near schools, hospitals and churches the limit may be 30kph

- 🚗 Compulsory
- All under 19s under 135 cm must wear an appropriate child restraint. Airbags must be deactivated if a rear-facing child seat is used in the front
- 🍷 0.049% △ Compulsory Recommended
- Recommended Compulsory ⊖ 18
- Only allowed with a hands-free kit
- ★ Cruise control must be deactivated on motorways where indicated
- ★ Dipped headlights mandatory at all times for motorcycles and advised during the day in poor conditions for other vehicles
- ★ On-the-spot fines imposed
- ★ Radar detectors prohibited
- ★ Sticker indicating maximum recommended speed for winter tyres must be displayed on dashboard if using them
- ★ Visibility vest compulsory

Bosnia & Herzegovina

Bosna i Hercegovina (BIH)

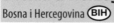

Area 51,197 km² (19,767 mi²)
Population 3,872,000 **Capital** Sarajevo (608,000)
Languages Bosnian/Croatian/Serbian
Currency Convertible Marka = 100 convertible pfenniga
Website www.fbihvlada.gov.ba/english/index.php

🏛	⚠	⚠	🏭
130	100	80	50

- 🚗 Compulsory if fitted
- Under 12s must sit in rear using an appropriate child restraint. Under-2s may travel in a rear-facing child seat in the front only if the airbags have been deactivated.
- 🍷 0.03% △ Compulsory
- Compulsory Compulsory
- Compulsory for LPG vehicles
- ⊖ 18
- Visa, International Driving Permit, green card
- Prohibited
- ★ Dipped headlights compulsory for all vehicles at all times
- ★ GPS must have fixed speed camera function deactivated; radar detectors prohibited.
- ★ On-the-spot fines imposed
- ★ Visibility vest, tow rope or tow bar compulsory
- ★ Spare wheel compulsory, except for two-wheeled vehicles
- ★ Winter tyres compulsory 15 Nov–15 Apr; snow chains recommended

---

Bulgaria Bulgariya (BG)

Area 110,912 sq km (42,822 sq miles)
Population 6,925,000 **Capital** Sofia (1,454,000)
Languages Bulgarian (official), Turkish
Currency Lev = 100 stotinki
Website www.government.bg

🏛	⚠	⚠	🏭
130	90	90	50

If towing trailer

100	70	70	50

- 🚗 Compulsory in front and rear seats
- Under 3s not permitted in vehicles with no child restraints; 3–10 year olds must sit in rear
- 🍷 0.05% △ Compulsory Compulsory
- Recommended Compulsory ⊖ 18
- Photo driving licence preferred; a paper licence must be accompanied by an International Driving Permit. Green card or insurance specific to Bulgaria.
- Only allowed with a hands-free kit
- ★ Dipped headlights compulsory
- ★ Fee at border
- ★ GPS must have fixed speed camera function deactivated; radar detectors prohibited
- ★ On-the-spot fines imposed
- ★ Road tax stickers (annual, monthly or weekly) must be purchased at the border and displayed prominently with the vehicle registration number written on them.
- ★ Snow chains should be carried from 1 Nov–1 Mar.
- ★ Visibility vest compulsory

Croatia Hrvatska (HR)

Area 56,538 km² (21,829 mi²)
Population 4,471,000 **Capital** Zagreb (1,111,000)
Languages Croatian **Currency** Kuna = 100 lipa
Website croatia.hr

🏛	⚠	⚠	🏭
130	110	90	50

Under 24

120	100	80	50

If towing

110	80	80	50

- 🚗 Compulsory if fitted
- Children under 12 not permitted in front seat and must use appropriate child seat or restraint in rear.
- 🍷 0.00% △ Compulsory
- Compulsory Compulsory
- Recommended ⊖ 18
- Green card recommended
- Only allowed with hands-free kit
- ★ Dipped headlights compulsory
- ★ Snow chains and shovel compulsory in winter
- ★ On-the-spot fines imposed
- ★ Radar detectors prohibited
- ★ Tow bar and rope compulsory
- ★ Visibility vest compulsory

Czech Republic

Česká Republica (CZ)

Area 78,864 sq km (30,449 sq miles)
Population 10,627,000
Capital Prague/Praha (1,211,000)
Languages Czech (official), Moravian
Currency Czech Koruna = 100 haler
Website www.vlada.cz/en/

🏛	⚠	⚠	🏭
130	90	90	50

If towing

80	80	80	50

- 🚗 Compulsory in front seats and, if fitted, in rear
- Children: Children under 36 kg and 150 cm must use appropriate child restraint. Only front-facing child retraints are permitted in the front in vehicles with airbags fitted. Airbags must be deactivated if a rear-facing child seat is used in the front.
- 🍷 0.00% △ Compulsory Compulsory
- Compulsory Compulsory
- ⊖ 18 (17 for motorcycles under 125 cc)
- Only allowed with a hands-free kit
- **LEZ** Two-stage LEZ in Prague for vehicles over 3.5 and 6 tonnes. Permit system.
- ★ Dipped headlights compulsory at all times
- ★ GPS must have fixed speed camera function deactivated; radar detectors prohibited
- ★ On-the-spot fines imposed
- ★ Replacement fuses must be carried
- ★ Spectacles or contact lens wearers must carry a spare pair in their vehicle at all times
- ★ Vignette needed for motorway driving, available for 1 year, 60 days, 15 days. Toll specific to lorries introduced 2006, those over 12 tonnes must buy an electronic tag
- ★ Visibility vest compulsory
- ★ Winter tyres or snow chains compulsory between Nov and Apr

---

Denmark Danmark (DK)

Area 43,094 sq km (16,638 sq miles)
Population 5,627,000 **Capital** Copenhagen / København (1,997,000) **Languages** Danish (official)
Currency Krone = 100 øre **Website** www.denmark.dk/en

🏛	⚠	⚠	🏭
110-130	80-90	80	50

If towing

80	70	70	50

- 🚗 Compulsory front and rear
- Under 135cm must use appropriate child restraint; in front permitted only in an appropriate rear-facing seat with any airbags disabled.
- 🍷 0.05% △ Compulsory
- Recommended Recommended
- Recommended ⊖ 18
- Only allowed with a hands-free kit
- **LEZ** Aalborg, Arhus, Copenhagen, Frederiksberg and Odense. Proofs of emissions compliance/compliant filter needed to obtain sticker. Non-compliant vehicles banned.
- ★ Dipped headlights must be used at all times
- ★ On-the-spot fines imposed
- ★ Radar detectors prohibited
- ★ Tolls apply on the Storebaeltsbroen and Oresundsbron bridges.
- ★ Visibility vest recommended

Estonia Eesti (EST)

Area 45,100 sq km (17,413 sq miles)
Population 1,314,000 **Capital** Tallinn (543,000)
Languages Estonian (official), Russian
Currency Euro = 100 cents **Website** valitsus.ee/en

🏛	⚠	⚠	🏭
n/a	90*	90	50

If full driving licence held for less than two years

*In summer, the speed limit on some dual carriageways may be raised to 100/110 kph

- 🚗 Compulsory if fitted
- Children too small for adult seatbelts must wear a seat restraint appropriate to their size. Rear-facing safety seats must not be used in the front if an air bag is fitted, unless this has been deactivated.
- 🍷 0.00% △ 2 compulsory
- Compulsory Recommended
- Compulsory ⊖ 18
- Only allowed with a hands-free kit
- ★ A toll system is in operation in Tallinn
- ★ Dipped headlights compulsory at all times
- ★ On-the-spot fines imposed
- ★ Winter tyres are compulsory from Dec–Mar. Studded winter tyres are allowed from 15 Oct–31 Mar, but this can be extended to start 1 October and/or end 30 April

---

inland Suomi (FIN)

ea 338,145 sq km (130,557 sq miles)
pulation 5,457,000 **Capital** Helsinki (1,403,000)
nguages Finnish, Swedish (both official)
rrency Euro = 100 cents
bsite http://valtioneuvosto.fi/en/frontpage

🛣	⩘	▲	🏙
120	100	80-100	20/50
ns, lorries and if towing			
80	80	60	20/50

0 in summer • If towing a vehicle by rope, cable or rod, x speed limit 60 kph • Maximum of 80 kph for vans and ies •Speed limits are often lowered in winter

Compulsory in front and rear
Below 135 cm must use a child restraint or seat
0.05% △ Compulsory ⊞ Recommended
Recommended 🧯 Recommended
18 (motorbikes below 125cc 16)
Only allowed with hands-free kit
Dipped headlights must be used at all times
On-the-spot fines imposed
Radar-detectors are prohibited
Visibility vest compulsory
Winter tyres compulsory Dec–Feb

ance (F)

a 551,500 sq km (212,934 sq miles)
oulation 66,616,000 **Capital** Paris (12,162,000)
guages French (official), Breton, Occitan
rency Euro = 100 cents
bsite www.diplomatie.gouv.fr/en/

🛣	⩘	▲	🏙
130	110	90	50
wet roads or if full driving licence held less than 2 yrs			
110	100	80	50
owing below / above 3.5 tonnes gross			
110/90	100/90	90/80	50

ph on all roads if fog reduces visibility to less than 50m ence will be lost and driver fined for exceeding speed t by over 40kph

Compulsory in front seats and, if fitted, in rear
In rear, 4 or under must have a child safety seat (rear facing if up to 9 months); if 5–10 must use an appropriate restraint system. Under 10 permitted in the front only if rear seats are fully occupied by other under 10s or there are no rear safety belts. In front, if child is in rear-facing child seat, any airbag must be deactivated.
0.05%. If towing or with less than 2 years with full driving licence, 0.00% • All drivers/motorcyclists must carry 2 unused breathalysers to French certification standards, showing an NF number.
Compulsory ⊞ Recommended
Recommended ⊖ 18
Use not permitted whilst driving
An LEZ operates in the Mont Blanc tunnel
Dipped headlights compulsory in poor daytime visibility and at all times for motorcycles
GPS must have fixed speed camera function deactivated; radar-detection equipment is prohibited
It is compulsory to carry a French-authority-recognised (NF) breathalyser.
On-the-spot fines imposed
Tolls on motorways. Electronic tag needed if using automatic tolls.
Visibility vests compulsory except for motorcyclists and passengers, who must have reflective stickers on their helmets (front, back and both sides).
Winter tyres recommended. Carrying snow chains recommended in winter as these may have to be fitted if driving on snow-covered roads, in accordance with signage.

ermany Deutschland (D)

a 357,022 sq km (137,846 sq miles)
ulation 80,716,000 **Capital** Berlin (6,000,000)
guages German (official) **Currency** Euro = 100 cents
bsite www.bundesregierung.de

🛣	⩘	▲	🏙
*	*	100	50
owing			
80	80	80	50

limit, 130 kph recommended

Compulsory
Under 150 cm and 12 or under must use an appropriate child seat or restraint. In front if child is in rear-facing child seat, airbags must be deactivated.
0.05%, 0.0% for drivers 21 or under or with less than two years full licence
Compulsory ⊞ Compulsory
Recommended 🧯 Recommended
18 (motorbikes: 16 if under 50cc)
Use permitted only with hands-free kit – also applies to drivers of motorbikes and bicycles
More than 60 cities have or are planning LEZs. Proof of compliance needed to acquire sticker. Non-compliant vehicles banned.
Dipped headlights compulsory in poor weather conditions and tunnels; recommended at other times
GPS must have fixed speed camera function deactivated; radar detectors prohibited
Motorcyclists must use dipped headlights at all times; other vehicles must use dipped headlights during poor daytime visibility.
On-the-spot fines imposed
Tolls on autobahns for lorries
Visibility vest compulsory
Winter tyres compulsory in all winter weather conditions; snow chains recommended

Greece Ellas (GR)

Area 131,957 sq km (50,948 sq miles)
Population 10,816,000
Capital Athens / Athina (3,758,000)
Languages Greek (official)
Currency Euro = 100 cents
Website www.primeminister.gr/english

	🛣	⩘	▲	🏙
⊙	130	110	90	50
Motorbikes, and if towing				
⊙	90	70	70	40

🔗 Compulsory in front seats and, if fitted, in rear
👶 Under 12 or below 135cm must use appropriate child restraint. In front if child is in rear-facing child seat, any airbag must be deactivated.
🍸 0.05%, 0.00% for drivers with less than 2 years' full licence and motorcyclists
△ Compulsory ⊞ Compulsory
💡 Recommended 🧯 Compulsory ⊖ 18
📱 Not permitted.
★ Dipped headlights compulsory during poor daytime visibility and at all times for motorcycles
★ On-the-spot fines imposed
★ Radar-detection equipment is prohibited
★ Snow chains permitted on ice- or snow-covered roads
★ Tolls on several newer motorways.

Hungary Magyarország (H)

Area 93,032 sq km (35,919 sq miles)
Population 9,879,000
Capital Budapest (3,284,000)
Languages Hungarian (official)
Currency Forint = 100 filler
Website www.kormany.hu/en

	🛣	⩘	▲	🏙
⊙	130	110	90	50
If towing				
⊙	80	70	70	50

🔗 Compulsory in front seats and if fitted in rear seats
👶 Under 135cm and over 3 must be seated in rear and use appropriate child restraint. Under 3 allowed in front only in rear-facing child seat with any airbags deactivated.
🍸 0.00% △ Compulsory ⊞ Compulsory
💡 Compulsory 🧯 Recommended ⊖ 17
📱 Only allowed with a hands-free kit
LEZ Budapest has vehicle restrictions on days with heavy dust and is planning an LEZ.
★ During the day dipped headlights compulsory outside built-up areas; compulsory at all times for motorcycles
★ Electronic vignette system in use for tolls on several motorways
★ Many motorways are toll and operate electronic vignette system with automatic number plate recognition, tickets are available for 4 days, 7 days, 1 month, 1 year
★ On-the-spot fines issued
★ Radar detectors prohibited
★ Snow chains compulsory where conditions dictate
★ Tow rope recommended
★ Visibility vest compulsory

Iceland Ísland (IS)

Area 103,000 sq km (39,768 sq miles)
Population 326,000
Capital Reykjavik (209,000)
Languages Icelandic
Currency Krona = 100 aurar
Website www.government.is/

	🛣	🚗	🚗	🏙
⊙	n/a	90	80	50

🔗 Compulsory in front and rear seats
👶 Under 12 or below 150cm not allowed in front seat and must use appropriate child restraint.
🍸 0.05% △ Compulsory ⊞ Compulsory
💡 Compulsory 🧯 Compulsory
⊖ 18; 21 to drive a hire car; 25 to hire a jeep
📱 Only allowed with a hands-free kit
★ Dipped headlights compulsory at all times
★ Driving off marked roads is forbidden
★ Highland roads are not suitable for ordinary cars
★ On-the-spot fines imposed
★ Winter tyres compulsory c.1 Nov–14 Apr (variable)

Ireland Eire (IRL)

Area 70,273 sq km (27,132 sq miles)
Population 4,593,000
Capital Dublin (1,804,000)
Languages Irish, English (both official)
Currency Euro = 100 cents
Website www.gov.ie/en/

	🛣	⩘	▲	🏙
⊙	120	100	80	50
If towing				
⊙	80	80	80	50

🔗 Compulsory where fitted. Driver responsible for ensuring passengers under 17 comply
👶 Children 3 and under must be in a suitable child restraint system. Airbags must be deactivated if a rear-facing child seat is used in the front. Those under 150 cm and 36 kg must use appropriate child restraint in cars with seatbelts.
🍸 0.05%, 0.02% for novice and professional drivers
△ Compulsory ⊞ Recommended
💡 Recommended 🧯 Recommended
⊖ 17 (16 for motorbikes up to 125cc; 18 for over 125cc; 18 for lorries; 21 bus/minibus)
📱 Only allowed with a hands-free kit
★ Dipped headlights compulsory for motorbikes at all times and in poor visibility for other vehicles
★ Driving is on the left
★ GPS must have fixed speed camera function deactivated; radar detectors prohibited
★ On-the-spot fines imposed
★ Tolls are being introduced on some motorways; the M50 Dublin has barrier-free tolling with number-plate recognition.

Italy Italia (I)

Area 301,318 sq km (116,338 sq miles)
Population 60,783,000 **Capital** Rome / Roma (4,194,000)
Languages Italian (official) **Currency** Euro = 100 cents
Website www.italia.it

	🛣	⩘	▲	🏙
⊙	130	110	90	50
If towing				
⊙	80	70	70	50
Less than three years with full licence				
⊙	100	90	90	50
When wet				
⊙	100	90	80	50

Some motorways with emergency lanes have speed limit of 150 kph

🔗 Compulsory in front seats and, if fitted, in rear
👶 Under 12 not allowed in front seats except in child safety seat; children under 3 must have special seat in the back. For foreign-registered cars, the country of origin's legislation applies.
🍸 0.05%, but 0.00% for professional drivers or with less than 3 years full licence
△ Compulsory
⊞ Recommended
💡 Compulsory
🧯 Recommended
⊖ 18 (14 for mopeds, 16 up to 125cc, 20 up to 350cc)
📱 Only allowed with hands-free kit
LEZ Most northern and several southern regions operate seasonal LEZs and many towns and cities have various schemes that restrict access. There is an LEZ in the Mont Blanc tunnel
★ Dipped headlights compulsory outside built-up areas, in tunnels, on motorways and dual carriageways and in poor visibility; compulsory at all times for motorcycles
★ On-the-spot fines imposed
★ Radar-detection equipment is prohibited
★ Snow chains compulsory where signs indicate 15 Oct–15 Apr
★ Tolls on motorways. Blue lanes accept credit cards; yellow lanes restricted to holders of Telepass pay-toll device.
★ Visibility vest compulsory

Kosovo Republika e Kosoves / Republika Kosovo (RKS)

Area 10,887 sq km (4203 sq miles)
Population 1,859,000
Capital Pristina (465,000)
Languages Albanian, Serbian (both official), Bosnian, Turkish, Roma
Currency Euro (Serbian dinar in Serb enclaves)
Website www.kryeministri-ks.net/?page=2,1

	🛣	⩘	▲	🏙
⊙	130	80	80	50

🔗 Compulsory
👶 Under 12 must sit in rear seats
🍸 0.03%, 0.00% for professional, business and commercial drivers
△ Compulsory
⊞ Compulsory
💡 Compulsory
🧯 Compulsory
⊖ 18 (16 for motorbikes less than 125 cc, 14 for mopeds)
🪪 International driving permit, locally purchased third-party insurance (green card is not recognised), documents with proof of ability to cover costs and valid reason for visiting. Visitors from many non-EU countries require a visa.
📱 Only allowed with a hands-free kit
★ Dipped headlights compulsory at all times
★ Winter tyres or snow chains compulsory in poor winter weather conditions

Latvia Latvija (LV)

Area 64,589 sq km (24,942 sq miles)
Population 1,998,000
Capital Riga (1,018,000)
Languages Latvian (official), Russian
Currency Euro = 100 cents
Website www.mk.gov.lv/en

	🛣	⩘	▲	🏙
⊙	n/a	100	90	50
If towing				
⊙	n/a	80	80	50

In residential areas limit is 20kph • If full driving licence held for less than two years, must not exceed 80 kph

🔗 Compulsory in front seats and if fitted in rear
👶 If under 12 years and 150cm must use child restraint in front and rear seats
🍸 0.05%, 0.02% with less than 2 years experience
△ Compulsory
⊞ Compulsory
💡 Recommended
🧯 Compulsory
⊖ 18
📱 Only allowed with hands-free kit
★ Dipped headlights must be used at all times all year round
★ On-the-spot fines imposed
★ Pedestrians have priority
★ Radar-detection equipment prohibited
★ Visibility vests compulsory
★ Winter tyres compulsory for vehicles up to 3.5 tonnes Dec–Feb, but illegal May–Sept

Lithuania Lietuva (LT)

Area 65,200 sq km (25,173 sq miles)
Population 2,944,000
Capital Vilnius (806,000)
Languages Lithuanian (official), Russian, Polish
Currency Euro = 100 cents
Website www.lrvk.lt/en

	🛣	⩘	▲	🏙
⊙	130	110	90	50
If towing				
⊙	n/a	70	70	50

In winter speed limits are reduced by 10–20 km/h

🔗 Compulsory in front seats and if fitted in rear seats
👶 Under 12 or below 135 cm not allowed in front seats unless in a child safety seat; under 3 must use appropriate child seat and sit in rear
🍸 0.04%, 0.02% for those with less than 2 years' full licence
△ Compulsory ⊞ Compulsory
💡 Recommended 🧯 Compulsory ⊖ 18
🪪 Licences without a photograph must be accompanied by photographic proof of identity, e.g. a passport
📱 Only allowed with a hands-free kit
★ Dipped headlights must be used at all times
★ On-the-spot fines imposed
★ Visibility vest compulsory
★ Winter tyres compulsory 10 Nov–1 Apr

Luxembourg (L)

Area 2,586 sq km (998 sq miles)
Population 550,000
Capital Luxembourg (165,000)
Languages Luxembourgian / Letzeburgish (official), French, German
Currency Euro = 100 cents
Website www.visitluxembourg.com

	🛣	⩘	▲	🏙
⊙	130/110	90	90	50
If towing				
⊙	90	75	75	50

If full driving licence held for less than two years, must not exceed 75 kph • In 20 km/h zones, pedestrians have right of way.

🔗 Compulsory
👶 Children under 3 must use an appropriate restraint system. Airbags must be disabled if a rear-facing child seat is used in the front. Children 3–8 and / or under 150 cm must use a restraint system appropriate to their size. If over 36kg a seatbelt may be used in the back only
🍸 0.05%, 0.02 for young drivers, drivers with less than 2 years experience and drivers of taxis and commercial vehicles
△ Compulsory ⊞ Compulsory (buses)
💡 Compulsory
🧯 Compulsory (buses, transport of dangerous goods)
⊖ 18
📱 Use permitted only with hands-free kit
★ Dipped headlights compulsory for motorcyclists and in poor visibility for other vehicles
★ On-the-spot fines imposed
★ Visibility vest compulsory
★ Winter tyres compulsory in winter weather

Macedonia Makedonija (MK)

Area 25,713 sq km (9,927 sq miles)
Population 2,100,000
Capital Skopje (669,000)
Languages Macedonian (official), Albanian
Currency Denar = 100 deni
Website www.vlada.mk/?language=en-gb

	🛣	⩘	▲	🏙
⊙	120	100	80	50
Newly qualified drivers or if towing				
⊙	100	80	60	50

🔗 Compulsory in front seats; compulsory if fitted in rear seats
👶 Under 12 not allowed in front seats
🍸 0.05%, 0.00% for business, commercial and professional drivers and with less than 2 years experience
△ Compulsory
⊞ Compulsory
💡 Compulsory
🧯 Recommended; compulsory for LPG vehicles
⊖ 18 (mopeds 16)
🪪 International driving permit; visa
📱 Use not permitted whilst driving
★ Dipped headlights compulsory at all times
★ GPS must have fixed speed camera function deactivated; radar detectors prohibited
★ Novice drivers may only drive between 11pm and 5am if there is someone over 25 with a valid licence in the vehicle.
★ On-the-spot fines imposed
★ Tolls apply on many roads
★ Tow rope compulsory
★ Visibility vest must be kept in the passenger compartment and worn to leave the vehicle in the dark outside built-up areas
★ Winter tyres or snow chains compulsory 15 Nov–15 Mar

Moldova (MD)

Area 33,851 sq km (13,069 sq miles)
Population 3,600,000 **Capital** Chisinau (801,000)
Languages Moldovan / Romanian (official)
Currency Leu = 100 bani **Website** www.moldova.md

	🛣	⛙	▲	🏙
⊙	90	90	90	60
If towing or if licence held under 1 year				
⊙	70	70	70	60

- 💺 Compulsory in front seats and, if fitted, in rear seats
- 👶 Under 12 not allowed in front seats
- 🍷 0.00% △ Compulsory ⊞ Compulsory
- 💡 Recommended 🧯 Compulsory
- ⊖ 18 (mopeds and motorbikes, 16; vehicles with more than eight passenger places, taxis or towing heavy vehicles, 21)
- ▣ International Driving Permit (preferred), visa
- 📱 Only allowed with hands-free kit
- ★ Motorcyclists must use dipped headlights at all times
- ★ Winter tyres recommended Nov–Feb

Montenegro Crna Gora (MNE)

Area 14,026 sq km, (5,415 sq miles)
Population 625,000
Capital Podgorica (186,000)
Languages Serbian (of the Ijekavian dialect)
Currency Euro = 100 cents
Website www.gov.me/en/homepage

	🛣	⛙	▲	🏙
⊙	n/a	100	80	50

80kph speed limit if towing a caravan

- 💺 Compulsory in front and rear seats
- 👶 Under 12 not allowed in front seats. Under-5s must use an appropriate child seat.
- 🍷 0.03 % △ Compulsory ⊞ Compulsory
- 💡 Compulsory 🧯 Compulsory
- ⊖ 18 (16 for motorbikes less than 125cc; 14 for mopeds)
- 📱 Prohibited
- ★ An 'eco' tax vignette must be obtained when crossing the border and displayed in the upper right-hand corner of the windscreen
- ★ Dipped headlights must be used at all times
- ★ From mid-Nov to March, driving wheels must be fitted with winter tyres
- ★ On-the-spot fines imposed
- ★ Tolls on some primary roads and in the Sozina tunnel between Lake Skadar and the sea
- ★ Visibility vest compulsory

Netherlands Nederland (NL)

Area 41,526 sq km (16,033 sq miles)
Population 16,820,000 **Capital** Amsterdam 2,400,000 • administrative capital 's-Gravenhage (The Hague) 1,051,000 **Languages** Dutch (official), Frisian
Currency Euro = 100 cents **Website** www.government.nl

	🛣	⛙	▲	🏙
⊙	130	80/100	80/100	50

- 💺 Compulsory
- 👶 Under 3 must travel in the back, using an appropriate child restraint; 3–18 and under 135cm must use an appropriate child restraint
- 🍷 0.05%, 0.02% with less than 5 years experience or moped riders under 24
- △ Compulsory ⊞ Recommended
- 💡 Recommended 🧯 Recommended
- ⊖ 18
- 📱 Only allowed with a hands-free kit
- LEZ About 20 cities operate or are planning LEZs. A national scheme is planned.
- ★ Dipped headlights compulsory for motorcycles and recommended in poor visibility and on open roads for other vehicles.
- ★ On-the-spot fines imposed
- ★ Radar-detection equipment is prohibited

Norway Norge (N)

Area 323,877 sq km (125,049 sq miles)
Population 5,138,000
Capital Oslo (1,503,000)
Languages Norwegian (official), Lappish, Finnish
Currency Krone = 100 øre
Website www.norway.org.uk

	🛣	⛙	▲	🏙
⊙	90/100	80	80	30/50
If towing trailer with brakes				
⊙	80	80	80	50
If towing trailer without brakes				
⊙	60	60	60	50

- 💺 Compulsory in front seats and, if fitted, in rear
- 👶 Children less than 150cm tall must use appropriate child restraint. Children under 4 must use child safety seat or safety restraint (cot)
- 🍷 0.01% △ Compulsory ⊞ Recommended
- 💡 Recommended 🧯 Recommended ⊖ 18 (heavy vehicles 18/21)
- 📱 Only allowed with a hands-free kit
- LEZ Planned for Bergen, Oslo and Trondheim
- ★ Dipped headlights must be used at all times
- ★ On-the-spot fines imposed
- ★ Radar-detectors are prohibited
- ★ Tolls apply on some bridges, tunnels and access roads into Bergen, Oslo, Trondheim and Stavangar. Several use electronic fee collection only.
- ★ Visibility vest compulsory
- ★ Winter tyres or summer tyres with snow chains compulsory for snow- or ice-covered roads

Poland Polska (PL)

Area 323,250 sq km (124,807 sq miles)
Population 38,545,000
Capital Warsaw / Warszawa (2,666,000)
Languages Polish (official)
Currency Zloty = 100 groszy
Website www.msz.gov.pl/en/

	🛣	⛙	▲	🏙
Motor-vehicle only roads[1], under/over 3.5 tonnes				
⊙	130[2]/80[2]	110/80	100/80	n/a
Motor-vehicle only roads[1] if towing				
⊙	n/a	80	80	n/a
Other roads, under 3.5 tonnes				
⊙	n/a	100	90	50/60[3]
Other roads, 3.5 tonnes or over				
⊙	n/a	80	70	50/60[3]
Other roads, if towing				
⊙	n/a	60	60	30

[1] Indicated by signs with white car on blue background. [2] Minimum speed 40 kph. [3] 50 kph 05.00–23.00; 60 kph 23.00–05.00; 20 kph in marked residential areas

- 💺 Compulsory in front seats and, if fitted, in rear
- 👶 Under 12 and below 150 cm must use an appropriate child restraint. Rear-facing child seats not permitted in vehicles with airbags.
- 🍷 0.02% △ Compulsory ⊞ Recommended
- 💡 Recommended 🧯 Compulsory
- ⊖ 18 (mopeds and motorbikes under 125cc – 16)
- 📱 Only allowed with a hands-free kit
- ★ Dipped headlights compulsory for all vehicles
- ★ On-the-spot fines imposed
- ★ Radar-detection equipment is prohibited
- ★ Snow chains permitted only on roads completely covered in snow
- ★ Vehicles over 3.5 tonnes (including cars towing caravans) must have a VIAbox for the electronic toll system
- ★ Visibility vests compulsory for drivers of Polish-registered vehicles

Portugal (P)

Area 88,797 sq km (34,284 sq miles)
Population 10,427,000 **Capital** Lisbon / Lisboa (3,035,000)
Languages Portuguese (official)
Currency Euro = 100 cents
Website www.portugal.gov.pt/en.aspx

	🛣	⛙	▲	🏙
⊙	120*	90/100	90	50/20
If towing				
⊙	100*	90	80	50

*40kph minimum; 90kph maximum if licence held under 1 year

- 💺 Compulsory in front seats; compulsory if fitted in rear seats
- 👶 Under 12 and below 135cm must travel in the rear in an appropriate child restraint; rear-facing child seats permitted in front only if airbags deactivated
- 🍷 0.05% 0.02% for drivers with less than 3 years with a full licence
- △ Compulsory ⊞ Recommended
- 💡 Recommended 🧯 Recommended
- ⊖ 18 (motorcycles under 50cc 17)
- ▣ MOT certificate for vehicles over 3 years old, photographic proof of identity (e.g. driving licence or passport) must be carried at all times.
- 📱 Only allowed with hands-free kit
- LEZ An LEZ prohibits vehicles without catalytic converters from certain parts of Lisbon. There are plans to extend the scheme to the whole of the city
- ★ Dipped headlights compulsory for motorcycles, compulsory for other vehicles in poor visibility and tunnels
- ★ On-the-spot fines imposed
- ★ Radar-detectors prohibited
- ★ Tolls on motorways; do not use green lanes, these are reserved for auto-payment users. Some motorways require an automatic toll device.
- ★ Visibility vest compulsory
- ★ Wearers of spectacles or contact lenses should carry a spare pair

Romania (RO)

Area 238,391 sq km (92,042 sq miles)
Population 20,122,000
Capital Bucharest / Bucuresti (2,272,000)
Languages Romanian (official), Hungarian
Currency Romanian leu = 100 bani
Website www.gov.ro

	🛣	⛙	▲	🏙
Cars and motorcycles				
⊙	120/130	100	90	50
Vans				
⊙	110	90	80	40
Motorcycles				
⊙	100	80	80	50

For motor vehicles with trailers or if full driving licence has been held for less than one year, speed limits are 20kph lower than those listed above • Jeep-like vehicles: 70kph outside built-up areas but 60kph in all areas if diesel. For mopeds, the speed limit is 45 kph.

- 💺 Compulsory
- 👶 Under 12s not allowed in front and must use an appropriate restraint in the rear
- 🍷 0.00% △ Compulsory ⊞ Compulsory
- 💡 Compulsory 🧯 Compulsory ⊖ 18
- 📱 Only allowed with hands-free kit
- ★ Dipped headlights compulsory outside built-up areas, compulsory everywhere for motorcycles
- ★ Electronic road tax system; price depends on emissions category and length of stay
- ★ Compulsory road tax can be paid for at the border, post offices and some petrol stations
- ★ It is illegal for vehicles to be dirty
- ★ On-the-spot fines imposed
- ★ Tolls on motorways
- ★ Visibility vest compulsory
- ★ Winter tyres compulsory Nov–Mar if roads are snow- or ice-covered, especially in mountainous areas

Russia Rossiya (RUS)

Area 17,075,000 sq km (6,592,800 sq miles)
Population 143,700,000
Capital Moscow / Moskva (11,511,000)
Languages Russian (official), and many others
Currency Russian ruble = 100 kopeks
Website government.ru/en/

	🛣	⛙	▲	🏙
⊙	110	90	90	60
If licence held for under 2 years				
⊙	70	70	70	60

- 💺 Compulsory if fitted
- 👶 Under 12 permitted in front seat only in an appropriate child restraint
- 🍷 0.03 % △ Compulsory ⊞ Compulsory
- 💡 Compulsory 🧯 Compulsory ⊖ 18
- ▣ International Driving Permit with Russian translation, visa, green card endorsed for Russia, International Certificate for Motor Vehicles
- 📱 Only allowed with a hands-free kit
- ★ Dipped headlights compulsory during the day
- ★ On-the-spot fines imposed
- ★ Picking up hitchhikers is prohibited
- ★ Radar detectors/blockers prohibited
- ★ Road tax payable at the border

Serbia Srbija (SRB)

Area 77,474 sq km, 29,913 sq miles
Population 7,187,000
Capital Belgrade / Beograd (1,659,000)
Languages Serbian
Currency Dinar = 100 paras
Website www.srbija.gov.rs

	🛣	⛙	▲	🏙
⊙	120	100	80	60

- 💺 Compulsory in front and rear seats
- 👶 Age 3–12 must be in rear seats and wear seat belt or appropriate child restraint; under 3 in rear-facing child seat permitted in front only if airbag deactivated
- 🍷 0.03%, but 0.0% for commercial drivers, motorcyclists or with less than one year with a full licence △ Compulsory ⊞ Compulsory
- 💡 Compulsory 🧯 Compulsory ⊖ 18 (16 for motorbikes less than 125cc; 14 for mopeds)
- ▣ International Driving Permit, green card or locally bought third-party insurance
- ★ 3-metre tow bar or rope
- ★ 80km/h speed limit if towing a caravan
- ★ Dipped headlights compulsory
- ★ Spare tyre compulsory
- ★ On-the-spot fines imposed
- ★ Radar detectors prohibited
- ★ Tolls on motorways and some primary roads
- ★ Visibility vest compulsory
- ★ Winter tyres compulsory Nov–Apr for vehicles up to 3.5 tonnes. Carrying snow chains recommended in winter as these may have to be fitted if driving on snow-covered roads, in accordance with signage.

Slovak Republic Slovenska Republika (SK)

Area 49,012 sq km (18,923 sq miles)
Population 5,416,000 **Capital** Bratislava (660,000)
Languages Slovak (official), Hungarian
Currency Euro = 100 cents
Website www.government.gov.sk

	🛣	⛙	▲	🏙
⊙	130/90	90	90	50

- 💺 Compulsory
- 👶 Under 12 or below 150cm must be in rear in appropriate child restraint
- 🍷 0.0% △ Compulsory ⊞ Compulsory
- 💡 Compulsory 🧯 Recommended
- ⊖ 18 (15 for mopeds)
- ▣ International driving permit, proof of health insurance
- 📱 Only allowed with a hands-free kit
- ★ Dipped headlights compulsory at all times
- ★ On-the-spot fines imposed
- ★ Radar-detection equipment is prohibited
- ★ Tow rope recommended
- ★ Vignette required for motorways, car valid for 1 year, 30 days, 7 days; lorry vignettes carry a higher charge.
- ★ Visibility vests compulsory
- ★ Winter tyres compulsory

Slovenia Slovenija (SLO)

Area 20,256 sq km (7,820 sq miles)
Population 2,062,000 **Capital** Ljubljana (275,000)
Languages Slovene **Currency** Euro = 100 cents
Website www.gov.si

	🛣	⛙	▲	🏙
⊙	130	90*	90*	50
If towing				
⊙	80	80*	80*	50

*70kph in urban areas

- 💺 Compulsory in front seats and, if fitted, in rear
- 👶 Under 12 and below 150cm must use appropriate ch restraint; babies must use child safety seat
- 🍷 0.05%, but 0.0% for commercial drivers, under 21s or with less than one year with a full licence
- △ Compulsory ⊞ Compulsory
- 💡 Compulsory 🧯 Recommended
- ⊖ 18 (motorbikes up to 125cc – 16, up to 350cc – 18)
- ▣ Licences without photographs must be accompanie by an International Driving Permit
- 📱 Only allowed with hands-free kit
- ★ Dipped headlights must be used at all times
- ★ On-the-spot fines imposed
- ★ Snow chains or winter tyres compulsory mid-Nov to mid-March, and in wintery conditions at other times
- ★ Vignettes valid for variety of periods compulsory for vehicles below 3.5 tonnes for toll roads. Write your vehicle registration number on the vignette before displaying it. For heavier vehicles electronic tolling system applies; several routes are cargo-traffic free during high tourist season.
- ★ Visibility vest compulsory

Spain España (E)

Area 497,548 sq km (192,103 sq miles)
Population 46,704,000 **Capital** Madrid (6,369,000)
Languages Castilian Spanish (official), Catalan, Galician, Basque **Currency** Euro = 100 cents
Website www.lamoncloa.gob.es

	🛣	⛙	▲	🏙
⊙	120*	100*	90	50
If towing				
⊙	80	80	70	50

* Motorways and dual carriageways in urban areas 80 kp

- 💺 Compulsory in front seats and if fitted in rear seats
- 👶 Under 135cm and below 12 must use appropriate ch restraint
- 🍷 0.05%, 0.03% if less than 2 years full licence or if vehic is over 3.5 tonnes or carries more than 9 passengers
- △ Two compulsory (one for in front, one for behind)
- ⊞ Recommended
- 💡 Compulsory 🧯 Recommended
- ⊖ 18 (21 for heavy vehicles; 16 for motorbikes up to 125
- 📱 Only allowed with hands-free kit
- ★ Dipped headlights compulsory for motorcycles and poor daytime visibility for other vehicles.
- ★ It is recommended that spectacles or contact lens wearers carry a spare pair.
- ★ Radar-detection equipment is prohibited
- ★ Snow chains recommended for mountainous areas i winter
- ★ Spare tyre compulsory
- ★ Tolls on motorways
- ★ Visibility vest compulsory

Sweden Sverige (S)

Area 449,964 sq km (173,731 sq miles)
Population 9,658,000
Capital Stockholm (2,127,000)
Languages Swedish (official), Finnish
Currency Swedish krona = 100 ore
Website www.sweden.gov.se

	🛣	⛙	▲	🏙
⊙	90–120	80	70–100	30–60
If towing trailer with brakes				
⊙	80	80	70	50

- 💺 Compulsory in front and rear seats
- 👶 Under 15 or below 135cm must use an appropriate child restraint and may sit in the front only if airbag is deactivated; rear-facing baby seat permitted in front only if airbag deactivated.
- 🍷 0.02% △ Compulsory ⊞ Recommended
- 💡 Recommended 🧯 Recommended ⊖ 18
- ▣ Licences without a photograph must be accompanie by photographic proof of identity, e.g. a passport
- LEZ Gothenberg, Helsingborg, Lund, Malmo, Mölndal and Stockholm have LEZs, progressively prohibiting vehicles 6 or more years old.
- ★ 1 Dec–31 Mar winter tyres, anti-freeze and shovel compulsory
- ★ Dipped headlights must be used at all times
- ★ On-the-spot fines imposed
- ★ Radar-detection equipment is prohibited

Switzerland Schweiz (CH)

Area 41,284 sq km (15,939 sq miles)
Population 8,014,000
Capital Bern (356,000)
Languages French, German, Italian, Romansch (all offici
Currency Swiss Franc = 100 centimes / rappen
Website www.admin.ch

	🛣	⛙	▲	🏙
⊙	120	80	80	50/30
If towing up to 1 tonne / over 1 tonne				
⊙	80	80	60/80	30/50

- 💺 Compulsory in front and, if fitted, in rear
- 👶 Up to 12 years or below 150 cm must use an appropriate child restraint. Children 6 and under mus sit in the rear.
- 🍷 0.05%, but 0.0% for commercial drivers or with less th three years with a full licence
- △ Compulsory ⊞ Recommended
- 💡 Recommended 🧯 Recommended
- ⊖ 18 (mopeds up to 50cc – 16)
- 📱 Only allowed with a hands-free kit
- ★ Dipped headlights compulsory
- ★ GPS must have fixed speed camera function deactivated; radar detectors prohibited

Motorways are all toll and for vehicles below 3.5 tonnes a vignette must be purchased at the border. The vignette is valid for one calendar year. Vehicles over 3.5 tonnes must have an electronic tag for travel on any road.

On-the-spot fines imposed

Pedestrians have right of way

Picking up hitchhikers is prohibited on motorways and main roads

Spectacles or contact lens wearers must carry a spare pair in their vehicle at all times

Winter tyres recommended Nov–Mar; snow chains compulsory in designated areas in poor winter weather

urkey Türkiye (TR)

ea 774,815 sq km (299,156 sq miles)
pulation 76,668,000
pital Ankara (5,045,000)
nguages Turkish (official), Kurdish
rrency New Turkish lira = 100 kurus
bsite www.mfa.gov.tr/default.en.mfa

120	90	90	50
owing			
80	80	80	40

Compulsory if fitted

Under 150 cm and below 36kg must use suitable child restraint. If above 136 cm may sit in the back without child restraint. Under 3s can only travel in the front in a rear facing seat if the airbag is deactivated. Children 3–12 may not travel in the front seat.

0.00%

Two compulsory (one in front, one behind)

Compulsory Compulsory

Compulsory 18

International driving permit advised, and required for use with licences without photographs; note that Turkey is in both Europe and Asia, green card/UK insurance that covers whole of Turkey or locally bought insurance, e-visa obtained in advance.

Prohibited

Spare tyre compulsory

Dipped headlights compulsory in daylight hours

On-the-spot fines imposed

Several motorways, and the Bosphorus bridges are toll roads

Tow rope and tool kit must be carried

kraine Ukraina (UA)

a 603,700 sq km (233,088 sq miles)
ulation 44,573,000
ital Kiev / Kyviv (3,275,000)
guages Ukrainian (official), Russian
rency Hryvnia = 100 kopiykas
bsite www.kmu.gov.ua/control/en

130	110	90	60
wing			
80	80	80	60

ed limit in pedestrian zone 20 kph

Compulsory in front and rear seats

Under 12 and below 145cm must use an appropriate child restraint and sit in rear

0.02% – if use of medication can be proved. Otherwise 0.00%

Compulsory Compulsory

Optional Compulsory 18

International Driving Permit, visa, International Certificate for Motor Vehicles, green card

No legislation

A road tax is payable on entry to the country.

Dipped headlights compulsory in poor daytime and from Oct–Apr

On-the-spot fines imposed

Tow rope and tool kit recommended

Winter tyres compulsory Nov–Apr in snowy conditions

nited Kingdom (GB)

a 241,857 sq km (93,381 sq miles)
ulation 63,705,000 **Capital** London (15,011,000)
guages English (official),
sh (also official in Wales), Gaelic
rency Sterling (pound) = 100 pence
bsite www.direct.gov.uk

112	112	96	48
wing			
96	96	80	48

Compulsory in front seats and if fitted in rear seats

Under 3 not allowed in front seats except with appropriate restraint, and in rear must use child restraint if available; in front 3–12 or under 135cm must use appropriate child restraint, in rear must use appropriate child restraint (or seat belt if no child restraint is available, e.g. because two occupied restraints prevent fitting of a third).

0.08% (England, Northern Ireland, Wales), 0.05% (Scotland)

Recommended Recommended

Recommended Recommended

17 (16 for mopeds)

Only allowed with hands-free kit

London's LEZ operates by number-plate recognition; non-compliant vehicles face hefty daily charges. Foreign-registered vehicles must register.

Driving is on the left

On-the-spot fines imposed

Smoking is banned in all commercial vehicles

Some toll motorways and bridges

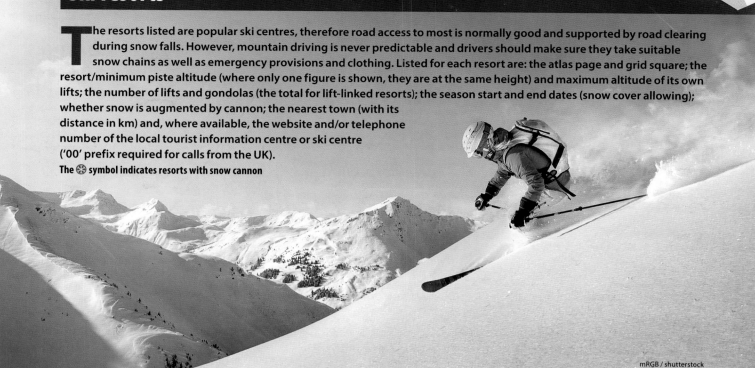

Ski resorts

The resorts listed are popular ski centres, therefore road access to most is normally good and supported by road clearing during snow falls. However, mountain driving is never predictable and drivers should make sure they take suitable snow chains as well as emergency provisions and clothing. Listed for each resort are: the atlas page and grid square; the resort/minimum piste altitude (where only one figure is shown, they are at the same height) and maximum altitude of its own lifts; the number of lifts and gondolas (the total for lift-linked resorts); the season start and end dates (snow cover allowing); whether snow is augmented by cannon; the nearest town (with its distance in km) and, where available, the website and/or telephone number of the local tourist information centre or ski centre ('00' prefix required for calls from the UK).

The ❆ symbol indicates resorts with snow cannon

mRGB / shutterstock

Andorra

Pyrenees

Pas de la Casa / Grau Roig 91 A4 ❆ 2050–2640m • 77 lifts • Dec–Apr • Andorra La Vella (30km) www.pasdelacasa-andorra.com • *Access via Envalira Pass (2407m), highest in Pyrenees, snow chains essential.*

Austria

Alps

Bad Gastein 72 A3 ❆ 1050/1100–2700m • 50 lifts • Dec–Mar • St Johann im Pongau (45km) +43 6432 3393 0 www.gastein.com

Bad Hofgastein 72 A3 ❆ 860–2295m • 50 lifts • Dec–Mar • St Johann im Pongau (40km) +43 6432 3393 0 www.gastein.com/en/region-orte/bad-hofgastein

Bad Kleinkirchheim 72 B3 ❆ 1070–2310m • 27 lifts • Dec–Mar • Villach (35km) +43 4240 8212 www.badkleinkirchheim.at

Ehrwald 71 A5 ❆ 1000–2965m • 24 lifts • Dec–Apr • Imst (30km) +43 5673 2395 www.wetterstein-bahnen.at/en

Innsbruck 71 A6 ❆ 574/850–3200m • 59 lifts • Dec–Apr • Innsbruck + 43 512 56 2000 www.innsbruck-pauschalen.com • *Motorway normally clear. The motorway through to Italy and through the Arlberg Tunnel are both toll roads.*

Ischgl 71 A5 ❆ 1340/1380–2900m • 101 lifts • Dec–May • Landeck (25km) +43 50990 100 www.ischgl.com • *Car entry to resort prohibited between 2200hrs and 0600hrs.*

Kaprun 72 A2 ❆ 885/770–3030m, • 53 lifts • Nov–Apr • Zell am See (10km) +43 6542 770 www.zellamsee-kaprun.com

Kirchberg in Tirol 72 A2 860–2000m • 60 lifts • Nov–Apr • Kitzbühel (6km) +43 57507 2000 www.kitzbueheler-alpen.com/en • *Easily reached from Munich International Airport (120 km)*

Kitzbühel (Brixen im Thale) 72 A2 ❆ 800/1210–2000m • 12 lifts • Dec–Apr • Wörgl (40km) +43 57057 2200 www.kitzbueheler-alpen.com/en

Lech/Oberlech 71 A5 ❆ 1450–2810m • 97 lifts • Dec–Apr • Bludenz (50km) +43 5583 2161 0 www.lechzuers.com • *Roads normally cleared but keep chains accessible because of altitude.*

Mayrhofen 72 A1 ❆ 630–2500m • 30 lifts • Dec–Apr • Jenbach (35km) +43 5285 6760 www.mayrhofen.at • *Chains rarely required.*

Obertauern 72 A3 ❆ 1740/1640–2350m • 26 lifts • Dec–Apr • Radstadt (20km) +43 6456 7252 www.obertauern.com • *Roads normally cleared but chain accessibility recommended. Camper vans and caravans not allowed; park these in Radstadt*

Saalbach Hinterglemm 72 A2 ❆ 1030/1100–2100m • 70 lifts • Nov–Apr • Zell am See (19km) +43 6541 6800-68 www.saalbach.com • *Both village centres are pedestrianised and there is a good ski bus service during the daytime*

St Anton am Arlberg 71 A5 ❆ 1300–2810m • 94 lifts • Dec–Apr • Innsbruck (104km) +43 5446 22690 www.stantonamarlberg.com

Schladming 72 A3 ❆ 745–1900m • 65 lifts • Dec–Mar • Schladming + 43 36 87 233 10 www.schladming-dachstein.at

Serfaus 71 A5 ❆ 1427/1200–2820m • 67 lifts • Dec–Apr • Landeck (30km) +43 5476 6239 www.serfaus-fiss-ladis.at • *Private vehicles banned from village. Use Dorfbahn Serfaus, an underground funicular which runs on an air cushion.*

Sölden 71 B6 ❆ 1380–3250m, • 33 lifts • Sep-Apr (glacier); Nov-Apr (main area) • Imst (50km) +43 57200 200 www.soelden.com • *Roads normally cleared but snow chains recommended because of altitude. The route from Italy and the south over the Timmelsjoch via Obergurgl is closed Oct–May and anyone arriving from the south should use the Brenner Pass motorway.*

Zell am See 72 A2 ❆ 750–1950m • 53 lifts • Dec–Mar • Zell am See +43 6542 770 www.zellamsee-kaprun.com • *Low altitude, so good access and no mountain passes to cross.*

Zell im Zillertal (Zell am Ziller) 72 A1 ❆ 580/930–2410m • 22 lifts • Dec–Apr • Jenbach (25km) +43 5282 7165–226 www.zillertalarena.com

Zürs 71 A5 ❆ 1720/1700–2450m • 97 lifts • Dec–Apr • Bludenz (30km) +43 5583 2245 www.lech-zuers.at • *Roads normally cleared but keep chains accessible because of altitude. Village has garage with 24-hour self-service gas/petrol, breakdown service and wheel chains supply.*

France

Alps

Alpe d'Huez 79 A5 ❆ 1860–3330m • 85 lifts • Dec–Apr • Grenoble (63km) www.alpedhuez.com • *Snow chains may be required on access road to resort.*

Avoriaz 70 B1 ❆ 1800/1100–2280m • 35 lifts • Dec–May • Morzine (14km) +33 4 50 74 72 72 www.morzine-avoriaz.com • *Chains may be required for access road from Morzine. Car-free resort, park on edge of village. Horse-drawn sleigh service available.*

Chamonix-Mont-Blanc 70 C1 ❆ 1035–3840m • 49 lifts • Dec–Apr • Martigny (38km) +33 4 50 53 75 50 www.chamonix.com

Chamrousse 79 A4 ❆ 1700–2250m • 26 lifts • Dec–Apr • Grenoble (30km) www.chamrousse.com • *Roads normally cleared, keep chains accessible because of altitude.*

Châtel 70 B1 ❆ 1200/1110–2200m • 41 lifts • Dec–Apr • Thonon-Les-Bains (35km) +33 4 50 73 22 44 http://info.chatel.com/english-version.html

Courchevel 70 C1 ❆ 1750/1300–2470m • 67 lifts • Dec–Apr • Moûtiers (23km) www.courchevel.com • *Roads normally cleared but keep chains accessible. Traffic 'discouraged' within the four resort bases.*

Flaine 70 B1 ❆ 1600–2500m • 26 lifts • Dec–Apr • Cluses (25km) +33 4 50 90 80 01 www.flaine.com • *Keep chains accessible for D6 from Cluses to Flaine. Car access for depositing luggage and passengers only. 1500-space car park outside resort. Near Sixt-Fer-á-Cheval.*

La Clusaz 69 C6 ❆ 1100–2600m • 55 lifts • Dec–Apr • Annecy (32km) +33 4 50 32 65 00 www.laclusaz.com • *Roads normally clear but keep chains accessible for final road from Annecy.*

La Plagne 70 C1 ❆ 2500/1250–3250m • 109 lifts • Dec–Apr Moûtiers (32km) +33 4 79 09 79 79 www.la-plagne.com • *Ten different centres up to 2100m altitude. Road access via Bozel, Landry or Aime normally cleared. Linked to Les Arcs by cablecar*

Les Arcs 70 C1 ❆ 1600/1200–3230m • 77 lifts • Dec–May • Bourg-St-Maurice (15km) +33 4 79 07 12 57 www.lesarcs.com • *Four base areas up to 2000 metres; keep chains accessible. Pay parking at edge of each base resort. Linked to La Plagne by cablecar*

Les Carroz d'Araches 70 B1 ❆ 1140–2500m • 80 lifts • Dec–Apr • Cluses (13km) + 33 4 50 90 00 04 www.lescarroz.com

Les Deux-Alpes 79 B5 ❆ 1650/1300–3600m • 55 lifts • Dec–Apr • Grenoble (75km) +33 4 76 79 22 00 www.les2alpes.com • *Roads normally cleared, however snow chains recommended for D213 up from valley road (D1091).*

Les Gets 70 B1 ❆ 1170/1000–2000m • 52 lifts • Dec–Apr • Cluses (18km) www.lesgets.com

Les Ménuires 69 C6 ❆ 1815/1850–3200m • 40 lifts • Dec–Apr • Moûtiers (27km) www.lesmenuires.com • *Keep chains accessible for D117 from Moûtiers.*

Les Sept Laux Prapoutel 69 C6 ❆ 1350–2400m, • 24 lifts • Dec–Apr • Grenoble (38km) www.les7laux.com • *Roads normally cleared, however keep chains accessible for mountain road up from the A41 motorway. Near St Sorlin d'Arves.*

Megève 69 C6 ❆ 1100/1050–2350m • 79 lifts • Dec–Apr • Sallanches (12km) +33 4 50 21 27 28 www.megeve.com • *Horse-drawn sleigh rides available.*

Méribel 69 C6 ❆ 1400/1100–2950m • 61 lifts • Dec–May • Moûtiers (18km) +33 4 79 08 60 01 www.meribel.net • *Keep chains accessible for 18km to resort on D90 from Moûtiers.*

Morzine 70 B1 ❆ 1000–2460m • 67 lifts, • Dec–Apr • Thonon-Les-Bains (30km) +33 4 50 74 72 72 www.morzine-avoriaz.com

Pra Loup 79 B5 ❆ 1600/1500–2500m • 53 lifts • Dec–Apr • Barcelonnette (10km) +33 4 92 84 10 04 www.praloup.com • *Roads normally cleared but chains accessibility recommended.*

Risoul 79 B5 ❆ 1850/1650–2750m • 59 lifts • Dec–Apr • Briançon (40km) +33 4 92 46 02 60 www.risoul.com • *Keep chains accessible. Near Guillestre. Linked with Vars Les Claux*

St-Gervais Mont-Blanc 70 C1 ❆ 850/1150–2350m • 27 lifts • Dec–Apr • Sallanches (10km) +33 4 50 47 76 08 www.st-gervais.com

Serre Chevalier 79 B5 ❆ 1350/1200–2800m • 77 lifts • Dec–Apr • Briançon (10km) + 33 4 92 24 98 98 www.serre-chevalier.com • *Made up of 13 small villages along the valley road, which is normally cleared.*

Tignes 70 C1 ❆ 2100/1550–3450m • 87 lifts • Jan–Dec • Bourg St Maurice (26km) +33 4 79 40 04 40 www.tignes.net • *Keep chains accessible because of altitude.*

Val d'Isère 70 C1 ❆ 1850/1550–3450m • 87 lifts • Dec–Apr • Bourg-St-Maurice (30km) +33 4 79 06 06 60 www.valdisere.com • *Roads normally cleared but keep chains accessible.*

Val Thorens 69 C6 ❆ 2300/1850–3200m • 29 lifts • Dec–Apr • Moûtiers (37km) www.valthorens.com • *Chains essential – highest ski resort in Europe. Obligatory paid parking on edge of resort.*

Valloire 69 C6 ❆ 1430–2600m • 34 lifts • Dec–Apr • Modane (20km) +33 4 79 59 03 96 www.valloire.net • *Road normally clear up to the Col du Galbier, to the south of the resort, which is closed from 1st November to 1st June. Linked to Valmeinier.*

Valmeinier 69 C6 ❆ 1500–2600m • 34 lifts • Dec–Apr • St Michel de Maurienne (47km) +33 4 79 59 53 69 www.valmeinier.com • *Access from north on D1006 / D902. Col du Galbier, to the south of the resort closed from 1st November to 1st June. Linked to Valloire.*

Valmorel 69 C6 ❆ 1400–2550m • 90 lifts • Dec–Apr • Moûtiers (15km) +33 4 79 09 85 55 www.valmorel.com • *Near St Jean-de-Belleville. Linked with ski areas of Doucy-Combelouvière and St François-Longchamp.*

Vars Les Claux 79 B5 ❆ 1850/1650–2750m • 59 lifts • Dec–Apr • Briançon (40km) +33 4 92 46 51 31 www.vars-ski.com • *Four base resorts up to 1850 metres. Keep chains accessible. Linked with Risoul.*

Villard de Lans 79 A4 ❆ 1050/1160–2170m • 28 lifts • Dec–Apr • Grenoble (32km) +33 4 76 95 10 38 www.villarddelans.com

Pyrenees

Font-Romeu 91 A5 ❆ 1800/1600–2200m • 25 lifts • Nov–Apr • Perpignan (87km) +33 4 68 30 68 30 www.font-romeu.fr • *Roads normally cleared but keep chains accessible.*

Saint-Lary Soulan 77 D3 ❆ 830/1650/1700–2515m • 31 lifts • Dec–Mar • Tarbes (75km) +33 5 62 39 50 81 www.saintlary.com • *Access roads constantly cleared of snow.*

Vosges

La Bresse-Hohneck 60 B2 ❆ 500/900–1350m • 33 lifts • Dec–Mar • Cornimont (6km) +33 3 29 25 41 29 www.labresse.net

Germany

Alps

Garmisch-Partenkirchen 71 A6 ✷ 700–2830m • 38 lifts • Dec–Apr • Munich (95km) • ☎ +49 8821 180 700 • 🖳 www.gapa.de • *Roads usually clear, chains rarely needed.*

Oberaudorf 62 C3 ✷ 480–1850m • 30 lifts • Dec–Apr • Kufstein (15km) 🖳 www.oberaudorf.de • *Motorway normally kept clear. Near Bayrischzell.*

Oberstdorf 71 A5 815m • 26 lifts • Dec–Apr • Sonthofen (15km) ☎ +49 8322 7000 • 🖳 http://oberstdorf.de

Rothaargebirge

Winterberg 51 B4 ✷ 700/620–830m • 19 lifts • Dec–Mar • Brilon (30km) ☎ +49 2981 925 00 🖳 www.winterberg.de • *Roads usually cleared, chains rarely required.*

Greece

Central Greece

Mount Parnassos: Kelaria-Fterolakka 116 D4 1640–2260m • 17 lifts • Dec–Apr • Amfiklia ☎ +30 22340 22694-5 🖳 www.parnassos-ski.gr

Mount Parnassos: Gerondovrahos 116 D4 1800–1900m • 3 lifts • Dec–Apr • Amfiklia ☎ +30 29444 70371

Peloponnisos

Mount Helmos: Kalavrita Ski Centre 117 D4 1650–2100m • 5 lifts • Dec–Mar • Kalavrita ☎ +30 26920 2261 🖳 www.kalavrita-ski.gr

Mount Menalo: Ostrakina 117 E4 1500–1600m • 4 lifts • Dec–Mar • Tripoli ☎ +30 27960 22227

Macedonia

Mount Falakro: Agio Pneuma 116 A6 1720/1620–2230m • 9 lifts • Dec–Apr • Drama ☎ +30 25210 23691 🖳 www.falakro.gr (Greek only)

Mount Vasilitsa: Vasilitsa 116 B3 1750/1800–2113m • 8 lifts • Dec–Mar • Konitsa ☎ +30 24620 24101 🖳 www.vasilitsa.com (Greek only)

Mount Vermio: Seli 116 B4 1500–1900m • 11 lifts • Dec–Mar • Kozani ☎ +30 23320 71234 🖳 www.seli-ski.gr (in Greek)

Mount Vermio: Tria-Pente Pigadia 116 B3 ✷ 1420–2005m • 7 lifts • Dec–Mar • Ptolemaida ☎ +30 23320 44464

Mount Verno: Vigla 116 B3 1650–1900m • 5 lifts • Dec–Mar • Florina ☎ +30 23850 22354 🖳 www.vigla-ski.gr (in Greek)

Mount Vrondous: Lailias 116 A5 1600–1850m • 3 lifts • Dec–Mar • Serres ☎ +30 23210 53790

Thessalia

Mount Pilio: Agriolefkes 116 C5 1300–1500m • 4 lifts • Dec–Mar • Volos ☎ +30 24280 73719

Italy

Alps

Bardonecchia 79 A5 ✷ 1312–2750m • 21 lifts • Dec–Apr • Bardonecchia ☎ +39 122 99032 🖳 www.bardonecchiaski.com • *Resort reached through the 11km Frejus tunnel from France, roads normally cleared.*

Bórmio 71 B5 ✷ 1200/1230–3020m • 24 lifts • Dec–Apr • Tirano (40km) 🖳 www.bormio.com • *Tolls payable in Ponte del Gallo Tunnel, open 0800hrs–2000hrs.*

Breuil-Cervinia 70 C2 ✷ 2050–3500m • 21 lifts • Jan–Dec • Aosta (54km) ☎ +39 166 944311 🖳 www.cervinia.it • *Snow chains strongly recommended. Bus from Milan airport.*

Courmayeur 70 C1 ✷ 1200–2760m • 21 lifts • Dec–Apr • Aosta (40km) ☎ +39 165 841612 🖳 www.courmayeurmontblanc.it • *Access through the Mont Blanc tunnel from France. Roads constantly cleared.*

Limone Piemonte 80 B1 ✷ 1000/1050–2050m • 29 lifts • Dec–Apr • Cuneo (27km) 🖳 www.limonepiemonte.it • *Roads normally cleared, chains rarely required.*

Livigno 71 B5 ✷ 1800–3000m • 31 lifts • Nov–May • Zernez (CH) ☎ +39 342 052200 🖳 www.livigno.eu • *Keep chains accessible. The direction of traffic through Munt la Schera Tunnel to/from Zernez is regulated on Saturdays. Check in advance.*

Sestrière 79 B5 ✷ 2035/1840–2840m • 92 lifts • Dec–Apr • Oulx (22km) ☎ +39 122 755444 🖳 www.visitsestriere.com • *One of Europe's highest resorts; although roads are normally cleared keep chains accessible.*

Appennines

Roccaraso – Aremogna 103 B7 ✷ 1285/1240–2140m • 24 lifts • Dec–Apr • Castel di Sangro (7km) ☎ +39 864 62210 🖳 www.roccaraso.net (in Italian)

Dolomites

Andalo – Fai della Paganella 71 B5 ✷ 1042/1050/2125m • 19 lifts • Dec–Apr • Trento (40km) 🖳 www.visitdolomitipaganella.it ☎ +39 461 585836

Arabba 72 B1 ✷ 1600/1450–2950m • 29 lifts • Dec–Mar • Brunico (45km) ☎ +39 436 780019 🖳 www.arabba.it • *Roads normally cleared but keep chains accessible.*

Cortina d'Ampezzo 72 B2 ✷ 1224/1050–2930m • 37 lifts • Dec–Apr • Belluno (72km) ☎ +39 436 869086 🖳 www.cortina.dolomiti.org • *Access from north on route 51 over the Cimabanche Pass may require chains.*

Corvara (Alta Badia) 72 B1 ✷ 1568–2500m • 56 lifts • Dec–Apr • Brunico (38km) ☎ +39 471 836176 🖳 www.altabadia.org • *Roads normally clear but keep chains accessible.*

Madonna di Campiglio 71 B5 ✷ 1550/1500–2600m • 72 lifts • Dec–Apr • Trento (60km) ☎ +39 465 447501 🖳 www.campigliodolomiti.it/homepage • *Roads normally cleared but keep chains accessible. Linked to Folgarida and Marilleva.*

Moena di Fassa (Sorte/Ronchi) 72 B1 ✷ 1184/1450–2520m • 8 lifts • Dec–Apr • Bolzano (40km) ☎ +39 462 609770 🖳 www.fassa.com

Selva di Val Gardena/Wolkenstein Groden 72 B1 ✷ 1563/1570–2450m • 81 lifts • Dec–Apr • Bolzano (40km) ☎ +39 471 777777 🖳 www.valgardena.it • *Roads normally cleared but keep chains accessible.*

Norway

Hemsedal 32 B5 ✷ 700/640–1450m • 24 lifts • Nov–May • Honefoss (150km) ☎ +47 32 055030 🖳 www.hemsedal.com • *Be prepared for extreme weather conditions.*

Slovak Republic

Chopok (Jasna-Chopok) 65 B5 ✷ 900/950–1840m • 17 lifts • Dec–Apr • Jasna ☎ +421 907 886644 🖳 www.jasna.sk (in Slovak only)

Donovaly 65 B5 ✷ 913–1360m • 17 lifts • Nov–Apr • Ruzomberok ☎ +421 48 4199900 🖳 www.parksnow.sk/zima

Martinské Hole 65 A4 1250/1150–1456m • 8 lifts • Nov–May • Zilina ☎ +421 43 430 6000 🖳 www.martinky.com

Plejsy 65 B6 470–912m • 9 lifts • Dec–Mar • Krompachy ☎ +421 53 429 8015 🖳 www.plejsy.sk

Strbske Pleso 65 A6 1380–1825m • 7 lifts • Dec–Mar • Poprad ☎ +421 917 682 260 🖳 www.vt.sk (in Slovak only)

Slovenia

Julijske Alpe

Kanin (Bovec) 72 B3 460/1600–2389m • 12 lifts • Dec–Apr • Bovec ☎ +386 5 384 1919 🖳 www.boveckanin.si

Kobla (Bohinj) 72 B3 ✷ 512/530–1495m • 6 lifts • Dec–Mar • Bohinjska Bistrica ☎ +386 4 5747 100 🖳 www.bohinj.si/kobla/en/naprave.html

Kranjska Gora 72 B3 ✷ 800–1210m • 19 lifts • Dec–Mar • Kranjska Gora ☎ +386 4 5809 440 🖳 www.kranjska-gora.si

Vogel 72 B3 570–1800m • 8 lifts • Dec–Apr • Bohinjska Bistrica ☎ +386 4 5729 712 🖳 www.vogel.si

Kawiniške Savinjske Alpe

Krvavec 73 B4 1450–1970m • 10 lifts • Dec–Apr • Kranj ☎ 386 4 25 25 911 🖳 www.rtc-krvavec.si

Pohorje

Rogla 73 B5 1517/1050–1500m • 13 lifts • Dec–Apr • Slovenska Bistrica ☎ +386 3 75 77 100 🖳 www.rogla.eu

Spain

Pyrenees

Baqueira-Beret/Bonaigua 90 A3 ✷ 1500–2500m • 33 lifts • Dec–Apr • Vielha (15km) ☎ +34 902 415 415 🖳 www.baqueira.es • *Roads normally clear but keep chains accessible. Near Salardú.*

Sistema Penibetico

Sierra Nevada 100 B2 ✷ 2100–3300m • 24 lifts • Dec–May • Granada (32km) ☎ +34 902 70 80 90 🖳 http://sierranevada.es • *Access road designed to be avalanche safe and is snow cleared.*

Sweden

Idre Fjäll 115 F9 590–890m • 33 lifts • Nov–Apr • Mora (140km) ☎ +46 253 41000 🖳 www.idrefjall.se • *Be prepared for extreme weather conditions.*

Sälen 34 A5 360m • 15 lifts • Nov–Apr • Malung (70km) ☎ +46 771 84 00 00 🖳 www.skistar.com/salen • *Be prepared for extreme weather conditions.*

Switzerland

Alps

Adelboden 70 B2 1353m • 55 lifts • Dec–Apr • Frutigen (15km) ☎ +41 33 673 80 80 🖳 www.adelboden.ch • *Linked with Lenk.*

Arosa 71 B4 1800m • 16 lifts • Dec–Apr • Chur (30km) ☎ +41 81 378 70 20 🖳 www.arosa.ch (German only) • *Roads cleared but keep chains accessible due to high altitude.*

Crans Montana 70 B2 ✷ 1500–3000m • 34 lifts • Dec–Apr, Jul–Oct • Sierre (15km) 🖳 www.crans-montana.ch • *Roads normally cleared but keep chains accessible for ascent from Sierre.*

Davos 71 B4 ✷ 1560/1100–2840m • 55 lifts • Nov–Apr • Davos. Linked with Klosters ☎ +41 81 415 21 21 🖳 www.davos.ch

Engelberg 70 B3 ✷ 1000/1050–3020m • 26 lifts • Nov–Apr • Luzern (39km) ☎ +41 41 639 77 77 🖳 www.engelberg.ch • *Straight access road normally cleared.*

Flums (Flumserberg) 71 A4 ✷ 1400/1000–2220m • 17 lifts • Dec–Apr • Buchs (25km) ☎ +41 81 720 18 18 🖳 www.flumserberg.ch • *Roads normally cleared, but 1000-metre vertical ascent; keep chains accessible.*

Grindelwald 70 B3 ✷ 1050–2950m • 20 lifts • Dec–Apr • Interlaken (20km) ☎ +41 33 854 12 50 🖳 www.jungfrauregion.ch

Gstaad – Saanenland 70 B2 ✷ 1050/950–3000m • 74 lifts • Dec–Apr • Gstaad ☎ +41 33 748 81 81 🖳 www.gstaad.ch • *Linked to Anzère.*

Klosters 71 B4 ✷ 1191/1110–2840m • 55 lifts • Dec–Apr • Davos (10km). Linked with Davos ☎ +41 81 410 20 20 🖳 www.davos.ch/klosters • *Roads normally clear but keep chains accessible.*

Leysin 70 B2 ✷ 2263/1260–2330m • 16 lifts • Dec–Apr • Aigle (6km) ☎ +41 24 493 33 00 🖳 www.leysin.ch

Mürren 70 B2 ✷ 1650–2970m • 12 lifts • Dec–Apr • Interlaken (18km) ☎ +41 33 856 86 86 🖳 www.mymuerren.ch • *No road access. Park in Stechelberg (1500 free places) and take a two-stage cable car.*

Nendaz 70 B2 ✷ 1365/1400–3300m • 20 lifts • Nov–Apr • Sion (16km) ☎ +41 27 289 55 89 🖳 www.nendaz.ch • *Roads normally cleared, however keep chains accessible for ascent from Sion. Near Vex.*

Saas-Fee 70 B2 ✷ 1800–3500m • 23 lifts • Jan–Dec • Brig (35km) ☎ +41 27 958 18 58 🖳 http://old.saas-fee.ch/en/ • *Roads normally cleared but keep chains accessible because of altitude.*

St Moritz 71 B4 ✷ 1856/1730–3300m • 24 lifts • Nov–May • Chur (89km) ☎ +41 81 837 33 33 🖳 www.stmoritz.ch • *Roads normally cleared but keep chains accessible.*

Samnaun 71 B5 ✷ 1846/1400–2900m • 40 lifts • Dec–Apr • Scuol (30km) ☎ +41 81 861 88 30 🖳 www.engadin.com • *Roads normally cleared but keep chains accessible.*

Verbier 70 B2 ✷ 1500–3330m • 17 lifts • Nov–Apr • Martigny (27km) ☎ +41 27 775 38 70 🖳 www.verbier.ch • *Roads normally cleared.*

Villars-Gryon 70 B2 ✷ 1253/1200–2100m • 16 lifts • Dec–Apr, Jun–Jul • Montreux (35km) ☎ +41 24 495 32 32 🖳 www.villars.ch • *Roads normally cleared but keep chains accessible for ascent from N9. Near Bex.*

Wengen 70 B2 ✷ 1270–2320m • 19 lifts • Dec–Apr • Interlaken (12km) ☎ +41 33 856 85 85 🖳 http://wengen.ch • *No road access. Park at Lauterbrunnen and take mountain railway.*

Zermatt 70 B2 ✷ 1620–3900m • 40 lifts, • all year • Brig (42km) ☎ +41 27 966 81 00 🖳 www.zermatt.ch • *Cars not permitted in resort, park in Täsch (3km) and take shuttle train.*

Turkey

North Anatolian Mountains

Uludag 118 B4 1770–2320m • 15 lifts • Dec–Mar • Bursa (36km) ☎ +90 224 285 21 11 🖳 http://skiingturkey.com/resorts/uludag.html

To the best of the Publisher's knowledge the information in this table was correct at the time of going to press. No responsibility can be accepted for any errors or their consequences.

Schladming ski resort, Austria
nikolpetr / Shutterstock

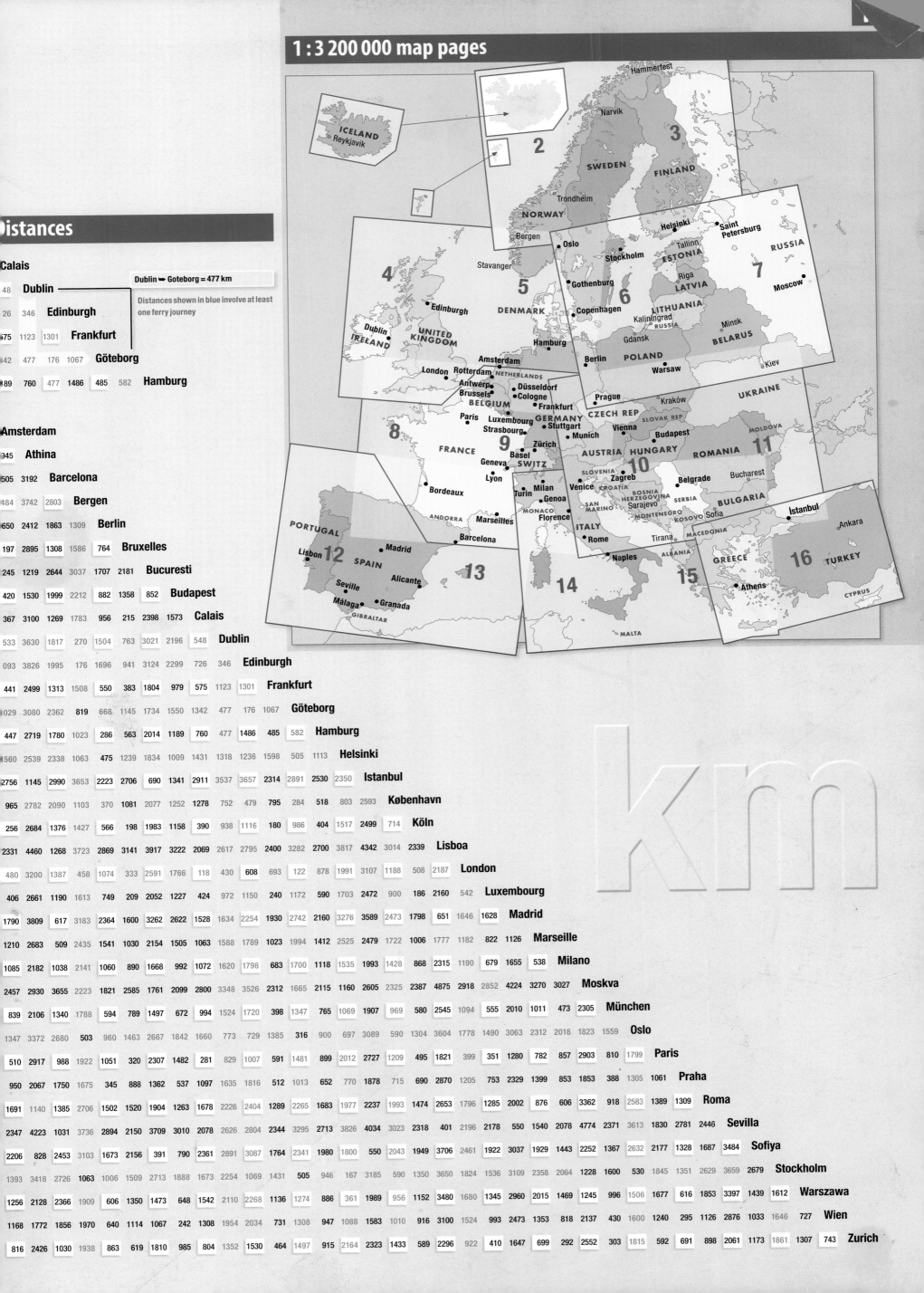

Distances

Calais

48				**Dublin**
26	346			**Edinburgh**
675	1123	1301		**Frankfurt**
42	477	176	1067	**Göteborg**
89	760	477	1486	485	582	**Hamburg**

Dublin ➡ Goteborg = 477 km

Distances shown in blue involve at least one ferry journey

Amsterdam

945 **Athina**
1505 3192 **Barcelona**
1484 3742 2803 **Bergen**
650 2412 1863 1309 **Berlin**
197 2895 1308 1586 764 **Bruxelles**
2245 1219 2644 3037 1707 2181 **Bucuresti**
1420 1530 1999 2212 882 1358 852 **Budapest**
367 3100 1269 1783 956 215 2398 1573 **Calais**
533 3630 1817 270 1504 763 3021 2196 548 **Dublin**
1093 3826 1995 176 1696 941 3124 2299 726 346 **Edinburgh**
441 2499 1313 1508 550 383 1804 979 575 1123 1301 **Frankfurt**
1029 3080 2362 819 668 1145 1734 1550 1342 477 176 1067 **Göteborg**
447 2719 1780 1023 286 563 2014 1189 760 477 1486 485 582 **Hamburg**
1560 2539 2338 1063 475 1239 1834 1009 1431 1318 1236 1598 505 1113 **Helsinki**
2756 1145 2990 3653 2223 2706 690 1341 2911 3537 3657 2314 2891 2530 2350 **Istanbul**
965 2782 2090 1103 370 1081 2077 1252 1278 752 479 795 284 518 803 2593 **København**
256 2684 1376 1427 566 198 1983 1158 390 938 1116 180 986 404 1517 2499 714 **Köln**
2331 4460 1268 3723 2869 3141 3917 3222 2069 2617 2795 2400 3282 2700 3817 4342 3014 2339 **Lisboa**
480 3200 1387 458 1074 333 2591 1766 118 430 608 693 122 878 1991 3107 1188 508 2187 **London**
406 2661 1190 1613 749 209 2052 1227 424 972 1150 240 1172 590 1703 2472 900 186 2160 542 **Luxembourg**
1790 3809 617 3183 2364 1600 3262 2622 1528 1634 2254 1930 2742 2160 3276 3589 2473 1798 651 1646 1628 **Madrid**
1210 2683 509 2435 1541 1030 2154 1505 1063 1588 1789 1023 1994 1412 2525 2479 1722 1006 1777 1182 822 1126 **Marseille**
1085 2182 1038 2141 1060 890 1668 992 1072 1620 1798 683 1700 1118 1535 1993 1428 868 2315 1190 679 1655 538 **Milano**
2457 2930 3655 2223 1821 2585 1761 2099 2800 3348 3526 2312 1665 2115 1160 2605 2325 2387 4875 2918 2852 4224 3270 3027 **Moskva**
839 2106 1340 1788 594 789 1497 672 994 1524 1720 398 1347 765 1069 1907 969 580 2545 1094 555 2010 1011 473 2305 **München**
1347 3372 2680 503 960 1463 2667 1842 1660 773 729 1385 316 900 697 3089 590 1304 3604 1778 1490 3063 2312 2018 1823 1559 **Oslo**
510 2917 988 1922 1051 320 2307 1482 281 829 1007 591 1481 899 2012 2727 1209 495 1821 399 351 1280 782 857 2903 810 1799 **Paris**
950 2067 1750 1675 345 888 1362 537 1097 1635 1816 512 1013 652 770 1878 715 690 2870 1205 753 2329 1399 853 1853 388 1305 1061 **Praha**
1691 1140 1385 2706 1502 1520 1904 1263 1678 2226 2404 1289 2265 1683 1977 2237 1993 1474 2653 1796 1285 2002 876 606 3362 918 2583 1389 1309 **Roma**
2347 4223 1031 3736 2894 2150 3709 3010 2078 2626 2804 2344 3295 2713 3826 4034 3023 2318 401 2196 2178 550 1540 2078 4774 2371 3613 1830 2781 2446 **Sevilla**
2206 828 2453 3103 1673 2156 391 790 2361 2891 3087 1764 2341 1980 1800 550 2043 1949 3706 2461 1922 3037 1929 1443 2252 1367 2632 2177 1328 1687 3484 **Sofiya**
1393 3418 2726 1063 1006 1509 2713 1888 1673 2254 1069 1431 505 946 167 3185 590 1350 3650 1824 1536 3109 2358 2064 1228 1600 530 1845 1351 2629 3659 2679 **Stockholm**
1256 2128 2366 1909 606 1350 1473 648 1542 2110 2268 1136 1274 886 361 1989 956 1152 3480 1680 1345 2960 2015 1469 1245 996 1506 1677 616 1853 3397 1439 1612 **Warszawa**
1168 1772 1856 1970 640 1114 1067 242 1308 1954 2034 731 1308 947 1088 1583 1010 916 3100 1524 993 2473 1353 818 2137 430 1600 1240 295 1126 2876 1033 1646 727 **Wien**
816 2426 1030 1938 863 619 1810 985 804 1352 1530 464 1497 915 2164 2323 1433 589 2296 922 410 1647 699 292 2552 303 1815 592 691 898 2061 1173 1861 1307 743 **Zurich**

km

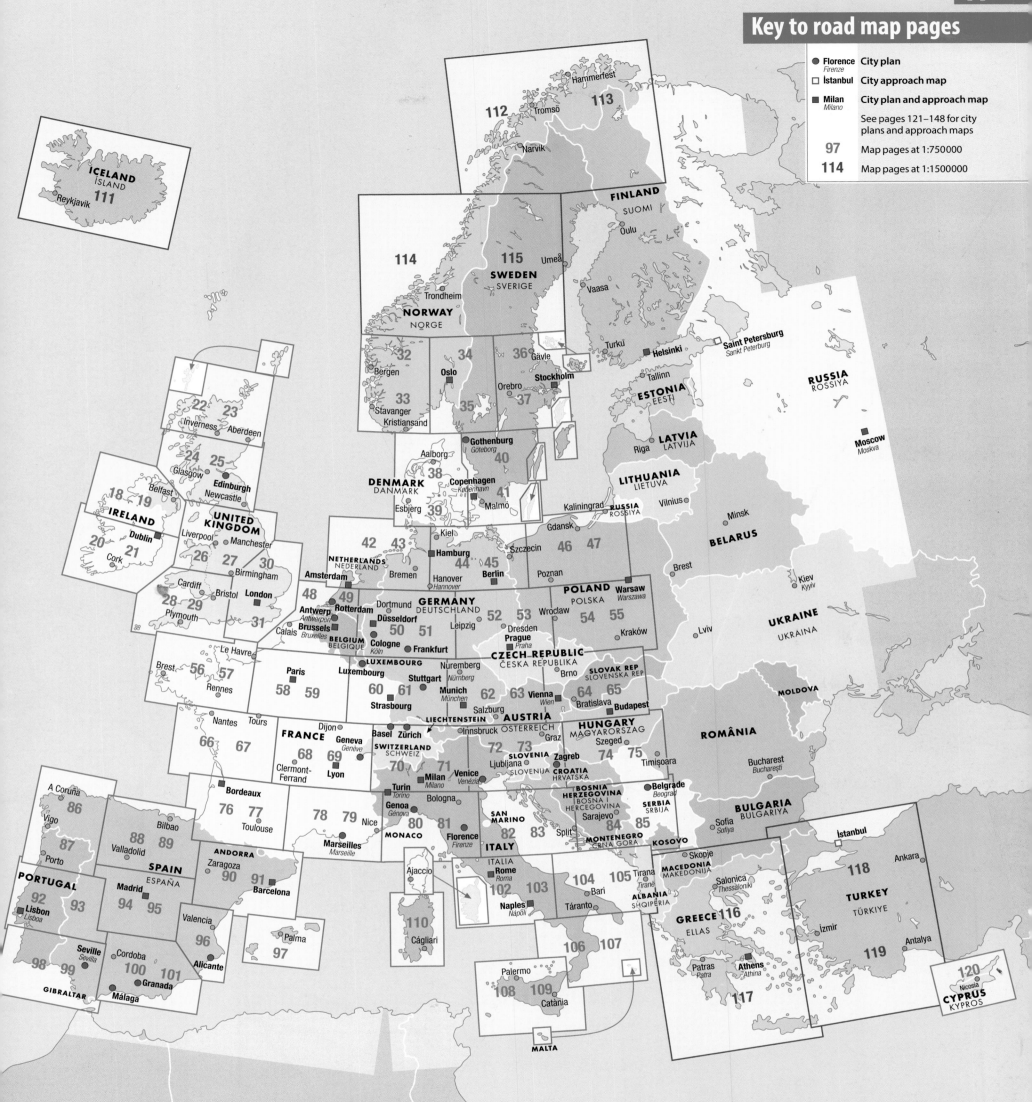

See pages 121–148 for city plans and approach maps

Key to road map pages

● Florence *Firenze*	City plan
□ İstanbul	City approach map
■ Milan *Milano*	City plan and approach map

97	Map pages at 1:750000
114	Map pages at 1:1500000

Motorway vignettes

Some countries require you to purchase (and in some cases display) a vignette before using motorways.

In Austria you will need to purchase and display a vignette on the inside of your windscreen. Vignettes are available for purchase at border crossings and petrol stations. More details from www.asfinag.at/toll/toll-sticker

In Belarus all vehicles over 3.5 tonnes and cars and vans under 3.5 tonnes registered outside the Eurasion Economic Union are required to have a *BelToll* unit installed. This device exchanges data with roadside gantries, enabling motorway tolls to be automatically deducted from the driver's account. www.beltoll.by/index.php/en/faq

In the Czech Republic, you can buy a vignette at the border and also at petrol stations. Make sure you write your vehicle registration number on the vignette before displaying it. The roads without toll are indicated by a traffic sign saying "Bez poplatku". More details from www.motorway.cz

In Hungary a new e-vignette system was introduced in 2008. It is therefore no longer necessary to display the vignette, though you should make doubly sure the information you give on your vehicle is accurate. Vignettes are sold at petrol stations throughout the country. Buy online at www.toll-charge.hu

In Slovakia, a vignette is also required to be purchased before using the motorways. This is sold in two kinds at the Slovak border and petrol stations. You will need to write your vehicle registration plate on the vignette before displaying it. www.slovakia.com/travel/car

In Switzerland, you will need to purchase and display a 'vignette' before you drive on the motorway. Bear in mind you will need a separate vignette if you are towing a caravan. www.ezv.admin.ch/zollinfo_privat/04338/index.html?lang=en

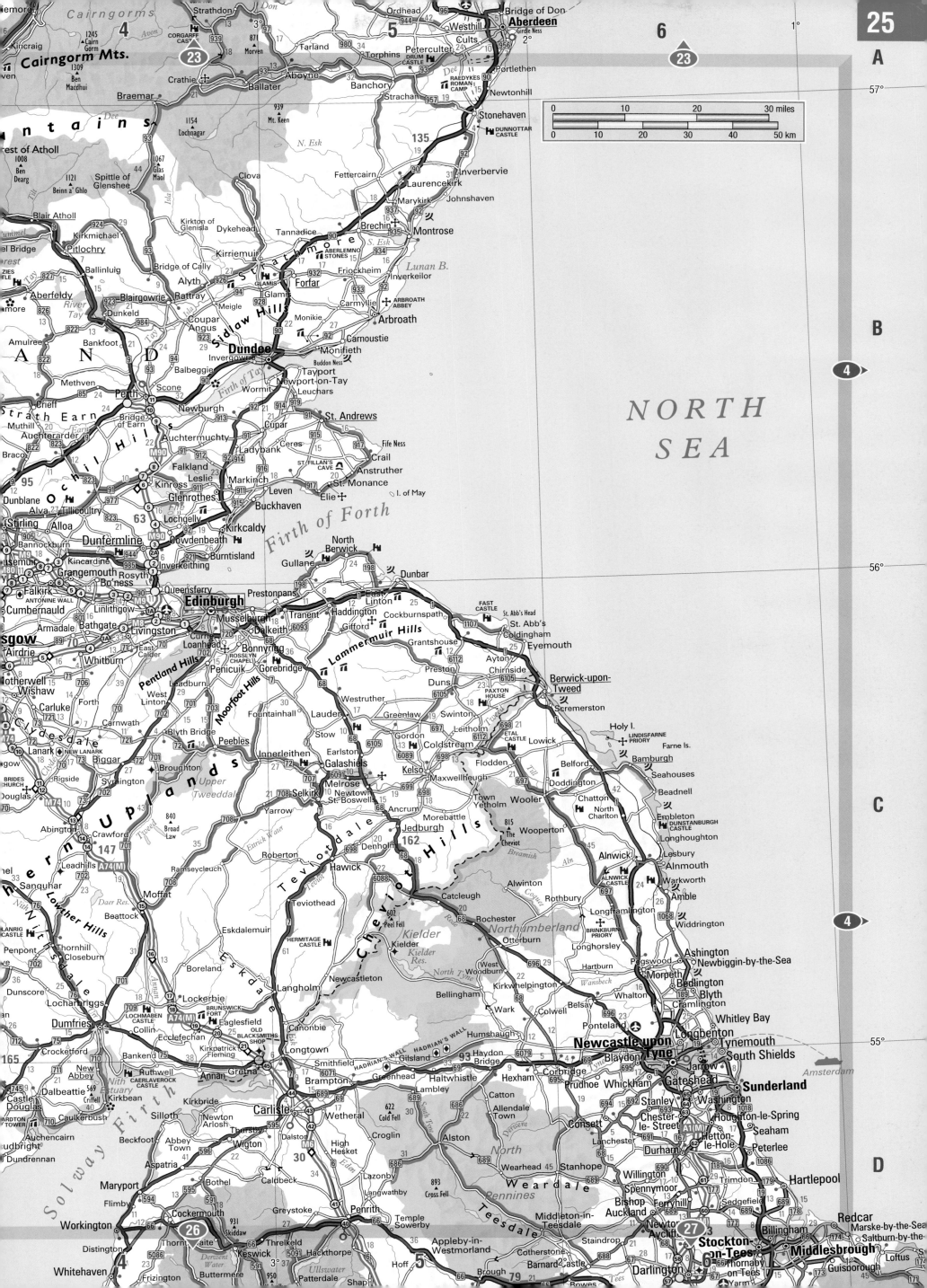

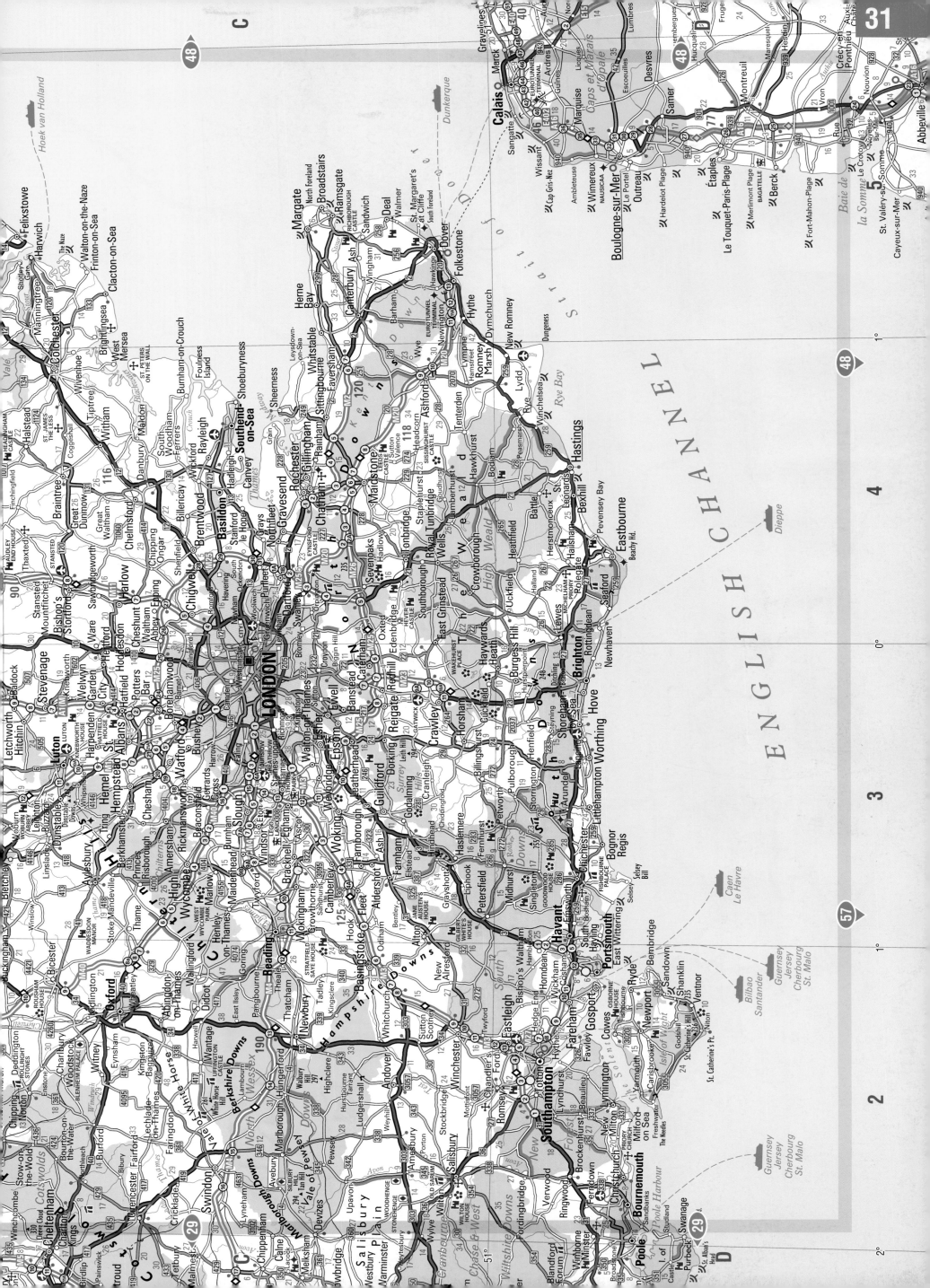

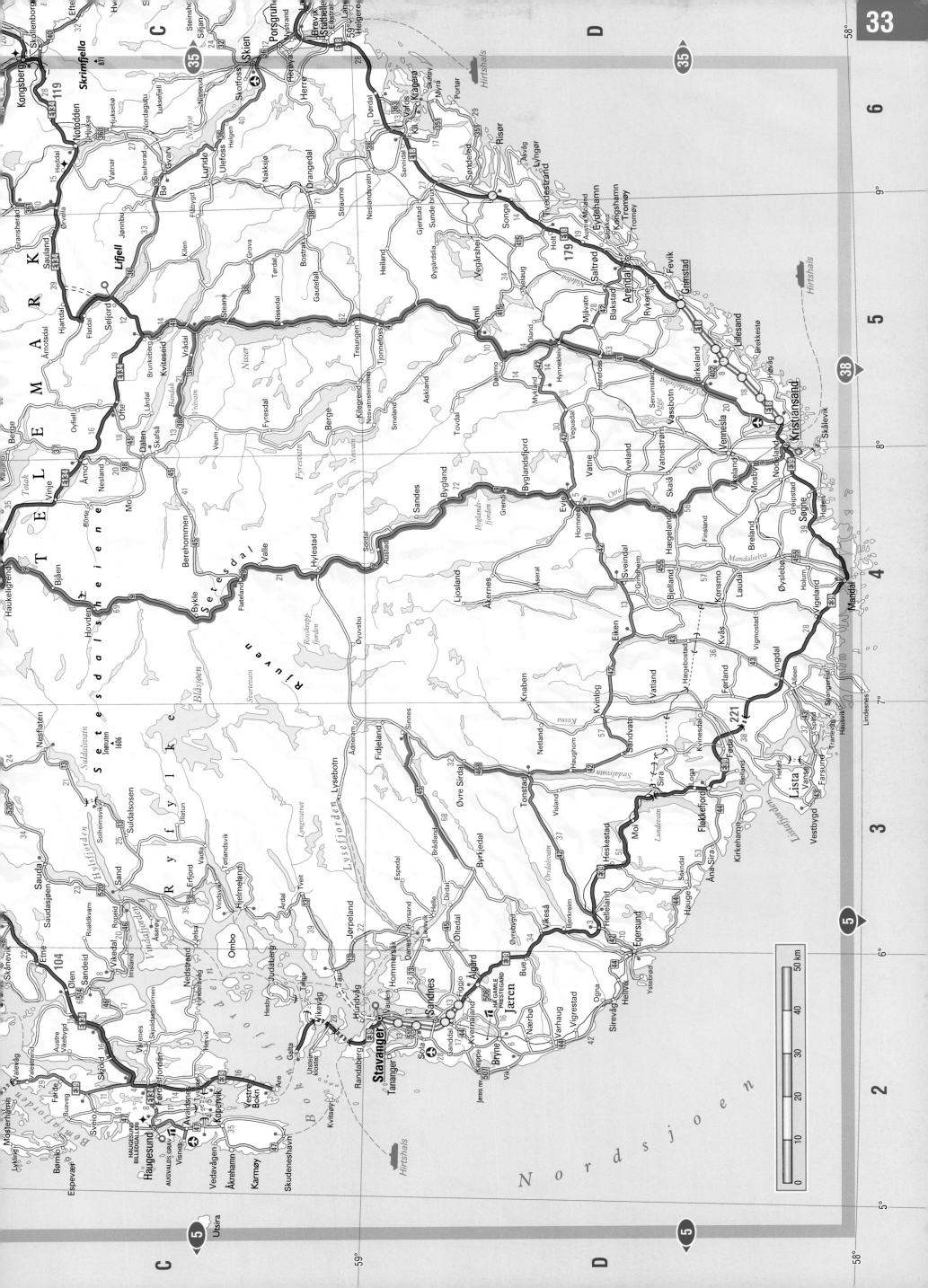

5°   1   4°   2   3°   3

28   29

0   10   20   30   40   50 km

A

Poole
Portsmouth

Guernsey   St. Sampson
Herm

St. Peter
Port

Cork
Rosslare

Plymouth

49°

Côte de Granit Rose

Sillon
de Talbert

Ploumanac'h   Plougrescant   Île de Bréhat
Perros-
Trégastel-Plage   Guirec   Pte. de l'Arcouest
Île de Batz   14   Pleubian   Ploubazlanec   Golfe de
Roscoff   Primel-   Pleumeur-   Tréguier   Lézardrieux   Paimpol
St-Pol-de-Léon   Trégastel   Bodou 9   786   31   Ploúézec   Côte d'
Brignogan-   Trébeurden   La Roche   Plouha
Plage   Cléder   10   788   Lannion   Derrien   786   St. Quay-
Kerlouan   Plouescat   Carantec   St.   St-Michel-   767   Pontrieux   Portrieux   Sables-d'Or-
Plouguerneau   16   Taulé   Lanmeur   Effiam   en-Grève   36   Bégard   Lanvollon   41   les-Pins
10   27   786   Plestin-   Plouaret   31   Binic   Étables-sur-Mer   Erquy
Lannilis   125 Lesneven   69   58   les-Grèves   138   E50   Guingamp   17   Baie de St. Brieuc
NOTRE DAME   CHÂTEAU   Plougasnou   Plouigneau   53   Belle-Isle-   Châtelaudren   Pordic   Les Rosaires   Pléneuf-
Portsall   Le Folgoet   DE KERJEAN   St.   Morlaix   Plougonven   en-Terre   Moustéru   24   Les Rosaires   Val-André
Ploudalmézeau   788   Plouzévédé   Thégonnec   Plougonver   Plouagat   St. Brieuc   786   768
Lanildut   68 168   26   56   Landivisiau   Plourin   787   Bourbriac   790   St. Brieuc   Plérin   Lamballe
Île d'Ouessant   Plabennec   712   Pleyber-   Lannéanou   Plougonver   Kérien   Quintin   38   Langueux   10
Lampaul   23   13 E50   12   764   30 11   Christ   785   Callac   Maël-Carhaix   St. Nicolas   767   Ploeuc-   38   Moncontour
St. Renan   Landerneau   Ploudiry   St.   51   du-Pélem   Corlay   sur-Lie   700   Collinée
789   Guipavas   770   Sizun   Sauveur   B   Mts. d'Arrée   Poullaouen   32 764   21   13   Uzel   31   Plouguenast
Brest   22   764   Huelgoat   Kerién   Plouévez-   767   700
Le Conquet   Plougastel-   Daoulas   18   Armorique   Brasparts   22   36   764   Carhaix-   Rostrenen   Quintin   24   Loudéac   Plémet
Pte. de St. Mathieu   Daoulas   165   Le   22   Plouguer   1064   Mûr-de-   19   Ménéac
Camaret-   TOUR   Faou   Pont-de-Buis   36   Spézet   Glomel   Gouarec   164   Bretagne   La Chèze   42   Merdr
sur-Mer   VAUBAN   791   lès-Quimerc'h   Playben   36   3   164   e   La Trinité-
Pte. de   Landévennec   44   785   Châteauneuf-   Mts.   Noires   53   782   Noyal-   Porhoët   Mar
Penhir   Crozon   887   du-Faou   27   Gourin   Ploúray   Cléguérec   18   Pontivy   Rohan
Mer d'Iroise   Morgat   84   Châteaulin   Roudouallec   1   764   L   154
887   164   Coray   Guiscriff   Le Faoüet   Guémené-Scorff   764   Pluméliau   32   Josselin
Baie de   Douarnenez   107   770   ST. RONAN   Briec   42   Kernascléden   768   20 767   24   166
Douarnenez   Locronan   165   Scaër   41   768   Moréac   22   Rie
Pte. du Raz   Plogoff   20   165   Quimper   15   Bubry   Bignan   St. Jean-   P10
Île de Sein   Audierne   765   Rosporden   765   Arzano   Plouay   Baud   Locminé   Brévelay   17
48°   784   Plouhinec   35   Llandudec   129   Bannalec   Scorff   Plumeliau   St. Anne-
Plozévet   784   Plogastel-   25   Concarneau   Pont-Aven   769   Quimperlé   Pont Scorff   768   24   Camors   d'Auray   Sérent
Plonéour-   St. Germain   34 783   165   E60   Moëlan-sur-Mer   Hennebont   768   Landévant   Pluvigner   28   Grand-Champ   767
Lanvern   785   Fouesnant   27   Tréguñc   783   Riec-   10   Baud   23   Elven
Pont-l'Abbé   28   Bénodet   Névez   sur-Bélon   Clohars-   Lanester   11   Ste. Anne-   Vannes
St. Guénolé   Loctudy   Port   Carnoêt   Ploemeur   Lorient   9 12   Auray   Questembert
Penmarch   Guilvinec   Manech   Le Pouldu   Port Louis   768   13
Pte. de Penmarch   Lesconil   Îles de Glénan   Larmor-Plage   16   Belz   781   Locmariaquer   165   Muzillac
Groix   12   14   18   Noyalo   La Roc
Île de Groix   Carnac   Le   26   Bern
66   St. Pierre   Sarzeau   Damgan   La Roc
Côte Sauvage   Presqu'île   de Quiberon   780   Pénestin
de Quiberon   Quiberon   St. Gildas-   Quiberon
C   de-Rhuys

5°   1   4°   2   3°   3

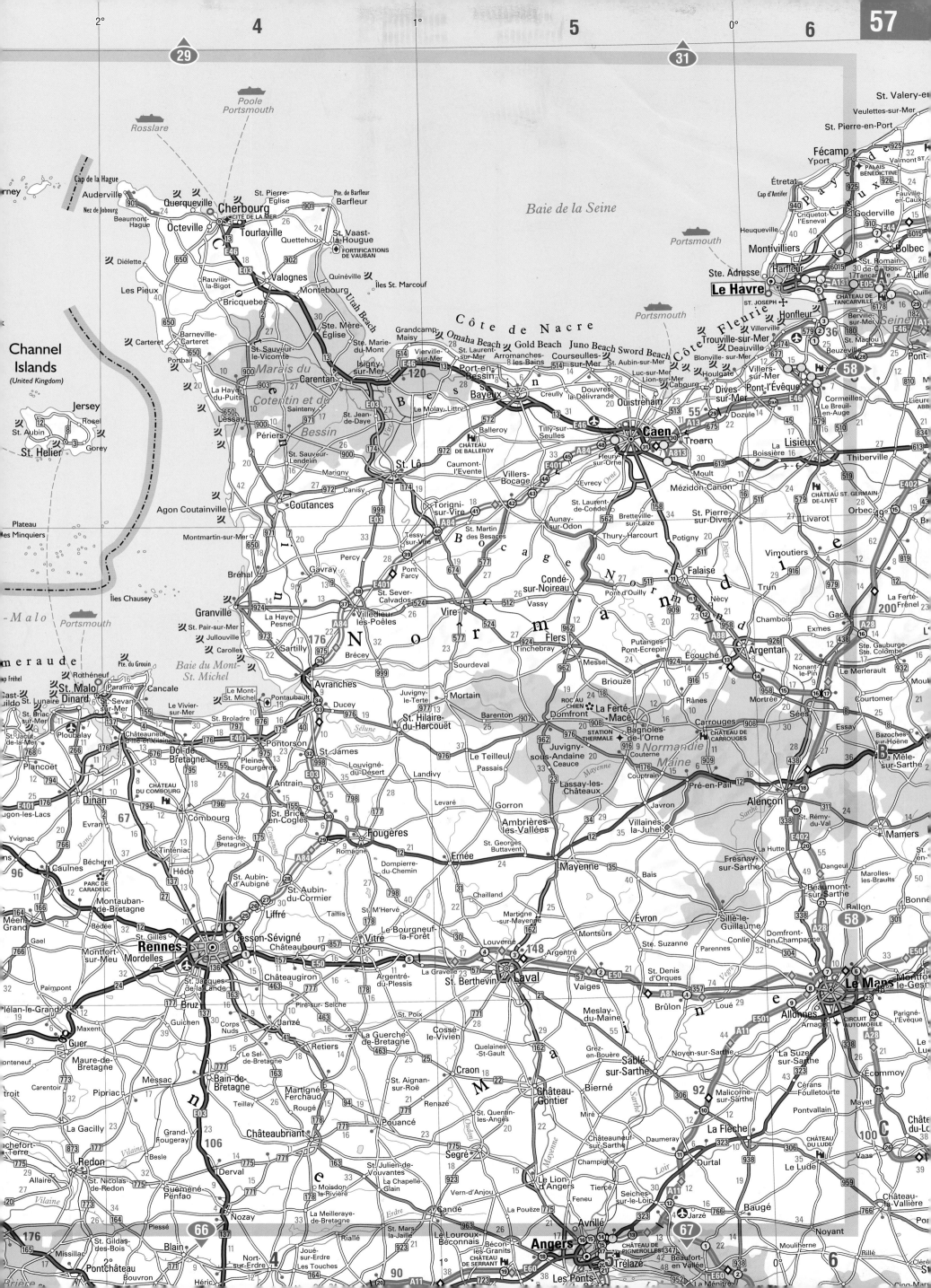

1 · 2 · 3

0 10 20 30 40 50 km

Newhaven

Le Tréport · Mers-les-Bains · Fressenville · Pont-Remy · Flixecourt · 50 · Albert
Criel-sur-Mer · Eu · Gamaches · Airaines · Amiens · Longueau · Corbie
Dieppe · Blangy-sur-Bresle · Oisemont · Picquigny · Ailly-sur-Somme · Villers-Bretonneux
St. Valery-en-Caux · Varengeville-sur-Mer · Envermeu · Hornoy-le-Bourg · Boves · Rosières-en-Santerre
Veulettes-sur-Mer · Offranville · Arques-la-Bataille · Aumale · Poix-de-Picardie · Conty · St. Just-en-Chaussée · Moreuil
St. Pierre-en-Port · Fontaine-le-Dun · Londinières · Les Grandes-Ventes · Grandvilliers · Breteuil · Montdidier
Fécamp · Yport · Cany-Barville · Tôtes · St. Saëns · Neufchâtel-en-Bray · Marseille-en-Beauvais · Crèvecœur-le-Grand
Étretat · Cap d'Antifer · Héricourt-en-Caux · Doudeville · Yerville · Forges-les-Eaux · Songeons · Cathédrale St. Étienne · Ferrières
Heuqueville · Criquetot-l'Esneval · Goderville · Yvetot · Clères · Buchy · Gournay-en-Bray · Beauvais · Clermont · Liancourt
Montivilliers · Bolbec · Caudebec-en-Caux · Barentin · Quincampoix · Malaunay · La Feuillie · Parc Saint Paul · Noailles · Mouy · Creil
Harfleur · St. Romain-de-Colbosc · Lillebonne · Abbaye St. Wandrille · Mont-St-Aignan · Lyons-la-Forêt · Auneuil · Sérifontaine · Ste. Maxence
Le Havre · St. Joseph · Château de Tancarville · Duclair · Maromme · Rouen · Étrépagny · Gisors · Méru · Chantilly · Senlis
Honfleur · Berville-sur-Mer · Jumièges · Abbaye de Jumièges · Le Grand-Quevilly · Boos · Fleury-sur-Andelle · Chaumont-en-Vexin · Neuilly-en-Thelle · Cathédrale Notre-Dame Senlis
Deauville · Pont-Audemer · Bourg-Achard · St. Étienne-du-Rouvray · Les Andelys · Les Thilliers-en-Vexin · L'Isle-Adam · Persan · Luzarches · Dammartin-en-Goële
Villers-sur-Mer · Pont-l'Évêque · Cormeilles · Le Breuil-en-Auge · Bourgtheroulde · Elbeuf · Château Gaillard · Magny-en-Vexin · Pontoise · Taverny · Sarcelles · Charles-de-Gaulle
Lisieux · Thiberville · Le Neubourg · Louviers · Pont-de-l'Arche · Acquigny · Gaillon · La Roche-Guyon · Marines · L'Isle-Adam · Cergy · Montmorency · St. Denis · Claye-Souilly
La Boissière · Brionne · Bernay · Beaumont-le-Roger · Évreux · Vernon · Giverny · Mantes-la-Jolie · Meulan · Les Mureaux · Argenteuil · Nanterre · Paris · Montreuil · Lagny-sur-Marne
Livarot · Orbec · Broglie · La Barre-en-Ouche · Conches-en-Ouche · Pacy-sur-Eure · Mantes-la-Ville · Maule · Septeuil · Poissy · St. Germain-en-Laye · Versailles · Vitry-sur-Seine · Créteil
Vimoutiers · La Neuve-Lyre · Damville · St. André-de-l'Eure · Ivry-la-Bataille · Château d'Anet · Anet · Houdan · Montfort-l'Amaury · Trappes · Palaiseau · Orsay · Brie-Comte-Robert
Trun · Rugles · Breteuil · Verneuil-sur-Avre · Nonancourt · Dreux · Chapelle Royale · Rambouillet · Élancourt · Versailles · Montlhéry · Évry · Melun
Argentan · La Ferté-Frênel · L'Aigle · Brezolles · Laons · Le Boullay-Mivoye · Nogent-le-Roi · Épernon · St. Arnoult · Arpajon · Brétigny-sur-Orge · Corbeil-Essonnes
Sées · Courtomer · Tourouvre · Ste. Anne · Châteauneuf-en-Thymerais · Maintenon · Gallardon · Dourdan · Étréchy · La Ferté-Alais · Dammarie-les-Lys
Le Mêle-sur-Sarthe · Mortagne-au-Perche · La Ferté-Vidame · Senonches · Digny · Cathédrale de Chartres · Ablis · Auneau · Étampes · Château de Courances · Fontainebleau
Mamers · Bellême · Rémalard · La Loupe · Courville · Mainvilliers · Chartres · Voise · Ouarville · Monnerville · Maisse · Avon
Marolles-les-Braults · Nogent-le-Rotrou · Thiron-Gardais · Illiers-Combray · Lucé · Sours · Plaine de la Beauce · Angerville · Sermaises · Malesherbes · La Chapelle-la-Reine · Nemours
Beaumont-sur-Sarthe · Ballon · La Ferté-Bernard · Authon-du-Perche · Brou · Bonneval · Voves · Charmont-en-Beauce · Puiseaux · Souppes-sur-Loing
Bonnétable · Montmirail · Chapelle Royale · Courtalain · Château de Châteaudun · Orgères-en-Beauce · Artenay · Pithiviers · Beaumont-du-Gâtinais · Château-Landon
Le Mans · Connerré · Vibraye · Arrou · Cloyes-sur-le-Loir · Châteaudun · Patay · Neuville-aux-Bois · Chilleurs-aux-Bois · Beaune-la-Rolande · Pannes
Allonnes · Parigné-l'Évêque · Bouloire · Mondoubleau · La Chapelle-Vicomtesse · Chevilly · Loury · Bellegarde · Ladon · Nogent-sur-Vernisson
Le Grand-Lucé · St. Calais · Morée · La Ferté-Villeneuil · Artenay · Fleury-les-Aubrais · Orléans · St-Jean-de-Braye · Châteauneuf-sur-Loire
Écommoy · Savigny-sur-Braye · Fréteval · Ouzouer-le-Marché · Olivet · Jargeau · Les Bordes · Sully-sur-Loire
Château-du-Loir · La Chartre-sur-le-Loir · Montoire-sur-le-Loir · Vendôme · Marchenoir · Meung-sur-Loire · Beaugency · Cléry-St-André · Château de Sully-sur-Loire · Gien
Le Lude · Montrichard · Villiers · Blois · Château de Chambord · Mer · La Ferté-St-Cyr · Vineuil · La Ferté-St-Aubin · Lamotte-Beuvron
Château-la-Vallière · Château-Renault · Herbault · Chaumont-sur-Loire · Cour-Cheverny · Neung-sur-Beuvron · Brinon-sur-Sauldre · Argent-sur-Sauldre
Tours · Vouvray · Amboise · Blois · Chambord · Château de Cheverny · Aubigny-sur-Nère · Châtillon-sur-Loire
St-Cyr-sur-Loire · Contres · Mur-de-Sologne · Millançay · Souesmes · Vailly-sur-Sauldre

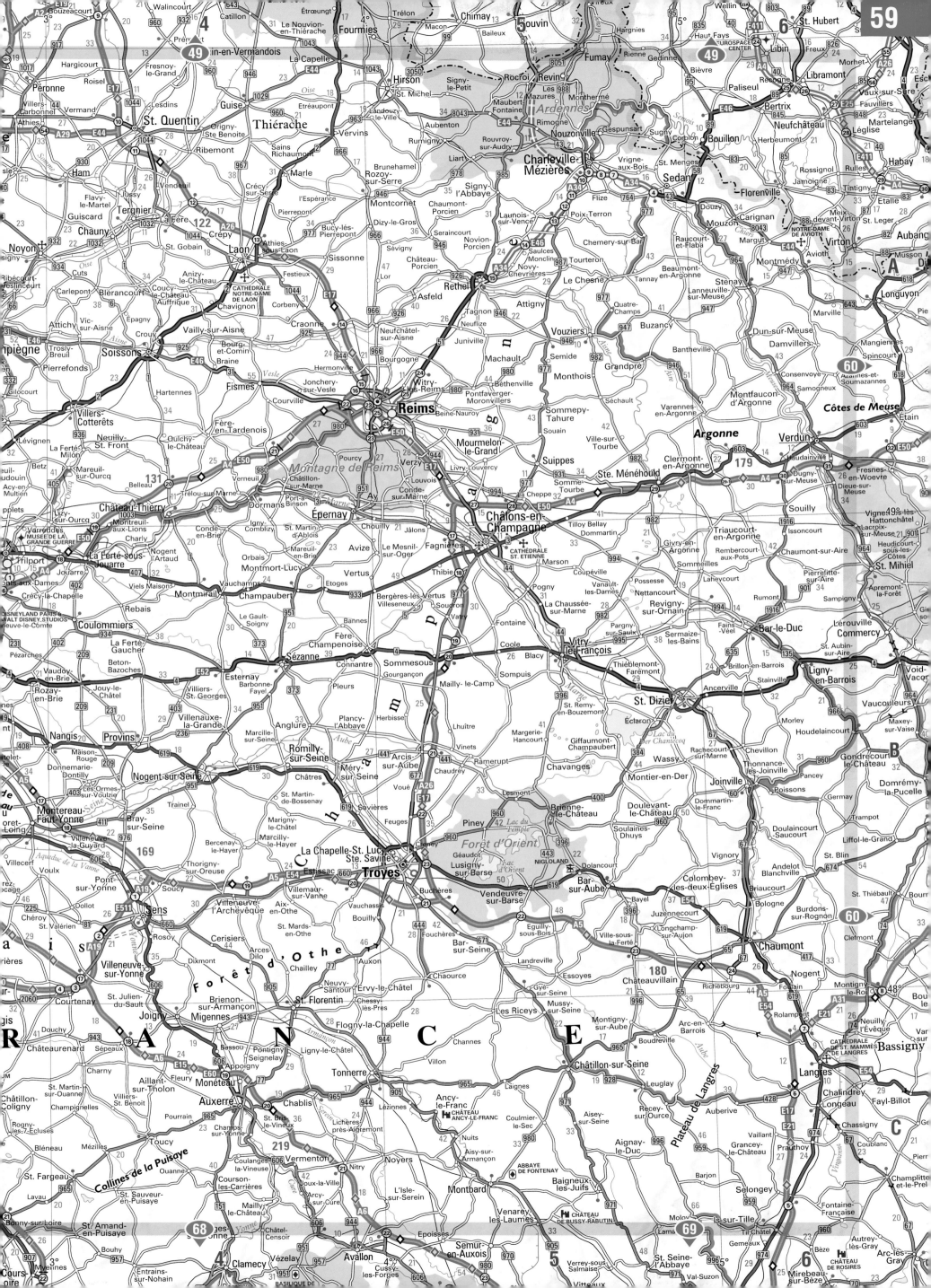

1   2   3

Hassfurt Zeil, Eltmann, Breitengussbach, Schesslitz, Memmelsdorf, Hollfeld, Bayreuth, Weidenberg, Bad Berneck, Schneeberg, Wunsiedel, Marktredwitz, Cheb, Slavkovský les, Touškov, Teplou

Bamberg, Stegaurach, Burgebrach, Hirschaid, Ebermannstadt, Fränkische Schweiz, Gössweinstein, Pegnitz, Speichersdorf, Kemnath, Erbendorf, Windischeschenbach, Neustadt, Floss, Weiden, Oberpfälzer Wald, Waldsassen, Mitterteich, Tirschenreuth, Mariánské Lázně, Planá, Tachov, Černošin

Steigerwald, Höchstadt, Forchheim, Baiersdorf, Gräfenberg, Hilpoltstein, Auerbach, Grafenwöhr, Pressath, Neustadt, Vohenstrauss, Waidhaus, Bor, Stříbro, Kladruby

Herzogenaurach, Erlangen, Eckental, Lauf, Schnaittach, Hersbruck, Sulzbach-Rosenberg, Hirschau, Amberg, Wernberg-Köblitz, Pfreimd, Nabburg, Oberviechtach, Horšovský Týn, Domažlice

Fürth, Zirndorf, Nürnberg, Nuremberg, Oberasbach, Feucht, Altdorf bei Nürnberg, Schwarzenfeld, Schwandorf, Neunburg vorm Wald, Rötz, Furth im Wald, Waldmünchen

Ansbach, Schwabach, Roth, Berg, Postbauer-Heng, Allersberg, Neumarkt, Velburg, Schmidmühlen, Burglengenfeld, Teublitz, Bruck, Roding, Cham, Chamerau, Kötzting, Viechtach

Windsbach, Merkendorf, Abenberg, Hiltpoltstein, Freystadt, Deining, Seubersdorf, Parsberg, Beratzhausen, Regenstauf, Nittenau, Wenzenbach, Wörth, Falkenstein, Bayerischer Wald

Gunzenhausen, Pleinfeld, Thalmässing, Greding, Beilngries, Berching, Dietfurt, Hemau, Regensburg, Obertraubling, Straubing, Bogen, Deggendorf

Weissenburg, Treuchtlingen, Rothenburg, Pappenheim, Kipfenberg, Pollenfeld, Denkendorf, Altmühltal, Kelheim, Bad Abbach, Schierling, Geiselhöring, Metten

Nördlingen, Monheim, Dollnstein, Eichstätt, Nassenfels, Köschung, Neustadt, Abensberg, Mindelstetten, Langquaid, Mallersdorf-Pfaffenberg, Plattling

Donauwörth, Tapfheim, Rennertshofen, Neuburg, Ingolstadt, Manching, Siegenburg, Rottenburg, Pilsting, Landau, Osterhofen

Höchstädt, Dillingen, Gundelfingen, Rain, Burgheim, Reichertshofen, Geisenfeld, Wolnzach, Mainburg, Essenbach, Dingolfing, Eichendorf

Burgau, Wertingen, Meitingen, Schrobenhausen, Pfaffenhofen, Pförring, Au, Obermünchen, Altdorf, Landshut, Arnstorf, Johanniskirchen

Gersthofen, Neusäss, Langweid, Aichach, Kühbach, Gerolsbach, Moosburg, Geisenhausen, Vilsbiburg, Pfarrkirchen, Eggenfelden

Augsburg, Friedberg, Petershausen, Allershausen, Freising, Neufahrn, Berglern, Taufkirchen, Velden, Neumarkt St. Veit

Zusmarshausen, Dinkelscherben, Bobingen, Mering, Markt Indersdorf, Erdweg, Unterschleissheim, Dachau, Erding, Dorfen, Ampfing, Mühldorf, Altötting, Neuötting, Burghausen

Krumbach, Schwabmünchen, Königsbrunn, Merching, Fürstenfeldbruck, Puchheim, Germering, Olching, Ismaning, Markt Schwaben, Isen, Haag, Wasserburg, Garching, Burgkirchen

Mindelheim, Türkheim, Buchloe, Landsberg, Gauting, München, Munich, Unterhaching, Ebersberg, Grafing, Assling, Kirchweidach, Simbach

Bad Wörishofen, Diessen, Starnberg, Herrsching, Sauerlach, Schäftlarn, Glonn, Rott, Obing, Trostberg, Tittmoning, Ostermiething

Obergünzburg, Kaufbeuren, Weilheim, Wolfratshausen, Holzkirchen, Geretsried, Feldkirchen-Westerham, Bad Aibling, Kolbermoor, Rosenheim, Prien, Traunreut, Freilassing

Schongau, Peiting, Penzberg, Miesbach, Hausham, Stephanskirchen, Chiemsee, Grassau, Bernau, Siegsdorf, Bad Reichenhall

Marktoberdorf, Murnau, Bad Tölz, Tegernsee, Rottach-Egern, Ruhpolding, Reit im Winkl, Berchtesgaden

Füssen, Garmisch-Partenkirchen, Oberammergau, Ettal, Lenggries, Bayrischzell, Oberaudorf, Kufstein, Kitzbühel, Saalfelden

Mittenwald, Achenkirch, Brandenberg, Wörgl, St. Johann in Tirol

156, 135, 132, 124, 125, 171, 176, 186, 109

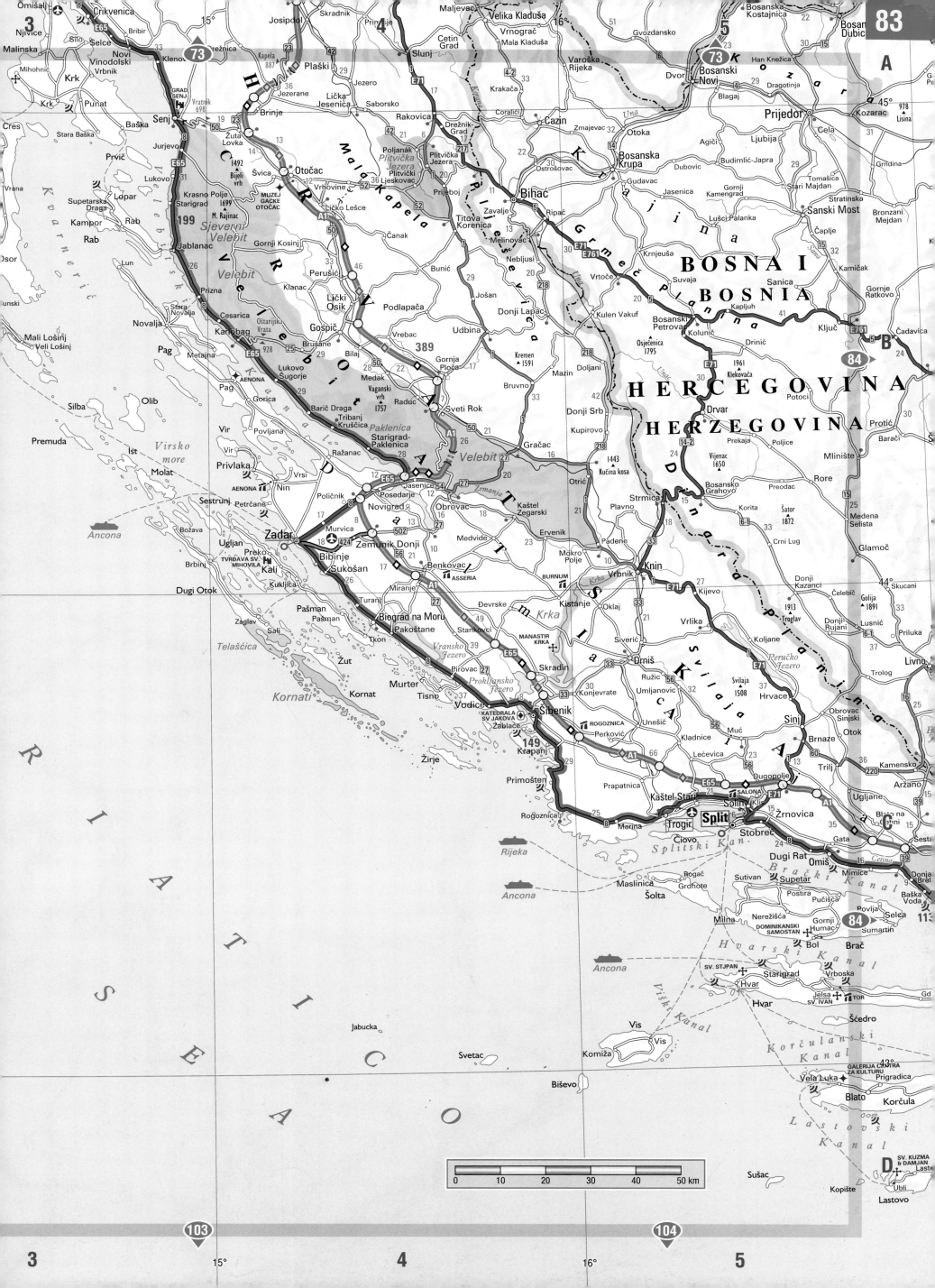

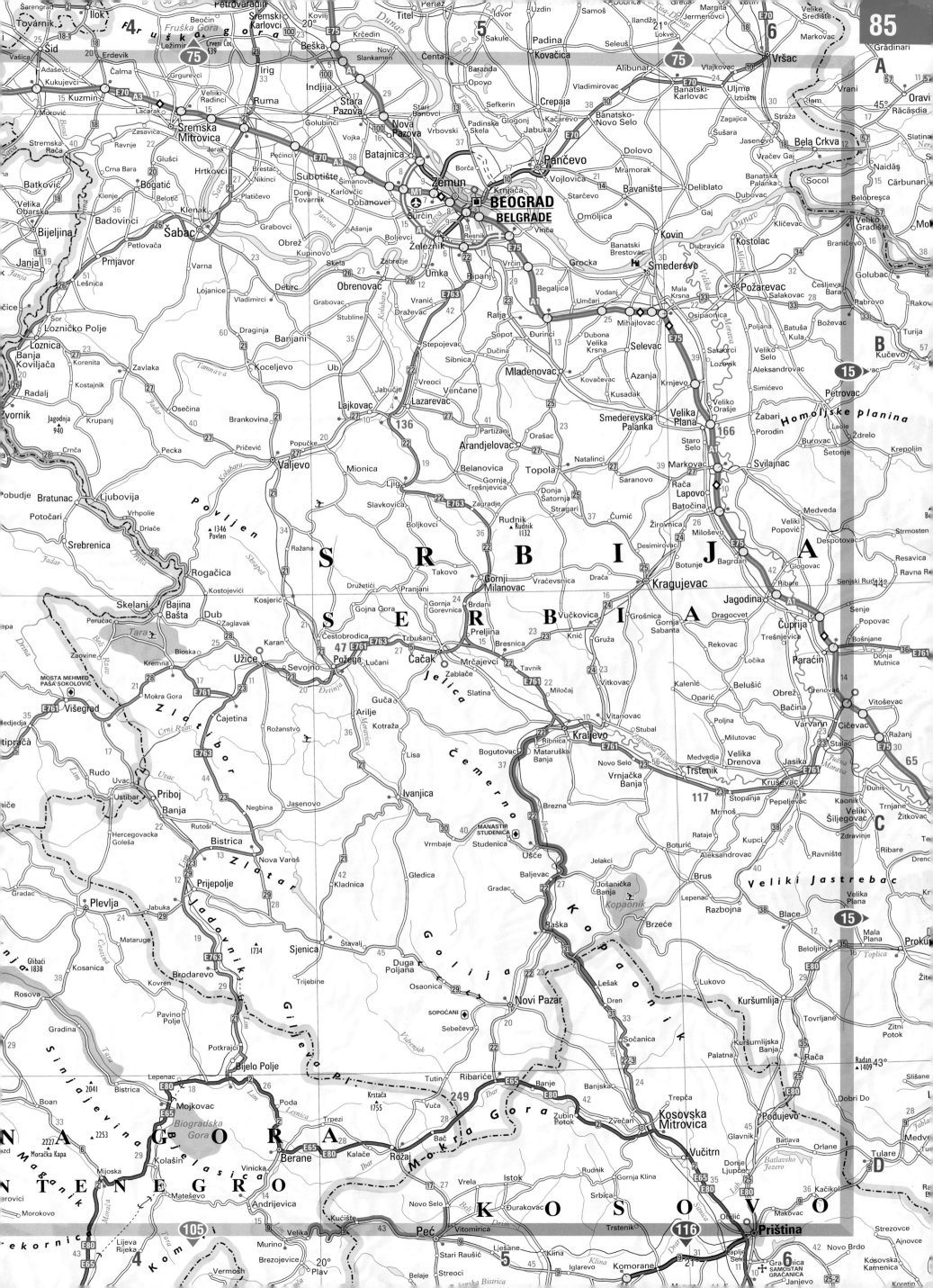

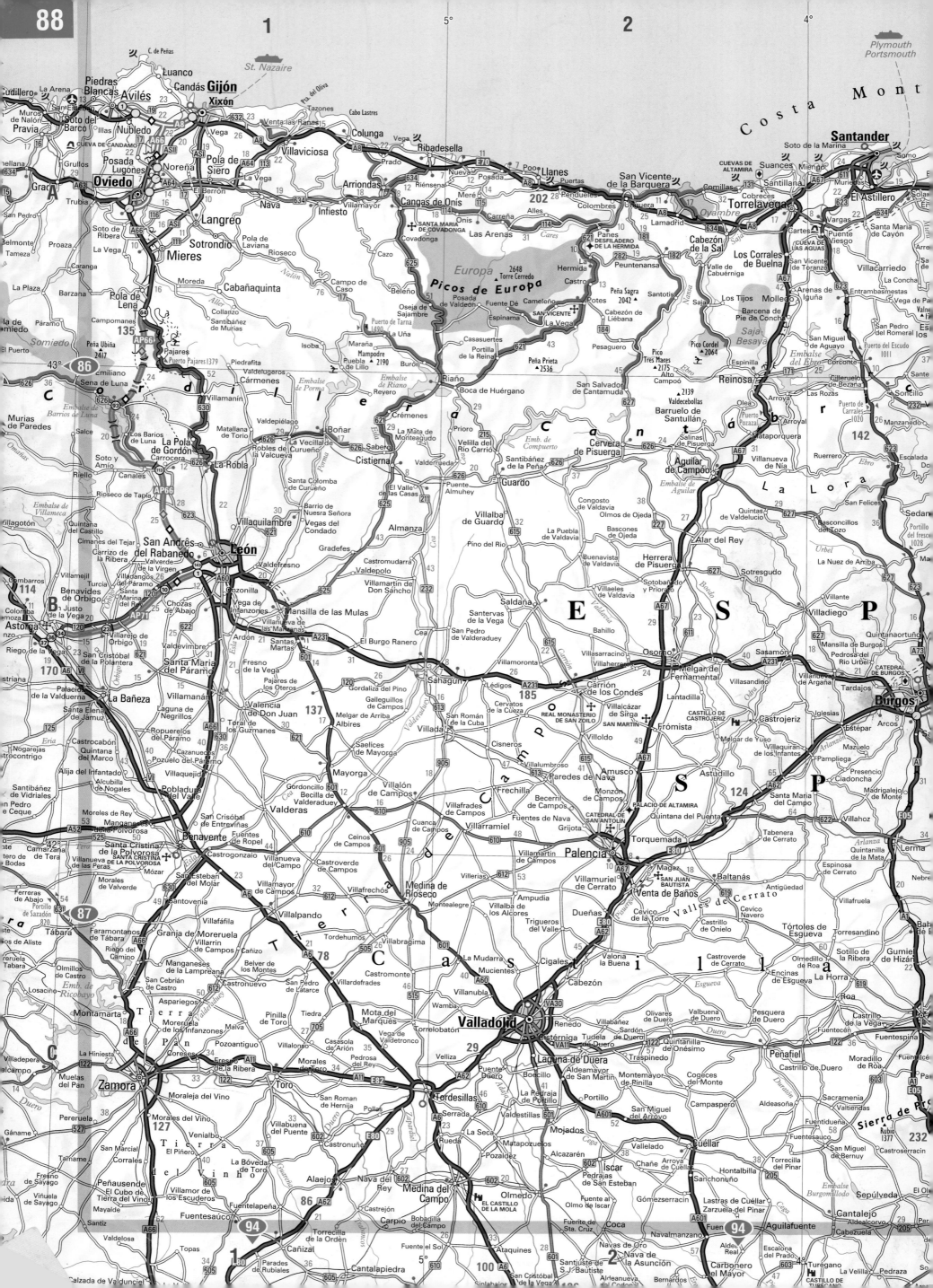

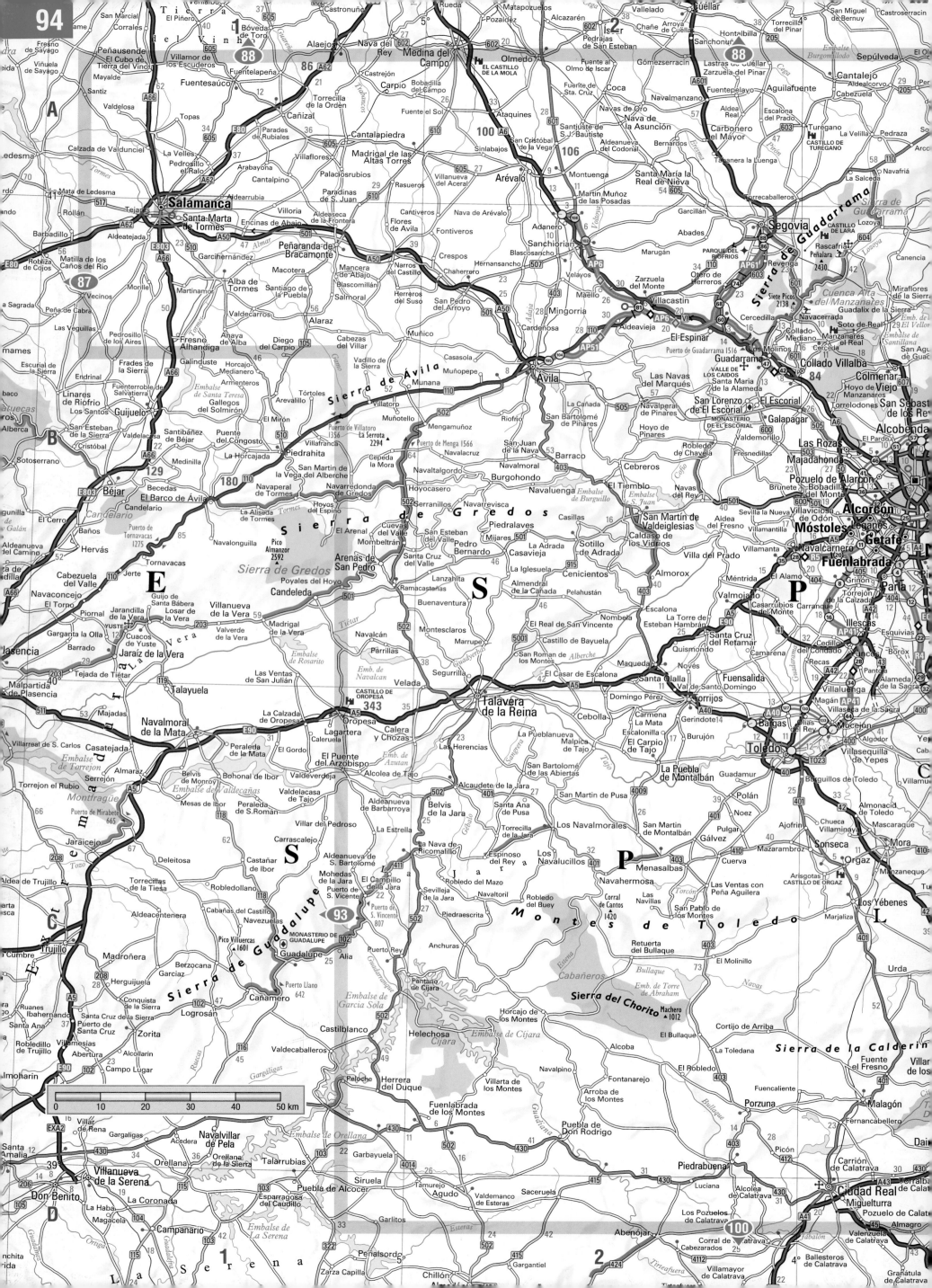

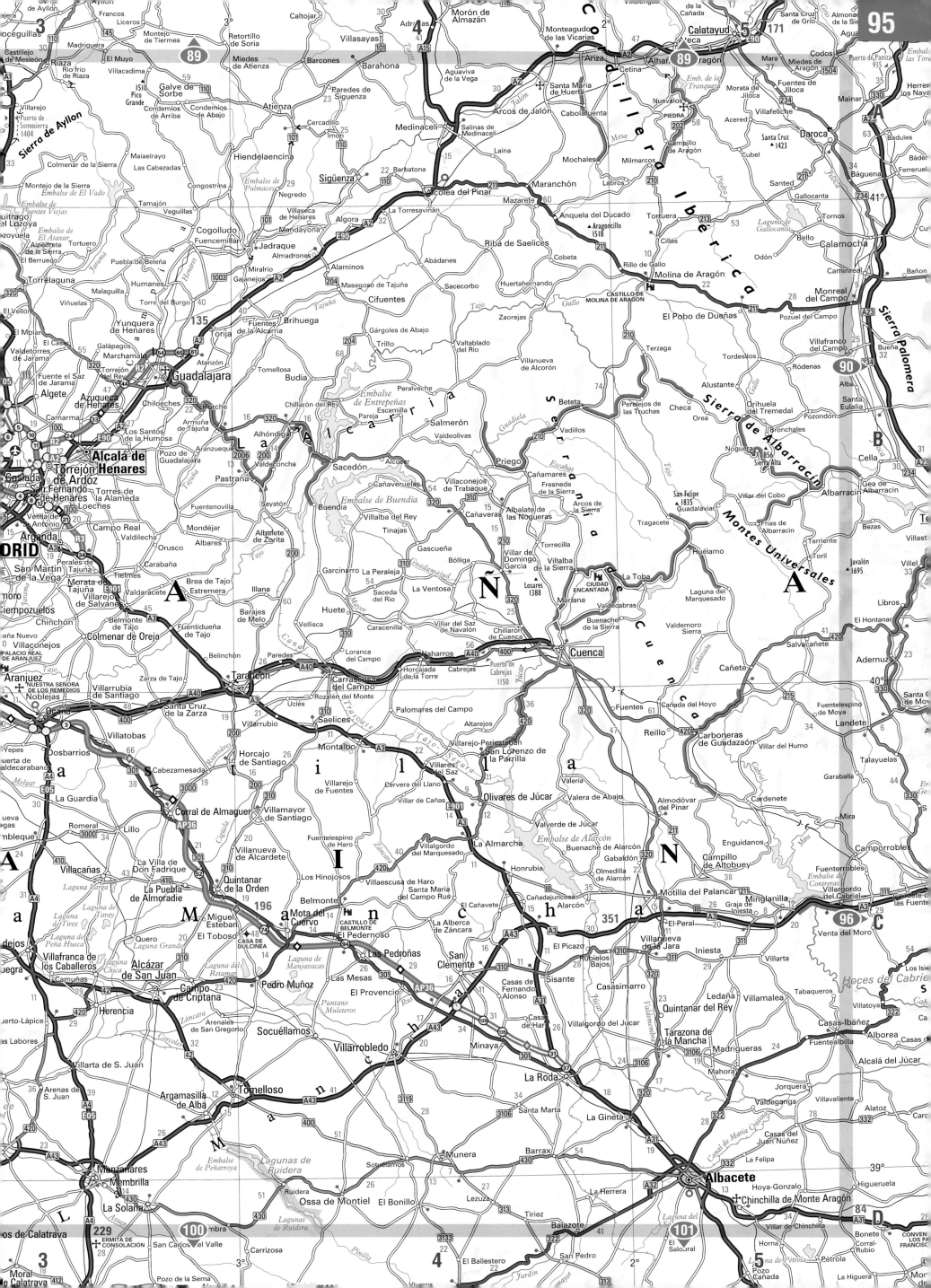

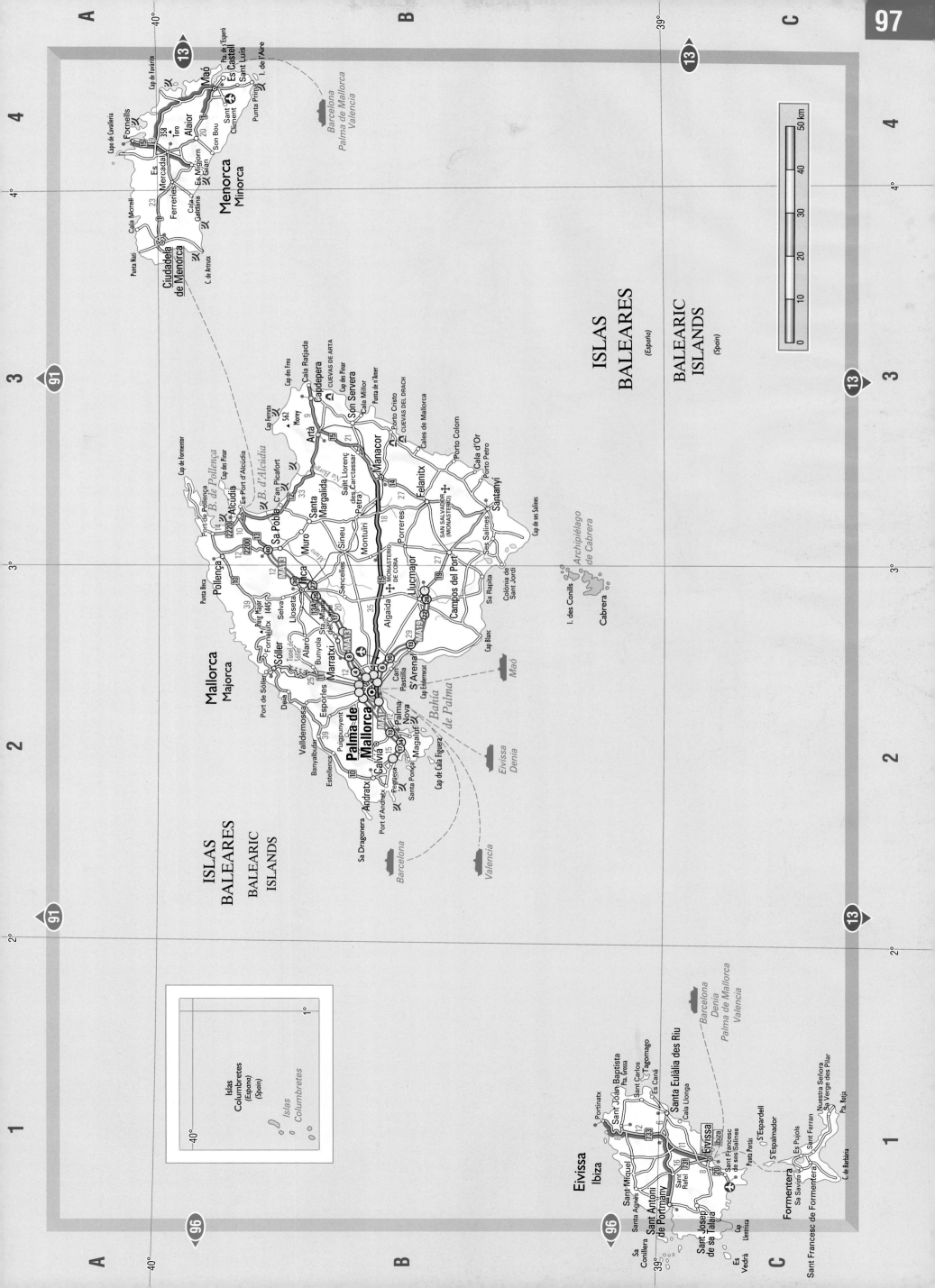

ISLAS
BALEARES
(España)

BALEARIC
ISLANDS
(Spain)

Menorca
Minorca

Mallorca
Majorca

ISLAS
BALEARES

BALEARIC
ISLANDS

Eivissa
Ibiza

Islas
Columbretes
(España)
(Spain)

Islas
Columbretes

Formentera

PARCO ARCHEOLOGICO
METAPONTO
Lido di Metaponto

Lizzano
Pulsano
Taranto
San Pancrazio
Salentino
Avetrana
Maruggio

San Cataldo
Campi
Salentina
Lecce
Monteroni di Lecce
San Cesário
di Lecce
San Foca
Vérnole
Melendugno
Torre dell'Orso

5

107

Veglie
Léquile
Leverano
Copertino
Calimera
Martano

Porto Cesáreo
Galatina
Soleto
Otranto

Nardó
Galátone
Maglie
Uggiano la Chiesa

Santa Maria al Bagno
Cutrofiano
Poggiardo

Gallípoli
Aléio
Parábita
Collepasso
Nociglia
Diso
Santa Cesárea Terme
GROTTA DI ROMANELLI
& ZINZULUSA

Sant'Andrea
Casarano
Miggiano
Castro

Taviano
Rácale
Taurisano
Tricase

Ugento
Presicce
Alessano

Marina di Nováglie
Gagliano del Capo

Castrignano del Capo
Marina di Léuca

C. Santa Maria di Léuca

A

40°

G o l f o
d i
T á r a n t o

Trionto
Cariati
Pta. Fiume Nicá

Campana
Crúcoli
Pta. Alice

Cirò
Cirò Marina

Umbriático
San Nicola
dell'Alto

vanni in Fiore
Strongoli

Vitravo
Neto

Cotronei
Santa Severina
Roccabernarda

Mesoraca
Scandale
Crotone

Cutro

Crópani
Ísola di Capo Rizzuto

Botricello
C. Colonna

C. Rizzuto

B

116

39°

M A R E

I O N I O

fo di
llace

I O N I A N

S E A

Gozo
San
Dimitri
Pt
Pozzallo

Victoriá
(Rabat)
Mgarr
Comino

Mellieha
San Pawl il-Bahar

Mosta
Sliema
Valletta
Birkirkara
Rabat
Paola

MALTA
Birzebbugia

Filfla
Benghisa Pt

14° 30'

14° 30'

117

C

38°

| 0 | 10 | 20 | 30 | 40 | 50 km |

D

15

15

17°

4

18°

5

19°

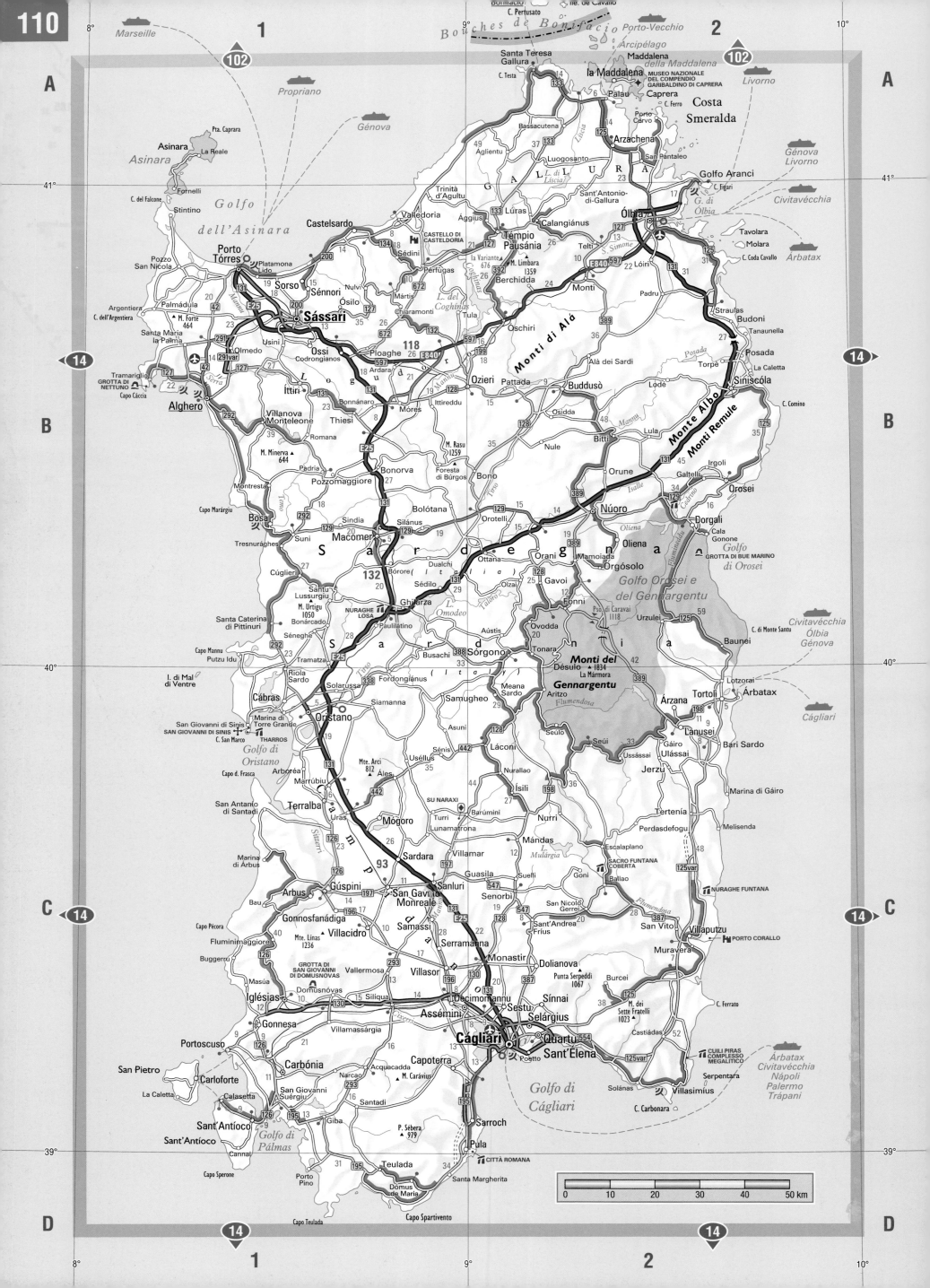

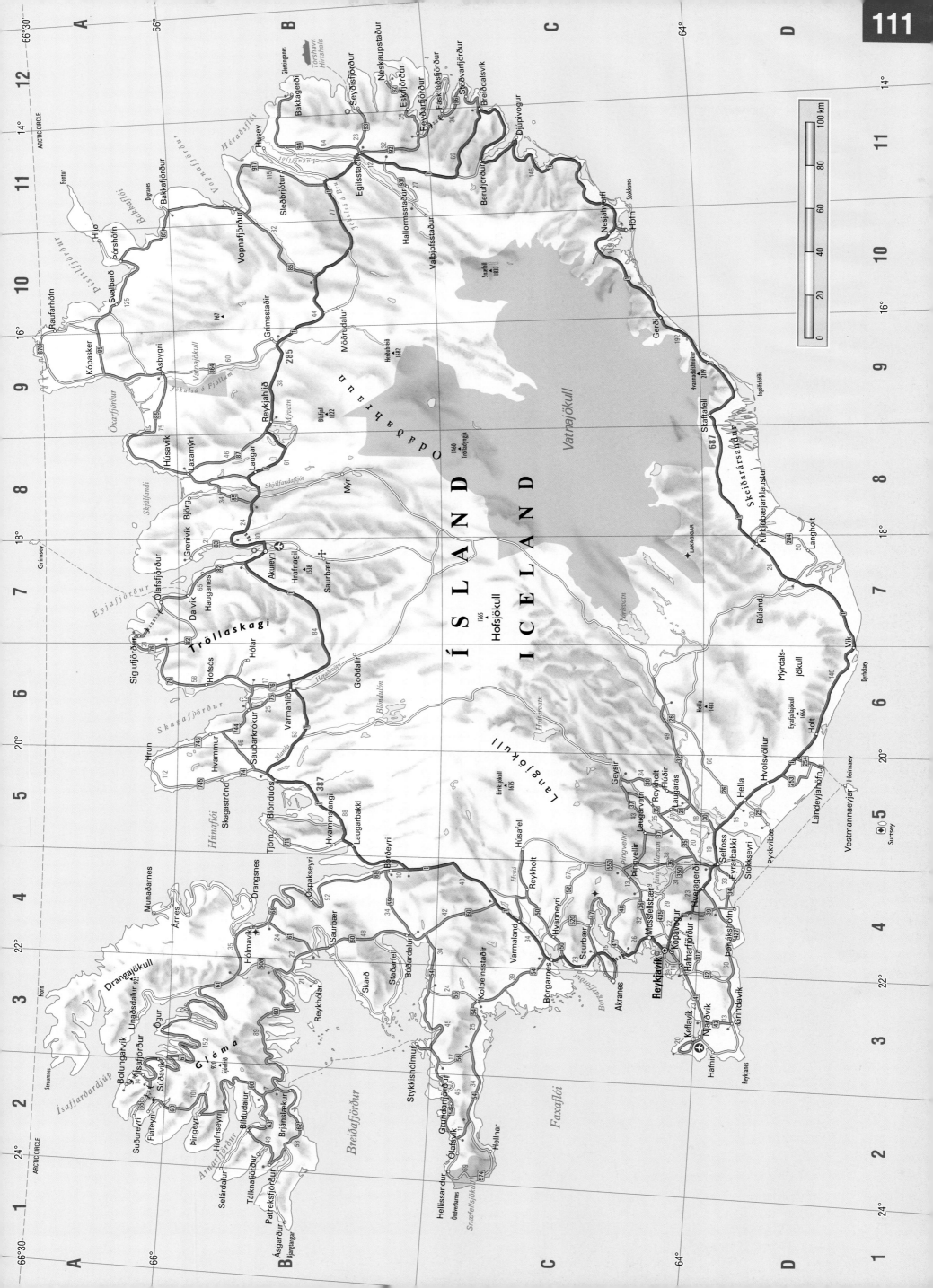

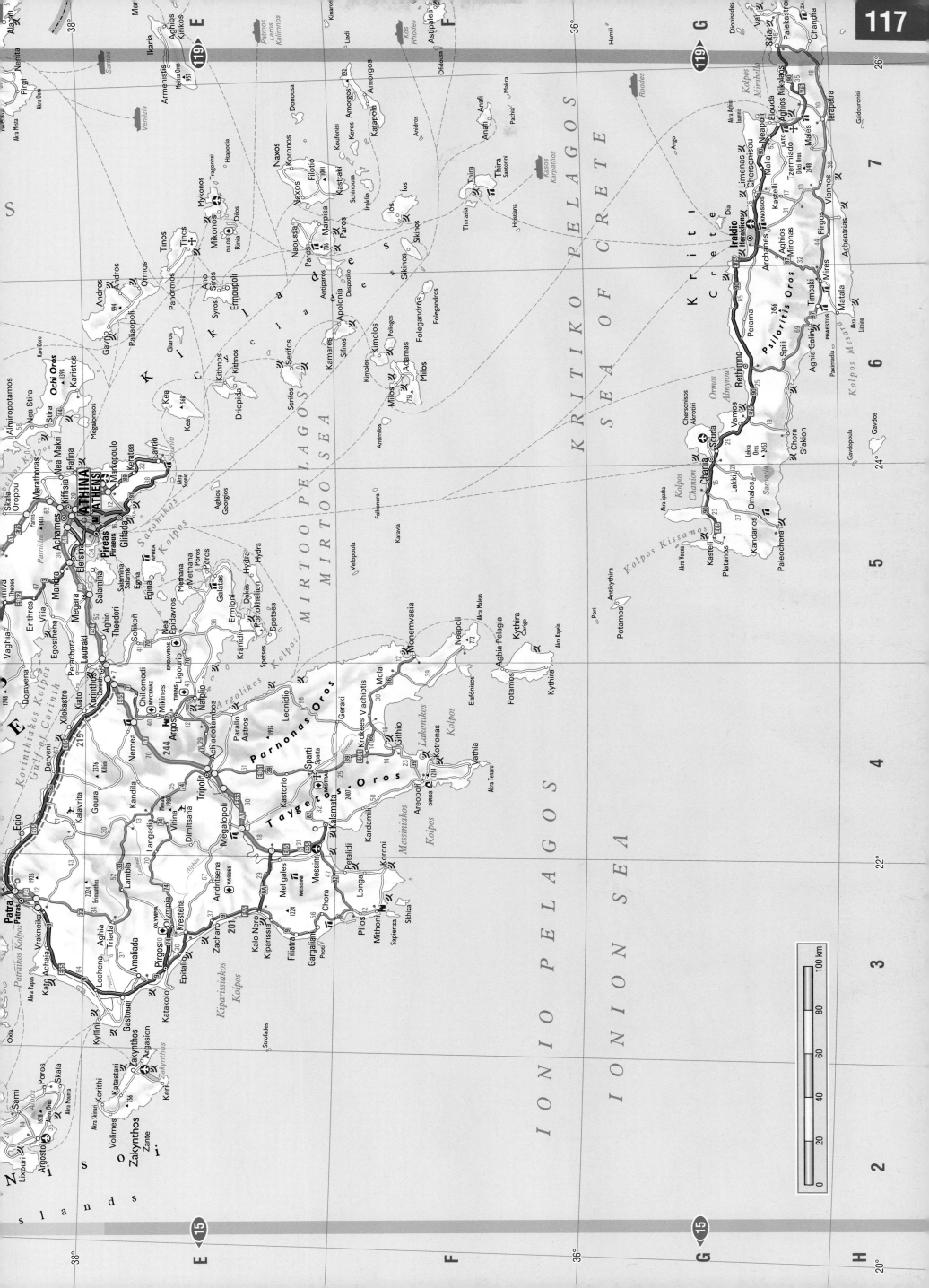

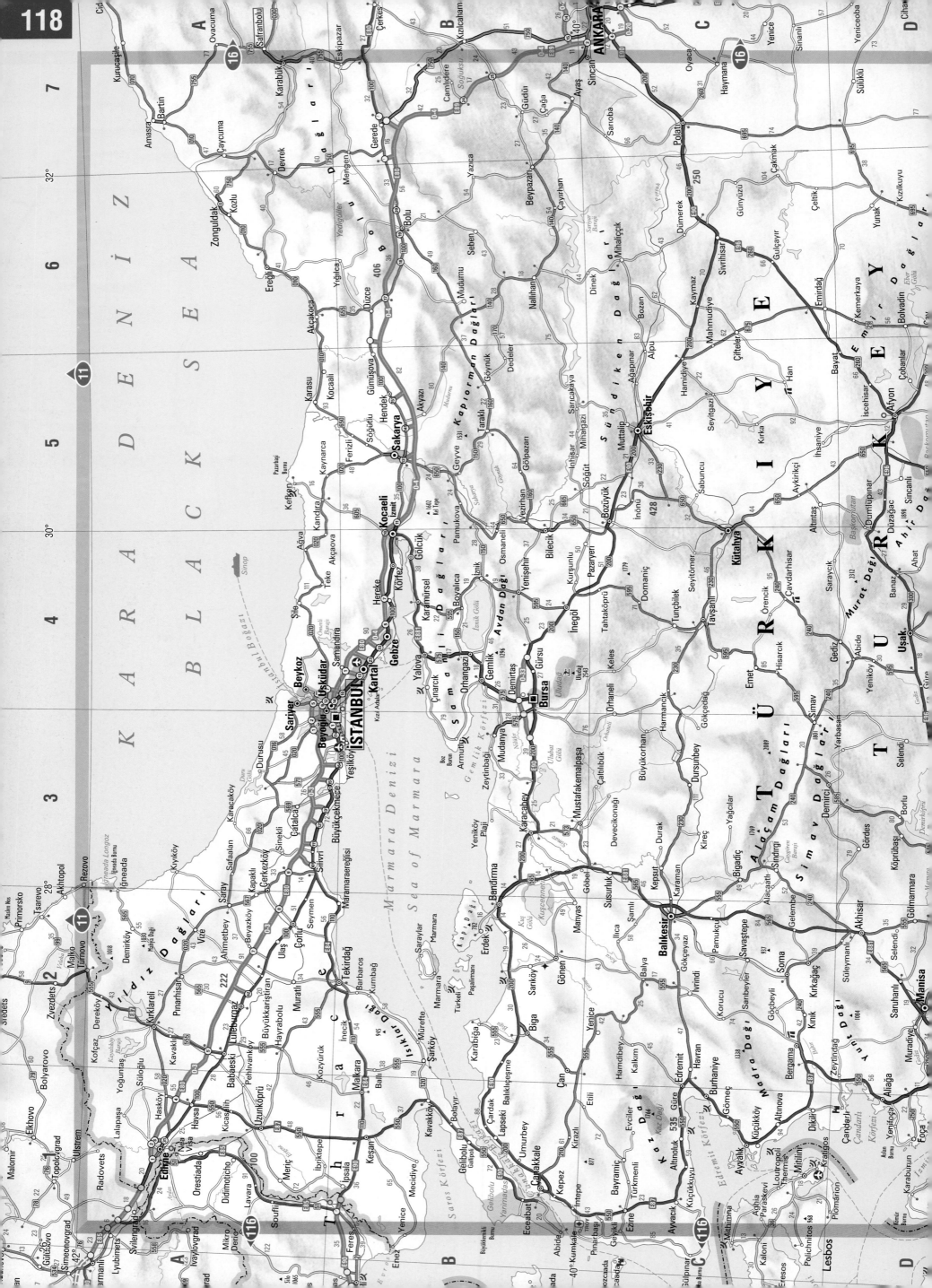

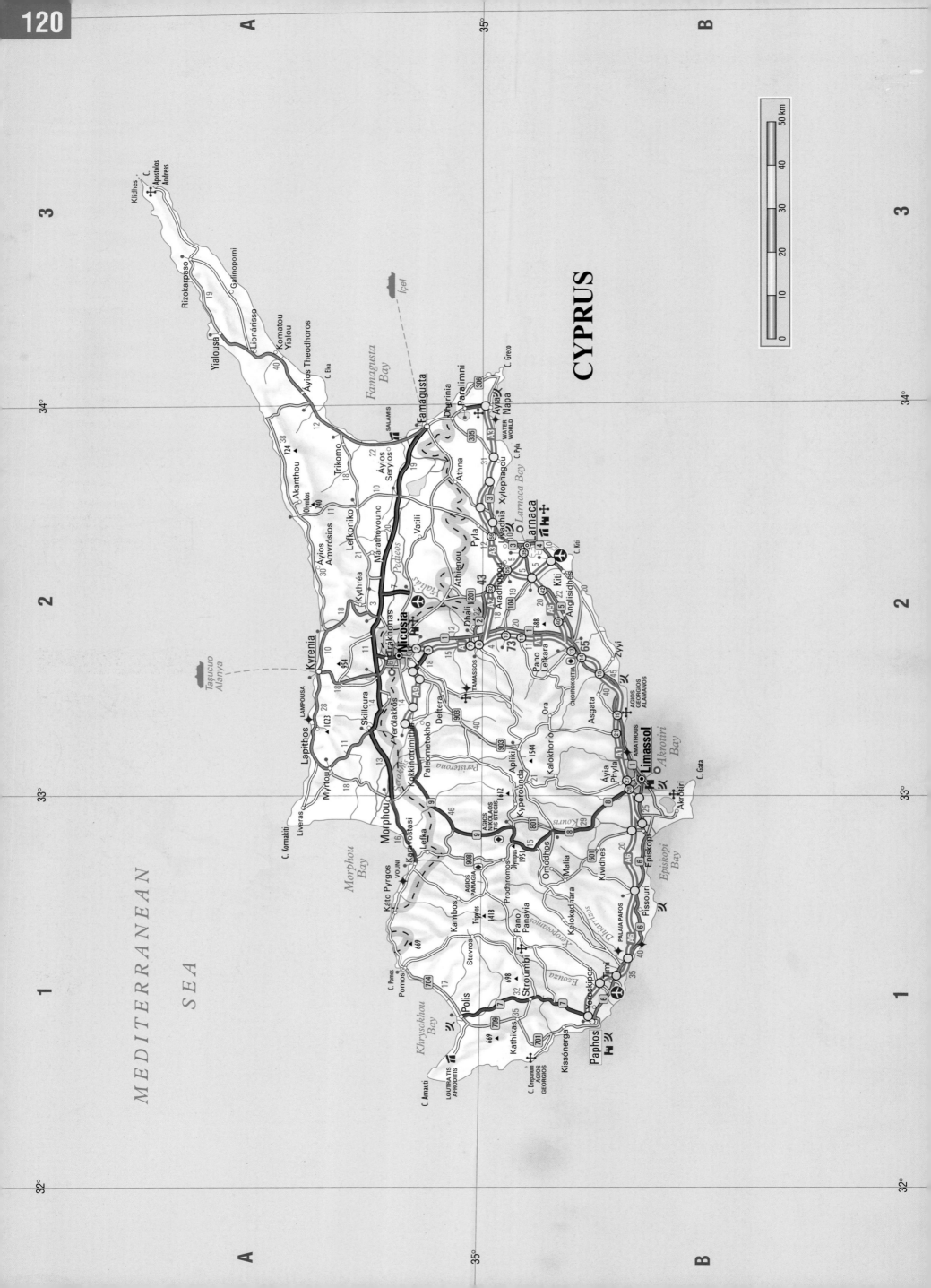

MEDITERRANEAN SEA

CYPRUS

50 km
40
30
20
10
0

Kilidhes C. Apostolos Andreas
Rizokarpaso
Galinoporni
Lionárisso
Komatou Yialou
Yialoúsa
Ayios Theodhoros
C. Eléa
Trikomo
Akanthou
Olymbos
Lefkoniko
Vatili
Ayios Seryios
SALAMIS
Famagusta
Famagusta Bay
Dherínia
Paralimni
Ayía Nápa
WATER WORLD
C. Greco
Athna
Xylophagou
Pyla
Athiénou
Livádhia
Larnaca
Larnaca Bay
Kíti
C. Kíti
Anglisídhes
Aradhíppou
Dhali
TAMASSOS
Tamassos
Pano Lefkara
Kythréa
Marathóvouno
Pedieos
Yialias
Nicosia
Trákhonas
Kyrenia
LAMPOUSA
Skilloura
Verólakkos
Dettera
Ora
Asgata
Zyyí
Choirokoitía
AGIOS GEORGIOS ALAMANOS
AMATHOUS
Limassol
Limassol Bay
Akrotiri
C. Gata
Akrotiri Bay
Ayia Phyla
Kalokhorió
Aplíki
Kyperoúnda
Ora
Peristerona
Paleometokho
Kokkinotrimithía
Morphou
Morphou Bay
Karavostasi
Lefka
Myrtou
Liveras
Lapithos
C. Kormakíti
AGIOS NIKOLAOS TIS STEGIS
Moutoullas
Agros
Kalokhorió
Kívidhes
Episkopi
Episkopi Bay
Pissouri
PALAIA PAFOS
Kíthima
Omodhos
Malia
Koúris
Diarizos
Ezoúsa
Kelokédhara
Xeropotamos
Pano Panayía
AGIOS PANAGIA
Olympus
Prodhromos
Pano Panayia
Tríplos
Kambos
Stavros
C. Pomos
Pomos
Polis
Khrysokhou Bay
Kathikas
Stroumbi
Kissónerga
Paphos
C. Arnaúti
LOUTRA TIS AFRODITIS
C. Drepanum
AGIOS GEORGIOS
Yeroskipos
Timi

Taşucuo Alanya
İçel

CYPRUS

City plans • Plans de villes
Stadtpläne • Piante di città

Motorway	Autoroute	Autobahn	Autostrada
Major through route	Route principale majeur	Hauptstrecke	Strada di grande communicazione
Through route	Route principale	Schnellstrasse	Strada d'importanza regionale
Secondary road	Route secondaire	Nebenstrasse	Strada d'interesse locale
Dual carriageway	Chaussées séparées		
Other road	Autre route	Zweispurig Schnellstrasse	Strada a carreggiate doppie
Tunnel	Tunnel	Nebenstrecke	Altra strada
Limited access / pedestrian road	Rue réglementée / rue piétonne	Tunnel	Galleria stradale
One-way street	Sens unique	Beschränkter Zugang / Fussgängerzone	Strada pedonale / a accesso limitato
Parking	Parc de stationnement	Einbahnstrasse	Senso unico
Motorway number	Numéro d'autoroute	Parkplatz	Parcheggio
National road number	Numéro de route nationale	Autobahnnummer	Numero di autostrada
European road number	Numéro de route européenne	Nationalstrassen- nummer	Numero di strada nazionale
Destination	Destination	Europäische Strassennummer	Numero di strada europea
Car ferry	Bac passant les autos	Ziel	Destinazione
Railway	Chemin de fer	Autofähre	Traghetto automobili
Rail / bus station	Gare / gare routière	Eisenbahn	Ferrovia
Underground, metro station	Station de métro	Bahnhof / Busstation	Stazione ferrovia / pullman
Cable car	Téléférique	U-Bahnstation	Metropolitano
Abbey, cathedral	Abbaye, cathédrale	Drahtseilbahn	Funivia
Church of interest	Église intéressante	Abtei, Kloster, Kathedrale	Abbazia, duomo
Synagogue	Synagogue	Interessante Kirche	Chiesa da vedere
Hospital	Hôpital	Synagoge	Sinagoga
Police station	Police	Krankenhaus	Ospedale
Post office	Bureau de poste	Polizeiwache	Polizia
Tourist information	Office de tourisme	Postamt	Ufficio postale
Place of interest	Autre curiosité	Informationsbüro	Ufficio informazioni turistiche
		Sonstige Sehenswürdigkeit	Luogo da vedere

Approach maps • Agglomérations
Carte régionale • Regionalkarte

Toll motorway – with motorway number	Autoroute à péage – avec numéro d'autoroute	Gebührenpflichtige Autobahn – mit Autobahnnummer	Autostrada a pedaggio – con numero
Toll-free motorway – with European road number	Autoroute – avec numéro de route européenne	Gebührenfreie Autobahn – Europäische Strassennummer	Autostrada – con numero di strada europea
Pre-pay motorway – vignette required	Autoroute – 'vignette'	Autobahn – 'vignette'	Autostrada – 'vignette'
Motorway services	Aire de service	Autobahnservice	Area di servizio autostradale
Motorway junction full access, restricted access	Échangeur d'autoroute – accès libre, accès reglémenté	Autobahnkreuz – voller/begrenzter Zugang	Raccordi autostradali – completo/parziali
Under construction	En construction	Im Bau	In construzione
Tunnel	Tunnel	Tunnel	Galleria stradale
Major route dual carriageway single carriageway	Route principale chausées séparées chausée sans séparation	Hauptstrecke – zweispurige Schnellstrasse	Strada di grande communicazione carreggiata doppia carreggiata unica
Secondary route dual carriageway single carriageway	Route secondaire chausées séparées chausée sans séparation	Nebenstrasse – zweispurige Schnellstrasse	Strada d'interesse locale – carreggiata doppia carreggiata unica
Other road	Autre route	Nebenstrecke	Altra strada
Car ferry	Bac passant les autos	Autofähre	Traghetto automobili
Destination	Destination	Ziel	Destinazione
Railway	Chemin de fer	Eisenbahn	Ferrovia
Railway station	Gare	Hauptbahnhof	Stazione ferrovia
Height – in metres	Altitude – en mètres	Höhe – über dem Meeresspiegel	Altezza in metri
Airport	Aéroport principal	Flughafen	Aeroporto
Airfield	Autre aéroport	Flugplatz	Aerodromo/ campo d'aviazione
City plan coverage area	Région de plan de ville	Vom Stadtplan abgedecktes Gebiet	Area della pianta della città

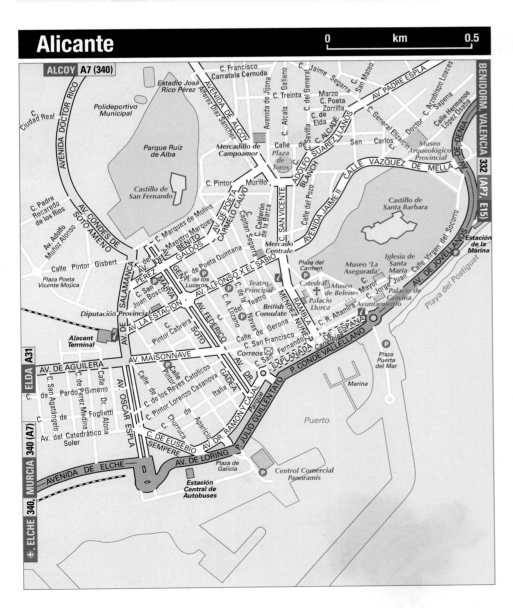

Alicante

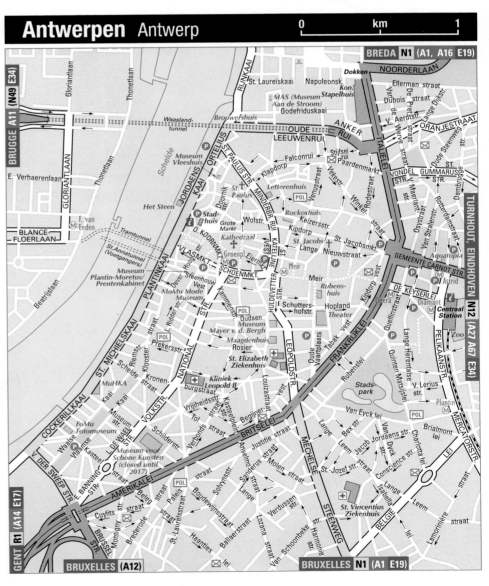

Antwerpen Antwerp

Amsterdam

0 km 2

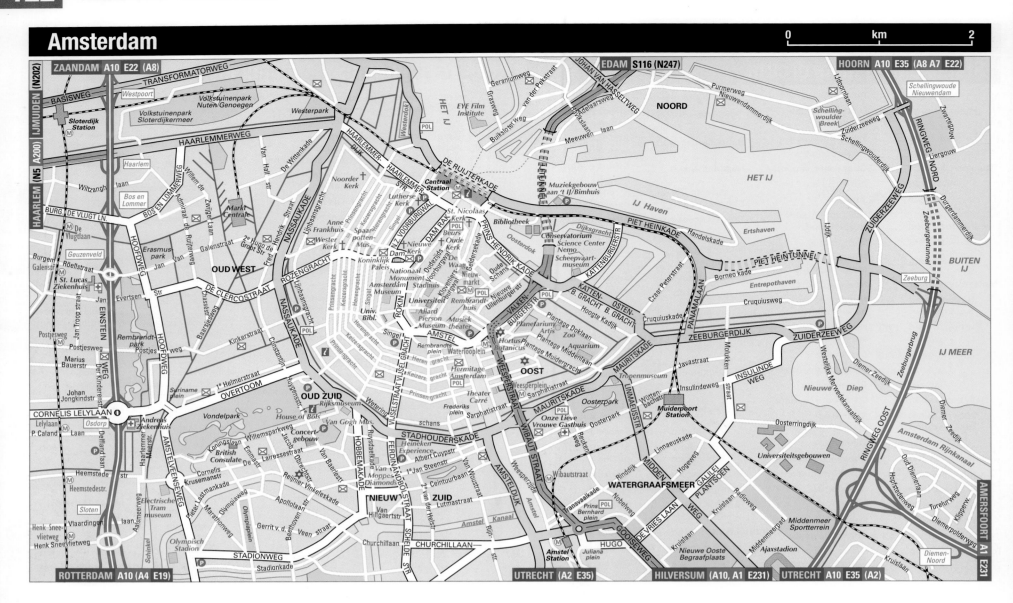

Amsterdam

0 km 5

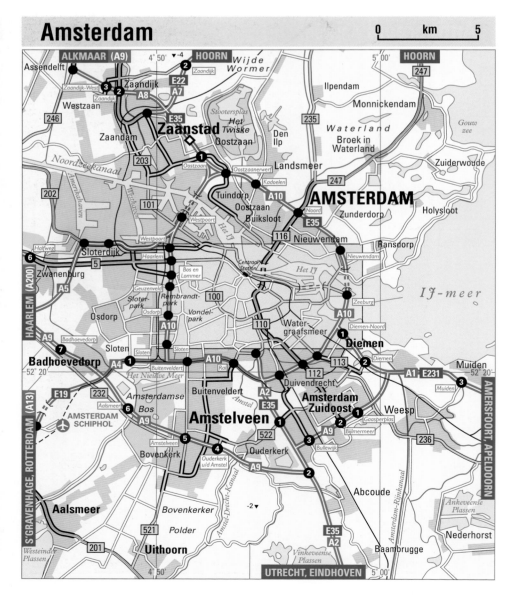

Athina Athens

0 km 5

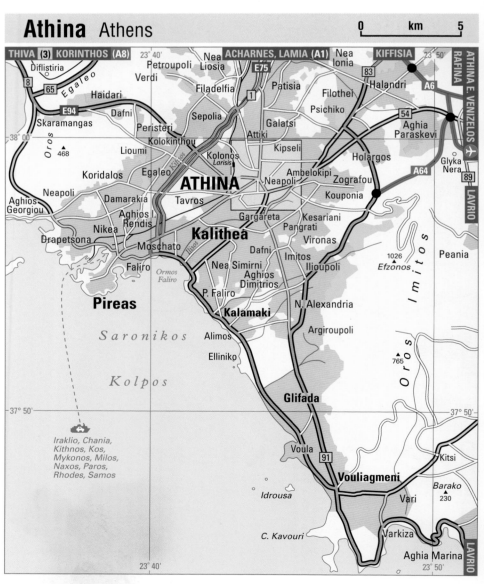

Athina Athens

0 km 1

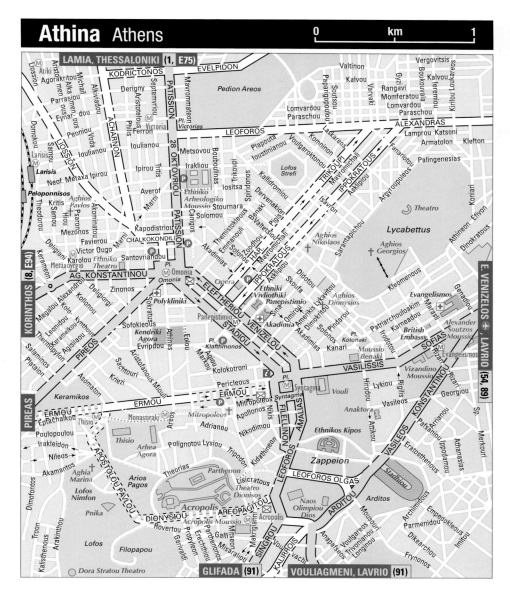

LAMIA, THESSALONIKI (1, E75)

KODRICTONOS
EVELPIDON
Pedion Areos
Valtinon
Kalvou
Vergovitsis
Soutzou
Papargiropoulou
Rangavi
Momferatou
Boukouvala
Parascho

ALEXANDRAS
Lomvardou
Lamprou Katsoni
Parascho
Armatolon
Klefton

Victoria

Metsovou
Ipirou
Iasiou
Stournara

KORINTHOS (8, E94)
PIREAS

Larisis
Neof. Metaxa Ipirou
Peloponnisos

AG. KONSTANTINOU
Omonia

Polykliniki

Lycabettus

Aghios
Nikolaos

Aghios
Georgios

ERMOU
VASILISSIS

Syntagma
Vouli

ERMOU
Mitropoleos

Thisio
Monastiraki

Zappeion

Acropolis
Parthenon

DIONYSIOU
Naos
Olimpiou
Dios
Stadiou

Filopapou

© Dora Stratou Theatre

GLIFADA (91)   VOULIAGMENI, LAVRIO (91)

Basel

0 km 0.5

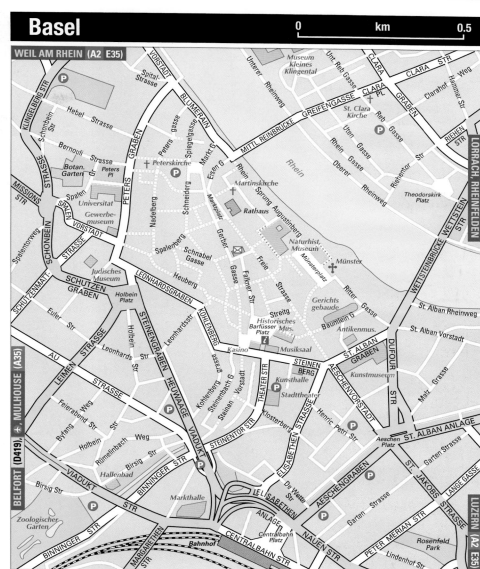

WEIL AM RHEIN (A2 E35)

Museum
kleines
Klingental

CLARA STR

St. Clara
Kirche

Rhein

Universität
Gewerbe-
museum

Rathaus

Münster

Judisches
Museum

Kasino
Musiksaal

Bahnhof

Centralbahn

LUZERN (A2 E35)

Barcelona

0 km 5

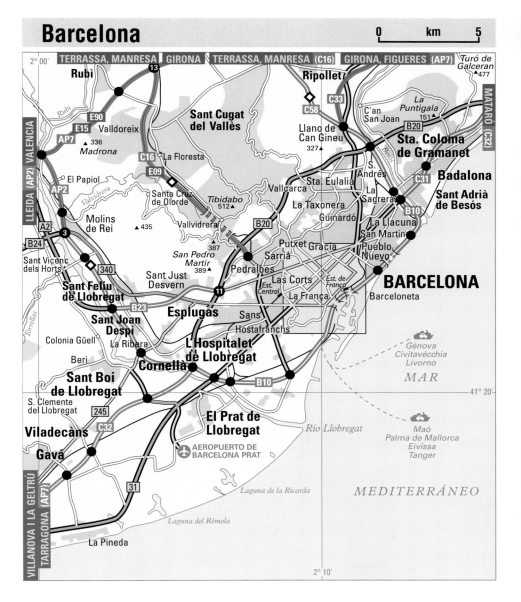

TERRASSA, MANRESA GIRONA TERRASSA, MANRESA (C16) GIRONA, FIGUERES (AP7)

Turó de
Galceran
477

Rubí
Ripollet

Sant Cugat
del Vallès

Valldoreix
C58
C33

Sta. Coloma
de Gramanet

Llano de
Can Gineu

Badalona

La Floresta

Vallcarca

Sta. Eulalia

Sant Adrià
de Besós

Santa Cruz
de Olorde

Tibidabo
512

La Taxonera
Guinardó

San Martín

Sarrià
Gracia

Pueblo
Nuevo

San Pedro
Martir

Pedralbes
Las Corts

BARCELONA
Barceloneta

Sant Feliu
de Llobregat

Sans
Hostafranchs

MAR

Esplugas

L'Hospitalet
de Llobregat

Cornellà

Génova
Civitavécchia
Livorno

Sant Boi
de Llobregat

Viladecans

El Prat de
Llobregat

Maó
Palma de Mallorca
Eivissa
Tanger

Gavá

AEROPUERTO DE
BARCELONA PRAT

MEDITERRÁNEO

La Pineda

Laguna de la Ricarda

Laguna del Rémola

Barcelona

0 km 1

MATARÓ (C32)

Sagrada
Familia

DIAGONAL

AVINGUDA

La Pedrera

MATARÓ (C32)

Parc
de la
Ciutadella

Parc
Zoológic

BARCELONA

Palau de
la Música
Catalana

Catedral

Estació
de França

Museu
Picasso

Sta. Maria
del Mar

Barceloneta

Plaça
d'Espanya

AVINGUDA DEL PARAL·LEL

World
Trade
Centre

Sant
Sebastià

Poble
Espanyol

Palau Nacional
Museu d'Art

Montjuïc

Parc de
Montjuïc

Castell de
Montjuïc

Palau
Sant Jordi

Estadi
Olympic

Mar
Mediterráneo

LLEIDA (AP7, AP2 E90), VALENCIA (C32, AP7 E15)

Berlin

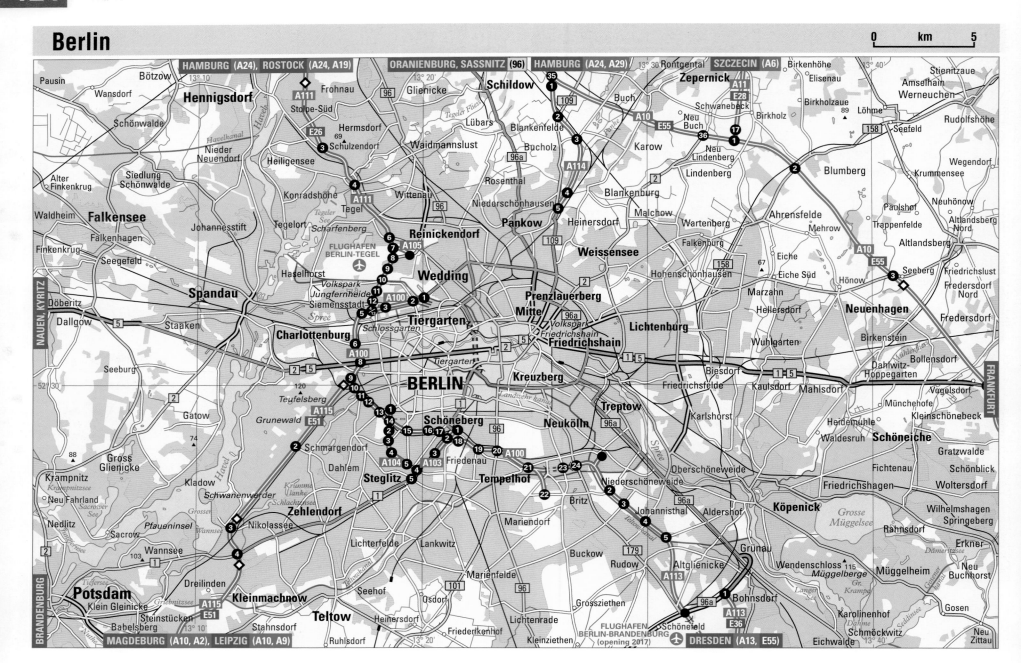

Berlin

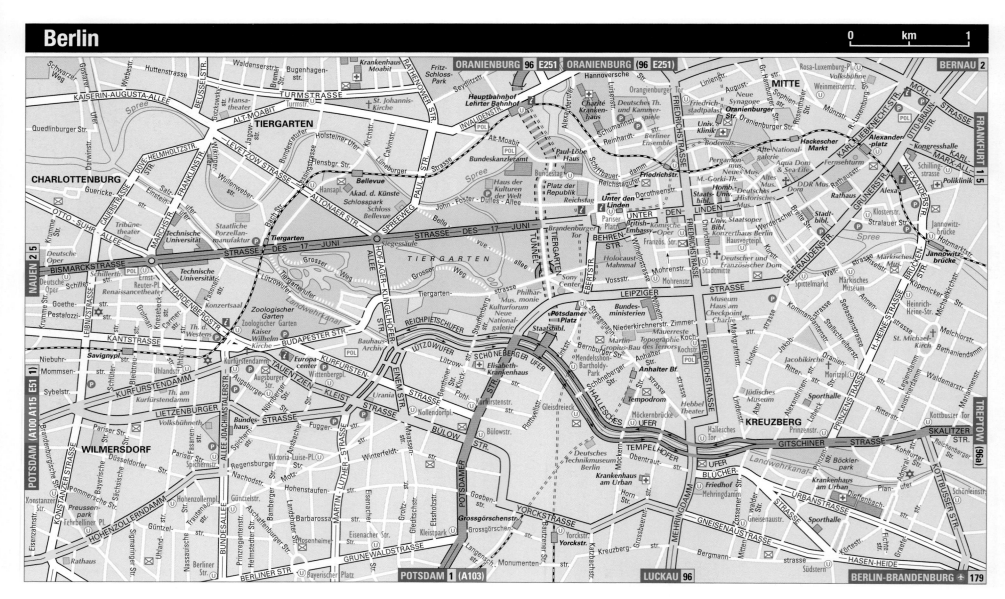

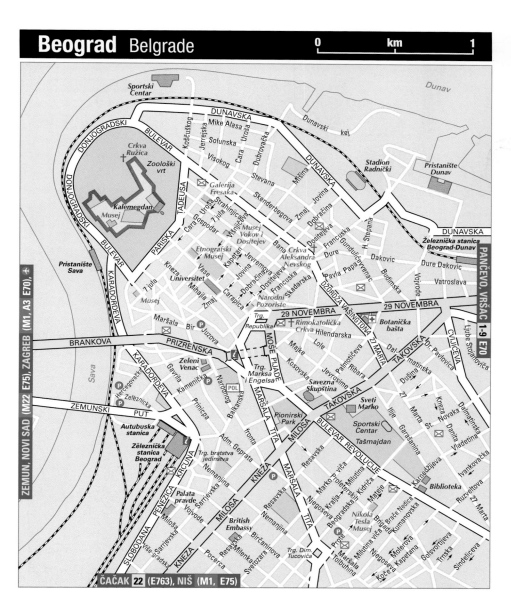

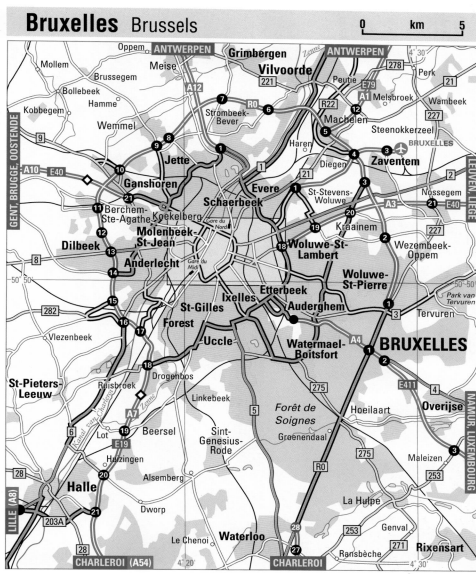

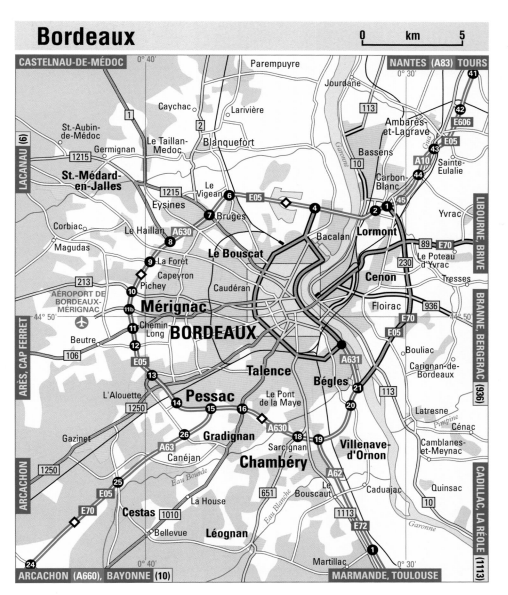

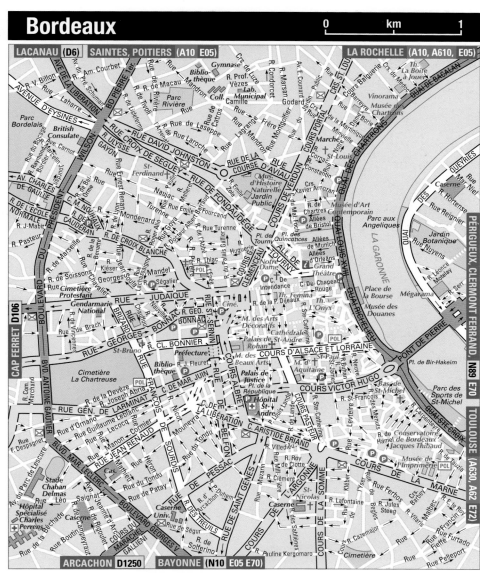

Bruxelles Brussels

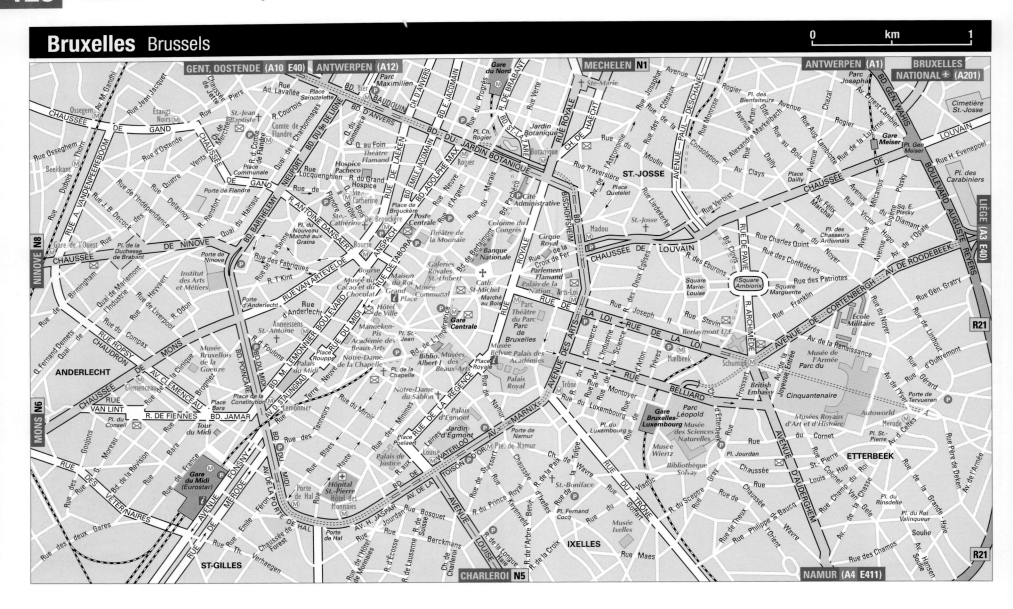

Budapest

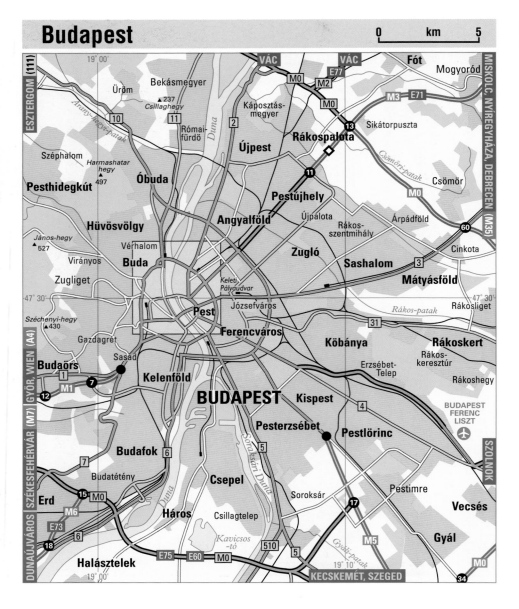

Budapest

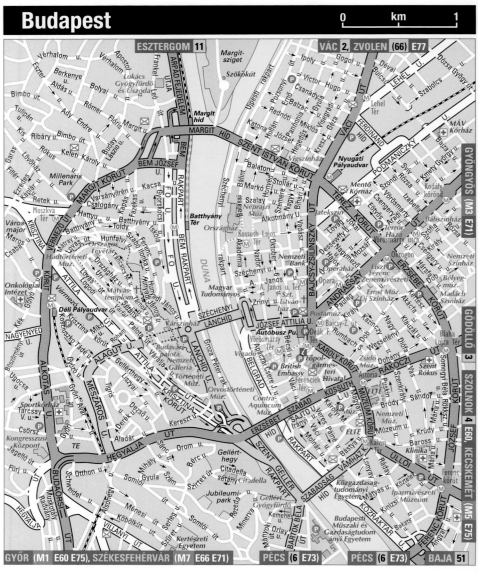

Dublin

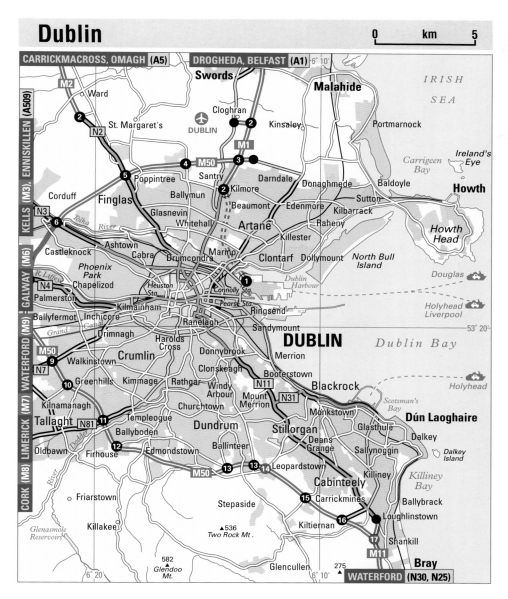

Dublin

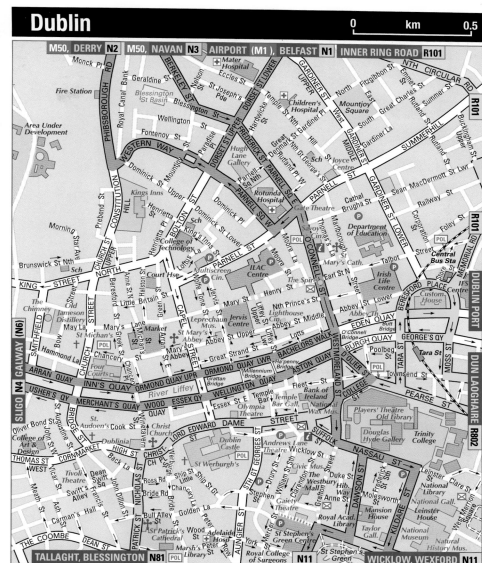

Düsseldorf

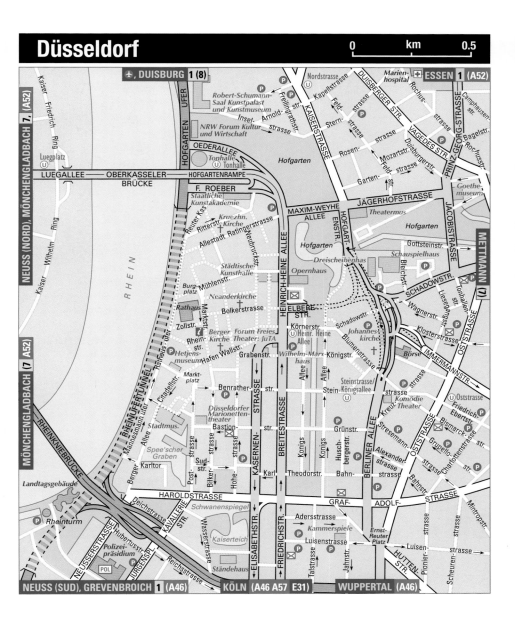

Edinburgh

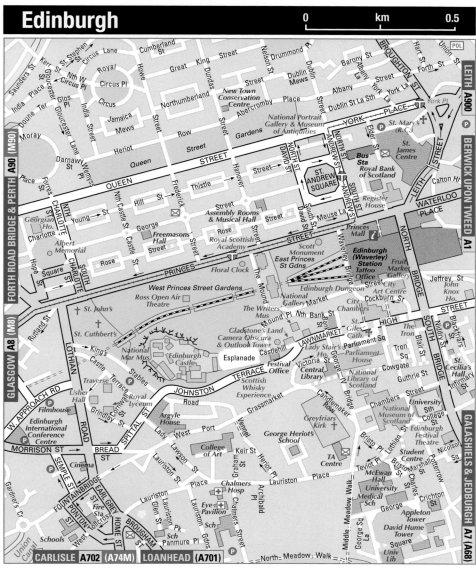

For **Cologne** see page 132
For **Copenhagen** see page 132

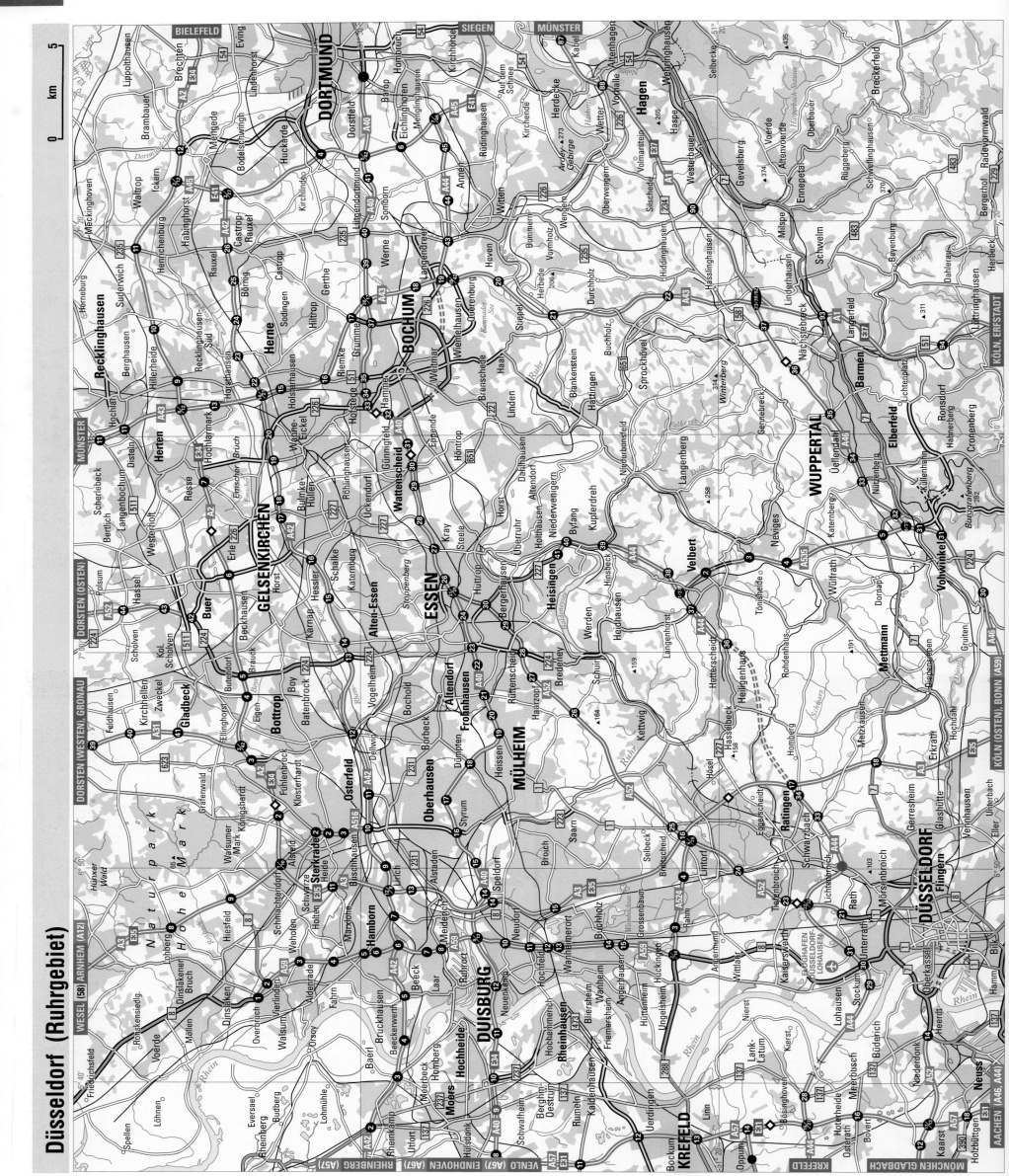

Firenze Florence

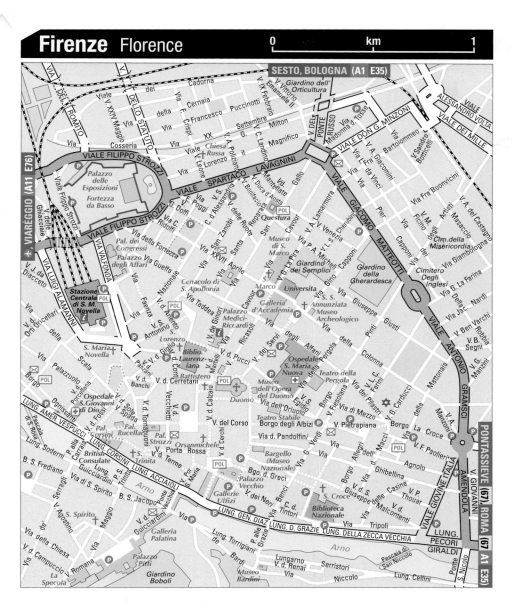

Frankfurt

Genève Geneva

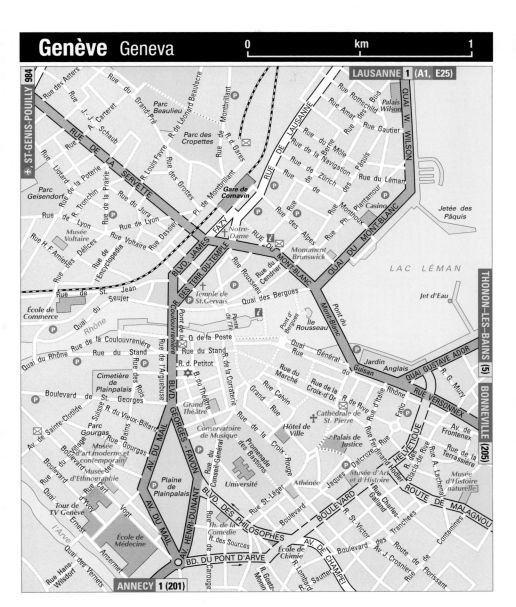

Génova Genoa

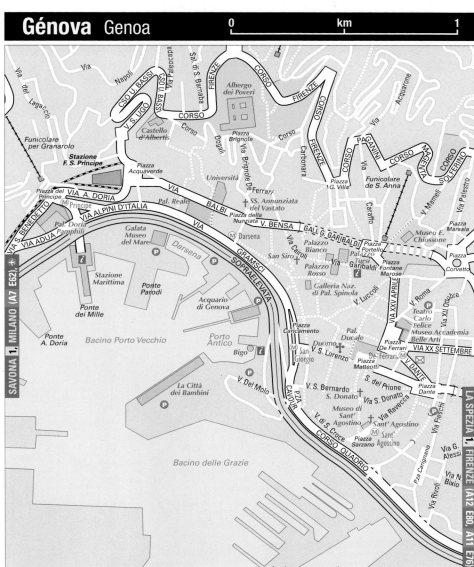

Granada

0   km   0.5

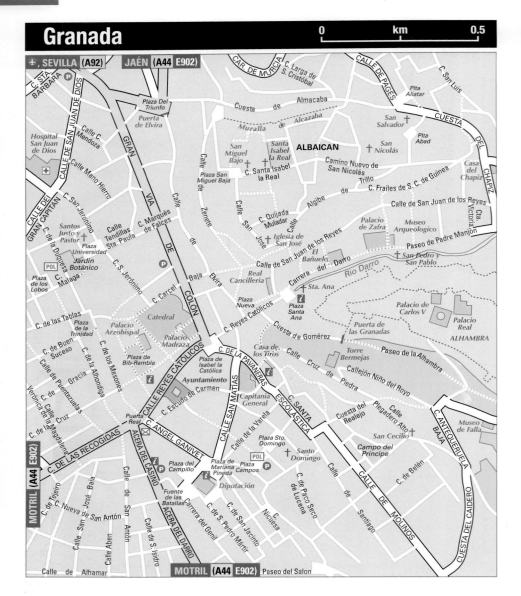

Göteborg Gothenburg

0   km   1

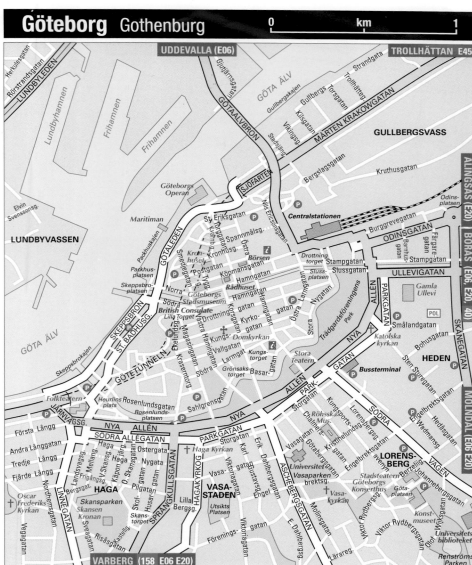

Hamburg

0   km   5

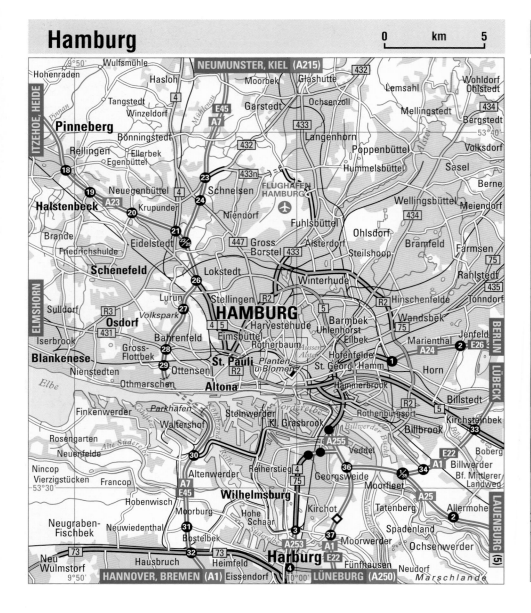

Hamburg

0   km   1

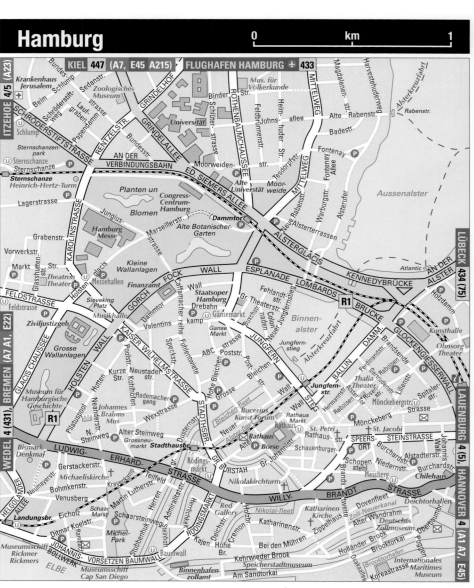

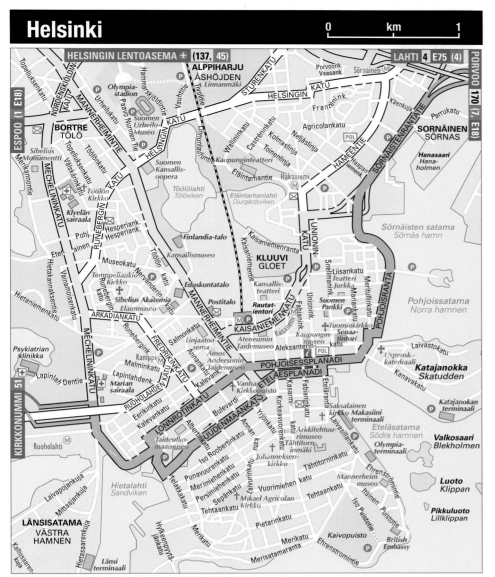

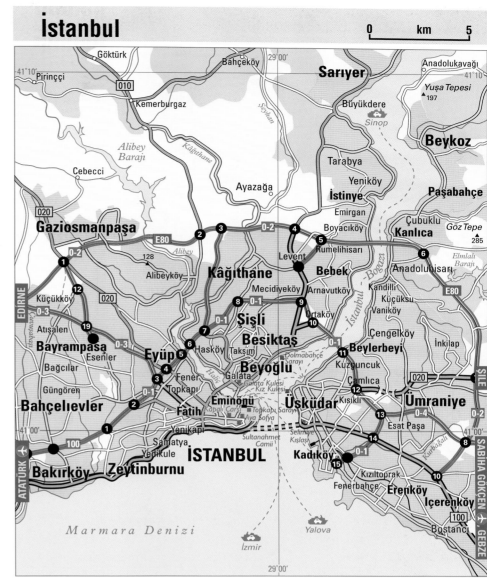

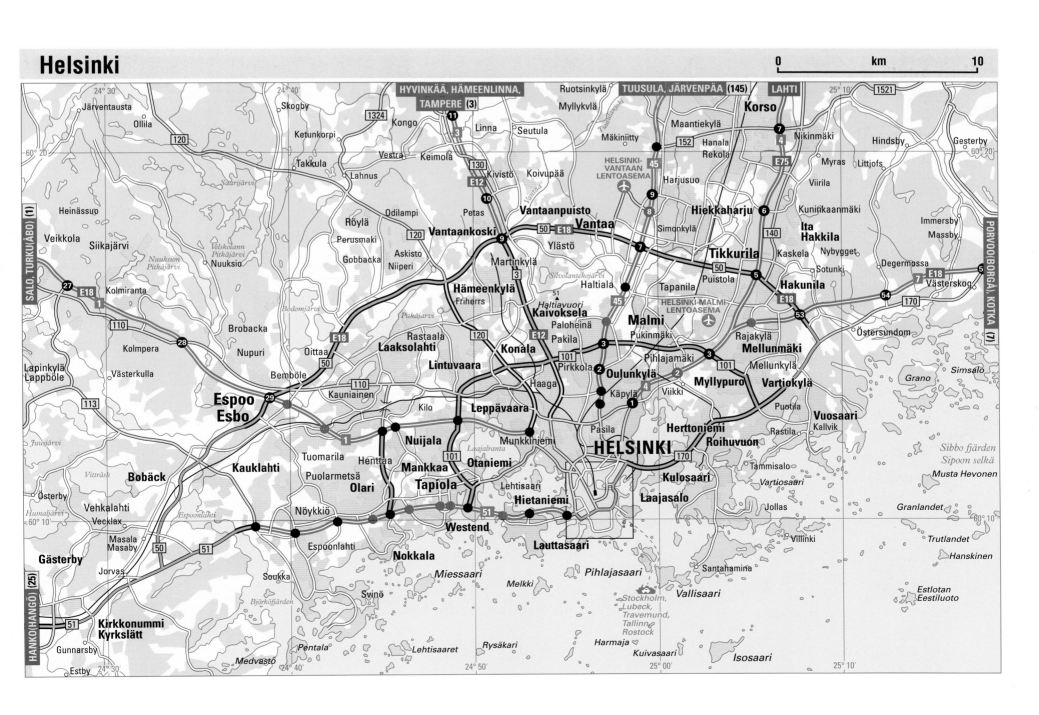

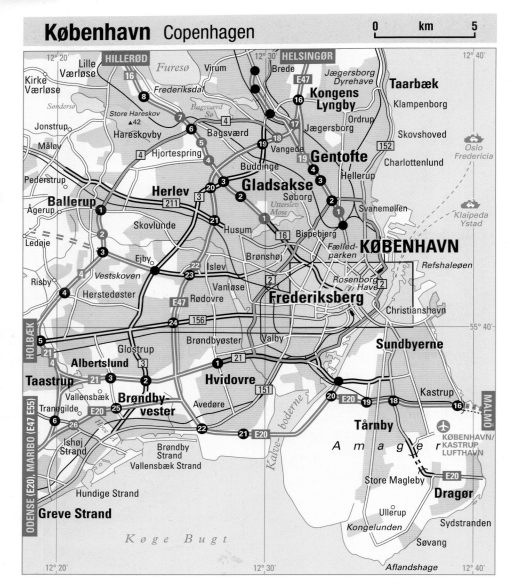

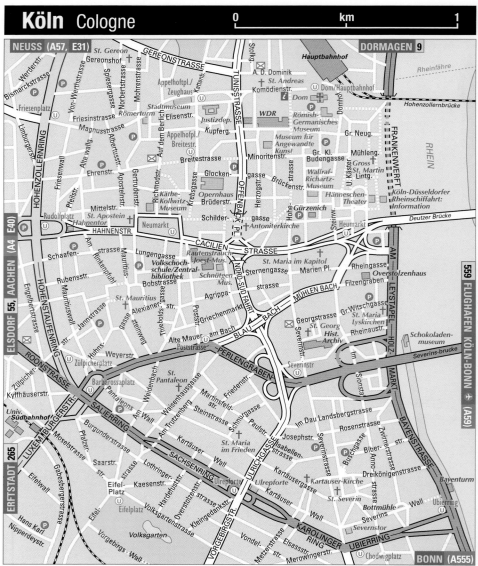

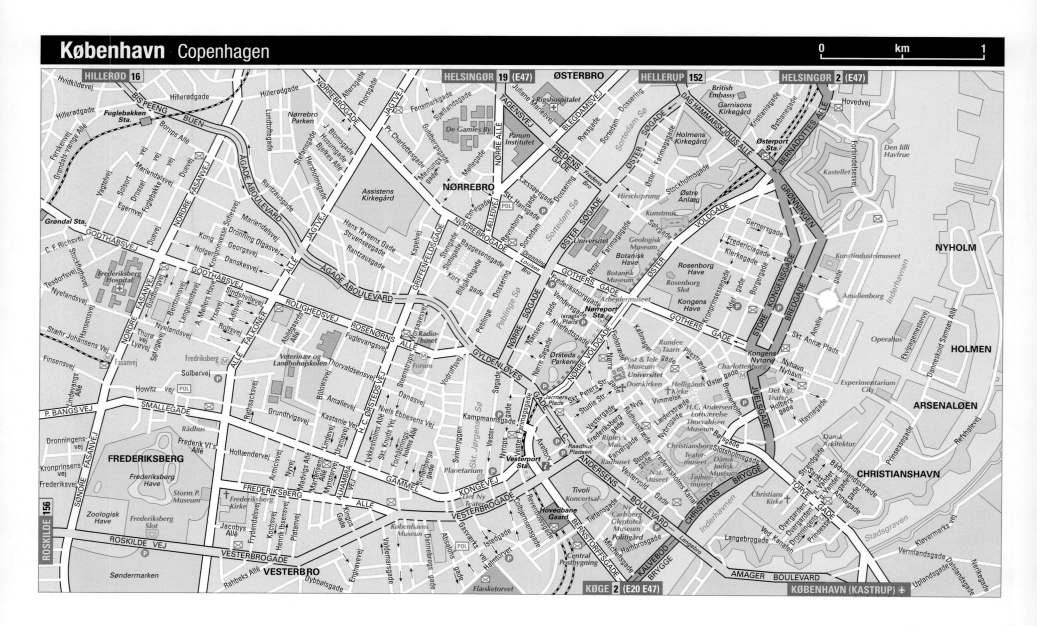

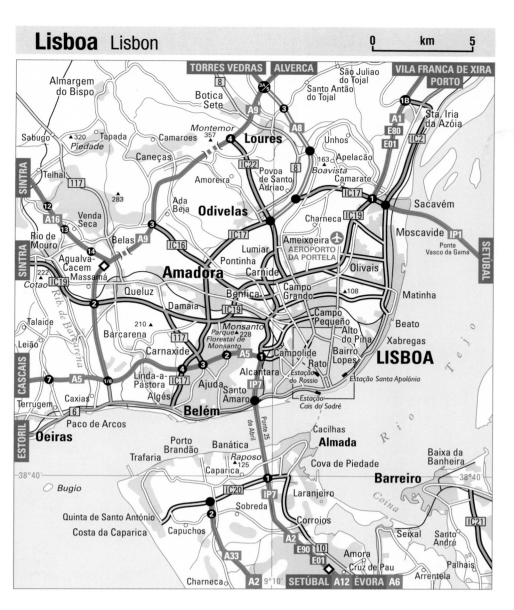

Lisboa Lisbon

0 km 5

Lisboa Lisbon

0 km 1

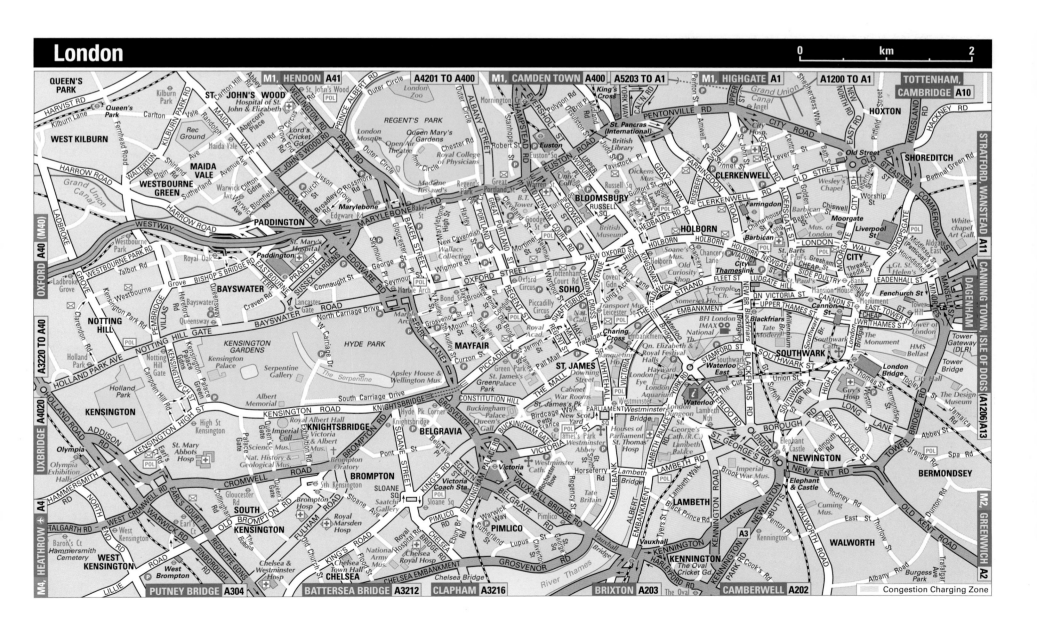

London

0 km 2

London

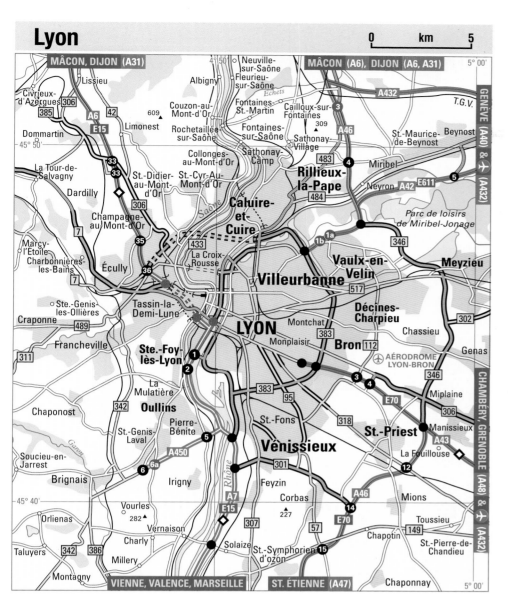

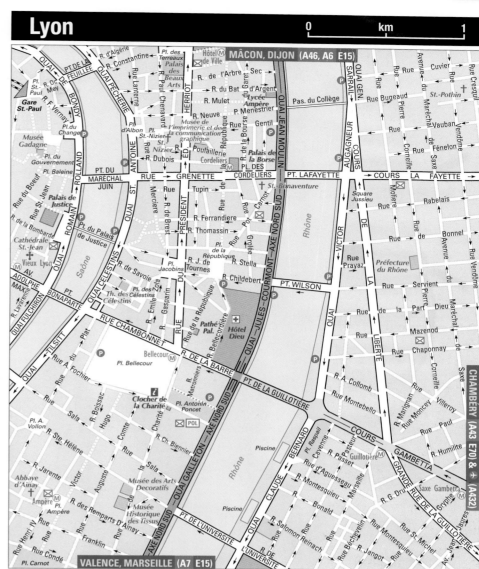

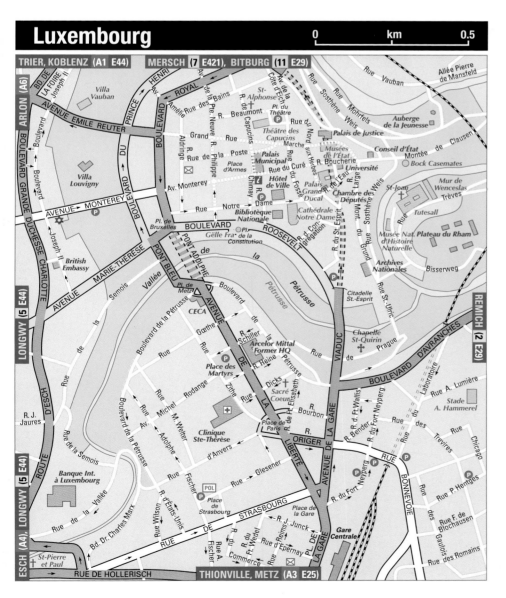

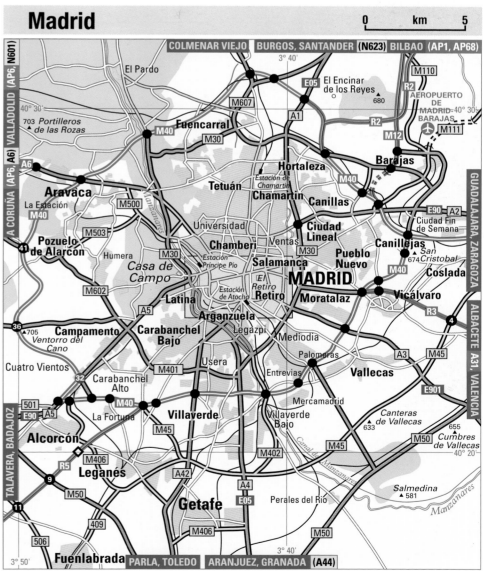

Madrid

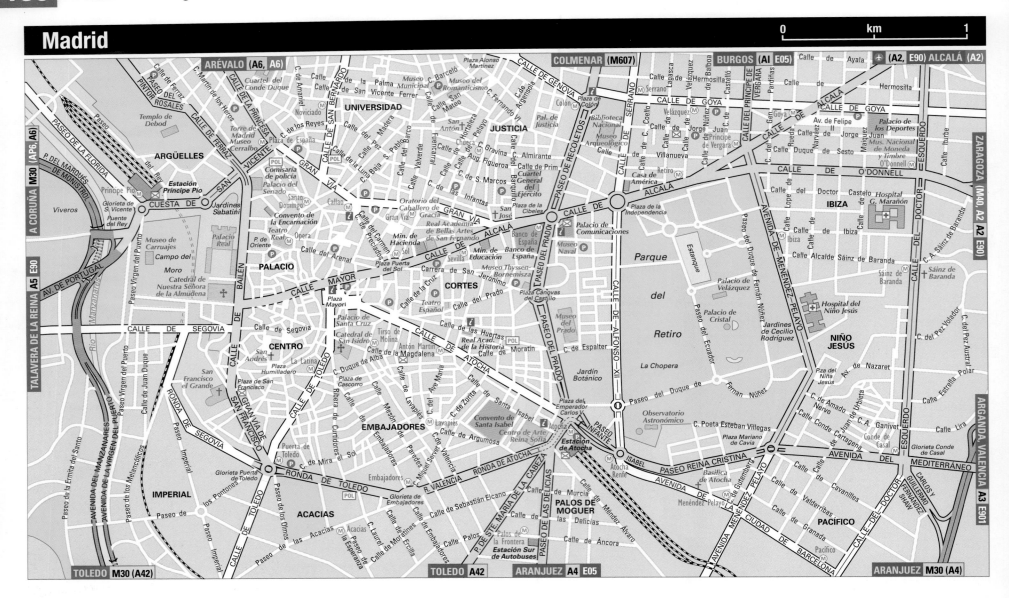

Málaga

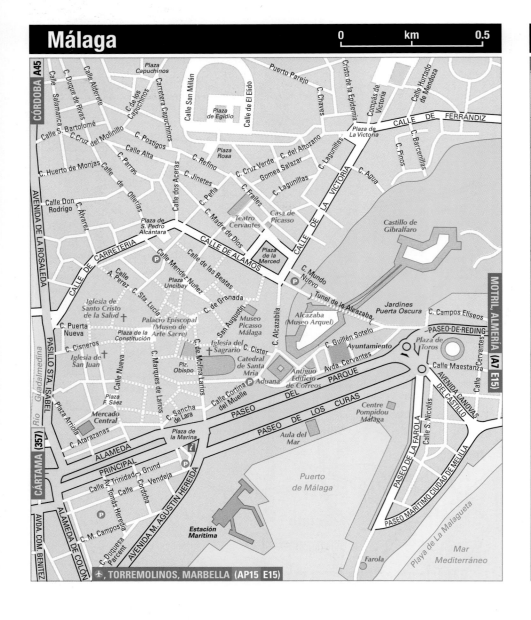

Marseille Marseilles

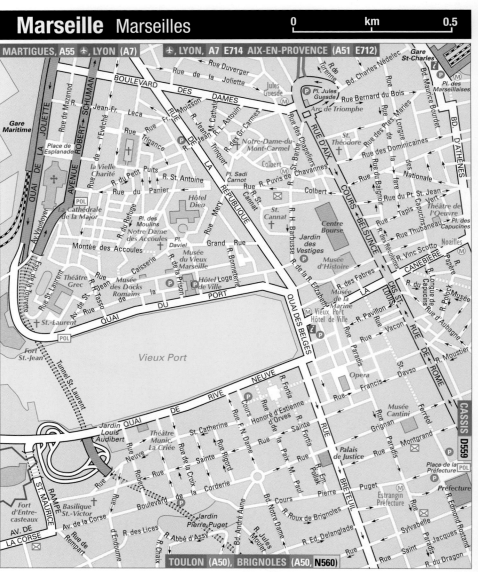

Milano

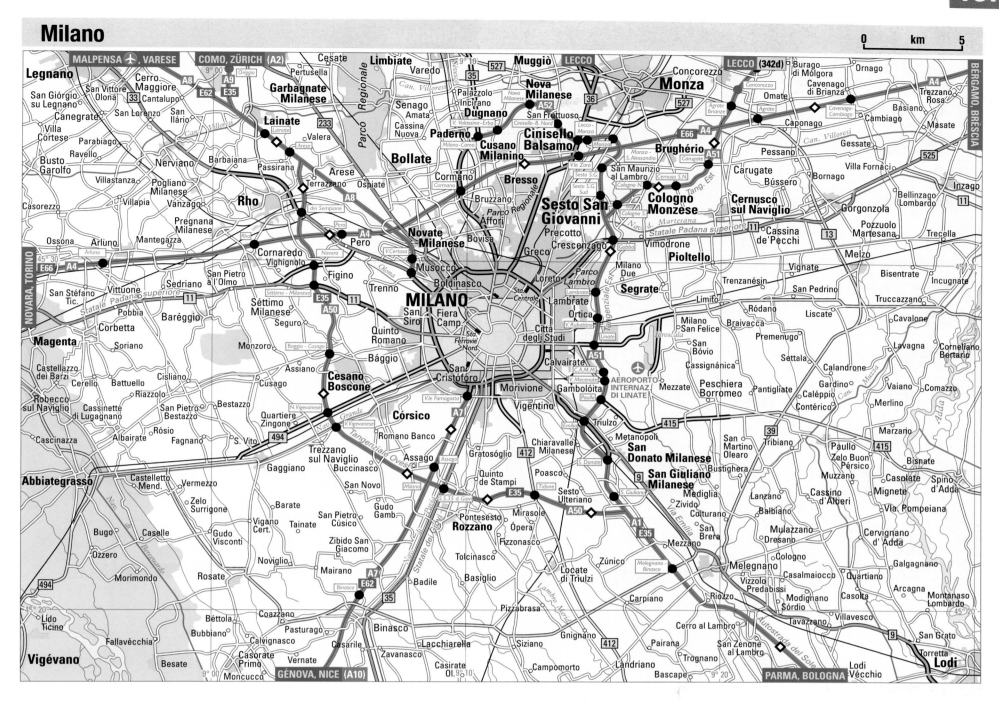

Milano Milan

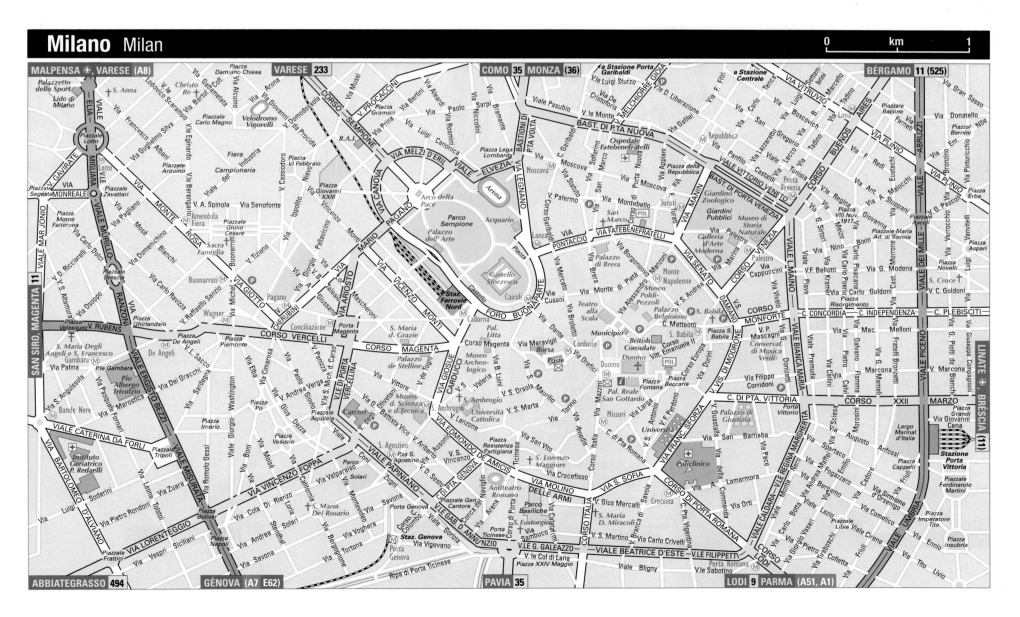

Moskva Moscow

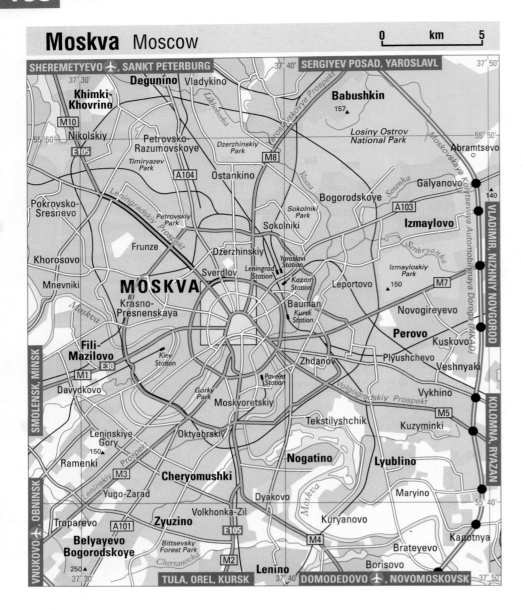

Moskva

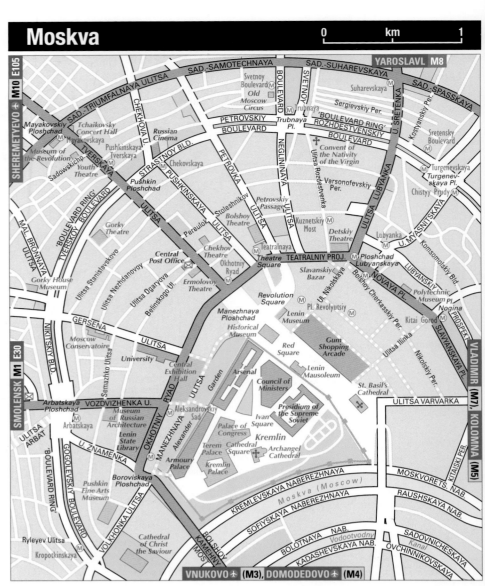

München Munich

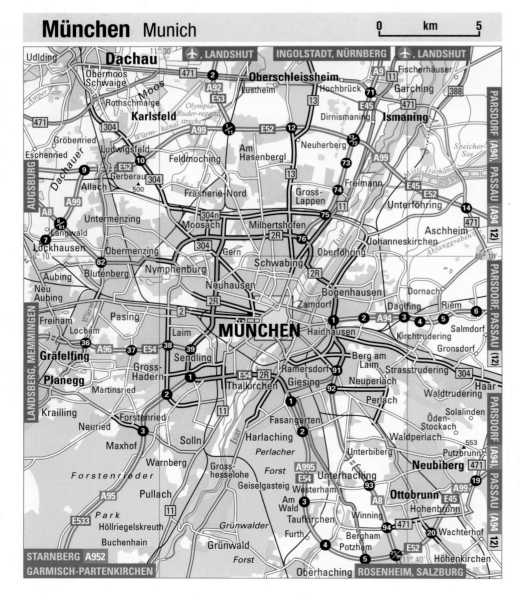

München Munich

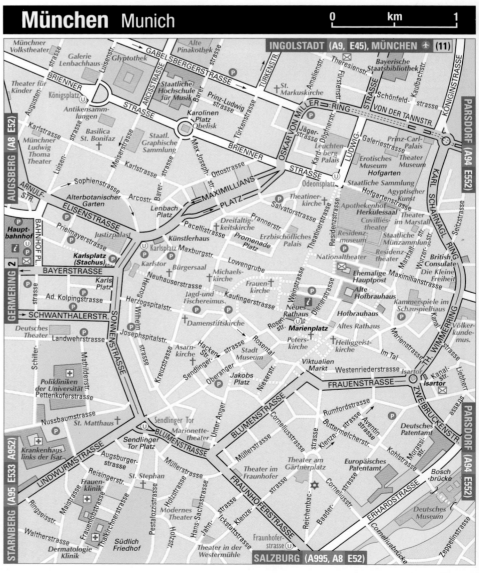

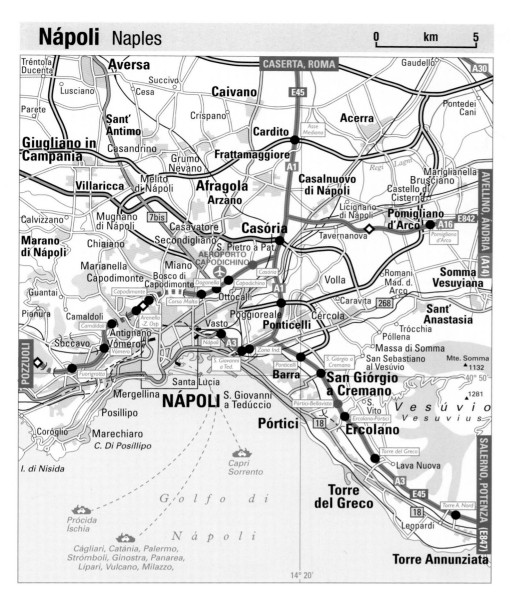

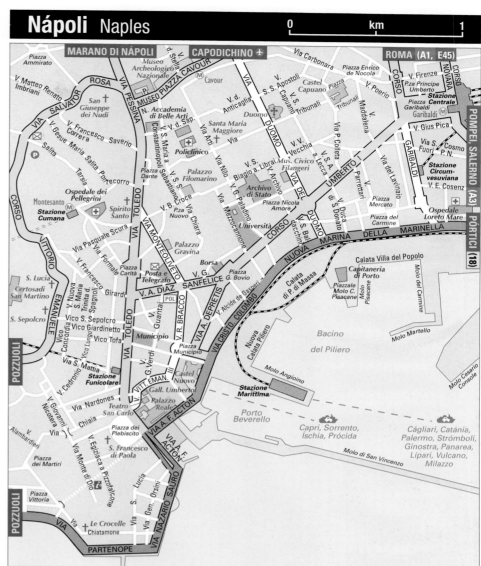

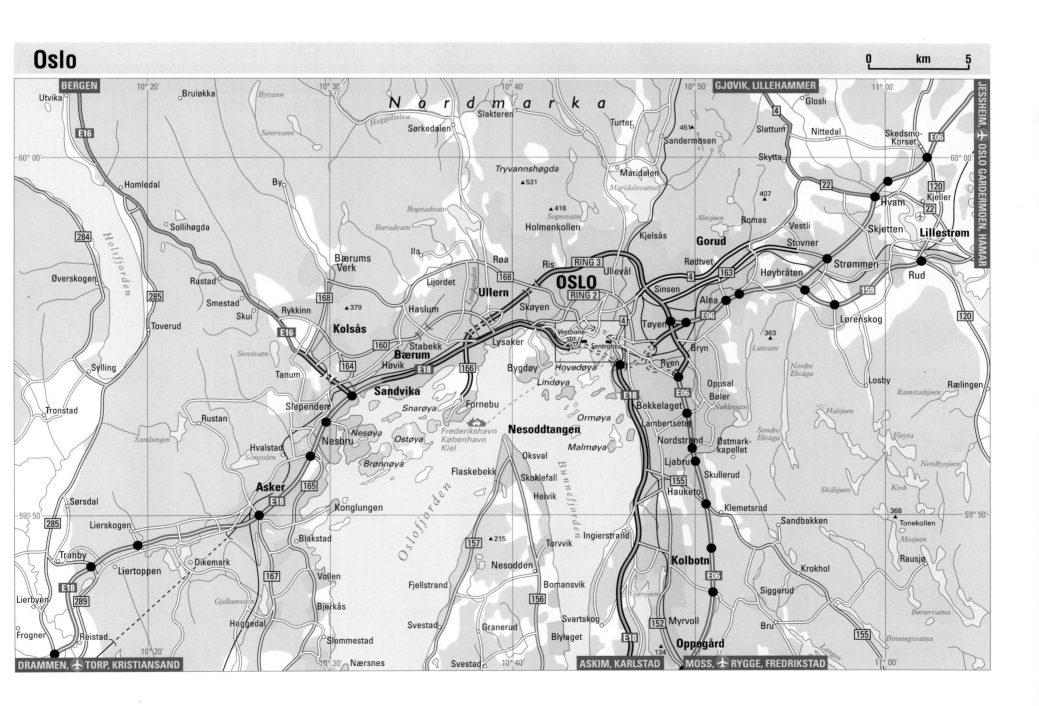

Oslo

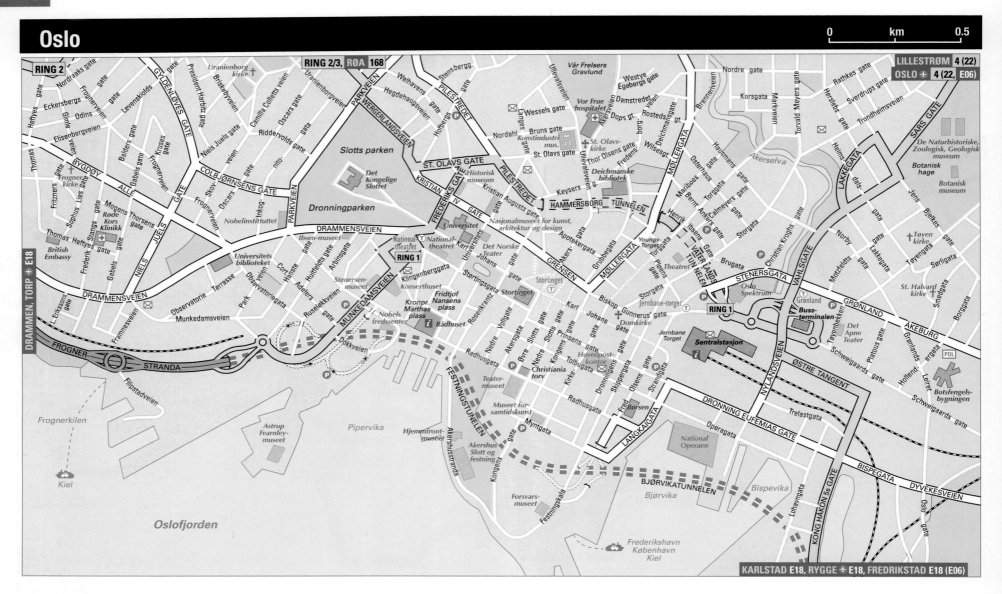

Paris

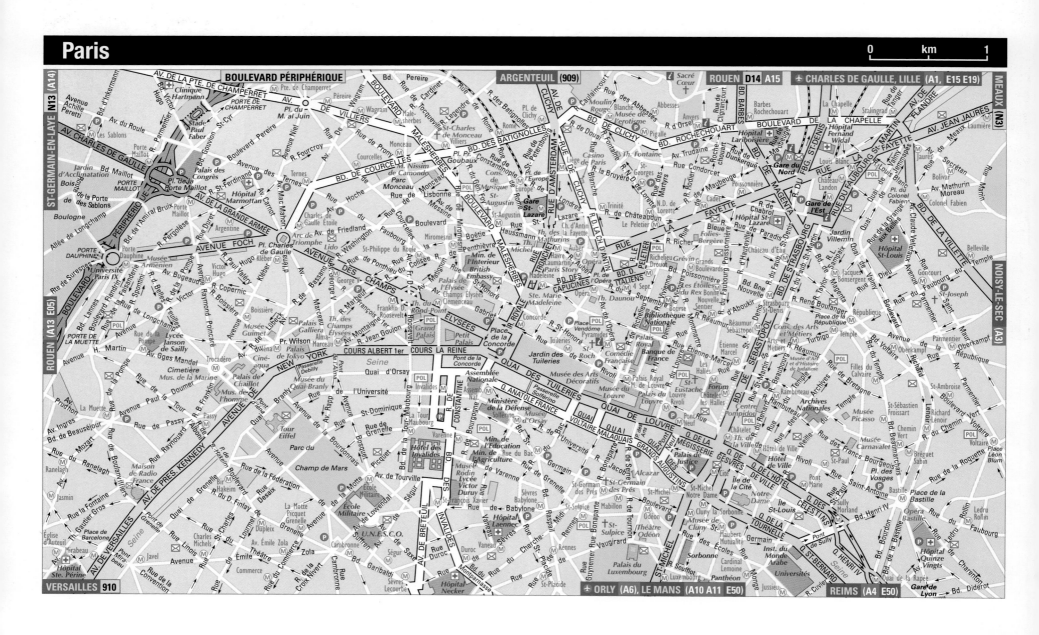

Paris

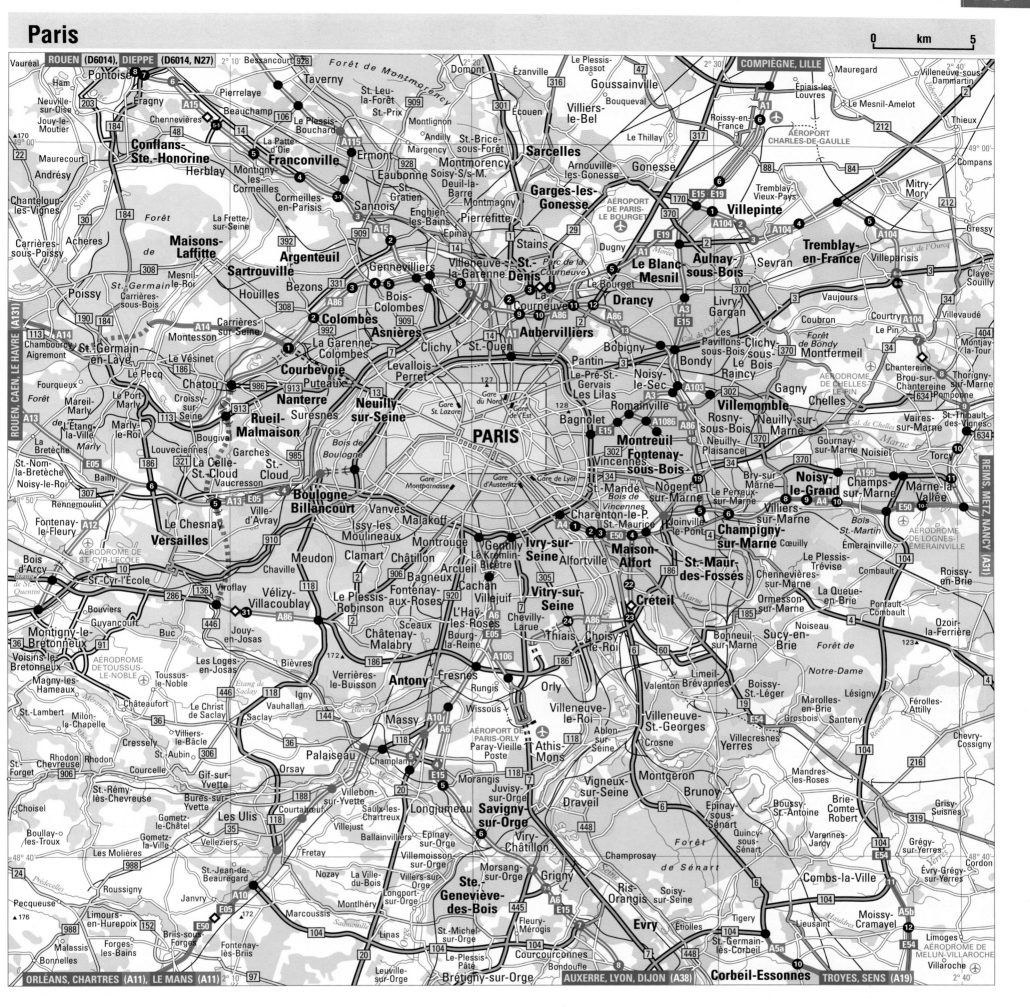

Praha Prague

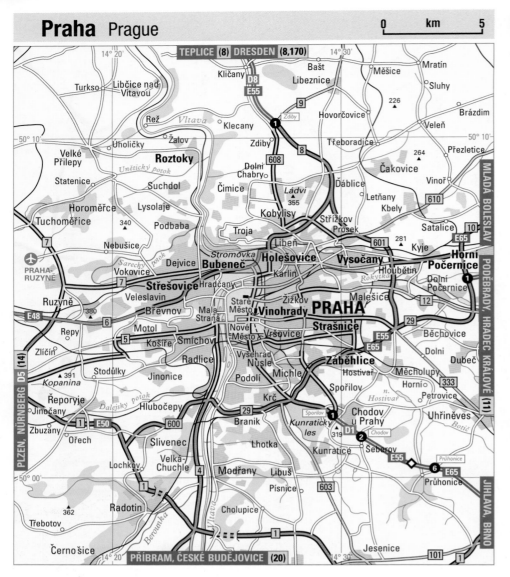

Praha Prague

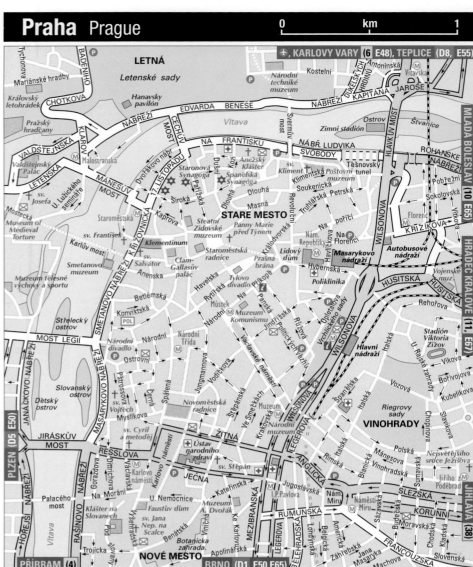

Rotterdam

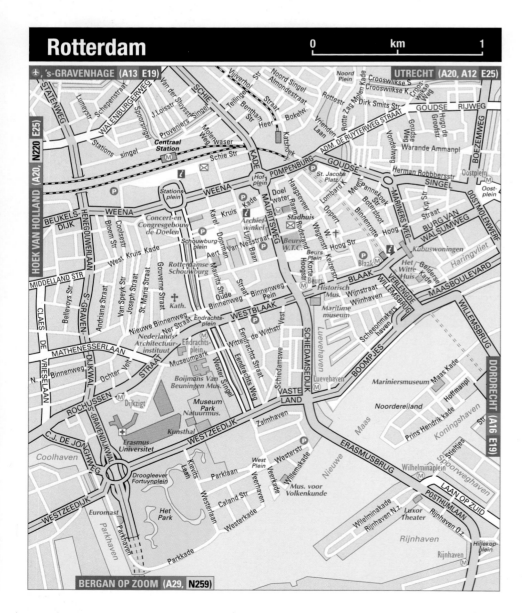

Sankt-Peterburg St. Petersburg

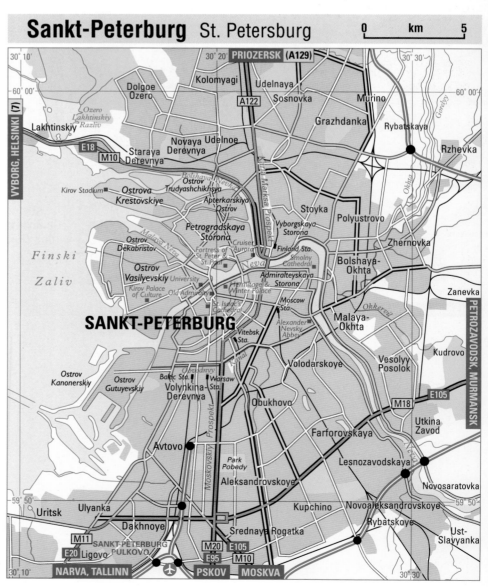

For **Rome** see page 143

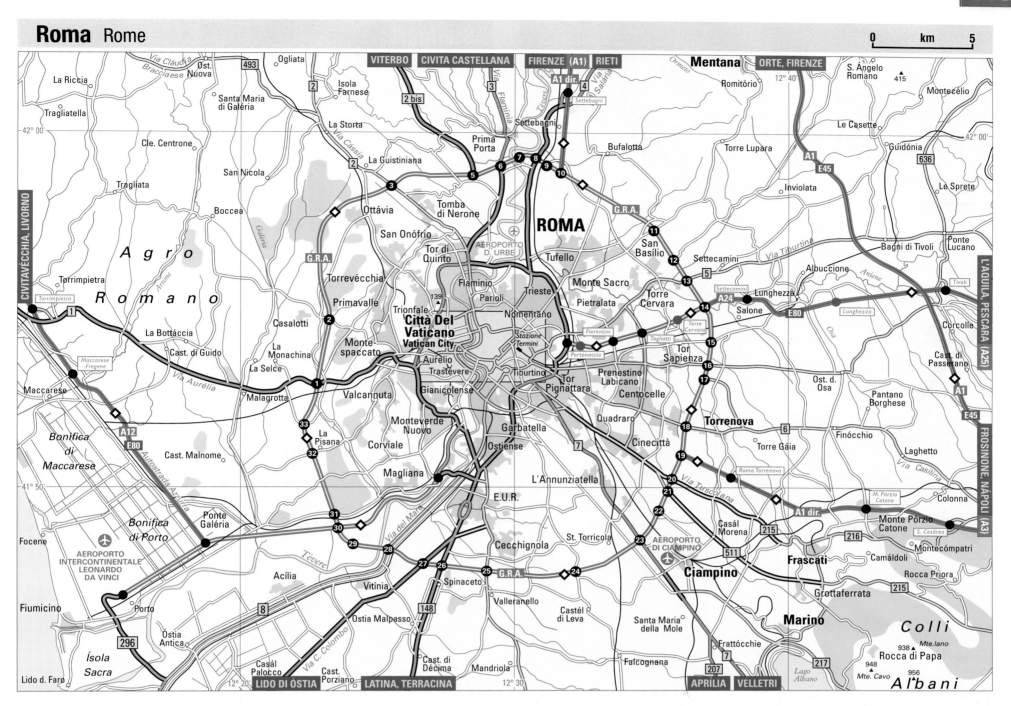

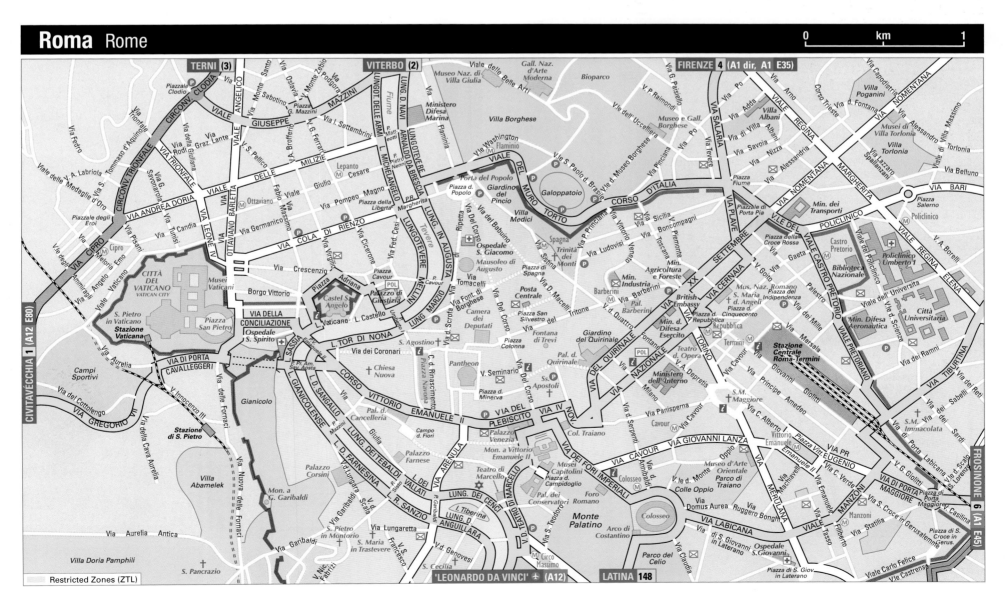

Restricted Zones (ZTL)

Sevilla Seville

0   km   0.5

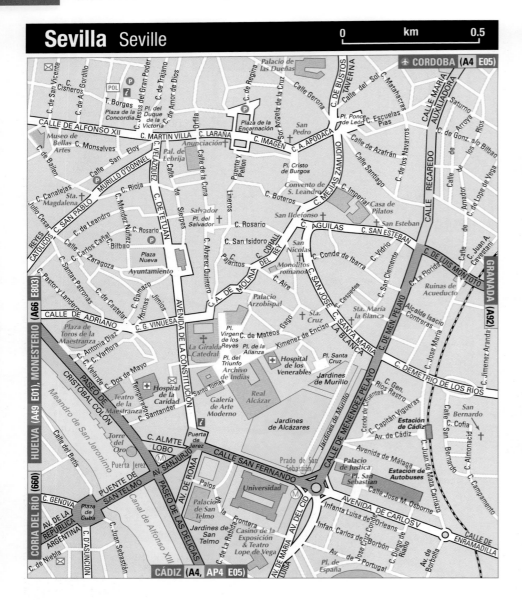

Stuttgart

0   km   0.5

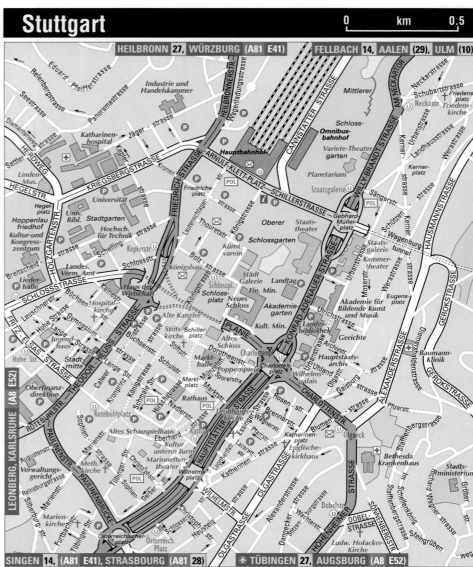

Strasbourg

0   km   5

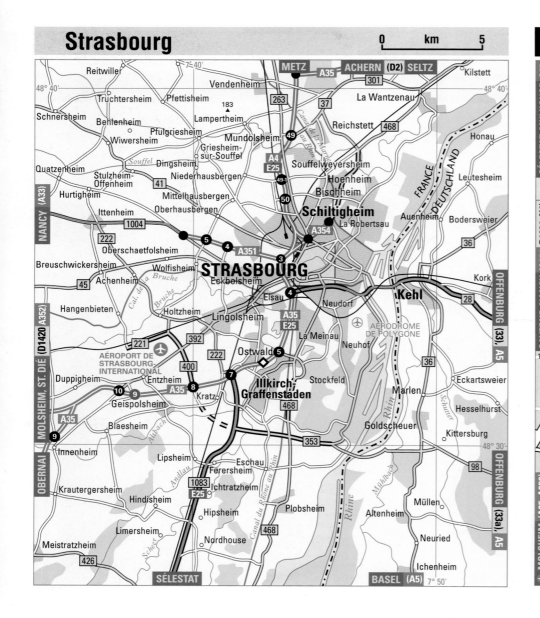

Strasbourg

0   km   0.5

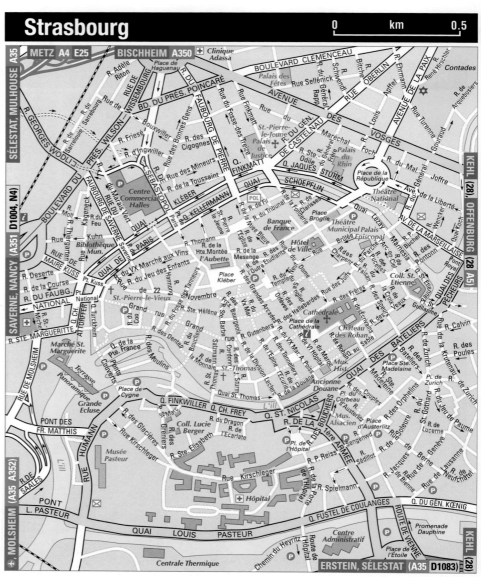

Stockholm

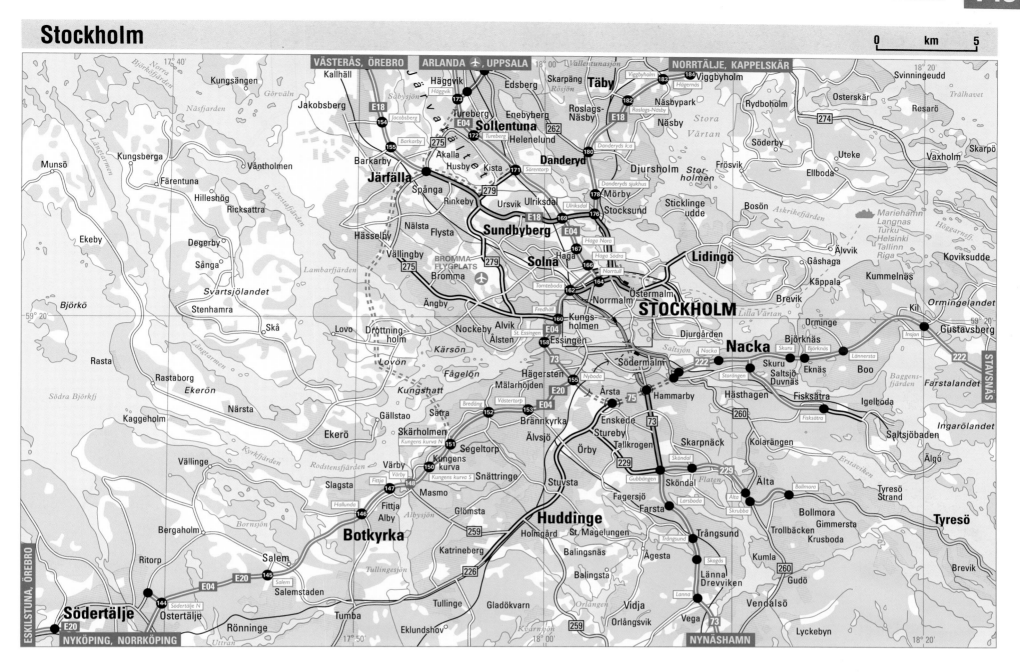

Stockholm

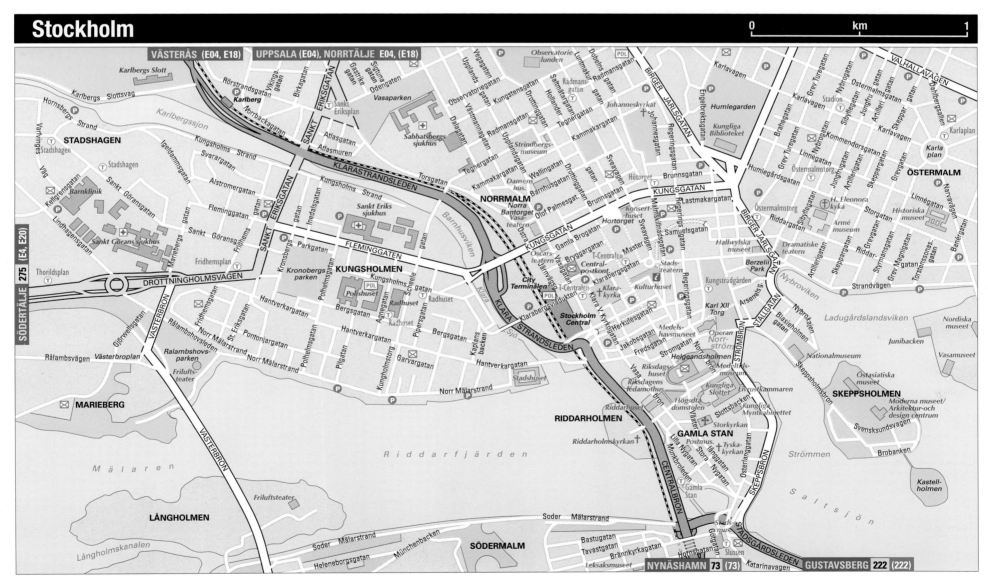

Torino Turin

0 km 5

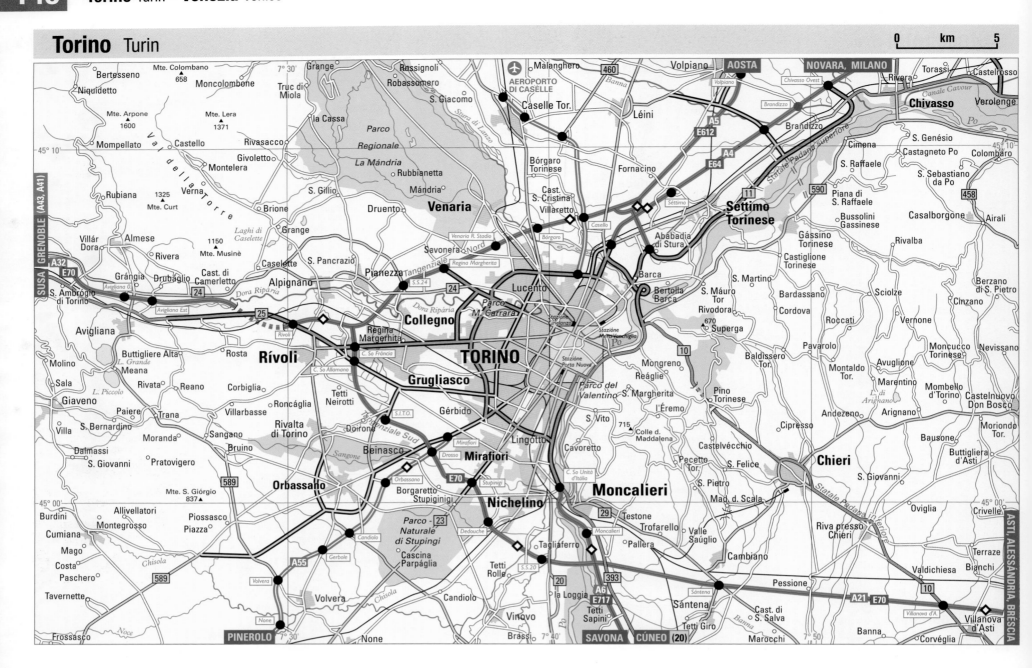

Venézia Venice

0 km 0.5

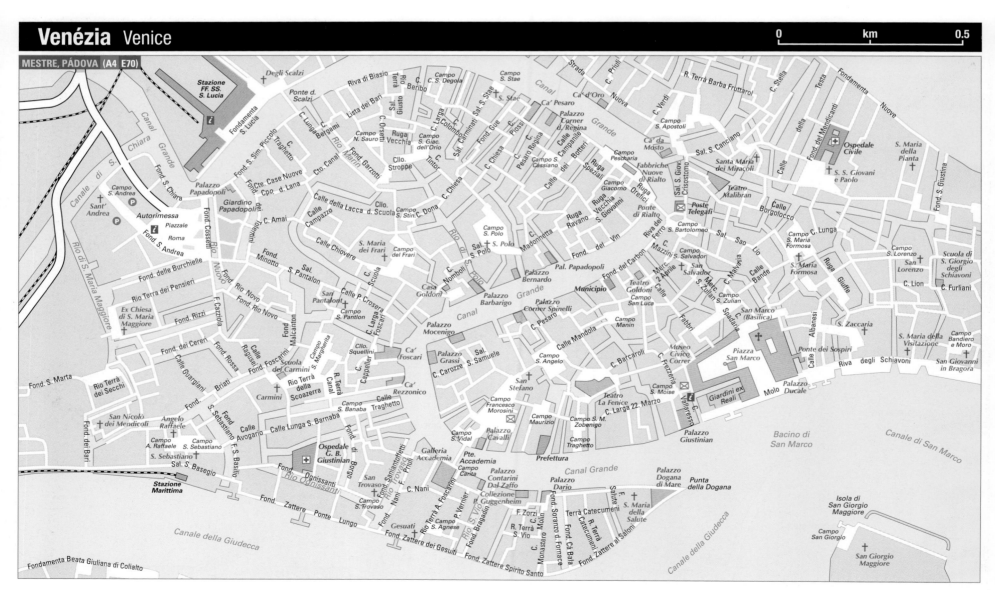

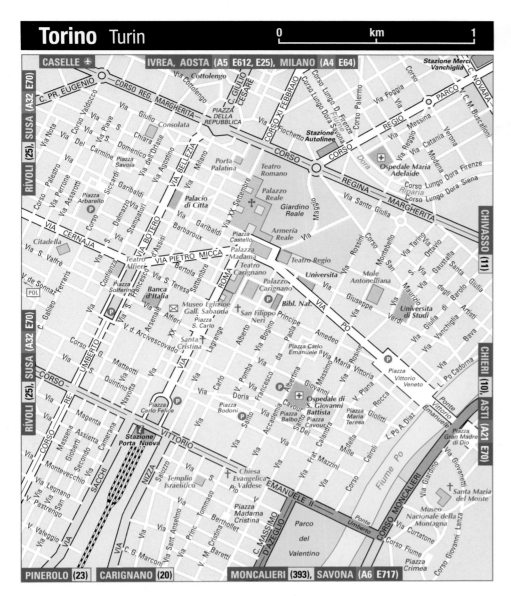

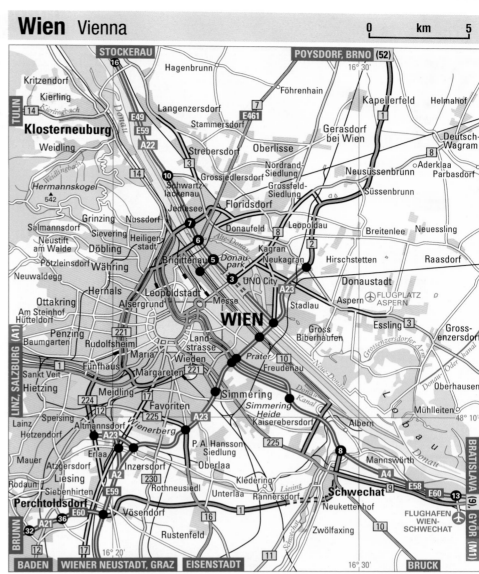

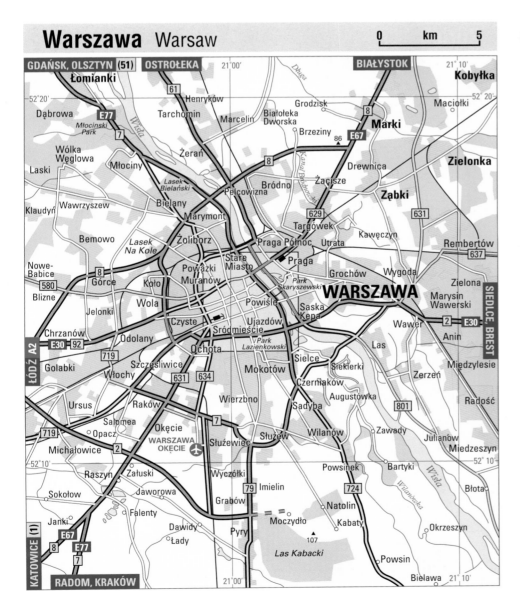

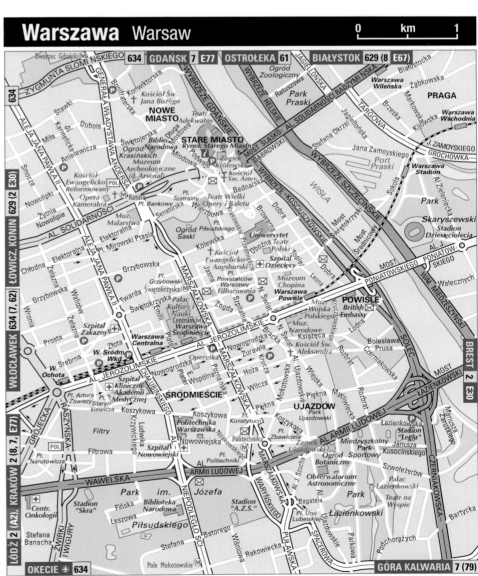

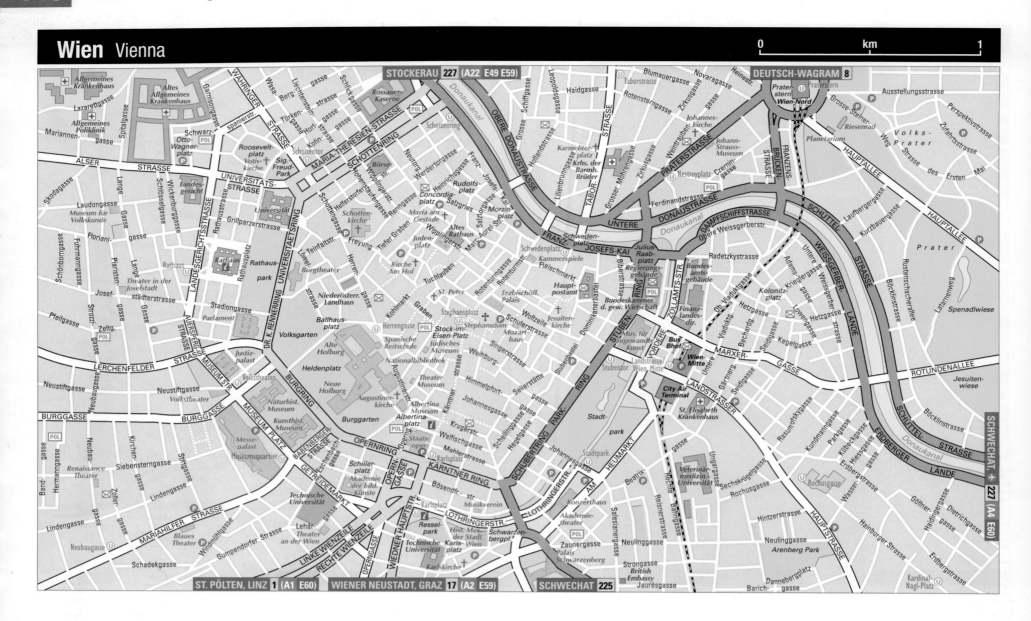

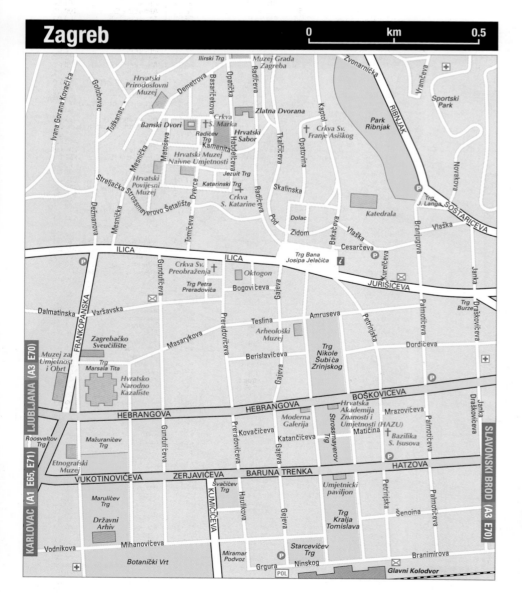

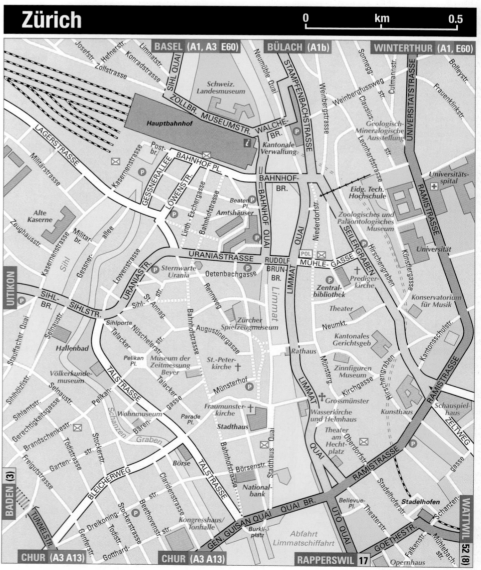

Index

Code	English	Français	Deutsch	Italiano
A	Austria	Autriche	Österreich	Austria
AL	Albania	Albanie	Albanien	Albania
AND	Andorra	Andorre	Andorra	Andorra
B	Belgium	Belgique	Belgien	Belgio
BG	Bulgaria	Bulgarie	Bulgarien	Bulgaria
BIH	Bosnia-Herzegovin	Bosnia-Herzegovine	Bosnien-Herzegowina	Bosnia-Herzegovina
BY	Belarus	Belarus	Weissrussland	Bielorussia
CH	Switzerland	Suisse	Schweiz	Svizzera
CY	Cyprus	Chypre	Zypern	Cipro
CZ	Czech Republic	République Tchèque	Tschechische Republik	Repubblica Ceca
D	Germany	Allemagne	Deutschland	Germania
DK	Denmark	Danemark	Dänemark	Danimarca
E	Spain	Espagne	Spanien	Spagna
EST	Estonia	Estonie	Estland	Estonia
F	France	France	Frankreich	Francia
FIN	Finland	Finlande	Finnland	Finlandia
FL	Liechtenstein	Liechtenstein	Liechtenstein	Liechtenstein
FO	Faeroe Islands	Îles Féroé	Färoër-Inseln	Isole Faroe
GB	United Kingdom	Royaume Uni	Grossbritannien und Nordirland	Regno Unito
GBZ	Gibraltar	Gibraltar	Gibraltar	Gibilterra
GR	Greece	Grèce	Greichenland	Grecia
H	Hungary	Hongrie	Ungarn	Ungheria
HR	Croatia	Croatie	Kroatien	Croazia
I	Italy	Italie	Italien	Italia
IRL	Ireland	Irlande	Irland	Irlanda
IS	Iceland	Islande	Island	Islanda
KOS	Kosovo	Kosovo	Kosovo	Kosovo
L	Luxembourg	Luxembourg	Luxemburg	Lussemburgo
LT	Lithuania	Lituanie	Litauen	Lituania
LV	Latvia	Lettonie	Lettland	Lettonia
M	Malta	Malte	Malta	Malta
MC	Monaco	Monaco	Monaco	Monaco
MD	Moldova	Moldavie	Moldawien	Moldavia
MK	Macedonia	Macédoine	Makedonien	Macedonia
MNE	Montenegro	Monténégro	Montenegro	Montenegro
N	Norway	Norvège	Norwegen	Norvegia
NL	Netherlands	Pays-Bas	Niederlande	Paesi Bassi
P	Portugal	Portugal	Portugal	Portogallo
PL	Poland	Pologne	Polen	Polonia
RO	Romania	Roumanie	Rumanien	Romania
RSM	San Marino	Saint-Marin	San Marino	San Marino
RUS	Russia	Russie	Russland	Russia
S	Sweden	Suède	Schweden	Svezia
SK	Slovak Republic	République Slovaque	Slowak Republik	Repubblica Slovacca
SLO	Slovenia	Slovénie	Slowenien	Slovenia
SRB	Serbia	Serbie	Serbien	Serbia
TR	Turkey	Turquie	Türkei	Turchia
UA	Ukraine	Ukraine	Ukraine	Ucraina

A

Aabenraa DK 39 D2
Aabybro DK 38 B2
Aach D 71 A4
Aachen D 50 C2
Aalborg DK 38 B2
Aalen D 61 B6
Aalestrup DK 38 C2
Aalsmeer NL 49 A5
Aalst B 49 C5
Aalten NL 50 B2
Aalter B 49 B4
Äänekoski FIN 3 E26
Aapajärvi FIN 113 E16
Ağağnar TR 118 C5
Aarau CH 70 A3
Aarberg CH 70 A2
Aarburg CH 70 A2
Aardenburg NL 49 B4
Aars DK 38 C2
Aarschot B 49 C5
Aarup DK 39 D3
Aba I 74 A3
Abádanes E 95 B4
Abades E 94 B2
Abadin E 86 A3
Abádszalók H 75 A5
Abaliget H 74 B3
Abana TR 16 A7
A Baña E 86 B2
Abanilla E 101 A4
Abano Terme I 72 C1
Abarán E 101 A4
Abasár H 65 C6
Abbadia San Salvatore I 81 D5
Abbase D 45 B5
Abbehausen D 43 B5
Abbekås S 41 D3
Abbeville F 48 C2
Abbey IRL 20 A3
Abbeydorney IRL 20 B2
Abbeyfeale IRL 20 B2
Abbeyleix IRL 21 B4
Abbey Town GB 25 C4
Abbiategrasso I 70 C3
Abborrträsk S 115 B16
Abbots Bromley GB 27 C4
Abbotsbury GB 29 C5
Abda H 64 C3
Abejar E 89 C4
Abela P 98 B2
Abelvær N 114 C8
Abenójar E 100 A1
Abensberg D 62 B2
Aberaeron GB 28 A3
Abercarn GB 29 B4
Aberchirder GB 23 D6
Abercynon GB 29 B4
Aberdare GB 29 B4
Aberdaron GB 26 C1
Aberdeen GB 23 D6
Aberdulais GB 28 B4
Aberdyfi GB 26 C1
Aberfeldy GB 25 B4
Aberffraw GB 26 B1
Aberfoyle GB 24 B3
Abergavenny GB 29 B4
Abergele GB 26 B2
AberGynolwyn GB 26 C2
Aberporth GB 28 A3
Abersoch GB 26 C1
Abertillery GB 29 B4
Abertura E 93 B5
Aberystwyth GB 26 C1
Abetone I 81 B4
Abfaltersbach A 72 B2
Abide
  Çanakkale TR 118 B1
  Kütahya TR 118 D4
Abiego E 90 A2
Abild DK 39 E1
Abingdon-on-Thames GB 31 C2
Abington GB 25 C4
Abisko S 112 D7
Abiul P 92 B2
Abla E 101 B3
Ablis F 58 B2
A Bola E 87 B3
Abondance F 70 B1
Abony H 75 A5
Abrantes P 92 B2
Abreiro P 87 C3
Abreschviller F 60 B3
Abrest F 68 B3
Abriès F 79 B5
Abrud RO 11 C7
Absdorf A 64 B1
Abtenau A 72 A3
Abtsgmünd D 61 B5
Abusejo E 93 A4
Aby
  Kronoberg S 40 B4
  Östergötland S 37 D3
Åbyggeby S 36 B4
Åbytorp S 37 C2
A Cañiza E 87 B2
A Capela E 86 A2
Acate I 109 B3
Accadia I 103 B8
Accéglio I 79 B5
Accettura I 104 C2
Acciaroli I 106 A2

Accous F 76 D2
Accrington GB 26 B3
Accúmoli I 82 D2
Acedera E 93 B5
Acehúche E 93 B4
Acered E 95 A5
Acerenza I 104 C1
Acerno I 103 C8
Acerra I 103 C7
Aceuchal E 93 C4
Acharacle GB 24 B2
Acharnes GR 117 D5
Achavanich GB 23 C5
Achene B 49 C6
Achenkirch A 72 A1
Achensee A 72 A1
Achenthal A 72 A1
Achentrias GR 117 H7
Achern D 61 B4
Acheux-en-Amienois F 48 C3
Achiltibuie GB 22 C3
Achim D 43 B6
Achladokambos GR 117 E4
Achnasheen GB 22 D3
Achnashellach GB 22 D3
Achosnich GB 24 B1
Aci Castello I 109 B4
Aci Catena I 109 B4
Acilia I 102 B5
Acipayam TR 119 E4
Acireale I 109 B4
Acle GB 30 B5
A Coruña E 86 A2
Acquacadda I 110 C1
Acqua Doria F 102 B1
Acquanegra sul Chiese I 71 C5
Acquapendente I 81 D5
Acquasanta Terme I 82 D2
Acquasparta I 102 A5
Acquaviva I 81 C5
Acquaviva delle Fonti I 104 C2
Acquaviva Picena I 82 D2
Acquigny F 58 A2
Acqui Terme I 80 B2
Acri I 106 B3
Acs H 64 C4
Acsa H 65 C5
Ácsteszér H 74 A2
Acy-le-Multien F 59 A3
Ada SRB 75 C5
Adak S 115 B15
Adalsbruk N 34 B3
Adamas GR 117 F6
Adamsfjord N 113 B15
Adamuz E 100 A1
Adana TR 16 C7
Adánd H 74 B3
Adare IRL 20 B3
Adaševci SRB 85 A4
Adeanueva de Ebro E 89 B5
Adelboden CH 70 B2
Adelebsen D 51 B5
Adélfia I 104 B2
Adelmannsfelden D 61 B6
Adelsheim D 61 A5
Adelsö S 37 C4
Ademuz E 96 A1
Adenau D 50 C2
Adendorf D 44 B2
Adinkerke B 48 B3
Adjud RO 11 C9
Adliswil CH 70 A3
Admont A 63 C5
Adneram N 33 C3
Adolfsström S 115 A13
Adony H 74 A3
Adorf
  Hessen D 51 B4
  Sachsen D 52 C2
Adra E 100 C2
Adradas E 89 C4
Adrall E 91 A4
Adrano I 109 B3
Adria I 82 A1
Adrigole IRL 20 C2
Adwick le Street GB 27 B4
Adzaneta E 96 A2
Aesch CH 70 A2
A Estrada E 86 B2
Afandou GR 119 F3
Affi I 71 C5
Affing D 62 B1
Affoltern CH 70 A3
Affric Lodge GB 22 D3
Afjord N 114 D7
Aflenz Kurort A 73 A5
A Fonsagrada E 86 A3
Afragola I 103 C7
Afritz A 72 B3
Afyon TR 118 D5
Agay F 79 C5
Agazzano I 80 B3
Agde F 78 C2
Agdenes N 114 D6
Agen F 77 B3
Ager E 90 B3
Agerbæk DK 39 D1
Agerskov DK 39 D2
Ageyevo RUS 7 D14
Agger DK 38 C1
Aggersund DK 38 B2
Aggius I 110 B2

Aggsbach Dorf A 63 B6
Aggsbach Markt A 63 B6
Aggtelek H 65 B6
Aghalee GB 19 B5
Aghia GR 116 C4
Aghia Anna GR 116 D5
Aghia Galini GR 117 G6
Aghia Marina GR 119 G1
Aghia Paraskevi GR 118 C1
Aghia Pelagia GR 117 F4
Aghia Triada GR 117 E3
Aghiokambos GR 116 C4
Aghios Efstratios GR 116 C6
Aghios Kirikos GR 119 E1
Aghios Mathaios GR 116 C1
Aghios Mironas GR 117 G7
Aghios Nikolaos GR 117 G7
Aghios Petros GR 116 D2
Aghio Theodori GR 117 E5
Agiá I 109 B3
Agira I 109 B3
Aglientu I 110 A2
Agnières F 79 B4
Agno CH 70 C3
Agnone I 103 B7
Agolada E 86 B2
Agon Coutainville F 57 A4
Ágordo I 72 B2
Agost E 96 C2
Agramón E 101 A4
Agramunt E 91 B4
Agreda E 89 C5
Agria GR 116 C5
Agrigento I 108 B2
Agrinio GR 116 D3
Agrón E 100 B2
Agrópoli I 103 C7
Aguadulce
  Almería E 101 C3
  Sevilla E 100 B1
Agualada E 86 A2
Agua Longa P 87 C2
A Guarda E 87 C2
Aguarón E 89 C5
Aguas E 90 A2
Aguas Belas P 92 B2
Aguas de Busot E 96 C2
Aguas de Moura P 92 C2
Aguas Frías P 87 C3
Aguas Santas P 87 C2
Aguaviva E 90 C2
Aguaviva de la Vega E 89 C4
A Gudiña E 87 B3
Agudo E 94 D2
Águeda P 92 A2
Aguessac F 78 B2
Agugliano I 82 C2
Aguiar P 92 C3
Aguiar da Beira P 87 D3
Aguilafuente E 94 A2
Aguilar de Campóo E 88 B2
Aguilar de la Frontera E 100 B1
Águilas E 101 B4
Agunnaryd S 40 C4
Ahat TR 118 D4
Ahaus D 50 A2
Åheim N 114 E2
Ahigal E 93 A4
Ahigal de Villarino E 87 C4
Ahillones E 99 A5
Ahlbeck
  Mecklenburg-Vorpommern D 45 B6
  Mecklenburg-Vorpommern D 45 B6
Ahlen D 50 B3
Ahlhorn D 43 C5
Ahmetbey TR 118 A2
Ahmetler TR 119 D4
Ahmetli TR 119 D2
Ahoghill GB 19 B5
Ahrensbök D 44 A2
Ahrensburg D 44 B2
Ahun F 68 B2
Åhus S 41 D4
Ahvenselkä FIN 113 F17
Aibar E 89 B5
Aich D 62 B3
Aicha D 63 B4
Aichach D 62 B2
Aidone I 109 B3
Aiello Cálabro I 106 B3
Aigen im Mühlkreis A 63 B4
Aigle CH 70 B1
Aignan F 76 C3
Aignay-le-Duc F 59 C5
Aigre F 67 C5
Aigrefeuille-d'Aunis F 66 B4
Aigrefeuille-sur-Maine F 66 A3
Aiguablava E 91 B6
Aiguebelle F 69 C6
Aigueperse F 68 B3
Aigues-Mortes F 78 C3
Aigues-Vives F 78 C1
Aiguilles F 79 B5
Aiguillon F 77 B3
Aigurande F 68 B1
Ailefroide F 79 B5
Aillant-sur-Tholon F 59 C4
Ailly-sur-Noye F 58 A3
Ailly-sur-Somme F 58 A3
Aimargues F 78 C3

Aime F 69 C6
Ainaži LV 6 C8
Ainet A 72 B2
Ainhoa F 76 C1
Ainsa E 90 A3
Airaines F 48 D2
Aird GB 24 B2
Aird Asaig Tairbeart GB 22 D2
Airdrie GB 25 C4
Aire-sur-l'Adour F 76 C2
Aire-sur-la-Lys F 48 C3
Airole I 80 C1
Airolo CH 70 B3
Airvault F 67 B4
Aisey-sur-Seine F 59 C5
Aïssey F 69 A6
Aisy-sur-Armançon F 59 C5
Aiterhofen D 62 B3
Aith
  Orkney GB 23 B6
  Shetland GB 22 A7
Aitona E 90 B3
Aix-en-Othe F 59 B4
Aix-en-Provence F 79 C4
Aixe-sur-Vienne F 67 C6
Aix-les-Bains F 69 C5
Aizenay F 66 B3
Aizkraukle LV 7 C8
Aizpute LV 6 C6
Ajac F 77 C5
Ajaccio F 102 B1
Ajain F 68 B1
Ajaureforsen S 115 B12
Ajdovščina SLO 72 C3
Ajka H 74 A2
Ajo E 89 A3
Ajofrin E 94 C3
Ajuda P 93 C3
Akanthou CY 120 A2
Akarca TR 118 D4
Akasztó H 75 B4
Akçakoca TR 118 A6
Akçaova TR 118 A4
Akçay TR 119 F4
Aken D 52 B2
Åkerby S 36 B4
Åkernes N 33 D4
Åkersberga S 37 C5
Åkers Styckebruk S 37 C4
Åkervik N 115 B10
Akhisar TR 118 D2
Akirkeby DK 41 D4
Akköy TR 119 E2
Akkrum NL 42 B2
Akören TR 119 E7
Akra N 32 C3
Akranes IS 111 C3
Akrehamn N 33 C2
Akréour CY 120 B1
Aksaray TR 16 B7
Akşehir TR 119 D6
Akseki TR 119 E6
Aksla N 32 A3
Aksu TR 119 F5
Aktsyabrski BY 7 E10
Akureyri IS 111 B7
Akvåg N 33 D6
Akyazı TR 118 B5
Al N 32 B5
Ala I 71 C6
Alaca TR 16 A7
Alacaatlı TR 118 C3
Alaçam TR 16 A7
Alaçatı TR 119 D1
Alaejos E 88 C1
Alagna Valsésia I 70 C2
Alagón E 90 B1
Alaior E 97 B4
Alájar E 99 B4
Alakurtti RUS 3 C29
Alalí FIN 113 E13
Alameda E 100 B1
Alameda de la Sagra E 94 B3
Alamedilla E 100 B2
Alamillo E 100 A1
Alaminos E 95 B4
Ala-Nampa FIN 113 F15
Alandroal P 92 C3
Alange E 93 C4
Alanís E 99 A5
Alanno I 103 A6
Alansbro S 115 E14
Alanya TR 119 F7
Alap H 74 B3
Alaquàs E 96 B2
Alarcón E 95 C4
Alar del Rey E 88 B2
Alaró E 97 B2
Alaşehir TR 119 D3
Alássio I 80 B2
Álava FIN 3 E25
Alba
  E 95 B5
  I 80 B2
Alba Adriática I 82 D2
Albacete E 95 D5

Alba de Tormes E 94 B1
Alba de Yeltes E 93 A4
Albaida E 96 C2
Albaida RO 11 C7
Albæk DK 38 B3
Albaladejo E 101 A3
Albala del Caudillo E 93 B4
Albalat E 96 B2
Albalate de Cinca E 90 B3
Albalate del Arzobispo E 90 B2
Albalete de Zorita E 95 B4
Alban F 77 C5
Albánchez E 101 B3
Albánchez de Ubeda E 100 B2
Albano Laziale I 102 B5
Albanyà E 91 A5
Albares E 95 B3
Albarracin E 95 B5
Albatana E 101 A4
Albatarrec E 90 B3
Albatera E 101 A5
Albbruck D 61 C4
Albedin E 100 B1
Albelda de Iregua E 89 B4
Albenga I 80 B2
Albens F 69 C5
Alberga
  Södermanland S 37 C3
  Södermanland S 37 D3
Albergaria-a-Nova P 87 D2
Albergaria-a-Velha P 92 A2
Albergaria dos Doze P 92 B2
Alberic E 96 B2
Albernoa P 98 B3
Alberobello I 104 C3
Alberoni I 72 C2
Albersdorf D 43 A6
Albersloh D 50 B3
Albert F 48 C3
Albertirsa H 75 A4
Albertville F 69 C6
Albi F 77 C5
Albidona I 106 B3
Albina I 71 C4
Albino I 71 C4
Albires E 88 B1
Albisola Marina I 80 B2
Albocácer E 90 C3
Albolote E 100 B2
Albondón E 100 C2
Alborea E 96 B1
Albox E 101 B3
Albrechtice nad Vltavou CZ 63 A5
Albstadt D 61 B5
Albufeira P 98 B2
Albuñol E 100 C2
Albuñuelas E 100 C2
Alburquerque E 93 B3
Alby
  Öland S 41 C6
  Västernorrland S 115 E12
Alcácer do Sal P 92 C2
Alcáçovas P 92 C2
Alcadozo E 101 A4
Alcafoces P 93 B3
Alcains P 92 B3
Alcalá de Guadaira E 99 B5
Alcalá de Gurrea E 90 A2
Alcalá de Henares E 95 B3
Alcalá de la Selva E 96 A2
Alcalá del Júcar E 96 C1
Alcalá de los Gazules E 99 C5
Alcalá del Río E 99 B5
Alcalá del Valle E 99 C5
Alcalá la Real E 100 B2
Álcamo I 108 B1
Alcampell E 90 B3
Alcanadre E 89 B4
Alcanar E 90 C3
Alcanede P 92 B2
Alcanena P 92 B2
Alcañices E 87 C4
Alcántara E 93 B4
Alcantarilla E 101 B4
Alcañiz E 90 B2
Alcaracejos E 100 A1
Alcara il Fusi I 109 A3
Alcaraz E 101 A3
Alcaria Ruiva P 98 B3
Alcarraz E 90 B3
Alcaudete E 100 B1
Alcaudete de la Jara E 94 C2
Alcázar de San Juan E 95 C3
Alcazarén E 88 C2
Alcester GB 29 A6
Alcoba E 94 C2
Alcobaça P 92 B1
Alcobendas E 94 B3
Alcocer E 95 B4
Alcochete P 92 C2
Alcoentre P 92 B2

Alcolea
  Almería E 100 C3
  Córdoba E 100 B1
Alcolea de Calatrava E 94 D2
Alcolea de Cinca E 90 B3
Alcolea del Pinar E 95 A4
Alcolea del Rio E 99 B5
Alcolea de Tajo E 93 B5
Alcollarín E 93 B5
Alconchel E 93 C3
Alconera E 93 C4
Alcóntar E 101 B3
Alcora E 96 A2
Alcorcón E 94 B3
Alcorisa E 90 C2
Alcossebre E 96 A3
Alcoutim P 98 B3
Alcover E 91 B4
Alcoy E 96 C2
Alcubierre E 90 B2
Alcubilla de Avellaneda E 89 C3
Alcubilla de Nogales E 88 B1
Alcublas E 96 B2
Alcúdia E 97 B3
Alcúdia de Guadix E 100 B2
Alcudia de Crespins E 96 C2
Aldea del Cano E 93 B4
Aldea del Fresno E 94 B2
Aldea del Obispo E 87 D4
Aldea del Rey E 100 A2
Aldea de Trujillo E 93 B5
Aldealcorvo E 94 A3
Aldealuenga de Santa Maria E 89 C3
Aldeamayor de San Martín E 88 C2
Aldeanueva de Barbarroya E 94 C1
Aldeanueva del Camino E 93 A5
Aldeanueva del Codonal E 94 A2
Aldeanueva de San Bartolomé E 94 C1
Aldeapozo E 89 C4
Aldeaquemada E 100 A2
Aldea Real E 94 A2
Aldearrubia E 94 A1
Aldeaseca de la Frontera E 94 B1
Aldeasoña E 88 C2
Aldeatejada E 94 B1
Aldeavieja E 94 B2
Aldeburgh GB 30 B5
Aldeia da Mata P 92 B3
Aldeia da Serra P 92 C3
Aldeia do Bispo P 93 A4
Aldeia do Mato P 92 B2
Aldeia Gavinha P 92 B1
Aldeire E 100 B2
Aldenhoven D 50 C2
Aldersbach D 62 B4
Aldershot GB 31 C3
Aldudes F 76 C1
Aled S 40 C2
Aledo E 101 B4
Alegria E 89 B4
Aleksa Šantić SRB 75 C4
Aleksandrovac
  Srbija SRB 85 B6
  Srbija SRB 85 C6
Aleksandrów Kujawski PL 47 C4
Aleksandrów Łódzki PL 55 B4
Ålem S 40 C6
Alençon F 57 B6
Alenquer P 92 B1
Alenya F 91 A5
Aléria F 102 A2
Alès F 78 B3
Alessándria I 80 B2
Alessándria della Rocca I 108 B2
Alessano I 107 B5
Ålesund N 114 E3
Alet-les-Bains F 77 D5
Alexandria
  GB 24 C3
  GR 116 B4
  RO 11 E8
Aleyrac F 78 B3
Alézio I 107 A5
Alfacar E 100 B2
Alfaiates P 93 A4
Alfajarin E 90 B2
Alfambra
  P 98 B2
  E 96 A1
Alfândega da Fé P 87 C4
Alfarela de Jafes P 87 C3
Alfarelos P 92 A2
Alfarim P 92 C1

Alfarnate E 100 C1
Alfaro E 89 B5
Alfarràs E 90 B3
Alfaz del Pi E 96 C2
Alfedena I 103 B7
Alfeizarão P 92 B1
Alfeld
  Bayern D 62 A2
  Niedersachsen D 51 B5
Alfena P 87 C2
Alferce P 98 B2
Alfhausen D 43 C4
Alford
  Aberdeenshire GB 23 D6
  Lincolnshire GB 27 B6
Alforja E 90 B3
Alfreton GB 27 B4
Alfta S 36 A3
Alfundão P 98 B2
Algaida E 97 B2
Algar E 99 C5
Ålgård N 33 D2
Algarinejo E 100 B1
Algarrobo E 100 C1
Algatocin E 99 C5
Algeciras E 99 C5
Algemesi E 96 B2
Algés P 92 C1
Algete E 95 B3
Alghero I 110 B1
Alginet E 96 B2
Algodonales E 99 C5
Algodor E 94 C3
Algora E 95 B4
Algoso P 87 C4
Algoz P 98 B2
Alguaire E 90 B3
Alguazas E 101 A4
Algutsrum S 41 C6
Algyö H 75 B5
Alhama de Almería E 101 C3
Alhama de Aragón E 89 C5
Alhama de Granada E 100 C2
Alhama de Murcia E 101 B4
Alhaurin de la Torre E 100 C1
Alhaurin el Grande E 100 C1
Alhendin E 100 B2
Alhóndiga E 95 B4
Aliaga
  TR 118 D1
  E 90 C2
Alíartos GR 116 D4
Alibunar SRB 85 A5
Alicante E 96 C2
Alicún de Ortega E 100 B2
Alife I 103 B7
Alija del Infantado E 88 B1
Alijó P 87 C3
Alimena I 109 B3
Alingsås S 40 B2
Alinyà E 91 A4
Aliseda E 93 B4
Ali Terme I 109 A4
Aliveri GR 116 D6
Alixan F 79 B4
Aljaraque E 99 B3
Aljezur P 98 B2
Aljorra E 101 B4
Aljubarrota P 92 B2
Aljucen E 93 B4
Aljustrel P 98 B2
Alken B 49 C6
Alkmaar NL 42 C1
Alkoven A 63 B5
Allaines F 58 B2
Allaire F 57 C3
Allanche F 68 C2
Alland A 64 B2
Allariz E 87 B3
Allassac F 67 C6
Allauch F 79 C4
Alleen N 33 D4
Alleghe I 72 B2
Allemont F 69 C6
Allendale Town GB 25 D5
Allendorf D 51 C4
Allentsteig A 63 B6
Allepuz E 90 C2
Aller N 114 B8
Alleuze F 68 C2
Allevard F 69 C6
Allgunnen S 40 B5
Allihies IRL 20 C1
Allingåbro DK 38 C3
Allmannsdorf D 61 C5
Allo E 89 B4
Alloa GB 25 B4
Allogny F 68 A2
Alloluokta S 112 E8
Allones
  Eure et Loire F 58 B2
  Maine-et-Loire F 67 A5
Allons F 76 B2
Allos F 79 B5
Allstedt D 52 B1
Alltwalis GB 28 B3
Allumiere I 102 A4
Almaceda P 92 B3
Almacelles E 90 B3
Almachar E 100 C1
Almada P 92 C1
Almadén E 100 A1
Almadén de la Plata E 99 B4
Almadenejos E 100 A1
Almadrones E 95 B4
Almagro E 100 A2
Almajano E 89 C4
Almansa E 96 C2
Almansil P 98 B2
Almanza E 88 B1
Almaraz E 93 B5
Almargen E 99 C5
Almarza E 89 C4
Almásfüzitő H 64 C4
Almassora E 96 A2
Almazán E 89 C4
Almazul E 89 C5
Alme D 51 B4
Almedina E 100 A3
Almedinilla E 100 B1
Almeida
  E 87 C4
  P 93 A4
Almeirim P 92 B2
Almelo NL 42 C3
Almenar E 90 B3
Almenara E 96 B2
Almenar de Soria E 89 C4
Almendra P 87 D3
Almendral E 93 C4
Almendral de la Cañada E 94 B2
Almendralejo E 93 C4
Almenno San Bartolomeo I 71 C4
Almere NL 42 C2
Almería E 101 C3
Almerimar E 100 C2
Almese I 70 C2
Almexial P 98 B3
Almhult S 40 C4
Almiropotamos GR 117 D6
Almiros GR 116 C4
Almodôvar P 98 B2
Almodóvar del Campo E 100 A1
Almodóvar del Pinar E 95 C5
Almodóvar del Río E 99 B5
Almofala P 87 D3
Almogia E 100 C1
Almoharin E 93 B4
Almonacid de la Sierra E 89 C5
Almonacid de Toledo E 94 C3
Almonaster la Real E 99 B4
Almondsbury GB 29 B5
Almonte E 99 B4
Almoradi E 101 A5
Almoraima E 99 C5
Almorox E 94 B2
Almoster P 92 B2
Almsele S 115 C14
Almsta S 36 C5
Almudévar E 90 A2
Almuñécar E 100 C2
Almunge S 36 C5
Almuradiel E 100 A2
Almussafes E 96 B2
Almvik S 40 B6
Alness GB 23 D4
Alnmouth GB 25 C6
Alnwick GB 25 C6
Aloppe S 36 C4
Álora E 100 C1
Alos d'Ensil E 91 A4
Alosno E 99 B3
Alozaina E 100 C1
Alpbach A 72 A1
Alpedrete de la Sierra E 95 B3
Alpedrinha P 92 B3
Alpen D 50 B2
Alpera E 96 C1
Alphen aan de Rijn NL 49 A5
Alpiarça P 92 B2
Alpignano I 70 C2
Alpirsbach D 61 B4
Alpu TR 118 C5

Alsóújlak H ... 74 A1
Alstad N ... 112 E4
Alstätte D ... 50 A2
Alsterbro S ... 40 C5
Alstermo S ... 40 C5
Alston GB ... 25 D5
Alsvåg N ... 112 D4
Alsvik N ... 112 E3
Alta N ... 113 C12
Älta S ... 37 C5
Altamura I ... 104 C2
Altarejos E ... 95 C4
Altaussee A ... 63 C4
Altavilla Irpina I ... 103 B7
Altavilla Silentina I ... 103 C8
Altdöbern D ... 53 B4
Altdorf
　CH ... 70 B3
　D ... 62 B3
Altdorf bei Nürnberg
　D ... 62 A2
Alte P ... 98 B2
Altea E ... 96 C2
Altedo I ... 81 B5
Altena D ... 50 B3
Altenau D ... 51 B6
Altenberg D ... 53 C3
Altenberge D ... 50 A3
Altenbruch D ... 43 B5
Altenburg D ... 52 C2
Altenfelden A ... 63 B4
Altengronau D ... 51 C5
Altenheim D ... 60 B3
Altenhundem D ... 50 B4
Altenkirchen
　Mecklenburg-
　Vorpommern D ... 45 A5
　Radom D ... 50 C3
Altenkunstadt D ... 52 C1
Altenmarkt
　A ... 63 C5
　D ... 62 B3
Altenmarkt im Pongau
　A ... 72 A3
Altensteig D ... 61 B4
Altentreptow D ... 45 B5
Altenwalde D ... 43 B5
Alten-weddingen D ... 52 A1
Alter do Chão P ... 92 B3
Altfraunhofen D ... 62 B3
Altheim
　A ... 63 B4
　D ... 61 A5
Althofen A ... 73 B4
Altholuk TR ... 118 C1
Altınova TR ... 118 C1
Altıntaş TR ... 118 C5
Altınyaka TR ... 119 F5
Altınyayla TR ... 119 E4
Altkirch F ... 60 C3
Altlandsberg D ... 45 C5
Altlewin D ... 45 C6
Altmannstein D ... 62 B2
Altmorschen D ... 51 B5
Altmünster A ... 63 C4
Altnaharra GB ... 23 C4
Alto Campoó E ... 88 A2
Altofonte I ... 108 A2
Altomonte I ... 106 B3
Alton
　Hampshire GB ... 31 C3
　Staffordshire GB ... 27 C4
Altopáscio I ... 81 C4
Altötting D ... 62 B3
Altreichenau D ... 63 B4
Alt Ruppin D ... 45 C4
Altshausen D ... 61 C5
Altstätten CH ... 71 A4
Altura E ... 96 B2
Altusried D ... 61 C6
Alūksne LV ... 7 C9
Alunda S ... 36 B5
Alustante E ... 95 B5
Alva GB ... 25 B4
Alvaiázere P ... 92 B2
Alvalade P ... 98 B2
Älvängen S ... 38 B5
Alvarenga P ... 87 D2
Alvares P ... 92 A2
Alvdal N ... 114 E7
Älvdalen S ... 34 A6
Alverca P ... 92 C1
Alversund N ... 32 B2
Alvesta S ... 40 C4
Alvignac F ... 77 B4
Alvik N ... 32 B3
Alvik S ... 36 B1
Alvimare F ... 58 A1
Alvobeira P ... 92 B2
Alvito P ... 98 A3
Älvkarleby S ... 36 B4
Älvkarleöbruk S ... 36 B4
Alvor P ... 98 B2
Alvorge P ... 92 B2
Alvøy N ... 32 B2
Alvros S ... 115 E11
Alvsbacka S ... 35 C5
Älvsbyn S ... 3 D24
Älvsered S ... 40 B2
Alwernia PL ... 55 C4
Alwinton GB ... 25 C5
Alyth GB ... 25 B4
Alytus LT ... 6 D8
Alzénau D ... 51 C5
Alzey D ... 61 A4
Alzira E ... 96 B2
Alzonne F ... 77 C5
Amadora P ... 92 C1
Åmål S ... 35 C4
Amalfi I ... 103 C7
Amaliada GR ... 117 E3
Amance F ... 60 C2
Amancey F ... 69 A6
Amándola I ... 82 D2
Amantea I ... 106 B3
Amarante P ... 87 C2
Amareleja P ... 98 A3
Amares P ... 87 C2
Amaseno I ... 103 B6
Amasra TR ... 118 A7
Amasya TR ... 16 A8
Amatrice I ... 103 A6
Amay B ... 49 C6
Ambarnyy RUS ... 3 D30
Ambazac F ... 67 C6
Ambelonas GR ... 116 C4
Ambérieu-en-Bugey
　F ... 69 C5
Ambérieux-en-Dombes
　F ... 69 B4
Ambert F ... 68 C3
Ambés F ... 76 A2
Ambjörby S ... 34 B5
Ambjörnarp S ... 40 B3
Amble GB ... 25 C6
Ambleside GB ... 26 A3
Ambleteuse F ... 48 C2
Amboise F ... 67 A5
Ambrières-les-Vallées
　F ... 57 B5
Amden CH ... 71 A4
Amel B ... 50 C2
Amélia I ... 102 A5
Amélie-les-Bains-Palalda
　F ... 91 A5
Amelinghausen D ... 44 B2
Amendoa P ... 92 B2
Amendoeira P ... 98 B3
Améndola I ... 104 B1
Amendolara I ... 106 B3
Amer E ... 91 A5
A Merca E ... 87 B3
Amerongen NL ... 49 A6
Amersfoort NL ... 49 A6
Amersham GB ... 31 C3
Amesbury GB ... 29 B6
Amfíklia GR ... 116 D4

Amfilochia GR ... 116 D3
Amfípoli GR ... 116 B5
Amfissa GR ... 116 D4
Amièira P ... 98 A3
Amiens F ... 58 A3
Amindeo GR ... 116 B3
Aminne S ... 40 B3
Åmli N ... 33 D5
Amlwch GB ... 26 B1
Ammanford GB ... 28 B4
Ammarnäs S ... 115 B13
Ammeberg S ... 37 D1
Amorbach D ... 61 A5
Amorebieta E ... 89 A4
Amorgos GR ... 117 F7
Amorosa P ... 87 C2
Amorosi I ... 103 B7
Amot
　Buskerud N ... 34 C1
　Telemark N ... 33 C4
　S ... 36 B3
Åmotfors S ... 34 C4
Åmotsdal N ... 33 C5
Amou F ... 76 C2
Ampezzo I ... 72 B2
Ampfing D ... 62 B3
Ampflwang A ... 63 B4
Amplepuis F ... 69 C4
Amposta E ... 90 C3
Ampthill GB ... 30 B3
Ampudia E ... 88 C2
Ampuero E ... 89 A3
Amriswil CH ... 71 A4
Amsele S ... 115 C16
Amstelveen NL ... 49 A5
Amsterdam NL ... 42 C1
Amstetten A ... 63 B5
Amtzell D ... 61 C5
Amulree GB ... 25 B4
Amurrio E ... 89 A4
Amusco E ... 88 B2
Anacapri I ... 103 C7
Anadia P ... 92 A2
Anadón E ... 90 C1
Anafi GR ... 117 F7
Anagni I ... 102 B6
Anamur TR ... 16 C6
Ananyiv UA ... 11 C10
Anascaul IRL ... 20 B1
Anäset S ... 3 D24
Ana-Sira N ... 33 D3
Anastázewo PL ... 47 C4
Ança P ... 92 A2
Ancaster GB ... 27 C5
Ancede P ... 87 C2
Ancenis F ... 66 A3
Ancerville F ... 59 B6
Anchuras E ... 94 C2
Ancona I ... 82 C2
Ancora P ... 87 C2
Ancrum GB ... 25 C5
Andalo I ... 71 B5
Andalsnes N ... 114 E4
Andance F ... 69 C4
Andau A ... 64 C3
Andebu N ... 35 C2
Andeer CH ... 71 B4
Andelfingen CH ... 61 C4
Andelot-Blancheville F ... 59 B6
Andelot-en-Montagne
　F ... 69 B5
Andenes N ... 112 C5
Andenne B ... 49 C6
Anderlues B ... 49 C5
Andermatt CH ... 70 B3
Andernach D ... 50 C3
Andernos-les-Bains F ... 76 B1
Anderslöv S ... 41 D3
Anderstorp S ... 40 B3
Andijk NL ... 42 C2
Andoain E ... 89 A4
Andocs H ... 74 B2
Andolsheim F ... 60 B3
Andorra E ... 90 C2
Andorra la Vella AND ... 91 A4
Andosilla E ... 89 B5
Andover GB ... 31 C2
Andratx E ... 97 B2
Andreapol RUS ... 7 C12
Andreas GB ... 26 A1
Andrespol PL ... 55 B4
Andrest F ... 76 C3
Andretta I ... 103 C8
Andrezieux-Bouthéon
　F ... 69 C4
Andria I ... 104 B2
Andrijevica MNE ... 85 D4
Andritsena GR ... 117 E3
Andros GR ... 117 E6
Andrychów PL ... 65 A5
Andselv N ... 112 C7
Andújar E ... 100 A1
Anduze F ... 78 B2
Aneby N ... 34 B2
Aneby S ... 40 B4
Añes E ... 89 A3
Anet F ... 58 B2
Anfo I ... 71 C5
Ang S ... 40 B4
Anga S ... 37 E5
Angaïs F ... 76 C2
Ange S ... 115 D11
Ånge S ... 115 E12
Angeja P ... 92 A2
Ängelholm S ... 41 C2
Angeli FIN ... 113 D14
Ängelsberg S ... 36 C3
Anger
　A ... 73 A5
　D ... 62 C3
Angera I ... 70 C3
Angermünde D ... 45 B6
Angern A ... 64 B2
Angers F ... 67 A4
Angerville F ... 58 B3
Anghiari I ... 82 C1
Angle GB ... 28 B2
Anglés E ... 91 B5
Anglés F ... 77 C5
Anglesola E ... 91 B4
Anglet F ... 76 C1
Anglisidhes CY ... 120 B2
Anglure F ... 59 B4
Angoulême F ... 67 C5
Angoulins F ... 66 B3
Angsö S ... 37 C3
Angues E ... 90 A2
Anguiano E ... 89 B4
Anguillara Sabazia I ... 102 A5
Anguillara Véneta I ... 72 C1
Anhée B ... 49 C5
Anholt DK ... 38 C4
Aniane F ... 78 C2
Aniche F ... 49 C4
Animskog S ... 35 D4
Anina RO ... 10 D6
Anixi GR ... 116 C3
Anizy-le-Château F ... 59 A4
Anjalankoski FIN ... 3 F27
Anjan S ... 115 D9
Ankara TR ... 118 C7
Ankaran SLO ... 72 C3
Ankarsrum S ... 40 B6
Ankerlia N ... 112 C9
Anklam D ... 45 B5
Ankum D ... 43 C4
Anlauftal A ... 72 A3
Anlezy F ... 68 B3
Ann S ... 115 D9
Annaberg A ... 63 C6
Annaberg-Buchholz
　D ... 52 C3
Annaberg im Lammertal
　A ... 72 A3
Annaburg D ... 52 B3
Annahütte D ... 53 B3
Annalong GB ... 19 B6

Annan GB ... 25 D4
Anndalsvågen N ... 115 B9
Anneberg
　Halland S ... 38 B5
　Jönköping S ... 40 B4
Annecy F ... 69 C6
Annelund S ... 40 B3
Annemasse F ... 69 B6
Annenskiy Most RUS ... 7 A14
Annerstad S ... 40 C3
Annestown IRL ... 21 B4
Annevoie-Rouillon B ... 49 C5
Annonay F ... 69 C4
Annot F ... 79 C5
Annweiler D ... 60 A3
Ano Poroia GR ... 116 A5
Añora E ... 100 A1
Ano Síros GR ... 117 E6
Anould F ... 60 B2
Anquela del Ducado
　E ... 95 B4
Anröchte D ... 51 B4
Ansager DK ... 39 D1
Ansbach D ... 62 A1
Anseroeul B ... 49 C4
Ansfelden A ... 63 B5
Ansião P ... 92 B2
Ansó E ... 76 D2
Ansoain E ... 76 D1
Anstruther GB ... 25 B5
Antas E ... 101 B4
Antegnate I ... 71 C4
Antequera E ... 100 B1
Anterselva di Mezzo I ... 72 B2
Antibes F ... 79 C6
Antigüedad E ... 88 C2
Antillo I ... 109 B4
Antirio GR ... 117 D3
An t-Ob GB ... 22 D1
Antoing B ... 49 C4
Antonin PL ... 54 B2
Antonín PL ... 54 B2
Antrain F ... 57 B4
Antrim GB ... 19 B5
Antrodoco I ... 102 A6
Antronapiana I ... 70 B3
Antronapiana GB ... 31 E11
Antuzede P ... 92 A2
Antwerp = Antwerpen
　B ... 49 B5
Antwerpen = Antwerp
　B ... 49 B5
Anversa d'Abruzzi I ... 103 B6
Anvin F ... 48 C3
Anzat-le-Luguet F ... 68 C3
Anzi I ... 104 C1
Ánzio I ... 102 B5
Anzola d'Emilia I ... 81 B5
Anzón E ... 89 C5
Aoiz E ... 76 D1
Aosta I ... 70 C2
Apalhão P ... 92 B3
Apátfalva H ... 75 B5
Apatin SRB ... 75 C4
Apatity RUS ... 3 C30
Apc H ... 65 C5
Apécchio I ... 82 C1
Apeldoorn NL ... 50 A1
Apen D ... 43 B4
Apenburg D ... 44 C3
Apensen D ... 43 B6
A Peroxa E ... 87 B3
Apiro I ... 82 C2
Apliki CY ... 120 B2
Apolda D ... 52 B1
Apolonia GR ... 117 F6
A Pontenova E ... 86 A3
Apostag H ... 75 B3
Appelbo S ... 34 B6
Appennino I ... 82 D2
Appenzell CH ... 71 A4
Appiano I ... 71 B6
Appingedam NL ... 42 B3
Appleby-in-Westmorland
　GB ... 26 A3
Applecross GB ... 22 D3
Appledore GB ... 28 B3
Appoigny F ... 59 C4
Apremont-la-Forêt F ... 60 B1
Aprica I ... 71 B5
Apricena I ... 103 B8
Aprigliano I ... 106 B3
Aprília I ... 102 B5
Apt F ... 79 C4
Apúlia P ... 87 C2
Aquiléia I ... 72 C3
Aquilónia I ... 103 C8
Aquino I ... 103 B6
Ar S ... 37 E5
Arabba I ... 72 B1
Arabayona E ... 94 A1
Aracena E ... 99 B4
Arachova GR ... 116 D4
Aračinovo MK ... 182 B3
Arad RO ... 75 B6
Aradac SRB ... 75 C5
Aradhippou CY ... 120 B2
Aragnouet F ... 76 D3
Aragona I ... 108 B2
Aramits F ... 76 C2
Aramon F ... 78 C3
Aranda de Duero E ... 88 C3
Aranda de Moncayo
　E ... 89 C5
Arandjelovac SRB ... 85 B5
Aranjuez E ... 95 B3
Arantzazu E ... 89 B4
Aranzueque E ... 95 B3
Aras de Alpuente E ... 96 B1
Arauzo de Miel E ... 89 C3
Arazede P ... 92 A2
Arbatax I ... 110 C2
Árbesbach A ... 63 B5
Arboga S ... 37 C2
Arbois F ... 69 B5
Arbon CH ... 71 A4
Arboréa I ... 110 C1
Árbol E ... 86 A2
Arbório I ... 70 C3
Arbostad N ... 112 D6
Arbrå S ... 36 A3
Arbroath GB ... 25 B5
Arbúcies E ... 91 B5
Arbuniel E ... 100 B2
Arbus I ... 110 C1
Arcachon F ... 76 B1
Arce I ... 103 B6
Arcen NL ... 50 B2
Arc-en-Barrois F ... 59 C5
Arces-Dilo F ... 59 B4
Arcévia I ... 82 C1
Arcey F ... 70 A1
Archanes GR ... 117 G7
Archangelos GR ... 119 F3
Archena E ... 101 A4
Archez E ... 100 C1
Archiac F ... 67 C4
Archidona E ... 100 B1
Archiestown GB ... 23 D5
Archivel E ... 101 A4
Arcidosso I ... 81 D5
Arcille I ... 81 D5
Arcis-sur-Aube F ... 59 B5
Arco I ... 71 C5
Arcos E ... 89 B3
Arcos de Jalón E ... 95 A4
Arcos de la Frontera
　E ... 99 C5
Arcos de la Sierra E ... 95 B4
Arcos de las Salinas
　E ... 96 B1
Arcos de Valdevez P ... 87 C2
Arcozelo P ... 92 A3
Arc-sur-Tille F ... 69 A5
Arcusa E ... 90 A3
Arcy-sur-Cure F ... 59 C4

Arcy-sur-Cure F ... 59 C4
Ardagh IRL ... 20 B2
Ardal N ... 33 C3
Ardales E ... 100 C1
Ardalstangen N ... 32 A4
Ardara
　I ... 110 B1
　IRL ... 18 B3
Ardarroch GB ... 22 D3
Ardbeg GB ... 24 C1
Ardcharnich GB ... 22 D3
Ardchyle GB ... 24 B3
Ardee IRL ... 19 C5
Arden DK ... 38 C2
Ardentes F ... 68 B1
Ardenza I ... 81 C4
Ardersier GB ... 23 D4
Ardes F ... 68 C3
Ardessie GB ... 22 D3
Ardez CH ... 71 B5
Ardfert IRL ... 20 B2
Ardgay GB ... 23 D4
Ardglass GB ... 19 B6
Ardgroom IRL ... 20 C2
Ardhasig GB ... 22 D2
Ardino BG ... 116 A7
Ardisa E ... 90 A2
Ardkearagh IRL ... 20 C1
Ardlui GB ... 24 B3
Ardlussa GB ... 24 B2
Ardón E ... 88 B1
Ardooie B ... 49 C4
Ardore I ... 106 C3
Ardre S ... 37 E5
Ardres F ... 48 C2
Ardrishaig GB ... 24 B2
Ardrossan GB ... 24 C3
Are N ... 33 C2
Åre S ... 115 D10
Areia Branca P ... 92 B1
Aremark N ... 35 C3
Arenales de San Gregorio
　E ... 95 C3
Arenas de Iguña E ... 88 A2
Arenas del Rey E ... 100 C2
Arenas de San Juan
　E ... 95 C3
Arenas de San Pedro
　E ... 94 B1
Arendal N ... 33 D5
Arendonk B ... 49 B6
Arengosse F ... 76 B2
Arentorp S ... 35 D4
Arenys de Mar E ... 91 B5
Arenys de Munt E ... 91 B5
Arenzano I ... 80 B2
Areo E ... 91 A4
Areópoli GR ... 117 F4
Ares E ... 86 A2
Arès F ... 76 B1
Ares del Maestrat E ... 90 C2
Aresvika N ... 114 D5
Arette F ... 76 C2
Aretxabaleta E ... 89 A4
Arevalillo E ... 93 A5
Arévalo E ... 94 A2
Arez P ... 92 B3
Arezzo I ... 81 C5
Arfeuilles F ... 68 B3
Argalasti GR ... 116 C5
Argallón E ... 99 A5
Argamasilla de Alba
　E ... 95 C3
Argamasilla de Calatrava
　E ... 100 A1
Arganda E ... 95 B3
Arganil P ... 92 A2
Argasion GR ... 117 E2
Argegno I ... 71 C4
Argelès-Gazost F ... 76 C2
Argelès-sur-Mer F ... 91 A6
Argenta I ... 81 B5
Argentan F ... 57 B5
Argentat F ... 77 A4
Argentera I ... 79 B5
Argenthal D ... 50 D3
Argentiera I ... 110 B1
Argentière F ... 70 C1
Argenton-Château F ... 67 B4
Argenton-sur-Creuse
　F ... 67 B6
Argentré F ... 57 B5
Argentré-du-Plessis
　F ... 57 B4
Argent-sur-Sauldre F ... 68 A2
Argirades GR ... 116 C1
Argithani TR ... 119 D6
Argos GR ... 117 E4
Argos Orestiko GR ... 116 B3
Argostoli GR ... 117 D2
Argote E ... 89 B4
Arguedas E ... 89 B5
Argueil F ... 58 A2
Arholma S ... 36 C6
Ariano Irpino I ... 103 B8
Ariano nel Polésine I ... 82 B1
Aribe E ... 76 D1
Aridea GR ... 116 B4
Arienzo I ... 103 B7
Arild S ... 41 C2
Arileod GB ... 24 B1
Arilje SRB ... 85 C5
Arinagour GB ... 24 B1
Ariño E ... 90 B2
Arinthod F ... 69 B5
Arisaig GB ... 24 B2
Arisgotas E ... 94 C3
Aritzo I ... 110 C2
Ariza E ... 89 C4
Årjäng S ... 35 C4
Arjeplog S ... 115 A14
Arjona E ... 100 B1
Arjonilla E ... 100 B1
Arkasa GR ... 119 G2
Arkelstorp S ... 41 C4
Arklow IRL ... 21 B5
Arkösund S ... 37 D3
Ärla S ... 37 C3
Arlanc F ... 68 C3
Arlanzón E ... 89 B3
Arlebosc F ... 78 A3
Arlena di Castro I ... 102 A4
Arles F ... 78 C3
Arles-sur-Tech F ... 91 A5
Arló H ... 65 B6
Arlon B ... 60 A1
Armação de Pera P ... 98 B2
Armadale
　Highland GB ... 23 C4
　West Lothian GB ... 25 C4
Armagh GB ... 19 B5
Armamar P ... 87 C3
Armenós E ... 70 C3
Armenis RO ... 10 D6
Armenistis GR ... 117 E8
Armentières F ... 48 C3
Armilla E ... 100 B2
Armiñón E ... 89 B4
Armoy GB ... 19 A5
Armuña de Tajuña E ... 95 B3
Armutlu
　Bursa TR ... 118 B3
　İzmir TR ... 119 D2
Arnac-Pompadour F ... 67 C6
Arnafjord N ... 32 A3
Arnage F ... 57 C6
Arnas F ... 69 B4
Arnäsvall S ... 115 D16
Árnes IS ... 111 A4
Arnes N ... 114 D8
Arnborg DK ... 39 C2
Arnedillo E ... 89 B4
Arnedo E ... 89 B4

Arneguy F ... 76 C1
Arnés E ... 90 C3
Arnes IS ... 111 A4
Årnes
　Akershus N ... 34 B3
　Troms N ... 112 C7
Arnfels A ... 73 B5
Arnhem NL ... 50 B1
Arnissa GR ... 116 B3
Arnö S ... 37 D4
Arnold GB ... 27 B4
Arnoldstein A ... 72 B3
Arnsberg D ... 50 B4
Arnschwang D ... 62 A3
Arnsdorf D ... 53 B3
Arnset N ... 114 D6
Arnside GB ... 26 A3
Arnstadt D ... 51 C6
Arnstein D ... 51 C5
Arnstorf D ... 62 B3
Arnum DK ... 39 D1
Aroche E ... 99 B4
Arola CH ... 70 B2
Arolla CH ... 70 B2
Arolsen D ... 51 B5
Arona I ... 70 C3
Aros N ... 35 C2
Arosa
　CH ... 71 B4
　P ... 87 C2
Æroskøbing DK ... 39 E3
Årøsund DK ... 39 D2
Arouca P ... 87 D2
Øreysund N ... 114 E3
Arpajon F ... 58 B3
Arpajon-sur-Cère F ... 77 B5
Arpino I ... 103 B6
Arquata del Tronto I ... 82 D2
Arques F ... 48 C3
Arques-la-Bataille F ... 58 A2
Arquillos E ... 100 A2
Arraia-Maeztu E ... 89 B4
Arraiolos P ... 92 C2
Arrancourt F ... 60 B2
Arras F ... 48 C3
Arrasate E ... 89 A4
Arre DK ... 39 D1
Arreau F ... 77 D3
Arredondo E ... 89 A3
Arrens-Marsous F ... 76 D2
Arriate E ... 99 C5
Arrifana P ... 98 B2
Arrigorriaga E ... 89 A4
Arriondas E ... 88 A1
Arroba de los Montes
　E ... 94 C2
Arrochar GB ... 24 B3
Arromanches-les-Bains
　F ... 57 A5
Arronches P ... 92 B3
Arroniz E ... 89 B4
Arronville F ... 58 A2
Arrou F ... 58 B2
Arroya E ... 88 B2
Arroya de Cuéllar E ... 88 C2
Arroyal E ... 88 B2
Arroyo de la Luz E ... 93 B4
Arroyo del Ojanco E ... 100 A2
Arroyo de San Servan
　E ... 93 C4
Arroyomolinos de León
　E ... 99 A4
Arroyomolinos de
　Montánchez E ... 93 B4
Arruda dos Vinhos P ... 92 C1
Arsac F ... 76 B2
Ars-en-Ré F ... 66 B3
Arsiè I ... 72 C1
Arsiero I ... 71 C6
Ársoli I ... 102 A6
Ars-sur-Moselle F ... 60 A2
Arsunda S ... 36 B3
Artà E ... 97 B3
Arta GR ... 116 C3
Artajona E ... 89 B5
Artegna I ... 72 B3
Artena I ... 102 B5
Artenay F ... 58 B2
Artern D ... 52 B1
Artés E ... 91 B4
Artesa de Segre I ... 91 B4
Arth CH ... 70 A3
Arthez-de-Béarn F ... 76 C2
Arthon-en-Retz F ... 66 A2
Arthurstown IRL ... 21 B5
Artieda E ... 90 A2
Artix F ... 76 C2
Artotina GR ... 116 D4
Artsyz UA ... 11 C10
A Rúa E ... 87 B3
Arudy F ... 76 C2
Arundel GB ... 31 D3
Arveyres F ... 76 B2
Arvidsjaur S ... 115 B16
Arvieux F ... 79 B5
Arvika S ... 35 C4
Aryd
　Blekinge S ... 41 C5
　Kronoberg S ... 40 C4
Arzachena I ... 110 A2
Arzacq-Arraziguet F ... 76 C2
Árzana I ... 110 C2
Arzano F ... 56 C2
Aržano HR ... 84 C1
Arzberg D ... 52 C2
Arzignano I ... 71 C6
Arzila P ... 92 A2
Arzl im Pitztal A ... 71 A5
Arzúa E ... 86 B2
As B ... 49 B6
Aš CZ ... 52 C2
As N ... 35 C2
Ås S ... 115 D11
Åsa S ... 38 B5
Åsane N ... 32 B2
Åsarna S ... 115 E11
Asarp S ... 40 A3
Asasp F ... 76 C2
Asbro S ... 37 C2
Asby S ... 40 B5
Asbygri IS ... 111 A9
Ascain F ... 76 C1
Ascea I ... 106 A2
Aschach an der Donau
　A ... 63 B5
Aschaffenburg D ... 51 D5
Aschau
　Bayern D ... 62 C3
　Bayern D ... 62 C2
Aschbach Markt A ... 63 B5
Ascheberg
　Nordrhein-
　Westfalen D ... 50 B3
　Schleswig-Holstein D ... 44 A2
Aschendorf D ... 43 B4
Aschersleben D ... 52 B1
Asciano I ... 81 C5
Ascó E ... 90 B3
Asco F ... 102 A2
Áscoli Piceno I ... 82 D2
Áscoli Satriano I ... 103 B8
Ascona CH ... 70 B3
Ascot GB ... 31 C3
Ascoux F ... 58 B3
Åseda S ... 40 B5
Asele S ... 115 C14
Åsen
　N ... 114 D8
　S ... 34 A5
Asendorf D ... 43 C6
Asenovgrad BG ... 11 E8
Asensbruk S ... 35 D4
Åseral N ... 33 D4
Asfeld F ... 59 A5
Åsgårdstrand N ... 35 C2
Ásgarður IS ... 111 B1
Asgate CY ... 120 B2

Ash
　Kent GB ... 31 C5
　Surrey GB ... 31 C3
Ashammar S ... 36 B3
Ashbourne
　GB ... 27 B4
　IRL ... 21 A5
Ashburton GB ... 28 C4
Ashby-de-la-Zouch
　GB ... 27 C4
Ashchurch GB ... 29 B5
Asheim N ... 114 F8
Ashford GB ... 31 C4
Ashington GB ... 25 C6
Ashley GB ... 26 C3
Ashmyany BY ... 7 D8
Ashton Under Lyne
　GB ... 26 B3
Ashwell GB ... 30 B3
Asiago I ... 71 C6
Asipovichy BY ... 7 E10
Aska FIN ... 113 E15
Askam-in-Furness
　GB ... 26 A2
Askeaton IRL ... 20 B3
Asker N ... 34 C2
Askersund S ... 37 D1
Åskilje S ... 115 C14
Askim
　N ... 35 C3
　S ... 38 B4
Askland N ... 33 D5
Asköping S ... 37 C3
Askola FIN ... 3 F26
Askvoll N ... 32 A2
Aslestad N ... 33 C4
Åsnes N ... 34 B4
Ås Neves E ... 87 B2
As Nogais E ... 86 B3
Asola I ... 71 C5
Asolo I ... 72 C1
Asos GR ... 116 D2
Asotthalom H ... 75 B4
Aspach A ... 63 B4
Aspang Markt A ... 64 C2
Aspariegos E ... 88 C1
Asparn an der Zaya
　A ... 64 B2
Aspatria GB ... 26 A2
Aspberg S ... 35 C5
Aspe E ... 101 A5
Aspet F ... 77 C3
Aspö S ... 41 C5
As Pontes de García
　Rodríguez E ... 86 A3
Aspres-sur-Buëch F ... 79 B4
Aspsele S ... 115 D15
Assafora P ... 92 C1
Asse B ... 49 C5
Assebakte N ... 113 C14
Assel D ... 43 B6
Asselborn L ... 50 C1
Assémini I ... 110 C1
Assen NL ... 42 C3
Assenede B ... 49 B4
Assens
　Aarhus Amt. DK ... 38 C3
　Fyns Amt. DK ... 39 D2
Assesse B ... 49 C6
Assisi I ... 82 C1
Assling D ... 62 C3
Asso I ... 71 C4
Asson F ... 76 C2
Åssøro I ... 109 B3
Assumar P ... 92 B3
Asta N ... 34 A3
Astaffort F ... 77 B3
Astakos GR ... 116 D3
Asten NL ... 50 B1
Asti I ... 80 B2
Astipalea GR ... 119 F1
Astorga E ... 86 B4
Astorp S ... 41 C2
Åström S ... 115 C16
Astráðsk S ... 115 C16
Astudillo E ... 88 B2
Asuni I ... 110 C1
Asvánÿráró H ... 64 C3
Aszód H ... 65 C5
Aszófő H ... 74 B2
Atabey TR ... 119 E5
Atalaia P ... 92 B3
Atalandi GR ... 116 D4
Atalho P ... 92 C2
Átány H ... 65 C6
Atanzón E ... 95 B3
Ataquines E ... 94 A2
Atarfe E ... 100 B2
Atça TR ... 119 E3
Ateca E ... 89 C5
A Teixeira E ... 87 B3
Atella I ... 104 C1
Atessa I ... 103 A7
Ath B ... 49 C4
Athboy IRL ... 19 C5
Athea IRL ... 20 B2
Athenry IRL ... 20 A3
Athens = Athina GR ... 117 E5
Atherstone GB ... 27 C4
Athienou CY ... 120 A2
Athies F ... 59 A4
Athies-sous-Laon F ... 59 A4
Athina = Athens GR ... 117 E5
Athleague IRL ... 20 A3
Athlone IRL ... 21 A4
Athy IRL ... 21 B5
Atienza E ... 95 A3
Atina I ... 103 B6
Atkár H ... 65 C6
Atlanti TR ... 119 D7
Atna N ... 114 F7
Atorp S ... 35 C6
Atrá N ... 33 C5
Åträn S ... 40 B3
Atri I ... 103 A6
Atripalda I ... 103 C7
Atsiki GR ... 116 C7
Attendorn D ... 50 B3
Attichy F ... 59 A4
Attigliano I ... 102 A5
Attigny F ... 59 A5
Attleborough GB ... 30 B5
Åtvidaberg S ... 37 D2
Atzendorf D ... 52 B1
Au
　Steiermark A ... 63 C6
　Vorarlberg A ... 71 A4
　Bayern D ... 62 B2
　Bayern D ... 62 C2
Aub D ... 61 A6
Aubagne F ... 79 C4
Aubange B ... 60 A1
Aubel B ... 50 C1
Aubenas F ... 78 B3
Aubenton F ... 59 A5
Auberive F ... 59 C6
Aubeterre-sur-Dronne
　F ... 67 C5
Aubiet F ... 77 C3
Aubigné F ... 67 B4
Aubigny F ... 66 B3
Aubigny-au-Bac F ... 49 C4
Aubigny-en-Artois F ... 48 C3
Aubigny-sur-Nère F ... 68 A2
Aubin F ... 77 B5
Aubonne CH ... 69 B6
Aubrac F ... 78 B1
Aubusson F ... 68 C2
Auch F ... 77 C3
Auchencairn GB ... 25 D4
Auchinleck GB ... 24 C3
Auchterarder GB ... 25 B4
Auchtermuchty GB ... 25 B4
Auchtertyre GB ... 22 D3
Auchy-au-Bois F ... 48 C3
Audenge F ... 76 B1
Auderville F ... 57 A4
Audierne F ... 56 B1
Audincourt F ... 70 A1
Audlem GB ... 26 C3
Audruicq F ... 48 C3
Audun-le-Roman F ... 60 A1
Audun-le-Tiche F ... 60 A1

Aue
　Nordrhein-Westfalen
　D ... 50 B4
　Sachsen D ... 52 C2
Auerbach
　Bayern D ... 62 A2
　Sachsen D ... 52 C2
Auffach A ... 72 A2
Augher GB ... 19 B4
Aughnacloy GB ... 19 B5
Aughrim IRL ... 21 B5
Augignac F ... 67 C5
Augsburg D ... 62 B1
Augusta I ... 109 B4
Augusten-borg DK ... 39 E2
Augustfehn D ... 43 B4
Augustów PL ... 6 E7
Aukrug D ... 44 A1
Auktsjaur S ... 115 B16
Auldearn GB ... 23 D5
Aulendorf D ... 61 C5
Auletta I ... 103 C8
Aulla I ... 81 B3
Aullène F ... 102 B2
Aulnay F ... 67 B4
Aulnoye-Aymeries F ... 49 C4
Ault F ... 48 C2
Aultbea GB ... 22 D3
Aulum DK ... 39 C1
Aulus-les-Bains F ... 77 D4
Auma D ... 52 C1
Aumale F ... 58 A2
Aumetz F ... 60 A1
Aumont-Aubrac F ... 78 B2
Aunay-en-Bazois F ... 68 A3
Aunay-sur-Odon F ... 57 A5
Aune N ... 115 C10
Auneau F ... 58 B2
Auneuil F ... 58 A2
Auning DK ... 39 C3
Aunsetra N ... 115 C9
Aups F ... 79 C5
Aura D ... 51 C5
Auray F ... 56 C3
Aurdal N ... 32 B6
Aure N ... 114 D5
Aurich D ... 43 B4
Aurignac F ... 77 C3
Aurillac F ... 77 B5
Auriol F ... 79 C4
Auritz-Burguette F ... 76 D1
Aurlandsvangen N ... 32 B4
Auronzo di Cadore I ... 72 B2
Auros F ... 76 B2
Auroux F ... 78 B2
Aurskog N ... 34 C3
Aursmoen N ... 34 C3
Ausónia I ... 103 B6
Ausservillgraton A ... 72 B2
Austad N ... 33 D4
Austbygda N ... 32 B5
Áustis I ... 110 B2
Austmarka N ... 34 B4
Austre Moland N ... 33 D5
Austre Vikebygd N ... 33 C2
Austrheim N ... 32 B1
Auterive F ... 77 C4
Authon F ... 79 B4
Authon-du-Perche F ... 58 B1
Autol E ... 89 B5
Autreville F ... 60 B1
Autrey-lès-Gray F ... 69 A5
Autun F ... 69 B4
Auty-le-Châtel F ... 58 C3
Auvelais B ... 49 C5
Auvillar F ... 77 B3
Auxerre F ... 59 C4
Auxi-le-Château F ... 48 C3
Auxon F ... 59 B4
Auxonne F ... 69 A5
Auxy F ... 69 B4
Auzances F ... 68 B2
Auzon F ... 68 C3
Availles-Limousine F ... 67 B5
Avaldsnes N ... 33 C2
Avallon F ... 68 A3
Avantas GR ... 116 B7
Avas GR ... 116 B7
Avavken S ... 115 B15
Avebury GB ... 29 B6
A Veiga E ... 87 B3
Aveiras de Cima P ... 92 B2
Aveiro P ... 92 A2
Avelgem B ... 49 C4
Avellino I ... 103 C7
Avenches CH ... 70 B2
A-Ver-o-Mar P ... 87 C2
Aversa I ... 103 C7
Avesnes-le-Comte F ... 48 C3
Avesnes-sur-Helpe F ... 49 C4
Avesta S ... 36 B3
Avetrana I ... 105 C3
Avezzano I ... 103 A6
Avià E ... 91 A4
Aviano I ... 72 B2
Aviemore GB ... 23 D5
Avigliana I ... 80 A1
Avigliano I ... 104 C1
Avignon F ... 78 C3
Ávila E ... 94 B2
Avilés E ... 88 A1
Avintes P ... 87 C2
Avinyo E ... 91 B4
Avio I ... 71 C5
Avioth F ... 59 A6
Avis P ... 92 B3
Avize F ... 59 B5
Avlonari GR ... 116 D6
Ávola I ... 109 C4
Avon F ... 58 B3
Avonmouth GB ... 29 B5
Avord F ... 68 A2
Avranches F ... 57 B4
Avril F ... 60 A1
Avrillé F ... 67 A4
Avtovac BIH ... 84 C3
Awans B ... 49 C6
Axams A ... 71 A6
Axat F ... 77 D5
Axbridge GB ... 29 B5
Axel NL ... 49 B4
Ax-les-Thermes F ... 77 D4
Axmarby S ... 36 B4
Axmarsbruk S ... 36 B4
Axminster GB ... 29 C4
Axvall S ... 35 D5
Ay F ... 59 A5
Aya E ... 89 A4
Ayamonte E ... 98 B3
Ayancık TR ... 16 A7
Ayas I ... 70 C2
Aydın TR ... 119 E2
Ayelo de Malferit E ... 96 C2
Ayer CH ... 70 B2
Ayerbe E ... 90 A2
Ayette F ... 48 C3
Ayia Napa CY ... 120 B2
Ayia Phyla CY ... 120 B2
Áyioi Omvrósioi
　CY ... 120 A2
Ayios Seryios CY ... 120 A2
Ayios Theodoros
　CY ... 120 A3
Aykirikçi TR ... 118 C5
Aylesbury GB ... 31 C2
Ayllón E ... 89 C3
Aylsham GB ... 30 B5
Ayna E ... 101 A3
Ayódar E ... 96 B2
Ayora E ... 96 C1
Ayr GB ... 24 C3
Ayrancı TR ... 16 C6
Ayrancılar TR ... 119 D2
Ayron F ... 67 B5
Aytos BG ... 11 E9
Ayton GB ... 25 C5
Aytré F ... 66 B3
Ayvacık TR ... 118 C1
Ayvalık TR ... 118 C1

Aywaille B ... 49 C6
Azaila E ... 90 B2
Azambuja P ... 92 B2
Azambujeira P ... 92 B2
Azanja SRB ... 85 B5
Azannes-et-Soumazannes
　F ... 60 A1
Azanúy-Alins E ... 90 A3
Azaruja P ... 92 C3
Azay-le-Ferron F ... 67 B6
Azay-le-Rideau F ... 67 A5
Azcoitia E ... 89 A4
Azé F ... 69 B4
Azeiteiros P ... 92 B3
Azenhas do Mar P ... 92 C1
Azinhaga P ... 92 B2
Azinheira dos Bairros
　P ... 98 A2
Azinhoso P ... 87 C4
Aznalcázar E ... 99 B4
Aznalcóllar E ... 99 B4
Azóia P ... 92 B2
Azpeitia E ... 89 A4
Azuaga E ... 99 A5
Azuara E ... 90 B2
Azuqueca de Henares
　E ... 95 B3
Azur F ... 76 C1
Azzano Décimo I ... 72 C2

B

Baad A ... 71 A5
Baamonde E ... 86 A3
Baar D ... 70 A3
Bağarası TR ... 119 E2
Baarle-Nassau B ... 49 B5
Baarn NL ... 49 A6
Babadag RO ... 11 D10
Babadag RO ... 11 D10
Babaeski TR ... 118 A2
Babayevo RUS ... 7 B13
Babenhausen
　Bayern D ... 61 B6
　Hessen D ... 51 D4
Babiak PL ... 54 A3
Babice PL ... 55 C4
Babigoszcz PL ... 45 B6
Babimost PL ... 53 A5
Babina Greda HR ... 84 A3
Babócsa H ... 74 B2
Bábolna H ... 64 C4
Baborów PL ... 54 C2
Baboszewo PL ... 47 C6
Babót H ... 64 C3
Babruysk BY ... 7 E10
Babsk PL ... 55 B5
Bač SRB ... 75 C4
　MNE ... 85 D5
　SRB ... 75 C4
Bacares E ... 101 B3
Bacău RO ... 11 C9
Baccarat F ... 60 B2
Bacharach D ... 50 C3
Bačina SRB ... 85 C6
Backa S ... 36 B2
Bačka Palanka SRB ... 75 C4
Backaryd S ... 41 C5
Bačka Topola SRB ... 75 C4
Backe S ... 115 D13
Bäckebo S ... 40 C6
Bäckefors S ... 35 D4
Bäckhammar S ... 35 C6
Bački Breg SRB ... 75 C3
Bački-Brestovac SRB ... 75 C4
Bački Monoštor SRB ... 75 C3
Bački Petrovac SRB ... 75 C4
Bački Sokolac SRB ... 75 C4
Backnang D ... 61 B5
Bačko Gradište SRB ... 75 C5
Bačko Novo Selo
　SRB ... 75 C4
Bačko Petrovo Selo
　SRB ... 75 C5
Bácoli I ... 103 C7
Bacqueville-en-Caux
　F ... 58 A2
Bácsalmás H ... 75 B4
Bácsbokod H ... 75 B4
Bad Abbach D ... 62 B3
Badacsonytomaj H ... 74 B2
Bad Aibling D ... 62 C3
Badajoz E ... 93 C4
Badalona E ... 91 B5
Badalucco I ... 80 C1
Bad Aussee A ... 63 C4
Bad Bederkesa D ... 43 B5
Bad Bentheim D ... 50 A3
Bad Bergzabern D ... 60 A3
Bad Berka D ... 52 C1
Bad Berleburg D ... 51 B4
Bad Berneck D ... 52 C1
Bad Bevensen D ... 44 B2
Bad Bibra D ... 52 B1
Bad Birnbach D ... 62 B4
Bad Blankenburg D ... 52 C1
Bad Bleiberg A ... 72 B3
Bad Brambach D ... 52 C2
Bad Bramstedt D ... 44 B1
Bad Breisig D ... 50 C3
Bad Brückenau D ... 51 C5
Bad Buchau D ... 61 B5
Bad Camberg D ... 50 C4
Badderen N ... 113 C11
Bad Doberan D ... 44 A3
Bad Driburg D ... 51 B5
Bad Düben D ... 52 B2
Bad Dürkheim D ... 61 A4
Bad Dürrenberg D ... 52 B2
Bad Dürrheim D ... 61 B4
Bad Elster D ... 52 C2
Bad Ems D ... 50 C3
Baden
　A ... 64 B2
　CH ... 70 A3
Bådenas E ... 90 B1
Baden-Baden D ... 61 B4
Bad Endorf D ... 62 C3
Badenweiler D ... 60 C3
Baderna HR ... 82 B3
Bad Essen D ... 50 A4
Bad Fischau A ... 64 C2
Bad Frankenhausen
　D ... 52 B1
Bad Freienwalde D ... 45 C6
Bad Friedrichshall D ... 61 A5
Bad Füssing D ... 63 B4
Bad Gandersheim D ... 51 B6
Bad Gastein A ... 72 A3
Bad Gleichenberg A ... 73 B5
Bad Goisern A ... 63 C4
Bad Gottleuba D ... 53 C3
Bad Hall A ... 63 B5
Bad Harzburg D ... 51 B6
Bad Herrenalb D ... 61 B4
Bad Hersfeld D ... 51 C5
Bad Hofgastein A ... 72 A3
Bad Homburg D ... 51 C4
Bad Honnef D ... 50 C3
Bad Hönningen D ... 50 C3
Badia Calavena I ... 71 C6
Badia Polésine I ... 81 A5
Badia Pratáglia I ... 81 C5
Badia Tedalda I ... 82 C1
Bad Iburg D ... 50 A4
Bad Ischl A ... 63 C4
Bad Karlshafen D ... 51 B5
Bad Kissingen D ... 51 C6
Bad Kleinen D ... 44 B3
Bad Kohlgrub D ... 62 C2
Bad König D ... 61 A5
Bad Königshofen D ... 51 C6
Bad Köstritz D ... 52 C2
Badkowo PL ... 47 C4
Bad Kreuzen A ... 63 B5

Bad Kreuznach D 60 A3
Bad Krozingen D 60 C3
Bad Laasphe D 51 C4
Bad Langensalza D 51 B6
Bad Lauchstädt D 52 B1
Bad Lausick D 52 B2
Bad Lauterberg D 51 B6
Bad Leonfelden A 63 B5
Bad Liebenwerda D 52 B3
Bad Liebenzell D 61 B4
Bad Lippspringe D 51 B4
Badljevina HR 74 C2
Bad Meinberg D 51 B4
Bad Mergentheim D 61 A5
Bad Mitterndorf A 72 A3
Bad Münder D 51 A5
Bad Münstereifel D 50 C2
Bad Muskau D 53 B4
Bad Nauheim D 51 C4
Bad Nenndorf D 43 C6
Bad Neuenahr-Ahrweiler
D 50 C3
Bad Neustadt D 51 C6
Bad Oeynhausen D 51 A4
Badolato I 106 C3
Badolatosa E 100 B1
Bad Oldesloe D 44 B2
Badonviller F 60 B2
Bad Orb D 51 C5
Badovinci SRB 85 B4
Bad Peterstal D 61 B4
Bad Pyrmont D 51 B5
Bad Radkersburg A 73 B5
Bad Ragaz CH 71 B4
Bad Rappenau D 61 A5
Bad Reichenhall D 62 C3
Bad Saarow-Pieskow
D 53 A4
Bad Sachsa D 51 B6
Bad Säckingen D 70 A2
Bad Salzdetfurth D 51 A6
Bad Salzig D 50 C3
Bad Salzuflen D 51 A4
Bad Salzungen D 51 C6
Bad Sankt Leonhard
A 73 B4
Bad Sassendorf D 50 B4
Bad Schandau D 53 C4
Bad Schmiedeberg D 52 B2
Bad Schönborn D 61 A4
Bad Schussenried D 61 B5
Bad Schwalbach D 50 C4
Bad Schwartau D 44 B2
Bad Segeberg D 44 B2
Bad Soden D 51 C4
Bad Soden-Salmünster
D 51 C5
Bad Sooden-Allendorf
D 51 B5
Bad Sulza D 52 B1
Bad Sülze D 45 A4
Bad Tatzmannsdorf A 73 A6
Bad Tennstedt D 51 B6
Bad Tölz D 62 C2
Badules E 90 B1
Bad Urach D 61 B5
Bad Vellach A 73 B4
Bad Vilbel D 51 C4
Bad Vöslau A 64 C2
Bad Waldsee D 61 C5
Bad Wiessee D 62 C2
Bad Wildungen D 51 B5
Bad Wilsnack D 44 C3
Bad Windsheim D 61 A6
Bad Wörishafen D 62 B1
Bad Wurzach D 61 C5
Bad Zwesten D 51 B5
Bad Zwischenahn D 43 B5
Baells E 90 B3
Baena E 100 B1
Baesweiler D 50 C2
Baeza E 100 B2
Baflo NL 42 B3
Bafra TR 16 A7
Baga E 91 A4
Bagaladi I 106 C2
Bagenkop DK 39 E3
Baggetorp S 37 C3
Bagh a Chaisteil GB 22 E1
Bagheria I 108 A2
Bagn N 32 B6
Bagnacavallo I 81 B5
Bagnáia I 102 A5
Bagnara Cálabra I 106 C2
Bagnasco I 80 B2
Bagnères-de-Bigorre
F 76 C3
Bagnères-de-Luchon
F 77 D3
Bagni del Másino I 71 B4
Bagni di Lucca I 81 B4
Bagni di Rabbi I 71 B5
Bagni di Tivoli I 102 B5
Bagno di Romagna I 81 C5
Bagnoles-de-l'Orne F 57 B5
Bagnoli dei Trigno I 103 B7
Bagnoli di Sopra I 72 C1
Bagnoli Irpino I 103 C8
Bagnolo Mella I 71 C5
Bagnols-en-Forêt F 79 C5
Bagnols-sur-Cèze F 78 B3
Bagnorégio I 102 A5
Bagolino I 71 C5
Bagrationovsk RUS 47 A6
Bagrdan SRB 85 B6
Báguena E 95 A5
Bahabón de Esgueva
E 88 C3
Bahillo E 88 B2
Báia delle Zágare I 104 B2
Báia Domizia I 103 B6
Baia Mare RO 11 C7
Baiano I 103 C7
Baião P 87 C2
Baiersbronn D 61 B4
Baiersdorf D 62 A2
Baignes-Ste Radegonde
F 67 C4
Baigneux-les-Juifs F 59 C5
Baildon GB 27 B4
Bailén E 100 A2
Băileşti RO 11 D7
Baileux B 49 C5
Bailieborough IRL 19 C5
Bailleul F 48 C3
Baillonville B 49 C6
Bailó E 90 A2
Bain-de-Bretagne F 57 C4
Bains F 78 A2
Bains-les-Bains F 60 B2
Bainton GB 27 B5
Baio E 86 A2
Baiona E 87 B2
Bais F 57 B5
Baiso I 81 B4
Baiuca P 92 A3
Baja H 75 B3
Bajánsenye H 73 B6
Bajina Bašta SRB 85 C4
Bajmok SRB 75 C4
Bajna H 65 C4
Bajovo Polje MNE 84 C3
Bajram Curri AL 105 A6
Bajša SRB 75 C4
Bajzë AL 105 A5
Bak H 74 B1
Bakar HR 73 C4
Bakewell GB 27 B4
Bakhmach UA 7 F12
Bakio E 89 A4
Bakırdaği TR 16 B7
Bakka N 32 C6
Bakkafjörður IS 111 A11
Bakkagerði IS 111 B12
Bække DK 39 D2
Bakken N 34 B3
Baklan TR 119 E4
Bækmarksbro DK 39 C1
Bakonybél H 74 A2
Bakonycsernye H 74 A3
Bakonyjákó H 74 A2
Bakonyszentkirály H 74 A2
Bakonyszombathely
H 74 A2
Bakov nad Jizerou
CZ 53 C4
Bąkowiec PL 55 B6
Baks H 75 B5
Baksa H 74 C3
Bakum D 43 C5
Bala GB 26 C2
Bâlâ TR 16 B6
Balaguer E 90 B3
Balassagyarmat H 65 B5
Balástya H 75 B5
Balatonakali H 74 B2
Balatonalmádi H 74 A3
Balatonboglár H 74 B2
Balatonbozsok H 74 B3
Balatonederics H 74 B2
Balatonfenyves H 74 B2
Balatonföldvár H 74 B2
Balatonfüred H 74 B2
Balatonfüzfö H 74 A3
Balatonkenese H 74 A3
Balatonkiliti H 74 B3
Balatonlelle H 74 B2
Balatonszabadi H 74 B3
Balatonszemes H 74 B2
Balatonszentgyörgy
H 74 B2
Balazote E 101 A3
Balbeggie GB 25 B4
Balbigny F 69 C4
Balboa E 86 B4
Balbriggan IRL 19 C5
Balchik BG 11 E10
Balçova TR 119 D2
Baldock GB 31 C3
Bale HR 82 A2
Baleira E 86 A3
Baleizao P 98 A3
Balen B 49 B6
Balerma E 100 C3
Balestrand N 32 A3
Balestrate I 108 A2
Balfour GB 23 B6
Bälganet S 41 C5
Balıkesir TR 118 C2
Balıklıçeşme TR 118 B2
Bälinge S 36 C4
Balingen D 61 B4
Balingsta S 36 C4
Balintore GB 23 D5
Balizac F 76 B2
Baljevac SRB 85 C5
Balk NL 42 C2
Balkbrug NL 42 C3
Balla IRL 18 C2
Ballachulish GB 24 B2
Ballaghaderreen IRL 18 C3
Ballancourt-sur-Essonne
F 58 B3
Ballantrae GB 24 C3
Ballao I 110 C2
Ballasalla GB 26 A1
Ballater GB 23 D5
Ballen DK 39 D3
Ballenstedt D 52 B1
Ballerias E 90 B2
Balleroy F 57 A5
Ballerup DK 41 D2
Ballesteros de Calatrava
E 100 A2
Ballı TR 118 B2
Ballina IRL 18 B2
Ballinalack IRL 19 C4
Ballinamore IRL 19 B4
Ballinascarty IRL 20 C3
Ballinasloe IRL 20 A3
Ballindine IRL 18 C3
Balling DK 38 C1
Ballingarry
Limerick IRL 20 B3
Tipperary IRL 21 B4
Ballingeary IRL 20 C2
Ballinhassig IRL 20 C3
Ballinluig GB 25 B4
Ballino I 71 C5
Ballinrobe IRL 18 C2
Ballinskelligs IRL 20 C1
Ballinspittle IRL 20 C3
Ballintra IRL 18 B3
Ballivor IRL 21 A5
Ballobar E 90 B3
Ballon
F 58 B1
IRL 21 B5
Ballószög H 75 B4
Ballsh AL 105 C5
Ballstad N 112 D2
Ballum DK 39 D1
Ballybay IRL 19 B5
Ballybofey IRL 19 B4
Ballybunion IRL 20 B2
Ballycanew IRL 21 B5
Ballycarry GB 19 B6
Ballycastle
GB 19 A5
IRL 18 B2
Ballyclare GB 19 B6
Ballyconneely IRL 18 C1
Ballycotton IRL 20 C3
Ballycroy IRL 18 B2
Ballydehob IRL 20 C2
Ballyferriter IRL 20 B1
Ballygawley GB 19 B4
Ballygowan GB 19 B6
Ballyhaunis IRL 18 C3
Ballyheige IRL 20 B2
Ballyjamesduff IRL 19 C4
Ballylanders IRL 20 B3
Ballylynan IRL 21 B4
Ballymahon IRL 21 A4
Ballymena GB 19 B5
Ballymoe IRL 18 C3
Ballymoney GB 19 A5
Ballymore IRL 21 A4
Ballymote IRL 18 B3
Ballynacorra IRL 20 C3
Ballynagore IRL 21 A4
Ballynahinch GB 19 B6
Ballynure GB 19 B6
Ballyragget IRL 21 B4
Ballysadare IRL 18 B3
Ballyshannon IRL 18 B3
Ballyvaughan IRL 20 A2
Ballyvourney IRL 20 C2
Ballywalter GB 19 B6
Balmaclellan GB 24 C3
Balmaseda E 89 A3
Balme I 70 C2
Balmedie GB 23 D6
Balmuccia I 70 C3
Balna-paling GB 23 D4
Balneario de Panticosa
E 76 D2
Balotaszállás H 75 B4
Balsa P 87 C3
Balsareny E 91 B4
Balsorano-Nuovo I 103 B6
Bålsta S 37 C4
Balsthal CH 70 A2
Balta UA 11 B10
Baltanás E 88 C2
Baltar E 87 C3
Baltasound GB 22 A8
Bălţi MD 11 C9
Baltimore IRL 20 C2
Baltinglass IRL 21 B5
Baltiysk RUS 47 A5
Baltów PL 55 B6
Balugães P 87 C2
Bælum DK 38 C3
Balve D 50 B3
Balvi LV 7 C9
Balvicar GB 24 B2
Balya TR 118 C2
Balzo I 82 D2
Bamberg D 62 A1
Bamburgh GB 25 C6
Banatska Palanka
SRB 85 B6
Banatski Brestovac
SRB 85 B5
Banatski Despotovac
SRB 75 C5
Banatski Dvor SRB 75 C5
Banatski-Karlovac
SRB 85 A6
Banatsko Arandjelovo
SRB 75 B5
Banatsko-Novo Selo
SRB 85 B5
Banaz TR 118 D4
Banbridge GB 19 B5
Banbury GB 30 B2
Banchory GB 23 D6
Bande
B 49 C6
E 87 B3
Bandholm DK 39 E4
Bandırma TR 118 B2
Bandol F 79 C4
Bandon IRL 20 C3
Bañeres E 96 C2
Banff GB 23 D6
Bangor
F 66 A1
Down GB 19 B6
Gwynedd GB 26 B1
IRL 18 B2
Bangsund N 114 C8
Banie PL 45 B6
Banja SRB 85 C4
Banja Koviljača SRB 85 B4
Banjaloka SLO 73 C4
Banja Luka BIH 84 B2
Banjani SRB 85 B4
Banja Vručica BIH 84 B2
Banje KOS 85 D5
Banjska KOS 85 D5
Banka SK 64 B3
Bankekind S 37 D2
Bankend GB 25 C4
Bankeryd S 40 B4
Bankfoot GB 25 B4
Banloc RO 75 C6
Bannalec F 56 C2
Bannes F 59 B4
Bannockburn GB 25 B4
Bañobárez E 87 D4
Bañon E 90 C1
Banon F 79 B4
Baños E 93 A5
Baños de Gigonza E 99 C5
Baños de la Encina
E 100 A2
Baños de Molgas E 87 B3
Baños de Rio Tobia
E 89 B4
Baños de Valdearados
E 89 C3
Bánov CZ 64 B3
Banova Jaruga HR 74 C1
Bánovce nad Bebravou
SK 64 B4
Banovići BIH 84 B3
Banoviči Selo BIH 84 B3
Bánréve H 65 B6
Bansin D 45 B6
Banská Belá SK 65 B4
Banská Bystrica SK 65 B5
Banská Štiavnica SK 65 B4
Banstead GB 31 C3
Banteer IRL 20 B3
Bantheville F 59 A6
Bantry IRL 20 C2
Bantzenheim F 60 C3
Banyalbufar E 97 B2
Banyoles E 91 A5
Banyuls-sur-Mer F 91 A6
Bapaume F 48 C3
Bar
MNE 105 A5
UA 11 B9
Barabhas GB 22 C2
Barači BIH 84 B1
Baracs H 74 B3
Baracska H 74 A3
Barahona E 89 C4
Barajes de Melo E 95 B4
Barakaldo E 89 A4
Baralla E 86 B3
Barañain E 76 D1
Baranavichy BY 7 E9
Báránd H 75 A6
Baranda SRB 85 A5
Baranello I 103 B7
Baranów Sandomierski
PL 55 C6
Baraqueville F 77 B5
Barasoain E 89 B5
Barbacena P 92 C3
Barbadás E 87 B3
Barbadillo E 94 B1
Barbadillo de Herreros
E 89 B3
Barbadillo del Mercado
E 89 B3
Barbadillo del Pez E 89 B3
Barban HR 82 A3
Barbarano Vicento I 71 C6
Barbariga HR 82 B2
Barbaros TR 118 B2
Barbastro E 90 A3
Barbate E 99 C5
Barbatona E 95 A4
Barbâtre F 66 B2
Barbazan F 77 C3
Barbeitos E 86 A3
Barbentane F 78 C3
Barberino di Mugello
I 81 B5
Barbezieux-St Hilaire
F 67 C4
Barbonne-Fayel F 59 B4
Barbotan-les-Thermes
F 76 C2
Barby D 52 B1
Bárcabo E 90 A3
Barca de Alva P 87 C4
Barcarrota E 93 C4
Barcellona-Pozzo di Gotto
I 109 A4
Barcelona E 91 B5
Barcelonette F 79 B5
Barcelos P 87 C2
Bárcena del Monasterio
E 86 A4
Barcena de Pie de
Concha E 88 A2
Barchfeld D 51 C6
Barcin PL 46 C3
Barcino PL 46 A2
Bárcis I 72 B2
Barco P 92 A3
Barcones E 89 C4
Barcs H 74 C2
Barcus F 76 C2
Barczewo PL 47 B6
Bardejov SK 10 B6
Bårdesø DK 39 D3
Bardi I 81 B3
Bardney GB 27 B5
Bardo PL 54 C1
Bardolino I 71 C5
Bardonécchia I 79 A5
Bardoňovo SK 65 B4
Barèges F 76 D3
Barenstein D 52 C3
Barentin F 58 A1
Barenton F 57 B5
Barevo BIH 84 B2
Barfleur F 57 A4
Barga I 81 B4
Bargas E 94 C2
Barge I 79 B6
Bargemon F 79 C5
Barghe I 71 C5
Bargoed GB 29 B4
Bargrennan GB 24 C3
Bargteheide D 44 B2
Barham GB 31 C5
Bari I 104 B2
Barič Draga HR 83 B4
Barilović HR 73 C5
Bari Sardo I 110 C2
Barisciano I 103 A6
Barjac F 78 B3
Barjols F 79 C4
Barjon F 59 C5
Bårkåker N 35 C2
Barkald N 114 F7
Barkowo
Dolnośląskie PL 54 B1
Pomorskie PL 46 B3
Bârlad RO 11 C9
Bar-le-Duc F 59 B6
Barles F 79 B5
Barletta I 104 B2
Barlinek PL 45 C7
Barmouth GB 26 C1
Barmstedt D 43 B6
Barnard Castle GB 27 A4
Barnarp S 40 B4
Bärnau D 62 A3
Bärnbach A 73 A5
Barneberg D 52 A1
Barnenitz D 45 C4
Barnet GB 31 C3
Barnetby le Wold GB 27 B5
Barneveld NL 49 A6
Barneville-Carteret F 57 A4
Barnoldswick GB 26 B3
Barnowko PL 45 C6
Barnsley GB 27 B4
Barnstädt D 52 B1
Barnstaple GB 28 B3
Barnstorf D 43 C5
Barntrup D 51 B5
Baron F 58 A3
Baronissi I 103 C7
Barqueiro P 92 B2
Barquinha P 92 B2
Barr
F 60 B3
GB 24 C3
Barra P 92 A2
Barracas E 96 A2
Barraco E 94 B2
Barrado E 93 A5
Barrafranca I 109 B3
Barranco do Velho P 98 B3
Barrancos P 99 A4
Barrax E 95 C4
Barrbaar D 62 B1
Barre-des-Cevennes
F 78 B2
Barreiro P 92 C1
Barreiros E 86 A3
Barrême F 79 C5
Barret-le-Bas F 79 B4
Barrhead GB 24 C3
Barrhill GB 24 C3
Barrio de Nuesra Señora
E 88 B1
Barrowford GB 26 B3
Barrow-in-Furness
GB 26 A2
Barrow upon Humber
GB 27 B5
Barruecopardo E 87 C4
Barruelo de Santullán
E 88 B2
Barruera E 90 A3
Barry GB 29 B4
Bårse DK 39 D4
Barsinghausen D 51 A5
Barssel D 43 B4
Bar-sur-Aube F 59 B5
Bar-sur-Seine F 59 B5
Barth D 45 A4
Bartholomä D 61 B5
Bartin TR 118 A7
Barton upon Humber
GB 27 B5
Bartoszyce PL 47 A6
Barúmini I 110 C1
Baruth D 52 A3
Barvaux B 49 C6
Barver D 43 C5
Barwatd PL 65 A5
Barwice PL 46 B2
Barysaw BY 7 D10
Barzana E 88 A1
Bârzava RO 10 C6
Bárzio I 71 C4
Bas E 91 A5
Bašaid SRB 75 C5
Basaluzzo I 80 B2
Basarabeasca MD 11 C10
Basauri E 89 A4
Baschi I 82 D1
Baschurch GB 26 C3
Basconcillos del Tozo
E 88 B3
Bascones de Ojeda E 88 B2
Basécles B 49 C4
Basel CH 70 A2
Basélice I 103 B7
Basildon GB 31 C4
Basingstoke GB 31 C2
Baška
CZ 65 A4
HR 83 B3
Baška Voda HR 84 C1
Bäsksjö S 115 C14
Baslow GB 27 B4
Başmakçı TR 119 E5
Basovizza I 72 C3
Bassacutena I 110 A2
Bassano del Grappa I 72 C1
Bassano Romano I 102 A5
Bassecourt CH 70 A2
Bassella E 91 A4
Bassevuovdde N 113 D14
Bassou F 59 C4
Bassoues F 76 C3
Bassum D 43 C5
Båstad S 40 C2
Bastardo I 82 D1
Bastelica F 102 A2
Bastelicaccia F 102 B1
Bastia
F 102 A2
I 82 C1
Bastogne B 50 C1
Baston GB 30 B3
Bastuträsk S 115 C17
Bata H 74 B3
Batajnica SRB 85 B5
Batalha P 92 B2
Bátaszék H 74 B3
Batea E 90 B3
Batelov CZ 63 A6
Bath GB 29 B5
Bathgate GB 25 C4
Batida H 75 B5
Batignano I 81 D5
Batina HR 74 C3
Bátka SK 65 B6
Batković BIH 85 B4
Batlava KOS 85 D6
Batley GB 27 B4
Batnfjordsøra N 114 E4
Batočina SRB 85 B6
Bátonyterenye H 65 C5
Batrina HR 74 C2
Båtsfjord N 113 B18
Battaglia Terme I 72 C1
Bätterkinden CH 70 A2
Battice B 50 C1
Battipáglia I 103 C7
Battle GB 31 D4
Battonya H 75 B6
Batuša SRB 85 B6
Bátya H 75 B3
Bau I 110 C1
Baud F 56 C2
Baudour B 49 C4
Baugé F 67 A4
Baugy F 68 A2
Bauma CH 70 A3
Baume-les-Dames F 69 A6
Baumholder D 60 A3
Baunatal D 51 B5
Baunei I 110 B2
Bauska LV 6 C8
Bautzen D 53 B4
Bavanište SRB 85 B5
Bavay F 49 C4
Bavilliers F 60 C2
Bavorov CZ 63 A5
Bawdsey GB 31 B5
Bawinkel D 43 C4
Bawtry GB 27 B4
Bayat TR 118 D5
Bayel F 59 B5
Bayeux F 57 A5
Bayındır TR 119 D2
Bayon F 60 B2
Bayonne F 76 C1
Bayons F 79 B5
Bayramiç TR 118 C1
Bayreuth D 52 D1
Bayrischzell D 62 C3
Baza E 101 B3
Bazas F 76 B2
Baziege F 77 C4
Bazoches-les-Gallerandes
F 58 B3
Bazoches-sur-Hoëne
F 58 B1
Bazzano I 81 B5
Beaconsfield GB 31 C3
Beade E 87 B2
Beadnell GB 25 C6
Beaminster GB 29 C5
Bearsden GB 24 C3
Beas E 99 B4
Beasain E 89 A4
Beas de Segura E 100 A3
Beattock GB 25 C4
Beaubery F 69 B4
Beaucaire F 78 C3
Beaufort
F 69 C6
IRL 20 B2
Beaufort-en Vallée F 67 A4
Beaugency F 58 C2
Beaujeu
Alpes-de-Haute-
Provence F 79 B5
Rhône F 69 B4
Beaulac F 76 B2
Beaulieu
F 68 A2
GB 31 D2
Beaulieu-sous-la-Roche
F 66 B3
Beaulieu-sur-Dordogne
F 77 B4
Beaulieu-sur-Mer F 80 C1
Beaulon F 68 B3
Beauly GB 23 D4
Beaumaris GB 26 B1
Beaumesnil F 58 A1
Beaumetz-lès-Loges
F 48 C3
Beaumont
B 49 C5
F 77 B3
Beaumont-de-Lomagne
F 77 C3
Beaumont-du-Gâtinais
F 58 B3
Beaumont-en-Argonne
F 59 A6
Beaumont-Hague F 57 A4
Beaumont-la-Ronce
F 58 C1
Beaumont-le-Roger F 58 A1
Beaumont-sur-Oise F 58 A3
Beaumont-sur-Sarthe
F 57 B6
Beaune F 69 A4
Beaune-la-Rolande F 58 B3
Beaupréau F 66 A4
Beauraing B 49 C5
Beaurepaire F 69 C5
Beaurepaire-en-Bresse
F 69 B5
Beaurières F 79 B4
Beauvais F 58 A3
Beauval F 48 C3
Beauville F 77 B3
Beauvoir-sur-Mer F 66 B2
Beauvoir-sur-Niort F 67 B4
Beba Veche RO 75 B5
Bebertal D 52 A1
Bebington GB 26 B2
Bebra D 51 C5
Bebrina HR 84 A2
Beccles GB 30 B5
Becedas E 93 A5
Beceite E 90 C3
Bečej SRB 75 C5
Becerreá E 86 B3
Becerril de Campos E 88 B2
Bécherel F 57 B4
Bechhofen D 61 A6
Bechyně CZ 63 A5
Bečići MNE 105 A4
Becilla de Valderaduey
E 88 B1
Beckfoot GB 25 D4
Beckingham GB 27 B5
Beckum D 50 B4
Beco P 92 B2
Bécon-les-Granits F 66 A4
Bečov nad Teplou CZ 52 C2
Becsehely H 74 B1
Bedale GB 27 A4
Bedames E 89 A3
Bédar E 101 B4
Bédarieux F 78 C2
Bédarrides F 78 B3
Bedburg D 50 C2
Beddgelert GB 26 B1
Beddingestrand S 41 D3
Bédée F 57 B4
Bedegkér H 74 B3
Beden TR 119 F7
Bedford GB 30 B3
Będków PL 55 B4
Bedlington GB 25 C6
Bedlno PL 55 A4
Bedmar E 100 B2
Bédoin F 79 B4
Bedónia I 80 B3
Bedretto CH 70 B3
Bedsted DK 38 C1
Bedum NL 42 B3
Bedwas GB 29 B4
Bedworth GB 30 B2
Będzin PL 55 C4
Beekbergen NL 50 A1
Beek en Donk NL 49 B6
Beelen D 50 B4
Beelitz D 52 A2
Beer GB 29 C4
Beerfelde D 45 C6
Beerfelden D 61 A4
Beernem B 49 B4
Beeskow D 53 A4
Beetsterzwaag NL 42 B3
Beetzendorf D 44 C3
Beflelay CH 70 A2
Begaljica SRB 85 B5
Bégard F 56 B2
Begejci SRB 75 C5
Begijar E 100 B2
Begijnendijk B 49 B5
Begndal N 34 B1
Begues E 91 B4
Beguildy GB 26 C2
Begur E 91 B6
Beho B 50 C1
Behringen D 51 B6
Beilen NL 42 C3
Beilngries D 62 A2
Beine-Nauroy F 59 A5
Beinwil CH 70 A3
Beiseförth D 51 B5
Beith GB 24 C3
Beitostølen N 32 A5
Beiuş RO 11 C7
Beja P 98 A3
Béjar E 93 A5
Bekçiler TR 119 F4
Békés H 75 B6
Békéscsaba H 75 B6
Bekilli TR 119 D4
Bekkarfjord N 113 B16
Bela SK 65 A4
Bélâbre F 67 B6
Bela Crkva SRB 85 B6
Belalcázar E 93 C5
Belánad Radbuzou
CZ 62 A3
Belanovica SRB 85 B5
Bélapátfalva H 65 B6
Bělápod Bezdězem
CZ 53 C4
Belcaire F 77 D4
Bełchatów PL 55 B4
Belchite E 90 B2
Bělčice CZ 63 A4
Belcoo GB 19 B4
Belecke D 51 B4
Beled H 74 A2
Belej HR 83 B3
Beleño E 88 A1
Bélesta F 77 D4
Belev RUS 7 E14
Belevi TR 119 D2
Belfast GB 19 B6
Belford GB 25 C6
Belfort F 60 C2
Belgentier F 79 C4
Belgern D 52 B3
Belgioioso I 71 C4
Belgodère F 102 A2
Belgooly IRL 20 C3
Belgorod RUS 7 F14
Belgrade = Beograd
SRB 85 B5
Belhade F 76 B2
Belica HR 74 B1
Beli Manastir HR 74 C3
Belin-Bèliet F 76 B2
Belinchón E 95 B3
Belišće HR 74 C3
Bělkovice-Lašťany
CZ 64 A3
Bella I 104 C1
Bellac F 67 B6
Bellágio I 71 C4
Bellananagh IRL 19 C4
Bellano I 71 B4
Bellária I 82 B1
Bellavary IRL 18 C2
Belleau F 59 A4
Belleek GB 18 B3
Bellegarde
Gard F 78 C3
Loiret F 58 C3
Bellegarde-en-Diois F 79 B4
Bellegarde-en-Marche
F 68 C2
Bellegarde-sur-Valserine
F 69 B5
Belle-Isle-en-Terre F 56 B2
Bellême F 58 B1
Bellenaves F 68 B3
Bellentre F 70 C1
Bellevaux F 69 B6
Bellevesvre F 69 B5
Belleville F 69 B4
Belleville-sur-Vie F 66 B3
Bellevue-la-Montagne
F 68 C3
Belley F 69 C5
Bellheim D 61 A4
Bellinge DK 39 D3
Bellingham GB 25 C5
Bellinzago Novarese
I 70 C3
Bellinzona CH 70 B4
Bell-lloc d'Urgell E 90 B3
Bello E 95 B5
Bellpuig d'Urgell E 91 B4
Bellreguart E 96 C2
Bellsbank GB 24 C3
Belltall E 91 B4
Belluno I 72 B2
Bellver de Cerdanya
E 91 A4
Bellvis E 90 B3
Bélmez E 93 C5
Belmez de la Moraleda
E 100 B2
Belmont GB 22 A8
Belmont-de-la-Loire F 69 B4
Belmonte
Asturias E 86 A4
Cuenca E 95 C4
P 92 A3
Belmonte de San José
E 90 C2
Belmonte de Tajo E 95 B3
Belmont-sur-Rance F 78 C1
Belmullet IRL 18 B2
Belobreşca RO 85 B6
Beloeil B 49 C4
Belogradchik BG 11 E7
Belokorovichi UA 11 A10
Beloljin SRB 85 C6
Belorado E 89 B3
Belotič SRB 85 B4
Bělotin CZ 64 A3
Belozersk RUS 7 B14
Belp CH 70 B2
Belpasso I 109 B3
Belpech F 77 C4
Belper GB 27 B4
Belsay GB 25 C6
Belsh AL 105 C5
Belsk Duzy PL 55 B5
Beltinci SLO 73 B6
Beltra IRL 18 C2
Belturbet IRL 19 B4
Beluša SK 64 A4
Belušić SRB 85 C6
Belvedere Maríttimo
I 106 B2
Belver de Cinca E 90 B3
Belver de los Montes
E 88 C1
Belvès F 77 B3
Belvezet F 78 B2
Belvis de la Jara E 94 C2
Belvis de Monroy E 93 B5
Belyy RUS 7 D12
Belz F 56 C2
Bełżec PL 11 A7
Belzig D 52 A2
Bembibre E 86 B4
Bembridge GB 31 D2
Bemmel NL 50 B1
Bemposta
Bragança P 87 C4
Santarém P 92 B2
Benabarre E 90 A3
Benacazón E 99 B4
Benaguacil E 96 B2
Benahadux E 101 C3
Benalmádena E 100 C1
Benalúa de Guadix
E 100 B2
Benalúa de las Villas
E 100 B2
Benalup E 99 C5
Benamargosa E 100 C1
Benamaurel E 101 B3
Benameji E 100 B1
Benamocarra E 100 C1
Benaocaz E 99 C5
Benaoján E 99 C5
Benarrabá E 99 C5
Benasque E 90 A3
Benátky nad Jizerou
CZ 53 C4
Benavente
E 88 B1
P 92 C2
Benavides de Órbigo
E 88 B1
Benavila P 92 B3
Bendorf D 50 C3
Benedikt SLO 73 B5
Benejama E 101 A5
Benejúzar E 101 A5
Benešov CZ 63 A5
Bénestroff F 60 B2
Benet F 67 B4
Bene Vagienna I 80 B1
Bénévent-l'Abbaye F 67 B6
Benevento I 103 B7
Benfeld F 60 B3
Benfica P 92 B2
Bengtsfors S 35 C4
Bengtsheden S 36 B2
Beničanci HR 74 C3
Benicarló E 90 C3
Benicássim E 96 A3
Benidorm E 96 C2
Benifaió E 96 B2
Beniganim E 96 C2
Benington GB 27 B6
Benisa E 96 C3
Benkovac HR 83 B4
Benllech GB 26 B1
Benneckenstein D 51 B6
Bénodet F 56 C1
Benquerencia de la
Serena E 93 C5
Bensafrim P 98 B2
Bensdorf D 44 C4
Benshausen D 51 C6
Bensheim D 61 A4
Bentley GB 31 C3
Bentwisch D 44 A4
Beočin SRB 75 C4
Beograd = Belgrade
SRB 85 B5
Beragh GB 19 B4
Berane MNE 85 D4
Beranga E 89 A3
Berat AL 105 C5
Bérat F 77 C4
Beratzhausen D 62 A2
Bérbaltavár H 74 A1
Berbegal E 90 B2
Berbenno di Valtellina
I 71 B4
Berberana E 89 B3
Bercedo E 89 A3
Bercel H 65 C5
Bercenay-le-Hayer F 59 B4
Berceto I 81 B3
Berchem B 49 C4
Berchidda I 110 B2
Berching D 62 A2
Berchtesgaden D 62 C4
Bérchules E 100 C2
Bercianos de Aliste E 87 C4
Berck F 48 C2
Berclaire d'Urgell E 90 B3
Berdoias E 86 A1
Berducedo E 86 A4
Berdún E 90 A2
Berdychiv UA 11 B10
Bere Alston GB 28 C3
Bereguardo I 70 C4
Berehommen N 33 C4
Berehove UA 11 B7
Berek BIH 84 A2
Beremend H 74 C3
Bere Regis GB 29 C5
Berestechko UA 11 A8
Berettyóújfalu H 10 C6
Berezhany UA 11 B8
Berezivka UA 11 C11
Berezna UA 7 F11
Berg
D 62 A2
N 114 B9
S 37 D3
Berga
Sachsen-Anhalt D 51 B7
Thüringen D 52 C2
E 91 A4
S 40 B6
Bergama TR 118 C2
Bérgamo I 71 C4
Bergara E 89 A4
Bergby S 36 B4
Berge
Brandenburg D 45 C4
Niedersachsen D 43 C4
Telemark N 33 C5
Telemark N 33 C5
Bergeforsen S 115 E14
Bergen
Mecklenburg-
Vorpommern D 45 A5
Niedersachsen D 44 C1
Niedersachsen D 44 C2
N 32 B2
NL 42 C1
Bergen op Zoom NL 49 B5
Bergerac F 77 B3
Bergères-lés-Vertus
F 59 B5
Bergeyk NL 49 B6
Berghausen D 61 B4
Bergheim D 50 C2
Berghem S 40 B2
Berg im Gau D 62 B2
Bergisch Gladbach D 50 C3
Bergkamen D 50 B3
Bergkvara S 41 C6
Berglern D 62 B2
Bergneustadt D 50 B3
Bergsäng S 34 B5
Bergshamra S 37 C5
Bergsjö S 115 F14
Bergs slussar S 37 D2
Bergtheim D 61 A6
Bergues F 48 C3
Bergum NL 42 B2
Bergün Bravuogn CH 71 B4
Bergwitz D 52 B2
Berhida H 74 A3
Beringel P 98 A3
Beringen B 49 B6
Berja E 100 C3
Berkåk N 114 E7
Berkeley GB 29 B5
Berkenthin D 44 B2
Berkhamsted GB 31 C3
Berkheim D 61 B6
Berkhof D 43 C6
Berkovići BIH 84 C3
Berkovitsa BG 11 E7
Berlanga E 99 A5
Berlanga de Duero E 89 C4
Berlevåg N 113 B18
Berlikum NL 42 B2
Berlin D 45 C5
Berlstedt D 52 B1
Bermeo E 89 A4
Bermillo de Sayago E 87 C4
Bern CH 70 B2
Bernalda I 104 C2
Bernardos E 94 A2
Bernartice
Jihočeský CZ 63 A5
Vychodočeský CZ 53 C5
Bernau
Baden-Württemberg
D 61 C4
Bayern D 62 C3
Brandenburg D 45 C5
Bernaville F 48 C3
Bernay F 58 A1
Bernburg D 52 B1
Berndorf A 64 C2
Berne D 43 B5
Bernecebarati H 65 B4
Bernhardsthal A 64 B2
Bernkastel-Kues D 60 A3
Bernolakovo SK 64 B3
Bernsdorf D 53 B4
Bernstadt D 53 B4
Bernstein A 73 A6
Bernués E 90 A2
Beromünster CH 70 A3
Beroun CZ 53 D4
Berovo MK 116 A4
Berre-l'Etang F 79 C4
Berriedale GB 23 C5
Berriew GB 26 C2
Berrocal E 99 B4
Bersenbrück D 43 C4
Bershad' UA 11 B10
Bertamiráns E 86 B2
Berthåga S 36 C4
Berthelming F 60 B2
Bertincourt F 48 C3
Bertinoro I 82 B1
Bertogne B 49 C6
Bertrix B 59 A6
Berufjörður IS 111 C11
Berville-sur-Mer F 58 A1
Berwick-upon-Tweed
GB 25 C5
Berzasca RO 10 D6
Berzence H 74 B2
Berzocana E 93 B5
Besalú E 91 A5
Besançon F 69 A6
Besenfeld D 61 B4
Besenyötelek H 65 C6
Besenyszög H 75 A5
Beshenkovichi BY 7 D10
Besigheim D 61 B5
Běšiny CZ 63 A4
Beška SRB 75 C5
Beşkonak TR 119 E6
Besle F 57 C4
Besnyö H 74 A3
Bessais-le-Fromental
F 68 B2
Bessan F 78 C2
Besse-en-Chandesse
F 68 C2
Bessèges F 78 B3
Bessé-sur-Braye F 58 C1
Bessines-sur-Gartempe
F 67 B6
Best NL 49 B6
Bestorp S 37 D2
Betanzos E 86 A2
Betelu E 76 C1
Bétera E 96 B2
Beteta E 95 B4
Béthenville F 59 A5
Bethesda GB 26 B1
Béthune F 48 C3
Beton-Bazoches F 59 B4
Bettembourg L 60 A2
Betterdorf L 60 A2
Bettna S 37 D3
Béttola I 80 B3
Bettona I 82 C1
Bettyhill GB 23 C4
Betws-y-Coed GB 26 B2
Betxi E 96 B2
Betz F 59 A3
Betzdorf D 50 C3
Beuil F 79 B5
Beulah GB 29 A4
Beuzeville F 58 A1
Bevagna I 82 D1
Bevens-bruk S 37 C2
Beveren B 49 B5
Beverley GB 27 B5
Bevern D 51 B5
Beverstedt D 43 B5
Beverungen D 51 B5
Beverwijk NL 42 C1
Bex CH 70 B2
Bexhill GB 31 D4
Beyazköy TR 118 A2
Beychevelle F 76 A2
Beydağ TR 119 D3
Beyeğaç TR 119 E3
Beykoz TR 118 A4
Beynat F 68 C1
Beyoğlu TR 118 A4
Beypazarı TR 118 B6
Beyşehir TR 119 E6
Bezas E 95 B5
Bezau A 71 A4
Bezdan SRB 75 C3
Bèze F 69 A5
Bezenet F 68 B2
Bezhetsk RUS 7 C14
Béziers F 78 C2
Bezzecca I 71 C5
Biadki PL 54 B2
Biała
Łódzkie PL 55 B4
Opolskie PL 54 C2
Białaczów PL 55 B5
Biała Podlaska PL 6 E7
Biała Rawska PL 55 B5
Biale Błota PL 46 B3
Białobłoty PL 54 A2
Białobrzegi PL 55 B5
Białogard PL 46 B1
Bialośliwie PL 46 B3
Białowąs PL 46 B2
Biały Bór PL 46 B2
Białystok PL 6 E7
Biancavilla I 109 B3
Bianco I 106 C3
Biandrate I 70 C3
Biar E 101 A5
Biarritz F 76 C1
Bias F 76 B1
Biasca CH 70 B3
Biatorbágy H 74 A3
Bibbiena I 81 C5
Bibbona I 81 C4
Biberach
Baden-Württemberg
D 61 B4
Baden-Württemberg
D 61 B5
Bibinje HR 83 B4
Bibione I 72 C3
Biblis D 61 A4
Bibury GB 29 B6
Bíccari I 103 B8
Bicester GB 31 C2
Bichl D 62 C2
Bichlbach A 71 A5
Bicorp E 96 B2
Bicos P 98 B2
Bicske H 74 A3
Bidache F 76 C1
Bidart F 76 C1
Biddinghuizen NL 42 C2
Biddulph GB 26 B3
Bideford GB 28 B3
Bidford-on-Avon GB 29 A6
Bidjovagge N 113 C11
Bie S 37 C3
Bieber D 51 C5
Biebersdorf D 53 B3
Biedenkopf D 51 C4
Biel E 90 A2
Bielany Wroclawskie
PL 54 B1
Bielawa PL 54 C1
Bielawy PL 55 A4
Biel/Bienne CH 70 A2
Bielefeld D 51 A4
Biella I 70 C3
Bielsa E 90 A3
Bielsk PL 47 C5
Bielsko-Biała PL 65 A5
Bielsk Podlaski PL 6 E7
Bienenbuttel D 44 B2
Bieniow PL 53 B5
Bienservida E 101 A3
Bienvenida E 93 C4
Bierdzany PL 54 C3
Bierné F 57 C5
Biersted DK 38 B2
Bierun PL 55 C4
Bierutów PL 54 B2
Bierwart B 49 C6
Bierzwina PL 46 B1
Bierzwnik PL 46 B1
Biescas E 90 A2
Biesenthal D 45 C5
Biesiekierz PL 46 A2

Bietigheim-Bissingen
D 61 B5
Bièvre B 49 D6
Bieżuń PL 47 C5
Biga TR 118 B2
Bigadiç TR 118 C3
Biganos F 76 B2
Bigas P 87 D3
Bigastro E 101 A5
Bigbury GB 28 C4
Biggar GB 25 C4
Biggin Hill GB 31 C4
Biggleswade GB 30 B3
Bignasco CH 70 B3
Biguglia F 102 A2
Bihać BIH 83 B4
Biharnagybajom H 75 A6
Bijela MNE 105 A4
Bijeljani BIH 84 C3
Bijeljina BIH 85 B4
Bijelo Polje MNE 85 C4
Bijuesca E 89 C5
Bilaj HR 83 B4
Bila Tserkva UA 11 B11
Bilbao E 89 A4
Bilcza PL 55 C5
Bíldudalur IS 111 B2
Bileća BIH 84 D3
Bilecik TR 118 B4
Biled RO 75 C5
Biłgoraj PL 11 A7
Bilhorod-Dnistrovskyy
UA 11 C11
Bílina CZ 53 C3
Bilisht AL 116 B2
Bilje HR 74 C3
Billdal S 38 B4
Billerbeck D 50 B3
Billericay GB 31 C4
Billesholm S 41 C2
Billingborough GB 30 B3
Billinge S 41 D3
Billingham GB 27 A4
Billinghay GB 27 B5
Billingsfors S 35 D4
Billingshurst GB 31 C3
Billom F 68 C3
Billsta S 115 D15
Billund DK 39 D2
Bilopillya UA 7 F13
Bílovec CZ 64 A4
Bilstein D 50 B4
Bilthoven NL 49 A6
Bilto N 112 C10
Bilzen B 49 C6
Bíňa SK 65 C4
Binaced E 90 B3
Binasco I 71 C4
Binbrook GB 27 B5
Binche B 49 C5
Bindlach D 52 D1
Bindslev DK 38 B3
Binefar E 90 B3
Bingen D 50 D3
Bingham GB 27 C5
Bingley GB 27 B4
Bingsjö S 36 A2
Binic F 56 B3
Binz D 45 A5
Bioče MNE 105 A5
Biograd na Moru HR 83 C4
Bionaz I 70 C2
Bioska SRB 85 C4
Birda RO 75 C6
Birdlip GB 29 B5
Biri N 34 B2
Birkeland N 33 D5
Birkenfeld
Baden-Württemberg D 61 B4
Rheinland-Pfalz D 60 A3
Birkenhead GB 26 B2
Birkerød DK 41 D2
Birkfeld A 73 A5
Birkirkara M 107 C5
Birmingham GB 27 C4
Birr IRL 21 A4
Birresborn D 50 C2
Birstein D 51 C5
Biržai LT 6 C8
Birzebbugia M 107 C5
Bisáccia I 103 B8
Bisacquino I 108 B2
Bisbal de Falset E 90 B3
Biscarosse F 76 B1
Biscarosse Plage F 76 B1
Biscarrués E 90 A2
Biscéglie I 104 B2
Bischheim F 60 B3
Bischofsheim D 51 C5
Bischofshofen A 72 A3
Bischofswerda D 53 B4
Bischofswiesen D 62 C3
Bischofszell CH 71 A4
Bischwiller F 60 B3
Bisenti I 103 A6
Bishop Auckland GB 27 A4
Bishop's Castle GB 26 C3
Bishops Lydeard GB 29 B4
Bishop's Stortford
GB 31 C4
Bishop's Waltham
GB 31 D2
Bisignano I 106 B3
Bisingen D 61 B4
Biskupice-Oławskie
PL 54 B2
Biskupiec PL 47 B5
Bismark D 44 C3
Bismo N 114 F5
Bispgården S 115 D13
Bispingen D 44 B1
Bissen L 60 A2
Bissendorf D 50 A4
Bisserup DK 39 D4
Bistango I 80 B2
Bistarac Donje BIH 84 B3
Bistrica
BIH 84 B2
MNE 85 D4
SRB 85 C4
Bistrica ob Sotli SLO 73 B5
Bistriţa RO 11 C8
Bisztynek PL 47 A6
Bitburg D 50 D2
Bitche F 60 A3
Bitetto I 104 B2
Bitola MK 116 A3
Bitonto I 104 B2
Bitschwiller F 60 C3
Bitterfeld D 52 B2
Bitti I 110 B2
Biville-sur-Mer F 48 D2
Bivona I 108 B2
Biwer L 60 A2
Bizeljsko SLO 73 B5
Bizovac HR 74 C3
Bjåen N 33 C4
Bjärnum S 41 C3
Bjärred S 41 D3
Bjästa S 115 D15
Bjelland
Vest-Agder N 33 D3
Vest-Agder N 33 D4
Bjelovar HR 74 C1
Bjerkreim N 33 D3
Bjerkvik N 112 D6
Bjerreby DK 39 E3
Bjerregrav DK 38 C2
Bjerringbro DK 39 C2
Bjøberg N 32 B5
Bjøllånes N 112 F3
Björbo S 36 B1
Bjordal N 32 A2
Björg IS 111 B8
Bjørkåsen N 112 D5
Björke
Gävleborg S 36 B4
Östergötland S 37 D2
Bjørkelangen N 34 C3
Björketorp S 40 B2
Björkholmen S 112 F8
Björkliden S 112 D7
Björklinge S 36 B4
Björko S 36 C6
Björkö S 38 B4
Björköby S 40 B4
Björkvik S 37 D3
Bjørn N 115 A9
Björna S 115 D15
Björneborg S 35 C6
Björnerod S 35 C3
Bjørnevatn N 113 C18
Björnlunda S 37 C4
Bjørnstad N 113 C19
Björsäter S 37 D3
Bjurberget S 34 B4
Bjurholm S 115 D16
Bjursås S 36 B2
Bjurtjärn S 35 C6
Bjuv S 41 C2
Blace SRB 85 C6
Blachownia PL 54 C3
Blackburn GB 26 B3
Blackpool GB 26 B2
Blackstad S 40 B6
Blackwater IRL 21 B5
Blackwaterfoot GB 24 C2
Blacy F 59 B5
Bladåker S 36 B5
Blaenau Ffestiniog
GB 26 C2
Blaenavon GB 29 B4
Blaengarw GB 29 B4
Blagaj
BIH 83 A5
BIH 84 C2
Blagdon GB 29 B5
Blagnac F 77 C4
Blagoevgrad BG 11 E7
Blaichach D 61 C6
Blain F 66 A3
Blainville-sur-l'Eau F 60 B2
Blair Atholl GB 25 B4
Blairgowrie GB 25 B4
Blajan F 77 C3
Blakeney GB 29 B5
Blakstad N 33 D5
Blâmont F 60 B2
Blanca E 101 A4
Blancos E 87 C3
Blandford Forum GB 29 C5
Blanes E 91 B5
Blangy-sur-Bresle F 58 A2
Blankaholm S 40 B6
Blankenberge B 49 B4
Blankenburg D 51 B6
Blankenfelde D 45 C5
Blankenhain D 52 C1
Blankenheim D 50 C2
Blanquefort F 76 B2
Blansko CZ 64 A2
Blanzac F 67 C5
Blanzy F 69 B4
Blaricum NL 49 A6
Blarney IRL 20 C3
Blascomillán E 94 B1
Blascosancho E 94 B2
Błaszki PL 54 B3
Blatná CZ 63 A4
Blatné SK 64 B3
Blatnice CZ 64 B3
Blatnika BIH 84 B2
Blato HR 84 D1
Blato na Cetini HR 84 C1
Blatten CH 70 B2
Blattnicksele S 115 B14
Blatzheim D 50 C2
Blaubeuren D 61 B5
Blaufelden D 61 A5
Blaustein D 61 B5
Blaydon GB 25 D6
Blaye F 76 A2
Blaye-les-Mines F 77 B5
Blázquez E 93 C5
Bleckede D 44 B2
Blecua E 90 A2
Bled SLO 73 B4
Bleiburg A 73 B4
Bleichenbach D 51 C5
Bleicherode D 51 B6
Bleik N 112 C4
Bleikvassli N 115 B10
Bléneau F 59 C3
Blentarp S 41 D3
Blera I 102 A5
Blérancourt F 59 A4
Bléré F 67 A5
Blesle F 68 C3
Blessington IRL 21 A5
Blet F 68 B2
Bletchley GB 31 C3
Bletterans F 69 B5
Blidö S 37 C5
Blidsberg S 40 B3
Blieskastel D 60 A3
Bligny-sur-Ouche F 69 A4
Blikstorp S 35 D6
Blinisht AL 105 B6
Blinja HR 73 C6
Blizanówek PL 54 B3
Bliżyn PL 55 B5
Blois F 58 C2
Blokhus DK 38 B2
Blokzijl NL 42 C2
Blombacka S 35 C5
Blomberg D 51 B5
Blomskog S 35 C4
Blomstermåla S 40 C6
Blomvåg N 32 B1
Blönduós IS 111 B5
Błonie PL 55 A5
Blonville-sur-Mer F 57 A6
Blötberget S 36 B2
Blovice CZ 63 A4
Bloxham GB 31 B2
Blšany CZ 52 C3
Bludenz A 71 A4
Bludov CZ 64 A2
Blumberg D 61 C4
Blyberg S 34 A6
Blyth
Northumberland GB 25 C6
Nottinghamshire GB 27 B4
Blyth Bridge GB 25 C4
Blythburgh GB 30 B5
Blythe Bridge GB 26 C3
Bø
Nordland N 112 D3
Telemark N 33 C6
Boal E 86 A4
Boan MNE 85 D4
Boario Terme I 71 C5
Boat of Garten GB 23 D5
Boa Vista P 92 B2
Boğazkale TR 16 A7
Boğazlıyan TR 16 B7
Boba H 74 A2
Bobadilla
Logroño E 89 B4
Málaga E 100 B1
Bobadilla del Campo
E 94 A1
Bobadilla del Monte
E 94 B3
Bóbbio I 80 B3
Bóbbio Pellice I 79 B6
Bobigny F 58 B3
Bobingen D 62 B1
Böblingen D 61 B5
Bobolice PL 46 B2
Boboras E 87 B2
Bobowa PL 65 A6
Bobrinets UA 11 B12
Bobrová CZ 64 A2
Bobrovitsa UA 11 A11
Bobrowice PL 53 B5
Bobrówko PL 46 C1
Boca de Huérgano E 88 B2
Bocairent E 96 C2
Bočar SRB 75 C5
Bocchigliero I 106 B3
Boceguillas E 89 C3
Bochnia PL 55 D5
Bocholt
B 49 B6
D 50 B2
Bochov CZ 52 C3
Bochum D 50 B3
Bockara S 40 B6
Bockenem D 51 A6
Bockfliess A 64 B2
Bockhorn D 43 B5
Bočna SLO 73 B4
Bocognano F 102 A2
Boconád H 65 C6
Boczów PL 45 C6
Boda S 36 A2
Böda S 41 B7
Boda
Stockholm S 36 B5
Värmland S 35 C5
Västernorrland S 115 E13
Bodafors S 40 B4
Boda Glasbruk S 40 C5
Bodajk H 74 A3
Boddam
Aberdeenshire GB 23 D7
Shetland GB 22 B7
Boddin D 44 B3
Bödefeld-Freiheit D 51 B4
Boden S 3 D24
Bodenmais D 62 A4
Bodenteich D 44 C2
Bodenwerder D 51 B5
Bodiam GB 31 C4
Bodinnick GB 28 C3
Bodio CH 70 B3
Bodjani SRB 75 C4
Bodmin GB 28 C3
Bodø N 112 E3
Bodonal de la Sierra
E 99 A4
Bodrum TR 119 E2
Bodstedt D 45 A4
Bodzanów PL 47 C6
Bodzanowice PL 54 C3
Bodzechów PL 55 C6
Bodzentyn PL 55 C5
Boecillo E 88 C2
Boëge F 69 B6
Boën F 68 C3
Bogács H 65 C6
Bogadmindszent H 74 C3
Bogajo E 87 D4
Bogarra E 101 A3
Bogarre E 100 B2
Bogatić SRB 85 B4
Bogatynia PL 53 C4
Bogdaniec PL 45 C7
Bogë AL 105 A5
Boge S 37 E5
Bogen
D 62 B3
Nordland N 112 D5
Nordland N 112 E4
S 34 B4
Bogense DK 39 D3
Bogetići MNE 84 D3
Bognanco Fonti I 70 B3
Bognelv N 113 B11
Bognes N 112 D5
Bogno CH 70 B4
Bognor Regis GB 31 D3
Bogoria PL 55 C6
Bograngen S 34 B4
Boguchwaly PL 47 B6
Bogumiłowice PL 55 B4
Boguslav UA 11 B11
Boguszów-Gorce PL 53 C6
Bogutovac SRB 85 C5
Bogyiszló H 74 B3
Bohain-en-Vermandois
F 49 D4
Böheimkirchen A 64 B1
Bohinjska Bistrica
SLO 72 B3
Böhlen D 52 B2
Böhmenkirch D 61 B5
Bohmte D 43 C5
Bohonal de Ibor E 93 B5
Böhönye H 74 B2
Bohumin CZ 65 A4
Boiro E 86 B2
Bois-d'Amont F 69 B6
Boisseron F 78 C3
Boitzenburg D 45 B5
Boixols E 91 A4
Boizenburg D 44 B2
Bojadła PL 53 B5
Bojano I 103 B7
Bojanowo PL 54 B1
Bøjden DK 39 D3
Bojkovice CZ 64 A3
Bojná SK 64 B4
Bojnice SK 65 B4
Boka SRB 75 C5
Böklund D 43 A6
Bokod H 74 A3
Böksholm S 40 B4
Boksitogorsk RUS 7 B12
Bol HR 83 C5
Bolaños de Calatrava
E 100 A2
Bolayır TR 118 B1
Bolbec F 58 A1
Bölcske H 75 B3
Bolderslev DK 39 E2
Boldog H 65 C5
Boldva H 65 B6
Bolea E 90 A2
Bolekhiv UA 11 B7
Bolesławiec PL 53 B5
Boleszkowice PL 45 C6
Bolewice PL 46 C2
Bólgheri I 81 C4
Bolhrad UA 11 D10
Boliden S 3 D24
Bolimów PL 55 A5
Boliqueime P 98 B2
Boljevci SRB 85 B5
Boljkovci SRB 85 B5
Bolkhov RUS 7 E14
Bolków PL 53 C6
Bollebygd S 40 B2
Bollène F 78 B3
Bólliga E 95 B4
Bollnäs S 36 A3
Bollstabruk S 115 E14
Bollullos E 99 B4
Bollullos par del Condado
E 99 B4
Bologna I 81 B5
Bologne F 59 B6
Bolognetta I 108 B2
Bolognola I 82 D2
Bologoye RUS 7 C13
Bolótana I 110 B1
Bolsena I 102 A4
Bolshaya Vradiyevka
UA 11 C11
Bolsover GB 27 B4
Bolstad S 35 D4
Bolsward NL 42 B2
Boltaña E 90 A3
Boltenhagen D 44 B3
Boltigen CH 70 B2
Bolton GB 26 B3
Bolu TR 118 B6
Bolungarvík IS 111 A2
Bolvadin TR 118 D6
Bóly H 74 C3
Bolzaneto I 80 B2
Bolzano I 71 B6
Bomba I 103 A7
Bombarral P 92 B1
Bömenzien D 44 C3
Bomlitz D 43 C6
Bømlo N 33 C2
Bøn N 34 B3
Bona F 68 A3
Bonaduz CH 71 B4
Bonanza E 99 C4
Boñar E 88 B1
Bonarbridge GB 23 D4
Bonárcado I 110 B1
Bonares E 99 B4
Bonäs S 36 A1
Bonassola I 80 B3
Bonawe GB 24 B2
Bondal N 32 C5
Bondeno I 81 B5
Bondorf D 61 B4
Bondstorp S 40 B3
Bon-Encontre F 77 B3
Bo'ness GB 25 B4
Bonete E 101 A4
Bonifacio F 102 B2
Bonigen CH 70 B2
Bonin PL 46 A2
Bonn D 50 C3
Bonnánaro I 110 B1
Bonnåsjøen N 112 E4
Bonnat F 68 B1
Bonndorf D 61 C4
Bonnétable F 58 B1
Bonnétage F 70 A1
Bonneuil-les-Eaux F 58 A3
Bonneuil-Matours F 67 B5
Bonneval F 58 B2
Bonneval-sur-Arc F 70 C2
Bonneville F 69 B6
Bonnières-sur-Seine
F 58 A2
Bonnieux F 79 C4
Bönnigheim D 61 A5
Bonnyrigg GB 25 C4
Bonny-sur-Loire F 68 A2
Bono
E 90 A3
I 110 B2
Bonorva I 110 B1
Bønsnes N 34 B2
Bonyhád H 74 B3
Boom B 49 B5
Boos F 58 A2
Boostedt D 44 A2
Bootle
Cumbria GB 26 A2
Merseyside GB 26 B2
Bopfingen D 61 B6
Boppard D 50 C3
Boqueixón E 86 B2
Bor
CZ 62 A3
S 40 B4
SRB 11 D7
TR 16 C7
Boran-sur-Oise F 58 A3
Borås S 40 B2
Borba P 92 C3
Borbona I 102 A6
Borča SRB 85 B5
Borci BIH 84 C3
Borculo NL 50 A2
Bordány H 75 B4
Bordeaux F 76 B2
Bordeira P 98 B2
Bordesholm D 44 A2
Borðeyri IS 111 B4
Bordighera I 80 C1
Bording DK 39 C2
Bordón E 90 C2
Bore I 81 B3
Borehamwood GB 31 C3
Borek Strzeliński PL 54 C2
Borek Wielkopolski
PL 54 B2
Boreland GB 25 C4
Borello I 82 B1
Borensberg S 37 D2
Borgafjäll S 115 C12
Borgarnes IS 111 C4
Borgentreich D 51 B5
Börger D 43 C4
Borger NL 42 C3
Borggård S 37 D2
Borghamn S 37 D1
Borghetta di Vara I 81 B3
Borghetto d'Arróscia
I 80 B1
Borghetto Santo Spirito
I 80 B2
Borgholm S 41 C6
Borghorst D 50 A3
Bórgia I 106 C3
Borgloon B 49 C6
Børglum DK 38 B2
Borgo F 102 A2
Borgo alla Collina I 81 C5
Borgo a Mozzano I 81 C4
Borgoforte I 81 A4
Borgofranco d'Ivrea I 70 C2
Borgomanero I 70 C3
Borgomasino I 70 C2
Borgonovo Val Tidone
I 80 A3
Borgo Pace I 82 C1
Borgorose I 102 A6
Borgo San Dalmazzo
I 80 B1
Borgo San Lorenzo I 81 C5
Borgosésia I 70 C3
Borgo Val di Taro I 81 B3
Borgo Valsugana I 71 B6
Borgo Vercelli I 70 C3
Borgstena S 40 B3
Borgue GB 24 D3
Borgund N 32 A4
Borgvik S 35 C4
Borisovka RUS 7 F14
Borja E 89 C5
Bork D 50 B3
Borken D 50 B2
Borkenes N 112 D5
Børkop DK 39 D2
Borkowice PL 55 B5
Borkowo PL 47 C6
Borkum D 42 B3
Borlänge S 36 B2
Borlu TR 118 D3
Bormes-les-Mimosas
F 79 C5
Bórmio I 71 B5
Bormujos E 99 B4
Borna D 52 B2
Borne NL 50 A2
Bornes P 87 C3
Borne Sulinowo PL 46 B2
Bornheim D 50 C2
Bornhöved D 44 A2
Börnicke D 45 C4
Bornos E 99 C5
Borobia E 89 C5
Borodino RUS 7 D13
Borohrádek CZ 53 C6
Boronów PL 54 C3
Bórore I 110 B1
Borosźow PL 54 C3
Borota H 75 B4
Boroughbridge GB 27 A4
Borovany CZ 63 B5
Borovichi RUS 7 B12
Borovnica SLO 73 C4
Borovo HR 75 C3
Borovsk RUS 7 D14
Borovy CZ 63 A4
Borowa PL 54 B2
Borowie PL 55 B6
Borox E 94 B3
Borrby S 41 D4
Borre
DK 41 E2
N 35 C2
Borredá E 91 A4
Borrenes E 86 B4
Borriol E 96 A2
Borris
DK 39 D1
IRL 21 B5
Borris-in-Ossory IRL 21 B4
Borrisokane IRL 20 B3
Borrisoleigh IRL 21 B4
Borrowdale GB 26 A2
Børrud N 34 C4
Borşa RO 11 C8
Borsdorf D 52 B2
Børselv N 113 B14
Borsfa H 74 B1
Borský Mikuláš SK 64 B3
Borsodivánka H 65 C6
Borsodnádasd H 65 B6
Börte N 33 C4
Borth GB 26 C1
Bort-les-Orgues F 68 C2
Börtnan S 115 E10
Børtnes N 32 B6
Borup DK 39 D4
Boryslav UA 11 B7
Boryspil UA 11 A11
Boryszyn PL 46 C1
Borzęciczki PL 54 B2
Borzęcin PL 55 A5
Borzna UA 7 F12
Borzonasca I 80 B3
Borzyszkowy PL 46 A3
Borzytuchom PL 46 A3
Bosa I 110 B1
Bošáca SK 64 B3
Bosanci HR 73 C5
Bosanska Dubica BIH 74 C1
Bosanska Gradiška
BIH 74 C2
Bosanska Kostajnica
BIH 74 C1
Bosanska Krupa BIH 83 B5
Bosanski Brod BIH 84 A2
Bosanski Novi BIH 83 A5
Bosanski Petrovac
BIH 83 B5
Bosanski Šamac BIH 84 A3
Bosansko Grahovo
BIH 83 B5
Bošany SK 64 B4
Bösárkány H 64 C3
Bosau D 44 A2
Bósca H 75 B4
Boscastle GB 28 C3
Bosco I 80 B2
Bosco Chiesanuova I 71 C6
Bösdorf D 44 A2
Bösel D 43 B4
Bosham GB 31 D3
Bösingfeld D 51 A5
Bosjön S 34 C5
Boskoop NL 49 A5
Boskovice CZ 64 A2
Bošnjaci HR 84 A3
Bošnjane SRB 85 C6
Bossast E 77 D3
Bossolasco I 80 B2
Boštanj SLO 73 B5
Boston GB 27 C5
Bostrak N 33 C5
Böszénfa H 74 B2
Bot E 90 B3
Botajica BIH 84 B3
Bøte By DK 44 A3
Bothel GB 26 A2
Boticas P 87 C3
Botilsäter S 35 C5
Botngård N 114 D6
Botoš SRB 75 C5
Botoşani RO 11 C9
Botricello I 107 C3
Bottendorf D 51 B4
Bottesford GB 27 C5
Bottnaryd S 40 B3
Bottrop D 50 B2
Botunje SRB 85 B6
Boturić SRB 85 C5
Bötzingen D 60 B3
Bouaye F 66 A3
Bouça P 87 C3
Boucau F 76 C1
Bouchain F 49 C4
Bouchoir F 58 A3
Boudreville F 59 C5
Boudry CH 70 B1
Bouesse F 67 B6
Bouguenais F 66 A3
Bouhy F 68 A3
Bouillargues F 78 C3
Bouillon B 59 A6
Bouilly F 59 B4
Bouin F 66 B3
Boulay-Moselle F 60 A2
Boulazac F 67 C5
Boule-d'Amont F 91 A5
Bouligny F 60 A1
Boulogne-sur-Gesse
F 77 C3
Boulogne-sur-Mer F 48 C2
Bouloire F 58 C1
Bouquemaison F 48 C3
Bourbon-Lancy F 68 B3
Bourbon l'Archambault
F 68 B3
Bourbonne-les-Bains
F 60 C1
Bourbourg F 48 C3
Bourbriac F 56 B2
Bourcefranc-le-Chapus
F 66 C3
Bourdeaux F 79 B4
Bouresse F 67 B5
Bourg F 76 A2
Bourg-Achard F 58 A1
Bourganeuf F 68 C1
Bourg-Argental F 69 C4
Bourg-de-Péage F 79 A4
Bourg-de-Thizy F 69 B4
Bourg-de-Visa F 77 B3
Bourg-en-Bresse F 69 B5
Bourges F 68 A2
Bourg-et-Comin F 59 A4
Bourg-Lastic F 68 C2
Bourg-Madame F 91 A4
Bourgneuf-en-Retz F 66 A3
Bourgogne F 59 A5
Bourgoin-Jallieu F 69 C5
Bourg-St Andéol F 78 B3
Bourg-St Maurice F 70 C1
Bourgtheroulde F 58 A1
Bourgueil F 67 A5
Bourmont F 60 B1
Bourne GB 30 B3
Bournemouth GB 29 C6
Bourneville F 58 A1
Bournezeau F 66 B3
Bourran F 77 B3
Bourret F 77 C4
Bourron-Marlotte F 58 B3
Bourton-on-The-Water
GB 29 B6
Boussac F 68 B2
Boussens F 77 C3
Boutersem B 49 C5
Bouttencourt F 48 D2
Bouvières F 79 B4
Bouvron F 66 A3
Bouxwiller F 60 B3
Bouzas E 87 B2
Bouzonville F 60 A2
Bova I 106 D2
Bovalino Marina I 106 C3
Bovallstrand S 35 D3
Bova Marina I 106 D2
Bovec SLO 72 B3
Bóveda E 86 B3
Bóvegno I 71 C5
Bovenau D 44 A1
Bovenden D 51 B5
Bøverdal N 114 F5
Boves F 58 A3
Bóves I 80 B1
Bovey Tracey GB 28 C4
Bovino I 103 B8
Bøvlingbjerg DK 38 C1
Bovolenta I 72 C1
Bovolone I 71 C6
Bowes GB 27 A4
Bowmore GB 24 C1
Bowness-on-Windermere
GB 26 A3
Box GB 29 B5
Boxberg
Baden-Württemberg D 61 A5
Sachsen D 53 B4
Boxholm S 37 D2
Boxmeer NL 50 B1
Boxtel NL 49 B6
Boyabat TR 16 A7
Boyalıca TR 118 B4
Boyle IRL 18 C3
Bozan TR 118 C6
Božava HR 83 B3
Bozburun TR 119 F3
Bozcaada TR 116 C8
Bozdoğan TR 119 E3
Bożepole Wielkie PL 46 A3
Boževac SRB 85 B6
Božice CZ 64 B2
Boži Dar CZ 52 C2
Bozkır TR 119 E7
Bozouls F 78 B1
Bozova TR 119 E5
Bozüyük TR 118 C5
Bózzolo I 81 A4
Bra I 80 B1
Braås S 40 B5
Brabrand DK 39 C3
Bracadale GB 22 D2
Bracciano I 102 A5
Bracieux F 67 A6
Bräcke S 115 E12
Brackenheim D 61 A5
Brackley GB 30 B2
Bracklin IRL 19 C5
Bracknell GB 31 C3
Brackwede D 51 B4
Braco GB 25 B4
Brad RO 11 C7
Bradford GB 27 B4
Bradford on Avon GB 29 B5
Bradina BIH 84 C3
Brådland N 33 D3
Brædstrup DK 39 D2
Brae GB 22 A7
Braemar GB 23 D5
Braemore GB 22 D3
Braga P 87 C2
Bragança P 87 C4
Brăila RO 11 D9
Braine F 59 A4
Braine-le-Comte B 49 C5
Braintree GB 31 C4
Braives B 49 C6
Brake D 43 B5
Brakel
B 49 C4
D 51 B5
Bräkne-Hoby S 41 C5
Brålanda S 35 D4
Bralin PL 54 B2
Brallo di Pregola I 80 B3
Bram F 77 C5
Bramafan F 79 C5
Bramberg am Wildkogel
A 72 A2
Bramdrupdam DK 39 D2
Bramming DK 39 D1
Brampton GB 25 D5
Bramsche D 43 C4
Branca I 82 C1
Brancaleone Marina
I 106 D3
Brancaster GB 30 B4
Brand
Nieder Östereich A 63 B6
Vorarlberg A 71 A4
Brandbu N 34 B2
Brande DK 39 D2
Brande-Hornerkirchen
D 43 B6
Brandenberg A 72 A1
Brandenburg D 45 C4
Brand-Erbisdorf D 52 C3
Brandis D 52 B2
Brando F 102 A2
Brandomil E 86 A2
Brandon GB 30 B4
Brandshagen D 45 A5
Brandval N 34 B4
Brandýs nad Labem
CZ 53 C4
Branice PL 54 C2
Braničevo SRB 85 B6
Braniewo PL 47 A5
Branik SLO 72 C3
Brankovina SRB 85 B4
Branky CZ 64 A3
Branne F 76 B2
Brannenburg-Degerndorf
D 62 C3
Brantôme F 67 C5
Branzi I 71 B4
Bras d'Asse F 79 C5
Braskereidfoss N 34 B3
Braslaw BY 7 D9
Braşov RO 11 D8
Brasparts F 56 B2
Brassac F 77 C5
Brassac-les-Mines F 68 C3
Brasschaat B 49 B5
Brastad S 35 D3
Břasy CZ 63 A4
Brąszewice PL 54 B3
Brataj AL 105 C5
Bratislava SK 64 B3
Brattfors S 35 C6
Brattvåg N 114 E3
Bratunac BIH 85 B4
Braubach D 50 C3
Braunau A 62 B4
Braunfels D 51 C4
Braunlage D 51 B6
Braunsbedra D 52 B1
Braunschweig D 51 A6
Bray IRL 21 A5
Bray Dunes F 48 B3
Bray-sur-Seine F 59 B4
Bray-sur-Somme F 48 D3
Brazatortas E 100 A1
Brazey-en-Plaine F 69 A5
Brbinj HR 83 B4
Brčko BIH 84 B3
Brdani SRB 85 C5
Brdów PL 47 C4
Brea de Tajo E 95 B3
Brécey F 57 B4
Brechen D 50 C4
Brechin GB 25 B5
Brecht B 49 B5
Brecketfeld D 50 B3
Břeclav CZ 64 B2
Brecon GB 29 B4
Brécy F 68 A2
Breda
E 91 B5
NL 49 B5
Bredaryd S 40 B3
Bredbyn S 115 D15
Breddin D 44 C4
Bredebro DK 39 D1
Bredelar D 51 B4
Bredenfelde D 45 B5
Bredsjö S 36 C1
Bredstedt D 43 A5
Bredsten DK 39 D2
Bredträsk S 115 D15
Bredviken S 115 A11
Bree B 49 B6
Bregana HR 73 C5
Breganze I 72 C1
Bregenz A 71 A4
Bréhal F 57 B4
Brehna D 52 B2
Breiðdalsvík IS 111 C11
Breidenbach F 60 A3
Breil-sur-Roya F 80 C1
Breisach D 60 B3
Breitenbach
CH 70 A2
D 51 C5
Breitenberg D 63 B4
Breitenfelde D 44 B2
Breitengussbach D 51 D6
Breivikbotn N 113 B11
Brejning DK 39 D2
Brekke N 32 A2
Brekken N 114 E8
Brekkestø N 33 D5
Brekkvasselv N 115 C10
Brekstad N 114 D6
Breland N 33 D4
Bremanger N 114 F1
Bremen D 43 B5
Bremerhaven D 43 B5
Bremervörde D 43 B6
Bremgarten CH 70 A3
Bremsnes N 114 D4
Brem-sur-Mer F 66 B3
Brenderup DK 39 D2
Brenes E 99 B5
Brengova SLO 73 B5
Brenna PL 65 A4
Breno I 71 C5
Brénod F 69 B5
Brensbach D 61 A4
Brentwood GB 31 C4
Brescello I 81 B4
Bréscia I 71 C5
Breskens NL 49 B4
Bresles F 58 A3
Bresnica SRB 85 C5
Bressana I 80 A3
Bressanone I 72 B1
Bressuire F 67 B4
Brest
BY 6 E7
F 56 B1
HR 72 C3
Brestač SRB 85 B4
Brestanica SLO 73 B5
Brestova HR 82 A3
Brestovac HR 74 C2
Bretenoux F 77 B4
Breteuil
Eure F 58 B1
Oise F 58 A3
Brétigny-sur-Orge F 58 B3
Bretten D 61 A4
Bretteville-sur-Laize
F 57 A5
Brettheim D 61 A6
Breuil-Cervínia I 70 C2
Breukelen NL 49 A6
Brevik
N 35 C1
Stockholm S 37 C5
Västra Götaland S 37 D1
Breza BIH 84 B3
Brežice SLO 73 C5
Bréziers F 79 B5
Brezna SRB 85 C5
Breznica HR 73 B6
Breznica Našička HR 74 C3
Březnice CZ 63 A4
Brezno SK 65 B5
Brezojevice MNE 85 D4
Brezolles F 58 B2
Březovánad Svitavou
CZ 64 A2
Brezovápod Bradlom
SK 64 B3
Brezovica
SK 65 A6
SLO 73 B4
Brezovo Polje Selo
BIH 84 B3
Briançon F 79 B5
Brianconnet F 79 C5
Briare F 58 C3
Briatexte F 77 C4
Briático I 106 C3
Briaucourt F 59 B6
Bribir HR 73 C4
Bricquebec F 57 A4
Bridgend
Argyll & Bute GB 24 C1
Bridgend GB 29 B4
Bridge of Cally GB 25 B4
Bridge of Don GB 23 D6
Bridge of Earn GB 25 B4
Bridge of Orchy GB 24 B3
Bridgnorth GB 26 C3
Bridgwater GB 29 B5
Břidličná CZ 64 A3
Bridlington GB 27 A5
Bridport GB 29 C5
Briec F 56 B1
Brie-Comte-Robert F 58 B3
Brienne-le-Château F 59 B5
Brienon-sur-Armançon
F 59 C4
Brienz CH 70 B3
Brienza I 104 C1
Briesen D 45 C6
Brieskow Finkenheerd
D 53 A4
Brietlingen D 44 B2
Brieva de Cameros E 89 B4
Briey F 60 A1
Brig CH 70 B3
Brigg GB 27 B5
Brighouse GB 27 B4
Brightlingsea GB 31 C5
Brighton GB 31 D3
Brignogan-Plage F 56 B1
Brignoles F 79 C5
Brigstock GB 30 B3
Brihuega E 95 B4
Brijuni HR 82 B2
Brillon-en-Barrois F 59 B6
Brilon D 51 B4
Brimnes N 32 B3
Brinches P 98 A3
Bríndisi I 105 C3
Brinje HR 83 A4
Brinon-sur-Beuvron
F 68 A3
Brinon-sur-Sauldre F 68 A2
Brinyan GB 23 B5
Brión E 86 B2
Briones E 89 B4
Brionne F 58 A1
Brioude F 68 C3
Brioux-sur-Boutonne
F 67 B4
Briouze F 57 B5
Briscous F 76 C1
Brisighella I 81 B5
Brissac-Quincé F 67 A4
Brissago CH 70 B3
Bristol GB 29 B5
Brive-la-Gaillarde F 67 C6
Briviesca E 89 B3
Brixham GB 29 C4
Brixlegg A 72 A1
Brjánslækur IS 111 B2
Brka BIH 84 B3
Brnaze HR 83 C5
Brněnec CZ 64 A2
Brno CZ 64 A2
Bro S 37 C4
Broadclyst GB 29 C4
Broadford
GB 22 D3
IRL 20 B3
Broad Haven GB 28 B2
Broadstairs GB 31 C5
Broadstone GB 29 C5
Broadway GB 29 A6
Broager DK 39 E2
Broaryd S 40 B3
Broby S 41 C4
Brobyværk DK 39 D3
Bročanac BIH 84 C2
Broćanac MNE 84 D3
Brocas F 76 B2
Brock D 50 A3
Brockel D 43 B6
Brockenhurst GB 31 D2
Broczyno PL 46 B2
Brod MK 116 A3
Brodalen S 35 D3
Brodarevo SRB 85 C4
Broddbo S 36 C3
Brodek u Přerova CZ 64 A3
Broden-bach D 50 C3
Brodick GB 24 C2
Brod na Kupi HR 73 C4
Brodnica PL 47 B5
Brodnica Graniczna
PL 47 A4
Brody
Lubuskie PL 53 A5
Lubuskie PL 53 B4
Mazowieckie PL 47 C6
UA 11 A8
Broglie F 58 B1
Brójce PL 53 A5
Brokind S 37 D2
Brolo I 109 A3
Brome D 44 C2
Bromley GB 31 C4
Bromölla S 41 C4
Bromont-Lamothe F 68 C2
Brömsebro S 41 C5
Bromsgrove GB 29 A5
Bromyard GB 29 A5
Bronchales E 95 B5
Bronco E 93 A4
Brønderslev DK 38 B2
Broni I 80 A3
Brønnøysund N 114 B9
Brøns DK 39 D1
Bronte I 109 B3
Bronzani Mejdan BIH 84 B1
Bronzolo I 71 B6
Broons F 57 B3
Broquies F 78 B1
Brora GB 23 C5
Brørup DK 39 D2
Brösarp S 41 D4
Brossac F 67 C4
Brostrud N 32 B5
Brotas P 92 C2
Brötjärna S 36 B2
Broto E 90 A2
Brottby S 37 C5
Brøttum N 34 A2
Brou F 58 B2
Brouage F 66 C3
Brough GB 26 A3
Broughshane GB 19 B5
Broughton GB 25 C4
Broughton-in-Furness
GB 26 A2
Broumov CZ 53 C6
Broût-Vernet F 68 B3
Brouvelieures F 60 B2
Brouwershaven NL 49 B4
Brovary UA 11 A11
Brovst DK 38 B2
Brownhills GB 27 C4
Brozas E 93 B4
Brozzo I 71 C5
Brtnice CZ 63 A6
Brtonigla HR 72 C3
Bruay-la-Buissière F 48 C3
Bruchhausen-Vilsen
D 43 C6
Bruchsal D 61 A4
Bruck D 62 A3
Brück D 52 A2
Bruck an der
Grossglocknerstrasse
A 72 A2
Bruck an der Leitha A 64 B2
Bruck an der Mur A 73 A5
Brückl A 73 B4
Bruckmühl D 62 C2
Brue-Auriac F 79 C4
Brüel D 44 B3
Bruen CH 70 B3
Bruère-Allichamps F 68 B2
Bruff IRL 20 B3
Bruflat N 32 B6
Brugg CH 70 A3
Brugge B 49 B4
Brüggen D 50 B2
Brühl D 50 C2
Bruinisse NL 49 B5
Brûlon F 57 C5
Brumano I 71 C4
Brumath F 60 B3
Brummen NL 50 A2
Brumov-Bylnice CZ 64 A4
Brumunddal N 34 B2
Brunau D 44 C3
Brunehamel F 59 A5
Brünen D 50 B2
Brunete E 94 B2
Brunflo S 115 D11
Brunico I 72 B1
Brunkeberg N 33 C5
Brunn D 45 B5
Brunnen CH 70 B3
Brunsbüttel D 43 B6
Brunssum NL 50 C1
Bruntál CZ 54 D2
Brus SRB 85 C6
Brušane HR 83 B4
Brusasco I 70 C3
Brusio CH 71 B5
Brusno SK 65 B5
Brusque F 78 C1
Brussels = Bruxelles
B 49 C5
Brusson I 70 C2
Brüssow D 45 B6
Brusy PL 46 B3
Bruton GB 29 B5
Bruvno HR 83 B4
Bruvoll N 34 B3
Bruxelles = Brussels
B 49 C5
Bruyères F 60 B2
Bruz F 57 B4
Bruzaholm S 40 B5
Brwinów PL 55 A5
Bryansk RUS 7 E13
Brynamman GB 28 B4
Bryncrug GB 26 C1
Bryne N 33 D2
Brynmawr GB 29 B4
Bryrup DK 39 C2
Brzeće SRB 85 C5
Brzeg PL 54 C2
Brzeg Dolny PL 54 B1
Brześć Kujawski PL 47 C4
Brzesko PL 55 D5
Brzeszcze PL 55 D4
Brzezie PL 46 B2
Brzeziny
Łódzkie PL 55 B4
Wielkopolskie PL 54 B3
Brzeźnica PL 53 B5
Brzežnica Nowa PL 55 B4
Brzeżno PL 46 B1
Brzotin SK 65 B6
Brzozie Lubawskie
PL 47 B5
Bua S 40 B2
Buarcos P 92 A2
Buaveg N 33 C2
Bubbio I 80 B2
Bubry F 56 C2
Buca TR 119 D2
Bucak TR 119 E5
Bučany SK 64 B3
Buccheri I 109 B3
Buccino I 103 C8
Bucelas P 92 C1
Buch
Bayern D 61 B6
Bayern D 62 B3
Buchach UA 11 B8
Bucharest = Bucureşti
RO 11 D9
Buchbach D 62 B3
Buchboden A 71 A4
Buchen D 61 A5
Büchen D 44 B2
Buchenberg D 61 C6
Buchères F 59 B5
Buchholz D 44 B1
Buchloe D 62 B1
Buchlovice CZ 64 A3

Buchlyvie GB 24 B3
Bucholz D 44 B4
Buchs CH 71 A4
Buchy F 58 A2
Bückeburg D 51 A5
Buckfastleigh GB 28 C4
Buckhaven GB 25 B4
Buckie GB 23 D6
Buckingham GB 31 B3
Bückwitz D 44 C4
Bučovice CZ 64 A3
Bucsa H 75 A6
Bucureşti = Bucharest
  RO 11 D9
Bucy-lés-Pierrepont
  F 59 A4
Buczek PL 55 B4
Bud N 114 E3
Budakalasz H 65 C5
Budakeszi H 75 A3
Budal N 114 E7
Budapest H 75 A3
Búðardalur IS 111 B4
Budča SK 65 B5
Buddusò I 110 B2
Bude GB 28 C3
Budel NL 50 B1
Büdelsdorf D 43 A6
Budens P 98 B2
Budia E 95 B4
Budimlić-Japra BIH . .83 B5
Büdingen D 51 C5
Budinščina HR 73 B6
Budišov CZ 64 A3
Budleigh Salterton
  GB 29 C4
Budmerice SK 64 B3
Budoni I 110 B2
Búdrio I 81 B5
Budva MNE 105 A4
Budyněnad Ohří CZ . .53 C4
Budziszewice PL 55 B4
Budzyń PL 46 C2
Bue N 33 D2
Bueña E 90 B1
Buenache de Alarcón
  E 95 C4
Buenache de la Sierra
  E 95 B5
Buenavista de Valdavia
  E 88 B2
Buendia E 95 B4
Bueu E 87 B2
Buezo E 89 B3
Bugarra E 96 B2
Bugeat F 68 C1
Buggerru I 110 C1
Bugojno BIH 84 B2
Bugøyfjord N 113 C18
Bugøynes N 113 C18
Bugyi H 75 A4
Buharkent TR 119 E3
Bühl
  Baden-Württemberg
  D 61 B4
  Bayern D 61 C6
Bühlertal D 61 B4
Bühlertann D 61 A5
Buia I 72 B3
Builth Wells GB 29 A4
Buin N 32 B6
Buis-les-Baronnies F .79 B4
Buitenpost NL 42 B3
Buitrago del Lozoya
  E 94 B3
Bujalance E 100 B1
Bujaraloz E 90 B2
Buje HR 72 C3
Bujedo E 89 B3
Bük H 74 A1
Buk PL 46 C2
Bükkösd H 74 B2
Bükkszérc H 65 C6
Bukovci SLO 73 B5
Bukowiec PL 53 A6
Bukowina Tatrzańska
  PL 65 A6
Bukownica PL 54 B3
Bukowno PL 55 C4
Bülach CH 70 A3
Buldan TR 119 D3
Bulgari BG 11 E9
Bulgnéville F 60 B1
Bulgurca TR 119 D2
Bülkau D 43 B5
Bulken N 32 B3
Bulkowo PL 47 C6
Bullas E 101 A4
Bullange B 50 C2
Büllingen B 50 C2
Bullmark S 115 A6
Buna BIH 84 C2
Bunahowen IRL 18 B2
Bunbeg IRL 18 A3
Bunclody IRL 21 B5
Buncrana IRL 19 A4
Bunde D 43 B4
Bünde D 51 A4
Bundoran IRL 18 B3
Bungay GB 30 B5
Bunge S 37 E6
Bunić HR 83 B4
Bunmahon IRL 21 B4
Bunnyconnellan IRL . .18 B2
Buño E 86 A2
Buñol E 96 B2
Bunratty IRL 20 B3
Bunsbeek B 49 C5
Buñuel E 89 C5
Bünyan TR 16 B7
Bunyola E 97 B2
Buonabitácolo I 104 C1
Buonalbergo I 103 B7
Buonconvento I 81 C5
Buonvicino I 106 B2
Burano I 72 C2
Burbach D 50 C4
Burcei I 110 C2
Burdons-sur-Rognon
  F 59 B6
Burdur TR 119 E5
Bureå S 3 D24
Büren D 51 B4
Büren an der Aare
  CH 70 A2
Burford GB 29 B6
Burg
  Cottbus D 53 B4
  Magdeburg D 52 A2
  Schleswig-Holstein D .43 B6
Burgas BG 11 E9
Burgau
  A 73 A6
  D 61 B6
Burg auf Fehmarn D . .44 A3
Burgbernheim D 61 A6
Burgdorf
  CH 70 A2
  D 44 C2
Burgebrach D 62 A1
Bürgel D 52 C1
Burgess Hill GB 31 D3
Burghaslach D 61 A6
Burghausen D 62 B3
Burghead GB 23 D5
Burgheim D 62 B2
Burgh le Marsh GB . .27 B6
Búrgio I 108 B2
Burgkirchen D 62 B3
Burgkunstadt D 52 C1
Burglengenfeld D . . .62 A3
Burgo P 87 D2
Burgoberbach D 61 A6
Burgohondo E 94 B2

Burgos E 88 B3
Burgsinn D 51 C5
Burgstädt D 52 C2
Burgstall D 44 C3
Burg Stargard D 45 B5
Burgsvik S 37 E5
Burgui E 76 D2
Burguillos E 99 B5
Burguillos del Cerro
  E 93 C4
Burguillos de Toledo
  E 94 C3
Burhaniye TR 118 C1
Burhave D 43 B5
Burie F 67 C4
Burjassot E 96 B2
Burk D 61 A6
Burkhardtsdorf D . . .52 C2
Burlada E 76 D1
Burladingen D 61 B5
Burness GB 23 B6
Burnham GB 31 C3
Burnham Market GB . .30 B4
Burnham-on-Crouch
  GB 31 C4
Burnham-on-Sea GB . .29 B5
Burniston GB 27 A5
Burnley GB 26 B3
Burntisland GB 25 B4
Buron E 88 A1
Buronzo I 70 C3
Burovac SRB 85 B6
Burow D 45 B5
Burravoe GB 22 A7
Burrel AL 105 B6
Burret F 77 D4
Burriana E 96 B2
Burry Port GB 28 B3
Bürs A 71 A4
Bursa TR 118 B4
Burseryd S 40 B3
Bürstadt D 61 A4
Burton GB 26 A3
Burton Agnes GB . . .27 B5
Burton Bradstock GB .29 C5
Burton Latimer GB . .31 B3
Burton upon Stather
  GB 27 B5
Burton upon Trent
  GB 27 C4
Burujón E 94 C2
Burwell GB 30 B4
Burwick GB 23 C6
Bury GB 26 B3
Buryn UA 7 F12
Bury St Edmunds GB .30 B4
Burzenin PL 54 B3
Busachi I 110 B1
Busalla I 80 B2
Busana I 81 B4
Busano I 70 C2
Busca I 80 B1
Busch D 44 C3
Busečvec HR 73 C6
Bushat AL 105 B5
Bushey GB 31 C3
Bushmills GB 19 A5
Bušince SK 65 B5
Buskhyttan S 37 D3
Busko-Zdrój PL 55 C5
Busot E 96 C2
Busovača BIH 84 B2
Busquistar E 100 C2
Bussang F 60 C2
Busseto I 81 B4
Bussière-Badil F 67 C5
Bussière-Poitevine F .67 B5
Bussolengo I 71 C5
Bussoleno I 70 C2
Bussum NL 49 A6
Busto Arsízio I 70 C3
Büsum D 43 A5
Butera I 109 B3
Butgenbach B 50 C2
Butler's Bridge IRL . .19 B4
Butryny PL 47 B6
Bütschwil CH 70 A4
Buttermere GB 26 A2
Buttevant IRL 20 B3
Buttle S 37 E5
Buttstädt D 52 B1
Butzbach D 51 C4
Bützfleth D 43 B6
Bützow D 44 B3
Buxières-les-Mines F .68 B2
Buxtehude D 43 B6
Buxton GB 27 B4
Buxy F 69 B4
Büyükçekmece TR . .118 A3
Büyükkariştiran TR . .118 A2
Büyükorhan TR 118 C3
Buzançais F 67 B6
Buzancy F 59 A5
Buzău RO 11 D9
Buzet HR 72 C3
Buzsák H 74 B2
Buzy F 76 C2
By S 36 B3
Byala BG 11 E8
Byaroza BY 6 E8
Bycyna PL 54 B3
Bydalen S 115 D10
Bydgoszcz PL 47 B4
Bygdin N 32 A5
Bygland N 33 D4
Byglandsfjord N 33 D4
Bygstad N 32 A2
Bykhaw BY 7 E11
Bykle N 33 C4
Bylderup-Bov DK . . .39 E2
Byrkjedal N 33 D3
Byrkjelo N 114 F3
Byrum DK 38 B3
Byšice CZ 53 C4
Byske S 3 D24
Byškovice CZ 64 A3
Byšlaw PL 46 B3
Bystré CZ 64 A2
Bystřice CZ 63 A5
Bystřice CZ 65 A4
Bystřice nad Pernštejnem
  CZ 64 A2
Bystrice pod Hostýnem
  CZ 64 A3
Bystrzyca Kłodzka
  PL 54 C1
Bytča SK 65 A4
Bytnica PL 53 A5
Bytom PL 54 C3
Bytom Odrzański PL .53 B5
Bytów PL 46 A3
Byxelkrok S 41 B7
Bzenec CZ 64 B3
Bzince SK 64 B3

C

Çağa TR 118 B7
Cabacos P 92 B2
Cabaj-Čápor SK 64 B4
Cabana E 86 A2
Cabanac-et-Villagrains
  F 76 B2
Cabañaquinta E 88 A1
Cabanas P 98 B3
Cabañas del Castillo
  E 93 B5
Cabañas de Yepes E .95 C3
Cabanelles E 91 A5
Cabanes E 96 A3
Cabanillas E 89 B5
Cabar HR 73 C4
Cabasse F 79 C5
Cabdella E 91 A4
Cabeceiras de Basto
  P 87 C2
Cabeço de Vide P . . .92 B3
Cabella Ligure I 80 B3
Cabeza del Buey E . .93 C5
Cabeza la Vaca E . . .99 A4

Cabezamesada E . .95 C3
Cabezarados E 100 A1
Cabezarrubias del Puerto
  E 100 A1
Cabezas del Villar E . .94 B1
Cabezas Rubias E . . .98 B3
Cabezón E 88 C2
Cabezón de la Sal E . .88 A2
Cabezón de Liébana
  E 88 A2
Cabezuela E 94 A3
Cabezuela del Valle E .93 A5
Cabo de Gata E 101 C3
Cabo de Palos E 101 B5
Cabolafuente E 95 A4
Cabourg F 57 A5
Cabra
  E 100 B1
  P 92 A3
Cabrach GB 23 D5
Cabra del Santo Cristo
  E 100 B2
Cabrela P 110 C1
Cabrillas E 89 A4
Cabuna HR 74 C2
Čačak SRB 85 C5
Cacabelos E 86 B4
Čačinci HR 74 C2
Cadafais P 92 C1
Cadalen F 77 C5
Cadalso E 93 A4
Cadaqués E 91 A6
Cadaval P 92 B1
Cadavedo E 86 A4
Čadavica BIH 84 B1
Čadca SK 65 A4
Cadéac F 77 D3
Cadelbosco di Sopra
  I 81 B4
Cadenazzo CH 70 B3
Cadenberge D 43 B6
Cadenet F 79 C4
Cadeuil F 66 C4
Cádiar E 100 C2
Cadillac F 76 B2
Cádiz E 99 C4
Čadjavica HR 74 C2
Cadouin F 77 B3
Cadours F 77 C4
Cadrete E 90 B2
Caen F 57 A5
Caerleon GB 29 B5
Caernarfon GB 26 B1
Caerphilly GB 29 B4
Caersws GB 26 C2
Cafede P 92 B3
Caggiano I 104 C1
Čaglin HR 74 C2
Cágliari I 110 C2
Čaglin HR 74 C2
Cagnano Varano I . . .104 B1
Cagnes-sur-Mer F . . .79 C6
Caher IRL 21 B4
Caherciveen IRL 20 C1
Caherdaniel IRL 20 C1
Cahors F 77 B4
Cahul MD 11 D10
Caiazzo I 103 B7
Caion E 86 A2
Cairndow GB 24 B3
Cairnryan GB 24 D2
Cairo Montenotte I . .80 B2
Caister-on-Sea GB . . .30 B5
Caistor GB 27 B5
Caivano I 103 C7
Cajarc F 77 B4
Čajetina SRB 85 C4
Čajniče BIH 84 C4
Çakırlar TR 119 F5
Çakmak TR 118 C6
Čakovec HR 73 B6
Cakran AL 105 C5
Çal TR 119 D4
Cala E 99 B4
Calabritto I 103 C8
Calaceite E 90 C3
Calacuccia F 102 A2
Cala d'Or E 97 B3
Calaf E 91 B4
Calafat RO 11 E7
Calafell E 91 B4
Cala Galdana E 97 B3
Calahonda
  Granada E 100 C2
  Málaga E 100 C1
Calahorra E 89 B5
Cala Llonga E 97 C1
Calalzo di Cadore I . .72 B2
Cala Millor E 97 B3
Calamocha E 95 B5
Calamonte E 93 C4
Cala Morell E 97 A3
Calanais GB 22 C2
Calañas E 99 B4
Calanda E 90 C2
Calangiánus I 110 B2
Călăraşi RO 11 D9
Cala Ratjada E 97 B3
Calascibetta I 109 B3
Calasetta I 110 C1
Calasparra E 101 A4
Calatafimi I 108 B1
Calatayud E 89 C5
Calatorao E 89 C5
Calau D 53 B3
Calbe D 52 B1
Calcena E 89 C5
Calcinelli I 82 C1
Calco I 71 C4
Caldarola I 82 C2
Caldas da Rainha P . .92 B1
Caldas de Malavella
  E 91 B5
Caldas de Reis E . . .86 B2
Caldas de San Jorge
  P 87 D2
Caldas de Vizela P . . .87 C2

Callander GB 24 B3
Callas F 79 C5
Calliano
  Piemonte I 80 A2
  Trentino Alto Adige I .71 C6
Callington GB 28 C3
Callosa de Ensarriá
  E 96 C2
Callosa de Segura E .101 A5
Čalma SRB 85 A4
Calmbach D 61 B4
Calne GB 29 B6
Calolziocorte I 71 C4
Calonge E 91 B6
Calovec SK 64 C3
Calpe E 96 C3
Caltabellotta I 108 B2
Caltagirone I 109 B3
Caltanissetta I 109 B3
Caltavuturo I 108 B2
Çaltılıbük TR 118 C3
Caltojar E 89 C4
Caluire-et-Cuire F . . .69 C4
Calvello I 104 C1
Calvi F 102 A1
Calvinet F 77 B5
Calvisson F 78 C3
Calvörde D 44 C3
Calw D 61 B4
Calzada de Calatrava
  E 100 A2
Calzada de Valdunciel
  E 94 A1
Calzadilla de los Barros
  E 93 C4
Cam GB 29 B5
Camaiore I 81 C4
Camarasa E 90 B3
Camarena E 94 B2
Camarès F 78 C1
Camaret-sur-Mer F . .56 B1
Camarillas E 90 C2
Camarma E 86 A1
Camarzana de Tera E .87 B4
Camas E 99 B4
Camastra I 108 B2
Cambados E 86 B2
Cambarinho P 92 A2
Camberley GB 31 C3
Cambil E 100 B2
Camblanes-et-Meynac
  F 76 C1
Cambo-les-Bains F . .76 C1
Camborne GB 28 C2
Cambrai F 49 C4
Cambre E 86 A2
Cambridge GB 30 B4
Cambrils E 91 B4
Cambs D 44 B3
Camburg D 52 B1
Camden GB 31 C3
Cameleño E 88 A2
Camelford GB 28 C3
Çamlıdere TR 118 B7
Çamoluk TR 16 A7
Camogli I 80 B3
Camors F 56 C3
Camp IRL 20 B2
Campagna I 103 C8
Campagnano di Roma
  I 102 A5
Campagnático I 81 D5
Campan F 76 C3
Campana I 107 B3
Campanario E 93 C5
Campanillas E 100 C1
Campano E 99 C4
Campaspero E 88 C2
Campbeltown GB . . .24 C2
Campello E 96 C2
Campelos P 92 B1
Campi Bisénzio I 81 C5
Campico López E . . .101 B4
Campíglia Maríttima I .81 C4
Campillo de Altobuey
  E 95 C5
Campillo de Aragón
  E 95 A5
Campillo de Arenas
  E 100 B2
Campillo de Llerena
  E 93 C5
Câmpina RO 11 D8
Campi Salentina I . . .105 C4
Campli I 82 D2
Campo E 90 A3
Campobasso I 103 B7
Campobello di Licata
  I 108 B2
Campobello di Mazara
  I 108 B1
Campo de Bacerros
  E 87 B3
Campo de Caso E . . .88 A1
Campo de Criptana E .95 C3
Campodolcino I 71 B4
Campofelice di Roccella
  I 108 B2
Campofiorito I 108 B2
Campofórmido I 72 B3
Campofranco I 108 B2
Campofrío E 99 B4
Campogalliano I 81 B4
Campo Ligure I 80 B2
Campo Maior P 92 B3
Campomanes E 88 A1
Campomarino I 103 B8
Campo Molino I 79 B6
Campomono F 102 B1
Campo Real E 95 B3
Camporeale I 108 B2
Camporeggiano I . . .82 C1
Camporrells E 90 B3
Camporrobles E 96 B1
Campos P 87 C3
Camposa P 87 C2
Camposampiero I . . .72 C1
Camposanto I 81 B5
Campos del Port E . .97 B3
Campotéjar E 100 B2
Campotosto I 103 A6
Campo Túres I 72 B1
Camprodón E 91 A5
Campsegret F 77 B3
Camrose GB 28 B2
Camuñas E 95 C3
Çamyolu TR 119 F7
Çan TR 118 B2
Cana I 81 D5
Cañada del Hoyo E . .95 C5
Cañadajuncosa E . . .95 C4
Cañada Rosal E 99 B5
Čanak HR 83 B4
Çanakkale TR 118 B1
Canale I 80 B1
Canales
  Asturias E 88 B1
  Castellón de la Plana
    E 96 B2
Canals E 96 C2

Canal San Bovo I . . .72 B1
Cañamares E 95 B4
Cañamero E 93 B5
Cañar E 100 C2
Cañate la Real E 99 C5
Cañaveral E 93 B4
Cañaveral de León E .99 A4
Cañaveras E 95 B4
Cañaveruelas E 95 B4
Canazei I 72 B1
Cancale F 57 B4
Cancellara I 104 C1
Cancello ed Arnone
  I 103 B7
Cancon F 77 B3
Candamil E 86 A3
Candanchu E 76 D2
Çandarlı TR 118 D1
Candas E 88 A1
Candasnos E 90 B3
Candé F 66 A3
Candela I 104 B1
Candelario E 93 A5
Candeleda E 93 A5
Cándia Lomellina I . .70 C3
Candide Casamazzagno
  I 72 B2
Candin E 86 B4
Candosa P 92 A3
Canecas P 92 C1
Canelli I 80 B2
Canena E 100 A2
Canencia E 94 B3
Canero E 86 A4
Canet de Mar E 91 B5
Canet d'en Berenguer
  E 96 B2
Cañete E 95 B5
Cañete de las Torres
  E 100 B1
Canet-Plage F 91 A6
Canfranc E 76 D2
Cangas
  Lugo E 86 A3
  Pontevedra E . . .87 B2
Cangas de Narcea E .86 A4
Cangas de Onís E . . .88 A1
Canha P 92 C2
Canhestros P 98 A2
Canicatti I 108 B2
Canicattini Bagni I . .109 B4
Canicosa de la Sierra
  E 89 C3
Caniles E 101 B3
Canino I 102 A4
Canisy F 57 A4
Cañizal E 94 A1
Canjáyar E 101 C3
Çankırı TR 16 A6
Cannai I 110 C1
Cannara I 82 C1
Cánnero Riviera I . . .70 B3
Cannes F 79 C6
Canneto
  Sicilia I 106 C1
  Toscana I 81 C4
Canneto sull'Oglio I . .71 C5
Cannich GB 22 D4
Cannóbio I 70 B3
Cannock GB 26 C3
Canonbie GB 25 C5
Canosa di Púglia I . . .104 B2
Can Pastilla E 97 B2
Can Picafort E 97 B3
Cantalapiedra E 94 A1
Cantalejo E 94 A3
Cantalgallo E 99 A4
Cantalice I 102 A5
Cantalpino E 94 A1
Cantalupo in Sabina
  I 102 A5
Cantanhede P 92 A2
Cantavieja E 90 C2
Čantavir SRB 75 C4
Canterbury GB 31 C5
Cantiano I 82 C1
Cantillana E 99 B5
Cantimpalos E 94 A3
Cantória E 101 B3
Cantù I 71 C4
Canvey GB 31 C4
Cany-Barville F 58 A1
Caol GB 24 B2
Cáorle I 72 C2
Caorso I 81 A3
Capáccio I 103 C8
Capáci I 108 A2
Capálbio I 102 A4
Capánnori I 81 C4
Caparde BIH 84 B3
Caparroso E 89 B5
Capbreton F 76 C1
Capdenac-Gare F . . .77 B5
Capdepera E 97 B3
Cap-de-Pin F 76 B1
Capel Curig GB 26 B2
Capellades E 91 B4
Capena I 102 A5
Capendu F 78 C1
Capestang F 78 C2
Capestrano I 103 A6
Cap Ferret F 76 B1
Capileira E 100 C2
Capinha P 92 A3
Ca'Pisani I 82 B1
Capistrello I 103 B6
Capizzi I 109 B3
Čaplje BIH 83 B5
Čapljina BIH 84 C2
Capo d'Orlando I . . .109 A3
Capoliveri I 81 D4
Capo Rizzuto I 107 C4
Caposile I 72 C2
Capoterra I 110 C1
Cappamore IRL 20 B3
Cappeln D 43 C5
Cappoquin IRL 21 B4
Capracotta I 103 B7
Capránica I 102 A5
Caprarola I 102 A5
Capretta I 82 D1
Capri I 103 C7
Capriati a Volturno I . .103 B7
Caprino Veronese I . .71 C5
Captieux F 76 B2
Cápua I 103 B7
Capurso I 104 B2
Caputh D 45 C5
Carabaña E 95 B3
Carabias E 89 C3
Caracal RO 11 D8
Caracenilla E 95 C4
Caráglio I 80 B1
Caraman F 77 C4
Caramánico Terme I . .103 A7
Caranga E 86 A4
Caransebeş RO 11 D7
Carantec F 56 B2
Carapelle I 104 B1
Carasco I 80 B3
Carate Brianza I 71 C4
Caravaca de la Cruz
  E 101 A4
Caravággio I 71 C4
Carbajal E 100 C1
Carbajo E 93 B3
Carballeda E 86 B3
Carballeda de Avia E .87 B2
Carballo E 86 A2
Carbis Bay GB 28 C2
Carbon-Blanc F 76 B2
Carbonera de Frentes
  E 89 C4
Carboneras E 101 C4
Carboneras de
  Guadazaón E . . .95 C5
Carbonero el Mayor E .94 A2

Carboneros E 100 A2
Carbónia I 110 C1
Carbonin I 72 B2
Carbonne F 77 C4
Carbost
  Highland GB 22 D2
  Highland GB 22 D2
Carcaboso E 93 A4
Carcabuey E 100 B1
Carcaixent E 96 B2
Carcans F 76 A1
Carcans-Plage F 76 A1
Carção P 87 C4
Carcar E 89 B5
Cárcare I 80 B2
Carcassonne F 77 C5
Carcastillo E 89 B5
Carcedo de Burgos E .89 B3
Carcelén E 96 B1
Carcès F 79 C5
Carchelejo E 100 B2
Çardak TR 119 D4
Cardeña E 100 A1
Cardenete E 95 C5
Cardeñosa E 94 B2
Cardeto I 109 A4
Cardiff GB 29 B4
Cardigan GB 28 A3
Cardona E 91 B4
Cardosos P 92 B2
Carei RO 11 C7
Carentan F 57 A4
Carentoir F 57 C3
Careri I 106 C3
Carevdar HR 74 B1
Cargèse F 102 A1
Carhaix-Plouguer F . .56 B2
Caria P 92 A3
Carignan F 59 A6
Carignano I 80 B1
Cariñena E 90 B1
Carini I 108 A2
Cariño E 86 A3
Carínola I 103 B6
Carisbrooke GB 31 D2
Carlabhagh GB 22 C2
Carlepont F 59 A4
Carlet E 96 B2
Carlingford IRL 19 B5
Carlisle GB 25 D5
Carloforte I 110 C1
Carlópoli I 106 B3
Carlow
  D 44 B2
  IRL 21 B5
Carlton GB 27 C4
Carluke GB 25 C4
Carmagnola I 80 B1
Carmarthen GB 28 B3
Carmaux F 77 B5
Carmena E 94 C2
Cármenes E 88 B1
Carmine I 80 B1
Carmona E 99 B5
Carmonita E 93 B4
Carmyllie GB 25 B5
Carnac F 56 C2
Carndonagh IRL 19 A4
Carnew IRL 21 B5
Carnforth GB 26 A3
Cárnia I 72 B3
Carnlough GB 19 B6
Carno GB 26 C2
Carnon Plage F 78 C2
Carnota E 86 B1
Carnoustie GB 25 B5
Carnwath GB 25 C4
Carolei I 106 B3
Carolinensiel D 43 B4
Carolles F 57 B4
Carona I 71 B4
Caronía I 109 A3
Carovigno I 104 C3
Carovilli I 103 B7
Carpaneto Piacentino
  I 81 B3
Carpegna I 82 C1
Carpenédolo I 71 C5
Carpentras F 79 B4
Carpi I 81 B4
Carpignano Sésia I . .70 C3
Cărpineni MD 11 C10
Carpineti I 81 B4
Carpineto Romano I . .102 B6
Cărpiniş RO 75 C5
Carpino I 104 B1
Carpinone I 103 B7
Carpio E 94 A1
Carquefou F 66 A3
Carqueiranne F 79 C5
Carral E 86 A2
Carranque E 94 B3
Carrapichana P 92 A3
Carrara I 81 B4
Carraroe IRL 20 A2
Carrascalejo E 93 B5
Carrascosa del Campo
  E 95 B4
Carratraca E 100 C1
Carrazeda de Ansiães
  P 87 C3
Carrazedo de Montenegro
  P 87 C3
Carrbridge GB 23 D5
Carregal do Sal P . . .92 A2
Carreña E 88 A2
Carrick IRL 18 B3
Carrickart IRL 19 A4
Carrickfergus GB . . .19 B6
Carrickmacross IRL . .19 C5
Carrick-on-Shannon
  IRL 18 C3
Carrick-on-Suir IRL . .21 B4
Carrigallen IRL 19 C4
Carrión E 99 B5
Carrión de Calatrava
  E 94 D3
Carrión de los Condes
  E 88 B2
Carrizo de la Ribera E .88 B1
Carrizosa E 95 D4
Carro F 79 C4
Carrocera E 88 B1
Carros F 79 C6
Carrouge CH 70 B1
Carrouges F 57 B5
Carrù I 80 B1
Carryduff GB 19 B6
Carry-le-Rouet F 79 C4
Carsóli I 102 A6
Carsphairn GB 24 C3
Cartagena E 101 B5
Cártama E 100 C1
Cartaxo P 92 B2
Cartaya E 98 B3
Carteret F 57 A4
Cartes E 88 A2
Carúnchio I 103 B7
Carviçães P 87 C4
Carvin F 48 C3
Carvoeira P 92 B1
Carvoeiro P 98 B2
Casabermeja E 100 C1
Casa Branca
  Portalegre P 92 C3
  Setúbal P 98 A2
Casacalenda I 103 B7
Casa Castalda I 82 C1
Casaio E 86 B3
Casa l'Abate I 105 C4
Casalarreina E 89 B4
Casalbordino I 103 A7
Casalbuono I 104 C1
Casalbuttano ed Uniti
  I 71 C4
Casàl di Principe I . . .103 B7
Casalécchio di Reno
  I 81 B5

Casale Monferrato I . .70 C3
Casalina I 82 D1
Casalmaggiore I 81 B4
Casalnuovo Monterotaro
  I 103 B8
Casaloldo I 71 C5
Casalpusterlengo I . . .71 C4
Casalromano I 71 C5
Casamássima I 104 C2
Casamicciola Terme
  I 103 C6
Casamozza F 102 A2
Casarabonela E 100 C1
Casarano I 107 A5
Casar de Cáceres E . .93 B4
Casar de Palomero E .93 A4
Casarejos E 89 C3
Casares E 99 C5
Casares de las Hurdes
  E 93 A4
Casariche E 100 B1
Casarrubios del Monte
  E 94 B2
Casas de Don Pedro
  E 93 B5
Casas de Fernando
  Alonso E 95 C4
Casas de Haro E 95 C4
Casas de Juan Gil E . .96 B1
Casas del Juan Núñez
  E 95 C5
Casas del Puerto E . .101 A4
Casas del Río E 96 B1
Casas de Millán E . . .93 B4
Casas de Reina E . . .99 A5
Casas de Ves E 96 B1
Casas-Ibáñez E 96 B1
Casasimarro E 95 C4
Casas Nuevas E 101 B4
Casasola E 94 B2
Casasola de Arión E . .88 C1
Casasuertes E 88 B2
Casatejada E 93 B5
Casavieja E 94 B2
Casazza I 71 C4
Cascais P 92 C1
Cascante E 89 C5
Cascante del Río E . . .96 A1
Cáscia I 82 D2
Casciana Terme I . . .81 C4
Cáscina I 81 C4
Cáseda E 89 B5
Casekow D 45 B6
Casella I 80 B3
Caselle Torinese I . . .70 C2
Casemurate I 82 B1
Casenove I 82 D1
Caseres E 90 B3
Caserío Benali E 96 B2
Caserta I 103 B7
Casével P 98 B2
Cashel IRL 21 B4
Casillas E 94 B2
Casillas de Coria E . . .93 B4
Casina I 81 B4
Casinos E 96 B2
Čáslav CZ 63 A6
Cásola Valsénio I 81 B5
Cásoli I 103 A7
Casola E 103 C7
Caspe E 90 B2
Cassàgnes-Bégonhès
  F 77 B5
Cassano allo Iónio I . .106 B3
Cassano d'Adda I . . .71 C4
Cassano delle Murge
  I 104 C2
Cassano Magnago I . .70 C3
Cassano Spínola I . . .80 B2
Cassel F 48 C3
Cassine I 80 B2
Cassino I 103 B6
Cassis F 79 C4
Cassolnovo I 70 C3
Cassuéjouls F 78 B1
Častá SK 64 B3
Castagnaro I 71 C6
Castagneto Carducci
  I 81 C4
Castanheira de Pêra
  P 92 A2
Cástano Primo I 70 C3
Castasegna CH 71 B4
Casteição P 87 D3
Casteggio I 80 A3
Casteição P 87 D3
Castejón E 89 B5
Castejón de Monegros
  E 90 B2
Castejón de Sos E . . .90 A3
Castejón de Valdejasa
  E 90 B2
Castèl Baronia I 103 B8
Castel Bolognese I . . .81 B5
Casteldaccia I 108 A2
Castel d'Aiano I 81 B4
Castel d'Ario I 71 C5
Castel de Cabra E . . .90 C2
Casteldelfino I 79 B6
Castél del Monte I . . .103 A6
Castel del Piano I . . .81 D5
Castel di Iúdica I 109 B3
Castel di Río I 81 B5
Castél di Sangro I . . .103 B7
Castél di Tora I 102 A5
Castelfidardo I 82 C2
Castelfiorentino I 81 C5
Castelforte I 103 B6
Castelfranco Emília I . .81 B5
Castelfranco in Miscano
  I 103 B8
Castelfranco Véneto
  I 72 C1
Castél Frentano I 103 A7
Casteljaloux F 76 B3
Castellabate I 103 C7
Castellammare del Golfo
  I 108 A1
Castellammare di Stábia
  I 103 C7
Castellamonte I 70 C2
Castellana Grotte I . . .104 C3
Castellane F 79 C5
Castellaneta I 104 C2
Castellaneta Marina
  I 104 C2
Castellar E 100 A2
Castellarano I 81 B4
Castellar de la Frontera
  E 99 C5
Castellar de la Ribera
  E 91 A4
Castellar del Vallès E .91 B5
Castellar de Santiago
  E 100 A2
Castell Arquato I 81 B3
Castell'Azzara I 81 D5
Castellbell i Villar E . . .91 B4
Castell de Cabres E . .90 C3
Castell de Castells E . .96 C2
Castelldefels E 91 B4
Castell de Ferro E . . .100 C2
Castellet E 91 B4
Castelli I 103 A6
Castellina in Chianti I . .81 C5
Castellina Maríttima I .81 C4
Castelló de Farfanya E .90 B3
Castelló de la Plana E .96 B2

Castello d'Empúries
  E 91 A6
Castello di Fiemme I . .71 B6
Castelloli E 91 B4
Castellón de Rugat E .96 C2
Castellote E 90 C2
Castello Tesino I 72 B1
Castelltercol E 91 B5
Castellúccio I 71 C5
Castellúccio de'Sáuri
  I 103 B8
Castelluccio Inferiore
  I 106 B2
Castelmassa I 81 A5
Castelmáuro I 103 B7
Castelmoron-sur-Lot
  F 77 B3
Castelnaudary F 77 C4
Castelnau-de-Médoc
  F 76 A2
Castelnau-de-Montmirail
  F 77 C4
Castelnau-Magnoac
  F 77 C3
Castelnau-Montratier
  F 77 B4
Castelnou E 90 B2
Castelnovo ne'Monti I .81 B4
Castelnuovo Berardenga
  I 81 C5
Castelnuovo della Dáunia
  I 103 B8
Castelnuovo di
  Garfagnana I 81 B4
Castelnuovo di Val di
  Cécina I 81 C4
Castelnuovo Don Bosco
  I 80 A1
Castelnuovo Scrívia I .80 B3
Castelo Branco
  Bragança P 87 C4
  Castelo Branco P . .92 B3
Castelo de Paiva P . . .87 C2
Castelo de Vide P . . .92 B3
Castelo do Neiva P . . .87 C2
Castelo Mendo P . . .93 A4
Castelraimondo I 82 C2
Castèl San Gimignano
  I 81 C5
Castèl San Giovanni I .80 A3
Castèl San Pietro Terme
  I 81 B5
Castelsantángelo I . . .82 D2
Castèl Sant'Elia I 102 A5
Castelsaraceno I 106 A2
Castelsardo I 110 B1
Castelsarrasin F 77 B4
Castelserás E 90 C2
Casteltérmini I 108 B2
Castelvecchio Subéquo
  I 103 A6
Castelvetrano I 108 B1
Castél Volturno I 103 B6
Castenédolo I 71 C5
Castets F 76 C1
Castiádas I 110 C2
Castiglioncello I 81 C4
Castiglione I 102 A6
Castiglione Chiavarese
  I 80 B3
Castiglione d'Adda I . .71 C4
Castiglione dei Pepoli
  I 81 B5
Castiglione del Lago
  I 82 C1
Castiglione della Pescáia
  I 81 D4
Castiglione delle Stiviere
  I 71 C5
Castiglione di Sicília
  I 109 B4
Castiglione d'Órcia I . .81 C5
Castiglione Messer
  Marino I 103 B7
Castiglione Messer
  Raimondo I 103 A6
Castiglion Fibocchi I . .81 C5
Castiglion Fiorentino
  I 81 C5
Castilblanco E 94 C1
Castilblanco de los
  Arroyos E 99 B5
Castil de Peones E . . .89 B3
Castilfrío de la Sierra
  E 89 C4
Castilgaleu E 90 A3
Castilisar E 90 A1
Castilleja E 99 B4
Castillejar E 101 B3
Castillejo de Martin Viejo
  E 93 A4
Castillejo de Mesleón
  E 89 C3
Castillejo de Robledo
  E 89 C3
Castillo de Bayuela E .94 B2
Castillo de Locubín
  E 100 B2
Castillon-la-Bataille F .76 B2
Castillonès F 77 B3
Castillonroy E 90 B3
Castilruiz E 89 C4
Castione CH 70 B3
Castions di Strada I . .72 C3
Castirla F 102 A2
Castlebar IRL 18 C2
Castlebellingham IRL .19 C5
Castleblayney IRL . . .19 B5
Castlebridge IRL 21 B5
Castle Cary GB 29 B5
Castlecomer IRL 21 B4
Castlederg GB 19 B4
Castledermot IRL . . .21 B5
Castle Douglas GB . . .25 D4
Castleford GB 27 B4
Castleisland IRL 20 B2
Castlemaine IRL 20 B2
Castlemartyr IRL 20 C3
Castlepollard IRL 19 C4
Castlerea IRL 18 C3
Castleton GB 27 B4
Castletown
  Highland GB 23 C5
  Isle of Man GB . . .26 A1
Castletown Bearhaven
  IRL 20 C2
Castletownroche IRL .20 B3
Castlewellan GB 19 B6
Casto I 71 C5
Castrejón E 88 C1
Castres F 77 C5
Castricum NL 42 C1
Castries F 78 C2
Castril E 101 B3
Castrillo de Duero E . .88 C3
Castrillo de la Vega E .88 C3
Castrillo de Onielo E . .88 C2
Castro
  E 88 A2
  I 107 A5
Castrocabón E 88 B1
Castro-Caldelas E . . .87 B3
Castrocaro Terme I . . .81 B5
Castrocontrigo E 87 B4
Castro Daire P 87 D3
Castro dei Volsci I . . .103 B6
Castro del Río E 100 B1
Castro de Rey E 86 A3
Castrofilippo I 108 B2
Castrogonzalo E 88 B1
Castrojeriz E 88 B2
Castro Laboreiro P . . .87 B2
Castro Marim P 98 B3
Castromonte E 88 C1

Castromudarra E 88 B1
Castronuevo E 88 C1
Castronuño E 88 C1
Castropol E 86 A3
Castroreale I 109 A4
Castroserracin E 88 C3
Castro-Urdiales E 89 A3
Castroverde E 86 A3
Castro Verde P 98 B2
Castroverde de Campos E 88 C1
Castroverde de Cerrato E 88 C2
Castrovillari I 106 B3
Castuera E 93 C5
Catadau E 96 B2
Cataéggio I 71 B4
Çatalca TR 118 A3
Çatallar TR 119 F5
Çatalzeytin TR 16 A7
Catánia I 109 B4
Catanzaro I 106 C3
Catanzaro Marina I 106 C3
Catarroja E 96 B2
Catarruchos P 92 A2
Catcleugh GB 25 C5
Catenanuova I 109 B3
Caterham GB 31 C3
Çati E 90 C3
Čatići BIH 84 B3
Catignano I 103 A6
Catillon F 49 C4
Catoira E 86 B2
Caton GB 26 A3
Catral E 101 A5
Catterick GB 27 A4
Cattólica I 82 C1
Cattólica Eraclea I 108 B2
Catton GB 25 D5
Caudebec-en-Caux F 58 A1
Caudete E 101 A5
Caudete de las Fuentes E 96 B1
Caudiel E 96 B2
Caudiès-de-Fenouillèdes F 77 D5
Caudry F 49 C4
Caulkerbush GB 25 D4
Caulnes F 57 B3
Caulónia I 106 C3
Caumont-l'Evente F 57 A5
Caunes-Minervois F 77 C5
Cauro F 102 B1
Caussade F 77 B4
Causse-de-la-Selle F 78 C2
Cauterets F 76 D2
Cava de Tirreni I 103 C7
Cavaglia I 70 C3
Cavaillon F 79 C4
Cavalaire-sur-Mer F 79 C5
Cavaleiro P 98 B2
Cavalese I 71 B6
Cavallermaggiore I 80 B1
Cavallino I 72 C2
Cavan IRL 19 C4
Cavárzere I 72 C2
Çavdarhisar TR 118 C4
Çavdır TR 119 E4
Cavernães P 87 D3
Cavezzo I 81 B5
Çavignac F 76 A2
Čavle HR 73 C4
Cavo I 81 D4
Cavour I 80 B1
Cavtat HR 84 D3
Cawdor GB 23 D5
Çay TR 118 D6
Çaycuma TR 118 A7
Çayeux-sur-Mer F 48 C2
Cayiralan TR 16 B7
Çayırhan TR 118 B6
Caylus F 77 B4
Cayres F 78 B2
Cazalilla E 100 B2
Cazalla de la Sierra E 99 B5
Cazals F 77 B4
Cazanuecos E 88 B1
Cazaubon F 76 C2
Cazaux F 76 B1
Cazavet F 77 C4
Cazères F 77 C4
Cazin BIH 83 B4
Çazis CH 71 B4
Čazma HR 74 C1
Cazo E 88 A1
Cazorla E 100 B3
Cazouls-lès-Béziers F 78 C2
Cea
León E 88 B1
Orense E 86 B3
Ceánuri E 89 A4
Ceauce F 57 B5
Çebolla E 94 C2
Čebovce SK 65 B5
Çebreros E 94 B2
Čečava BIH 84 B2
Ceccano I 103 B6
Cece H 74 B3
Čecenowo PL 46 A3
Čechtice CZ 63 A6
Čechtin CZ 64 A1
Cécina I 81 C4
Ceclavín E 93 B4
Cedégolo I 71 B5
Cedeira E 86 A2
Cedillo E 92 B3
Cedillo del Condado E 94 B3
Cedrillas E 90 C2
Cedynia PL 45 C6
Cée E 86 B1
Cefalù I 109 A3
Céggia I 72 C2
Cegléd H 75 A4
Ceglédbercel H 75 A4
Céglie Messápica I 104 C3
Cehegín E 101 A4
Ceilhes-et-Rocozels F 78 C2
Ceinos de Campos E 88 B1
Çeira P 92 A2
Čejč CZ 64 B2
Cekcyn PL 47 B4
Çela BIH 83 B5
Čelákovice CZ 53 C4
Celano I 103 A6
Celanova E 87 B3
Çelbridge IRL 21 A5
Čelebič BIH 83 C5
Çelenza Valfortore I 103 B7
Čelić BIH 84 B3
Čelinac BIH 84 B2
Celje SLO 73 B5
Cella E 95 B5
Celldömölk H 74 A2
Celle D 44 C2
Celle Ligure I 80 B2
Celles B 49 C5
Celles-sur-Belle F 67 B4
Cellino San Marco I 105 C3
Celorico da Beira P 92 A3
Celorico de Basto P 87 C2
Çeltik TR 118 C6
Çeltikçi TR 119 E5
Cemaes GB 26 B1
Çembra I 71 B6
Čemerno BIH 84 C3
Cenad RO 75 B5
Cencenighe Agordino I 72 B1
Cenei RO 75 C5
Ceneselli I 81 A5
Cenicero E 89 B4
Cenicientos E 94 B2
Çenseau F 69 B6
Čenta SRB 85 A5
Centallo I 80 B1
Centelles E 91 B5
Cento I 81 B5
Centúripe I 109 B3
Cepeda la Mora E 94 B1
Çépet F 77 C4
Çepin HR 74 C3
Čepinski Martinci HR 74 C3
Cepovan SLO 72 B3
Çeprano I 103 B6
Čeralije HR 74 C2
Cerami I 109 B3
Cerano I 70 C3
Cérans Foulletourte F 57 C6
Ceraso I 106 A2
Cerbaia I 81 C5
Cerbère F 91 A6
Cercadillo E 95 A4
Cercal
Lisboa P 92 B1
Setúbal P 98 B2
Čerčany CZ 63 A5
Cerceda E 94 B3
Cercedilla E 94 B2
Cercemaggiore I 103 B7
Cercs E 91 A4
Cercy-la-Tour F 68 B3
Cerda I 108 B2
Cerdedo E 86 B2
Cerdeira P 93 A3
Cerdon F 58 C3
Cerea I 71 C6
Ceres
GB 25 B5
I 70 C2
Cerese I 81 A4
Ceresole-Reale I 70 C2
Cereste F 79 C4
Céret F 91 A5
Cerezo de Abajo E 95 A3
Cerezo de Riotirón E 89 B3
Cerfontaine B 49 C5
Cergy F 58 A3
Cerignola I 104 B1
Cérilly F 68 B2
Cerisiers F 59 B4
Cerizay F 67 B4
Çerkeş TR 16 A6
Çerkezköy TR 118 A3
Cerkije SLO 73 B4
Cerknica SLO 73 C4
Cerkno SLO 72 B3
Cerkwica PL 45 A7
Çermë-Proshkë AL 105 B5
Çerna HR 74 C3
Černá Hora CZ 64 A2
Cernavodă RO 11 D10
Cernay F 60 C3
Cerne Abbas GB 29 C5
Cernégula E 89 B3
Cernik HR 74 C2
Çernóbbio I 70 C4
Černošin CZ 62 A3
Cernovice CZ 63 A5
Cérons F 76 B2
Cerovlje HR 73 C4
Cerovo SK 65 B5
Cerqueto I 82 D1
Cerralbo E 87 D4
Cerreto d'Esi I 82 C1
Cerreto Sannita I 103 B7
Cerrigydrudion GB 26 B2
Cërrik AL 105 B5
Cerro Muriano E 100 A1
Certaldo I 81 C5
Certosa di Pésio I 80 B1
Cerva P 87 C3
Cervaro I 103 B6
Cervatos de la Cueza E 88 B2
Červena Řečice CZ 63 A6
Červená-Skala SK 65 B6
Červená Voda CZ 54 C1
Cerveny Kostelec CZ 53 C6
Cervera E 91 B4
Cervera de la Cañada E 89 C5
Cervera del Llano E 95 C4
Cervera del Río Alhama E 89 B5
Cervera de Pisuerga E 88 B2
Cervéteri I 102 B5
Cérvia I 82 B1
Cerviáde les Garriques E 90 B3
Cervignano del Friuli I 72 C3
Cervinara I 103 B7
Cervione F 102 A2
Cervo E 86 A3
Cervon F 68 A3
Cesana Torinese I 79 B5
Cesarica HR 83 B4
Cesarò I 109 B3
Cesena I 82 B1
Cesenático I 82 B1
Çēsis LV 7 C8
Česká Belá CZ 63 A6
Česká Kamenice CZ 53 C4
Česká Lípa CZ 53 C4
Česká Třebová CZ 64 A2
České Budějovice CZ 63 B5
České Velenice CZ 63 B5
Český Brod CZ 53 C4
Český Dub CZ 53 C4
Český Krumlov CZ 63 B5
Český Těšín CZ 65 A4
Češljeva Bara SRB 85 B6
Çeşme TR 119 D1
Cessenon F 78 C2
Cesson-Sévigné F 57 B4
Çestas F 76 B2
Čestobrodica SRB 85 C5
Cesuras E 86 A2
Cetina E 89 C5
Cetin Grad HR 73 C5
Cetinje MNE 105 A4
Cetraro I 106 B2
Ceuta E 99 D5
Ceuti E 101 A4
Ceva I 80 B2
Cevico de la Torre E 88 C2
Cevico Navero E 88 C2
Cevins F 69 C6
Cévio CH 70 B3
Çevizli TR 119 E6
Čevo MNE 105 A4
Cewice PL 46 A3
Ceyhan TR 16 C7
Ceylan TR 119 F4
Ceyrat F 68 C3
Ceyzériat F 69 B5
Chaam NL 49 B5
Chabanais F 67 C5
Chabeuil F 79 B4
Chabielice PL 55 B4
Chablis F 59 C4
Châbons F 69 C5
Chabówka PL 65 A5
Chabreloche F 68 C3
Chabris F 67 A6
Chagford GB 28 C4
Chagny F 69 B4
Chagoda RUS 7 B13
Chaherrero E 94 B2
Chailland F 57 B5
Chaillé-les-Marais F 66 B3
Chailles F 67 A6
Chailley F 59 B4
Chalabre F 77 D5
Chalais F 67 C5
Chalamont F 69 C5
Châlette-sur-Loing F 58 B3
Chalindrey F 59 C6
Chalkida GR 116 D5
Challacombe GB 28 B4
Challans F 66 B3
Challes-les-Eaux F 69 C5
Chalmazel F 68 C3
Chalmoux F 68 B3
Chalonnes-sur-Loire F 66 A4
Châlons-en-Champagne F 59 B5
Chalon-sur-Saône F 69 B4
Chalupy PL 47 A4
Châlus F 67 C5
Cham
CH 70 A3
D 62 A3
Chamberet F 68 C1
Chambéry F 69 C5
Chambilly F 68 B4
Chambley F 60 A1
Chambly F 58 A3
Chambois F 57 B6
Chambon-sur-Lac F 68 C2
Chambon-sur-Voueize F 68 B2
Chambord F 58 C2
Chamborigaud F 78 B2
Chamboulive F 68 C1
Chamerau D 62 A3
Chamonix-Mont Blanc F 70 C1
Chamoux-sur-Gelon F 69 C6
Champagnac-le-Vieux F 68 C3
Champagney F 60 C2
Champagnole F 69 B5
Champagny-Mouton F 67 B5
Champaubert F 59 B4
Champdeniers-St Denis F 67 B4
Champdieu F 68 C4
Champdôtre F 69 A5
Champeix F 68 C3
Champéry CH 70 B1
Champigne F 57 C5
Champignelles F 59 C4
Champigny-sur-Veude F 67 A5
Champlitte-et-le-Prelot F 60 C1
Champoluc I 70 C2
Champoly F 68 C3
Champorcher I 70 C2
Champrond-en-Gâtine F 58 B2
Champs-sur-Tarentaine F 68 C2
Champs-sur-Yonne F 59 C4
Champtoceaux F 66 A3
Chamrousse F 69 C5
Chamusca P 92 B2
Chanac F 78 B2
Chanaleilles F 78 B2
Chandler's Ford GB 31 D2
Chandra GR 117 G8
Chandrexa de Queixa E 87 B3
Chañe E 88 C2
Changy F 68 B3
Chania GR 117 G6
Channes F 59 C5
Chantada E 86 B3
Chantelle F 68 B3
Chantenay-St Imbert F 68 B3
Chanteuges F 78 A2
Chantilly F 58 A3
Chantonnay F 66 B3
Chão de Codes P 92 B2
Chaource F 59 B5
Chapa E 86 B2
Chapareillan F 69 C5
Chapel en le Frith GB 27 B4
Chapelle Royale F 58 B2
Chapelle-St Laurent F 67 B4
Charbonnat F 68 B4
Chard GB 29 C5
Charenton-du-Cher F 68 B2
Charlbury GB 31 C2
Charleroi B 49 C5
Charlestown
GB 28 C3
IRL 18 C3
Charlestown of Aberlour GB 23 D5
Charleville IRL 20 B3
Charleville-Mézières F 59 A5
Charlieu F 68 B4
Charlottenberg S 34 C4
Charlton Kings GB 29 B5
Charly F 59 B4
Charmes F 60 B2
Charmes-sur-Rhône F 78 B3
Charmey CH 70 B2
Charminster GB 29 C5
Charmont-en-Beauce F 58 B3
Charny F 59 C4
Charolles F 69 B4
Chârost F 68 B2
Charquemont F 70 A1
Charrin F 68 B3
Charroux F 67 B5
Chartres F 58 B2
Charzykow PL 46 B3
Chasseneuil-sur-Bonnieure F 67 C5
Chassigny F 59 C6
Château-Arnoux F 79 B5
Châteaubernard F 67 C4
Châteaubourg F 57 B4
Châteaubriant F 57 C4
Château-Chinon F 68 A3
Château-d'Oex CH 70 B2
Château-d'Olonne F 66 B3
Château-du-Loir F 58 C1
Châteaudun F 58 B2
Châteaugiron F 57 B4
Château-Gontier F 57 C5
Château-Landon F 58 B3
Château-la-Vallière F 67 A5
Château-l'Evêque F 67 C5
Châteaulin F 56 B1
Châteaumeillant F 68 B2
Châteauneuf
Nièvre F 68 A3
Saône-et-Loire F 69 B4
Châteauneuf-de-Randon F 78 B2
Châteauneuf-d'Ille-et-Vilaine F 57 B4
Châteauneuf-du-Faou F 56 B2
Châteauneuf-du-Pape F 78 B3
Châteauneuf-en-Thymerais F 58 B2
Châteauneuf la-Forêt F 67 C6
Châteauneuf-le-Rouge F 79 C4
Châteauneuf-sur-Charente F 67 C4
Châteauneuf-sur-Cher F 68 B2
Châteauneuf-sur-Loire F 58 C3
Châteauneuf-sur-Sarthe F 57 C5
Châteauponsac F 67 B6
Château-Porcien F 59 A5
Châteauredon F 79 B5
Châteaurenard
Bouches du Rhône F 78 C3
Loiret F 59 C3
Château-Renault F 58 C1
Châteauroux F 68 B1
Châteauroux-les-Alpes F 79 B5
Château-Salins F 60 B2
Château-Thierry F 59 A4
Châteauvillain F 59 B5
Châtel F 70 B1
Châtelaillon-Plage F 66 B3
Châtelaudren F 56 B3
Châtel-Censoir F 68 A3
Châtel-de-Neuvre F 68 B3
Châtelet B 49 C5
Châtelguyon F 68 C3
Châtellerault F 67 B5
Châtel-Montagne F 68 B3
Châtel-St Denis CH 70 B1
Châtel-sur-Moselle F 60 B2
Châtelus-Malvaleix F 68 B2
Châtenois F 60 B1
Châtenois-les-Forges F 70 A1
Chatham GB 31 C4
Châtillon I 70 C2
Châtillon-Coligny F 59 C3
Châtillon-en-Bazois F 68 A3
Châtillon-en-Diois F 79 B4
Châtillon-sur Chalaronne F 69 B4
Châtillon-sur-Indre F 67 B6
Châtillon-sur-Loire F 58 C3
Châtillon-sur-Marne F 59 A4
Châtillon-sur-Seine F 59 C5
Châtres F 59 B4
Chatteris GB 30 B4
Chatton GB 25 C6
Chauchina E 100 B2
Chaudes-Aigues F 78 B2
Chaudrey F 59 B5
Chauffailles F 69 B4
Chaulnes F 58 A3
Chaument Gistoux B 49 C5
Chaumergy F 69 B5
Chaumont F 59 B6
Chaumont-en-Vexin F 58 A2
Chaumont-Porcien F 59 A5
Chaumont-sur-Aire F 59 B6
Chaumont-sur-Loire F 67 A6
Chaunay F 67 B5
Chauny F 59 A4
Chaussin F 69 B5
Chauvigny F 67 B5
Chavagnes-en-Paillers F 66 B3
Chavanges F 59 B5
Chaves P 87 C3
Chavignon F 59 A4
Chazelles-sur-Lyon F 69 C4
Chazey-Bons F 69 C5
Cheadle
Greater Manchester GB 26 B3
Staffordshire GB 27 C4
Cheb CZ 52 C2
Chebsara RUS 7 B15
Checa E 95 B5
Chęciny PL 55 C5
Cheddar GB 29 B5
Cheddleton GB 26 B3
Chef-Boutonne F 67 B4
Chekalin RUS 7 D14
Chekhovo RUS 47 A6
Cheles E 93 C3
Chella E 96 B2
Chelles F 58 B3
Chełm PL 11 A7
Chełmno
Kujawsko-Pomorskie PL 47 B4
Wielkopolskie PL 54 A3
Chelmsford GB 31 C4
Chelmża PL 47 B4
Cheltenham GB 29 B5
Chelva E 96 B1
Chémery F 67 A6
Chemery-sur-Bar F 59 A5
Chemillé F 67 A4
Chemin F 69 B5
Chemnitz D 52 C2
Chénerailles F 68 B2
Cheniménil F 60 B2
Chenonceaux F 67 A6
Chenôve F 69 A4
Chepelare BG 116 A6
Chepstow GB 29 B5
Chera E 96 B2
Cherasco I 80 B1
Cherbonnières F 67 C4
Cherbourg F 57 A4
Cherchiara di Calábria I 106 B3
Cherepovets RUS 7 B14
Cherkasy UA 11 B12
Chernihiv UA 7 F11
Chernivtsi UA 11 B8
Chernobyl = Chornobyl UA 7 F11
Chernyakhovsk RUS 6 D6
Chéroy F 59 B3
Cherven BY 7 E10
Chervonohrad UA 11 A8
Cherykaw BY 7 E11
Chesham GB 31 C3
Cheshunt GB 31 C3
Chessy-lès-Pres F 59 B4
Cheste E 96 B2
Chester GB 26 B3
Chesterfield GB 27 B4
Chester-le-Street GB 25 D6
Chevagnes F 68 B3
Chevanceaux F 67 C4
Chevillon F 59 B6
Chevilly F 58 B2
Chew Magna GB 29 B5
Chézery-Forens F 69 B5
Chialamberto I 70 C2
Chiampo I 71 C6
Chianale I 79 B6
Chianciano Terme I 81 C5
Chiaramonte Gulfi I 109 B3
Chiaramonti I 110 B1
Chiaravalle I 82 C2
Chiaravalle Centrale I 106 C3
Chiaréggio I 71 B4
Chiari I 71 C4
Chiaromonte I 106 A3
Chiasso CH 70 C4
Chiávari I 80 B3
Chiavenna I 71 B4
Chiché F 67 B4
Chichester GB 31 D3
Chiclana de la Frontera E 99 C4
Chiclana de Segura E 100 A2
Chiddingfold GB 31 C3
Chieri I 80 A1
Chiesa in Valmalenco I 71 B4
Chieti I 103 A7
Chieti Scalo I 103 A7
Chiéuti I 103 B8
Chigirin UA 11 B12
Chigwell GB 31 C4
Chiliomodi GR 117 E4
Chillarón de Cuenca E 95 B4
Chillarón del Rey E 95 B4
Chilleurs-aux-Bois F 58 B3
Chillón E 100 A1
Chilluevar E 100 B2
Chiloeches E 95 B3
Chimay B 49 C5
Chimeneas E 100 B2
Chinchilla de Monte Aragón E 96 C1
Chinchón E 95 B3
Chingford GB 31 C4
Chinon F 67 A5
Chióggia I 72 C2
Chiomonte I 79 A5
Chipiona E 99 C4
Chippenham GB 29 B5
Chipping Campden GB 29 A6
Chipping Norton GB 31 C2
Chipping Ongar GB 31 C4
Chipping Sodbury GB 29 B5
Chirac F 78 B2
Chirbury GB 26 C2
Chirens F 69 C5
Chirivel E 101 B3
Chirk GB 26 C2
Chirnside GB 25 C5
Chişinău = Khisinev MD 11 C10
Chişineu Criş RO 10 C6
Chissey-en-Morvan F 69 A4
Chiusa I 71 B6
Chiusa di Pésio I 80 B1
Chiusaforte I 72 B3
Chiusa Scláfani I 108 B2
Chiusi I 81 C5
Chiva E 96 B2
Chivasso I 70 C2
Chlewiska PL 55 B5
Chludowo PL 46 C2
Chlumec nad Cidlinou CZ 53 C5
Chlum u Třeboně CZ 63 B5
Chmielnik PL 55 C5
Chobienia PL 54 B1
Chobienice PL 53 A5
Choceň CZ 53 D6
Choceń PL 47 C5
Chochołów PL 65 A5
Chocianów PL 53 B5
Chociw PL 55 B4
Chociwel PL 46 B1
Choczewo PL 46 A3
Chodaków PL 55 A5
Chodecz PL 47 C5
Chodov CZ 52 C2
Chodzież PL 46 C2
Chojna PL 45 C6
Chojnice PL 46 B3
Chojno
Kujawsko-Pomorskie PL 47 C5
Wielkopolskie PL 46 C2
Chojnów PL 53 B5
Cholet F 66 A4
Chomérac F 78 B3
Chomutov CZ 52 C3
Chop UA 11 B7
Chora GR 117 E3
Chora Sfakion GR 117 G6
Chorges F 79 B5
Chorley GB 26 B3
Chornobyl = Chernobyl UA 7 F11
Chortkiv UA 11 B8
Chorzew PL 54 B3
Chorzów PL 54 C3
Choszczno PL 46 B1
Chotcza-Józefów PL 55 B6
Chotěboř CZ 63 A6
Chouilly F 59 A5
Chouto P 92 B2
Chouzy-sur-Cisse F 67 A6
Chozas de Abajo E 88 B1
Chrast CZ 64 A1
Chrást CZ 63 A4
Chrastava CZ 53 C4
Chřibská CZ 53 C4
Christchurch GB 29 C6
Christiansfeld DK 39 D2
Chroberz PL 55 C5
Chropyně CZ 64 A3
Chrudim CZ 53 D5
Chrzanów PL 55 C4
Chtelnica SK 64 B3
Chudovo RUS 7 B11
Chueca E 94 C3
Chulmleigh GB 28 C4
Chur CH 71 B4
Church Stretton GB 26 C3
Churriana E 100 C1
Churwalden CH 71 B4
Chvalšiny CZ 63 B5
Chwaszczyno PL 47 A4
Chynava CZ 53 C4
Chýnov CZ 63 A5
Ciacova RO 75 C6
Ciadîr-Lunga MD 11 C10
Ciadoncha E 88 B3
Cianciana I 108 B2
Ciano d'Enza I 81 B4
Ciążen PL 54 A2
Cibakhaza H 75 B5
Ciborro P 92 C2
Cicagna I 80 B3
Cicciano I 103 C7
Cičevac SRB 85 C6
Ciciliano I 102 B5
Cicognolo I 71 C5
Cidadelhe P 87 D3
Cide TR 16 A6
Cidones E 89 C4
Ciechanów
Dolnośląskie PL 54 B1
Mazowieckie PL 47 C6
Ciechocinek PL 47 C4
Cielądz PL 55 B5
Ciemnik PL 46 B1
Ciempozuelos E 95 B3
Çiepielów PL 55 B6
Čierny Balog SK 65 B5
Cierp-Gaud F 77 D3
Cierpice PL 47 C4
Ciervana E 89 A3
Cierznie PL 46 B3
Cieslé PL 47 C6
Cieszyn PL 65 A4
Cieutat F 76 C3
Cieza E 101 A4
Cifer SK 64 B3
Çifteler TR 118 C6
Cifuentes E 95 B4
Cigales E 88 C2
Cigliano I 70 C3
Çihanbeyli TR 16 B6
Čilipi HR 105 A4
Cillas E 95 B5
Cilleros E 93 A4
Cilleruelo de Arriba E 88 C3
Cilleruelo de Bezana E 88 B3
Cimalmotto CH 70 B3
Cimanes del Tejar E 88 B1
Ciminna I 108 B2
Cimişlia MD 11 C10
Cimoláis I 72 B2
Cîmpulung RO 11 D8
Çınarcık TR 118 B4
Cinctorres E 90 C2
Cinderford GB 29 B5
Çine TR 119 E3
Činěves CZ 53 C5
Ciney B 49 C6
Cinfães P 87 C2
Cingia de Botti I 81 A4
Cíngoli I 82 C2
Cinigiano I 81 D5
Cinobaňa SK 65 B5
Cinq-Mars-la-Pile F 67 A5
Cinquefrondí I 106 C3
Cintegabelle F 77 C4
Cintruénigo E 89 B5
Ciółkowo PL 47 C5
Ciperez E 87 D4
Cirat E 96 A2
Cirella I 106 B2
Cirencester GB 29 B6
Cirey-sur-Vezouze F 60 B2
Ciria E 89 C5
Ciriè I 70 C2
Cirigliano I 104 C2
Cirò I 107 B4
Cirò Marina I 107 B4
Ciry-le-Noble F 69 B4
Cislău RO 11 D9
Cismon del Grappa I 72 C1
Cisneros E 88 B2
Çissac-Médoc F 66 C4
Čista CZ 52 C3
Cisterna di Latina I 102 B5
Cistérniga E 88 C2
Cisternino I 104 C3
Çistierna E 88 B1
Čitluk BIH 84 C2
Cítov CZ 53 C4
Cittadella I 72 C1
Cittàdella Pieve I 81 D6
Cittádel Vaticano = Vatican City I 102 B5
Cittàdi Castello I 82 C1
Cittaducale I 102 A5
Cittanova I 106 C3
Città Sant'Angelo I 103 A7
Ciudadela de Menorca E 97 B3
Ciudad Real E 94 D3
Ciudad Rodrigo E 93 A4
Ciutadilla E 91 B4
Cividale del Friuli I 72 B3
Cívita I 102 A6
Cívita Castellana I 102 A5
Civitanova Alta I 82 C2
Civitanova Marche I 82 C2
Civitavécchia I 102 A4
Civitella di Romagna I 81 B5
Civitella di Tronto I 82 D2
Civitella Roveto I 103 B6
Civray F 67 B5
Çivril TR 119 D4
Čizur Mayor E 76 D1
Clabhach GB 24 B1
Clachan GB 22 D2
Clachan na Luib GB 22 D1
Clacton-on-Sea GB 31 C5
Cladich GB 24 B2
Claggan GB 24 B2
Clairvaux-les-Lacs F 69 B5
Clamecy F 68 A3
Claonaig GB 24 C2
Clarecastle IRL 20 B3
Claregalway IRL 20 A3
Claremorris IRL 18 C2
Clarinbridge IRL 20 A3
Clashmore
GB 23 D4
IRL 21 B4
Claudy GB 19 B4
Clausthal-Zellerfeld D 51 B6
Cláut I 72 B2
Clay Cross GB 27 B4
Claye-Souilly F 58 B3
Cléder F 56 B1
Cleethorpes GB 27 B5
Clefmont F 60 B1
Cléguérec F 56 B2
Clelles F 79 B4
Clenze D 44 C2
Cleobury Mortimer GB 29 A5
Cléon-d'Andran F 78 B3
Cléré-les-Pins F 67 A5
Clères F 58 A2
Clermont F 58 A3
Clermont-en-Argonne F 59 A6
Clermont-Ferrand F 68 C3
Clermont-l'Hérault F 78 C2
Clerval F 69 A6
Clervaux L 50 C2
Clèry-St André F 58 C2
Cles I 71 B6
Clevedon GB 29 B5
Cleveleys GB 26 B2
Cley GB 30 B5
Clifden IRL 18 C1
Clifford GB 29 A4
Clisson F 66 A3
Clitheroe GB 26 B3
Clogh IRL 21 B4
Cloghan
Donegal IRL 19 B4
Offaly IRL 21 A4
Clogheen IRL 21 B4
Clogher GB 19 B4
Cloghjordan IRL 20 B3
Clohars-Carnoët F 56 C2
Clonakilty IRL 20 C3
Clonaslee IRL 21 A4
Clondalkin IRL 21 A5
Clones IRL 19 B4
Clonmany IRL 19 A4
Clonmel IRL 21 B4
Clonmellon IRL 19 C4
Clonord IRL 21 A4
Clonroche IRL 21 B5
Cloone IRL 19 C4
Cloppenburg D 43 C5
Closeburn GB 25 C4
Clough GB 19 B6
Clova GB 25 B4
Clovelly GB 28 C3
Clowne GB 27 B4
Cloyes-sur-le-Loir F 58 C2
Cloyne IRL 20 C3
Cluis F 68 B1
Cluj-Napoca RO 11 C7
Clun GB 26 C2
Clunes GB 24 B3
Cluny F 69 B4
Cluses F 69 B6
Clusone I 71 C4
Clydach GB 28 B4
Clydebank GB 24 C3
Coachford IRL 20 C3
Coagh GB 19 B5
Coalisland GB 19 B5
Coalville GB 27 C4
Coaña E 86 A4
Çobanlar TR 118 D5
Čobas E 86 A2
Cobertelade E 89 C4
Cobeta E 95 B4
Cóbh IRL 20 C3
Cobreces E 88 A2
Coburg D 51 C6
Coca E 94 A2
Cocentaina E 96 C2
Cochem D 50 C3
Cockburnspath GB 25 C5
Cockermouth GB 26 A2
Codigoro I 82 B1
Codogno I 71 C4
Codos E 89 C5
Codróipo I 72 C2
Codrongianos I 110 B1
Coelhoso P 87 C4
Coesfeld D 50 B3
Coevorden NL 42 C3
Cofrentes E 96 B1
Cogeces del Monte E 88 C2
Coggeshall GB 31 C4
Cognac F 67 C4
Cogne I 70 C2
Cognin F 69 C5
Cogolin F 79 C5
Cogollos de Guadix E 100 B2
Cogollos-Vega E 100 B2
Cogolludo E 95 B3
Coimbra P 92 A2
Coín E 100 C1
Çoirós E 86 A2
Čoka SRB 75 C5
Col SLO 73 C4
Colares P 92 C1
Cölbe D 51 C4
Colbitz D 52 A1
Colchester GB 31 C4
Coldingham GB 25 C5
Colditz D 52 B2
Coldstream GB 25 C5
Colebrooke GB 28 C4
Colera E 91 A6
Coleraine GB 19 A5
Colfiorito I 82 C1
Cólico I 71 B4
Coligny F 69 B5
Colindres E 89 A3
Collado-Mediano E 94 B2
Collado Villalba E 94 B3
Collagna I 81 B4
Collanzo E 88 A1
Collat F 68 C3
Coll de Nargó E 91 A4
Collécchio I 81 B4
Colledimezzo I 103 B7
Colle di Val d'Elsa I 81 C5
Colleferro I 102 B6
Colle Isarco I 71 B6
Collelongo I 103 B6
Collepasso I 107 A5
Collepepe I 82 D1
Collesalvetti I 81 C4
Colle Sannita I 103 B7
Collesano I 108 B2
Colli a Volturno I 103 B7
Collin GB 25 C4
Collinée F 56 B3
Collingham
Nottinghamshire GB 27 B5
West Yorkshire GB 27 B4
Collinghorst D 43 B4
Cóllio I 71 C5
Collobrières F 79 C5
Collon IRL 19 C5
Collooney IRL 18 B3
Colmar F 60 B3
Colmars F 79 B5
Colmenar E 100 C1
Colmenar de la Sierra E 95 A3
Colmenar de Oreja E 95 B3
Colmenar Viejo E 94 B3
Colmonel GB 24 C3
Colne GB 26 B3
Colobraro I 106 A3
Cologna Véneta I 71 C6
Cologne = Köln D 50 C2
Cologne F 77 C3
Cologne al Serio I 71 C4
Colombey-les-Belles F 60 B1
Colombey-les-deux-Églises F 59 B5
Colombres E 88 A2
Colomera E 100 B2
Colomers E 91 A5
Colomiers F 77 C4
Colònia de Sant Jordi E 97 B3
Colorno I 81 B4
Colos P 98 B2
Cölpin D 45 B5
Colpy GB 23 D6
Colsterworth GB 30 B3
Coltishall GB 30 B5
Colunga E 88 A1
Colwell GB 25 C5
Colwyn Bay GB 26 B2
Colyford GB 29 C4
Comácchio I 82 B1
Coma-ruga E 91 B4
Combarros E 86 B4
Combeaufontaine F 60 C1
Comber GB 19 B6
Comblain-au-Pont B 49 C6
Combloux F 70 C1
Combourg F 57 B4
Combronde F 68 C3
Comeglians I 72 B2
Comillas E 88 A2
Comines F 49 C4
Cómiso I 109 C3
Comloşu Mare RO 75 C5
Commensacq F 76 B2
Commentry F 68 B2
Commerau D 53 B4
Commercy F 60 B1
Como I 71 C4
Cómpeta E 100 C2
Compiègne F 58 A3
Comporta P 92 C2
Comps-sur-Artuby F 79 C5
Comrat MD 11 C10
Comrie GB 25 B4
Comunanza I 82 D2
Cona
Emilia Romagna I 81 B5
Veneto I 72 C2
Concarneau F 56 C2
Conceição P 98 B2
Conches-en-Ouche F 58 B1
Concordia Sagittária I 72 C2
Concordia sulla Sécchia I 81 B4
Concots F 77 B4
Condat F 68 C2
Condé-en-Brie F 59 B4
Condeixa P 92 A2
Condemios de Abajo E 95 A3
Condemios de Arriba E 95 A3
Condé-sur-l'Escaut F 49 C4
Conde-sur-Marne F 59 A5
Condé-sur-Noireau F 57 B5
Condino I 71 C5
Condom F 77 C3
Condove I 70 C2
Condrieu F 69 C4
Conegliano I 72 C2
Conflans-sur-Lanterne F 60 C2
Confolens F 67 B5
Conforto E 86 A3
Cong IRL 18 C2
Congleton GB 26 B3
Congosto E 86 B4
Congosto de Valdavia E 88 B2
Congostrina E 95 A3
Conil de la Frontera E 99 C4
Coningsby GB 27 B5
Coniston GB 26 A2
Conlie F 57 B5
Conliège F 69 B5
Conna IRL 20 B3
Connah's Quay GB 26 B2
Connantre F 59 B4
Connaugh IRL 20 B3
Connaux F 78 B3
Connel GB 24 B2
Connerré F 58 B1
Çononbridge GB 23 D4
Čonoplja SRB 75 C4
Conques F 77 B5
Conques-sur-Orbiel F 77 C5
Conquista E 100 A1
Conquista de la Sierra E 93 B5
Consándolo I 81 B5
Consélice I 81 B5
Conselve I 72 C1
Consenvoye F 59 A6
Consett GB 25 D6
Consolacão P 92 B1
Constancia P 92 B2
Constanco E 86 A2
Constanța RO 11 D10
Constanti E 91 B4
Constantina E 99 B5
Consuegra E 95 C3
Consuma I 81 C5
Contarina I 82 A1
Contay F 48 D3
Conthey CH 70 B2
Contigliano I 102 A5
Contis-Plage F 76 B1
Contrada I 103 C7
Contres F 67 A6
Contrexéville F 60 B1
Controne I 103 C8
Contursi Termi I 103 C8
Conty F 58 A3
Conversano I 104 C3
Conwy GB 26 B2
Cookstown GB 19 B5
Coole F 59 B5
Coolgreany IRL 21 B5
Cooneen GB 19 B4
Cootehill IRL 19 B4
Cope E 101 B4
Copenhagen = København DK 41 D2
Copertino I 105 C4
Copparo I 81 B5
Coppenbrugge D 51 A5
Corabia RO 11 E8
Córaci I 106 B3
Coralići BIH 83 B4
Corato I 104 B2
Coray F 56 B2
Corbeil-Essonnes F 58 B3
Corbeny F 59 A4
Corbera E 96 B2
Corbie F 58 A3
Corbigny F 68 A3
Corbion B 59 A5
Corbridge GB 25 D5
Corby GB 30 B3
Corconte E 88 A3
Corcubión E 86 B1
Corcumello I 103 A6
Cordenòns I 72 C2
Cordes-sur-Ciel F 77 B4
Córdoba E 100 B1
Cordobilla de Lácara E 93 B4
Cordovado I 72 C2
Corella E 89 B5
Coreses E 88 C1
Corfe Castle GB 29 C5
Corga de Lobão P 87 D2
Cori I 102 B5
Coria E 93 B4
Coria del Río E 99 B4
Corigliano Cálabro I 106 B3
Corinaldo I 82 C1
Corinth = Korinthos GR 117 E4
Cório I 70 C2
Coripe E 99 C5
Cork IRL 20 C3
Corlay F 56 B2
Corleone I 108 B2
Corleto Monforte I 103 C8
Corleto Perticara I 104 C2
Çorlu TR 118 A2
Čormainville F 58 B2
Cormatin F 69 B4
Cormeilles F 58 A1
Cormery F 67 A5
Cormòns I 72 C3
Cormoz F 69 B5
Cornago E 89 B4
Cornberg D 51 B5
Cornellana E 86 A4
Corneşti MD 11 C10
Corníglio I 81 B4
Cornimont F 60 C2
Corniolo I 81 C5
Cornuda I 72 C2
Cornudella de Montsant E 90 B3
Cornudilla E 89 B3
Cornus F 78 C2
Çorovodë AL 116 B2
Čorpach GB 24 B2
Corps F 79 B4
Corps Nuds F 57 C4
Corral de Almaguer E 95 C3
Corral de Ayllon E 89 C3
Corral de Calatrava E 100 A1
Corrales E 88 C1
Corral-Rubio E 101 A4
Corran GB 24 B2
Corredoiras E 86 A2
Corréggio I 81 B4
Corrèze F 68 C1
Corridónia I 82 C2
Corris GB 26 C2
Corrubedo E 86 B1
Córsico I 71 C4
Corsock GB 25 C4
Corte F 102 A2
Corteconcepción E 99 B4
Corte de Peleas E 93 C4
Cortegaca P 87 D2
Cortegada E 87 B2
Cortegana E 99 B4
Cortemaggiore I 81 B3
Cortemilia I 80 B2
Corte Pinto P 98 B3
Cortes E 89 C5
Cortes de Aragón E 90 C2
Cortes de Arenoso E 96 A2
Cortes de Baza E 101 B3
Cortes de la Frontera E 99 C5
Cortes de Pallás E 96 B2
Cortiçadas P 92 C2
Cortico P 87 C3
Cortijo de Arriba E 94 C2
Cortijos Nuevos E 101 A3
Cortina d'Ampezzo I 72 B2
Corton GB 30 B5
Cortona I 81 C5
Coruche P 92 C2
Corullón E 86 B4
Çorum TR 16 A7
Čorvara in Badia I 72 B1
Corvera E 101 B4
Corwen GB 26 C2
Cosenza I 106 B3
Cosham GB 31 D2
Coslada E 95 B3
Cosne-Cours-sur-Loire F 68 A2
Cosne d'Allier F 68 B2
Cospeito E 86 A3
Cossato I 70 C3
Cossaye F 68 B3
Cossé-le-Vivien F 57 C5
Cossonay CH 69 B6
Costa da Caparica P 92 C1
Costa de Santo André P 98 A2
Costalpino I 81 C5
Costa Nova P 92 A2
Costaros F 78 B2
Costeşti RO 11 D8
Costigliole d'Asti I 80 B2
Costigliole Saluzzo I 80 B1
Coswig
Sachsen D 52 B3
Sachsen-Anhalt D 52 B2
Cotherstone GB 27 A4
Cotronei I 107 B3
Cottbus D 53 B4
Cottenham GB 30 B4
Cottingham GB 27 B5
Coublanc F 60 C1
Couches F 69 B4
Couço P 92 C2
Coucouron F 78 B2
Coucy-le-Château-Auffrique F 59 A4
Couëron F 66 A3
Couflens F 77 D4
Couhé F 67 B5
Couiza F 77 D5
Coulags GB 22 D3
Coulanges F 68 B3
Coulanges-la-Vineuse F 59 C4
Coulanges-sur-Yonne F 68 A3
Couleuvre F 68 B2
Coulmier-le-Sec F 59 C5
Coulommiers F 59 B4
Coulonges-sur-l'Autize F 67 B4
Coulounieix-Chamiers F 67 C5
Coulport GB 24 B3
Coupar Angus GB 25 B4
Coupéville F 59 B5
Couptrain F 57 B5
Coura P 87 C2
Courcelles B 49 C5
Courcelles-Chaussy F 60 A2

Courchevel F 70 C1
Cour-Cheverny F . . .67 A6
Courçôme F 67 C5
Courçon F 66 B4
Cour-et-Buis F 69 C4
Courgenay CH 70 A2
Courmayeur I 70 C1
Courniou F 78 C1
Cournon d'Auvergne
 F 68 C3
Cournonterral F . . .78 C2
Courpière F 68 C3
Coursan F 78 C2
Courseulles-sur-Mer
 F 57 A5
Cours-la-Ville F . . .69 B4
Courson-les-Carrières
 F 59 C4
Courtalain F 58 B2
Courtenay F 59 B4
Courtomer F 58 B1
Courville
 Eure-et-Loire F . .58 B2
 Marne F 59 A4
Coussac-Bonneval F .67 C6
Coutances F 57 B4
Couterne F 57 B5
Coutras F 76 A2
Couvet CH 70 B1
Couvin F 49 C5
Couzon F 68 B3
Covadonga E 88 A1
Covaleda E 89 C4
Covarrubias E 89 C3
Covas P 87 C2
Cove GB 22 D3
Coventry GB 30 B2
Coverack GB 28 C2
Covigliáio I 81 B5
Covilhã P 92 A3
Cowbridge GB 29 B4
Cowdenbeath GB . .25 B4
Cowes GB 31 D2
Cox F 77 C4
Cózar E 100 A2
Cozes F 66 C4
Cozzano F 102 B2
Craco I 104 C2
Craibstone GB 23 D6
Craighouse GB . . .24 C2
Craignure GB 24 B2
Crail GB 25 B5
Crailsheim D 61 A6
Craiova RO 11 D7
Cramlington GB . . .25 C6
Cranleigh GB 31 C3
Craon F 57 C5
Craonne F 59 A4
Craponne F 69 C4
Craponne-sur-Arzon
 F 68 C3
Crathie GB 23 D5
Crato P 92 B3
Craughwell IRL . . .20 A3
Craven Arms GB . .26 C3
Crawford GB 25 C4
Crawinkel D 51 C6
Crawley GB 31 C3
Creag Ghoraidh GB .22 D1
Crecente E 87 B2
Crèches-sur-Saône F .69 B4
Crécy-en-Ponthieu F .48 C2
Crécy-la-Chapelle F .59 B3
Crécy-sur-Serre F . .59 A4
Crediton GB 29 C4
Creeslough IRL . . .19 A4
Creetown GB 24 D3
Creeve GB 19 B5
Creglingen D 61 A6
Creil F 58 A3
Creissels F 78 B2
Crema I 71 C4
Cremaux F 68 C3
Cremenes E 88 B1
Crémieu F 69 C5
Cremlingen D 51 A6
Cremona I 81 A4
Creney F 59 B5
Črenšovci SLO 73 B6
Créon F 76 B2
Crepaja SRB 85 A5
Crépey F 60 B1
Crépy F 59 A4
Crépy-en-Valois F . .59 A3
Cres HR 83 B3
Crescentino I 70 C3
Crespino I 81 B5
Crespos E 94 B2
Cressage GB 26 C3
Cressensac F 77 A4
Cressia F 69 B5
Crest F 79 B4
Cresta CH 71 B4
Créteil F 58 B3
Creully F 57 A5
Creussen D 62 A2
Creutzwald F 60 A2
Creuzburg D 51 B6
Crevalcore I 81 B5
Crèvecoeur-le-Grand
 F 58 A3
Crevillente E 101 A5
Crévola d'Ossola I . .70 B3
Crewe GB 26 B3
Crewkerne GB 29 C5
Criales E 89 B3
Crianlarich GB 24 B3
Criccieth GB 26 C1
Crickhowell GB . . .29 B4
Cricklade GB 29 B6
Crieff GB 25 B4
Criel-sur-Mer F . . .48 C2
Crikvenica HR 73 C4
Crillon F 58 A2
Crimmitschau D . . .52 C2
Crimond GB 23 D7
Crinitz D 53 B3
Cripán E 89 B4
Criquetot-l'Esneval F .57 A6
Crispiano I 104 C3
Crissolo I 79 B6
Cristóbal E 93 A5
Crivitz D 44 B3
Črna SLO 73 B4
Crna Bara
 Srbija SRB 85 B4
 Vojvodina SRB . . .75 C5
Crnac HR 74 C2
Crnča SRB 85 B4
Crni Lug
 BIH 83 B5
 HR 73 C4
Črni Vrh SLO 73 B4
Crnjelovo Donje BIH .85 B4
Črnomelj SLO 73 C5
Crocketford GB . . .25 C4
Crocq F 68 C2
Crodo I 70 B3
Croglin GB 25 D5
Crolly IRL 18 A3
Cromarty GB 23 D4
Cromer GB 30 B5
Cronat F 68 B3
Crookhaven IRL . . .20 C2
Crookstown IRL . . .20 C3
Croom IRL 20 B3
Cropalati I 106 B3
Cropani I 107 C3
Crosbost GB 22 C2
Crosby GB 26 B2
Crosia I 106 B3
Crossakiel IRL 19 C4
Cross-Hands GB . .28 B3
Crosshaven IRL . . .20 C3
Crosshill GB 24 C3
Crossmolina IRL . .18 B2
Crotone I 107 B4
Crottendorf D 52 C2
Crouy F 59 A4
Crowborough GB . .31 C4
Crowland GB 30 B3

Crowthorne GB . . .31 C3
Croyde GB 28 B3
Croydon GB 31 C3
Crozon F 56 B1
Cruas F 78 B3
Crúcoli I 107 B4
Cruden Bay GB . . .23 D7
Crudgington GB . . .26 C3
Cruis F 79 B4
Crumlin GB 19 B5
Cruseilles F 69 B6
Cruz de Incio E . . .86 B3
Crvenka SRB 75 C4
Crveny Kamen SK . .64 A4
Csabacsüd H 75 B5
Csabrendek H 74 A2
Csákánydoroszló H .74 B1
Csákvár H 74 A3
Csanádapáca H . . .75 B5
Csanádpalota H . . .75 B5
Csány H 65 C5
Csanytelek H 75 B5
Csapod H 74 A1
Császár H 74 A3
Császártöltés H . . .75 B4
Csávoly H 75 B4
Csemö H 75 A4
Csengöd H 75 B4
Csépa H 75 B5
Cserkeszölö H 75 B5
Csernely H 65 B6
Csesztreg H 74 B1
Csökmö H 75 A6
Csököly H 74 B2
Csokonyavisonta H .74 B2
Csólyospálos H . . .75 B4
Csongrád H 75 B5
Csopak H 74 B2
Csorna H 64 C3
Csorvás H 75 B5
Csurgo H 74 B2
Cuacos de Yuste E .93 A5
Cualedro E 87 C3
Cuanca de Campos E .88 B1
Cuba P 98 A3
Cubel E 95 A5
Cubelles E 91 B4
Cubillas del Sil E . .86 B4
Cubjac F 67 C5
Cubo de la Solana E .89 C4
Çubuk TR 16 A6
Cuckfield GB 31 C3
Cucuron F 79 C4
Cudillero E 86 A4
Cuéllar E 88 C2
Cuenca E 95 B4
Cuers F 79 C5
Cuerva E 94 C2
Cueva de Ágreda E .89 C5
Cuevas Bajas E . .100 B1
Cuevas del Almanzora
 E 101 B4
Cuevas del Becerro E .99 C5
Cuevas del Campo
 E 100 B3
Cuevas del Valle E .94 B1
Cuevas de San Clemente
 E 89 B3
Cuevas de San Marcos
 E 100 B1
Cuges-les-Pins F . .79 C4
Cúglieri I 110 B1
Cugnaux F 77 C4
Cuijk NL 50 B1
Cuinzier F 69 B4
Cuiseaux F 69 B5
Cuisery F 69 B5
Culan F 68 B2
Culemborg NL 49 B6
Cúllar E 101 B3
Cullaville GB 19 B5
Cullera E 96 B2
Cullivoe GB 22 A7
Cullompton GB . . .29 C4
Cully CH 70 B1
Culoz F 69 C5
Cults GB 23 D6
Cumbernauld GB . .25 C4
Cumbres de San
 Bartolomé E 99 A4
Cumbres Mayores E .99 A4
Cumiana I 80 B1
Ćumić SRB 85 B5
Cumnock GB 24 C3
Çumra TR 16 C6
Cúneo I 80 B1
Cunhat F 68 C3
Ćunski HR 83 B3
Cuntis E 86 B2
Cuorgné I 70 C2
Cupar GB 25 B4
Cupello I 103 A7
Cupra Maríttima I . .82 C2
Cupramontana I . . .82 C2
Čuprija SRB 85 C6
Curek I 86 B3
Curinga I 106 C3
Currelos E 86 B3
Currie GB 25 C4
Curtea de Argeş RO .11 D8
Curtici RO 75 B6
Curtis E 86 A2
Curtis Santa Eulalia E .86 A2
Çürüg SRB 75 C5
Cusano Mutri I . . .103 B7
Cushendall GB 19 A5
Cusset F 68 B3
Cussy-les-Forges F .68 A4
Custines F 60 B2
Cutanda E 90 C1
Cutro I 107 B3
Cutrofiano I 107 A5
Cuts F 59 A4
Cuvilly F 58 A3
Cuxhaven D 43 B5
Čvikov CZ 53 C4
Cwmbran GB 29 B4
Cybinka PL 53 A4
Czaczk PL 54 A1
Czajków PL 54 B3
Czaplinek PL 46 B2
Czarlin PL 47 A4
Czarna-Dąbrówka PL .46 A3
Czarna Woda PL . .47 B4
Czarnca PL 55 C4
Czarne PL 46 B2
Czarnków PL 46 C2
Czarnowąsy PL . . .54 C2
Czarnozyly PL 54 B3
Czarny Bór PL 53 C6
Czarny Dunajec PL .65 A5
Czarny Las PL 54 B2
Czchów PL 55 D5
Czechowice-Dziedzice
 PL 65 A4
Czempiń PL 54 A1
Czermno PL 55 B5
Czernichów PL 46 C3
Czerniejewo PL . . .47 C4
Czersk PL 46 B3
Czerwieńsk PL 53 A5
Czerwionka-Leszczyny
 PL 54 C3
Czerwonka PL 47 C6
Częstochowa PL . .55 C4
Czeszewo PL 54 B2
Człopa PL 46 B2
Człuchów PL 46 B3
Czołpino PL 46 A3

D

Dabo F 60 B3
Dabrowa PL 46 C3
Dabrowa Górnicza
 PL 55 C4
Dabrowa Tarnowska
 PL 55 C5
Dabrowice PL 55 A4
Dabrowno PL 47 B6
Dachau D 62 B2
Dačice CZ 63 A6
Daday TR 16 A6
Dagali N 32 B5
Dägebüll D 39 E1
Dahlen D 52 B2
Dahlenburg D 44 B2
Dahme D 52 B3
Dahn D 60 A3
Dähre D 44 C2
Daikanvik S 115 B13
Dail bho Dheas GB .22 C2
Dailly GB 24 C3
Daimiel E 95 C3
Daingean IRL 21 A4
Ðakovica KOS 10 E6
Ðakovo HR 74 C3
Dal
 Akershus N 34 B3
 Telemark N 32 C5
Dalaas A 71 A5
Dalabrog GB 22 D1
Dala-Floda S 36 B1
Dala-Husby S 36 B2
Dala-Järna S 36 B1
Dalaman TR 119 F3
Dalarö S 37 C5
Dalbeattie GB 25 D4
Dalby
 DK 39 D3
 Skåne S 41 D3
 Uppsala S 37 C4
 Värmland S 34 B4
Dale
 Pembrokeshire GB .28 B2
 Shetland GB 22 A7
 Hordaland N 33 C5
 Sogn og Fjordane N .32 A2
Dalen
 Akershus N 34 C3
 Telemark N 33 C5
Daleszyce PL 55 C5
Dalhalvaig GB 23 C5
Dalholm L 60 A2
Dalhem S 37 E5
Dalías E 100 C3
Dalj HR 75 C3
Dalkeith GB 25 C4
Dalkey IRL 21 A5
Dalmally GB 24 B3
Dalmellington GB . .24 C3
Dalmose DK 39 D4
Daløy N 32 A1
Dalry
 Dumfries & Galloway
 GB 24 C3
 North Ayrshire GB .24 C3
Dalrymple GB 24 C3
Dalseter N 32 A6
Dalsjöfors S 40 B3
Dalskog S 35 D4
Dals Långed S 35 D4
Dals Rostock S . . .35 D4
Dalston GB 25 D5
Dalstorp S 40 B3
Dalton-in-Furness GB .26 A2
Dalton GB 25 D4
Dalum
 D 43 C4
 S 40 B3
Dalvík IS 111 B7
Dalwhinnie GB 24 B3
Dalyan TR 119 F3
Damasi GR 116 C4
Damasławek PL . . .46 C3
Damazan F 76 B3
Dambach F 60 B3
Damësi AL 105 C5
Damgan F 56 C3
Dammarie-les-Lys F .58 B3
Dammartin-en-Goële
 F 58 A3
Damme
 B 49 B4
 D 43 C5
Dammen N 35 C2
Damnica PL 46 A3
Dampierre F 69 A5
Dampierre-sur-Salon
 F 69 A5
Damülls A 71 A4
Damville F 58 B2
Damvillers F 59 A6
Damwoude NL 42 B2
Danasjö S 115 B13
Danbury GB 31 C4
Dångebo S 40 C5
Dangé-St Romain F .67 B5
Dångeul F 58 B1
Danilovgrad MNE . .105 A5
Danischenhagen D .44 A2
Daniszyn PL 54 B2
Danjoutin F 60 C2
Dannas S 40 B3
Dannemarie F 60 C3
Dannemora S 36 B4
Dannenberg D 44 B3
Dánszentmiklós H . .75 A4
Daoulas F 56 B1
Darabani RO 11 B9
Darány H 74 C2
Darda HR 74 C3
Dardesheim D 51 B6
Darfeld D 50 A3
Darfo I 71 C5
Dargin PL 46 A2
Dargun D 45 B4
Darlington GB 27 A4
Darłowo PL 46 A2
Darmstadt D 61 A4
Darney F 60 B2
Daroca E 95 A5
Darque P 87 C2
Darragh IRL 20 B2
Dartford GB 31 C4
Dartington GB 28 C4
Dartmouth GB 29 C4
Darton GB 27 B4
Daruvar HR 74 C2
Darvas H 75 A6
Darvel GB 24 C3
Darwen GB 26 B3
Dassel D 51 B5
Dassow D 44 B2
Datça TR 119 F2
Datteln D 50 B3
Dattenfeld D 50 C3
Dáver HR 39 D2
Daventry GB 30 B2
Davor HR 84 A2
Davos CH 71 B4
Davutlar TR 119 E2
Davyd Haradok BY . .7 E9
Dawlish GB 29 C4
Dax F 76 C1
Dazkırı TR 119 E4
Deba E 89 A4
Debar MK 116 A2
Debe PL 47 C6
Dębe Wielkie PL . .55 A6
Debica PL 55 C6
Dęblin PL 55 B6
Debnica Kaszubska
 PL 46 A3
Dębno PL 45 C6
Dębołęka PL 54 B3
Dębowa Łąka PL . .47 B5
Debrc SRB 85 B4
Debrecen H 10 C6
Debrznica PL 53 A5
Debrzno PL 46 B3

Debstedt D 43 B5
Decazeville F 77 B5
Dechtice SK 64 B3
Decima I 102 B5
Decimomannu I . . .110 C1
Děčín CZ 53 C4
Decize F 68 B3
De Cocksdorp NL . .42 B1
Decollatura I 106 B3
Decs H 74 B3
Dedaj AL 105 A5
Deddington GB . . .31 C2
Dedeler TR 118 B5
Dedelow D 45 B5
Dedemli TR 119 E7
Dedemsvaart NL . . .42 C3
Dédestapolcsány H .65 B6
Dedovichi RUS 7 C10
Deeping St Nicholas
 GB 30 B3
Deftera CY 120 A2
Dęg H 74 B3
Degaña E 86 B4
Degeberga S 41 D4
Degerby FIN 36 B7
Degerfors S 37 C1
Degerhamn S 41 C6
Degerndorf D 62 C3
Deggendorf D 62 B3
Deggingen D 61 B5
Dego I 80 B2
Degolados P 93 B3
De Haan B 49 B4
Dehesa de Guadix
 E 100 B2
Dehesas Viejas E . .100 B2
Deia E 97 B2
Deining D 62 B2
Deinze B 49 C4
Déiva Marina I 80 B3
Dej RO 11 C7
Deje S 35 C5
De Koog NL 42 B1
Delabole GB 28 C3
Delary S 40 C3
Delbrück D 51 B4
Dikili TR 118 C1
Diksmuide B 48 B3
Delden NL 50 A2
Deleitosa E 93 B5
Delekovec HR 74 B1
Delémont CH 70 A2
Delft NL 49 A5
Delfzijl NL 42 B3
Délia I 108 B2
Delianuova I 106 C2
Deliblato SRB 85 B6
Delice TR 16 B6
Deliceto I 103 B8
Delitzsch D 52 B2
Dellach A 72 B3
Delmen-horst D . . .43 B5
Delnice HR 73 C4
Delsbo S 115 E13
Delvin IRL 19 C4
Delvinë AL 116 C2
Demandice SK 65 B4
Demen D 44 B3
Demidov RUS 7 D11
Demigny F 69 B4
Demirci TR 118 C3
Demirköy TR 118 A2
Demirtaş TR 118 B4
Demmin D 45 B5
Demonte I 79 B6
Demyansk RUS 7 C12
Denain F 49 C4
Denbigh GB 26 B2
Den Burg NL 42 B1
Denekamp NL 42 C3
Den Ham NL 42 C3
Den Helder NL 42 C1
Denholm GB 25 C5
Denia E 96 C3
Denizli TR 119 E4
Denkendorf D 62 B2
Denklingen D 50 C3
Denny GB 25 B4
Den Oever NL 42 C2
Deols F 68 B1
De Panne B 48 B3
Derby GB 27 C4
Dereköy TR 118 A2
Derenberg D 51 B6
Derinkuyu TR 16 B7
Dermbach D 51 C6
Dermulo I 71 B6
Deronje SRB 75 C4
Derrygonnelly GB . .19 B4
Derrylin GB 19 B4
Derry/Londonderry
 GB 19 B4
Dersingham GB . . .30 B4
Deruta I 82 D1
Dervaig GB 24 B1
Derval F 57 C4
Derveni GR 117 D4
Derventa BIH 84 B2
Dervock GB 19 A5
Desana I 70 C3
Descartes F 67 B5
Desenzano del Garda
 I 71 C5
Deševa BIH 84 C3
Desfina GR 116 D4
Desimirovac SRB . .85 B5
Désio I 71 C4
Deskati GR 116 C3
Deskle SLO 72 B3
Despetal D 51 A5
Despotovac SRB . . .85 B6
Despotovo SRB . . .75 C4
Dessau D 52 B2
Deštná CZ 63 A5
Destriana E 88 B1
Désulo I 110 B2
Desvres F 48 C2
Deszk H 75 B5
Deta RO 75 C6
Detmold D 51 B4
Dětřichov CZ 64 A3
Dettelbach D 61 A6
Dettingen
 Baden-Württemberg
 D 61 B5
 Baden-Württemberg
 D 61 B5
Dettwiller F 60 B3
Detva SK 65 B5
Deurne NL 50 B1
Deutschkreutz A . . .64 C2
Deutschlandsberg A .73 B5
Deutsch Wagram A . .64 B2
Deva RO 11 D7
Dévaványa H 75 A5
Devecikonağı TR . .118 C3
Devecser H 74 A2
Devene BG 11 E7
Deventer NL 50 A2
Devil's Bridge GB . .28 A4
Devínska Nová Ves
 SK 64 B2
Devizes GB 29 B6
Devonport GB 28 C3
Devrek TR 118 A6
Devrske HR 83 C4
Dewsbury GB 27 B4
Deza E 89 C4
Dezzo I 71 C5
Dhali CY 120 A2
Dherinia CY 120 A2
Dhèrmi AL 116 C2
Diamante I 106 B2

Dianalund DK 39 D4
Diano d'Alba I 80 B2
Diano Marina I 80 C2
Dicomano I 81 C5
Didcot GB 31 C2
Didima GR 117 E5
Didimoticho GR . . .118 A1
Die F 79 B4
Diebling F 60 A2
Dieburg D 61 A4
Diego del Carpio E .93 A5
Diekirch L 60 A2
Diélette F 57 A4
Diémoz F 69 C5
Dienheim D 61 A4
Dienten am Hochkönig
 A 72 A2
Diepenbeck B 49 C6
Diepholz D 43 C5
Dieppe F 58 A2
Dierberg D 45 B4
Dierdorf D 50 C3
Dieren NL 50 A2
Dierhagen D 44 A4
Diesdorf D 44 C2
Diessen D 62 C2
Diest B 49 C6
Dietenheim D 61 B6
Dietfurt D 62 A2
Dietikon CH 70 A3
Dietzenbach D 51 C4
Dieue-sur-Meuse F .60 A1
Dieulefit F 79 B4
Dieulouard F 60 B2
Dieuze F 60 B2
Diever NL 42 C3
Diez D 50 C4
Diezma E 100 B2
Differdange L 60 A1
Digermulen N 112 D4
Dignac F 67 C5
Dignano I 72 C2
Digne-les-Bains F . .79 B5
Digny F 58 B2
Digoin F 68 B3
Dijon F 69 A5
Dikanäs S 115 B13
Dikili TR 118 C1
Diksmuide B 48 B3
Dilar E 100 B2
Dillenburg D 50 C4
Dillingen
 Bayern D 61 B6
 Saarland D 60 A2
Dilsen B 50 B1
Dimaro I 71 B5
Dimitrovgrad BG . . .11 E8
Dimitsana GR 117 E4
Dinami I 106 C3
Dinan F 57 B3
Dinant B 49 C5
Dinar TR 119 D5
Dinard F 57 B3
Dinek TR 118 C5
Dingden D 50 B2
Dingelstädt D 51 B6
Dingle
 IRL 20 B1
 S 35 D3
Dingolfing D 62 B3
Dingtuna S 37 C3
Dingwall GB 23 D4
Dinkelsbühl D 61 A6
Dinkelscherben D . .62 B1
Dinklage D 43 C5
Dinslaken D 50 B2
Dinxperlo NL 50 B2
Dió S 40 C4
Diósgyör H 65 B6
Diósjenö H 65 B5
Diou F 68 B3
Dippen GB 24 C2
Dipperz D 51 C5
Dippoldiswalde D . .53 C3
Dirdal N 33 D3
Dirksland NL 49 B5
Dirlewang D 61 C6
Dischingen D 61 B6
Diso I 107 A5
Diss GB 30 B5
Dissen D 50 A4
Distington GB 26 A2
Ditzingen D 61 B5
Ditzum D 43 B4
Divača SLO 72 C3
Dives-sur-Mer F . . .57 A5
Divín SK 65 B5
Divišov CZ 63 A5
Divjakë AL 105 C5
Divonne les Bains F .69 B6
Dixmont F 59 B4
Dizy-le-Gros F 59 A5
Djupivogur IS 111 C11
Djupvasshytta N . .114 F4
Djura S 36 B1
Djurås S 36 B2
Djurmo S 36 B2
Djursdala S 40 B5
Dlouhá Loucka CZ .64 A3
Długowola PL 55 B6
Dmitriev Lgovskiy
 RUS 7 E13
Dmitrov RUS 7 C14
Dmitrovsk-Orlovskiy
 RUS 7 E13
Dno RUS 7 C10
Doade E 87 B3
Doğanhisar TR . . .119 D6
Dobanovci SRB . . .85 B5
Dobbertin D 44 B4
Dobbiaco I 72 B2
Dobczyce PL 55 D5
Dobele LV 6 C7
Döbeln D 52 B3
Doberlug-Kirchhain D .52 B3
Dobern D 53 B4
Dobersberg A 63 B6
Dobiegniew PL 46 C1
Doboj BIH 84 B3
Dobošnica BIH 84 B3
Doboz H 75 B6
Dobra
 Wielkopolskie PL . .54 B3
 Zachodnio-Pomorskie
 PL 45 B7
 Zachodnio-Pomorskie
 PL 46 B1
Dobra Niva SK 65 B5
Dobřany CZ 63 A4
Dobre
 Kujawsko-Pomorskie
 PL 47 C4
 Mazowieckie PL . .55 A6
Dobre Miasto PL . .47 B6
Dobri H 74 B1
Dobrica SRB 85 A5
Dobri Do SRB 85 D6
Dobriš CZ 63 A5
Dobro E 89 B3
Döbrököz H 74 B3
Dobromierz PL 53 C6
Dobronin CZ 63 A6
Dobrosołovo PL . . .54 A3
Dobroszyce PL 54 B2
Dobrovnik SLO 73 B6
Dobrush BY 7 E11
Dobruška CZ 53 C6
Dobrzany PL 45 B7
Dobrzen Wielki PL . .54 C2
Dobrzyca
 Wielkopolskie PL . .46 B2
 Wielkopolskie PL . .54 B2
 Zachodnio-Pomorskie
 PL 46 A1
Dobrzyń nad Wisłą
 PL 47 C5

Dobšiná SK 65 B6
Dobwalls GB 28 C3
Dochamps B 49 C6
Docking GB 30 B4
Docksta S 115 D15
Doddington GB . . .25 C5
Döderhult S 40 B6
Doesburg NL 50 A2
Doetinchem NL 50 B2
Dogliani I 80 B2
Dogueno P 98 B3
Doische B 49 C5
Dois Portos P 92 B1
Dokka N 34 B2
Dokkedal DK 38 C3
Dokkum NL 42 B2
Dokležovje SLO . . .73 B6
Doksy CZ 53 C4
Dol-de-Bretagne F . .57 B4
Dole F 69 A5
Dølemo N 33 D5
Dolenja vas SLO . .73 C4
Dolenjske Toplice
 SLO 73 C4
Dolfor GB 26 C2
Dolgarrog GB 26 B2
Dolgellau GB 26 C2
Dolianá GR 116 C2
Dolianova I 110 C2
Dolice PL 45 B7
Doljani HR 83 B5
Döllach im Mölltal A .72 B2
Dolle D 44 C3
Dollnstein D 62 B2
Dollot F 59 B4
Döllstädt D 51 B6
Dolná Strehová SK . .65 B5
Dolné Saliby SK . . .64 B3
Dolní Benešov CZ . .64 A4
Dolní Bousov CZ . .53 C5
Dolní Kounice CZ . .64 A2
Dolní Kralovice CZ . .63 A6
Dolní Újezd CZ 64 A2
Dolní Žandov CZ . .52 C2
Dolný Kubín SK . . .65 A5
Dolo I 72 C2
Dolores E 101 A5
Dolovo SRB 85 B5
Dölsach A 72 B2
Dolsk PL 54 B2
Dolwyddelan GB . . .26 B2
Dolynska UA 11 B12
Domaljevac BIH . . .84 A3
Domanić TR 118 C4
Domaniža SK 65 A4
Domanovići BIH . . .84 C2
Domašov CZ 64 A3
Domaszék H 75 B4
Domaszków PL 54 C1
Domaszowice PL . .54 B2
Domat-Ems CH . . .71 B4
Domažlice CZ 62 A3
Dombås N 114 E6
Dombasle-sur-Meurthe
 F 60 B2
Dombegyház H 75 B6
Dombóvár H 74 B3
Domène F 69 C5
Domérat F 68 B2
Domfessel F 60 B3
Domfront F 57 B5
Domfront-en-Champagne
 F 57 B6
Domingão P 92 B2
Domingo Pérez
 Granada E 100 B2
 Toledo E 94 C2
Dömitz D 44 B3
Dommartin-le-Franc
 F 59 B5
Domme F 77 B4
Dommitzsch D 52 B2
Domodóssola I 70 B3
Domokos GR 116 C4
Domoszló H 65 C6
Dompaire F 60 B2
Dompierre-du-Chemin
 F 57 B4
Dompierre-sur-Besbre
 F 68 B3
Dompierre-sur-Mer F .66 B3
Domrémy-la-Pucelle
 F 60 B1
Dömsöd H 75 A4
Domsure F 69 B5
Dómus de Maria I . .110 D1
Domusnóvas I 110 C1
Domvena GR 117 D4
Domžale SLO 73 B4
Donado E 87 B4
Donaghadee GB . .19 B6
Don Álvaro E 93 C4
Doña Mencia E . . .100 B1
Donaueschingen D .61 C4
Donauwörth D 62 B1
Don Benito E 93 C5
Doncaster GB 27 B4
Donegal IRL 18 B3
Donestebe-Santesteban
 E 76 C1
Donges F 66 A2
Dongo I 71 B4
Donington GB 30 B3
Doniños E 86 A2
Donja Bebrina HR . .84 A3
Donja Brela HR . . .84 C2
Donja Dubica HR . .84 A3
Donja Dubrava HR . .74 B1
Donja Kupčina HR . .73 C5
Donja Mutnica SRB .85 C6
Donja Šatornja SRB .85 B5
Donja Stubica HR . .73 C5
Donje Brišnik BIH . .84 C2
Donje Biljane HR . .83 B4
Donje Ljupče KOS . .85 D6
Donji Andrijevci HR .74 C3
Donji Kazanci BIH . .84 C1
Donji Koričani BIH . .84 B2
Donji Lapac HR . . .83 B5
Donji Malovan BIH . .84 C2
Donji Miholjac HR . .74 C3
Donji Mosti HR 74 B1
Donji Poloj HR 73 C5
Donji Rujani BIH . . .84 C1
Donji Srb HR 83 B5
Donji Svilaj BIH . . .84 A3
Donji Tovarnik SRB .85 B4
Donji Vakuf BIH . . .84 B2
Donnalucata I 109 C3
Donnemarie-Dontilly
 F 59 B4
Donnersbach A 73 A4
Donnersbachwald A .73 A4
Donnerskirchen A . .64 C2
Donorático I 81 C4
Donostia-San Sebastián
 E 76 C1
Donovaly SK 65 B5
Donzenac F 67 C6
Donzère F 78 B3
Donzy F 68 A3
Doonbeg IRL 20 B2
Doorn NL 49 A6
Dor E 86 A1
Dorchester GB 29 C5
Dørdal N 33 D6
Dordrecht NL 49 B5
Dörenthe D 50 A3
Dores GB 23 D4
Dorfen D 62 B3
Dorfgastein A 72 A3
Dorfmark D 43 C6
Dorf Mecklenburg D .44 B3
Dorgali I 110 B2
Dorking GB 31 C3
Dormagen D 50 B2
Dormánd H 65 C6

Dormans F 59 A4
Dornava SLO 73 B5
Dornbirn A 71 A4
Dornburg D 52 B1
Dorndorf D 51 C6
Dornecy F 68 A3
Dornes F 68 B3
Dornhan D 61 B4
Dornie GB 22 D3
Dornoch GB 23 D4
Dornum D 43 B4
Dorog H 65 C4
Dorogobuzh RUS . . .7 D12
Dorohoi RO 11 C9
Dorotea S 115 C13
Dorotowo PL 47 B6
Dörpen D 43 C4
Dorsten D 50 B2
Dortan F 69 B5
Dortmund D 50 B3
Doruchów PL 54 B3
Dorum D 43 B5
Dörverden D 43 C6
Dörzbach D 61 A5
Dos Aguas E 96 B2
Dosbarrios E 95 C3
Döşemealtı TR . . .119 E5
Dos Hermanas E . .99 B5
Dospat BG 116 A6
Dos-Torres E 100 A1
Dötlingen D 43 C5
Dottignies B 49 C4
Döttingen CH 70 A3
Douai F 49 C4
Douarnenez F 56 B1
Douchy F 59 A4
Douchy-les-Mines F .49 C4
Doucier F 69 B5
Doudeville F 58 A1
Doué-la-Fontaine F . .67 A4
Douglas
 Isle of Man GB . .26 A1
 South Lanarkshire
 GB 25 C4
Doulaincourt-Saucourt
 F 59 B6
Doulevant-le-Château
 F 59 B5
Doullens F 48 C3
Dounby GB 23 B5
Doune GB 24 B3
Dounreay GB 23 C5
Dour B 49 C4
Dourdan F 58 B3
Dourgne F 77 C5
Douro Calvo P 87 D3
Douvaine F 69 B6
Douvres-la-Délivrande
 F 57 A5
Douzy F 59 A6
Dover GB 31 C5
Dovje SLO 72 B3
Dovre N 114 F6
Downham Market GB .30 B4
Downhill GB 19 A5
Downpatrick GB . . .19 B6
Dowra IRL 18 B3
Dozule F 57 A5
Drača SRB 85 B5
Dračevo MNE 84 D3
Drachten NL 42 B3
Dragalovci BIH 84 B2
Draganić HR 73 C5
Dragaš SRB 10 E6
Drăgăşani RO 11 D8
Dragatuš SLO 73 C5
Dragichyn BY 7 E8
Draginja SRB 85 B4
Dragocvet SRB 85 C6
Dragolovci BIH 84 B2
Dragoni I 103 B7
Dragør DK 41 D2
Dragotina HR 73 C6
Dragotinja BIH 83 A5
Dragozetići HR 83 A3
Draguignan F 79 C5
Drahnsdorf D 52 B3
Drahonice CZ 63 A5
Drahovce SK 64 B3
Drama GR 116 A6
Drammen N 35 C2
Drangedal N 33 C6
Drangsnes IS 111 B4
Dransfeld D 51 B5
Dranske D 45 A5
Draperstown GB . . .19 B5
Drassburg A 64 C2
Dravaszabolcs H . . .74 C3
Dravograd SLO 73 B5
Drawno PL 46 B1
Drawsko Pomorskie
 PL 46 B1
Drayton GB 30 B5
Draženov CZ 62 A3
Draževac SRB 85 B5
Dražice HR 73 C4
Drebkau D 53 B4
Dreieich D 51 C4
Dreisen D 61 A4
Dren KOS 85 D5
Drena I 71 C5
Drenovac SRB 85 C6
Drenovci HR 84 B3
Drensteinfurt D 50 B3
Dresden D 53 B3
Dretyń PL 46 A2
Dreux F 58 B2
Dřevohostice CZ . . .64 A3
Drevsjø N 114 F9
Drezdenko PL 46 C1
Drežnica HR 83 A4
Drežnik-Grad HR . .83 B4
Drietona SK 64 B3
Driffield GB 27 B5
Drimnin GB 24 B2
Drimoleague IRL . . .20 C2
Dringenberg D 51 B5
Drinić BIH 84 B1
Drinjača BIH 84 B3
Drinovci BIH 84 C2
Driva N 114 E6
Drlače SRB 85 B4
Drnholec CZ 64 B2
Drniš HR 83 C5
Drnje HR 74 B1
Drnovice CZ 64 A2
Dro I 71 C5
Drøbak N 35 C2
Drobin PL 47 C5
Drochia MD 11 B9
Drochtersen D 43 B6
Drogheda IRL 19 C5
Drohobych UA 11 B7
Droitwich Spa GB . .29 A5
Drołtowice PL 54 B2
Dromahair IRL 18 B3
Dromcolliher IRL . . .20 B3
Dromore
 Down GB 19 B5
 Tyrone GB 19 B4
Dromore West IRL . .18 B3
Dronero I 79 B6
Dronfield GB 27 B4
Drongan GB 24 C3
Dronninglund DK . . .38 B3
Dronrijp NL 42 B2
Dronten NL 42 C2
Drosendorf A 63 B6
Drösing A 64 B2
Drottningholm S . . .37 C4
Droué F 58 B2
Drulingen F 60 B3
Drumbeg GB 22 C3
Drumcliff IRL 18 B3
Drumgask GB 24 A3
Drumkeeran IRL . . .18 B3
Drummore GB 24 D3
Drumnadrochit GB . .23 D4
Drumquin GB 19 B4

Drumshanbo IRL . .18 B3
Drumsna IRL 19 C4
Drunen NL 49 B6
Druskininkai LT 6 D7
Druten NL 49 B6
Druya BY 7 D9
Družetići SRB 85 B5
Drvar BIH 83 B5
Drvenik HR 84 C2
Drwalew PL 55 B6
Drymen GB 24 B3
Drynoch GB 22 D2
Drzewce PL 46 B2
Drzewiany PL 46 B2
Drzewica PL 55 B5
Dualchi I 110 B1
Duas Igrejas P 87 C4
Dub SRB 85 C4
Dubá CZ 53 C4
Dübásari MD 11 C10
Duben D 53 B3
Dübendorf CH 70 A3
Dubí CZ 53 C3
Dubica HR 84 A1
Dublin IRL 21 A5
Dubna RUS 7 C14
Dubňany CZ 64 B2
Dubnica nad Váhom
 SK 64 B4
Dubnik SK 65 C4
Dubno UA 11 A8
Dubodiel SK 64 B4
Dubona SRB 85 B5
Dubovac SRB 85 B6
Dubovic BIH 73 C5
Dubranec HR 73 C5
Dubrava HR 74 C1
Dubrave BIH 84 B3
Dubravica
 HR 73 C5
 SRB 85 B6
Dubrovnik HR 84 D3
Dubrovytsya UA 7 F9
Ducey F 57 B4
Duchcov CZ 53 C3
Ducherow D 45 B5
Dučina SRB 85 B5
Duclair F 58 A1
Dudar H 74 A2
Duddington GB . . .30 B3
Duderstadt D 51 B6
Dudeştii Vechi RO . .75 B5
Dudley GB 26 C3
Dueñas E 88 C2
Duesund N 32 B2
Dueville I 72 C1
Duffel B 49 B5
Duffield GB 27 C4
Dufftown GB 23 D5
Duga Poljana SRB . .85 C5
Duga Resa HR 73 C5
Dugi Rat HR 83 C5
Dugny-sur-Meuse F .59 A6
Dugo Selo HR 73 C6
Duino I 72 C3
Duisburg D 50 B2
Dukat AL 105 C5
Dukhovshchina RUS .7 D12
Dukovany CZ 64 A2
Duleek IRL 19 C5
Dülken D 50 B2
Dülmen D 50 B3
Dulovo BG 11 E9
Dulpetorpet N 34 B4
Dulverton GB 29 B4
Dumbarton GB 24 C3
Dümerek TR 118 C6
Dumfries GB 25 C4
Dümmer D 44 C3
Dümpelfeld D 50 C2
Dunaföldvár H 74 B3
Dunajská Streda SK .64 C3
Dunakeszi H 65 C5
Dunakömlöd H 74 B3
Dunapataj H 75 B3
Dunaszekcsö H . . .74 B3
Dunaszentgyörgy H .74 B3
Dunatetétlen H 75 B4
Dunaújváros H 74 B3
Dunavecse H 75 B3
Dunbar GB 25 B5
Dunblane GB 25 B4
Dunboyne IRL 21 A5
Dundalk IRL 19 B5
Dundee GB 25 B5
Dundrennan GB . . .25 D4
Dundrum GB 19 B6
Dunfanaghy IRL . . .19 A4
Dunfermline GB . . .25 B4
Dungannon GB 19 B5
Dungarvan IRL 21 B4
Dungiven GB 19 B5
Dunglow IRL 18 B3
Dunholme GB 27 B5
Dunkeld GB 25 B4
Dunker S 37 C3
Dunkerque = Dunkirk
 F 48 B3
Dunkineely IRL 18 B3
Dunkirk = Dunkerque
 F 48 B3
Dún Laoghaire IRL . .21 A5
Dunlavin IRL 21 A5
Dunleer IRL 19 C5
Dun-le-Palestel F . .67 B6
Dun-les-Places F . .68 A4
Dunlop GB 24 C3
Dunmanway IRL . . .20 C2
Dunmore IRL 18 C3
Dunmore East IRL . .21 B5
Dunmurry GB 19 B5
Dunnet GB 23 C5
Dunningen D 61 B4
Dunoon GB 24 C3
Dunscore GB 25 C4
Dunsford GB 29 C4
Dunshaughlin IRL . .21 A5
Dunstable GB 31 C3
Dunster GB 29 B4
Dun-sur-Auron F . . .68 B2
Dun-sur-Meuse F . .59 A6
Dunure GB 24 C3
Dunvegan GB 22 D2
Duplek SLO 73 B5
Dupnitsa BG 11 E7
Durach D 61 C6
Durağan TR 16 A7
Durak TR 118 C3
Ðurakovac KOS . . .85 D5
Durana E 89 B4
Durance F 76 B3
Durango E 89 A4
Durankulak BG 11 E10
Duras F 76 B3
Durban-Corbières F .78 D1
Dürbheim D 61 B4
Durbuy B 49 C6
Dúrcal E 100 C2
Ðurdenovac HR . . .74 C2
Ðurdevac HR 74 B1
Ðurdevik BIH 84 B3
Düren D 50 C2
Durham GB 25 D6
Ðurinci SRB 85 B5
Durlach D 61 B4
Ðurmanec HR 73 B5
Durness GB 22 C3
Dürnkrut A 64 B2
Durón E 95 B4
Durrës AL 105 B5
Dürrboden CH 71 B4

Dürrenboden CH 70 B3
Durrës AL 105 B5
Durrow IRL 21 B4
Durrus IRL 20 C2
Dursunbey TR 118 C3
Durtal F 57 C5
Durup DK 38 C1
Durusu TR 118 A3
Dusina BIH 84 C2
Dusnok H 75 B3
Dusocin PL 47 B4
Düsseldorf D 50 B2
Dusslingen D 61 B5
Duszniki PL 46 C2
Duszniki-Zdrój PL 54 C1
Dutovlje SLO 72 C3
Duvebo S 40 A4
Duved S 115 D9
Düzağac TR 118 D5
Düzce TR 118 B6
Dvärsätt S 115 D11
Dvor HR 83 A5
Dvorce CZ 64 A3
Dvorníky SK 64 B3
Dvory nad Žitavou SK 64 C4
Dvůr Královénad Labem CZ 53 C5
Dyatkovo RUS 7 E13
Dybvad DK 38 B3
Dyce GB 23 D6
Dygowo PL 46 A1
Dykehead GB 25 B4
Dymchurch GB 31 C5
Dymer UA 11 A11
Dyrnes N 114 D4
Dywity PL 47 B6
Džanići BIH 84 C2
Dziadowa Kłoda PL 54 B2
Działdowo PL 47 B6
Działoszyce PL 55 C5
Działoszyn PL 54 B3
Dziemiany PL 46 A3
Dzierżąźnia PL 47 C6
Dzierzgoń PL 47 B5
Dzierzgowo PL 47 B6
Dzierżoniów PL 54 C1
Dzisna BY 7 D10
Dziwnów PL 45 A6
Dzyarzhynsk BY 7 E9
Dzyatlava BY 7 E8

E

Ea E 89 A4
Eaglesfield GB 25 C4
Ealing GB 31 C3
Eardisley GB 29 A4
Earls Barton GB 30 B3
Earl Shilton GB 30 B2
Earlston GB 25 C5
Easington GB 27 B6
Easky IRL 18 B3
Eastbourne GB 31 D4
East Calder GB 25 C4
East Dereham GB 30 B4
Easter Skeld GB 22 A7
East Grinstead GB 31 C4
East Ilsley GB 31 C2
East Kilbride GB 24 C3
Eastleigh GB 31 D2
East Linton GB 25 C5
East Markham GB 27 B5
Easton GB 29 C5
East Wittering GB 31 D3
Eaton Socon GB 30 B3
Eaux-Bonnes F 76 D2
Eauze F 76 C3
Ebberup DK 39 D2
Ebbs A 62 C3
Ebbw Vale GB 29 B4
Ebeleben D 51 B6
Ebeltoft DK 39 C3
Ebene Reichenau A 72 B3
Eben im Pongau A 72 A3
Ebensee A 63 C4
Ebensfeld D 51 C6
Eberbach D 61 A4
Ebergötzen D 51 B6
Ebermann-Stadt D 62 A2
Ebern D 51 C6
Eberndorf A 73 B4
Ebersbach D 53 B4
Ebersberg D 62 B2
Ebersdorf
Bayern D 52 C1
Niedersachsen D 43 B6
Eberstein A 73 B4
Eberswalde D 45 C5
Ebnat-Kappel CH 71 A4
Éboli I 103 C8
Ebrach D 61 A6
Ebreichsdorf A 64 C2
Ebreuil F 68 B3
Ebstorf D 44 B2
Ecclefechan GB 25 C4
Eccleshall GB 26 C3
Eceabat TR 118 B1
Echallens CH 69 B6
Echauri E 76 D1
Echinos GR 116 A7
Echiré F 67 B4
Échirolles F 69 C5
Echourgnac F 76 A3
Echt NL 50 B1
Echte D 51 B6
Echternach L 60 A2
Ecija E 99 B5
Ečka SRB 75 C5
Eckartsberga D 52 B1
Eckelshausen D 51 C4
Eckental D 62 A2
Eckernförde D 44 A1
Eckerö FIN 36 B6
Eckington GB 27 B4
Éclaron F 59 B5
Écommoy F 58 C1
Écouché F 57 B5
Ecouis F 58 A2
Ecséd H 65 C5
Ecsegfalva H 75 A5
Écueillé F 67 A6
Ed S 35 D3
Eda S 34 C4
Eda glasbruk S 34 C4
Edam NL 42 C2
Edane S 35 C4
Edderton GB 23 D4
Ede NL 49 A6
Edebäck S 34 B5
Edebo S 36 B5
Edelény H 65 B6
Edelschrott A 73 A5
Edemissen D 44 C2
Edenbridge GB 31 C4
Edenderry IRL 21 A4
Edenkoben D 61 A4
Edesheim D 61 A4
Edessa GR 116 B4
Edewecht D 43 B4
Edgeworthstown IRL 19 C4
Edinburgh GB 25 C4
Edinet MD 11 B9
Edirne TR 118 A1
Edland N 33 C4
Edolo I 71 B5
Edøy N 114 D5
Edremit TR 118 C2
Edsbro S 36 C5
Edsbruk S 40 A6
Edsbyn S 36 A2
Edsele S 115 D13
Edsleskog S 35 C4
Edsvalla S 35 C5
Eekloo B 49 B4
Eemshaven NL 42 B3
Eerbeek NL 50 A2
Eersel NL 49 B6
Eferding A 63 B5
Effiat F 68 B3
Efteløt N 35 C1
Egeln D 52 B1
Eger H 65 C6
Egerbakta H 65 C6
Egernsund DK 39 E2
Egersund N 33 D3
Egerszólát H 65 C6
Egervár H 74 B1
Egg
A 71 A4
D 61 B6
Eggby S 35 D5
Eggedal N 32 B6
Eggenburg A 64 B1
Eggenfelden D 62 B3
Eggesin D 45 B6
Eggum N 112 D2
Egham GB 31 C3
Éghezée B 49 C5
Egiertowo PL 47 A4
Egilsstaðir IS 111 B11
Egina GR 117 E5
Eginio GR 116 B4
Egio GR 117 D4
Égletons F 68 C2
Egling D 62 C2
Eglinton GB 19 A4
Eglisau CH 61 C4
Égliseneuve-d'Entraigues F 68 C2
Eglofs D 61 C5
Egmond aan Zee NL 42 C1
Egna I 71 B6
Egosthena GR 117 D5
Egremont GB 26 A2
Egtved DK 39 D2
Eguilles F 79 C4
Eguilly-sous-Bois F 59 B5
Éguzon-Chantôme F 67 B6
Egyek H 65 C6
Egyházasrádóc H 74 A1
Ehekirchen D 62 B2
Ehingen D 61 B5
Ehra-Lessien D 44 C2
Ehrang D 60 A2
Ehrenfriedersdorf D 52 C2
Ehrenhain D 52 C2
Ehrenhausen A 73 B5
Ehringshausen D 51 C4
Ehrwald A 71 A5
Eibar E 89 A4
Eibelstadt D 61 A6
Eibenstock D 52 C2
Eibergen NL 50 A2
Eibiswald A 73 B5
Eichenbarleben D 52 A1
Eichendorf D 62 B3
Eichstätt D 62 B2
Eickelborn D 50 B4
Eide
Hordaland N 32 B3
Møre og Romsdal N 114 E4
Eidet N 112 C7
Eidfjord N 32 B4
Eidsberg N 35 C3
Eidsbugarden N 32 A5
Eidsdal N 114 E4
Eidsfoss N 35 C2
Eidskog N 34 B4
Eidsvåg
Hordaland N 32 B2
Møre og Romsdal N 114 E5
Eidsvoll N 34 B3
Eikefjord N 114 F2
Eikelandsosen N 32 C2
Eiken N 33 D4
Eikesdal N 114 E5
Eikstrand N 35 C1
Eilenburg D 52 B2
Eilsleben D 52 A1
Eina N 34 B2
Einbeck D 51 B5
Eindhoven NL 49 B6
Einsiedeln CH 70 A3
Einville-au-Jard F 60 B2
Eisenach D 51 C6
Eisenberg
Rheinland-Pfalz D 61 A4
Thüringen D 52 C1
Eisenerz A 73 A4
Eisenhüttenstadt D 53 A4
Eisenkappel A 73 B4
Eisenstadt A 64 C2
Eisentratten A 72 B3
Eisfeld D 51 C6
Eisleben D 52 B1
Eislingen D 61 B5
Eitensheim D 62 B2
Eiterfeld D 51 C5
Eitorf D 50 C3
Eivindvik N 32 B2
Eivissa = Ibiza E 97 C1
Eixo P 92 A2
Ejby DK 39 D2
Ejea de los Caballeros E 90 A1
Ejstrupholm DK 39 D2
Ejulve E 90 C2
Eke B 49 C4
Ekeby
Gotland S 37 E5
Skåne S 41 D2
Uppsala S 36 B5
Ekeby-Almby S 37 C2
Ekenäs S 35 D5
Ekenässjön S 40 B5
Ekerö S 37 C4
Eket S 41 C3
Eketorp S 41 C6
Ekevik S 40 A6
Ekkerøy N 113 B19
Ekshärad S 34 B5
Eksingedal N 32 B2
Eksjö S 40 B4
Eksta S 37 E5
Ektrask S 115 C16
El Alamo
Madrid E 94 B3
Sevilla E 99 B4
El Algar E 101 B5
El Almendro E 98 B3
El Alquián E 101 C3
Élancourt F 58 B2
El Arahal E 99 B5
El Arenal E 94 B1
El Arguellite E 101 A3
Elassona GR 116 C4
El Astillero E 88 A3
Elati GR 116 C3
Želazno PL 54 C1
El Ballestero E 101 A3
El Barco de Ávila E 93 A5
Elbasan AL 116 A2
El Berrón E 88 A1
El Berrueco E 95 B3
Elbeuf F 58 A1
Elbingerode D 51 B6
Elbląg PL 47 A5
El Bodón E 93 A4
El Bonillo E 95 D4
El Bosque E 99 C5
El Bullaque E 94 C2
Elburg NL 42 C2
El Burgo E 100 C1
El Burgo de Ebro E 90 B2
El Burgo de Osma E 89 C3
El Burgo Ranero E 88 B1
El Buste E 89 C5
El Cabaco E 93 A4
El Callejo E 89 A3
El Campillo E 99 B4
El Campillo de la Jara E 94 C1
El Cañavete E 95 C4
El Carpio E 100 B1
El Carpio de Tajo E 94 C2
El Casar E 95 B3
El Casar de Escalona E 94 B2
El Castillo de las Guardas E 99 B4
El Centenillo E 100 A2
El Cerro E 93 A5
El Cerro de Andévalo E 99 B4
Elche E 96 C2
Elche de la Sierra E 101 A3
Elchingen D 61 B6
El Comenar E 99 C5
El Coronil E 99 B5
El Crucero E 86 A4
El Cubo de Tierra del Vino E 88 C1
El Cuervo E 99 C4
Elda E 101 A5
Eldena D 44 B3
Eldingen D 44 C2
Elefsina GR 117 D5
El Ejido E 101 C3
Elek H 75 B6
Elemir SRB 75 C5
El Escorial E 94 B2
El Espinar E 94 B2
Eleutheroupoli GR 116 B6
El Frago E 90 A2
El Franco E 86 A4
El Frasno E 89 C5
Elgå N 114 E8
El Garrobo E 99 B4
El Gastor E 99 C5
Elgin GB 23 D5
Elgoibar E 89 A4
Elgol GB 22 D2
El Gordo E 93 B5
El Grado E 90 A3
El Granado E 98 B3
El Grao de Castelló E 96 B3
El Grau E 96 C2
Elgshøa N 34 A4
El Higuera E 100 B1
El Hijate E 101 B3
El Hontanar E 96 A1
El Hoyo E 100 A2
Elie GB 25 B5
Elizondo E 76 C1
Ełk PL 6 E7
Elkhovo BG 11 E9
Ellenberg D 61 A6
Ellesmere GB 26 C3
Ellesmere Port GB 26 B3
Ellezelles B 49 C4
Ellingen D 62 A1
Ellmau A 72 A2
Ellon GB 23 D6
Ellös S 35 D3
Ellrich D 51 B6
Ellwangen D 61 B6
Elm
CH 71 B4
D 43 B6
Elmadağ TR 16 B6
El Madroño E 99 B4
El Maillo E 93 A4
Elmalı TR 119 F4
El Masnou E 91 B5
El Mirón E 93 A5
El Molar E 95 B3
El Molinillo E 94 C2
El Morell E 91 B4
Elmshorn D 43 B6
Elmstein D 60 A3
El Muyo E 89 C3
Elne F 91 A5
Elnesvågen N 114 E4
El Olmo E 88 C3
Elorrio E 89 A4
Elöszállás H 74 B3
Elouda GR 117 G7
Éloyes F 60 B2
El Palo E 100 C1
El Pardo E 94 B3
El Payo E 93 A4
El Pedernoso E 95 C4
El Pedroso E 99 B5
El Peral E 95 C5
El Perelló
Tarragona E 90 C3
Valencia E 96 B2
Elphin GB 22 C3
El Picazo E 95 C4
El Pinell de Bray E 90 B3
El Piñero E 88 C1
El Pla de Santa Maria E 91 B4
El Pobo E 90 C2
El Pobo de Dueñas E 95 B5
El Pont d'Armentera E 91 B4
El Port de la Selva E 91 A6
El Port de Llançà E 91 A6
El Port de Sagunt E 96 B2
El Prat de Llobregat E 91 B5
El Provencio E 95 C4
El Puente E 89 A3
El Puente del Arzobispo E 93 B5
El Puerto E 86 A4
El Puerto de Santa María E 99 C4
El Real de la Jara E 99 B4
El Real de San Vincente E 94 B2
El Robledo E 94 C2
El Rocío E 99 B4
El Rompido E 99 B3
El Ronquillo E 99 B4
El Royo E 89 C4
El Rubio E 100 B1
El Sabinar E 101 A3
El Saler E 96 B2
El Salobral E 101 A4
El Saucejo E 99 B5
Els Castells E 91 A4
Elsdorf D 50 C2
Elsenfeld D 61 A5
El Serrat AND 91 A4
Elsfleth D 43 B5
Elspeet NL 50 A1
Elst NL 50 B1
Elstead GB 31 C3
Elster D 52 B2
Elsterberg D 52 C2
Elsterwerda D 52 B3
Elstra D 53 B4
El Temple E 90 B2
El Tiemblo E 94 B2
Eltmann D 51 D6
El Toboso E 95 C4
El Tormillo E 90 B2
El Torno E 93 A5
Eltville D 50 C4
El Valle de las Casas E 88 B1
Elvas P 93 C3
Elvebakken N 113 C12
El Vellón E 95 B3
Elven F 56 C3
El Vendrell E 91 B4
Elverum N 34 B3
El Villar de Arnedo E 89 B4
Elvington GB 27 B5
El Viso E 100 A1
El Viso del Alcor E 99 B5
Elxleben D 51 B6
Ely GB 30 B4
Elzach D 61 B4
Elze D 51 A5
Emådalen S 36 A1
Embleton GB 25 C6
Embonas GR 119 F2
Embrun F 79 B5
Embún E 90 A2
Emden D 43 B4
Emecik TR 119 F2
Emet TR 118 C4
Emirdağ TR 118 C6
Emlichheim D 42 C3
Emmaboda S 40 C5
Emmaljunga S 41 C3
Emmeloord NL 42 C2
Emmen
CH 70 A3
NL 42 C3
Emmendingen D 60 B3
Emmer-Compascuum NL 43 C4
Emmerich D 50 B2
Emmern D 51 A5
Emöd H 65 C6
Empoli I 81 C4
Emsbüren D 43 C4
Emsdetten D 50 A3
Emsfors S 40 B6
Emskirchen D 62 A1
Emstek D 43 C5
Emsworth GB 31 D3
Emyvale IRL 19 B5
Enafors S 115 D9
Enånger S 115 F14
Encamp AND 91 A4
Encarnação P 92 C1
Encinas de Abajo E 94 B1
Encinas de Esgueva E 88 C2
Encinasola E 99 A4
Encinas Reales E 100 B1
Encio E 89 B3
Enciso E 89 B4
Enden N 114 F7
Endingen D 60 B3
Endrinal E 93 A5
Endröd H 75 B5
Enebakk N 34 C3
Eneryda S 40 C4
Enese H 64 C3
Enez TR 116 B8
Enfield IRL 21 A5
Eng A 72 A1
Engelberg CH 70 B3
Engelhartszell A 63 B4
Engelskirchen D 50 C3
Engen D 61 C4
Enger N 34 B2
Engerdal N 114 F8
Engerneset N 34 A4
Enge-sande D 39 E1
Engesvang DK 39 C2
Enghien B 49 C5
Engstingen D 61 B5
Engter D 43 C5
Enguera E 96 C2
Enguidanos E 95 C5
Enkenbach D 60 A3
Enkhuizen NL 42 C2
Enklinge FIN 36 B7
Enköping S 37 C4
Enna I 109 B3
Ennezat F 68 C3
Ennigerloh D 50 B4
Enningdal N 35 D3
Ennis IRL 20 B3
Enniscorthy IRL 21 B5
Enniskean IRL 20 C3
Enniskillen GB 19 B4
Ennistimon IRL 20 B2
Enns A 63 B5
Eno FIN 3 E29
Enontekiö FIN 113 D12
Ens NL 42 C2
Enschede NL 50 A2
Ensdorf D 62 A2
Ensisheim F 60 C3
Enstaberga S 37 D3
Enstone GB 31 C2
Entlebuch CH 70 A3
Entrácque I 80 B1
Entradas P 98 B2
Entrains-sur-Nohain F 68 A3
Entrambasaguas E 88 A3
Entrambasmestas E 88 A3
Entraygues-sur-Truyère F 77 B5
Entre-os-Rios P 87 C2
Entrevaux F 79 C5
Entrin Bajo E 93 C4
Entroncamento P 92 B2
Entzheim F 60 B3
Envermeu F 58 A2
Enviken S 36 B2
Enying H 74 B3
Enzingerboden A 72 A2
Enzklösterle D 61 B4
Épagny F 59 A4
Epalinges CH 70 B1
Epannes F 67 B4
Epanomi GR 116 B4
Epe
D 50 A3
NL 42 C2
Épernay F 59 A4
Épernon F 58 B2
Epfig F 60 B3
Épierre F 69 C6
Épila E 90 B1
Épinac F 69 B4
Épinal F 60 B2
Episcopia I 106 A3
Episkopi CY 120 B1
Epitalio GR 117 E3
Epoisses F 69 A4
Eppenbrunn D 60 A3
Eppendorf D 52 C3
Epping GB 31 C4
Eppingen D 61 A4
Epsom GB 31 C3
Epworth GB 27 B5
Eraclea I 72 C2
Eraclea Mare I 72 C2
Erba I 71 C4
Erbach
Baden-Württemberg D 61 B5
Hessen D 61 A4
Erbalunga F 102 A2
Erbendorf D 62 A3
Érchie I 105 C3
Ercolano I 103 C7
Ercsi H 74 A3
Érd H 74 A3
Erdek TR 118 B2
Erdemli TR 16 C7
Erdevik SRB 85 A4
Erding D 62 B2
Erdőtelek H 65 C6
Erdut HR 75 C4
Erdweg D 62 B2
Ereğli
Konya TR 16 C7
Zonguldak TR 118 A6
Erenkaya TR 119 E7
Eresfjord N 114 E5
Eresos GR 116 C7
Eretria GR 116 D5
Erfde D 43 A6
Erfjord N 33 C3
Erfstadt D 50 C2
Erfurt D 52 C1
Ergli LV 7 C8
Ergoldsbach D 62 B3
Eriboll GB 22 C4
Érice I 108 A1
Ericeira P 92 C1
Eğridir TR 119 E5
Eriksberg S 115 B12
Eriksmåla S 40 C5
Eringsboda S 40 C5
Eriswil CH 70 A2
Erithres GR 117 D5
Erkelenz D 50 B2
Erkner D 45 C5
Erkrath D 50 B2
Erla E 90 A2
Erlangen D 62 A2
Erli I 80 B2
Erlsbach A 72 B2
Ermelo NL 49 A6
Ermenak TR 16 C6
Ermenonville F 58 A3
Ermezinde P 87 C2
Ermidas P 98 A2
Ermioni GR 117 E5
Ermoupoli GR 117 E6
Ermsleben D 52 B1
Erndtebrück D 50 C4
Ernée F 57 B5
Ernestinovo HR 74 C3
Ernstbrunn A 64 B2
Erolzheim D 61 B6
Erquelinnes B 49 C5
Erquy F 56 B3
Erra P 92 C2
Erratzu E 76 C1
Errindlev DK 44 A3
Erro E 76 D1
Ersa F 102 A2
Érsekcsanád H 75 B3
Ersekë AL 116 B2
Érsekvadkert H 65 C5
Erstein F 60 B3
Erstfeld CH 70 B3
Ertebølle DK 38 C2
Ertingen D 61 B5
Ervedal
Coimbra P 92 A2
Portalegre P 92 B3
Ervenik HR 83 B4
Ervidel P 98 B2
Ervy-le-Châtel F 59 B4
Erwitte D 51 B4
Erxleben D 52 A1
Erzsébet H 74 B3
Esbjerg DK 39 D1
Esbly F 58 B3
Escacena del Campo E 99 B4
Escairón E 86 B3
Escalada E 88 B3
Escalante E 89 A3
Escalaplano I 110 C2
Escalona E 94 B2
Escalona del Prado E 94 A2
Escalonilla E 94 C2
Escalos de Baixo P 92 B3
Escalos de Cima P 92 B3
Escamilla E 95 B4
Es Caná E 97 B1
Escañuela E 100 B1
Es Castell E 97 B4
Escatrón E 90 B2
Eschach D 61 C5
Eschau D 61 A5
Eschede D 44 C2
Eschenau D 62 A2
Eschenbach D 62 A2
Eschenz CH 61 C4
Eschershausen D 51 B5
Esch-sur-Alzette L 60 A1
Esch-sur-Sûre L 60 A1
Eschwege D 51 B6
Eschweiler D 50 C2
Escobasa de Almazán E 89 C4
Escoeuilles F 48 C2
Escombreras E 101 B5
Escos F 76 C1
Escource F 76 B1
Escragnolles F 79 C5
Escrick GB 27 B4
Escurial E 93 B5
Escurial de la Sierra E 93 A5
Esens D 43 B4
Esgos E 87 B3
Esher GB 31 C3
Eskdalemuir GB 25 C4
Eskifjörður IS 111 B12
Eskilhem S 37 E5
Eskilsäter S 35 D5
Eskilstrup DK 39 E4
Eskilstuna S 37 C3
Eskipazar TR 118 B7
Eskişehir TR 118 C5
Eslarn D 62 A3
Eslava E 89 B5
Eslida E 96 B2
Eslohe D 50 B4
Eslöv S 41 D3
Eşme TR 119 D3
Es Mercadal E 97 B4
Es Migjorn Gran E 97 B4
Espa N 34 B3
Espalion F 78 B1
Esparragalejo E 93 C4
Esparragosa del Caudillo E 93 C5
Esparragossa de la Serena E 93 C5
Esparreguera E 91 B4
Esparron F 79 C4
Espe N 32 B3
Espedal N 33 D3
Espejo
Alava E 89 B3
Córdoba E 100 B1
Espeland N 32 B2
Espelkamp D 43 C5
Espeluche F 78 B3
Espeluy E 100 A2
Espera E 99 C5
Esperança P 93 B3
Espéraza F 77 D5
Espéria I 103 B6
Espevær N 33 C2
Espiel E 99 A5
Espinama E 88 A2
Espiñaredo E 86 A3
Espinasses F 79 B5
Espinelves E 91 B5
Espinhal P 92 A2
Espinho P 87 C2
Espinilla E 88 A2
Espinosa de Cerrato E 88 C3
Espinosa de los Monteros E 89 A3
Espinoso del Rey E 94 C2
Espirito Santo P 98 B3
Espluga de Francolí E 91 B4
Esplús E 90 B3
Espolla E 91 A5
Espoo FIN 6 A8
Esporles E 97 B2
Es Port d'Alcúdia E 97 B3
Esposende P 87 C2
Espot E 91 A4
Es Pujols E 97 C1
Esquedas E 90 A2
Esquivias E 94 B3
Essay F 57 B6
Essen
B 49 B5
Niedersachsen D 43 C4
Nordrhein-Westfalen D 50 B3
Essenbach D 62 B3
Essertaux F 58 A3
Essingen D 61 B6
Esslingen D 61 B5
Es Soleràs E 90 B3
Essoyes F 59 B5
Estacas E 87 B2
Estadilla E 90 A3
Estagel F 78 D1
Estaires F 48 C3
Estang F 76 C2
Estarreja P 87 D2
Estartit E 91 A6
Estavayer-le-Lac CH 70 B1
Este I 72 C1
Esteiro E 86 A2
Estela P 87 C2
Estella E 89 B4
Estellencs E 97 B2
Estepa E 100 B1
Estépar E 88 B3
Estepona E 99 C5
Esternay F 59 B4
Esterri d'Aneu E 91 A4
Esterwegen D 43 C4
Estissac F 59 B4
Estivadas E 87 B3
Estivareilles F 68 B2
Estivella E 96 B2
Estói P 98 B3
Estopiñán E 90 B3
Estoril P 92 C1
Estoublon F 79 C5
Estrée-Blanche F 48 C3
Estrées-St Denis F 58 A3
Estrela P 98 A3
Estremera E 95 B3
Estremoz P 92 C3
Estuna S 36 C5
Esyres F 67 A5
Esztergom H 65 C4
Étables-sur-Mer F 56 B3
Étain F 60 A1
Étalans F 69 A6
Etalle B 60 A1
Étampes F 58 B3
Étang-sur-Arroux F 69 B4
Étaples F 48 C2
Etauliers F 67 C4
Etili TR 118 C1
Etna N 34 B1
Etne N 33 C2
Etoges F 59 B4
Etoliko GR 116 D3
Eton GB 31 C3
Etréaupont F 59 A4
Étréchy F 58 B3
Étrépagny F 58 A2
Étretat F 57 A6
Étroeungt F 49 C4
Étroubles I 70 C2
Ettal D 62 C2
Ettelbruck L 60 A2
Etten NL 49 B5
Ettenheim D 60 B3
Ettington GB 29 A6
Ettlingen D 61 B4
Ettringen D 62 B1
Etuz F 69 A5
Etxarri-Aranatz E 89 B4
Etyek H 74 A3
Eu F 48 C2
Euerdorf D 51 C6
Eulate E 89 B4
Eupen B 50 C2
Europoort NL 49 B5
Euskirchen D 50 C2
Eutin D 44 A2
Evanger N 32 B3
Évaux-les-Bains F 68 B2
Evciler
Afyon TR 119 D4
Çanakkale TR 118 C1
Evenskjær N 112 D5
Evenstad N 34 A3
Evercreech GB 29 B5
Evergem B 49 B4
Everöd S 41 D4
Eversberg D 51 B4
Everswinkel D 50 B3
Evertsberg S 34 A5
Evesham GB 29 A6
Évian-les-Bains F 69 B6
Evisa F 102 A1
Evje N 33 D4
Evolène CH 70 B2
Évora P 92 C3
Evoramonte P 92 C3
Evran F 57 B4
Evrecy F 57 A5
Évreux F 58 A2
Évron F 57 B5
Évry F 58 B3
Ewell GB 31 C3
Ewersbach D 50 C4
Excideuil F 67 C6
Exeter GB 29 C4
Exmes F 57 B6
Exminster GB 29 C4
Exmouth GB 29 C4
Eydehamn N 33 D5
Eye
Peterborough GB 30 B3
Suffolk GB 30 B5
Eyemouth GB 25 C5
Eyguians F 79 B4
Eyguières F 79 C4
Eygurande F 68 C2
Eylie F 77 D3
Eymet F 77 B3
Eymoutiers F 68 C1
Eynsham GB 31 C2
Eyrarbakki IS 111 D4
Eystrup D 43 C6
Ezaro E 86 B1
Ezcaray E 89 B4
Ezcároz E 76 D1
Ezine TR 118 C1
Ezmoriz P 87 D2

F

Fabara E 90 B3
Fábbrico I 81 B4
Fåberg N 34 A2
Fabero E 86 B4
Fábiánsebestyén H 75 B5
Fåborg DK 39 D3
Fabrègues F 78 C2
Fabriano I 82 C1
Fabrizia I 106 C3
Facha P 87 C2
Facinas E 99 C5
Fačkov SK 65 A4
Fadagosa P 92 B3
Fadd H 74 B3
Faédis I 72 B3
Faenza I 81 B5
Fafe P 87 C2
Fagagna I 72 B3
Făgăraş RO 11 D8
Fågelberget S 115 C11
Fågelfors S 40 B5
Fågelmara S 41 C5
Fågelsta S 37 D2
Fagerås S 35 C5
Fagerheim N 32 B4
Fagerhøy N 34 A1
Fagerhult S 40 B5
Fagernes
Oppland N 32 B6
Troms N 112 C8
Fagersanna S 35 D6
Fagersta S 36 B2
Fåglavik S 35 D5
Fagnano Castello I 106 B3
Fagnières F 59 B5
Faido CH 70 B3
Fains-Véel F 59 B6
Fairford GB 29 B6
Fairlie GB 24 C3
Fajsz H 74 B3
Fakenham GB 30 B4
Fåker S 115 D11
Fakse DK 39 D5
Fakse Ladeplads DK 41 D2
Falaise F 57 B5
Falcade I 72 B1
Falcarragh IRL 18 A3
Falces E 89 B5
Fălciu RO 11 C10
Falconara I 109 B3
Falconara Marittima I 82 C2
Falcone I 109 A4
Faldingworth GB 27 B5
Falerum S 37 D3
Fălești MD 11 C9
Falkenberg
Bayern D 62 A3
Bayern D 62 B3
Brandenburg D 52 B3
S 40 C2
Falkensee D 45 C5
Falkenstein
Bayern D 62 A3
Sachsen D 52 C2
Falkenthal D 45 C5
Falkirk GB 25 B4
Falkland GB 25 B4
Falköping S 35 D5
Fall D 62 C2
Falla S 37 D2
Fallingbostel D 43 C6
Falmouth GB 28 C2
Falset E 90 B3
Fălticeni RO 11 C9
Falun S 36 B2
Famagusta CY 120 A2
Fammestad N 32 B2
Fana N 32 B2
Fanano I 81 B4
Fanari GR 116 C3
Fanjeaux F 77 C5
Fano I 82 C2
Fântânele RO 75 B6
Fão P 87 C2
Fara in Sabina I 102 A5
Faramontanos de Tábara E 88 C1
Fara Novarese I 70 C3
Farasdues E 90 A1
Fårbo S 40 B6
Fareham GB 31 D2
Färentuna S 37 C4
Färgelanda S 35 D3
Färila S 115 F12
Faringdon GB 31 C2
Faringe S 36 C5
Farini I 80 B3
Fariza E 87 C4
Färjestaden S 41 C6
Farkadona GR 116 C4
Farkasfa H 73 B6
Farlete E 90 B2
Färlöv S 41 C4
Farmos H 75 A4
Farnă SK 65 C4
Färnäs S 36 B1
Farnborough GB 31 C3
Farnese I 102 A4
Farnham GB 31 C3
Farnroda D 51 C6
Faro P 98 B3
Fåro S 37 E6
Fårösund S 37 E6
Farra d'Alpago I 72 B2
Farranfore IRL 20 B2
Farre DK 39 C2
Farsala GR 116 C4
Farsø DK 38 C2
Farsund N 33 D3
Farum DK 41 D2
Fårup DK 38 C2
Fasana I 103 C8
Fasano I 104 C3
Fáskrúðsfjörður IS 111 C11
Fassberg D 44 C2
Fastiv UA 11 A10
Fastnäs S 34 B5
Fatesh RUS 7 E13
Fátima P 92 B2
Fatmomakke S 115 B12
Fättjaur S 115 B12
Faucogney-et-la-Mer F 60 C2
Fauguerolles F 76 B3
Faulenrost D 45 B4
Faulquemont F 60 A2
Fauquembergues F 48 C3
Fauske N 112 E4
Fauville-en-Caux F 58 A1
Fauvillers B 60 A1
Fåvang N 34 A2
Favara
E 96 B2
I 108 B2
Faverges F 69 C6
Faverney F 60 C2
Faversham GB 31 C4
Favignana I 108 B1
Fawley GB 31 D2
Fay-aux-Loges F 58 C3
Fayence F 79 C5
Fayet F 78 C1
Fayl-Billot F 60 C1
Fayón E 90 B3
Fearn GB 23 D5
Fécamp F 58 A1
Feda N 33 D3
Fedje N 32 B1
Feeny GB 19 B4
Fegen S 40 B3
Fegyvernek H 75 A5
Fehrbellin D 45 C4
Fehring A 73 B6
Feichten A 71 A5
Feiring N 34 B3
Feistritz im Rosental A 73 B4
Feke TR 16 C7
Feketić SRB 75 C4
Felanitx E 97 B3
Feld am See A 72 B3
Feldbach A 73 B5
Feldberg D 45 B5
Feldkirch A 71 A4
Feldkirchen in Kärnten A 73 B4
Feldkirchen-Westerham D 62 C2
Felgueiras P 87 C2
Felitto I 103 C8
Félix E 101 C3
Felixstowe GB 31 C5
Felizzano I 80 B2
Felletin F 68 C2
Fellingsbro S 37 C2
Felnac RO 75 B6
Felnémet H 65 C6
Felpéc H 74 A2
Fels am Wagram A 64 B1
Felsberg D 51 B5
Felsönyék H 74 B3
Felsöszentiván H 75 B4
Felsöszentmárton H 74 C2
Felsözsolca H 65 B6
Felsted DK 39 E2
Feltre I 72 B1
Femsjö S 40 C3
Fenagh IRL 19 B4
Fene E 86 A2
Fenestrelle I 79 A6
Fénétrange F 60 B3
Feneu F 57 C5
Fengersfors S 35 D4
Fenit IRL 20 B2
Fensmark DK 39 D4
Fenwick GB 24 C3
Feolin Ferry GB 24 C1
Ferbane IRL 21 A4
Ferdinandovac HR 74 B2
Ferdinandshof D 45 B5
Fère-Champenoise F 59 B4
Fère-en-Tardenois F 59 A4
Ferentillo I 102 A5
Ferentino I 103 B6
Feres GR 116 B8
Férez E 101 A3
Feria E 93 C4
Feričanci HR 74 C2
Ferizli TR 118 B5
Ferla I 109 B3
Ferlach A 73 B4
Ferleiten A 72 A2
Fermil P 87 C3
Fermo I 82 C2
Fermoselle E 87 C4
Fermoy IRL 20 B3
Fernancabellero E 94 C3
Fernán Nuñéz E 100 B1
Fernán Peréz E 101 C3
Fernão Ferro P 92 C1
Fernay-Voltaire F 69 B6
Ferndown GB 29 C6
Ferness GB 23 D5
Fernhurst GB 31 C3
Ferns IRL 21 B5
Ferpécle CH 70 B2
Ferrals-les-Corbières F 78 C1
Ferrandina I 104 C2
Ferrara I 81 B5
Ferrara di Monte Baldo I 71 C5
Ferreira E 86 A3
Ferreira do Alentejo P 98 A2
Ferreira do Zêzere P 92 B2
Ferreras de Abajo E 87 C4
Ferreras de Arriba E 87 C4
Ferreries E 97 B4
Ferreruela E 90 B1
Ferreruela de Tabara E 87 C4
Ferret CH 70 C2
Ferrette F 70 A2
Ferriere I 80 B3
Ferrière-la-Grande F 49 C4
Ferrières
Hautes-Pyrénées F 76 C2
Loiret F 58 B3
Oise F 58 A3
Ferrières-sur-Sichon F 68 B3
Ferrol E 86 A2
Ferryhill GB 27 A4
Fertőrákos H 64 C2
Fertőszentmiklós H 64 C2
Ferwerd NL 42 B2
Festieux F 59 A4
Festøy N 114 E3
Festvåg N 112 E3
Feteşti RO 11 D9
Fethard
Tipperary IRL 21 B4
Wexford IRL 21 B5
Fethiye TR 119 F4
Fetsund N 34 C3
Fettercairn GB 25 B5
Feucht D 62 A2
Feuchtwangen D 61 A6
Feudingen D 50 C4
Feuges F 59 B5
Feuquières F 58 A2
Feurs F 69 C4
Fevik N 33 D5
Ffestiniog GB 26 C2
Fiamignano I 102 A6
Fiano I 70 C2
Ficarazzi I 108 A2
Ficarolo I 81 B5
Fichtelberg D 52 C1
Ficulle I 82 D1
Fidenza I 81 B4
Fidjeland N 33 D3
Fieberbrunn A 72 A2
Fier AL 105 C5
Fiera di Primiero I 72 B1
Fierzë AL 105 A6
Fiesch CH 70 B3
Fiesso Umbertiano I 81 B5
Figari F 102 B2
Figeac F 77 B5
Figeholm S 40 B6
Figgjo N 33 D2
Figline Valdarno I 81 C5
Figols E 90 A3
Figueira da Foz P 92 A2
Figueira de Castelo Rodrigo P 87 D4
Figueira dos Caveleiros P 98 A2
Figueiredo P 92 B3
Figueiredo de Alva P 87 D3
Figueiródos Vinhos P 92 B2
Figueres E 91 A5
Figueroles E 96 A2
Figueruela de Arriba E 87 C4
Filadélfia I 106 C3
Fil'akovo SK 65 B5
Filderstadt D 61 B5
Filey GB 27 A5
Filiaşi RO 11 D7
Filiates GR 116 C2
Filiatra GR 117 E3
Filipstad S 35 C6
Filisur CH 71 B4
Fillan N 114 D5
Filotio GR 117 E7
Filottrano I 82 C2
Filskov DK 39 D2
Filton GB 29 B5
Filtvet N 35 C2
Filzmoos A 72 A3
Finale Emilia I 81 B5
Finale Ligure I 80 B2
Fiñana E 101 B3
Finby FIN 36 B7
Fincham GB 30 B4
Finchingfield GB 31 C4
Findhorn GB 23 D5
Findochty GB 23 D6
Finike TR 119 F5
Finkenberg A 72 A1
Finnea IRL 19 C4
Finneidfjord N 115 A10
Finnerödja S 37 D1
Finnskog N 34 B4
Finnsnes N 112 C7
Finntorp S 35 C4
Finócchio I 102 B5
Finsjö S 40 B6
Finsland N 33 D4
Finspång S 37 D2
Finsterwalde D 53 B3
Finsterwolde NL 43 B4
Finstown GB 23 B5
Fintona GB 19 B4
Fionnphort GB 24 B1
Fiorenzuola d'Arda I 81 B3
Firenze = Florence I 81 C5
Firenzuola I 81 B5
Firmi F 77 B5
Firminy F 69 C4
Firmo I 106 B3
Fischamend Markt A 64 B2
Fischbach
A 73 A5
D 60 A3
Fischbeck D 44 C4
Fischen D 71 A5
Fishbourne GB 31 D2
Fishguard GB 28 B3
Fiskardo GR 116 D2
Fiskebäckskil S 35 D3
Fiskebøl N 112 D3
Fismes F 59 A4
Fisterra E 86 B1
Fitero E 89 B5
Fitjar N 32 C2
Fiuggi I 102 B6
Fiumata I 102 A6
Fiumefreddo Brúzio I 106 B3
Fiumefreddo di Sicília I 109 B4
Fiumicino I 102 B5
Fivemiletown GB 19 B4
Fivizzano I 81 B4
Fjälkinge S 41 C4
Fjällåsen S 112 E9
Fjällbacka S 35 D3
Fjæra N 32 C3
Fjärdhundra S 36 C3
Fjellerup DK 38 C3
Fjerritslev DK 38 B2
Fjordgard N 112 C6
Fjugesta S 37 C1
Flå N 32 B6
Flåbygd N 33 C5
Flaça E 91 A5
Flace F 69 B4
Fladungen D 51 C6
Flaine F 70 B1
Flaka FIN 36 B7
Flåm N 32 B4
Flamatt CH 70 B2
Flamborough GB 27 A5

Flammersfeld D 50 C3
Flassans-sur-Issole F 79 C5
Flatdal N 33 C5
Flatebø N 32 B3
Flateby N 34 C3
Flateland N 33 C4
Flateyri IS 111 A2
Flatøydegard N 32 B6
Flatråker N 32 C2
Flattach A 72 B3
Flatvarp S 37 E3
Flauenskjold DK 38 B3
Flavigny-sur-Moselle F . .60 B2
Flavy-le-Martel F 59 A4
Flawil CH 71 A4
Flayosc F 79 C5
Flechtingen D 44 C3
Fleckeby D 44 A1
Fleet GB 31 C3
Fleetmark D 44 C3
Fleetwood GB 26 B2
Flehingen D 61 A4
Flekke N 32 A2
Flekkefjord N 33 D3
Flen S 37 D3
Flensburg D 39 E2
Fleringe S 37 E5
Flerohopp S 40 C5
Flers F 57 B5
Flesberg N 32 C6
Fleurance F 77 C3
Fleuré F 67 B5
Fleurier CH 69 B6
Fleurus B 49 C5
Fleury
  Hérault F 78 C2
  Yonne F 59 C4
Fleury-les-Aubrais F . .58 C2
Fleury-sur-Andelle F . .58 A2
Fleury-sur-Orne F 57 A5
Flieden D 51 C5
Flimby GB 26 A2
Flims CH 71 B4
Flines-lèz-Raches F . .49 C4
Flint GB 26 B2
Flirey F 60 B1
Flirsch A 71 A5
Flisa N 34 B4
Flisby S 40 B4
Fliseryd S 40 B6
Flix E 90 B3
Flixecourt F 48 C3
Flize F 59 A5
Flobecq B 49 C4
Floby S 35 D5
Floda S 40 B2
Flodden GB 25 C5
Flogny-la-Chapelle F . .59 C4
Flöha D 52 C3
Flonheim D 61 A4
Florac F 78 B2
Floreffe B 49 C5
Florence = Firenze I . .81 C5
Florennes B 49 C5
Florensac F 78 C2
Florentin F 77 C5
Florenville B 59 A6
Flores de Avila E 94 B1
Floresta I 109 B3
Floreşti MD 11 C10
Floridia I 109 B4
Florina GR 116 B3
Florø N 114 F2
Flörsheim D 51 C4
Floss D 62 A3
Fluberg N 34 B2
Flúðir IS 111 C5
Flühli CH 70 B3
Flumet F 69 C6
Fluminimaggiore I . . .110 C1
Flums CH 71 A4
Flyeryd S 41 C5
Flygsfors S 40 C5
Foča BIH 84 C3
Foga TR 118 D1
Fochabers GB 23 D5
Focşani RO 11 D9
Foel GB 26 C2
Foeni RO 75 C5
Fogdö S 37 C3
Fóggia I 104 B1
Foglianise I 103 B7
Föglö FIN 36 B7
Fohnsdorf A 73 A4
Foiano della Chiana I . .81 C6
Foix F 77 D4
Fojnica
  BIH 84 C2
  BIH 84 C3
Fokino RUS 7 E13
Fokstua N 114 E6
Földeák H 75 B5
Foldereid N 114 C9
Földes H 75 A6
Folegandros GR 117 F6
Folelli F 102 A2
Folgaria I 71 C6
Folgosinho P 92 A3
Folgoso de la Ribera E . .86 B4
Folgoso do Courel E. .86 B3
Foligno I 82 D1
Folkärna S 36 B3
Folkestad N 114 E3
Folkestone GB 31 C5
Follafoss N 114 D8
Folldal N 114 E6
Follebu N 34 A2
Follina I 72 C2
Föllinge S 115 D11
Follónica I 81 D4
Fölsbyn S 35 C4
Foncebadón E 86 B4
Foncine-le-Bas F 69 B6
Fondevila E 87 C2
Fondi I 103 B6
Fondo I 71 B6
Fonelas E 100 B2
Fonfría
  Teruel E 90 C1
  Zamora E 87 C4
Fonnes N 32 B1
Fonni I 110 B2
Fontaine F 59 B5
Fontaine-Française F . .69 A5
Fontaine de Vaucluse F . .79 C4
Fontaine-le-Dun F . . .58 A1
Fontan F 80 B1
Fontanarejo E 94 C2
Fontane I 80 B1
Fontanélice I 81 B5
Fontanières F 68 B2
Fontanosas E 100 A1
Fonteblanda I 102 A4
Fontenay-le-Comte F . .66 B4
Fontenay-Trésigny F . .59 B3
Fontevraud-l'Abbaye F . .67 A5
Fontiveros E 94 B2
Fontoy F 60 A1
Fontpédrouse F 91 A5
Font-Romeu F 91 A5
Fontstown IRL 21 A5
Fonyód H 74 B2
Fonz E 90 A3
Fónzaso I 72 B1
Fóppolo I 71 B4
Föra S 41 B6
Forbach
  D 61 B4
  F 60 A2
Forcall E 90 C2
Forcalquier F 79 C4
Forcarei E 86 B2
Forchheim D 62 A2
Forchtenau A 64 C2
Forchtenberg D 61 A5
Ford GB 24 B2

Førde
  Hordaland N 33 C2
  Sogn og Fjordane N . 32 A2
Fördersteð D 52 B1
Førdesfjorden N 33 C2
Fordham GB 30 B4
Fordingbridge GB . . .29 C6
Fordon PL 47 B4
Fordongiánus I 110 C1
Forenza I 104 C1
Foresta di Búrgos I . . .110 B1
Forfar GB 25 B5
Forges-les-Eaux F . . .58 A2
Foria I 106 A2
Forjães P 87 C2
Førland N 33 D4
Forl ì I 81 B6
Forlimpopoli I 82 B1
Formazza I 70 B3
Formby GB 26 B2
Formerie F 58 A2
Fórmia I 103 B6
Formigine I 81 B4
Formigliana I 70 C3
Formiguères F 91 A5
Formiultx E 97 D2
Fornás a S 37 D2
Fornelli I 110 B1
Fornells E 97 A4
Fornelos de Montes E . .87 B2
Fornes E 100 C2
Forneset N 112 C8
Forni Avoltri I 72 B2
Forni di Sopra I 72 B2
Forni di Sotto I 72 B2
Forno
  Piemonte I 70 C3
  Piemonte I 79 A6
Forno Alpi-Gráie I . . .70 C2
Forno di Zoldo I 72 B2
Fornovo di Taro I 81 B4
Foros do Arrão P 92 B2
Forráskút H 75 B4
Forres GB 23 D5
Forríolo E 87 B3
Fors S 36 B3
Forsand N 33 D3
Forsbacka S 36 B3
Forserum S 40 B4
Forshaga S 35 C5
Forsheda S 40 B3
Forsinain GB 23 C5
Forslev DK 39 D4
Förslöv S 41 C2
Forsmark
  Uppsala S 36 B5
  Västerbotten S 115 B12
Forsmo S 115 D14
Forsnäs S 115 A15
Forsnes N 114 D5
Forssa FIN 3 F25
Forssjöbruk S 37 D3
Forst D 53 B4
Forsvik S 37 D1
Fortanete E 90 C2
Fort Augustus GB . . .22 D4
Forte dei Marmi I 81 C4
Fortezza I 72 B1
Forth GB 25 C4
Fort-Mahon-Plage F . .48 C2
Fortrie GB 23 D6
Fortrose GB 23 D4
Fortun N 32 A4
Fortuna E 101 A4
Fortuneswell GB 29 C5
Fort William GB 24 B2
Forvik N 115 B9
Fos F 77 D3
Fosdinovo I 81 B4
Fossa I 103 A7
Fossacésia I 103 A7
Fossano I 80 B1
Fossato di Vico I 82 C1
Fossbakken N 112 D6
Fosse-la-Ville B 49 C5
Fossombrone I 82 C1
Fos-sur-Mer F 78 C3
Fot H 75 A4
Fouchères F 59 B5
Fouesnant F 56 C1
Foug F 60 B1
Fougères F 57 B4
Fougerolles F 60 C2
Foulain F 59 B6
Fountainhall GB 25 C5
Fouras F 66 C3
Fourchambault F 68 A3
Fourmies F 49 C5
Fourna GR 116 C3
Fournels F 78 B2
Fourni GR 119 E1
Fournols F 68 C3
Fourques F 91 A5
Fourquevaux F 77 C4
Fours F 68 B3
Fowey GB 28 C3
Foxdale GB 26 A1
Foxford IRL 18 C2
Foyers GB 23 D4
Foynes IRL 20 B2
Foz E 86 A3
Foz do Arelho P 92 B1
Foz do Giraldo P 92 B3
Frabosa Soprana I . . .80 B1
Frades da Sierra E . . .93 A5
Fraga E 90 B3
Fragagnano I 104 C3
Frailes E 100 B2
Fraire B 49 C5
Fraize F 60 B2
Framlingham GB 30 B5
Frammersbach D 51 C5
Framnes N 35 C2
França P 87 C4
Francaltroff F 60 B2
Francavilla al Mare I . .103 A7
Francavilla di Sicília I . .109 B4
Francavilla Fontana I . .104 C3
Francavilla in Sinni I . .106 A3
Francescas F 77 B3
Franco P 87 C3
Francofonte I 109 B3
Francos E 89 C3
Frändefors S 35 D4
Franeker NL 42 B2
Frangy F 69 B5
Frankenau D 51 B4
Frankenberg
  Hessen D 51 B4
  Sachsen D 52 C3
Frankenburg A 63 B4
Frankenfels A 63 C6
Frankenmarkt A 63 C4
Frankenthal D 61 A4
Frankfurt
  Brandenburg D 45 C6
  Hessen D 51 C4
Frankowo PL 47 A6
Frankrike S 115 D10
Fränsta S 115 E13
František ovy Lázně CZ . .52 C2
Franzburg D 45 A4
Frascati I 102 B5
Frasdorf D 62 C3
Fraserburgh GB 23 D6
Frashër AL 116 B2
Frasne F 69 B6
Frasnes-lez-Anvaing F . .49 C4
Frasso Telésino I 103 B7
Frastanz A 71 A4
Fratel P 92 B3
Fratta Todina I 82 D1
Frauenau D 63 B4

Frauenfeld CH 70 A3
Frauenkirchen A 64 C2
Frauenstein D 52 C3
Frauental A 73 B5
Frayssinet F 77 B4
Frayssinet-le-Gélat F . .77 B4
Frechas P 87 C3
Frechen D 50 C2
Frechilla E 88 B2
Freckenhorst D 50 B3
Fredeburg D 50 B4
Fredelsloh D 51 B5
Fredeng N 34 B2
Fredensborg DK 41 D2
Frederícia DK 39 D2
Frederiks DK 39 C2
Frederikshavn DK 38 B3
Frederikssund DK 39 D5
Frederiksværk DK 39 D5
Fredrika S 115 C15
Fredriksberg S 36 B6
Fredriksdal S 40 B4
Fredrikstad N 35 C2
Fregenal de la Sierra E . .99 A4
Fregene I 102 B5
Freiberg D 52 C3
Freiburg
  Baden-Württemberg D . .60 C3
  Niedersachsen D . . .43 B6
Freienhagen D 51 B5
Freienhufen D 53 B3
Freiensteinau D 51 C5
Freihung D 62 A2
Freilassing D 62 C3
Freisen D 60 A3
Freising D 62 B2
Freistadt A 63 B5
Freital D 52 B3
Freixedas P 93 A3
Freixo de Espada à Cinta P . .87 C4
Fréjus F 79 C5
Frémdingen D 61 B6
Frenštát pod Radhoštěm CZ . .64 A4
Freren D 43 C4
Freshford IRL 21 B4
Freshwater GB 31 D2
Fresnay-sur-Sarthe F . 57 B6
Fresne-St Mamès F . .69 A5
Fresno Alhándiga E . .94 B1
Fresno de Ebro E 90 B2
Fresno de la Ribera E . .88 C1
Fresno de la Vega E . . .88 B1
Fresno de Sayago E . .87 C5
Fresnoy-Folny F 58 A2
Fresnoy-le-Grand F . . .59 A4
Fressenville F 48 C2
Fresvik N 32 A3
Fréteval F 58 C2
Fretigney F 69 A5
Freudenberg
  Baden-Württemberg D . .61 A5
  Nordrhein-Westfalen D . .50 C3
Freudenstadt D 61 B4
Freux B 49 D6
Frévent F 48 C3
Freyburg D 52 B1
Freyenstein D 44 B4
Freyming-Merlebach F . .60 A2
Freystadt D 62 A2
Freyung D 63 B4
Frías de Albarracin E . .95 B5
Fribourg CH 70 B2
Frick CH 70 A3
Fridafors S 41 C4
Fridaythorpe GB 27 A5
Friedberg
  Bayern D 62 B1
  Hessen D 51 C4
Friedeburg D 43 B4
Friedewald D 51 C5
Friedland
  Brandenburg D 53 A4
  Mecklenburg-Vorpommern D . .45 B5
  Niedersachsen D . . .51 B5
Friedrichroda D 51 C6
Friedrichsdorf D 51 C4
Friedrichshafen D 61 C5
Friedrichskoog D 43 A5
Friedrichstadt D 43 A6
Friedrichswalde D 45 B5
Friesach A 73 B4
Friesack D 45 C4
Friesenheim D 60 B3
Friesoythe D 43 B4
Friggesund S 115 F13
Frigiliana E 100 C2
Frihetsli N 112 D8
Frillesås S 40 B2
Frinnaryd S 40 B4
Frinton-on-Sea GB . . .31 C5
Friockheim GB 25 B5
Friol E 86 A3
Fristad S 40 B2
Fritsla S 40 B2
Frittzlar D 51 B5
Frizington GB 26 A2
Frödinge S 40 B6
Froges F 69 C5
Frohburg D 52 B2
Frohnhausen D 51 C4
Frohnleiten A 73 A5
Froissy F 58 A3
Frombork PL 47 A5
Frome GB 29 B5
Frómista E 88 B2
Fröndenberg D 50 B3
Fronsac F 76 B2
Front I 70 C2
Fronteira P 92 B3
Frontenay-Rohan-Rohan F . .67 B4
Frontenhausen D 62 B3
Frontignan F 78 C2
Fronton F 77 C4
Fröseke S 40 C5
Frosinone I 103 B6
Frosolone I 103 B7
Frosta N 114 D7
Frøstrup DK 38 B1
Frosunda S 37 C5
Frouard F 60 B2
Frøyset N 32 B2
Frøyrland N 33 D3

Fuentealbilla E 96 B1
Fuente al Olmo de Iscar E . .88 C2
Fuentecén E 88 C3
Fuente Dé E 88 A2
Fuente de Cantos E . .99 A4
Fuente de Arco E 99 A5
Fuente del Conde E . .100 B1
Fuente del Maestre E . .93 C4
Fuente de Santa Cruz E . .94 A2
Fuente el Fresno E . . .94 C3
Fuente el Saz de Jarama E . .95 B3
Fuente el Sol E 94 A2
Fuenteguinaldo E 93 A4
Fuentelapeña E 88 C1
Fuentelcésped E 89 C3
Fuentelespino de Haro E . .95 C4
Fuentelespino de Moya E . .96 B1
Fuentenovilla E 95 B3
Fuente Obejuna E 99 A5
Fuente Palmera E 99 B5
Fuentepelayo E 94 A2
Fuentepinilla E 89 C4
Fuenterroble de Salvatierra E . .93 A5
Fuenterrobles E 96 B1
Fuentes E 95 C4
Fuentesaúco E 88 C2
Fuentesaúco E 94 A1
Fuentes de Andalucía E . .99 B5
Fuentes de Ebro E . . .90 B2
Fuentes de Jiloca E . .89 C5
Fuentes de la Alcarria E . .95 B4
Fuentes de León E . . .99 A4
Fuentes de Nava E . . .88 B2
Fuentes de Oñoro E . .93 A4
Fuentes de Ropel E . .88 B1
Fuentespalda E 90 C3
Fuentespina E 89 C3
Fuente-Tójar E 100 B1
Fuente Vaqueros E . .100 B2
Fuentidueña E 88 C3
Fuentidueña de Tajo E . .95 B3
Fuerte del Rey E 100 B2
Fügen A 72 A1
Fuglebjerg DK 39 D4
Fuglevik N 35 C2
Fuhrberg D 44 C1
Fulda D 51 C5
Fulgatore I 108 B1
Fully CH 70 B2
Fulnek CZ 64 A3
Fülöpszállás H 75 B4
Fulpmes A 71 A6
Fulunäs S 34 A5
Fumay F 49 D5
Fumel F 77 B3
Funäsdalen S 115 E9
Fundão P 92 A3
Fundrup DK 38 B3
Funzie GB 22 A8
Furadouro P 87 D2
Fürstenau D 43 C4
Furtei I 110 C2
Furth im Wald D 62 A3
Furtwangen D 61 B4
Furuby S 40 C5
Furudal S 36 A2
Furuflaten N 112 C9
Furulund S 41 D3
Furusjö S 40 B3
Fusa N 32 B2
Fuscaldo I 106 B3
Fusch an der Grossglocknerstrasse A . .72 A2
Fushë Arrëz AL 105 A6
Fushë-Krujë AL 105 B5
Fusina I 72 C2
Fusio CH 70 B3
Füssen D 62 C1
Fustiñana E 89 B5
Futog SRB 75 C4
Futrikelv N 112 C8
Füzesabony H 65 C6
Füzesgyarmat H 75 A6
Fužine HR 73 C4
Fylaxak A 73 B4
Fylling s S 40 C2
Fynshav DK 39 E2
Fyresdal N 33 C5

G

Gaaldorf A 73 A4
Gabaldón E 95 C5
Gabarret F 76 C3
Gabčíkovo SK 64 C3
Gabin PL 47 C5
Gabriac F 78 B1
Gabrovo BG 11 E8
Gaby I 70 C2
Gacé F 58 B1
Gacko BIH 84 C3
Gäddede S 115 C11
Gadebusch D 44 B3
Gadmen CH 70 B3
Gádor E 101 C3
Gádoros H 75 B5
Gael F 57 B3
Gǽrum DK 38 B3
Găești RO 11 D8
Gaeta I 103 B6
Gaflenz A 63 C5
Gagarin RUS 7 D13
Gaggenau D 61 B4
Gaglianico I 70 C3
Gagliano Castelferrato I . .109 B3
Gagliano del Capo I . .107 B5
Gagnet S 36 B2
Gaibanella I 81 B5
Gaildorf D 61 B5
Gaillac F 77 C4
Gaillefontaine F 58 A2
Gaillon F 58 A2
Gainsborough GB 27 B5
Gairloch GB 22 D3
Gairlochy GB 24 B3
Gáiro I 110 C2
Gaj
  HR 74 C2
  SRB 85 B6
Gaja-la-Selve F 77 C4
Gajanejos E 95 B4
Gajary SK 64 B2
Ga|dobra SRB 75 C4
Galan F 77 C3
Galanta SK 64 B3
Galapagar E 94 B2
Galápagos E 95 B3
Galaroza E 99 B4
Galashiels GB 25 C5
Galatas GR 117 E5
Galati RO 11 D10
Galatina I 107 A5
Galatista GR 116 B5
Galátone I 107 A5
Galaxidi GR 117 D4
Galdakao E 89 A4
Galeata I 81 C5
Galende E 87 B4
Galera E 101 B3
Galéria F 102 A1
Galgamácsa H 65 C5

Galgon F 76 B2
Galinduste E 93 A5
Galiniporni CY 120 A3
Galisteo E 93 B4
Galizes P 92 A3
Galków PL 55 B4
Gallarate I 70 C3
Gallardon F 58 B2
Gallareta E 94 A2
Galleno I 81 C4
Galliate I 70 C3
Gallicano I 81 B4
Gallipoli = Gelibolu TR . .118 B1
Gallípoli I 107 A4
Gällivare S 112 E9
Gallizien A 73 B4
Gallneukirchen A 63 B5
Gällö S 115 E12
Gallocanta E 95 B5
Gällstad S 40 B3
Gallur E 90 B1
Galmisdale GB 24 B1
Galmpton GB 29 C4
Galston GB 24 C3
Galtelli I 110 B2
Galten DK 39 C2
Galtür A 71 B5
Galve de Sorbe E 95 A3
Galveias P 92 B2
Galway IRL 20 A2
Gamaches F 48 D2
Gámbara I 71 C5
Gambárie I 106 C2
Gambassi Terme I 81 C4
Gambatesa I 103 B7
Gambolò I 70 C3
Gaming A 63 C6
Gamla Uppsala S 36 C4
Gamleby S 40 B6
Gammelgarn S 37 E5
Gammelstad S 3 D25
Gammertingen D 61 B5
Gams CH 71 A4
Gamvik
  Finnmark N 113 A17
  Finnmark N 113 B11
Gan F 76 C2
Gáname F 87 C4
Ganda di Martello I . . .71 B5
Gandarela P 87 C2
Ganddal N 33 D2
Ganderkesee D 43 B5
Gandesa E 90 B3
Gandía E 96 C2
Gandino I 71 C4
Gandrup DK 38 B3
Ganges F 78 C2
Gånghester S 40 B3
Gangi I 109 B3
Gangkofen D 62 B3
Gannat F 68 B3
Gannay-sur-Loire F . . .68 B3
Gänserndorf A 64 B2
Ganzlin D 44 B4
Gap F 79 B5
Gara H 75 B4
Garaballa E 96 B1
Garaguso I 104 C2
Garbayuela E 94 C1
Garbhallt GB 24 B2
Garbsen D 43 C6
Garching D 62 B3
Garciaz E 93 B5
Garcihernández E 94 B1
Garcillán E 94 B2
Garcisobaco E 99 C5
Garda I 71 C5
Gardanne F 79 C4
Gårdås S 34 B5
Gårdby S 41 C6
Gardeja PL 47 B4
Gardelegen D 44 C3
Gardermoen N 34 B3
Gardíki GR 116 D3
Garding D 43 A5
Gardone Riviera I 71 C5
Gardone Val Trómpia I . .71 C5
Gárdony H 74 A3
Gardouch F 77 C4
Gårdsjö S 37 D1
Gårdskär S 36 B4
Gards Köpinge S 41 D4
Garein F 76 B2
Garelochhead GB 24 B3
Garéoult F 79 C4
Gares = Puente la Reina E . .89 B5
Garešnica HR 74 C1
Garéssio I 80 B2
Garforth GB 27 B4
Gargaliani GR 117 E3
Gargaligas E 93 B5
Gargallo E 90 C2
Garganta la Olla E . . .93 A5
Gargantiel E 100 A1
Gargellen A 71 A4
Gargilesse-Dampierre F . .67 B6
Gargnano I 71 C5
Gargnäs S 115 B14
Gárgoles de Abajo E . .95 B4
Gargrave GB 26 B3
Garitz D 52 B2
Garlasco I 70 C3
Garlieston GB 24 D3
Garlin F 76 C2
Garlitos E 94 D1
Garmisch-Partenkirchen D . .71 A6
Garnat-sur-Engièvre F . .68 B3
Garpenberg S 36 B3
Garphyttan S 37 C1
Garray E 89 C4
Garrel D 43 C5
Garriguella E 91 A6
Garrison GB 18 B3
Garrovillas E 93 B4
Garrucha E 101 B4
Gars-am-Kamp A 63 B6
Garsås S 36 B1
Garsdale Head GB . . .26 A3
Gärsnäs S 41 D4
Garstang GB 26 B3
Gartow D 44 B3
Gartz D 45 B6
Gǽrum DK 38 B3
Garvagh GB 19 B5
Garváo P 98 B2
Garwolin PL 55 B6
Garz D 45 A5
Gàsawa PL 46 C3
Gåsborn S 34 C6
Gaschurn A 71 A4
Gascueña E 95 B4
Gasny F 58 A2
Gasocin PL 47 C6
Gastes F 76 B1
Gastouni GR 117 E3
Gastouri GR 116 C1
Gata
  E 93 A4
  HR 83 C5
Gata de Gorgos E 96 C3
Gatchina RUS 7 B11
Gátova E 96 B2

Gattendorf A 64 B2
Gatteo a Mare I 82 B1
Gattinara I 70 C3
Gattorna I 80 B3
Gaucín E 99 C5
Gaugeac F 33 C3
Gaulstad N 114 D9
Gaupne N 32 A4
Gautefall N 33 C5
Gauting D 62 B2
Gauto S 115 A13
Gava E 91 B5
Gavardo I 71 C5
Gavarnie F 76 D2
Gavi I 80 B2
Gavião P 92 B3
Gavirate I 70 C3
Gävle S 36 B4
Gavoi I 110 B2
Gavorrano I 81 D4
Gavray F 57 B4
Gavrio GR 117 E6
Gâvros GR 116 B3
Gavsele S 115 C14
Gaworzyce PL 53 B5
Gawroniec PL 46 B2
Gaydon GB 30 B2
Gayton GB 30 B4
Gazipaşa TR 119 F7
Gazoldo degli Ippoliti I . .71 C5
Gazzuolo I 81 A4
Gbelce SK 65 C4
Gdánsk PL 47 A4
Gdinj HR 84 C1
Gdov RUS 7 B9
Gdów PL 65 A6
Gdynia PL 47 A4
Gea de Albarracín E . .95 B5
Geary GB 22 D2
Geaune F 76 C2
Gebesee D 51 B6
Gebiz TR 119 E5
Gebze TR 118 B4
Gedern D 51 C5
Gedinne B 49 D5
Gediz TR 118 D4
Gèdre F 76 D3
Gedser DK 44 A3
Gedsted DK 38 C2
Geel B 49 B5
Geesthacht D 44 B2
Geetbets B 49 C6
Gefell D 52 C1
Gehrden D 51 A5
Gehren D 52 C1
Geilenkirchen D 50 C2
Geilo N 32 B5
Geinsheim D 61 A4
Geisa D 51 C5
Geiselhöring D 62 B3
Geiselwind D 61 A6
Geisenfeld D 62 B2
Geisenhausen D 62 B3
Geisenheim D 50 D4
Geising D 53 C3
Geisingen D 61 C4
Geislingen D 61 B5
Geistthal A 73 A5
Geiterygghytta N 32 B4
Geithain D 52 B2
Geithus N 34 C1
Gela I 109 B3
Geldermalsen NL 49 B6
Geldern D 50 B2
Geldrop NL 49 B6
Geldwil CH 50 C1
Gelemic TR 118 C4
Gelendost TR 119 D6
Gelibolu = Gallipoli TR . .118 B1
Gelida E 91 B4
Gelnhausen D 51 C5
Gelnica SK 65 B6
Gelsa E 90 B2
Gelse H 74 B1
Gelsenkirchen D 50 B3
Gelsted DK 39 D2
Geltendorf D 62 B2
Gelterkinden CH 70 A2
Gelting D 39 E2
Gelu RO 75 B6
Gelves E 99 B4
Gembloux B 49 C5
Gemeaux F 69 A5
Gémenos F 79 C4
Gemerská Poloma SK . .65 B6
Gemerská Ves SK 65 B6
Gemert NL 50 B1
Gemla S 40 C4
Gemlik TR 118 B4
Gemmenich B 50 C1
Gemona del Friuli I . . .72 B2
Gémozac F 67 C4
Gemund D 50 C2
Gemünden
  Bayern D 51 C5
  Hessen D 51 B4
  Rheinland-Pfalz D . .60 A3
Genappe B 49 C5
Génave E 101 A3
Genazzano I 102 B5
Gençay F 67 B5
Gendringen NL 50 B2
Genelard F 69 B4
Genemuiden NL 42 C3
Generalski Stol HR . . .73 C5
Geneva = Genève CH . .69 B6
Genevad S 40 C3
Genève = Geneva CH . .69 B6
Geneviéres F 60 C1
Gengenbach D 61 B4
Genillé F 67 A6
Genk B 49 C6
Genlis F 69 A5
Gennep NL 50 B1
Genner DK 39 D2
Gennes F 67 A4
Genoa = Génova I 80 B2
Genola I 80 B1
Génova = Genoa I 80 B2
Genowefa PL 54 A3
Gensingen D 60 A3
Gent = Ghent B 49 B4
Genthin D 44 C4
Gentioux F 68 C1
Genzano di Lucánia I . .104 C2
Genzano di Roma I . .102 B5
Georgenthal D 51 C6
Georgsmarienhütte D . .50 A4
Gera D 52 C2
Geraards-bergen B . .106 C3
Geraci Sículo I 109 B3
Geráki GR 117 F4
Gérardmer F 60 B2
Geras A 63 B6
Gerbéviller F 60 B2
Gerbini I 109 B3
Gerbstedt D 52 B1
Gerði IS 111 D7
Gerede TR 118 C7
Gerena E 99 B4
Geretsried D 62 C2
Gérgal E 101 B3
Gergy F 69 B4
Gerindote E 94 C2
Gerjen H 74 B3
Gerlos A 72 A2
Germay F 60 B1
Germencik TR 119 E2
Germering D 62 B2
Germersheim D 61 A4
Gernika-Lumo E 89 A4
Gernrode D 52 B1
Gernsbach D 61 B4
Gernsheim D 61 A4

Geroda D 51 C5
Gerola Alta I 71 B4
Geroldsgrün D 52 C1
Gerolsbach D 62 B2
Gerolstein D 50 C2
Gerolzhofen D 61 A6
Gerpinnes B 49 C5
Gerrards Cross 31 C3
Gersfeld D 51 C5
Gerstetten D 61 B6
Gersthofen D 62 B1
Gerstungen D 51 C6
Gerswalde D 45 B5
Gerzat F 68 C3
Gerze TR 16 A7
Gerzen D 62 B3
Gescher D 50 B3
Geseke D 51 B4
Geslau D 61 A6
Gespunsart F 59 A5
Gesté F 66 A3
Gestorf D 51 A5
Gesualda I 103 C8
Gesunda S 36 B1
Geta FIN 36 B6
Getafe E 94 B3
Getinge S 40 C2
Getxo E 89 A4
Geversdorf D 43 B6
Gevgelija MK 116 A4
Gevrey-Chambertin F . .69 A4
Gex F 69 B6
Gey D 50 C2
Geyikli TR 118 C1
Geysir IS 111 C5
Gevre TR 118 B5
Gföhl A 63 B6
Ghedi I 71 C5
Ghent = Gent B 49 B4
Gheorgheni RO 11 C8
Ghigo I 79 B6
Ghilarza I 110 B1
Ghisonaccia F 102 A2
Ghisoni F 102 A2
Gialtra GR 116 D4
Gialova GR 117 E3
Gianitsa GR 116 B4
Giardinetto Vécchio I . .103 B8
Giardini Naxos I 109 B4
Giarratana I 109 B3
Giarre I 109 B4
Giat F 68 C2
Giaveno I 80 A1
Giazza I 71 C6
Giba I 110 C1
Gibellina Nuova I 108 B1
Gibostad N 112 C7
Gibraléon E 99 B4
Gibraltar GBZ 99 C5
Gic H 74 A2
Gideå S 115 D16
Gideåkroken S 115 C14
Gidle PL 55 B4
Giebelstadt D 61 A5
Gieboldehausen D . . .51 B6
Gielniów PL 55 B5
Gielow D 45 B4
Gien F 58 C3
Giengen D 61 B6
Giens F 79 C5
Giera RO 75 C5
Gieselwerder D 51 B5
Giessen D 51 C4
Gieten NL 42 B3
Giethoorn NL 42 C3
Giffaumont-Champaubert F . .59 B5
Gifford GB 25 C5
Gifhorn D 44 C2
Gige H 74 B2
Giglio Porto I 102 A3
Gignod I 70 C2
Gijón = Xixón E 88 A1
Gilena E 100 B1
Gilford GB 19 B5
Gillberga S 35 C4
Gilleleje DK 41 C2
Gilley GB 69 A6
Gilley-sur-Loire F 68 B3
Gillingham
  Dorset GB 29 B5
  Medway GB 31 C4
Gilocourt F 59 A3
Gilserberg D 51 C5
Gilsland GB 25 D5
Gilze NL 49 B5
Gimåt S 115 D15
Gimo S 36 B5
Gimont F 77 C3
Ginasservis F 79 C4
Gingelom B 49 C6
Gingst D 45 A5
Ginosa I 104 C2
Ginzling A 72 A1
Giões P 98 B3
Gióia dei Marsi I 103 B6
Gióia del Colle I 104 C2
Gióia Sannitica I 103 B7
Gióia Táuro I 106 C2
Gioiosa Iónica I 106 C3
Gioiosa Marea I 109 A3
Giosla GB 22 C2
Giovinazzo I 104 B2
Girifalco I 106 C3
Giromagny F 60 C2
Girona E 91 B5
Gironcourt-sur-Vraine F . .60 B1
Gironella E 91 A4
Gironville-sous-les-Côtes F . .60 B1
Girvan GB 24 C3
Gislaved S 40 B3
Gislev DK 39 D3
Gisors F 58 A2
Gissi I 103 A7
Gistad S 37 D2
Gistel B 48 B3
Gistrup DK 38 C3
Giswil CH 70 B3
Githio GR 117 F4
Giugliano in Campania I . .103 C7
Giulianova I 82 D2
Giulvăz RO 75 C5
Giurgiu RO 11 E8
Give DK 39 D2
Givet F 49 C5
Givors F 69 C4
Givry
  B 49 C5
  F 69 B4
Givry-en-Argonne F . . .59 B5
Givskud DK 39 D2
Gizałki PL 54 A2
Gizeux F 67 A5
Giźycko PL 47 A6
Gizzeria I 106 C3
Gizzeria Lido I 106 C3
Gjedved DK 39 D2
Gjegjan AL 105 A6
Gjendesheim N 32 A5
Gjerde N 32 B3
Gjerlev DK 38 C3
Gjermundshamn N . . .32 B2
Gjerrild DK 38 C3
Gjerstad N 33 D5
Gjesås N 34 B4
Gjesvær N 113 A14
Gjirokastër AL 116 B2
Gjøfjell N 35 C2
Gjøl DK 38 B2
Gjøra N 114 E6
Gjøvdal N 33 D5
Gjøvik N 34 B2
Gladbeck D 50 B2
Gladenbach D 50 C4
Gladstad N 115 B8
Glamis GB 25 B5

Glamoč BIH 84 B1
Glamsbjerg DK 39 D3
Gland CH 69 B6
Glandorf D 50 A3
Glanegg A 73 B4
Glanshammar S 37 C2
Glarus CH 70 A4
Glasgow GB 24 C3
Glashütte
  Bayern D 62 C2
  Sachsen D 53 C3
Glastonbury GB 29 B5
Glatzau A 73 B5
Glauchau D 52 C2
Glava S 35 C4
Glavatičevo BIH 84 C3
Glavičice BIH 85 B4
Glavnik KOS 85 C5
Gledica SRB 85 C5
Glein
  A 73 A4
  N 115 A9
Gleinstätten A 73 B5
Gleisdorf A 73 A5
Glenamoy IRL 18 B2
Glenarm GB 19 B6
Glenavy GB 19 B5
Glenbarr GB 24 C2
Glenbeigh IRL 20 B2
Glenbrittle GB 22 D2
Glencoe GB 24 B2
Glencolumbkille IRL . .18 B3
Glendalough IRL 21 A5
Glenealy IRL 21 B5
Glenelg GB 22 D3
Glenfinnan GB 24 B2
Glengarriff IRL 20 C2
Glenluce GB 24 D3
Glenmaddy IRL 18 C3
Glenrothes GB 25 B4
Glenties IRL 18 B3
Glesborg DK 38 C3
Glesien D 52 B2
Gletsch CH 70 B3
Glewitz D 45 A4
Glifa GR 117 E5
Glimåkra S 41 C4
Glin IRL 20 B2
Glina HR 73 C6
Glinde D 44 B2
Glinojeck PL 47 C6
Glinsk IRL 20 A2
Gliwice PL 54 C3
Glödnitz A 73 B4
Gloggnitz A 63 C6
Głogoczów PL 65 A5
Glogonj SRB 85 B5
Glogovac SRB 85 B6
Głogów PL 53 B6
Głogówek PL 54 C2
Glomel F 56 B2
Glomfjord N 112 F2
Glommen S 40 C2
Glommersträsk S 115 B16
Glonn D 62 C2
Glorenza I 71 B5
Gloria P 92 B2
Glosa GR 116 C5
Glossop GB 27 B4
Gloucester GB 29 B5
Głowaczów PL 55 B6
Głowczyce PL 46 A3
Glöwen D 44 C4
Głowno PL 55 A4
Gložan SRB 75 C4
Glubczyce PL 54 C2
Głuchołazy PL 54 C2
Głuchów PL 55 B5
Głuchowo PL 53 A5
Glücksburg D 39 E2
Glückstadt D 43 B6
Glumina BIH 84 B4
Glumsö DK 39 D4
Glušci SRB 85 B4
Glusk BY 7 E10
Głuszyca PL 53 C6
Glyn Ceirog GB 26 C2
Glyngøre DK 38 C1
Gmünd
  Kärnten A 72 B3
  Nieder Österreich A . .63 B5
Gmund D 62 C2
Gmunden A 63 C4
Gnarp S 115 E14
Gnarrenburg D 43 B6
Gnesau A 72 B3
Gnesta S 37 C4
Gniechowice PL 54 B1
Gniew PL 47 B4
Gniewkowo PL 47 C4
Gniezno PL 46 C3
Gnoien D 45 B4
Gnojnice BIH 84 C2
Gnojno PL 55 C5
Gnosall GB 26 C3
Gnosjö S 40 B3
Göbel TR 118 C3
Göçbeyli TR 118 C2
Goch D 50 B2
Gochsheim D 51 C6
Göd H 65 C5
Godalming GB 31 C3
Godby FIN 36 B6
Godeanu RO 11 D7
Godegård S 37 D2
Godelheim D 51 B5
Goderville F 58 A1
Godiasco I 80 B3
Godič SLO 73 B4
Godkowo PL 47 A5
Godmanchester GB . . .30 B3
Gödöllő H 65 C5
Gödre H 74 B2
Goes NL 49 B4
Goetzenbrück F 60 B3
Göflis A 71 A4
Gogolin PL 54 C3
Göhren D 45 A5
Goirle NL 49 B5
Góis P 92 A2
Goizueta E 89 A5
Gójar E 100 B2
Gójsk PL 47 C5
Goja Gora SRB 85 C5
Golańcz PL 46 C3
Gölbaşı TR 23 B8
Gölby FIN 36 B6
Gölcük
  Kocaeli TR 118 B4
  Niğde TR 16 B7
Golčův Jenikov CZ . . .63 A6
Golczewo PL 45 B6
Goldach CH 71 A4
Goldbach D 51 C5
Goldberg D 44 B4
Goldelund D 43 A6
Goldenstedt D 43 C5
Golega P 92 B2
Goleniów PL 45 B6
Golfo Aranci I 110 B2
Golina PL 54 A3

Gölle H 74 B3
Göllersdorf A 64 B2
Golling an der Salzach
A 63 C4
Gölmarmara TR 118 D2
Golnice PL 53 B5
Golnik SLO 73 B4
Gölova TR 119 F5
Gölpazarı TR 118 B5
Gols A 64 C2
Golspie GB 23 D5
Golssen D 52 B3
Golubac SRB 85 B6
Golub-Dobrzyń PL 47 B5
Golubinci SRB 85 B5
Golubovci MNE 105 A5
Goluchów PL 54 B2
Golzow D 52 A2
Gomagoi I 71 B5
Gómara E 89 C4
Gomaringen D 61 B5
Gömbe TR 119 F4
Gömeç TR 118 C1
Gomel = Homyel BY 7 E11
Gomes Aires P 98 B2
Gómezserracin E 88 C2
Gommern D 52 A1
Gomulin PL 55 B4
Gonäs S 36 B2
Goncelin F 69 C5
Gończyce PL 55 B6
Gondomar
E 87 B2
P 87 C2
Gondrecourt-le-Château
F 60 B1
Gondrin F 76 C3
Gönen
Balıkesir TR 118 B2
İsparta TR 119 E5
Gonfaron F 79 C5
Goñi E 76 D1
Goni
GR 116 C4
I 110 C2
Gonnesa I 110 C1
Gonnosfanádiga I 110 C1
Gönyü H 64 C3
Gonzaga I 81 B4
Goodrich GB 29 B5
Goodwick GB 28 A2
Gooik B 49 C5
Goole GB 27 B5
Goor NL 50 A2
Göpfritz an der Wild
A 63 B6
Goppenstein CH 70 B2
Göppingen D 61 B5
Gor E 100 B3
Góra
Dolnośląskie PL 54 B1
Mazowieckie PL 47 C6
Gorafe E 100 B2
Góra Kalwaria PL 55 B6
Gorawino PL 46 B1
Goražde BIH 84 C3
Gordaliza del Pino E 88 B1
Gördes TR 118 D3
Gørding DK 39 D1
Górdola CH 70 B3
Gordon GB 25 C5
Gordoncillo E 88 B1
Gorebridge GB 25 C4
Gorenja Vas SLO 73 B4
Gorenje Jelenje HR 73 C4
Gorey
GB 57 A3
IRL 21 B5
Gorgonzola I 71 C4
Gorica HR 83 B4
Gorican HR 74 B1
Gorinchem NL 49 B5
Goring GB 31 C2
Goritsy RUS 7 C14
Göritz D 45 B5
Gorízia I 72 C3
Górki PL 47 C5
Gorleben D 44 B3
Gorleston-on-sea GB 30 B5
Gørlev DK 39 D4
Görlitz D 53 B4
Górliz E 89 A4
Görmin D 45 B5
Górna Grupa PL 47 B4
Gorna Oryakhovitsa
BG 11 E8
Gornja Gorevnica
SRB 85 C5
Gornja Klina KOS 85 D5
Gornja Ploča HR 83 B4
Gornja Radgona SLO 73 B5
Gornja Sabanta SRB 85 C6
Gornja Trešnjevica
SRB 85 B5
Gornja Tuzla BIH 84 B3
Gornje Polje MNE 84 D3
Gornje Ratkovo BIH 84 B1
Gornji Grad SLO 73 B4
Gornji Humac HR 83 C5
Gornji Jasenjani BIH 84 C2
Gornji Kamengrad
BIH 83 B5
Gornji Kneginec HR 73 B6
Gornji Kokoti MNE 105 A5
Gornji Kosinj HR 83 B4
Gornji Milanovac
SRB 85 B5
Gornji Podgradci BIH 84 A2
Gornji Ravno BIH 84 C2
Gornji Sjenicak HR 73 C5
Gornji Vakuf BIH 84 C2
Górno PL 55 C5
Görömböly H 65 B6
Górowo Iławeckie
PL 47 A6
Gorran Haven GB 28 C3
Gorredijk NL 42 B3
Gorron F 57 B5
Gorseinon GB 28 B3
Gort IRL 20 A3
Gortin GB 19 B4
Görzke D 52 A2
Gorzkowice PL 55 B4
Górzno
Kujawsko-Pomorskie
PL 47 B5
Zachodnio-Pomorskie
PL 46 B1
Gorzów Śląski PL 54 B3
Gorzów Wielkopolski
PL 45 C7
Górzyca PL 45 C6
Gorzyce PL 54 D3
Górzyn PL 53 B4
Gorzyń PL 46 C1
Gorzyno PL 46 A3
Gosaldo I 72 B1
Gosau A 63 C4
Gosberton GB 30 B3
Gościcino PL 47 A4
Gościęcin PL 54 C3
Gościm PL 46 C1
Gościno PL 46 A1
Gosdorf A 73 B5
Gosforth GB 26 A2
Goslar D 51 B6
Goslice PL 47 C5
Gospič HR 83 B4
Gosport GB 31 D2
Gössäter S 35 D5
Gossau CH 71 A4
Goss Ilsede D 51 A6
Gössnitz D 52 C2
Gössweinstein D 62 A2
Gostimë AL 105 C6
Gostkow PL 55 B4
Göstling an der Ybbs
A 63 C5
Gostomia PL 46 B2
Gostycyn PL 46 B3
Gostyń PL 54 B2
Gostynin PL 47 C5
Goszczyn PL 55 B5
Göta S 35 D4
Göteborg = Gothenburg
S 38 B4
Götene S 35 D5
Gotha D 51 C6
Gothem S 37 E5
Gothenburg = Göteborg
S 38 B4
Gotse Delchev BG 116 A5
Gottersdorf D 62 B3
Göttingen D 51 B5
Gottne S 115 D15
Götzis A 71 A4
Gouarec F 56 B2
Gouda NL 49 A5
Goudhurst GB 31 C4
Goumenissa GR 116 B4
Goura GR 117 E4
Gourdon F 77 B4
Gourgançon F 59 B5
Gourin F 56 B2
Gournay-en-Bray F 58 A2
Gourock GB 24 C3
Gouveia P 92 A3
Gouvy B 50 C1
Gouzeacourt F 49 C4
Gouzon F 68 B2
Govedari HR 84 D2
Govérnolo I 81 A4
Gowarczów PL 55 B5
Gowerton GB 28 B3
Gowidlino PL 46 A3
Gowran IRL 21 B4
Goyatz D 53 A4
Göynük
TR 118 B5
Antalya TR 119 F5
Gozdnica PL 53 B5
Gozdowo PL 47 C5
Gozee B 49 C5
Graal-Müritz D 44 A4
Grab BIH 84 D3
Grabenstätt D 62 C3
Grabhair GB 22 C2
Gråbo S 38 B5
Grabovac
HR 84 C1
SRB 85 B5
Grabovci SRB 85 B4
Grabow D 44 B3
Grabów PL 55 A4
Grabow nad Pilicą PL 55 B6
Grabów nad Prosną
PL 54 B3
Grabowno PL 46 B3
Grabs CH 71 A4
Gračac HR 83 B4
Gračanica
BIH 84 B3
KOS 85 D6
Graçay F 68 A1
Gracen AL 105 B5
Grad SLO 73 B6
Gradac
BIH 84 D3
HR 84 C2
MNE 85 C4
SRB 85 C5
Gradačac BIH 84 B3
Gradec HR 74 C1
Gradefes E 88 B1
Grades A 73 B4
Gradil P 92 C1
Gradina
HR 74 C2
MNE 85 C4
Gradisca d'Isonzo I 72 C3
Gradište HR 74 C3
Grado
E 86 A4
I 72 C3
Grafenau D 63 B4
Gräfenberg D 62 A2
Gräfenhainichen D 52 B2
Grafenschlag A 63 B6
Grafenstein A 73 B4
Gräfenthal D 52 C1
Grafentonna D 51 B6
Grafenwöhr D 62 A2
Grafing D 62 B2
Grafling D 62 B3
Gräfsnäs S 40 A2
Gragnano I 103 C7
Grahovo
MNE 84 D3
SLO 72 B3
Graiguenamanagh
IRL 21 B5
Grain GB 31 C4
Grainau D 71 A6
Graja de Iniesta E 95 C5
Grajera E 89 C3
Gram DK 39 D2
Gramais A 71 A5
Gramat F 77 B4
Gramatneusiedl A 64 B2
Grambow D 45 B6
Grammichele I 109 B3
Gramsh AL 116 B2
Gramzow D 45 B6
Gran N 34 B2
Granada E 100 B2
Granard IRL 19 C4
Grañas E 86 A3
Granátula de Calatrava
E 100 A2
Grancey-le-Château
F 59 C6
Grandas de Salime E 86 A4
Grandcamp-Maisy F 57 A4
Grand-Champ F 56 C3
Grand Couronne F 58 A2
Grand-Fougeray F 57 C4
Grândola P 98 A2
Grandpré F 59 A5
Grandrieu
B 49 C5
F 78 B2
Grandson CH 70 B1
Grandvillars F 70 A1
Grandvilliers F 58 A2
Grañén E 90 B2
Grangärde S 36 B1
Grange IRL 18 B3
Grangemouth GB 25 B4
Grange-over-Sands
GB 26 A3
Grängesberg S 36 B1
Granges-de Crouhens
F 77 D3
Granges-sur-Vologne
F 60 B2
Gräningen D 44 C4
Granitola-Torretta I 108 B1
Granja
Évora P 98 A3
Porto P 87 C2
Granja de Moreruela
E 88 C1
Granja de Torrehermosa
E 93 C5
Gränna S 40 A4
Grannäs
Västerbotten S 115 B13
Västerbotten S 115 B14
Granö S 115 C16
Granollers E 91 B5
Granowiec PL 54 B2
Granowo PL 54 A1
Gransee D 45 B5
Gransherad N 33 C6
Grantham GB 27 C5
Grantown-on-Spey
GB 23 D5
Grantshouse GB 25 C5
Granville F 57 B4
Granvin N 32 B3
Grærup Strand DK 39 D1
Gräsås S 40 C2
Grasbakken N 113 B17
Grasberg D 43 B6
Grasmere GB 26 A2
Gräsmyr S 115 D16
Grasö S 36 B5
Grassano I 104 C2
Grassau D 62 C3
Grasse F 79 C5
Grassington GB 27 A4
Græsted DK 41 C2
Gråsten DK 39 E2
Grästorp S 35 D4
Gratkorn A 73 A5
Gråträsk S 115 B16
Gratwein A 73 A5
Graulhet F 77 C4
Graus E 90 A3
Grávalos E 89 B5
Gravberget N 34 B4
Grave NL 50 B1
Gravedona I 71 B4
Gravelines F 48 B3
Gravellona Toce I 70 C3
Gravendal S 36 B1
Gravens DK 39 D2
Gravesend GB 31 C4
Graveson F 78 C3
Gravina in Púglia I 104 C2
Gray F 69 A5
Grayrigg GB 26 A3
Grays GB 31 C4
Grayshott GB 31 C3
Grayvoron RUS 7 F13
Graz A 73 A5
Grazalema E 99 C5
Grążawy PL 47 B5
Grazzano Visconti I 80 B3
Greåker N 35 C3
Great Dunmow GB 31 C4
Great Malvern GB 29 A5
Great Torrington GB 28 C3
Great Waltham GB 31 C4
Great Yarmouth GB 30 B5
Grebbestad S 35 D3
Grebenstein D 51 B5
Grębocice PL 53 B6
Grębocin PL 47 B4
Greding D 62 A2
Gredstedbro DK 39 D1
Greencastle IRL 19 A4
Greenhead GB 25 D5
Greenisland GB 19 B6
Greenlaw GB 25 C5
Greenock GB 24 C3
Greenway GB 28 B3
Greenwich GB 31 C4
Grefrath D 50 B2
Greifenburg A 72 B3
Greiffenberg D 45 B5
Greifswald D 45 A5
Grein A 63 B5
Greipstad N 33 D4
Greiz D 52 C2
Grenaa DK 39 C3
Grenade F 77 C4
Grenade-sur-l'Adour
F 76 C2
Grenchen CH 70 A2
Grendi N 33 D4
Grenivík IS 111 B7
Grenoble F 69 C5
Gréoux-les-Bains F 79 C4
Gresenhorst D 44 A4
Gressoney-la-Trinité
I 70 C2
Gressoney-St-Jean I 70 C2
Gressthal D 51 C6
Gressvik N 35 C2
Gresten A 63 C6
Gretna GB 25 D4
Greussen D 51 B6
Greve in Chianti I 81 C5
Greven
Mecklenburg-Vorpommern D 44 B2
Nordrhein-Westfalen D 50 A3
Grevena GR 116 B3
Grevenbroich D 50 B2
Grevenbrück D 50 B4
Grevenmacher L 60 A2
Grevesmühlen D 44 B3
Grevestrand DK 41 D2
Grevie S 41 C2
Greystoke GB 26 A3
Greystones IRL 21 A5
Grez-Doiceau B 49 C5
Grèzec F 77 B4
Grez-en-Bouère F 57 C5
Grezzana I 71 C6
Grgar SLO 72 B3
Grgurevci SRB 85 A4
Gries A 71 A6
Griesbach D 63 B4
Griesheim D 61 A4
Gries in Sellrain A 71 A6
Grieskirchen A 63 B4
Griffen A 73 B4
Grignan F 78 B3
Grignano I 72 C3
Grigno I 72 B1
Grignols F 76 B2
Grignon F 69 C6
Grijota E 88 B2
Grijpskerk NL 42 B3
Gril AL 105 A5
Grillby S 37 C4
Grimaud F 79 C5
Grimbergen B 49 C5
Grimma D 52 B2
Grimmen D 45 A5
Grimmialp CH 70 B2
Grimsås S 40 B3
Grimsby GB 27 B5
Grimslöv S 40 C4
Grímsstaðir IS 111 B9
Grimstad N 33 D5
Grimstorp S 40 B4
Grindavík IS 111 D3
Grindelwald CH 70 B3
Grindheim N 33 D4
Grindsted DK 39 D1
Griñón E 94 B3
Gripenberg S 40 B4
Gripsholm S 37 C4
Grisolles F 77 C4
Grisslehamn S 36 B5
Gritley GB 23 C6
Grizebeck GB 26 A2
Grndina BIH 84 B1
Gröbming A 72 A3
Gröbzig D 52 B1
Grocka SRB 85 B5
Gröditz D 52 B3
Gródki PL 47 B6
Grodków PL 54 C2
Grodziec PL 54 A3
Grodzisk Mazowiecki
PL 55 A5
Grodzisk Wielkoposki
PL 54 A1
Groenlo NL 50 A2
Groesbeek NL 50 B1
Grohote HR 83 C5
Groitzsch D 52 B2
Groix F 56 C2
Grójec PL 55 B5
Grom PL 47 B6
Gromiljca BIH 84 C3
Grömitz D 44 A2
Gromnik PL 65 A6
Gromo I 71 C4
Gronau
Niedersachsen D 51 A5
Nordrhein-Westfalen
D 50 A3
Grønbjerg DK 39 C1
Grönenbach D 61 C6
Grong N 114 C9
Grönhögen S 41 C6
Groningen
D 52 B1
NL 42 B3
Grønnestrand DK 38 B2
Grono CH 71 B4
Grönskåra S 40 B5
Grootegast NL 42 B3
Gropello Cairoli I 70 C3
Grorud N 34 C2
Grósio I 71 B5
Grošnica SRB 85 C5
Grossalmerode D 51 B5
Grossarl A 72 A3
Gross Beeren D 45 C5
Gross Berkel D 51 A5
Grossbodungen D 51 B6
Gross-botwar D 61 B5
Grossburgwedel D 44 C1
Grosschönau D 53 C4
Gross-Dölln D 45 B5
Grossenbrode D 44 A3
Grossenehrich D 51 B6
Grossengottern D 51 B6
Grossenhain D 52 B3
Grossenkneten D 43 C5
Grossenlüder D 51 C5
Grossensee D 44 B2
Grossenzersdorf A 64 B2
Grosseto I 81 D5
Gross-Gerau D 61 A4
Grossgerungs A 63 B5
Grossglobnitz A 63 B6
Grosshabersdorf D 62 A1
Grossharras A 64 B2
Grosshartmansdorf
D 52 C3
Grosshöchstetten
CH 70 B2
Gross Kreutz D 45 C4
Grosskrut A 64 B2
Gross Lafferde D 51 A6
Gross Leutheb D 53 A4
Grosslohra D 51 B6
Grossmehring D 62 B2
Gross Muckrow D 53 A4
Gross Oesingen D 44 C2
Grossostheim D 61 A5
Grosspertholz A 63 B5
Grosspetersdorf A 73 A6
Grosspostwitz D 53 B4
Grossraming A 63 C5
Grossräschen D 53 B4
Gross Reken D 50 B3
Grossrinderfeld D 61 A5
Grossröhrsdorf D 53 B4
Gross Sarau D 44 B2
Gross Särchen D 53 B4
Grossschirma D 52 C3
Gross Schönebeck D 45 C5
Grossschweinbarth A 64 B2
Grosssiegharts A 63 B6
Grosssölk A 72 A3
Gross Umstadt D 61 A4
Grosswarasdorf A 74 A1
Gross Warnow D 44 B3
Gross-Weikersdorf A 64 B1
Gross-Welle D 44 B4
Grosswilfersdorf A 73 A5
Gross Wokern D 44 B4
Grostenquin F 60 B2
Grosuplje SLO 73 C4
Grotli N 114 E4
Grötlingbo S 37 E5
Grottáglie I 104 C3
Grottaminarda I 103 B8
Grottammare I 82 D2
Grotte di Castro I 81 D5
Grotteria I 106 C3
Gróttole I 104 C2
Grouw NL 42 B2
Grov N 112 D6
Grova N 33 C5
Grove E 86 B2
Grua N 34 B2
Grube D 44 A3
Grubišno Polje HR 74 C2
Gruda HR 105 A4
Grude BIH 84 C2
Grudusk PL 47 B6
Grudziądz PL 47 B4
Grue N 34 B4
Gruissan F 78 C2
Grullos E 86 A4
Grumo Áppula I 104 B2
Grums S 35 C5
Grünau im Almtal A 63 C4
Grünberg D 51 C4
Grünburg A 63 C5
Grundarfjörður IS 111 C2
Gründau D 51 C5
Gründelhardt D 61 A5
Grundforsen S 34 A4
Grundlsee A 63 C4
Grundsund S 35 D3
Grunewald D 53 B3
Grungedal N 33 C4
Grunow D 53 A4
Grünstadt D 61 A4
Gruvberget S 36 A3
Gruyères CH 70 B2
Gruža SRB 85 C5
Grybów PL 65 A6
Grycksbo S 36 B2
Gryfice PL 45 B7
Gryfino PL 45 B6
Gryfów Śląski PL 53 B5
Gryllefjord N 112 C6
Grymyr N 34 B2
Gryt S 37 D3
Grytgöl S 37 D2
Grythyttan S 37 C1
Grytnäs S 37 D4
Grzmiąca PL 46 B2
Grzybno PL 45 B6
Grzywna PL 47 B4
Gschnitz A 71 A6
Gschwend D 61 B5
Gstaad CH 70 B2
Gsteig CH 70 B2
Guadahortuna E 100 B2
Guadalajara E 95 B3
Guadalaviar E 95 B5
Guadalcanal E 99 A5
Guadalcázar E 100 B1
Guadalix de la Sierra
E 94 B3
Guadálmez E 100 A1
Guadalupe E 93 B5
Guadamur E 94 C2
Guadarrama E 94 B2
Guadiaro E 99 C5
Guadix E 100 B2
Guagnano I 105 C3
Guagno F 102 A1
Guajar-Faragüit E 100 C2
Gualchos E 100 C2
Gualdo Tadino I 82 C1
Gualtieri I 81 B4
Guarcino I 103 B6
Guarda P 92 A3
Guardamar del Segura
E 96 C2
Guardão P 92 A2
Guardavalle I 106 C3
Guardea I 102 A5
Guárdia I 103 C8
Guardiagrele I 103 A7
Guardiarégia I 103 B7
Guárdia Sanframondi
I 103 B7
Guardias Viejas E 100 C3
Guardiola de Bergueda
E 91 A4
Guardo E 88 B2
Guareña E 93 C4
Guaro E 100 C1
Guarromán E 100 A2
Guasila I 110 C2
Guastalla I 81 B4
Gubbhögen S 115 C12
Gúbbio I 82 C1
Guben D 53 B4
Gubin PL 53 B4
Guča SRB 85 C5
Gudå N 114 D8
Gudavac BIH 83 B5
Guddal N 32 A2
Güderup DK 39 E2
Gudhem S 35 D5
Gudhjem DK 41 D4
Gudovac HR 74 C1
Gudow D 44 B2
Güdüı TR 118 B7
Gudvangen N 32 B3
Guebwiller F 60 C3
Guéjar-Sierra E 100 B2
Guéméné-Penfao F 57 C4
Guéméné-sur-Scorff
F 56 B2
Güeñes E 89 A3
Guer F 57 C3
Guérande F 66 A2
Guéret F 68 B1
Guérigny F 68 A3
Guesa E 76 D1
Gueugnon F 68 B4
Guglionesi I 103 B7
Gühlen Glienicke D 45 B4
Guia P 92 B2
Guichen F 57 C4
Guidizzolo I 71 C5
Guidónia-Montecélio
I 102 B5
Guiglia I 81 B4
Guignes F 58 B3
Guijo E 100 A1
Guijo de Coria E 93 A4
Guijo de Santa Bábera
E 93 A5
Guijuelo E 93 A5
Guildford GB 31 C3
Guillaumes F 79 B5
Guillena E 99 B4
Guillestre F 79 B5
Guillos F 76 B2
Guilsfield GB 26 C2
Guilvinec F 56 C1
Guimarães P 87 C2
Guincho P 92 C1
Guînes F 48 C2
Guingamp F 56 B2
Guipavas F 56 B1
Guisborough GB 27 A4
Guiscard F 59 A4
Guiscriff F 56 B2
Guise F 59 A4
Guisona E 91 B4
Guitiriz E 86 A3
Guîtres F 76 A2
Gujan-Mestras F 76 B1
Gulbene LV 7 C9
Gulçayır TR 118 C6
Guldborg DK 39 E4
Gullabo S 40 C5
Gullane GB 25 B5
Gullbrå N 32 B3
Gullbrandstorp S 40 C2
Gulleråsen S 36 A2
Gullhaug N 35 C2
Gullringen S 40 B5
Gullspång S 35 D6
Gullstein N 114 D5
Güllük TR 119 E2
Gülnar TR 16 C6
Gülpınar TR 116 C8
Gülşehir TR 16 B7
Gulsvik N 34 B1
Gumiel de Hizán E 88 C3
Gummersbach D 50 B3
Gümüldür TR 119 D2
Gümüşhaciköy TR 16 A7
Gümüşova TR 118 B5
Gundelfingen D 61 B6
Gundel-fingen D 60 B3
Gundelsheim D 61 A5
Gunderschoffen F 60 B3
Gundertshausen A 62 B3
Gundinci HR 74 C3
Gündoğmuş TR 119 F7
Güney
Burdur TR 119 E4
Denizli TR 119 D4
Gunja HR 84 B3
Günlüce TR 119 F3
Gunnarn S 115 B14
Gunnarskog S 34 C4
Gunnebo S 40 B6
Gunnislake GB 28 C3
Günselsdorf A 64 C2
Guntersblum D 61 A4
Guntersdorf A 64 B2
Guntin E 86 B3
Günyüzü TR 118 C6
Günzburg D 61 B6
Gunzenhausen D 62 A1
Güre
Balıkesir TR 118 C1
Uşak TR 118 D4
Gurk A 73 B4
Gurrea de Gállego E 90 A2
Gürsu TR 118 B4
Gušće HR 74 C1
Gusev RUS 6 D7
Gusinje MNE 105 A5
Gusmar AL 105 C5
Gúspini I 110 C1
Gusselby S 37 C2
Güssing A 73 A6
Gusswerk A 63 C6
Gustav Adolf S 34 B5
Gustavsberg S 37 C5
Gustavsfors S 35 C4
Güstrow D 44 B4
Gusum S 37 D3
Gutcher GB 22 A7
Gutenstein A 64 C1
Gütersloh D 51 B4
Guttannen CH 70 B3
Guttaring A 73 B4
Guttau D 53 B4
Güttingen CH 61 C5
Gützkow D 45 B5
Guzów PL 55 A5
Gvardeysk RUS 6 D6
Gvarv N 33 C6
Gvozd MNE 85 D4
Gvozdansko HR 73 C6
Gwda Wielka PL 46 B2
Gwennap GB 28 C2
Gy F 69 A5
Gyál H 75 A4
Gyarmat H 74 A2
Gyékényes H 74 B2
Gyé-sur-Seine F 59 B5
Gylling DK 39 D3
Gyoma H 75 B5
Gyömöre H 74 A2
Gyömrö H 75 A4
Gyón H 75 A4
Gyöngyfa H 74 C2
Gyöngyös H 65 C5
Gyöngyöspata H 65 C5
Gyönk H 74 B3
Györ H 64 C3
Györszemere H 74 A2
Gypsera CH 70 B2
Gysinge S 36 B3
Gyttorp S 37 C1
Gyula H 75 B6
Gyulafirátót H 74 A2
Gyulaj H 74 B3

H

Haacht B 49 C5
Haag
Nieder Östereich A 63 B5
Ober Östereich A 63 B4
D 62 B3
Haaksbergen NL 50 A2
Haamstede NL 49 B4
Haan D 50 B3
Haapajärvi FIN 3 E26
Haapsalu EST 6 B7
Haarlem NL 42 C1
Habas F 76 C2
Habay B 60 A1
Habo S 40 B4
Håbol S 35 D4
Habry CZ 63 A6
Habsheim F 60 C3
Hachenburg D 50 C3
Hacıbektaş TR 16 B7
Hacılar TR 16 B7
Hacinas E 89 C3
Hackås S 115 E11
Hacketstown IRL 21 B5
Hackthorpe GB 26 A3
Hadamar D 50 C4
Hädanberg S 115 D15
Haddington GB 25 C5
Hadersdorf am Kamp
A 63 B6
Haderslev DK 39 D2
Haderup DK 39 C1
Hadım TR 119 F7
Hadleigh
Essex GB 31 C4
Suffolk GB 30 B4
Hadlow GB 31 C4
Hadmersleben D 52 A1
Hadsten DK 39 C3
Hadsund DK 38 C3
Hadyach UA 7 F13
Hadžići BIH 84 C3
Hafnarfjörður IS 111 C4
Hafnir IS 111 D3
Hafslo N 32 A4
Haganj HR 74 C1
Hagby S 40 C6
Hage D 43 B4
Hægebostad N 33 D4
Hægeland N 33 D4
Hagen
Niedersachsen D 43 B5
Nordrhein-Westfalen
D 50 B3
Hagenbach D 61 A4
Hagenow D 44 B3
Hagetmau F 76 C2
Hagfors S 34 B5
Häggenås S 115 D11
Hagondange F 60 A2
Hagsta S 36 B4
Haguenau F 60 B3
Hahnbach D 62 A2
Hahnslätten D 50 C4
Hahót H 74 B1
Haiger D 50 C4
Haigerloch D 61 B4
Hailsham GB 31 D4
Hainburg A 64 B2
Hainfeld A 64 B1
Hainichen D 52 C3
Hajdúböszörmény H 10 C6
Hajdučica SRB 75 C5
Hajdúszoboszló H 75 A6
Hajnáčka SK 65 B5
Hajnówka PL 6 E7
Hajós H 75 B4
Håkafot S 115 C11
Hakkas S 113 F10
Håksberg S 36 B2
Halaszi H 64 C3
Halberstadt D 52 B1
Halberton GB 29 C4
Hald Ege DK 39 C2
Haldem D 43 C5
Halden N 35 C3
Haldensleben D 52 A1
Halenbeck D 44 B4
Halesowen GB 26 C3
Halesworth GB 30 B5
Halfing D 62 C3
Halhjem N 32 B2
Håliden S 34 B5
Halifax GB 27 B4
Häljelöt S 37 D3
Halkirk GB 23 C5
Hall S 37 E5
Hälla S 115 D14
Hallabro S 41 C5
Hällabrottet S 37 C2
Halland GB 31 D4
Hällaryd S 41 C4
Hallaryd S 40 C3
Hällberga S 37 C3
Hällbybrunn S 37 C3
Halle
B 49 C5
Nordrhein-Westfalen
D 51 A4
Sachsen-Anhalt D 52 B1
Hålleberga S 40 C5
Hällefors S 36 C1
Hälleforsnäs S 37 C3
Hallein A 62 C4
Hällekis S 35 D5
Hallen S 115 D11
Hållen S 36 B4
Hallenberg D 51 B4
Hällestad S 37 D2
Hällevadsholm S 35 D3
Hällevik S 41 C4
Hälleviksstrand S 35 D3
Hallingby N 34 B2
Hallingeberg S 40 B6
Hallingen N 32 B6
Hall in Tirol A 71 A6
Hällnäs S 115 A15
Hållnäs S 36 B4
Hällnäs S 115 C16
Hallormsstaður IS 111 B11
Hallsberg S 37 C2
Hållsta S 37 C3
Hallstahammar S 37 C3
Hallstatt A 72 A3
Hallstavik S 36 B5
Halltorp S 40 C6
Halluin F 49 C4
Hallviken S 115 D12
Hallworthy GB 28 C3
Halmstad S 40 C2
Hals DK 38 B3
Halsa N 114 D5
Halstead GB 31 C4
Haltdalen N 114 E8
Haltern D 50 B3
Haltwhistle GB 25 D5
Halvarsgårdarna S 36 B2
Halver D 50 B3
Halvrimmen DK 38 B2
Ham F 59 A4
Hamar N 34 B3
Hamarhaug N 32 B2
Hamarøy N 112 D4
Hambach F 60 A3
Hambergen D 43 B5
Hambergsund S 35 D3
Hambledon GB 31 D2
Hambuhren D 44 C1
Hamburg D 44 B2
Hamdibey TR 118 C2
Hamdorf D 43 A6
Hämeenlinna FIN 3 F26
Hameln = Hamlin D 51 A5
Hamersleben D 52 A1
Hamidiye TR 118 C5
Hamilton GB 24 C3
Hamina FIN 7 A9
Hamlagrø N 32 B3
Hamlin = Hameln D 51 A5
Hamm D 50 B3
Hammar S 37 D1
Hammarland FIN 36 B6
Hammarö S 35 C5
Hammarstrand S 115 D13
Hamme B 49 B5
Hammel DK 39 C2
Hammelburg D 51 C5
Hammelspring D 45 B5
Hammenhög S 41 D4
Hammerdal S 115 D12
Hammerfest N 113 B12
Hammershøj DK 38 C2
Hammerum DK 39 C2
Hamminkeln D 50 B2
Hamnavoe GB 22 A7
Hamneda S 40 C3
Hamningberg N 113 B19
Hamoir B 49 C6
Hamont B 49 B6
Hámor H 65 B6
Hamra
Gävleborg S 115 F12
Gotland S 37 F5
Hamrångefjärden S 36 B4
Hamstreet GB 31 C4
Hamsund N 112 D4
Han
MNE 84 D3
TR 118 C5
Hanaskog S 41 C4
Hanau D 51 C4
Händelöp S 40 B6
Handlová SK 65 B4
Hanerau-Hademarschen
D 43 A6
Hånger S 40 B3
Hanhimaa FIN 113 E14
Han i Hotit AL 105 A5
Hanken S 37 D1
Hankensbüttel D 44 C2
Han Knežica BIH 83 A5
Hanko FIN 6 B7
Hannover D 43 C6
Hannut B 49 C6
Han Pijesak BIH 84 B3
Hansnes N 112 C8
Hanstedt D 44 B2
Hanstholm DK 38 B1
Hantsavichy BY 7 E9
Hanušovice CZ 54 C1
Haparanda S 3 D26
Haradok BY 7 D10
Harads S 3 C24
Häradsbäck S 40 C4
Häradsbygden S 36 B2
Harbo S 36 B4
Harboør DK 38 C1
Harburg
Bayern D 62 B1
Hamburg D 44 B1
Hårby DK 39 D3
Harc H 74 B3
Hardegarijp NL 42 B2
Hardegsen D 51 B5
Hardelot Plage F 48 C2
Hardenbeck D 45 B5
Hardenberg NL 42 C3
Harderwijk NL 42 C2
Hardheim D 61 A5
Hardt D 61 B4
Hareid N 114 E3
Haren
D 43 C4
NL 42 B3
Harestua N 34 B2
Harfleur F 57 A6
Harg S 36 B5
Hargicourt F 49 D4
Hargnies F 49 C5
Hargshamn S 36 B5
Härja S 40 A3
Harkány H 74 C3
Härkeberga S 37 C4
Harkebrügge D 43 B4
Harlech GB 26 C1
Harleston GB 30 B5
Hårlev DK 41 D2
Harlingen NL 42 B2
Harlösa S 41 D3
Harlow GB 31 C4
Harmancık TR 118 C4
Harmånger S 115 F14
Härnevi S 37 C4
Härnösand S 115 E14
Haro E 89 B4
Haroldswick GB 22 A8
Háromfa H 74 B2
Haroué F 60 B2
Harpenden GB 31 C3
Harplinge S 40 C2
Harpstedt D 43 C5
Harrogate GB 27 A4
Harrow GB 31 C3
Härryda S 40 B2
Harsefeld D 43 B6
Harsewinkel D 50 B4
Hârşova RO 11 D9
Harstad N 112 D5
Harsum D 51 A5
Harsvik N 114 C7
Harta H 75 B4
Hartberg A 73 A5
Hartburn GB 25 C6
Hartennes F 59 A4
Hartest GB 30 B4
Hartha D 52 B2
Hartland GB 28 C3
Hartlepool GB 27 A4
Hartmanice CZ 63 A4
Hartmannsdorf A 73 A5
Harvassdal N 115 B11
Harwell GB 31 C2
Harwich GB 31 C5
Harzgerode D 52 B1
Häselgehr A 71 A5
Haselünne D 43 C4
Hasköy TR 118 A1
Haslach D 61 B4
Haslach an der Mühl
A 63 B5
Hasle DK 41 D4
Haslemere GB 31 C3
Haslev DK 39 D4
Hasloch D 61 A5
Hasparren F 76 C1
Hassela S 115 E13
Hasselfelde D 51 B6
Hasselfors S 37 C1
Hasselt
B 49 C6
NL 42 C3
Hassfurt D 51 C6
Hassleben D 45 B5
Hässleholm S 41 C3
Hasslö S 41 C5
Hassloch D 61 A4
Hästbo S 36 B4
Hastersboda FIN 36 B7
Hästholmen S 37 D1
Hastière-Lavaux B 49 C5
Hastigrow GB 23 C5
Hastings GB 31 D4
Hästveda S 41 C3
Hasvik N 113 B11
Hatfield
Hertfordshire GB 31 C3
South Yorkshire GB 27 B5
Hatherleigh GB 28 C3
Hathersage GB 27 B4
Hatlestrand N 32 B2
Hattem NL 42 C3
Hatten
D 43 B5
F 60 B3
Hattfjelldal N 115 B10
Hatting DK 39 D2
Hattingen D 50 B3
Hattstadt F 60 B3
Hattstedt D 43 A6
Hatvan H 65 C5
Hatvik N 32 B2
Hau D 50 B2
Haudainville F 59 A6
Hauganes IS 111 B7
Haugastøl N 32 B4
Hauge N 33 D3
Haugesund N 33 C2
Haughom N 33 D3
Haugsdal N 32 B2
Haugsdorf A 64 B2
Haukedal N 32 A3
Haukeland N 32 B2
Haukeligrend N 33 C4
Haukeliseter N 32 C4
Haukipudas FIN 3 D26
Haulerwijk NL 42 B3
Haunersdorf D 62 B3
Haus N 32 B2
Hausach D 61 B4
Hausham D 62 C2
Hausmannstätten A 73 B5
Hausvik N 33 D3
Hautajärvi FIN 113 F18
Hautefort F 67 C6
Hauterives F 69 C5
Hauteville-Lompnès
F 69 C5
Haut-Fays B 49 C6
Hautmont F 49 C4
Hautrage B 49 C4
Hauzenberg D 63 B4
Havant GB 31 D3
Havdhem S 37 E5
Havdrup DK 39 D5
Havelange B 49 C6
Havelberg D 44 C4
Havelte NL 42 C3
Haverfordwest GB 28 B3
Haverhill GB 30 B4
Havering GB 31 C4
Håverud S 35 D4
Havířov CZ 65 A4
Havixbeck D 50 B3
Havlíčkův Brod CZ 63 A6
Havndal DK 38 C3
Havneby DK 39 D1
Havnebyen DK 39 D4
Havnsø DK 39 D4
Havøysund N 113 A13
Havran TR 118 C2
Havrebjerg DK 39 D4
Havsa TR 118 A1
Havstenssund S 35 D3
Havza TR 16 A7
Hawes GB 26 A3
Hawick GB 25 C5
Hawkhurst GB 31 C4
Hawkinge GB 31 C5
Haxey GB 27 B5
Hayange F 60 A2
Haydarlı TR 119 D5
Haydon Bridge GB 25 D5
Hayle GB 28 C2
Haymana TR 118 C7
Hay-on-Wye GB 29 A4
Hayrabolu TR 118 A2
Haysyn UA 11 B10
Hayvoron UA 11 B10
Haywards Heath GB 31 D3
Hazebrouck F 48 C3
Hazlov CZ 52 C2
Heacham GB 30 B4
Headcorn GB 31 C4
Headford IRL 20 A2
Heanor GB 27 B4
Héas F 76 D3
Heathfield GB 31 D4
Hebden Bridge GB 26 B3
Heberg S 40 C2
Heby S 36 C3
Hechingen D 61 B4
Hechlingen D 62 B1
Hecho E 76 D2
Hechtel B 49 B6
Hechthausen D 43 B6
Heckelberg D 45 C5
Heckington GB 27 C5
Hecklingen D 52 B1
Hed S 37 C2
Hedalen N 34 B1
Hedared S 40 B2
Heddal N 33 C6
Hédé F 57 B4
Hede S 115 E10
Hedekas S 35 D3
Hedemora S 36 B2
Hedensted DK 39 D2
Hedersleben D 52 B1
Hedesunda S 36 B4
Hedge End GB 31 D2
Hedon GB 27 B5
Heede D 43 C4
Heek D 50 A3
Heemstede NL 42 C1
Heerde NL 42 C3
Heerenveen NL 42 C2
Heerhugowaard NL 42 C1
Heerlen NL 50 C1
Heeze NL 49 B6
Heggenes N 32 A6
Hegra N 114 D8
Hegyeshalom H 64 C3
Hegyközség H 74 A1
Heia N 114 C9
Heide D 43 A6
Heidelberg D 61 A4
Heiden D 50 B2
Heidenau D 53 C3
Heidenheim D 61 B6
Heidenreichstein A 63 B6
Heikendorf D 44 A2
Heilam GB 22 C4
Heiland N 33 D5
Heilbad Heiligenstadt
D 51 B6
Heilbronn D 61 A5
Heiligenblut A 72 A2
Heiligendamn D 44 A3
Heiligendorf D 44 C2
Heiligengrabe D 44 B4
Heiligenhafen D 44 A2
Heiligenhaus D 50 B2
Heiligenkreuz A 73 B6
Heiligenstadt D 62 A2
Heiloo NL 42 C1
Heilsbronn D 62 A1
Heim N 114 D6
Heimburg D 51 B6
Heimdal N 114 D7
Heinerscheid L 50 C2
Heinersdorf D 45 C6
Heining D 63 B4
Heiningen D 61 B5
Heinola FIN 3 F27
Heinsberg D 50 B2
Heist-op-den-Berg B 49 B5
Hejde S 37 E5
Hejdeby S 37 E5
Hejls DK 39 D2
Hejnice CZ 53 C5
Hel PL 47 A4
Helchteren B 49 B6
Heldburg D 51 C6
Heldrungen D 52 B1
Helechosa E 94 C2
Helensburgh GB 24 B3
Helfenberg A 63 B5
Helgen N 33 C6
Helgeroa N 35 D1
Hella
IS 111 D5
N 32 A3
Helland N 112 D5
Hellas S 35 D4
Helle N 33 D3
Helleland N 33 D3
Hellendoorn NL 42 C3
Hellenthal D 50 C2
Hellesøy N 32 B1
Hellesylt N 114 E3
Hellevoetsluis NL 49 B5
Helligskogen N 112 C9
Hellín E 101 A4
Hellissandur IS 111 C2
Hellnar IS 111 C2
Hellum DK 38 B3
Hellvi S 37 E5
Hellvik N 33 D2
Helm-brechts D 52 C1
Helmond NL 49 B6
Helmsdale GB 23 C5
Helmsley GB 27 A4
Helmstedt D 51 A6
Hel'pa SK 65 B5
Helsa D 51 B5
Helsby GB 26 B3

Helsingborg S 41 C2
Helsinge DK 41 C2
Helsingør DK 41 C2
Helsinki FIN 6 A8
Helston GB 28 C2
Hemau D 62 A2
Hemavan S 115 B12
Hemel Hempstead GB 31 C3
Hemer D 50 B3
Héming F 60 B2
Hemmet DK 39 D1
Hemmingstedt D 43 A6
Hemmoor D 43 B6
Hemnes N 35 C3
Hemnesberget N 115 A10
Hemse S 37 E5
Hemsedal N 32 B5
Hemslingen D 43 B6
Hemsworth GB 27 B4
Hen N 34 B2
Henån S 35 D3
Hendaye F 76 C1
Hendek TR 118 B5
Hendungen D 51 C6
Henfield GB 31 D3
Hengelo
Gelderland NL 50 A2
Overijssel NL 50 A2
Hengersberg D 62 B4
Hengoed GB 29 B4
Hénin-Beaumont F 48 C3
Henley-on-Thames GB 31 C3
Hennan S 115 E12
Henneberg D 51 C6
Hennebont F 56 C2
Henne Strand DK 39 D1
Hennigsdorf D 45 C5
Hennset N 114 D5
Hennstedt
Schleswig-Holstein D 43 A6
Schleswig-Holstein D 43 A6
Henrichemont F 68 A2
Henryków PL 54 C2
Henrykowo PL 47 A6
Hensås N 32 A5
Henstedt-Ulzburg D 44 B1
Heppenheim D 61 A4
Herad
Buskerud N 32 B6
Vest-Agder N 33 D3
Heradsbygd N 34 B3
Heraklion = Iraklio GR 117 G7
Herálec CZ 64 A2
Herand N 32 B3
Herbault F 58 C2
Herbern D 50 B3
Herbertstown IRL 20 B3
Herbeumont B 59 A6
Herbignac F 66 A2
Herbisse F 59 B5
Herbitzheim F 60 A3
Herbolzheim D 60 B3
Herborn D 50 C4
Herbrechtingen D 61 B6
Herby PL 54 C3
Herceg-Novi MNE 105 A4
Hercegovać HR 74 C2
Hercegovacka Goleša SRB 85 C4
Hercegszántó H 75 C3
Herchen D 50 C3
Heréd H 65 C5
Hereford GB 29 A5
Herefoss N 33 D5
Hereke TR 118 B4
Herencia E 95 C3
Herend H 74 A2
Herent B 49 C5
Herentals B 49 B5
Hérépian F 78 C2
Herfølge DK 41 D2
Herford D 51 A4
Herguijuela E 93 B5
Héric F 66 A3
Héricourt F 60 C2
Héricourt-en-Caux F 58 A1
Hérimoncourt F 70 A1
Heringsdorf D 44 A3
Herisau CH 71 A4
Hérisson F 68 B2
Herk-de-Stad B 49 C6
Herlufmagle DK 39 D4
Hermagor A 72 B3
Hermannsburg D 44 C2
Hermansverk N 32 A3
Heřmanův Městec CZ 53 D5
Herment F 68 C2
Hermeskeil D 60 A2
Hermisende E 87 C4
Hermonville F 59 A4
Hermsdorf D 52 C1
Hernani E 76 C1
Hernansancho E 94 B2
Herne D 50 B3
Herne Bay GB 31 C5
Hernes N 34 B3
Herning DK 39 C1
Herøya N 35 C1
Herramelluri E 89 B3
Herräng S 36 B5
Herre N 33 C6
Herrenberg D 61 B4
Herrera E 100 B1
Herrera de Alcántara E 92 B3
Herrera del Duque E 94 C1
Herrera de los Navarros E 90 B1
Herrera de Pisuerga E 88 B2
Herreros del Suso E 94 B1
Herrestad S 35 D3
Herrhamra S 37 D4
Herritslev DK 44 A3
Herrlisheim F 60 B3
Herrljunga S 40 A3
Herrnhut D 53 B4
Herrsching D 62 B2
Hersbruck D 62 A2
Hersby S 37 C5
Herscheid D 50 B3
Herselt B 49 B5
Herso GR 116 A4
Herstal B 49 C6
Herstmonceux GB 31 D4
Herten D 50 B3
Hertford GB 31 C3
Hervás E 93 A5
Hervik N 33 C2
Herxheim D 61 A4
Herzberg
Brandenburg D 45 C4
Brandenburg D 52 B3
Niedersachsen D 51 B6
Herzebrock D 50 B4
Herzfelde D 45 C5
Herzlake D 43 C4
Herzogen-aurach D 62 A1
Herzogenbuchsee CH 70 A2
Herzogenburg A 63 B6
Herzsprung D 44 B4
Hesby N 33 C2
Hesdin F 48 C3
Hesel D 43 B4
Heskestad N 33 D3
Hessdalen N 114 E8
Hesselager DK 39 D3
Hesseng N 113 C18
Hessisch Lichtenau D 51 B5
Hessisch-Oldendorf D 51 A5
Hestra S 40 B3
Heswall GB 26 B2
Hetlevik N 32 B2
Hettange-Grande F 60 A2
Hetton-le-Hole GB 25 D6
Hettstedt D 52 B1
Heuchin F 48 C3
Heudicourt-sous-les-Côtes F 60 B1
Heunezel F 60 B2
Heuqueville F 57 A6
Heves H 65 C6
Héviz H 74 B2
Hexham GB 25 D5
Heysham GB 26 A3
Heytesbury GB 29 B5
Hidas H 74 B3
Hieflau A 63 C5
Hiendelaencina E 95 A4
Hiersac F 67 C5
High Bentham GB 26 A3
Highclere GB 31 C2
High Hesket GB 25 D5
Highley GB 26 C3
High Wycombe GB 31 C3
Higuera de Arjona E 100 B2
Higuera de Calatrava E 100 B1
Higuera de la Serena E 93 C5
Higuera de la Sierra E 99 B4
Higuera de Vargas E 93 C4
Higuera la Real E 99 A4
Higuers de Llerena E 93 C4
Higueruela E 96 C1
Híjar E 90 B2
Hilchenbach D 50 B4
Hildburghausen D 51 C6
Hilden D 50 B2
Hilders D 51 C5
Hildesheim D 51 A5
Hilgay GB 30 B4
Hillared S 40 B3
Hille D 51 A4
Hillegom NL 49 A5
Hillerød DK 41 D2
Hillerstorp S 40 B3
Hillesheim D 50 C2
Hillestad N 35 C2
Hillmersdorf D 52 B3
Hillsborough GB 19 B5
Hillswick GB 22 A7
Hilpoltstein D 62 A2
Hiltpoltstein D 62 A2
Hilvarenbeek NL 49 B6
Hilversum NL 49 A6
Himarë AL 116 B1
Himbergen D 44 B2
Himesháza H 74 B3
Himmelberg A 73 B4
Himmelpforten D 43 B6
Himód H 74 A2
Hinckley GB 30 B2
Hindås S 40 B2
Hindelang D 71 A5
Hindelbank CH 70 A2
Hinderavåg N 33 C2
Hindhead GB 31 C3
Hinjosa del Valle E 93 C4
Hinnerup DK 39 C3
Hinneryd S 40 C3
Hinojal E 93 B4
Hinojales E 99 B4
Hinojos E 99 B4
Hinojosa del Duque E 93 C5
Hinojosas de Calatrava E 100 A1
Hinterhornbach A 71 A5
Hinterriss A 71 A6
Hintersee
A 63 C4
D 45 B6
Hinterstoder A 63 C5
Hintertux A 72 A1
Hinterweidenthal D 60 A3
Hinwil CH 70 A3
Hios GR 116 D8
Hippolytushoef NL 42 C1
Hirschaid D 62 A1
Hirschau D 62 A2
Hirschfeld D 52 B3
Hirschhorn D 61 A4
Hirsingue F 60 C3
Hirson F 59 A5
Hirtshals DK 38 B2
Hirzenhain D 51 C5
Hisarcık TR 118 C4
Hishult S 41 C3
Hitchin GB 31 C3
Hitra N 114 D5
Hittarp S 41 C2
Hittisau A 71 A4
Hittun N 32 A1
Hitzacker D 44 B3
Hjallerup DK 38 B3
Hjällstad S 34 B5
Hjältevad S 40 B5
Hjärnarp S 41 C2
Hjartdal N 33 C5
Hjellestad N 32 B2
Hjelmeland N 33 C3
Hjelset N 114 E4
Hjerkinn N 114 E6
Hjerm DK 38 C1
Hjerpsted DK 39 D1
Hjerting DK 39 D1
Hjo S 35 D6
Hjordkær DK 39 D2
Hjørring DK 38 B2
Hjorted S 40 B6
Hjortkvarn S 37 D2
Hjortnäs S 36 B1
Hjortsberga S 40 C4
Hjukse N 33 C6
Hjuksebø N 33 C6
Hjulsjö S 36 C1
Hliník nad Hronom SK 65 B4
Hlinsko CZ 64 A1
Hlío IS 111 A10
Hlohovec SK 64 B3
Hlubokánad Vltavou CZ 63 A5
Hlučín CZ 64 A4
Hlukhiv UA 7 F12
Hlyboka UA 11 B8
Hlybokaye BY 7 D9
Hniezdne SK 65 A6
Hnilec SK 65 B6
Hnúšt'a SK 65 B5
Hobol H 74 B2
Hobro DK 38 C2
Hobscheid L 60 A1
Hocalar TR 119 D4
Hochdonn D 43 A6
Hochdorf CH 70 A3
Hochfelden F 60 B3
Hochspeyer D 60 A3
Höchstädt D 61 B6
Höchstadt D 62 A1
Hochstenbach D 50 C3
Höchst im Odenwald D 61 A5
Höckendorf D 52 C3
Hockenheim D 61 A4
Hoddesdon GB 31 C3
Hodejov SK 65 B5
Hodenhagen D 43 C6
Hodkovice CZ 53 C5
Hódmezövásárhely H 75 B5
Hodnet GB 26 C3
Hodonín CZ 64 B3
Hodslavice CZ 64 A4
Hoedekenskerke NL 49 B4
Hoegaarden B 49 C5
Hoek van Holland NL 49 B5
Hoenderlo NL 50 A1
Hof
D 52 C1
N 35 C2
Hofbieber D 51 C5
Hoff GB 26 A3
Hofgeismar D 51 B5
Hofheim
Bayern D 51 C6
Hofheim *continued*
Hessen D 51 C4
Hofkirchen im Mühlkreis A 63 B4
Höfn IS 111 C10
Hofors S 36 B3
Hofsós IS 111 B6
Hofstad N 114 C7
Höganäs S 41 C2
Högbo S 36 B3
Hogdal S 35 C3
Høgebru N 32 A4
Högfors S 36 C2
Högklint S 37 E5
Högsäter S 35 D4
Högsby S 40 B6
Högsjö S 37 C2
Hogstad S 37 D2
Högyész H 74 B3
Hohenau A 64 B2
Hohenberg A 63 C6
Hohenbucko D 52 B3
Hohenburg D 62 A2
Hohendorf D 45 A4
Hohenems A 71 A4
Hohenhameln D 51 A6
Hohenhausen D 51 A4
Hohenkirchen D 43 B4
Hohenlinden D 62 B2
Hohenlockstedt D 43 B6
Hohenmölsen D 52 B2
Hohennauen D 44 C4
Hohen Neuendorf D 45 C5
Hohenseeden D 52 A2
Hohentauern A 73 A4
Hohentengen D 70 A3
Hohenwepel D 51 B5
Hohenwestedt D 43 A6
Hohenwutzen D 45 C6
Hohenzieritz D 45 B5
Hohn D 43 A6
Hohne D 44 C2
Hohnstorf D 44 B2
Højer DK 39 E1
Højslev Stby DK 38 C2
Hok S 40 B4
Hökerum S 40 B3
Hökhuvud S 36 B5
Hokksund N 34 C1
Hökön S 40 C4
Hol N 32 B5
Hola Pristan UA 11 C12
Hólar IS 111 B6
Holašovice CZ 63 B5
Holbæk
Aarhus Amt. DK 38 C3
Vestsjællands Amt. DK 39 D4
Holbeach GB 30 B4
Holdenstedt D 44 C2
Holdhus N 32 B2
Holdorf D 43 C5
Holeby DK 44 A3
Hølen N 35 C2
Hølervasseter N 32 B6
Holešov CZ 64 A3
Holguera E 93 B4
Holíč SK 64 B3
Holice
CZ 53 C5
SK 64 C3
Höljes S 34 B4
Hollabrunn A 64 B2
Hollandstoun GB 23 B6
Høllen N 33 D4
Hollfeld D 52 D1
Hollókő H 65 C5
Hollstadt D 51 C6
Hollum NL 42 B2
Höllviksnäs S 41 D2
Holm N 114 B9
Hólmavík IS 111 B4
Holmbukt N 113 B10
Holmedal S 35 C3
Holmegil N 35 C3
Holmen N 34 B2
Holme-on-Spalding-Moor GB 27 B5
Holmes Chapel GB 26 B3
Holmestrand N 35 C2
Holmfirth GB 27 B4
Holmfoss N 113 C19
Holmsbu N 35 C2
Holmsjö S 41 C5
Holmsund S 3 E24
Holmsveden S 36 A3
Holmudden S 37 E6
Hölö S 37 C4
Holøydal N 114 E8
Holsbybrunn S 40 B5
Holseter N 34 A1
Holsljunga S 40 B2
Holstebro DK 39 C1
Holsted DK 39 D1
Holsworthy GB 28 C3
Holt
D 39 E2
Norfolk GB 30 B5
Wrexham GB 26 B3
IS 111 D6
N 33 D5
Holten NL 50 A2
Holtwick D 50 A3
Holum N 33 D4
Holwerd NL 42 B2
Holycross IRL 21 B4
Holyhead GB 26 B1
Holýšov CZ 62 A4
Holywell GB 26 B2
Holywood GB 19 B6
Holzdorf D 52 B3
Holzhausen D 51 A4
Holzheim D 61 B6
Holzkirchen D 62 C2
Holzminden D 51 B5
Holzthaleben D 51 B6
Homberg
Hessen D 51 B5
Hessen D 51 C5
Homburg D 60 A3
Hommelstø N 115 B9
Hommersåk N 33 D2
Homokmegy H 75 B4
Homokszentgyörgy H 74 B2
Homrogd H 65 B6
Homyel = Gomel BY 7 E11
Honaz TR 119 E4
Hondarribia E 76 C1
Hondón de los Frailes E 101 A5
Hondschoote F 48 C3
Hönebach D 51 C5
Hønefoss N 34 B2
Honfleur F 57 A6
Høng DK 39 D4
Honiton GB 29 C4
Hönningen D 50 C2
Honningsvåg N 113 B14
Hönö S 38 B4
Honrubia E 95 C4
Hontalbilla E 88 C2
Hontheim D 50 C2
Hontianske-Nemce SK 65 B4
Hontoria de la Cantera E 88 B3
Hontoria del Pinar E 89 C3
Hontoria de Valdearados E 89 C3
Hoofddorp NL 49 A5
Hoogerheide NL 49 B5
Hoogeveen NL 42 C3
Hoogezand-Sappemeer NL 42 B3
Hoogkarspel NL 42 C2
Hoogkerk NL 42 B3
Hoogstede D 42 C3
Hoogstraten B 49 B5
Hook GB 31 C3
Hooksiel D 43 B5
Höör S 41 D3
Hoorn NL 42 C2
Hope GB 26 B2
Hopen N 112 E4
Hope under Dinmore GB 29 A5
Hopfgarten A 72 A2
Hopfgarten in Defereggen A 72 B2
Hopseidet N 113 B16
Hopsten D 43 C4
Hoptrup DK 39 D2
Hora Svatého Sebestiána CZ 52 C3
Horaždóvice CZ 63 A4
Horb am Neckar D 61 B4
Horbelev DK 39 E5
Hørby DK 38 B3
Hörby S 41 D3
Horcajada de la Torre E 95 B4
Horcajo de los Montes E 94 C2
Horcajo de Santiago E 95 C3
Horcajo-Medianero E 93 A5
Horche E 95 B3
Horda S 40 B4
Hordabø N 32 B1
Hordalia N 32 C3
Hordvik N 32 B2
Hořesedly CZ 52 C3
Horezu RO 11 D8
Horgen CH 70 A3
Horgoš SRB 75 B4
Hořice CZ 53 C5
Horjul SLO 73 B4
Horka D 53 B4
Hörken S 36 B1
Horki BY 7 D11
Hörle S 40 B4
Horn
A 63 B6
D 51 B4
N 34 B2
S 40 B5
Horna E 101 A4
Hornachos E 93 C4
Hornachuelos E 99 B5
Horná Mariková SK 64 A4
Hornanes N 32 C2
Horná Streda SK 64 B3
Horná Štrubna SK 65 B4
Horná Súča SK 64 B3
Hornbæk
Aarhus Amt. DK 38 C2
Frederiksværk DK 41 C2
Hornberg D 61 B4
Hornburg D 51 A6
Horncastle GB 27 B5
Horndal S 36 B3
Horndean GB 31 D2
Horne
Fyns Amt. DK 39 D3
Ribe Amt. DK 39 D1
Hörnebo S 35 D6
Horneburg D 43 B6
Hörnefors S 115 D16
Horní Bečva CZ 64 A4
Horni Benešov CZ 64 A3
Horni Cerekev CZ 63 A6
Horní Jiřetín CZ 52 C3
Horní Lomná CZ 65 A4
Horni Maršov CZ 53 C5
Hornindal N 114 F3
Hørning DK 39 C3
Hörningsholm S 37 C4
Horní Planá CZ 63 B5
Horni Slavkov CZ 52 C2
Horni Vltavice CZ 63 B4
Hornnes N 33 D4
Horno D 53 B4
Hornos E 101 A3
Hornoy-le-Bourg F 58 A2
Hornsea GB 27 B5
Hornsjø N 34 A2
Hornslet DK 39 C3
Hornstein A 64 C2
Hörnum D 39 E1
Hornum DK 38 C2
Horný Tisovnik SK 65 B5
Horodenka UA 11 B8
Horodnya UA 7 F11
Horodok
Khmelnytskyy UA 11 B9
Lviv UA 11 B7
Horodyshche UA 11 B11
Horokhiv UA 11 A8
Horovice CZ 63 A4
Horred S 40 B2
Hörröd S 41 D4
Hörsching A 63 B5
Horsens DK 39 D2
Horsham GB 31 C3
Hørsholm DK 41 D2
Horslunde DK 39 E4
Horšovský Týn CZ 62 A3
Horst NL 50 B2
Horstel D 50 A3
Horsten D 43 B4
Horstmar D 50 A3
Hort H 65 C5
Horta P 87 C3
Horten N 35 C2
Hortezuela E 89 C4
Hortiguela E 89 B3
Hortobágy H 75 A6
Horton in Ribblesdale GB 26 A3
Hørve DK 39 D4
Hörvik S 41 C4
Horwich GB 26 B3
Hosanger N 32 B2
Hösbach D 51 C5
Hosena D 53 B4
Hosenfeld D 51 C5
Hosingen L 50 C2
Hospental CH 70 B3
Hospital IRL 20 B3
Hossegor F 76 C1
Hosszuhetény H 74 B3
Hostal de Ipiés E 90 A2
Hoštálkova CZ 64 A3
Hostalric E 91 B5
Hostens F 76 B2
Hostěradice CZ 64 B2
Hostinné CZ 53 C5
Hostomice CZ 63 A5
Hostouň CZ 62 A3
Hotagen S 115 D11
Hoting S 115 C13
Hotolisht AL 116 A2
Hotton B 49 C6
Houdain F 48 C3
Houdan F 58 B2
Houdelaincourt F 60 B1
Houeillès F 76 B3
Houffalize B 50 C1
Houghton-le-Spring GB 25 D6
Houlberg DK 39 C2
Houlgate F 57 A5
Hounslow GB 31 C3
Hourtin F 66 C3
Hourtin-Plage F 66 C3
Houthalen B 49 B6
Houyet B 49 C5
Hov
DK 39 D3
N 34 B2
Hova S 35 D6
Høvåg N 33 D5
Hovborg DK 39 D1
Hovda N 32 B6
Hovden N 33 C4
Hove GB 31 D3
Hovedgård DK 39 D2
Hovelhof D 51 B4
Hoven DK 39 D1
Hovet N 32 B5
Hovingham GB 27 A5
Hovmantorp S 40 C5
Hovsta S 37 C2
Howden GB 27 B5
Howe D 44 B2
Höxter D 51 B5
Hoya D 43 C6
Hoya de Santa Maria E 99 B4
Hoya-Gonzalo E 95 D5
Høyanger N 32 A3
Hoyerswerda D 53 B4
Høyjord N 35 C2
Hoylake GB 26 B2
Høylandet N 114 C9
Hoym D 52 B1
Høymyr N 32 C6
Hoyocasero E 94 B2
Hoyo de Manzanares E 94 B3
Hoyo de Pinares E 94 B2
Hoyos E 93 A4
Hoyos del Espino E 93 A5
Hrabusiče SK 65 B6
Hradec Králové CZ 53 C5
Hradec nad Moravicí CZ 64 A3
Hrádek CZ 64 B2
Hrádek nad Nisou CZ 53 C4
Hradište SK 65 B4
Hrafnagil IS 111 B7
Hrafnseyri IS 111 B2
Hranice
Severomoravsky CZ 64 A3
Západočeský CZ 52 C2
Hranovnica SK 65 B6
Hrasnica BIH 84 C3
Hrastnik SLO 73 B5
Hrebenka UA 11 A12
Hřensko CZ 53 C4
Hriňová SK 65 B5
Hrisoupoli GR 116 B6
Hrochov CZ 64 A2
Hrochův Tynec CZ 53 D5
Hrodna BY 6 E7
Hrodzyanka BY 7 E10
Hronov CZ 53 C6
Hronský Beňadik SK 65 B4
Hrotovice CZ 64 A2
Hrtkovci SRB 85 B4
Hrun IS 111 A5
Hrušov SK 65 B5
Hrušovany nad Jevišovkou CZ 64 B2
Hřuštin SK 65 A5
Hrvaćani BIH 84 B2
Hrvace HR 83 C5
Hrymayliv UA 11 B9
Huben A 72 B2
Hückel-hoven D 50 B2
Hückeswagen D 50 B3
Hucknall GB 27 B4
Hucqueliers F 48 C2
Huddersfield GB 27 B4
Huddinge S 37 C4
Huddunge S 36 B3
Hude D 43 B5
Hudiksvall S 115 F14
Huélago E 100 B2
Huélamo E 95 B5
Huelgoat F 56 B2
Huelma E 100 B2
Huelva E 99 B4
Huéneja E 100 B3
Huércal de Almeria E 101 C3
Huércal-Overa E 101 B4
Huerta de Abajo E 89 B3
Huerta del Rey E 89 C3
Huerta de Valdecarabanos E 95 C3
Huertahernando E 95 B4
Huesa E 100 B2
Huesca E 90 A2
Huéscar E 101 B3
Huete E 95 B4
Huétor Tájar E 100 B1
Hüfingen D 61 C4
Hufthamar N 32 B2
Hugh Town GB 28 D1
Huglfing D 62 C2
Huissen NL 50 B1
Huittinen FIN 3 F25
Huizen NL 49 A6
Hulín CZ 64 A3
Hüls D 50 B2
Hulsig DK 38 B3
Hulst NL 49 B5
Hult S 40 B5
Hulta S 40 A6
Hulteby S 35 C6
Hulterstad S 41 C6
Hultsfred S 40 B5
Humanes E 95 B3
Humberston GB 27 B5
Humble DK 39 E3
Humenné SK 10 B6
Humilladero E 100 B1
Humlebæk DK 41 D2
Humlum DK 38 C1
Hummelsta S 37 C3
Humpolec CZ 63 A6
Humshaugh GB 25 C5
Hundåla N 115 B9
Hundested DK 39 D4
Hundvåg N 33 C2
Hundvin N 32 B2
Hunedoara RO 11 D7
Hünfeld D 51 C5
Hungen D 51 C4
Hungerford GB 31 C2
Hunndalen N 34 B2
Hunnebostrand S 35 D3
Hunstanton GB 30 B4
Huntingdon GB 30 B3
Huntley GB 29 B5
Huntly GB 23 D6
Hünxe D 50 B2
Hurbanovo SK 64 C4
Hürbel D 61 B5
Hurdal N 34 B3
Hurezani RO 11 D7
Hurlford GB 24 C3
Hurstbourne Tarrant GB 31 C2
Hurstpierpoint GB 31 D3
Hürth D 50 C2
Hurum N 32 A5
Hurup DK 38 C1
Húsafell IS 111 C5
Húsavík IS 111 A8
Husbands Bosworth GB 30 B2
Husby
D 39 E2
DK 39 C1
Husey IS 111 B11
Huşi RO 11 C10
Husina BIH 84 B3
Husínec CZ 63 A4
Husinish GB 22 D1
Huskvarna S 40 B4
Husnes N 32 C2
Husøy N 112 C6
Hustad N 114 E4
Hüsten D 50 B3
Hustopeče CZ 64 B2
Hustopeče nad Bečvou CZ 64 A3
Husum
D 43 A6
S 115 D16
Husvika N 115 B9
Huta PL 46 C2
Hutovo BIH 84 D2
Hüttenberg A 73 B4
Hüttlingen D 61 B6
Huttoft GB 27 B6
Hutton Cranswick GB 27 B5
Hüttschlag A 72 A3
Huttwil CH 70 A2
Huy B 49 C6
Hüyük TR 119 E6
Hval N 34 B2
Hvåle N 32 B6
Hvaler N 35 C3
Hvalpsund DK 38 C2
Hvammstangi IS 111 B5
Hvammur IS 111 B6
Hvanneyri IS 111 C4
Hvar HR 83 C5
Hvarnes N 35 C1
Hveragerði IS 111 D4
Hvidbjerg DK 38 C1
Hvide Sande DK 39 D1
Hvittingfoss N 35 C2
Hvolsvöllur IS 111 D5
Hybe SK 65 A5
Hycklinge S 40 B5
Hydra GR 117 E5
Hyen N 114 F2
Hyères F 79 C5
Hyéres Plage F 79 C5
Hylestad N 33 C4
Hylke DK 39 D2
Hyllestad N 32 A2
Hyllstofta S 41 C3
Hyltebruk S 40 B3
Hynish GB 24 B1
Hynnekleiv N 33 D5
Hythe
Hampshire GB 31 D2
Kent GB 31 C5
Hyvinkää FIN 3 F26

I

Iam RO 85 A6
Iaşi RO 11 C9
Iasmos GR 116 A7
Ibahernando E 93 B5
Iballë AL 105 A5
Ibarranguelua E 89 A4
Ibbenbüren D 50 A3
Ibeas de Juarros E 89 B3
Ibestad N 112 D6
Ibi E 96 C2
Ibiza = Eivissa E 97 C1
İbradı TR 119 E6
İbriktepe TR 118 A1
Ibros E 100 A2
Ibstock GB 27 C4
İçel TR 16 C7
Ichenhausen D 61 B6
Ichnya UA 11 A12
Ichtegem B 49 B4
Ichtershausen D 51 C6
Idanha-a-Novo P 93 B3
Idar-Oberstein D 60 A3
Idd N 35 C3
Idiazábal E 89 B4
Idivuoma S 113 D10
Idkerberget S 36 B2
Idön S 36 B5
Idre S 115 F9
Idrija SLO 73 C4
Idritsa RUS 7 C10
Idstein D 50 C4
Idvor SRB 75 C5
Iecca Mare RO 75 C5
Ielsi I 103 B7
Ieper = Ypres B 48 C3
Ierapetra GR 117 G7
Ierissos GR 116 B5
Ifjord N 113 B16
Ig SLO 73 C4
Igal H 74 B2
Igalo MNE 105 A4
Igea E 89 B4
Igea Marina I 82 B1
Igelfors S 37 D2
Igersheim D 61 A5
Iggesund S 115 F14
Iglarevo KOS 85 D5
Iglesias E 88 B3
Iglésias I 110 C1
Igls A 71 A6
Igny-Comblizy F 59 A4
Igorre E 89 A4
Igoumenitsa GR 116 C2
Igries E 90 A2
Igualada E 91 B4
Igüeña E 86 B4
Iguerande F 68 B4
Iharosberény H 74 B2
Ihl'any SK 65 A6
Ihlienworth D 43 B5
Ihringen D 60 B3
Ihrlerstein D 62 B2
İhsaniye TR 118 C5
Ii FIN 3 D26
Iijärvi FIN 113 C16
Iisalmi FIN 3 E27
IJmuiden NL 42 C1
IJsselmuiden NL 42 C2
IJzendijke NL 49 B4
Ikast DK 39 C2
Ikervár H 74 A1
Ilandža SRB 75 C5
Ilanz CH 71 B4
Ilava SK 64 B4
Iława PL 47 B5
il Castagno I 81 C4
Ilche E 90 B3
Ilchester GB 29 C5
Ilfeld D 51 B6
Ilfracombe GB 28 B3
Ilgaz TR 16 A6
Ilgın TR 119 D6
Ílhavo P 92 A2
Ilica TR 118 C2
Ilidža BIH 84 C3
Ilijaš BIH 84 C3
Ilirska Bistrica SLO 73 C4
Ilkeston GB 27 C4
Ilkley GB 27 B4
Illana E 95 B4
Illano E 86 A4
Illar E 101 C3
Illas E 88 A1
Illats F 76 B2
Illertissen D 61 B6
Illescas E 94 B3
Ille-sur-Têt F 91 A5
Illfurth F 60 C3
Illichivsk UA 11 C11
Illiers-Combray F 58 B2
Illkirch-Graffenstaden F 60 B3
Illmersdorf D 52 B3
Illmitz A 64 C2
Íllora E 100 B2
Illueca E 89 C5
Ilmajoki FIN 3 E25
Ilmenau D 51 C6
Ilminster GB 29 C5
Ilok HR 75 C4
Ilomantsi FIN 3 E29
Iłow PL 47 C6
Iłowa PL 53 B5
Iłowo-Osada PL 47 B6
Ilsenburg D 51 B6
Ilshofen D 61 A5
Ilz A 73 A5
Iłża PL 55 B6
İmamoğlu TR 16 C7
Imatra FIN 3 F28
Imielin PL 55 C4
Imingen N 32 B5
Immeln S 41 C4
Immenhausen D 51 B5
Immenstadt D 61 C6
Immingham GB 27 B5
Ímola I 81 B5
Imon E 95 A4
Imotski HR 84 C2
Impéria I 80 C2
Imphy F 68 B3
İmroz TR 116 B7
Imsland N 33 C2
Imst A 71 A5
Inagh IRL 20 B2
Inari FIN 113 D15
Inca E 97 B2
Inchnadamph GB 22 C4
Incinillas E 89 B3
Indal S 115 E14
Indjija SRB 85 A5
Indre Arna N 32 B2
Indre Billefjord N 113 B14
Indre Brenna N 113 B14
İğneada TR 118 A2
İnebolu TR 16 A6
İnecik TR 118 B2
İnegöl TR 118 B4
Inerthal CH 70 A3
Infiesto E 88 A1
Ingatorp S 40 B5
Ingedal N 35 C3
Ingelheim D 50 D4
Ingelmunster B 49 C4
Ingelstad S 40 C4
Ingleton GB 26 A3
Ingolfsland N 32 C5
Ingolstadt D 62 B2
Ingrandes
Maine-et-Loire F 66 A4
Vienne F 67 B5
Ingwiller F 60 B3
Inhisar TR 118 B5
Inhulec UA 11 C12
Iniesta E 95 C5
Inishannon IRL 20 C3
Inishcrone IRL 18 B2
Inke H 74 B2
Inndyr N 112 E3
Innellan GB 24 C3
Innerleithen GB 25 C4
Innermessan GB 24 D3
Innertkirchen CH 70 B3
Innervillgraten A 72 B2
Innsbruck A 71 A6
Innset N 112 D7
Innvik N 114 F3
İnönü TR 118 C5
Inowłódz PL 55 B5
Inowrocław PL 47 C4
Ins CH 70 A2
Insch GB 23 D6
Insjön S 36 B2
Ińsko PL 46 B1
Instow GB 28 B3
İntepe TR 118 B1
Interlaken CH 70 B2
Intragna CH 70 B3
Introbio I 71 C4
Inverallochy GB 23 D7
Inveran
GB 23 D4
IRL 20 A2
Inveraray GB 24 B2
Inverbervie GB 25 B5
Invergarry GB 22 D4
Invergordon GB 23 D4
Invergowrie GB 25 B4
Inverkeilor GB 25 B5
Inverkeithing GB 25 B4
Invermoriston GB 22 D4
Inverness GB 23 D4
Inveruno I 70 C3
Inverurie GB 23 D6
Ioannina GR 116 C2
Iolanda di Savoia I 81 B5
Ion Corvin RO 11 D9
Ióppolo I 106 C2
Ios GR 117 F7
Ipati GR 116 D4
İpsala TR 118 B1
Ipswich GB 30 B5
Iraklia GR 116 A5
Iraklio = Heraklion GR 117 G7
Irdning A 73 A4
Iregszemcse H 74 B3
Irgoli I 110 B2
Irig SRB 85 A4
Ironbridge GB 26 C3
Irpin UA 11 A11
Irrel D 60 A2
Irsina I 104 C2
Irsta S 37 C3
Irthlingborough GB 30 B3
Iruela E 87 B4
Irún E 76 C1
Irurita E 76 C1
Irurzun E 76 D1
Irvine GB 24 C3
Irvinestown GB 19 B4
Isaba E 76 D2
Isabela E 100 A2
Ísafjörður IS 111 A2
Isane N 114 F2
Isaszeg H 75 A4
Isbister GB 22 A7
Íscar E 88 C2
İscehisar TR 118 D5
Ischgl A 71 A5
Íschia I 103 C6
Ischia di Castro I 102 A4
Ischitella I 104 B1
Isdes F 58 C3
Ise N 35 C3
Iselle I 70 B3
Iseltwald CH 70 B2
Isen D 62 B3
Isenbüttel D 44 C2
Iseo I 71 C5
Iserlohn D 50 B3
Isérnia I 103 B7
Isfjorden N 114 E4
Ishëm AL 105 B5
Isigny-sur-Mer F 57 A4
Işıklı TR 119 D4
Ísili I 110 C2
İskilip TR 16 A7
Isla Canela E 98 B3
Isla Cristina E 98 B3
Islares E 89 A3
Isleham GB 30 B4
Isle of Whithorn GB 24 D3
Ismaning D 62 B2
Isna P 92 B3
Isnestoften N 113 B11
Isny D 61 C6
Isoba E 88 A1
Isokylä
FIN 113 F16
S 113 E11
Isola F 79 B6
Isola d'Asti I 80 B2
Isola del Gran Sasso d'Itália I 103 A6
Ísola della Scala I 71 C6
Isola delle Fémmine I 108 A2
Ísola del Liri I 103 B6
Ísola di Capo Rizzuto I 107 C4
Isona E 91 A4
Ispagnac F 78 B2
Isparta TR 119 E5
Isperikh BG 11 E9
Íspica I 109 C3
Isselburg D 50 B2
Issigeac F 77 B3
Issogne I 70 C2
Issoire F 68 C3
Issoncourt F 59 B6
Issoudun F 68 B2
Issum D 50 B2
Is-sur-Tille F 69 A5
Issy-l'Evêque F 68 B3
Istán E 100 C1
İstanbul TR 118 A3
Istebna PL 65 A4
Ístia d'Ombrone I 81 D5
Istiea GR 116 D5
Istok KOS 85 D5
Istres F 78 C3
Istvándi H 74 B2
Itea GR 116 D4
Ithaki GR 117 D2
Itoiz E 76 D1
Ítrabo E 100 C2
Itri I 103 B6
Ittireddu I 110 B1
Íttiri I 110 B1
Itzehoe D 43 B6
Ivalo FIN 113 D16
Iván H 74 A1
Ivanava BY 7 E8
Ivančice CZ 64 A2
Ivančna Gorica SLO 73 C4
Iváncsa H 74 A3
Ivanec HR 73 B6
Ivanić Grad HR 73 C6
Ivanjica SRB 85 C5
Ivanjska BIH 84 B2
Ivanka SK 64 B4
Ivankovo HR 74 C3
Ivano-Frankivsk UA 11 B8
Ivanovice na Hané CZ 64 A3
Ivanska HR 74 C1
Ivatsevichy BY 7 E8
Ivaylovgrad BG 116 A8
Iveland N 33 D4
Ivoz Ramet B 49 C6
Ivrea I 70 C2
İvrindi TR 118 C2
Ivry-en-Montagne F 69 A4
Ivry-la-Bataille F 58 B2
Ivybridge GB 28 C4
Iwaniska PL 55 C6
Iwiny PL 53 B5
Iwuy F 49 C4
Ixworth GB 30 B4
Izarra E 89 B4
Izbica Kujawska PL 47 C4
Izbište SRB 85 A6
Izeda P 87 C4
Izegem B 49 C4
Izernore F 69 B5
Izmayil UA 11 D10
İzmir TR 119 D2
İzmit = Kocaeli TR 118 B4
Iznájar E 100 B1
Iznalloz E 100 B2
Iznatoraf E 100 A2
İznik TR 118 B4
Izola SLO 72 C3
Izsák H 75 B4
Izsófalva H 65 B6
Izyaslav UA 11 A9

J

Jabalquinto E 100 A2
Jablanac HR 83 B3
Jablanica BIH 84 C2
Jablonec nad Jizerou CZ 53 C5
Jablonec nad Nisou CZ 53 C5
Jablonica SK 64 B3
Jablonka PL 65 A5
Jabłonna PL 55 A5
Jablonnénad Orlicí CZ 54 C1
Jablonne Podještědi CZ 53 C4
Jablonov nad Turňou SK 65 B6
Jabłonowo Pomorskie PL 47 B5
Jablúnka CZ 64 A3
Jablunkov CZ 65 A4
Jabučje SRB 85 B5
Jabugo E 99 B4
Jabuka
Srbija SRB 85 C4
Vojvodina SRB 85 B5
Jabukovac HR 73 C6
Jaca E 90 A2
Jáchymov CZ 52 C2
Jacobidrebber D 43 C5
Jade D 43 B5
Jäderfors S 36 B3
Jädraås S 36 B3
Jadraque E 95 B4
Jaén E 100 B2
Jagare BIH 84 B2
Jagel D 43 A6
Jagenbach A 63 B6
Jægerspris DK 39 D4
Jagodina SRB 85 C6
Jagodnjak HR 74 C3
Jagodzin PL 53 B5
Jagstheim D 61 A6
Jagstzell D 61 A6
Jahodna SK 64 B3
Jajce BIH 84 B2
Ják H 74 A1
Jakabszálbs H 75 B4
Jäkkvik S 115 A14
Jaklovce SK 65 B6
Jakobsnes N 113 C19
Jakovlje HR 73 C5
Jakšic HR 74 C2
Jakubany SK 65 A6
Jalance E 96 B1
Jalasjärvi FIN 3 E25
Jalhay B 50 C1
Jaligny-sur-Besbre F 68 B3
Jallais F 66 A4
Jalón E 96 C2
Jâlons F 59 B5
Jamena SRB 84 B4
Jamilena E 100 B2
Jämjö S 41 C5
Jamnička Kiselica HR 73 C5
Jamno PL 46 A2
Jamoigne B 59 A6
Jämsä FIN 3 F26
Jämshög S 41 C4
Janakkala FIN 3 F26
Jandelsbrunn D 63 B4
Jänickendorf D 52 A3
Janikowo PL 47 C4
Janja BIH 85 B4
Janjina HR 84 D2
Janki
Łódzkie PL 55 B4
Mazowieckie PL 55 A5
Jankov CZ 63 A5
Jankowo Dolne PL 46 C3
Jánoshalma H 75 B4
Jánosháza H 74 A2
Jánoshida H 75 A5
Jánossomorja H 64 C3
Janovice nad Uhlavou CZ 63 A4
Janów PL 55 C4
Janowiec Wielkopolski PL 46 C3
Janowo PL 47 B6
Jänsmässholmen S 115 D10
Janville F 58 B2
Janzé F 57 C4
Jarabá SK 65 B5
Jaraczewo PL 54 B2
Jarafuel E 96 B1
Jaraicejo E 93 B5
Jaraíz de la Vera E 93 A5
Jarak SRB 85 B4
Jarandilla de la Vera E 93 A5
Jaray E 89 C4
Järbo S 36 B3
Jard-sur-Mer F 66 B3
Jaren N 34 B2
Jargeau F 58 C3
Jarkovac SRB 75 C5
Järlåsa S 36 C4
Jarmen D 45 B5
Järna S 37 C4
Jarnac F 67 C4
Järnäs S 115 D16
Järnforsen S 40 B5
Jarny F 60 A1
Jarocin PL 54 B2
Jaroměř CZ 53 C5

Jaroměřice nad Rokytnou CZ....64 A1
Jaroslav CZ....53 C6
Jaroslavice CZ....64 B2
Jaroslaw PL....11 A7
Jarosław PL....46 A2
Jarošov nad Nežarkou CZ....63 A6
Järpås S....35 A5
Järpen S....115 D10
Jarrow GB....25 D6
Järso FIN....36 B6
Järvenpää FIN....115 F13
Jarvorník CZ....54 C1
Järvsö S....115 F13
Jarze F....67 A4
Jaša Tomic SRB....75 C5
Jasenak HR....73 C5
Jasenica BIH....83 B5
Jasenica SRB....85 C5
Jasenovac HR....74 C1
Jasenovo
  Srbija SRB....85 C4
  Vojvodina SRB....85 B6
Jasień PL....53 B5
Jasienica PL....53 C6
Jasika SRB....85 C6
Jasło PL....10 B6
Jásova SK....65 C4
Jasseron F....69 B5
Jastarnia PL....47 A4
Jastrebarsko HR....73 C5
Jastrowie PL....46 B2
Jastrzębia-Góra PL....47 A4
Jastrzębie Zdrój PL....54 D3
Jászals-Lószentgyörgy H....75 A5
Jászapáti H....75 A5
Jászárokszállás H....65 C5
Jászberény H....75 A4
Jászdózsa H....65 C6
Jászfényszaru H....75 A4
Jászjákóhalma H....75 A5
Jászkarajenő H....75 A5
Jászkisér H....75 A5
Jászladány H....75 A5
Jászszentlászló H....75 B4
Jásztelek H....75 A5
Játar E....100 C2
Jättendal S....115 F14
Jatznick D....45 B5
Jaun CH....70 B2
Jausiers F....79 B5
Jávea E....96 C3
Jävenitz D....44 C3
Javerlhac F....67 C5
Javier E....90 A1
Javorani BIH....84 B2
Javorina SK....65 A6
Javron F....57 B5
Jawor PL....53 B6
Jaworzno PL....55 C4
Jaworzyna Śl. PL....54 C1
Jayena E....100 C2
Jazów PL....53 B5
Jebel RO....75 C6
Jebjerg DK....38 C2
Jedburgh GB....25 C5
Jedlinsk PL....55 B6
Jednia Letnisko PL....55 B6
Jedovnice CZ....64 A2
Jedrychów PL....47 B5
Jędrzejów PL....55 C5
Jedwabno PL....47 B6
Jeesiö FIN....113 E15
Jegłownik PL....47 A5
Jegun F....77 C3
Jēkabpils LV....7 C8
Jektvik N....32 C2
Jektvik N....112 F2
Jelakci SRB....85 C5
Jelcz-Laskowice PL....54 B2
Jelenec SK....64 B4
Jelenia Góra PL....53 C5
Jelka SK....64 B3
Jelling DK....39 D2
Jels DK....39 D2
Jelsa
  HR....83 C5
Jelšava SK....65 B6
Jemgum D....43 B4
Jemnice CZ....64 A1
Jena D....52 C1
Jenaz CH....71 B4
Jenbach A....72 A1
Jenikow PL....45 B7
Jennersdorf A....73 B6
Jenny S....40 B6
Jerchel D....44 C3
Jeres del Marquesado E....100 B2
Jerez de la Frontera E....99 C4
Jerez de los Caballeros E....99 A4
Jerica E....96 B2
Jerichow D....44 C4
Jerka PL....54 A1
Jermenovci SRB....75 C6
Jerslev DK....38 B3
Jerte E....93 A5
Jerup DK....38 B3
Jerxheim D....51 A6
Jerzmanowice PL....55 C5
Jerzu I....110 C2
Jerzwald PL....47 B5
Jesberg D....51 C5
Jesenice
  Středočeský CZ....52 C3
  Středočeský CZ....53 C4
  SLO....73 B4
Jeseník CZ....54 C2
Jesenské SK....65 B6
Jesi I....82 C2
Jésolo I....72 C2
Jessen D....52 B2
Jessenitz D....44 B3
Jessheim N....34 B3
Jessnitz D....52 B2
Jesteburg D....44 B1
Jeumont F....49 C5
Jeven-stedt D....43 A6
Jever D....43 B4
Jevičko CZ....64 A2
Jevišovice CZ....64 B1
Jevnaker N....34 B2
Jezerane HR....83 A4
Jezero
  BIH....84 B2
  HR....83 A4
Jeziorany PL....47 B6
Jeżów PL....55 B5
Jičín CZ....53 C5
Jičiněves CZ....53 C5
Jihlava CZ....63 A6
Jijona E....96 C2
Jilemnice CZ....53 C5
Jílové CZ....52 B2
Jílové u Prahy CZ....63 A5
Jimbolia RO....75 C5
Jimena E....100 B2
Jimena de la Frontera E....99 C5
Jimera de Libar E....99 C5
Jimramov CZ....64 A2
Jince CZ....63 A5
Jindřichovice CZ....52 C2
Jindřichův Hradec CZ....63 A6
Jirkov CZ....52 C3
Jistebnice CZ....63 A5
Joachimsthal D....45 C5
João da Loura P....92 C2
Jobbágyi H....65 C5
Jochberg A....72 A2
Jockfall S....113 F11

Jódar E....100 B2
Jodoigne B....49 C5
Joensuu FIN....3 E28
Joesjö S....115 B11
Joeuf F....60 A1
Jõgeva EST....7 B9
Johanngeorgenstadt D....52 C2
Johannishus S....41 C5
Johanniskirchen D....62 B3
Johansfors S....40 C5
John o'Groats GB....23 C5
Johnshaven GB....25 B5
Johnstone GB....24 C3
Johnstown IRL....21 B4
Jõhvi EST....7 B9
Joigny F....59 C4
Joinville F....59 B6
Jokkmokk S....112 F8
Jöllenbeck D....51 A4
Jomala FIN....36 B6
Jönåker S....37 D3
Jonava LT....6 D8
Jonchery-sur-Vesle F....59 A4
Jondal N....32 B3
Jondalen N....33 C6
Joniškis LT....6 C7
Jönköping S....40 B4
Jonkowo PL....47 B6
Jonnu N....33 C6
Jonsberg S....37 D3
Jonsered S....38 B5
Jonstorp S....41 C2
Jonzac F....67 C4
Jorba E....91 B4
Jordanów PL....65 A5
Jordanowo PL....46 C1
Jordanów Śląski PL....54 C1
Jordbro S....37 C5
Jordbrua N....115 A11
Jördenstorf D....45 B4
Jordet N....34 A4
Jordøse DK....39 D3
Jork D....43 B6
Jörlanda S....38 B4
Jormlien S....115 C10
Jormvattnet S....115 C11
Jörn S....115 B17
Jørpeland N....33 C3
Jorquera E....96 B1
Jošan HR....83 B4
Jošavka Banja SRB....85 C5
Jošavka BIH....84 B2
Josipdol HR....73 C5
Josipovac HR....74 C3
Jössefors S....35 C4
Josselin F....56 C3
Jøssund N....114 C7
Jostedal N....114 F4
Jósvafő H....65 B6
Jou P....87 C3
Jouarre F....59 B4
Joué-lès-Tours F....67 A5
Joué-sur-Erdre F....66 A3
Joure NL....42 C2
Joutseno FIN....3 F28
Joutsijärvi FIN....113 F16
Joux-la-Ville F....59 C4
Jouy F....58 B2
Jouy-le-Châtel F....59 B4
Jouy-le-Potier F....58 C2
Joyeuse F....78 B3
Joze F....68 C3
Józefów PL....55 A6
Juankoski FIN....3 E28
Juan-les-Pins F....79 C6
Juban AL....105 A5
Jübek D....43 A6
Jubera E....89 B4
Jubrique E....99 C5
Jüchsen D....51 C6
Judaberg N....33 C2
Judenburg A....73 A4
Juelsminde DK....39 D3
Jugon-les-Lacs F....56 B3
Juillac F....67 C6
Juillan F....76 C3
Juist D....43 B4
Jukkasjärvi S....112 E9
Jule N....115 C10
Julianadorp NL....42 C1
Julianstown IRL....21 A5
Jülich D....50 C2
Jullouville F....57 B4
Jumeaux F....68 C3
Jumièges F....58 A1
Jumilhac-le-Grand F....67 C6
Jumilla E....101 A4
Juncosa E....90 B3
Juneda E....90 B3
Jung S....35 D5
Jungingen D....61 B5
Junglingster L....60 A2
Juniville F....59 A5
Junosuando S....113 E11
Junqueira P....87 C3
Junsele S....115 D13
Juoksengi S....113 F12
Juoksenki FIN....113 F12
Juprelle B....49 C6
Jurata PL....47 A4
Jurbarkas LT....6 D7
Jurbise HR....83 B3
Jurjevo HR....83 B3
Jūrmala LV....6 C7
Juromenha P....93 C3
Jursla S....37 D3
Jussac F....77 B5
Jussey F....60 C1
Jussy F....59 A4
Juta H....74 B2
Jüterbog D....52 B3
Juuka FIN....3 E28
Juuma FIN....113 F17
Juvigny-le-Terte F....57 B4
Juvigny-sous-Andaine F....57 B5
Juzennecourt F....59 B5
Jyderup DK....39 D4
Jyväskylä FIN....3 E26

K

Kaamanen FIN....113 C16
Kaamasmukka FIN....113 C15
Kaaresuvanto FIN....113 D11
Kaarssen D....44 B2
Kaatsheuvel NL....49 B6
Kaba H....75 A6
Kåbdalis S....115 A17
Kačarevo SRB....85 B5
Kačikol KOS....85 D6
Kács H....65 C6
Kadaň CZ....52 C3
Kadarkút H....74 B2
Kadıköy TR....118 B1
Kåfalla S....37 C2
Kåfjord N....113 C13
Kåfjordbotn N....112 C9
Kågeröd S....41 D3
Kahl D....51 C5
Kahla D....52 C1
Kainach bei Voitsberg A....73 A5
Kaindorf A....73 A5
Kainulasjärvi S....113 F11
Kairala FIN....113 E16
Kaisepakte S....112 E8
Kaisersesch D....50 C2
Kaiserslautern D....60 A3
Kaisheim D....62 B1
Kajaani FIN....3 D27
Kajárpéc H....74 A2
Kajdacs H....74 B3
Kakanj BIH....84 B3
Kaklik TR....119 E4
Kalajoki FIN....3 D25
Kalak N....113 B16
Kalamata GR....117 E4
Kalambaka GR....116 C3
Kalamria GR....116 B4
Kalandra GR....116 C5
Kalarne S....115 E13
Kalavárda GR....119 F2
Kalavryta GR....117 D4
Kalbe D....44 C3
Kalce SLO....73 C4
Káld H....74 A2
Kale
  Antalya TR....119 F4
  Denizli TR....119 E3
Kalecik TR....16 A6
Kalefeld D....51 B6
Kalenić SRB....85 C5
Kalesija BIH....84 B3
Kalety PL....54 C3
Kalevala RUS....3 D29
Kali HR....83 B4
Kalimnos GR....119 F2
Kalinkavichy BY....7 E10
Kalinovac HR....74 B2
Kalinovik BIH....84 C3
Kalinovo SK....65 B5
Kalirachi GR....116 B6
Kaliska
  Pomorskie PL....47 A4
  Pomorskie PL....47 B4
Kalisko PL....55 B4
Kalisz PL....54 B3
Kalisz Pomorski PL....46 B1
Kalix S....3 D25
Kaljord N....112 D4
Kalkan TR....119 F4
Kalkar D....50 B2
Kalkim TR....118 C2
Kall
  D....50 C2
  S....115 D10
Kållby S....35 D5
Kållered S....38 B5
Kållerstad S....40 B4
Kallham A....63 B4
Kallinge S....41 C5
Kallmeti i Madh AL....105 B5
Kallmünz D....62 A2
Kallo FIN....113 E13
Kallsedet S....115 D9
Kallvik S....37 D4
Kalmar S....40 C6
Kalmthout B....49 B5
Kalná SK....65 B4
Kalocsa H....75 B3
Kalokhorio CY....120 B2
Kalo Nero GR....117 E3
Kaloni GR....116 C8
Kalói I....72 A2
Kalsdorf A....73 B5
Kaltbrunn CH....70 A4
Kaltenbach A....72 A1
Kaltennordheim D....51 C6
Kaltenkirchen D....44 B1
Kaltental D....61 B6
Kaluga RUS....7 D14
Kalundborg DK....39 D4
Kalush UA....11 B8
Kaluszyn PL....55 A6
Kalv S....40 B3
Kalvåg N....114 F1
Kalvehave DK....41 D2
Kalwang A....73 A4
Kalwaria-Zebrzydowska PL....65 A5
Kalyazin RUS....7 C14
Kam H....74 A1
Kaman TR....16 B6
Kamares GR....117 F6
Kambos CY....120 A1
Kamen D....50 B3
Kamenice nad Lipou CZ....63 A6
Kamenný Most SK....65 C4
Kamenný Ujezd CZ....63 B5
Kamenska HR....74 C2
Kamensko HR....84 C1
Kamenz D....53 B4
Kamičak BIH....83 B5
Kamień PL....55 B5
Kamieniec Zabk PL....54 C1
Kamienka SK....65 A6
Kamień Krajeński PL....46 B3
Kamienna Góra PL....53 C6
Kamień Pomorski PL....45 B6
Kamiennik PL....54 C2
Kaminia UA....11 B12
Kamiros Skala GR....119 F2
Kamnik SLO....73 B4
Kampen NL....42 C2
Kampinos PL....55 A5
Kamp-Lintfort D....50 B2
Kamyanets-Podil's'kyy UA....11 B9
Kamyanka-Buz'ka UA....11 A8
Kamýk nad Vltavou CZ....63 A5
Kanal SLO....72 B3
Kanalia GR....116 C4
Kandalaksha RUS....3 C30
Kandanos GR....117 G5
Kandel D....61 A4
Kandern D....60 C3
Kandersteg CH....70 B2
Kandila GR....117 E3
Kandıra TR....118 A5
Kanfanar HR....82 A2
Kangasala FIN....3 F26
Kangos S....113 E11
Kangosjärvi FIN....113 E12
Kaninë AL....105 C5
Kaniów PL....53 B4
Kanjiža SRB....75 B5
Kankaanpää FIN....3 F25
Kannus FIN....3 E25
Kanturk IRL....20 B3
Kaonik
  BIH....84 B2
  SRB....85 C6
Kapaklı TR....118 A2
Kapellen
  A....63 C6
  B....49 B5
Kapellskär S....37 C6
Kapfenberg A....73 A5
Kapfenstein A....73 B5
Kaplice CZ....63 B5
Kapljuh BIH....83 B5
Kápolna H....65 C6
Kápolnásnyék H....74 A3
Kaposfö H....74 B2
Kaposszekcsö H....74 B3
Kaposvár H....74 B2
Kapp N....34 B2
Kappel D....60 B3
Kappeln D....44 A1
Kappelshamn S....37 E5
Kappl A....71 A5
Kaprun A....72 A2
Kaptol HR....74 C2
Kapuvár H....64 C2
Karaadilli TR....119 D5
Karabiğa TR....118 B1
Karabük TR....118 A7
Karaburun TR....118 D1
Karacabey TR....118 B3
Karacaköy TR....118 A3
Karacasu TR....119 E3
Karachev RUS....7 E13
Karácsond H....65 C6
Karád H....74 B2
Karahallı TR....119 D4
Karaisali TR....16 C7
Karaman
  Balıkesir TR....118 C3
  Karaman TR....16 C6
Karamanlı TR....119 E4
Karamürsel TR....118 B4

Karan SRB....85 C4
Karancslapujto H....65 B5
Karaova TR....119 E2
Karapınar TR....16 C6
Karasjok N....113 C14
Karasu TR....118 A5
Karataş
  Adana TR....16 C7
  Manisa TR....119 D3
Karatoprak TR....119 E2
Karavostasi CY....120 A1
Karbenning S....36 B3
Kårberg S....37 D1
Kårböle S....115 F12
Karby
  D....44 A1
  DK....38 C1
Kårby S....40 B6
Karcag H....75 A5
Karczew PL....55 A6
Karczów PL....54 C2
Karczowiska PL....53 B6
Kardamena GR....119 E2
Kardamili GR....117 F4
Kardašova Rečice CZ....63 A5
Kardis S....113 F12
Karditsa GR....116 C3
Kárdla EST....6 B7
Kardoskút H....75 B5
Karesuando S....113 D11
Kargı TR....16 A7
Kargowa PL....53 A5
Karigasniemi FIN....113 C14
Karise DK....41 D2
Karistos GR....117 D6
Karkkila FIN....6 A8
Karlholmsbruk S....36 B4
Karlino PL....46 A1
Karl Liebknecht RUS....7 F13
Karlobag HR....83 B4
Karlovac HR....73 C5
Karlovasi GR....119 E1
Karlovčic SRB....85 B5
Karlovice CZ....54 C2
Karlovo BG....11 E8
Karlovy Vary CZ....52 C2
Karlsborg S....37 D1
Karlshamn S....41 C4
Karlshöfen D....43 B6
Karlshus N....35 C2
Karlskoga S....37 C1
Karlskrona S....41 C5
Karlsrud N....32 B5
Karlsruhe D....61 A4
Karlstad S....35 C5
Karlstadt D....51 D5
Karlstetten A....63 B6
Karlstift A....63 B5
Karlstorp S....40 B5
Karmacs H....74 B2
Kärna S....38 B4
Karnobat BG....11 E9
Karojba HR....72 C3
Karow
  Brandenburg D....52 A2
  Mecklenburg-Vorpommern D....45 A5
Karpacz PL....53 C5
Karpathos GR....119 G2
Karpenisi GR....116 D3
Karpuzlu TR....119 E2
Karrebæksminde DK....39 D4
Karshult S....40 B3
Karsin PL....46 B3
Kärstädt D....44 B3
Kartal TR....118 B4
Kartitsch A....72 B2
Kartuzy PL....47 A4
Karviná CZ....65 A4
Kås DK....38 B2
Kaş TR....119 F4
Kasaba TR....119 F4
Kašava CZ....64 A3
Kasejovice CZ....63 A4
Kashin RUS....7 C14
Kasina-Wielka PL....65 A6
Kaskinen FIN....3 E24
Kašperské Hory CZ....63 A4
Kassándrino GR....116 B5
Kassel D....51 B5
Kassiopi GR....116 C1
Kastamonu TR....16 A6
Kastav HR....73 C4
Kasteli GR....117 G5
Kastellaun D....50 C3
Kastelli GR....117 G7
Kastel-Stari HR....83 C4
Kaštel Zegarski HR....83 B4
Kasterlee B....49 B5
Kastl D....62 A2
Kastlösa S....41 C6
Kastorf D....44 B2
Kastoria GR....116 B3
Kastorio GR....117 E4
Kastraki GR....117 F7
Kastrosikia GR....116 C2
Kastsyukovichy BY....7 E12
Kaszaper H....75 B5
Katakolo GR....117 E3
Katapola GR....117 F7
Katastari GR....117 E2
Katerbow D....45 C4
Katerini GR....116 B4
Kathikas CY....120 B1
Kätkesuando S....113 D12
Katlenburg-Lindau D....51 B6
Kato Achaia GR....117 D3
Káto Pyrgos CY....120 A1
Katouna GR....116 D3
Katovice CZ....63 A4
Katowice PL....54 C3
Katrineberg S....36 A3
Katrineholm S....37 D3
Kattarp S....41 C2
Kattavia GR....119 G2
Katthammarsvik S....37 E5
Kattilstorp S....40 A3
Katwijk NL....49 A5
Katymár H....75 B4
Katzenelnbogen D....50 C3
Katzhütte D....52 C1
Kaub D....50 C3
Kaufbeuren D....62 C1
Kauhajoki FIN....3 E25
Kauhava FIN....3 E25
Kaukonen FIN....113 E13
Kaulsdorf D....52 C1
Kaunas LT....6 D7
Kaunisvaara S....113 E12
Kaupanger N....32 A4
Kautokeino N....113 C12
Kautzen A....63 B6
Kavadarci MK....116 A4
Kavajë AL....105 B5
Kavakköy TR....118 B1
Kavaklıdere TR....119 E3
Kavala GR....116 B6
Kavarna BG....11 E10
Kävlinge S....41 D3

Kazincbarcika H....65 B6
Kazmierz PL....46 C2
Kcynia PL....46 B3
Kdyně CZ....62 A4
Kea GR....117 E6
Keadew IRL....18 B3
Keady GB....19 B5
Kecel H....75 B4
Keçiborlu TR....119 E5
Kecskemét H....75 B4
Kedainiai LT....6 D8
Kędzierzyn-Koźle PL....54 C3
Keel IRL....18 C1
Keenagh IRL....19 C4
Keerbergen B....49 B5
Kefalos GR....119 F1
Kefken TR....118 A5
Keflavík IS....111 C3
Kegworth GB....27 C4
Kehl D....60 B3
Kehrigk D....53 A3
Keighley GB....27 B4
Keila EST....6 B8
Keillmore GB....24 C2
Keiss GB....23 C5
Keith GB....23 D6
Kelberg D....50 C2
Kelbra D....51 B7
Kelč CZ....64 A3
Kelchsau A....72 A2
Keld GB....26 A3
Kelebia H....75 B4
Këlcyrë AL....116 B2
Kelheim D....62 B2
Kell D....60 A2
Kellas GB....23 D5
Kellinghusen D....43 B6
Kelloselkä FIN....113 F17
Kells
  GB....19 C5
  IRL....19 C5
Kelmis B....50 C2
Kelokedhara CY....120 B1
Kelottijärvi FIN....113 D11
Kelsall GB....26 B3
Kelso GB....25 C5
Kelsterbach D....51 C4
Keltneyburn GB....24 B3
Kelujärvi FIN....113 E16
Kemaliye TR....119 D3
Kemalpaşa TR....119 D2
Kematen A....71 A6
Kemberg D....52 B2
Kemer
  Antalya TR....119 F5
  Burdur TR....119 F5
  Muğla TR....119 F4
Kemeten A....73 A6
Kemi FIN....3 D26
Kemijärvi FIN....113 F16
Keminmaa FIN....3 D26
Kemnath D....62 A2
Kemnay GB....23 D6
Kemnitz D
  Brandenburg D....52 A2
  Mecklenburg-Vorpommern D....45 A5
Kempen D....50 B2
Kempsey GB....29 A5
Kempten D....61 C6
Kemptthal CH....70 A3
Kendal GB....26 A3
Kenderes H....75 A5
Kengyel H....75 A5
Kenilworth GB....30 B2
Kenmare IRL....20 C2
Kenmore GB....25 B4
Kennacraig GB....24 C2
Kenyeri H....74 A2
Kenzingen D....60 B3
Kepez TR....118 B1
Kępice PL....46 A2
Kępno PL....54 B3
Kepsut TR....118 C3
Keramoti GR....116 B6
Kerasochori GR....116 C3
Keratea GR....117 E5
Kerava FIN....7 A8
Kerecsend H....65 C6
Kerekegyhaza H....75 B4
Kerepestarcsa H....75 A4
Keri GR....117 E2
Kérien F....56 B2
Kerkafalva H....73 B6
Kerken D....50 B2
Kerkrade NL....50 C2
Kerkyra GR....116 C1
Kerlouan F....56 B1
Kernascléden F....56 B2
Kernhof A....63 C6
Kerns CH....70 B3
Kerpen D....50 C2
Kerrysdale GB....22 D3
Kerta H....74 A2
Kerteminde DK....39 D3
Kerzers CH....70 B2
Keşan TR....118 B1
Kesgrave GB....30 B5
Kesh GB....19 B4
Keskin TR....16 B6
Kesselfall A....72 A2
Kestenga RUS....3 D29
Keswick GB....26 A2
Keszthely H....74 B2
Kétegyháza H....75 B6
Kéthely H....74 B2
Kętrzyn PL....6 D6
Kettering GB....30 B3
Kettlewell GB....26 A3
Kęty PL....65 A5
Ketzin D....45 C4
Keula D....51 B6
Keuruu FIN....3 E26
Kevelaer D....50 B2
Kevermes H....75 B6
Kevi SRB....75 C4
Keyingham GB....27 B5
Keynsham GB....29 B5
Kežmarok SK....65 A6

Kihlanki
  FIN....113 E12
  S....113 E12
Kiistala FIN....113 E14
Kije PL....55 C5
Kijevo HR....83 C5
Kikallen N....32 B2
Kikinda SRB....75 C5
Kil
  N....33 D6
  Örebro S....37 C2
  Värmland S....35 C5
Kila S....35 A3
Kilafors S....36 A3
Kilbaha IRL....20 B2
Kilbeggan IRL....21 A4
Kilberry IRL....19 C5
Kilbirnie GB....24 C3
Kilboghamn N....112 F2
Kilbotn N....112 D6
Kïlb Rabenstein A....63 B6
Kilchattan GB....24 C2
Kilchoan GB....24 B1
Kilcock IRL....21 A5
Kilconnell IRL....20 A3
Kilcormac IRL....21 A4
Kilcreggan GB....24 C3
Kilcullen IRL....21 B5
Kilcurry IRL....19 B5
Kildare IRL....21 A5
Kildinstroy RUS....3 B30
Kildonan GB....20 B3
Kildorrery IRL....20 B3
Kilegrend N....33 C5
Kilen N....33 C5
Kilgarvan IRL....20 C2
Kiliya UA....11 D10
Kilkee IRL....20 B2
Kilkeel GB....19 B5
Kilkelly IRL....18 C3
Kilkenny IRL....21 B4
Kilkieran IRL....20 A2
Kilkinlea IRL....20 B2
Kilkis GR....116 A4
Kill IRL....21 B4
Killadysert IRL....20 B3
Killala IRL....18 B2
Killaloe IRL....20 B3
Killarney IRL....20 B2
Killashandra IRL....19 B4
Killashee IRL....19 C4
Killearn GB....24 B3
Killeberg S....40 C4
Killeigh IRL....21 A4
Killenaule IRL....21 B4
Killimor IRL....20 A3
Killin GB....24 B3
Killinaboy IRL....20 B3
Killinge S....112 E9
Killinick IRL....21 B5
Killorglin IRL....20 B2
Killucan IRL....21 A4
Killybegs IRL....18 B3
Killyleagh GB....19 B6
Kilmacolm GB....24 C3
Kilmacrenan IRL....19 A4
Kilmacthomas IRL....21 B4
Kilmaine IRL....18 C2
Kilmallock IRL....20 B3
Kilmarnock GB....24 C3
Kilmartin GB....24 B2
Kilmaurs GB....24 C3
Kilmeadan IRL....21 B4
Kilmeedy IRL....20 B3
Kilmelford GB....24 B2
Kilmore Quay IRL....21 B5
Kilmuir GB....23 D4
Kilninver GB....24 B2
Kilpisjärvi FIN....112 C9
Kilrea GB....19 B5
Kilrush IRL....20 B2
Kilsmo S....37 C2
Kilsyth GB....24 C3
Kiltoom IRL....20 A3
Kilwinning GB....24 C3
Kimasozero RUS....3 D30
Kími GR....116 D6
Kimolos GR....117 F6
Kimovsk RUS....7 D14
Kimratshofen D....61 C6
Kimry RUS....7 C14
Kimstad S....37 D2
Kinbrace GB....23 C5
Kincardine GB....25 B4
Kincraig GB....23 D5
Kindberg A....73 A5
Kindelbruck D....52 B1
Kingarrow IRL....18 B3
Kingisepp RUS....7 B10
Kingsbridge GB....28 C4
Kingsclere GB....31 C2
Kingscourt IRL....19 C5
King's Lynn GB....30 B4
Kingston
  Greater London GB....31 C3
  Moray GB....23 D5
Kingston Bagpuize GB....31 C2
Kingston upon Hull GB....27 B5
Kingswear GB....29 C4
Kingswood GB....29 B5
Kington GB....29 A4
Kingussie GB....23 D4
Kınık
  Antalya TR....119 F4
  İzmir TR....118 C2
Kinloch
  Highland GB....22 C4
  Highland GB....22 D2
Kinlochbervie GB....22 C3
Kinlochewe GB....22 D3
Kinlochleven GB....24 B3
Kinlochmoidart GB....24 B2
Kinloch Rannoch GB....24 B3
Kinloss GB....23 D5
Kinlough IRL....18 B3
Kinn N....32 B2
Kinna S....40 B2
Kinnared S....40 C3
Kinnarp S....35 D5
Kinnegad IRL....21 A4
Kinne-Kleva S....35 D5
Kinnitty IRL....21 A4
Kinrooi B....50 B1
Kinross GB....25 B4
Kinsale IRL....20 C3
Kinsarvik N....32 B3
Kintarvie GB....22 C2
Kintore GB....23 D6
Kinvarra IRL....20 A3
Kioni GR....116 D2
Kiparissia GR....117 E3
Kipfenburg D....62 B2
Kippen GB....24 B3
Kiraz TR....119 D3
Kirazlı TR....118 B1
Kirberg D....50 C4
Kircasalih TR....118 A1
Kirchbach in Steiermark A....73 B5
Kirchberg
  CH....70 A2
  Baden-Württemberg D....61 A5
  Rheinland-Pfalz D....60 A3
Kirchberg am Wechsel A....64 C1
Kirchberg an der Pielach A....63 B6
Kirchberg in Tirol A....72 A2
Kirchbichl A....72 A2
Kirchdorf
  Bayern D....63 B4
  Mecklenburg-Vorpommern D....44 B3
  Niedersachsen D....43 C5
Kirchdorf an der Krems A....63 C5
Kirchenlamitz D....52 C1
Kirchenthumbach D....62 A2

Kirchhain D....51 C4
Kirchheim
  Baden-Württemberg D....61 B5
  Bayern D....61 B6
  Hessen D....51 C5
Kirchheimbolanden D....61 A4
Kirchhundem D....50 B4
Kirchlintein D....43 C6
Kirchschlag A....73 A6
Kirchweidach D....62 B3
Kirchzarten D....60 C3
Kircubbin GB....19 B6
Kireç TR....118 C3
Kırka TR....118 C6
Kırkağaç TR....118 C2
Kirkbean GB....25 D4
Kirkbride GB....25 D4
Kirkby GB....26 B3
Kirkby Lonsdale GB....26 A3
Kirkby Malzeard GB....27 A4
Kirkbymoorside GB....27 A5
Kirkby Stephen GB....26 A3
Kirkcaldy GB....25 B4
Kirkcolm GB....24 D2
Kirkconnel GB....24 C3
Kirkcowan GB....24 D3
Kirkcudbright GB....24 D3
Kirkehamn N....33 D3
Kirke Hyllinge DK....39 D4
Kirkenær N....34 B4
Kirkenes N....113 C19
Kirkham GB....26 B3
Kirkintilloch GB....24 C3
Kirkjubæjarklaustur IS....111 D7
Kirkkonummi FIN....6 A8
Kırklareli TR....118 A2
Kirkmichael GB....25 B4
Kirk Michael GB....26 A1
Kirkoswald GB....24 D3
Kirkpatrick Fleming GB....25 C4
Kirkton of Glenisla GB....25 B4
Kirkwall GB....23 C6
Kirkwhelpington GB....25 C6
Kirn D....60 A3
Kiro AL....105 A5
Kirovohrad UA....11 B12
Kirovsk RUS....3 C30
Kirriemuir GB....25 B5
Kırşehir TR....16 B7
Kirton GB....30 B4
Kirton in Lindsey GB....27 B5
Kirtorf D....51 C5
Kiruna S....112 E9
Kisa S....40 B5
Kisbér H....74 A3
Kiseljak BIH....84 C3
Kisielice PL....47 B5
Kisköre H....75 A5
Kiskőrös H....75 B4
Kiskunfélegyháza H....75 B4
Kiskunhalas H....75 B4
Kiskunlacháza H....75 A3
Kiskunmajsa H....75 B4
Kisláng H....74 B3
Kißlegg D....61 C5
Kissónerga CY....120 B1
Kist D....61 A5
Kistanje HR....83 C4
Kistelek H....75 B4
Kisterenye H....65 B5
Kisújszállás H....75 A5
Kisvárda H....11 B7
Kisvejke H....74 B3
Kiszkowo PL....46 C3
Kiszombor H....75 B5
Kitee FIN....3 E29
Kithnos GR....117 E6
Kiti CY....120 B2
Kitkiöjärvi S....113 E12
Kitkiöjoki S....113 E12
Kittelfjäll S....115 B13
Kittendorf D....45 B4
Kittilä FIN....113 E13
Kittlitz D....53 B4
Kittsee A....64 B3
Kitzbühel A....72 A2
Kitzingen D....61 A6
Kiuruvesi FIN....3 E27
Kivertsi UA....11 A8
Kividhes CY....120 B1
Kivik S....41 D4
Kivotos GR....116 B3
Kiwity PL....47 A6
Kıyıköy TR....118 A3
Kızılcabölük TR....119 E4
Kızılcadağ TR....119 E5
Kızılcahamam TR....16 A6
Kızılırmak TR....16 A6
Kızılkaya TR....119 E5
Kızılkuyu TR....118 D6
Kızılören
  Afyon TR....119 D5
  Konya TR....119 E7
Kjøllefjord N....113 B16
Kjøpmannskjær N....35 C2
Kjøpsvik N....112 E6
Kl'ačno SK....65 B4
Kladanj BIH....84 B3
Kläckeberga S....40 C6
Kladnice HR....83 C5
Kladno CZ....53 C4
Kladruby CZ....62 A3
Klädesholmen S....38 B4

Klewki PL....47 B6
Kličevac SRB....85 B6
Kliening A....73 B4
Klietz D....44 C4
Klikuszowa PL....65 A5
Klimkovice CZ....54 D3
Klimontów PL....55 C6
Klimpfjäll S....115 B11
Klin RUS....7 C14
Klina KOS....85 D5
Klinča Sela HR....73 C5
Klingenbach A....64 C2
Klingenberg D....61 A5
Klingenmünster D....60 A3
Klingenthal D....52 C2
Klinken D....44 B3
Klintehamn S....37 E5
Klintsy RUS....7 E11
Kliplev DK....39 E2
Klippan S....41 C3
Klis HR....83 C5
Klitmøller DK....38 B1
Klitten D....53 B4
Klixbüll D....39 E1
Kljajićevo SRB....75 C4
Ključ BIH....84 B1
Klobouky CZ....64 B2
Kłobuck PL....54 C3
Kłodawa
  Lubuskie PL....45 C7
  Wielkopolskie PL....54 A3
Kłodzko PL....54 C1
Kløfta N....34 B3
Klokkarvik N....32 B2
Klokkerholm DK....38 B3
Klokočov SK....65 A4
Klomnice PL....55 C4
Klonowa PL....54 B3
Kloosterzande NL....49 B5
Klopot PL....53 A4
Klos AL....116 A2
Kloštar Ivanić HR....73 C6
Kloster
  D....45 A5
  D....39 C1
Klösterle A....71 A5
Klostermansfeld D....52 B1
Klosterneuburg A....64 B2
Klosters CH....71 B4
Kloten CH....70 A3
Klötze D....44 C3
Klövsjö S....115 E11
Kluczbork PL....54 C3
Kluczewo PL....46 B1
Kluisbergen B....49 C4
Klundert NL....49 B5
Klutz D....44 B3
Klwów PL....55 B5
Klyetsk BY....7 E9
Knaben N....33 D3
Knaften S....115 C15
Knapstad N....35 C3
Knäred S....40 C3
Knaresborough GB....27 A4
Knarvik N....32 B2
Knebel DK....39 C3
Knebworth GB....31 C3
Knesebeck D....44 C2
Knesselare B....49 B4
Knežak SLO....73 C4
Kneževi Vinogradi HR....74 C3
Kneževo HR....74 C3
Knić SRB....85 C5
Knighton GB....29 A4
Knin HR....83 B5
Knislinge S....41 C4
Knittelfeld A....73 A4
Knivsta S....37 C4
Knock IRL....18 C3
Knocktopher IRL....21 B4
Knokke-Heist B....49 B4
Knowle GB....30 B2
Knurów PL....54 C3
Knutby S....36 C5
Knutsford GB....26 B3
Kobarid SLO....72 B3
København
  Copenhagen DK....41 D2
Kobenz A....73 A4
Kobersdorf A....64 C2
Kobierzyce PL....54 C1
Kobiór PL....54 C3
Koblenz
  CH....61 C4
  D....50 C3
Kobryn BY....11 A8
Kobylanka PL....45 B6
Kobylin PL....54 B2
Kobylnica PL....46 A2
Kocaali TR....118 A5
Kocaaliler TR....119 E5
Kocaeli = İzmit TR....118 B4
Kočani MK....11 F7
Koçarlı TR....119 E2
Koceljevo SRB....85 B4
Kočevje SLO....73 C4
Kočevska Reka SLO....73 C4
Kochel am See D....62 C2
Kocs H....64 C4
Kocsér H....75 A4
Kocsola H....74 B3
Koczała PL....46 B2
Kodal N....35 C2
Kode S....38 B4
Kodersdorf D....53 B4
Kodrab PL....55 B4
Koekelare B....48 B3
Köfçaz TR....118 A2
Köflach A....73 A5
Køge DK....41 D2
Kohila EST....6 B8
Kohtla-Järve EST....7 B9
Köinge S....40 B2
Kojetín CZ....64 A3
Kökar FIN....36 C7
Kokkinotrimithia CY....120 B2
Kokkola FIN....3 E25
Kokori BIH....84 B2
Kokoski PL....47 A4
Koksijde B....48 B3
Kola
  BIH....84 B2
  RUS....3 B30
Köla S....34 C4
Kołacin PL....55 B4
Kolari
  FIN....113 E12
  S....113 E12
Kolárovo SK....64 C3
Kolašin MNE....85 D4
Kolbäck S....37 C3
Kolbacz PL....45 B6
Kolbeinsstaðir IS....111 C3
Kolbermoor D....62 C3
Kolbnitz A....72 B3
Kolbotn N....35 C2
Kolbu N....34 B2
Kolby Kås DK....39 D3
Kolczewo PL....45 B6
Kolczygłowy PL....46 A2
Kolding DK....39 D2
Kölesd H....74 B3
Kolgrov N....32 A1
Koli FIN....3 E28
Kolín CZ....53 C5
Kolind DK....39 C3
Kolindrós GR....116 B4
Kolínec CZ....63 A4
Koljane HR....83 C5
Kølkær DK....39 C2
Kölleda D....52 B1
Köln = Cologne D....50 C2
Koło PL....54 A3
Kołobrzeg PL....46 A1
Kolochau D....52 B3

Kolomyya UA 11 B8
Kolonje AL 105 C5
Kolonowskie PL 54 C3
Koloveč CZ 62 A4
Kolpino RUS 7 B11
Kolpny RUS 7 E14
Kolrep D 44 B4
Kölsillre S 115 E12
Kolsko PL 53 B5
Kolsva S 37 C2
Kolta SK 65 B4
Kolunič BIH 83 B5
Koluszki PL 55 B4
Kolut SRB 75 C3
Kolvereid N 114 C8
Kølvrå DK 39 C2
Komagvær N 113 B19
Koman AL 105 A5
Komarica BIH 84 B2
Komárno SK 64 C4
Komárom H 64 C4
Komatou Yialou CY 120 A3
Komboti GR 116 C3
Komen SLO 72 C3
Komin HR 84 C2
Komiža HR 83 C5
Komjáti H 65 B6
Komjatice SK 64 B4
Komletinci HR 75 C3
Komló H 74 B3
Kömlo H 65 C6
Komoča SK 64 C4
Komorane KOS 85 D5
Komorniki PL 54 A1
Komorzno PL 54 B3
Komotini GR 116 A7
Konak SRB 75 C5
Konakovo RUS 7 C14
Konary PL 55 B6
Konarzyny PL 46 B3
Kondias GR 116 C7
Kondorfa H 73 B6
Kondoros H 75 B5
Kondrovo RUS 7 D13
Køng DK 39 D4
Konga S 40 C5
Köngäs FIN 113 E13
Kongerslev DK 38 C3
Kongsberg N 35 C1
Kongshamn N 33 D5
Kongsmark DK 39 D1
Kongsmoen N 115 C9
Kongsvik N 112 D5
Kongsvinger N 34 B4
Konice CZ 64 A2
Konie PL 55 B5
Koniecpol PL 55 C4
Königsberg D 51 C6
Königsbronn D 61 B6
Königsbrück D 53 B3
Königsbrunn D 62 B1
Königsdorf D 62 C2
Königsee D 52 C1
Königshorst D 45 C4
Königslutter D 51 A6
Königssee D 62 C3
Königstein
Hessen D 51 C4
Sachsen D 53 C4
Königstetten A 64 B2
Königswartha D 53 B4
Königswiesen A 63 B5
Königswinter D 50 C3
Königs Wusterhausen
D 52 A3
Konin PL 54 A3
Konispol AL 116 C2
Konitsa GR 116 B2
Köniz CH 70 B2
Konjevići BIH 85 B4
Konjevrate HR 83 C5
Konjic BIH 84 C2
Konjščina HR 73 B6
Könnern D 52 B1
Konnerud N 35 C2
Konopiska PL 54 C3
Konotop
PL 53 B5
UA 7 F12
Końskie PL 55 B5
Konsmo N 33 D4
Konstancin-Jeziorna
PL 55 A6
Konstantynów Łódzki
PL 55 B4
Konstanz D 61 C5
Kontich B 49 B5
Kontiolahti FIN 3 E28
Konya TR 119 E7
Konz D 60 A2
Kópasker IS 111 A9
Kópavogur IS 111 C4
Kopčany SK 64 B3
Koper SLO 72 C3
Kopervik N 33 C2
Kópháza H 64 C2
Kopice PL 54 C2
Kopidlno CZ 53 C5
Köping S 37 C2
Köpingebro S 41 D3
Köpingsvik S 41 C6
Koplik AL 105 A5
Köpmanholmen S 115 D15
Koppang N 34 A3
Koppangen N 112 C9
Kopparberg S 36 C1
Koppelo FIN 113 D16
Koppom S 35 C4
Koprivlen BG 116 A5
Koprivna BIH 84 B3
Koprivnica HR 74 B1
Kopřivnice CZ 64 A4
Köprübaşı TR 118 D3
Koprzywnica PL 55 C6
Kopstal L 60 A2
Kopychyntsi UA 11 B8
Kopytkowo PL 47 B4
Korbach D 51 B4
Körbecke D 50 B4
Korçë AL 116 B2
Korčula HR 84 D2
Korczyców PL 53 A4
Korenevo RUS 7 F13
Korenita SRB 85 B4
Korets UA 11 A9
Korfantów PL 54 C2
Körfez TR 118 B4
Korgen N 115 A10
Korinth DK 39 D3
Korinthos = Corinth
GR 117 E4
Korita
BIH 83 B5
HR 84 D2
Korithi GR 117 E2
Korkuteli TR 119 E5
Körmend H 74 A1
Korne PL 46 A3
Korneuburg A 64 B2
Kornevo RUS 47 A6
Kórnik PL 54 A2
Kornsjø N 35 D3
Környe H 74 A3
Koromačno HR 82 B3
Koroni GR 117 F3
Koronos GR 117 E7
Koronowo PL 46 B3
Körösladány H 75 B6
Köröstarcsa H 75 B6
Korosten UA 11 A10
Korostyshev UA 11 A10
Korpilombolo S 113 F12
Korsberga
Jönköping S 40 B5
Skaraborg S 35 D6
Korshavn N 35 C2
Korskrogen S 115 F12
Korsnäs S 36 B2
Korsør DK 39 D4
Korsun Shevchenkovskiy
UA 11 B11
Kortrijk B 49 C4
Korucu TR 118 C2
Koryčany CZ 64 A3
Koryukovka UA 7 F12
Korzeńsko PL 54 B1
Korzybie PL 46 A2
Kos GR 119 F2
Kosakowo PL 47 A4
Kosanica MNE 85 C4
Kosaya Gora RUS 7 D14
Kösching D 62 B2
Kościan PL 54 A1
Kościelec PL 54 A3
Kościerzyna PL 46 A3
Koserow D 45 A5
Košetice CZ 63 A6
Košice SK 10 B6
Kosjerić SRB 85 C4
Koška HR 74 C3
Koskullskulle S 112 E9
Kosovska Mitrovica
KOS 85 D5
Kosta S 40 C5
Kostajnica HR 74 C1
Kostajnik SRB 85 B4
Kostanica MNE 105 A5
Kostanjevica SLO 73 C5
Kostelec nad Černými
Lesy CZ 53 D4
Kostelec na Hané CZ 64 A3
Kostice CZ 53 C3
Kostkowo PL 47 A4
Kostojevići SRB 85 B4
Kostolac SRB 85 B6
Kostomłoty PL 54 B1
Kostopil UA 11 A9
Kostów PL 54 B3
Kostrzyn
Lubuskie PL 45 C6
Wielkopolskie PL 46 C3
Koszalin PL 46 A2
Koszęcin PL 54 C3
Kőszeg H 74 A1
Koszwaly PL 47 A4
Koszyce PL 55 C5
Kot SLO 73 C5
Kotala FIN 113 E17
Kotë AL 105 C5
Kötelek H 75 A5
Köthen D 52 B1
Kotka FIN 7 A9
Kotomierz PL 47 B4
Kotor MNE 105 A4
Kotoriba HR 74 B1
Kotorsko BIH 84 B3
Kotor Varoš BIH 84 B2
Kotovsk UA 11 C10
Kotraža SRB 85 C5
Kotronas GR 117 F4
Kötschach A 72 B2
Kötzting D 62 A3
Koudum NL 42 C2
Kouřim CZ 53 C4
Kout na Šumave CZ 62 A4
Kouvola FIN 3 F27
Kovačevac SRB 85 B5
Kovačica SRB 85 A5
Kovdor RUS 3 C29
Kovel' UA 11 A8
Kovilj SRB 75 C5
Kovin SRB 85 B5
Kovren MNE 85 C4
Kowal PL 47 C5
Kowalewo Pomorskie
PL 47 B4
Kowalów PL 45 C6
Kowary PL 53 C5
Köyceğiz TR 119 F3
Kozan TR 16 C7
Kozani GR 116 B3
Kozarac
BIH 84 B1
HR 73 C5
Kozárovce SK 65 B4
Kozelets UA 11 A11
Kozelsk RUS 7 D13
Kozica HR 84 C2
Koziegłowy PL 55 C4
Kozienice PL 55 B6
Kozina SLO 72 C3
Kozje SLO 73 B5
Kozlu TR 118 A6
Kozluk BIH 85 B4
Koźmin PL 54 B2
Koźminek PL 54 B3
Kozolupy CZ 63 A4
Kożuchów PL 53 B5
Kožuhe BIH 84 B3
Kozyatyn UA 11 B10
Kozyörük TR 118 A1
Krackow D 45 B6
Kraddsele S 115 B13
Krąg PL 46 A2
Kragenæs DK 39 E4
Kragerø N 33 D6
Kragi PL 46 B2
Kragujevac SRB 85 B5
Kraiburg D 62 B3
Krajenka PL 46 B2
Krajišnik SRB 75 C5
Krajková CZ 52 C2
Krajné SK 64 B3
Krajnik Dolny PL 45 B6
Krakača BIH 83 A4
Kråklingbo S 37 E5
Kraków = Cracow PL 55 C4
Krakow am See D 44 B4
Králíky CZ 54 C1
Kraljevica HR 73 C4
Kraljevo SRB 85 C5
Kral'ovany SK 65 A5
Král'ov Brod SK 64 B3
Kralovice CZ 52 D3
Kralupy nad Vltavou
CZ 53 C4
Králův Dvůr CZ 63 A5
Kramfors S 115 E14
Kramsach A 72 A1
Kramsk PL 54 A3
Kråmvik N 32 C5
Kranenburg D 50 B2
Krania GR 116 C3
Krania Elasonas GR 116 C4
Kranichfeld D 52 C1
Kranidi GR 117 E5
Kranj SLO 73 B4
Kranjska Gora SLO 72 B3
Krapanj HR 83 C4
Krapina HR 73 B5
Krapje HR 74 C1
Krapkowice PL 54 C2
Kraselov CZ 63 A4
Krašić HR 73 C5
Krāslava LV 7 D9
Kraslice CZ 52 C2
Krasna PL 55 B5
Krasna Lipa CZ 53 C4
Krasnik PL 11 A7
Krašnja SLO 73 B4
Krásno SK 65 A4
Krásnohorské Podhradie
SK 65 B6
Krasno Polje HR 83 B4
Krasnozavodsk RUS 7 C15
Krasnystaw PL 11 A7
Krasnyy RUS 7 D11
Krasnyy Kholm RUS 7 B14
Krasocin PL 55 C5
Kraszewice PL 54 B3
Kraszkowice PL 54 B3
Kratigos GR 118 C1
Kraubath A 73 A4
Krausnick D 53 A3
Krautheim D 61 A5
Kravaře CZ 53 C4
Kraváre CZ 64 A4
Kravarsko HR 73 C6
Kraznějov CZ 63 A4
Krčedin SRB 75 C5
Kŭrdzhali BG 116 A7
Krefeld D 50 B2
Kregme DK 39 D5
Krembz D 44 B3
Kremenchuk UA 11 B12
Kremenets UA 11 A8
Kremmen D 45 C5
Kremna SRB 85 C4
Kremnica SK 65 B4
Krempe D 43 B6
Krems A 63 B6
Kremsbrücke A 72 B3
Kremsmünster A 63 B5
Křemže CZ 63 B5
Křenov CZ 64 A2
Krepa PL 54 B3
Krępa Krajeńska PL 46 B2
Krepsko PL 46 B2
Kreševo BIH 84 C3
Kressbronn D 61 C5
Krestena GR 117 E3
Kretinga LT 6 D6
Krettsy RUS 7 B12
Kreuth D 62 C2
Kreuzau D 50 C2
Kreuzlingen CH 61 C5
Kreuztal D 50 C3
Krewelin D 45 C5
Krezluk BIH 84 B2
Krieglach A 73 A5
Kriegsfeld D 60 A3
Kriens CH 70 A3
Krimml A 72 A2
Krimpen aan de IJssel
NL 49 B5
Křinec CZ 53 C5
Kristdala S 40 B6
Kristiansand N 33 D5
Kristianstad S 41 C4
Kristiansund N 114 D4
Kristiinankaupunki
FIN 3 E24
Kristinefors S 34 B4
Kristinehamn S 35 C6
Kriváň SK 65 B5
Křivoklát CZ 53 C3
Krivoy Rog = Kryvyy Rih
UA 11 C12
Križ HR 74 C1
Křižanov CZ 64 A2
Križevci HR 74 B1
Krk HR 83 A3
Krka SLO 73 C4
Krnjača SRB 85 B5
Krnjak HR 73 C5
Krnjeuša BIH 83 B5
Krnjevo SRB 85 B6
Krnov CZ 54 C2
Krobia PL 54 B1
Kroczyce PL 55 C4
Krøderen N 34 B1
Krokees GR 117 F4
Krokek S 37 D3
Krokom S 115 D11
Krokowa PL 47 A4
Krokstad-elva N 34 C1
Kroksund N 35 C3
Kroměříž CZ 64 A3
Krommenie NL 42 C1
Krompachy SK 65 B6
Kromy RUS 7 E13
Kronach D 52 C1
Kronshagen D 44 A2
Kronshtadt RUS 7 B10
Kröpelin D 44 A3
Kropp D 43 A6
Kroppenstedt D 52 B1
Kropstädt D 52 B2
Krościenko nad
Dunajcem PL 65 A6
Kröslin D 45 A5
Krośnice PL 54 B2
Krośniewice PL 55 A4
Krosno PL 10 B6
Krosno Odrzańskie
PL 53 A5
Krostitz D 52 B2
Krotoszyn PL 54 B2
Krottendorf A 73 A5
Krouna CZ 64 A2
Krowiarki PL 54 C3
Krrabë AL 105 B5
Kršan HR 73 C4
Krško SLO 73 C5
Krstac MNE 84 C3
Krstur SRB 75 B5
Křtiny CZ 64 A2
Kruft D 50 C3
Kruishoutem B 49 C4
Krujë AL 105 B5
Krulyewshchyna BY 7 D9
Krumbach
A 73 A6
D 61 B6
Krumovgrad BG 116 A7
Krün D 71 A6
Krupá CZ 53 C3
Krupa na Vrbasu BIH 84 B2
Krupanj SRB 85 B4
Krupina SK 65 B5
Krupka CZ 53 C3
Krupki BY 7 D10
Kruså DK 39 E2
Kruščica BIH 84 B2
Kruševac SRB 85 C6
Kruševo MK 116 A3
Kruszwica PL 47 C4
Kruszyn PL 47 C5
Krute MNE 105 A5
Krychaw BY 7 E11
Krynica PL 65 A6
Krynica Morska PL 47 A5
Kryvyy Rih = Krivoy Rog
UA 11 C12
Krzęcin PL 46 B1
Krzelów PL 54 B1
Krzepice PL 54 C3
Krzepielów PL 53 B6
Krzeszowice PL 55 C4
Krzeszyce PL 45 C7
Krzynowlaga Mała
PL 47 B6
Krzywiń PL 54 B1
Krzyżanowice PL 54 D3
Krzyżowa PL 65 A5
Krzyż Wielkopolski
PL 46 C2
Ksiaz Wielkopolski
PL 55 C5
Książ Wielkopolski
PL 54 A2
Kłębowiec PL 46 B2
Kübekháza H 75 B5
Küblis CH 71 B4
Kuç AL 105 C5
Kuchary PL 54 B2
Kuchl A 63 C4
Kucice PL 47 C6
Kuciste HR 84 D2
Kućište KOS 85 D5
Kuçovë AL 105 C5
Küçükbahçe TR 118 D1
Küçükköy TR 118 C1
Küçükkuyu TR 118 C1
Kucura SRB 75 C4
Kuczbork-Osada PL 47 B6
Kuddby S 37 D3
Kudowa-Zdrój PL 53 C6
Kufstein A 62 C3
Kuggeboda S 41 C5
Kuggörana S 115 F14
Kühbach D 62 B2
Kuhmo FIN 3 D28
Kuhmoinen FIN 3 F26
Kuhnsdorf A 73 B4
Kuhstedt D 43 B5
Kuinre NL 42 C2
Kuivastu EST 6 B7
Kukës AL 105 A6
Kuklin PL 47 B6
Kukljica HR 83 B4
Kukujevci SRB 85 A4
Kula
Srbija SRB 85 B6
Vojvodina SRB 75 C4
Kula *continued*
TR 119 D3
Kuldīga LV 6 C6
Kulen Vakuf BIH 83 B5
Kulina BIH 84 B3
Kullstedt D 51 B6
Kulmain D 62 A2
Kulmbach D 52 C1
Kulu TR 16 B6
Kumafşarı TR 119 E4
Kumane SRB 75 C5
Kumanovo MK 10 E6
Kumbağ TR 118 B2
Kumdanlı TR 119 D5
Kumkale TR 118 C1
Kumla S 37 C2
Kumlakyrkby S 36 C3
Kumlinge FIN 36 B7
Kumluca TR 119 F5
Kumrovec HR 73 B5
Kunadacs H 75 B4
Kunágota H 75 B6
Kunbaja H 75 B4
Kunda EST 7 B9
Kundl A 72 A1
Kunes N 113 B15
Kunfehértó H 75 B4
Kungälv S 38 B4
Kungsängen S 37 C4
Kungsäter S 40 B2
Kungsbacka S 38 B5
Kungsgården S 36 B3
Kungshamn S 35 D3
Kungs-Husby S 37 C4
Kungsör S 37 C3
Kunhegyes H 75 A5
Kunmadaras H 75 A5
Kunovice CZ 64 A3
Kunów PL 55 C6
Kunowo
Wielkopolskie PL 54 B2
Zachodnio-Pomorskie
PL 45 B6
Kunštát CZ 64 A2
Kunszállás H 75 B4
Kunszentmárton H 75 B5
Kunszentmiklós H 75 A4
Kunžak CZ 63 A6
Künzelsau D 61 A5
Kuolayarvi RUS 113 F18
Kuopio FIN 3 E27
Kuosku FIN 113 E17
Kup
H 74 A2
PL 54 C2
Kupa H 65 B6
Kupari HR 84 D3
Kupci SRB 85 C6
Kupferzell D 61 A5
Kupinec HR 73 C5
Kupinečki Kraljevac
HR 73 C5
Kupinovo SRB 85 B5
Kupirovo HR 83 B5
Kupjak HR 73 C4
Kuppenheim D 61 B4
Kupres BIH 84 C2
Küps D 52 C1
Kurbnesh AL 105 B6
Kurd H 74 B3
Küre TR 16 A6
Kuressaare EST 6 B7
Kurikka FIN 3 E25
Kuřim CZ 64 A2
Kuřivody CZ 53 C4
Kurki PL 47 B6
Kurort Oberwiesenthal
D 52 C2
Kurort Schmalkalden
D 51 C6
Kurort Stolberg D 51 B6
Kurort Wippra D 52 B1
Kurów PL 11 A7
Kurowice PL 55 B4
Kurravaara S 112 E9
Kursk RUS 7 F14
Kursu FIN 113 F17
Kuršumlija SRB 85 C6
Kuršumlijska Banja
SRB 85 C6
Kurşunlu
Bursa TR 118 B4
Çankırı TR 16 A6
Kurtakko FIN 113 E13
Kürten D 50 B3
Kurucaşile TR 16 A6
Kurzelów PL 55 C4
Kusadak SRB 85 B5
Kuşadası TR 119 E2
Kusel D 60 A3
Kusey D 44 C3
Küsnacht CH 70 A3
Kütahya TR 118 C4
Kutenholz D 43 B6
Kutina HR 74 C1
Kutjevo HR 74 C2
Kutná Hora CZ 53 D5
Kutno PL 55 A4
Kuttara FIN 113 D15
Küttingen CH 70 A3
Kúty SK 64 B3
Kuusamo FIN 3 D28
Kuusankoski FIN 3 F27
Kuvshinovo RUS 7 C13
Kuyucak TR 119 E3
Kuzmin SRB 85 A4
Kuźnia Raciborska
PL 54 C3
Kuźnica Czarnkowska
PL 46 C2
Kuźnica Żelichowska
PL 46 C2
Kvalsyletta N 112 C7
Kvalsund N 113 B12
Kvam
Nord-Trøndelag N 114 C8
Oppland N 114 F6
Kvamsøy N 32 A3
Kvænangsbotn N 113 C11
Kvanndal N 32 B3
Kvänum S 35 D5
Kværndrup DK 39 D3
Kvås N 33 D4
Kvasice CZ 64 A3
Kvelde N 35 C1
Kvenna N 114 E5
Kvernaland N 33 D2
Kvibille S 40 C2
Kvicksund S 37 C3
Kvidinge S 41 C3
Kvikkjokk S 112 F6
Kvikne N 114 E7
Kvilda CZ 63 A4
Kville S 35 D3
Kvillsfors S 40 B5
Kvinesdal N 33 D3
Kvinlog N 33 D3
Kvinnherad N 32 C3
Kvissel DK 38 B3
Kvissleby S 115 E14
Kviteseid N 33 C5
Kvitsøy N 33 C2
Kwakowo PL 46 A3
Kwidzyn PL 47 B4
Kwilcz PL 46 C2
Kyjov CZ 64 B3
Kyleakin GB 22 D3
Kyle of Lochalsh GB 22 D3
Kylerhea GB 22 D3
Kylestrome GB 22 C3
Kyllburg D 50 C2
Kyllini GR 117 E3
Kynšperk nad Ohří
CZ 52 C2
Kyperounda CY 120 B1
Kyrenia CY 120 A2
Kyritz D 44 C4
Kyrkesund S 38 A4
Kyrkhult S 41 C4
Kyrksæterøra N 114 D6
Kysucké Nové Mesto
SK 65 A4
Kythira GR 117 F4
Kythréa CY 120 A2
Kyustendil BG 11 E7
Kyyiv = Kiev UA 11 A11
Kyyjärvi FIN 3 E26

L

Laa an der Thaya A 64 B2
La Adrada E 94 B2
Laage D 44 B4
La Alameda E 100 A2
La Alberca E 93 A4
La Alberca de Záncara
E 95 C4
La Albergueria de
Argañán E 93 A4
La Albuera E 93 C4
La Aldea del Portillo del
Busto E 89 B3
La Algaba E 99 B4
La Aliseda de Tormes
E 93 A5
La Almarcha E 95 C4
La Almolda E 90 B2
La Almunia de Doña
Godina E 89 C5
Laanila FIN 113 D16
La Antillas E 98 B3
La Arena E 86 A4
Laatzen D 51 A5
La Aulaga E 99 B4
La Balme-de-Sillingy
F 69 C6
Laban IRL 20 A3
La Bañeza E 88 B1
La Barca de la Florida
E 99 C5
La Barre-de-Monts F 66 B2
La Barre-en-Ouche F 58 B1
La Barrosa E 99 C4
La Barthe-de-Neste F 77 C3
La Bassée F 48 C3
La Bastide-de-Sèrou
F 77 C4
La Bastide-des-Jourdans
F 79 C4
Labastide-Murat F 77 B4
La Bastide-Puylaurent
F 78 B2
Labastide-Rouairoux
F 77 C5
Labastide-St Pierre F 77 C4
La Bathie F 69 C6
Lábatlan H 65 C4
La Baule-Escoublac
F 66 A2
La Bazoche-Gouet F 58 B1
La Bégude-de-Mazenc
F 78 B3
Labenne F 76 C1
La Bernerie-en-Retz F 66 A2
Labin HR 82 A3
La Bisbal d'Empordà
E 91 B6
Łabiszyn PL 46 C3
Lablachère F 78 B3
Lábod H 74 B2
Laboe D 44 A2
La Boissière F 57 A6
Labouheyre F 76 B2
La Bourboule F 68 C2
La Bóveda de Toro E 88 C1
Łabowa PL 65 A6
La Brède F 76 B2
La Bresse F 60 B2
La Bridoire F 69 C5
La Brillanne F 79 C4
Labrit F 76 B2
Labros E 95 A5
La Bruffière F 66 A3
Labruguière F 77 C5
Labrujo P 87 C2
L'Absie F 67 B4
La Bussière F 58 C3
Laç AL 105 B5
La Caillère F 66 B4
Lacalahorra E 100 B2
La Caletta
Cágliari I 110 C1
Núoro I 110 B2
La Calmette F 78 C3
La Calzada de Oropesa
E 93 B5
La Campana E 99 B5
La Cañada E 94 B2
Lacanau F 76 B1
Lacanau-Océan F 76 A1
Lacanche F 69 A4
La Canourgue F 78 B2
La Capelle F 49 D4
Lacapelle-Marival F 77 B4
Laćarak SRB 85 A4
La Cardanchosa E 99 A5
La Caridad E 86 A4
La Carlota E 100 B1
La Carolina E 100 A2
Lacaune F 78 C1
La Cava E 90 C3
La Cavalerie F 78 B2
Laceby GB 27 B5
Lacedónia I 103 B8
La Celle-en-Moravan
F 69 A4
La Celle-St Avant F 67 A5
La Cerca E 89 B3
Láces I 71 B5
La Chaise-Dieu F 68 C3
La Chaize-Giraud F 66 B3
La Chaize-le-Vicomte
F 66 B3
La Chambre F 69 C6
Lachania GR 119 G2
La Chapelaude F 68 B2
La Chapelle-d'Angillon
F 68 A2
La Chapelle-en-
Aalgaudémar F 79 B5
La Chapelle-en-Vercors
F 79 B4
La Chapelle-Glain F 57 C4
La Chapelle-la-Reine
F 58 B3
La Chapelle-Laurent
F 68 C3
La Chapelle-St Luc F 59 B5
La Chapelle-sur-Erdre
F 66 A3
La Chapelle-Vicomtesse
F 58 C2
La Charce F 79 B4
La Charité-sur-Loire
F 68 A3
La Chartre-sur-le-Loir
F 58 C1
La Châtaigneraie F 67 B4
La Châtre F 68 B1
La Chaussée-sur-Marne
F 59 B5
La Chaux-de-Fonds
CH 70 A1
Lachen CH 70 A3
Lachendorf D 44 C2
La Cheppe F 59 A5
La Chèze F 56 B3
Lachowice PL 65 A5
La Ciotat F 79 C4
Łąck PL 47 C5
Läckeby S 40 C6
Läckö S 35 D5
La Clayette F 69 B4
La Clusaz F 69 C6
Lacock GB 29 B5
La Codosera E 93 B3
La Concha E 88 A3
La Condamine-Châtelard
F 79 B5
Láconi I 110 C2
La Contienda E 99 A4
La Coquille F 67 C5
La Coronada E 93 C5
La Côte-St André F 69 C5
La Cotinière F 66 C3
La Courtine F 68 C2
Lacq F 76 C2
La Crau F 79 C5
La Crèche F 67 B4
La Croix F 67 A5
Lacroix-Barrez F 77 B5
Lacroix-St Ouen F 58 A3
Lacroix-sur-Meuse F 60 B1
La Croix-Valmer F 79 C5
La Cumbre E 93 B5
Łącznik PL 54 C2
Lad H 74 B2
Ladbergen D 50 A3
Lądek-Zdrój PL 54 C1
Ladelund D 39 E2
Ladendorf A 64 B2
Ladignac-le-Long F 67 C6
Ladispoli I 102 B5
Ladoeiro P 93 B3
Ladon F 58 C3
La Douze F 77 A3
Ladushkin RUS 47 A6
Ladybank GB 25 B4
Laer D 50 A3
La Espina E 86 A4
La Estrella E 94 C1
La Farga de Moles E 91 A4
La Fatarella E 90 B3
La Felipa E 95 C5
La Fère F 59 A4
La Ferrière
Indre-et-Loire F 58 C1
Vendée F 66 B3
La Ferrière-en-Parthenay
F 67 B4
La-Ferté-Alais F 58 B3
La Ferté-Bernard F 58 B1
La Ferté-Frênel F 58 B1
La Ferté-Gaucher F 59 B4
La Ferté-Imbault F 68 A1
La Ferté-Macé F 57 B5
La Ferté-Milon F 59 A4
La Ferté-sous-Jouarre
F 59 B4
La Ferté-St-Aubin F 58 C2
La Ferté-St-Cyr F 58 C2
La Ferté-Vidame F 58 B1
La Ferté Villeneuil F 58 C2
La Feuillie F 58 A2
Lafkos GR 116 C5
La Flèche F 57 C5
La Flotte F 66 B3
Lafnitz A 73 A6
La Font de la Figuera
E 101 A5
La Fouillade F 77 B5
Lafrançaise F 77 B4
La Fregeneda E 87 D4
La Fresneda E 90 C3
La Fuencubierta E 99 B6
La Fuente de San Esteban
E 87 D4
La Fulioala E 91 B4
La Gacilly F 57 C3
La Galera E 90 C3
Lagan S 40 C3
Laganadi I 109 A4
Lagarde F 77 C4
La Garde-Freinet F 79 C5
Lagares
Coimbra P 92 A3
Porto P 87 C2
La Garnache F 66 B3
Lagaro I 81 B5
La Garriga E 91 B5
La Garrovilla E 93 C4
Lagartera E 93 B5
La Gaubretière F 66 B3
Lägbol S 36 B5
Lage D 51 B4
Lägerdorf D 43 B6
Lagg GB 24 C2
Laggan GB 22 D4
Laggartorp S 35 C6
Łagiewniki PL 54 C1
La Gineta E 95 C4
Láglio I 71 C4
Lagnieu F 69 C5
Lagny-sur-Marne F 58 B3
Lago
Calabria I 106 B3
Veneto I 72 C2
Lagôa P 98 B2
Lagoaça P 87 C4
Lagonegro I 106 A2
Lagos
GR 116 A7
P 98 B2
Lagosanto I 82 B1
Łagów
Lubuskie PL 46 C1
Świętokrzyskie PL 55 C6
La Granadella
Alicante E 96 C3
Lleida E 90 B3
La Grand-Combe F 78 B3
La Grande-Croix F 69 C4
La Grande-Motte F 78 C3
La Granja d'Escarp E 90 B3
La Granjuela E 93 C5
Lagrasse F 77 C5
La Grave F 79 A5
La Gravelle F 57 B4
Laguardia E 89 B4
La Guardia E 95 C3
La Guardia de Jaén
E 100 B2
Laguarres E 90 A3
Laguenne F 68 C1
Laguépie F 77 B4
La Guerche-de-Bretagne
F 57 C4
La Guerche-sur-l'Aubois
F 68 B2
La Guérinière F 66 B2
Laguiole F 78 B1
Laguna de Duera E 88 C2
Laguna del Marquesado
E 95 B5
Laguna de Negrillos
E 88 B1
Lagundo I 71 B6
Lagunilla E 93 A4
La Haba E 93 C5
Laharie F 76 B2
La Haye-du-Puits F 57 A4
La Haye-Pesnel F 57 B4
Lahden D 43 C4
La Herlière F 48 C3
La Hermida E 88 A2
La Herrera E 95 D4
Laheycourt F 59 B6
La Higuera E 101 A4
La Hiniesta E 88 C1
Lahnstein D 50 C3
Laholm S 40 C3
La Horcajada E 93 A5
La Horra E 88 C3
Lahr D 60 B3
Lahti FIN 3 F26
La Hulpe B 49 C5
La Hutte F 57 B6
Laichingen D 61 B5
L'Aigle F 58 B1
La Iglesuela E 94 B2
La Iglesuela del Cid E 90 C2
Laignes F 59 C5
Laiguéglia I 80 C2
L'Aiguillon-sur-Mer F 66 B3
Laimbach am Ostrong
A 63 B6
Laina E 95 A4
Lainio S 113 E11
Lairg GB 23 C4
La Iruela E 100 B2
Laissac F 78 B1
Laisvall S 115 A14
Láives I 71 B6
La Javie F 79 B5
Lajkovac SRB 85 B5
La Jonchère-St Maurice
F 67 B6
La Jonquera E 91 A5
Lajoskomárom H 74 B3
Lajosmizse H 75 A4
Lak H 65 B6
Lakenheath GB 30 B4
Lakitelek H 75 B5
Lakki GR 117 G5
Lakolk DK 39 D1
Łąkorz PL 47 B5
Lakšárska Nová Ves
SK 64 B3
Lakselv N 113 B13
Laksfors N 115 B10
Laktaši BIH 84 B2
La Lantejuela E 99 B5
Lalapaşa TR 118 A1
L'Albagès E 90 B3
Lalbenque F 77 B4
L'Alcudia E 96 B2
L'Aldea E 90 C3
Lalëz AL 105 B5
Lalín E 86 B2
Lalinde F 77 B3
La Línea de la
Concepción E 99 C5
Lalizolle F 68 B3
La Llacuna E 91 B4
Lalley F 79 B4
Lalling D 62 B4
Lalm N 114 F6
La Londe-les-Maures
F 79 C5
La Loupe F 58 B2
La Louvière B 49 C5
L'Alpe-d'Huez F 79 A5
La Luisiana E 99 B5
Laluque F 76 C1
Lam D 62 A4
La Machine F 68 B3
la Maddalena I 110 A2
Lama dei Peligni I 103 A7
Lamadrid E 88 A2
Lamagistère F 77 B3
La Mailleraye-sur-Seine
F 58 A1
La Malène F 78 B2
Lama Mocogno I 81 B4
La Mamola E 100 C2
La Manresana dels Prats
E 91 B4
Lamarche F 60 B1
Lamarche-sur-Saône
F 69 A5
Lamargelle F 69 A4
Lamarosa P 92 B2
Lamarque F 76 A2
Lamas P 92 A2
La Masadera E 90 B2
Lamas de Moaro P 87 B2
Lamastre F 78 B3
La Mata E 94 C2
La Mata de Ledesma
E 94 A1
La Mata de Monteagudo
E 88 B1
Lambach A 63 B4
Lamballe F 56 B3
Lamberhurst GB 31 C4
Lambesc F 79 C4
Lambia GR 117 E3
Lambley GB 25 D5
Lambourn GB 31 C2
Lamego P 87 C3
La Meilleraye-de-Bretagne
F 66 A3
La Ménitré F 67 A4
L'Ametlla de Mar E 90 C3
Lamia GR 116 D4
Lammhult S 40 B4
La Mojonera E 101 C3
La Mole F 79 C5
La Molina E 91 A4
La Monnerie-le-Montel
F 68 C3
La Morera E 93 C4
La Mothe-Achard F 66 B3
Lamothe-Cassel F 77 B4
Lamothe-Montravel F 76 B3
La Mothe-St Héray F 67 B4
Lamotte-Beuvron F 58 C3
La Motte-Chalançon
F 79 B4
La Motte-du-Caire F 79 B5
La Motte-Servolex F 69 C5
Lampertheim D 61 A4
Lampeter GB 28 A3
L'Ampolla E 90 C3
Lamprechtshausen A 62 C3
Lamsfeld D 53 B4
Lamspringe D 51 B6
Lamstedt D 43 B6
La Mudarra E 88 C2
La Muela E 90 B1
La Mure F 79 B4
Lamure-sur-Azergues
F 69 B4
Lana I 71 B6
Lanaja E 90 B2
Lanarce F 78 B2
Lanark GB 25 C4
La Nava E 99 B4
La Nava de Ricomalillo
E 94 C2
La Nava de Santiago
E 93 B4
Lancaster GB 26 A3
Lanchester GB 25 D6
Lanciano I 103 A7
Lancing GB 31 D3
Lançon-Provence F 79 C4
Lancova Vas SLO 73 B5
Landau
Bayern D 62 B3
Rheinland-Pfalz D 61 A4
Landeck A 71 A5
Landen B 49 C6
Landerneau F 56 B1
Landeryd S 40 B3
Landesbergen D 43 C6
Landete E 96 B1
Landévant F 56 C2
Landévennec F 56 B1
Landeyjahöfn IS 111 D5
Landivisiau F 56 B1
Landivy F 57 B4
Landl A 62 C3
Landön S 115 D11
Landos F 78 B2
Landouzy-le-Ville F 59 A5
Landquart CH 71 B4
Landrecies F 49 C4
Landreville F 59 B5
Landriano I 71 C4
Landsberg D 62 B1
Lands-berg D 52 B2
Landsbro S 40 B4
Landscheid D 50 D2
Landshut D 62 B3
Landskrona S 41 D2
Landstuhl D 60 A3
Lanesborough IRL 19 C4
Lanester F 56 C2
Lanestosa E 89 A3
La Neuve-Lyre F 58 B1
La Neuveville CH 70 A2
Langå DK 39 C2
Langadas GR 116 B5
Langa de Duero E 89 C3
Langadia GR 117 E4
Langangen N 35 C1
Långared S 40 A2
Långaröd S 41 D3
Långaryd S 40 B3
Långås S 40 C2
Långasjö S 40 C5
Langau A 63 B6
Langeac F 78 A2
Langeais F 67 A5
Langedijk NL 42 C1
Langeln D 51 B6
Langelsheim D 51 B6
Langemark-Poelkapelle
B 48 C3
Langen
Hessen D 51 D4
Niedersachsen D 43 B5
Langenau D 61 B6
Langenberg D 50 B4
Langenbruck CH 70 A2
Langenburg D 61 A5
Längenfeld A 71 A5
Langenfeld D 50 B2
Langenhorn D 43 A5
Langenlois A 63 B6
Langenlonsheim D 60 A3
Langennaudorf D 52 B3
Langenneufnach D 62 B1
Langenthal CH 70 A2
Langenzenn D 62 A1
Langeoog D 43 B4
Langeskov DK 39 D3
Langesund N 35 C1
Langewiesen D 51 C6
Långflon S 34 A4
Langförden D 43 C5
Langhagen D 44 B4
Länghem S 40 B3
Langhirano I 81 B4
Langholm GB 25 C5
Langholt IS 111 D7
Långlöt S 41 C6
Langnau CH 70 B2
Langø DK 39 E4
Langogne F 78 B2
Langon F 76 B2
Langquaid D 62 B3
Långrådna S 37 D3
Langreo E 88 A1
Langres F 59 C6
Långsele S 115 D14
Långserud S 35 C4
Langset N 34 B3
Långshyttan S 36 B3
Langstrand N 113 B12
Långträsk S 115 B17
Langueux F 56 B3
Languidic F 56 C2
Längvik S 37 C5
Langwarden D 43 B5
Langwathby GB 26 A3
Langwedel D 43 C6
Langweid D 62 B1
Langwies CH 71 B4
Lanheses P 87 C2
Lanięta PL 47 C5
Lanildut F 56 B1
Lanjarón E 100 C2
Lanmeur F 56 B2
Lanna
Jönköping S 40 B3
Örebro S 37 C1
Lännaholm S 36 C4
Lannavaara S 113 D10
Lannéanou F 56 B2
Lannemezan F 77 C3
Lanneuville-sur-Meuse
F 59 A6
Lannilis F 56 B1
Lannion F 56 B2
La Nocle-Maulaix F 68 B3
Lanouaille F 67 C6
Lansjärv S 113 F11
Lanškroun CZ 64 A2
Lanslebourg-Mont-Cenis
F 70 C1
Lanta F 77 C4
Lantadilla E 88 B2
Lanton F 76 B1
Lantosque F 79 C6
La Nuez de Arriba E 88 B3
Lanusei I 110 C2
Lanúvio I 102 B5
Lanvollon F 56 B3
Lánycsók H 74 B3
Lanz D 44 B3
Lanza E 86 A2
Lanzada E 86 B2
Lanzahita E 94 B2
Lanžhot CZ 64 B2
Lanzo Torinese I 70 C2
Laole SRB 85 B6
Laon F 59 A4
Laons F 58 B2
La Paca E 101 B4
La Pacaudière F 68 B3
Lapalisse F 68 B3
La Palma d'Ebre E 90 B3
La Palma del Condado
E 99 B4
La Palme F 78 D2
La Palmyre F 66 C3
La Parra E 93 C4
Łapczyna Wola PL 55 C4
La Pedraja de Portillo
E 88 C2
La Peraleja E 95 B4
La Petit-Pierre F 60 B3
Lapeyrade F 76 B2
Lapeyrouse F 68 B2
Lapford GB 28 C4
La Pinilla E 101 B4
Lapithos CY 120 A2
La Plagne F 70 C1
La Plaza E 86 A4
Laplje Selo KOS 85 D6
Laplume F 77 B3
La Pobla de Lillet E 91 A4
La Pobla de Vallbona
E 96 B2
La Pobla Llarga E 96 B2
La Pola de Gordón E 88 B1
la Porta F 102 A2
La Pouëze F 66 A4
Lapoutroie F 60 B3
La Póveda de Soria
E 89 B4
Lapovo SRB 85 B6
Läppe S 37 C2
Lappeenranta FIN 3 F28
Lappoluobbal N 113 C12
La Preste F 91 A5
La Primaube F 77 B5
Lapseki TR 118 B1
Lapua FIN 3 E25
La Puebla de Almoradie
E 95 C3
La Puebla de Cazalla
E 99 B5
La Puebla de los Infantes
E 99 B5
La Puebla del Río E 99 B4
La Puebla de Montalbán
E 94 C2
La Puebla de Roda E 90 A3
La Puebla de Valdavia
E 88 B2
La Puebla de Valverde
E 96 A2
La Pueblanueva E 94 C2
La Puerta de Segura
E 101 A3
La Punt CH 71 B4
L'Áquila I 103 A6
La Quintana E 100 B1
La Quintera E 99 B5
La Rábita
Granada E 100 C2
Jaén E 100 B1
Laracha E 86 A2
Laragh IRL 21 A5
Laragne-Montéglin F 79 B4
La Rambla E 100 B1
l'Arboç E 91 B4
L'Arbresle F 69 C4
Lärbro S 37 E5
Larceveau F 76 C1

Larche
  Alpes-de-Haute-
  Provence F 79 B5
  Corrèze F 77 A4
Lårdal N 33 C5
Lardosa P 92 B3
La Reale I 110 A1
Laredo E 89 A3
La Redondela E 86 B1
La Réole F 76 B2
Largentière F 78 B3
L'Argentière-la-Bessée
  F 79 B5
Largs GB 24 C3
Lari I 81 C4
La Riera de Gaià E . . 91 B4
La Rinconada E 99 B4
Lariño E 86 B1
Larino I 103 B7
Larisa GR 116 C4
La Rivière-Thibouville
  F 58 A1
Larkhall GB 25 C4
Larkollen N 35 C2
Larmor-Plage F 56 C2
Larnaca CY 120 B2
Larne GB 19 B6
La Robla E 88 B1
La Roca de la Sierra
  E 93 B4
La Roche CH 70 B2
La Rochebeaucourtet-
  Argentine F 67 C5
La Roche-Bernard F . 66 A2
La Roche-Canillac F . 68 C1
La Roche-Chalais F . 67 C5
La Roche Derrien F . 56 B2
La Roche-des-Arnauds
  F 79 B4
La Roche-en-Ardenne
  B 49 C6
La Roche-en-Brénil F 69 A4
La Rochefoucauld F . 67 C5
La Roche-Guyon F . . 58 A2
La Rochelle F 66 B3
La Roche-Posay F . . 67 B5
La Roche-sur-Foron
  F 69 B6
La Roche-sur-Yon F . 66 B3
La Rochette F 60 A2
La Rochette I 79 B4
La Roda
  Albacete E 95 C4
  Oviedo E 86 A4
La Roda de Andalucía
  E 100 B1
Laroquebrou F 77 B5
La Roquebrussanne
  F 79 C4
Laroque d'Olmes F . . 77 D4
La Roque-Gageac F . 77 B4
La Roque-Ste Marguerite
  F 78 B2
Laroque-Timbaut F . . 77 B3
Larouco E 87 B3
Larraga E 89 B5
Larrau F 76 C2
Larraaet F 77 C4
Larsnes N 114 E2
La Rubia E 89 C4
Larva E 100 B2
Larvik N 35 C2
La Sagrada E 87 D4
La Salceda E 94 A3
Lasalle F 78 B2
La Salle F 79 B5
la Salute di Livenza I . 72 C2
La Salvetat-Peyralés
  F 77 B5
La Salvetat-sur-Agout
  F 78 C1
Las Arenas E 88 A2
La Sarraz CH 69 B6
Lasarte E 89 A4
Låsby DK 39 C2
Las Cabezadas E . . . 95 A3
Las Cabezas de San Juan
  E 99 C5
Las Correderas E . . 100 A2
Las Cuevas de Cañart
  E 90 C2
La Seca E 88 C1
La Selva del Camp E 91 B4
La Senia E 90 C3
La Serra E 91 B4
La Seu d'Urgell E . . . 91 A4
La Seyne-sur-Mer F . 79 C4
Las Gabias E 100 B2
Las Herencias E . . . 94 C2
Las Herrerias E 98 B3
Łasin PL 47 B5
Lask PL 55 B4
Laska PL 46 B3
Łaskarzew PL 55 B6
Laško SLO 73 B5
Laskowice PL 47 B4
Las Labores E 95 C3
Las Mesas E 95 C4
Las Minas E 101 A4
Las Navas E 100 B1
Las Navas de la
  Concepción E . . . 99 B5
Las Navas del Marqués
  E 94 B2
Las Navillas E 94 C2
Las Negras E 101 C4
La Solana E 95 C3
La Souterraine F . . . 67 B6
Las Pajanosas E . . . 99 B4
Laspaules E 90 A3
Las Pedroñas E 95 C4
La Spézia I 81 B3
Las Planes d'Hostoles
  E 91 A5
Laspuña E 90 A3
Las Rozas
  Cantabria E 88 B2
  Madrid E 94 B3
Lassan D 45 B5
Lassay-les-Châteaux
  F 57 B5
Lasseube F 76 C2
Lassigny F 58 A3
La Storta I 102 B5
Lastovo HR 84 D2
Lastras de Cuéllar E . 88 C2
Låstringe S 37 D4
Lastrup D 43 C4
Lastva BIH 84 D3
La Uces E 87 C4
La Suze-sur-Sarthe F 57 C6
Las Veguillas E 94 B1
Las Ventas con Peña
  Aguilera E 94 C2
Las Ventas de San Julián
  E 93 A5
Las Villas E 92 B1
Latasa E 76 D1
Látera I 102 A4
Laterza I 104 C2
La Teste F 79 B1
Lathen D 43 C4
Latheron GB 23 C5
La Thuile I 70 C1
Latiano I 105 C3
Latina I 102 B5
Latisana I 72 C2
Látky SK 65 B5
La Toba E 95 B5
La Toledana E 94 C2
La Torre de Cabdella
  E 90 A3
La Torre de Esteban
  Hambrán E 94 B2
La Torre del l'Espanyol
  E 90 B3

La Torresaviñán E . . 95 B4
La Tour d'Aigues F . . 79 C4
La Tour de Peilz CH . 70 B1
La Tour-du-Pin F . . . 69 C5
Latowicz PL 55 A6
La Tranche-sur-Mer F 66 B3
La Tremblade F 66 C3
La Trimouille F 67 B6
La Trinité F 56 C2
La Trinité-Porhoët F . 56 B3
Latrónico I 106 A3
Latronquière F 77 B5
Latterbach CH 70 B2
La Turballe F 66 A2
Laubach D 51 C4
Laubert F 78 B2
Laucha D 52 B1
Lauchhammer D . . . 53 B3
Lauchheim D 61 B6
Lauda-Königshofen
  D 61 A5
Laudal N 33 D4
Lauder GB 25 C5
Lauenau D 51 A5
Lauenburg D 44 B2
Lauf D 62 A2
Laufach D 51 C5
Laufen
  CH 70 A2
  D 62 C3
Lauffen D 61 A5
Laugar IS 111 B8
Laugarás IS 111 C5
Laugarbakki IS . . . 111 B5
Laugarvatn IS 111 C5
Laugharne GB 28 B3
Lauingen D 61 B6
Laujar de Andarax E 100 C3
Laukaa FIN 3 E26
Lauker S 115 B16
Laukvik N 112 E3
Launceston GB 28 C3
La Unión E 101 B5
Launois-sur-Vence F 59 A5
Laupheim D 61 B5
Lauragh IRL 20 C2
Laureana di Borrello
  I 106 C3
Laurencekirk GB . . . 25 B5
Laurencetown IRL . . 20 A3
Laurenzana I 104 C1
Lauria I 106 A2
Laurière F 67 B6
Laurieston GB 24 D3
Laurino I 103 C8
Lausanne CH 69 B6
Laussonne F 78 B3
Lauta D 53 B4
Lautenthal D 51 B6
Lauterach A 71 A4
Lauterbach D 51 C5
Lauterbrunnen CH . . 70 B2
Lauterecken D 60 A3
Lauterhofen D 62 A2
Lautrec F 77 C5
Lauvsnes N 114 C7
Lauvvik N 33 D3
Lauzerte F 77 B4
Lauzès F 77 B4
Lauzun F 77 B3
Lavagna I 80 B3
Lavaur F 57 B5
La Vall d'Uixó E 96 B2
Lavamünd A 73 B4
Lavara GR 118 A1
Lavardac F 76 B3
Lavaris P 92 A2
Lavarone I 71 C6
Lavau F 59 C3
Lavaur F 77 C4
La Vecilla de Curueño
  E 88 B1
La Vega
  Asturias E 88 A1
  Asturias E 88 A1
  Cantabria E 77 D4
Lavelanet F 77 D4
La Velilla E 94 A3
La Velles E 94 A1
Lavello I 104 B1
Lavelsloh D 43 C5
Lavenham GB 30 B4
Laveno I 70 C3
La Ventosa E 95 B4
Lavezzola I 81 B5
Laviano I 103 C8
La Victoria E 100 B1
La Vid E 89 C3
Lavik N 32 A2
La Vilavella E 96 B2
La Vilella Baixa E . . . 90 B3
La Villa de Don Fadrique
  E 95 C3
Lavilledieu F 78 B3
La Villedieu F 67 B4
La Ville Dieu-du-Temple
  F 77 B4
Lavinio-Lido di Enea
  I 102 B5
Lav is I 71 B6
Lavit F 77 C3
Lavoncourt F 60 C1
Lavos P 92 A2
La Voulte-sur-Rhône
  F 78 B3
Lavoûte-Chilhac F . . 68 C3
Lavradio P 92 C1
Lavre P 92 C2
Lavrio GR 117 E5
La Wantzenau F . . . 60 B3
Lawers GB 24 B3
Ławy PL 45 C6
Laxá S 37 D1
Laxamýri IS 111 B8
Laxe E 86 A2
Laxey GB 26 A1
Laxford Bridge GB . . 22 C3
Laxhall S 35 D5
Laxsjö S 115 D11
Laxtjarn S 34 B6
Laxvik S 40 C2
Laxviken S 115 D11
La Yesa E 96 B2
Laza E 87 B3
Lazarevac SRB 85 B5
Lazarev Krst MNE . . 84 D3
Lazarevo SRB 75 C5
Łaziska Grn. PL 54 C3
Lazkao E 89 A4
Lázně Bělohrad CZ . 53 C5
Lázně Bohdaneč CZ . 53 C5
Lázně Kynžvart CZ . . 52 C2
Lazonby GB 26 A3
La Zubia E 100 B2
Lazy PL 46 A2
Lazzaro I 109 B4
Lea GB 27 B5
Leadburn GB 25 C4
Leadhills GB 25 C4
Leap IRL 20 C2
Leatherhead GB . . . 31 C3
Leba PL 46 A3
Lebach D 60 A2
Le Barp F 76 B2
Le Bar-sur-Loup F . . 79 C6
Le Beausset F 79 C4
Lebedyn UA 7 F13
Lébény H 64 C3
Le Bessat F 69 C4
Le Blanc F 67 B6
Le Bleymard F 78 B2

Le Bourget-du-Lac F . 69 C5
Le Bourgneuf-la-Forêt
  F 57 B5
Le Bousquet d'Orb F 78 C2
Le Brassus CH 69 B6
Le Breuil F 68 B3
Le Breuil-en-Auge F . 57 A6
Lebrija E 99 C4
Lebring A 73 B5
Le Brusquet F 79 B5
Le Bry CH 70 B2
Le Bugue F 77 B3
Le Buisson F 77 B3
Lebus D 45 C6
Lebusa D 52 B3
Le Caloy F 76 C2
Le Cap d'Agde F . . . 78 C2
Le Caylar F 78 C2
Le Cayrol F 78 B1
Lecce I 105 C4
Lecco I 71 C4
Lécera E 90 B2
Lećevica HR 83 C5
Lech A 71 A5
Le Chambon-Feugerolles
  F 69 C4
Le Chambon-sur-Lignon
  F 78 A3
Le Château d'Oléron
  F 66 C3
Le Châtelard F 69 C6
Le Châtelet F 68 B2
Le Châtelet-en-Brie F 58 B3
Lechbruck D 62 C1
Lechena GR 117 E3
Le Chesne F 59 A5
Le Cheylard F 78 B3
Lechlade GB 29 B6
Lechovice CZ 64 B2
Leciñena E 90 B2
Le Collet-de-Deze F . 78 B2
Le Conquet F 56 B1
Le Creusot F 69 B4
Le Croisic F 66 A2
Le Crotoy F 48 C2
Lectoure F 77 C3
Łęczyca
  Łódzkie PL 55 A4
  Zachodnio-Pomorskie
  PL 45 B7
Ledaña E 95 C5
Ledbury GB 29 A5
Lede B 49 C4
Ledečnad Sazavou
  CZ 63 A6
Ledenice CZ 63 B5
Le Deschaux F 69 B5
Ledesma E 87 C4
Lédignan F 78 C3
Lédigos E 88 B1
Ledmore GB 22 C4
Lednice CZ 64 B2
Lednogóra PL 46 C3
Le Donjon F 68 B3
Le Dorat F 67 B6
Łędyczek PL 46 B2
Lędziny PL 55 C4
Leeds GB 27 B4
Leek
  GB 26 B3
  NL 42 B3
Leende NL 49 B6
Leer D 43 B4
Leerdam NL 49 B6
Leerhafen D 43 B4
Leese D 43 C6
Leeuwarden NL 42 B2
Leezen D 44 B2
Le Faou F 56 B1
Le Faoüet F 56 B2
Lefkada GR 116 D2
Lefkimis GR 116 C2
Lefkoniko CY 120 A2
Le Folgoet F 56 B1
Le Fossat F 77 C4
Le Fousseret F 77 C4
Le Fuget F 79 B5
Leganés E 94 B3
Le Gault-Soigny F . . 59 B4
Legbąd PL 46 B3
Legé F 66 B3
Lège-Cap-Ferret F . . 76 B1
Legionowo PL 55 A5
Léglise B 60 A1
Legnago I 71 C6
Legnano I 70 C3
Legnaro I 72 C1
Legnica PL 53 B6
Łęgowo PL 47 A4
Legrad HR 74 B1
Le Grand-Bornand F . 69 C6
Le-Grand-Bourg F . . 67 B6
Le Grand-Lucé F . . . 58 C1
Le Grand-Pressigny
  F 67 B5
Le Grand-Quevilly F . 58 A2
Le Grau-du-Roi F . . . 78 C3
Léguevin F 77 C4
Legutiano E 89 B4
Le Havre F 57 A6
Le Hohwald F 60 B3
Le Houga F 76 C2
Lehrberg D 61 A6
Lehre D 51 A6
Lehrte D 44 C1
Lehsen D 44 B3
Leibnitz A 73 B5
Leicester GB 30 B2
Leiden NL 49 A5
Leidschendam NL . . 49 A5
Leigh GB 26 B3
Leighlinbridge IRL . . 21 B5
Leighton Buzzard GB 31 C3
Leignon B 49 C6
Leikanger N 114 F2
Leimen D 61 A4
Leinefelde D 51 B6
Leinfelden GB 61 B5
Leirada N 114 F2
Leíramoen N 112 F3
Leiria P 92 B2
Leirvik
  Hordaland N 32 C2
  Sogn og Fjordane N 32 A2
Leisach A 72 B2
Leiston GB 30 B5
Leitholm GB 25 C5
Leitrim IRL 18 C3
Leitza E 76 C1
Leitzkau D 52 A1
Łękawa PL 55 B4
Lekawica PL 65 A5
Lekeberga S 37 C2
Lekeitio E 89 A4
Leknes N 112 D2
Leknica PL 53 B4
Leksand S 36 B1
Leksvik N 114 D7
Lekvattnet S 34 B4
Le Lardin-St Lazare F 67 C6
Le Lauzet-Ubaye F . . 79 B5

Le Lavandou F 79 C5
Le Lion-d'Angers F . . 57 C5
Lelkowo PL 47 A6
Le Locle CH 70 A1
Le Loroux-Botereau
  F 66 A3
Le Louroux-Béconnais
  F 66 A4
Lelów PL 55 C4
Le Luc F 79 C5
Le Lude F 57 C6
Lelystad NL 42 C2
Lem
  Ringkøbing DK . . . 39 C1
  Viborg Amt. DK . . . 38 C1
Le Malzieu-Ville F . . 78 B2
Le Mans F 57 B6
Le Mas-d'Azil F 77 C4
Le Massegros F 78 B2
Le Mayet-de-Montagne
  F 68 B3
Le May-sur-Èvre F . . 66 A4
Lembach F 60 A3
Lemberg F 60 A3
Lembèye F 76 C2
Lemelerveld NL 42 C3
Le Mêle-sur-Sarthe F 58 B1
Le Ménil F 60 B2
Le Merlerault F 57 B6
Le Mesnil-sur-Oger F 59 B5
Lemförde D 43 C5
Lemgo D 51 A4
Le Miroir F 69 B5
Lemland FIN 36 B7
Lemmer NL 42 C2
Le Molay-Littry F . . . 57 A5
Le Monastier-sur-Gazeille
  F 78 B2
Le Mont-Dore F 68 C2
Le Montet F 68 B3
Le Mont-St Michel F . 57 B4
Lempdes F 68 C3
Le Muret F 76 B2
Le Muy F 79 C5
Lemvig DK 38 C1
Lemwerder D 43 B5
Lena N 34 B2
Lénart SLO 73 B5
Lenartovce SK 65 B6
Lencloître F 67 B5
Lend A 72 A3
Lendalfoot GB 24 C3
Lendava SLO 73 B6
Lendery RUS 3 E29
Lendinara I 81 A5
Lendorf A 72 B3
Lendum DK 38 B3
Le Neubourg F 58 A1
Lengefeld D 52 C3
Lengerich
  Niedersachsen D . . 43 C4
  Nordrhein-Westfalen
  D 50 A3
Lenggries D 62 C2
Lengyeltóti H 74 B2
Lenhovda S 40 C5
Lenk CH 70 B2
Lennartsfors S 35 C3
Lennestadt D 50 B4
Lennoxtown GB 24 C3
Leno I 71 C5
Lénola I 103 B6
Le Nouvion-en-Thiérache
  F 49 C4
Lens
  B 49 C4
  F 48 C3
Lensahn D 44 A2
Lens Lestang F 69 C5
Lensvik N 114 D6
Lentellais F 87 B3
Lentföhrden D 44 B1
Lenti H 74 B1
Lentini I 109 B3
Lenungshammar S . . 35 C4
Lenzburg CH 70 A3
Lenzen D 44 B3
Lenzerheide CH . . . 71 B4
Leoben A 73 A5
Leogang A 72 A2
Leominster GB 29 A5
León E 88 B1
León E 76 C1
Leonberg D 61 B5
Léoncel F 79 B4
Leonding A 63 B5
Leonessa I 103 A6
Leonforte I 109 B3
Leonidio GR 117 E4
Leopoldsburg B 49 B6
Leopoldsdorf im
  Marchfeld A 64 B2
Leopoldshagen D . . 45 B5
Leova MD 11 C10
Le Palais F 56 C2
Le Parcq F 48 C3
Le Péage-de-Roussillon
  F 69 C4
Le Pellerin F 66 A3
Lepenac
  MNE 85 D4
  SRB 85 C6
Lepoglava HR 116 D3
Le Perthus F 91 A5
Le Petit-Bornand F . 69 C6
Lephin GB 22 D2
L'Épine F 79 B4
Le Poët F 79 B4
Lepoglava HR 73 B6
Le Poire-sur-Vie F . . 66 B3
Le Pont CH 69 B6
Le Pont-de-Montvert
  F 78 B2
Le Porge F 76 B1
Le Porge-Océan F . . 76 B1
Le Portel F 48 C2
Le Pouldu F 56 C2
Le Pouliguen F 66 A2
Leppäjärvi FIN 113 D12
Leppävirta FIN 3 E27
Leppin D 44 C3
le Rayol F 79 C5
Lercara Friddi I 108 B2
Léré F 68 A2
Lérici I 81 B3
Lerin E 89 B5
Lerma E 88 B3
Lermoos A 71 A5
Le Roeulx B 49 C5
Le Rouget F 77 B5
Lerouville F 60 B1
Le Rozier F 78 B2
Le Russey F 70 A1
Lervik N 35 C2
Lerwick GB 22 A7
Lés
  East Yorkshire GB . 27 B5
  Fife GB 25 B4
Les Abrets F 69 C5
Leśak KOS 85 C5
Lesaka E 76 C1
Les Aix-d'Angillon F . 68 A2
Les Andelys F 58 A2
Les Ancizes-Comps
  F 68 C2
Les Arcs
  Savoie F 70 C1
  Var F 79 C5
Les-Aubiers F 67 B4

Les Baux-de-Provence
  F 78 C3
Les Bézards F 58 C3
Les Bois CH 70 A1
Les Bordes F 58 C3
Les Borges del Camp
  E 90 B3
Les Borges Blanques
  E 91 B4
Les Brunettes F 68 B3
Lesbury GB 25 C6
Les Cabannes F . . . 77 D4
L'Escala E 91 A6
Lescar F 76 C2
Lesce SLO 73 B4
Lescheraines F 69 C6
Lesconil F 56 C1
Les Contamines-Montjoie
  F 70 C1
les Coves de Vinroma
  E 90 C3
Les Déserts F 69 C5
Les Deux-Alpes F . . 79 B5
Les Diablerets CH . . 70 B2
Lesdins F 59 A4
Les Echelles F 69 C5
Le Sel-de-Bretagne F 57 C4
Le Sentier CH 69 B6
Les Escaldes AND. . 91 A4
Les Estables F 78 B3
Les Eyzies-de-Tayac
  F 77 B4
Les Gets F 70 B1
Les Grandes-Ventes
  F 58 A2
Les Haudères CH . . 70 B2
Les Herbiers F 66 B3
Les Hôpitaux-Neufs
  F 69 B6
Lesično SLO 73 B5
Lésina I 103 B8
Lesjaskog N 114 E5
Lesjöfors S 34 C6
Lešké SLO 73 C5
Les Mages F 78 B3
Lesmahagow GB . . . 25 C4
Les Mazures F 59 A5
Les Mées F 79 B4
Les Mureaux F 58 B2
Lesna PL 53 B5
Lešná CZ 64 A3
Lešnica PL 54 C3
Lešnica SRB 85 B4
Lesneven F 56 B1
Leśniów Wielkoplski
  PL 53 B5
Lesnoye RUS 7 B13
Les Omergues F . . . 79 B4
Les Ormes-sur-Voulzie
  F 59 B4
Les Orres F 79 B5
Le Souquet F 76 C1
Lesparre-Médoc F . . 66 C4
l'Espérance F 59 A4
l'Esperou F 78 B2
Les Pieux F 57 A4
Lesponne F 76 C3
Les Ponts-de-Cé F . . 67 A4
Les Ponts-de-Martel
  CH 70 B1
Le Praz F 70 C1
L'Espunyola E 91 A4
Les Riceys F 59 C5
Les Roches F 69 C4
Les Rosaires F 56 B3
Les Rosiers F 67 A4
Les Rousses F 69 B6
Les Sables-d'Olonne
  F 66 B3
Lessach A 72 A3
Lessay F 57 A4
Lessebo S 40 C5
Les Settons F 68 A4
Lessines B 49 C4
L'Estany E 91 B5
Les Ternes F 78 A1
Lesterps F 67 B5
Les Thilliers en-Vexin
  F 58 A2
Les Touches F 66 A3
Les Trois Moûtiers F . 67 A5
Les Vans F 78 B3
Les Verrières CH . . . 69 B6
Les Vignes F 78 B2
Leswalt GB 24 D2

Lévignen F 59 A3
le Ville I 82 C1
Levinovac HR 74 C2
Le Vivier-sur-Mer F . 57 B4
Levoča SK 65 A6
Levroux F 67 B6
Lewes GB 31 D4
Lewin Brzeski PL . . . 54 C2
Lewisham GB 31 C3
Leyburn GB 27 A4
Leyland GB 26 B3
Leysdown-on-Sea GB 31 C4
Leysin CH 70 B2
Lezajsk PL 11 A7
Lézardrieux F 56 B2
Lézat-sur-Lèze F . . . 77 C4
Lezay F 67 B4
Lezhë AL 105 B5
Lézignan-Corbières
  F 78 C1
Lézignan-la-Cèbe F . 78 C2
Ležimir SRB 85 A4
Lézinnes F 59 C5
Lezoux F 68 C3
Lezuza E 95 C4
Lgov RUS 7 F13
Lhenice CZ 63 B5
Lherm F 77 C4
Lhommaizé F 67 B5
L'Hospitalet F 91 A4
L'Hospitalet de l'Infant
  E 90 C3
L'Hospitalet de Llobregat
  E 91 B5
L'Hospitalet-du-Larzac
  F 78 C2
Lhuître F 59 B5
Liancourt F 58 A3
Liart F 59 A5
Liatorp S 40 C4
Liatrie GR 22 D4
Libán CZ 53 C5
Libčeves CZ 53 C3
Liběchov CZ 53 C4
Liber E 86 B3
Libiąž PL 55 C4
Libina CZ 64 A3
Libochovice CZ 53 C4
Libofshë AL 105 C5
Libohovë AL 116 B2
Libourne F 76 B2
Libramont B 49 D6
Librazhd AL 116 A2
Librilla E 101 B4
Libros E 96 A1
Licata I 108 B2
Licciana Nardi I 81 B4
Licenza I 102 A5
Liceros E 89 C3
Lich D 51 C4
Lichères-près-Aigremont
  F 59 C4
Lichfield GB 27 C4
Lichtenau
  A 63 B6
  D 51 B4
Lichtenberg D 52 C1
Lichtenfels D 52 C1
Lichtensteig CH 71 A4
Lichtenstein D 52 C2
Lichtenvoorde NL . . 50 B2
Lichtervelde B 49 B4
Lička Jesenica HR . . 83 A4
Lickershamn S 37 E5
Lički Osik HR 83 B4
Ličko Lešce HR 83 B4
Licodia Eubéa I . . . 109 B3
Licques F 48 C2
Lida BY 7 E8
Lidar N 32 A6
Lidečko CZ 64 A4
Liden S 115 E13
Lidhult S 40 C3
Lidköping S 35 D5
Lido I 72 C2
Lido Azzurro I 104 C3
Lido degli Estensi I . 82 B1
Lido degli Scacchi I . 82 B1
Lido della Nazioni I . 82 B1
Lido di Camaiore I . . 81 C4
Lido di Casalbordino
  I 103 A7
Lido di Castél Fusano
  I 102 B5
Lido di Cincinnato I . 102 B5
Lido di Classe I 82 B1
Lido di Fermo I 82 C2
Lido di Fondi I 103 B6
Lido di Jésolo I 72 C2
Lido di Licola I 103 C6
Lido di Metaponto I 104 C2
Lido di Ostia I 102 B5
Lido di Policoro I . . 106 A3
Lido di Savio I 82 B1
Lido di Scanzano I . 104 C2
Lido di Siponto I . . 104 B1
Lido di Volano I 82 B1
Lido Riccio I 103 A7
Lidoríki GR 116 D4
Lido Silvana I 104 C3
Lidsjöberg S 115 C12
Lidzbark PL 47 B5
Lidzbark Warmiński
  PL 47 A6
Liebenau
  A 63 B5
  D 43 C6
Liebenwalde D 45 C5
Lieberose D 53 B4
Liebling RO 75 C6
Lieboch A 73 B5
Liège B 49 C6
Lieksa FIN 3 E29
Lienen D 50 A3
Lienz A 72 B2
Liepāja LV 6 C6
Lier B 49 B5
Lierbyen N 34 C2
Liérganes E 88 A3
Liernais F 69 A4
Liesing A 72 B2
Liestal CH 70 A2
Liétor E 101 A4
Lieurac F 77 D4
Lieurey F 57 A6
Liévin F 48 C3
Liezen A 63 C5
Liffol-le-Grand F . . . 60 B1
Liffré F 57 B4
Ligardes F 77 B3
Lignano Sabbiadoro I 72 C3
Ligne F 66 A3
Lignières F 68 B2
Ligny-en-Barrois F . . 59 B6
Ligny-le-Châtel F . . . 59 C4
Ligourió GR 117 E4
Ligowo PL 47 C5
Ligueil F 67 A5
Ljeva Rijeka MNE . . 85 D4
Likavka SK 65 A5
Likenäs S 34 B5
Likhoslavl RUS 7 C13
Lild Strand DK 38 B2
Lilienfeld A 63 B6
Lilienthal D 43 B5
Lilla Edet S 35 D4
Lilla Tjärby S 40 C3
Lille
  B 49 B5
  F 49 C4
Lillebonne F 57 A6
Lillehammer N 34 A2
Lillerød DK 41 D2
Lillers F 48 C3
Lillesand N 33 D5
Lillestrøm N 34 C3

Lillhärdal S 115 F11
Lillkyrka S 37 C4
Lillo E 95 C3
Litija SLO 73 B4
Lit-et-Mixe F 76 B1
Lithnes H 65 B5
Litlabø N 32 C2
Litóchoro GR 116 B4
Litomerice CZ 53 C4
Litoměřice CZ 53 C4
Litomyšl CZ 64 A2
Litovel CZ 64 A3
Litschau A 63 B6
Littlehampton GB . . . 31 D3
Littleborough GB . . . 30 B4
Littleton IRL 21 B4
Little Walsingham GB 30 B4
Littleport GB 30 B4
Litvinov CZ 52 C3
Livadero GR 116 B3
Livadhia CY 120 B2
Livadia GR 116 D4
Livarot F 57 B6
Liveras CY 120 A1
Livernon F 77 B4
Liverpool GB 26 B3
Livigno I 71 B5
Livingston GB 25 C4
Livno BIH 84 C1
Livold SLO 73 C4
Livorno I 81 C4
Livorno Ferraris I . . . 70 C3
Livron-sur-Drôme F . 78 B3
Livry-Louvercy F . . . 59 A5
Lixheim F 60 B3
Lixouri GR 117 D2
Lizard GB 28 D2
Lizy-sur-Ourcq F . . . 59 A4
Lizzano I 104 C3
Lizzano in Belvedere
  I 81 B4
Ljesane KOS 85 D5
Ljig SRB 85 B5
Ljørdalen N 34 A4
Ljosland N 33 D4
Ljubija BIH 83 B5
Ljubinje BIH 84 D3
Ljubljana SLO 73 B4
Ljubno ob Savinji
  SLO 73 B4
Ljubovija SRB 85 B4
Ljubuški BIH 84 C2
Ljugarn S 37 E5
Ljung S 40 B3
Ljunga S 37 D3
Ljungaverk S 115 E13
Ljungby S 40 C3
Ljungbyhed S 41 C3
Ljungbyholm S 40 C6
Ljungdalen S 115 E9
Ljungsarp S 40 B3
Ljungsbro S 37 D2
Ljungskile S 35 D3
Ljusdal S 115 F13
Ljusfallshammar S . . 37 D2
Ljusne S 36 A4
Ljusterö S 37 C5
Ljutomer SLO 73 B6
Lladurs E 91 A4
Llafranc E 91 B6
Llagostera E 91 B5
Llanaelhaiarn GB . . . 26 C1
Llanarth GB 28 A3
Llanbedr GB 26 C1
Llanberis GB 26 B1
Llanbister GB 29 A4
Llanbrynmair GB . . . 26 C2
Llandeilo GB 28 B4
Llandissilio GB 28 B3
Llandovery GB 28 B4
Llandrillo GB 26 C2
Llandrindod Wells
  GB 29 A4
Llandudec GB 56 B1
Llandudno GB 26 B2
Llandysul GB 28 A3
Llanelli GB 28 B3
Llanerchymedd GB . . 26 B1
Llanes E 88 A2
Llanfair Caereinion
  GB 26 C2
Llanfairfechan GB . . 26 B2
Llanfyllin GB 26 C2
Llangadog GB 28 B4
Llangefni GB 26 B1
Llangollen GB 26 C2
Llangranog GB 28 A3
Llanidloes GB 26 C2
Llanilar GB 28 A3
Llanrhystud GB 28 A3
Llanrwst GB 26 B2
Llansannan GB 26 B2
Llansawel GB 28 A4
Llanstephan GB . . . 28 B3
Llanteno E 89 A3
Llanthony GB 29 B4
Llantrisant GB 29 B4
Llanuwchllyn GB . . . 26 C2
Llanwddyn GB 26 C2
Llanwrda GB 28 B4
Llanwrtyd Wells GB . 29 A4
Llanybydder GB 28 A4
Llanymynech GB . . . 26 C2
Llavorsi E 91 A4
Lleida E 90 B3
Llera E 93 C4
Llerena E 93 C4
Lles E 91 A4
Llessui E 91 A4
Llinars E 91 A4
Lliria E 96 B2
Llodio E 89 A4
Lloret de Mar E 91 B5
Llosa de Ranes E . . 96 B2
Lloseta E 97 B2
Llucena del Cid E . . 96 A2
Lluçmajor E 97 B2
Llutxent E 96 C2
Llwyngwril GB 26 C1
Llysnes N 32 C2
Lnáře CZ 63 A4
Loanhead GB 25 C4
Loano I 80 B2
Loarre E 90 A2
Löbau D 53 B4
Löbejün D 52 B1
Lobenstein D 52 C1
Löberöd S 41 D3
Łobez PL 45 B7
Löbnitz D 45 A4
Lobón E 93 C4
Loburg D 52 A2
Łobżenica PL 46 B3
Locana I 70 C2
Locarno CH 70 B3
Loccum D 43 C6
Loče SLO 73 B5
Lochailort GB 24 B2
Lochaline GB 24 B2
Lochans GB 24 D2
Locharbriggs GB . . . 25 C4
Lochau A 71 A4
Loch Baghasdail GB 22 D1
Lochcarron GB 22 D3
Lochearnhead GB . . 24 B3
Lochem NL 50 A2
Loches F 67 A5
Lochgelly GB 25 B4
Lochgilphead GB . . . 24 B2
Lochgoilhead GB . . . 24 B3
Loch nam Madadh
  GB 22 D1
Lochranza GB 24 C2
Locharbriggs SRB . . 85 C5
Lockenhaus A 73 A6
Lockerbie GB 25 C4
Löcknitz D 45 B6
Locmaria F 56 C2

Massa I 81 B4
Massa Fiscáglia I 81 B6
Massafra I 104 C3
Massa Lombarda I 81 B6
Massa Lubrense I 103 C7
Massamagrell E 96 B2
Massa Marittima I 81 C4
Massa Martana I 82 D1
Massanassa E 96 B2
Massarosa I 81 C4
Massat F 77 D4
Massay F 68 A2
Massbach D 51 C6
Masseret F 67 C6
Masseube F 77 C3
Massiac F 68 C3
Massignac F 67 C5
Massing D 62 B3
Massmechelen B 50 C1
Masterud N 34 B4
Mästocka S 40 C3
Masty BY 6 E8
Masúa I 110 C1
Masueco E 87 C4
Masugnsbyn S 113 E11
Masun SLO 73 C4
Maszewo
    Lubuskie PL 53 A4
    Zachodnio-Pomorskie
    PL 45 B7
Mata de Alcántara E . .93 B4
Matala GR 117 H6
Matalebreras E 89 C4
Matallana de Torio E 88 B1
Matamala E 89 C4
Mataporquera E 88 B2
Matapozuelos E 88 C2
Mataró E 91 B5
Matarocco I 108 B1
Mataruge MNE 85 C4
Mataruška Banja
    SRB 85 C5
Matelica I 82 C2
Matera I 104 C2
Mateševo MNE 85 D4
Mátészalka H 11 C7
Matet E 96 B2
Matfors S 115 E14
Matha F 67 C4
Mathay F 70 A1
Matignon F 57 B3
Matilla de los Caños del
    Rio E 94 B1
Matlock GB 27 B4
Matosinhos P 87 C2
Matour F 69 B4
Mátrafüred H 65 C5
Mátraterenye H 65 B5
Matre
    Hordaland N 32 B2
    Hordaland N 32 C2
Matrei am Brenner A . .71 A6
Matrei in Osttirol A 72 A2
Matrica I 103 B7
Matsdal S 115 B12
Mattarello I 71 B6
Mattersburg A 64 C2
Mattighofen A 62 B4
Mattinata I 104 B2
Mattos P 92 B2
Mattsee A 62 C4
Mattsmyra S 36 A2
Matulji HR 73 C4
Maubert-Fontaine F . .59 A5
Maubeuge F 49 C4
Maubourguet F 76 C3
Mauchline GB 24 C3
Maud GB 23 D6
Mauer-kirchen A 62 B4
Mauern D 62 B2
Mauguio F 78 C3
Maule F 58 B2
Mauléon F 67 B4
Mauléon-Barousse F . .77 D3
Mauléon-Licharre F . .76 C2
Maulévrier F 66 A4
Maum IRL 18 C2
Maurach A 72 A1
Maure-de-Bretagne F . .57 C3
Maureilhan F 78 C2
Mauriac F 68 C2
Mauron F 57 B3
Maury F 77 D5
Maussane-les-Alpilles
    F 78 C3
Mautern A 63 B6
Mauterndorf A 72 A3
Mautern im Steiermark
    A 73 A4
Mauthausen A 63 B5
Mauthen A 72 B2
Mauvezin F 77 C3
Mauzé-sur-le-Mignon
    F 67 B4
Maxent F 57 C3
Maxey-sur-Vaise F 60 B1
Maxial P 92 B1
Maxieira P 92 B2
Maxwellheugh GB 25 C5
Mayalde E 88 C1
Maybole GB 24 C3
Mayen D 50 C3
Mayenne F 57 B5
Mayet F 58 C1
Mayorga E 88 B1
Mayres F 78 B3
Mayrhofen A 72 A1
Mazagón E 99 B4
Mazaleón E 90 B3
Mazamet F 77 C5
Mazan F 79 B4
Mazara del Vallo I . . .108 B1
Mazaramroz E 104 C2
Mazarete E 95 B4
Mazaricos E 86 B2
Mazarrón E 101 B4
Mažeikiai LT 6 C7
Mazères F 77 C4
Mazères-sur-Salat F . .77 C3
Mazières-en-Gâtine F . .67 B4
Mazin HR 83 B4
Mazuelo E 88 B3
Mazyr BY 7 E10
Mazzarino I 109 B3
Mazzarrà Sant'Andrea
    I 109 A4
Mazzo di Valtellina I . .71 B5
Mdzewo PL 47 C6
Mealabost GB 22 C2
Mealhada P 92 A2
Méan B 49 C6
Meana Sardo I 110 C2
Meaulne F 68 B2
Meaux F 59 B3
Mebonden N 114 D8
Mecerreyes E 89 B3
Mechelen B 49 B5
Mechernich D 50 C2
Mechnica PL 54 C3
Mechowo PL 45 B7
Mechterstädt D 51 C6
Mecidiye TR 118 B1
Mecikal PL 46 B3
Mecina-Bombarón
    E 100 C2
Meckenbeuren D 61 C5
Meckenheim
    Rheinland-Pfalz D . . .50 C3
    Rheinland-Pfalz D . . .61 A4
Meckesheim D 61 A4
Mecseknádasd H 74 B3
Meda
    I 71 C4
    P 87 D3
Medak HR 83 B4
Mede I 80 A2

Medebach D 51 B4
Medelim P 93 A3
Medemblik NL 42 C2
Medena Selista BIH . . .84 B1
Medesano I 81 B4
Medevi S 37 D1
Medgidia RO 11 D10
Medgyesháza H 75 B6
Mediaş RO 11 C8
Medicína I 81 B5
Medinaceli E 95 A4
Medina de las Torres
    E 93 C4
Medina del Campo E . .88 C2
Medina de Pomar E 89 B3
Medina de Rioseco E . .88 C1
Medina Sidonia E 99 C5
Medinilla E 93 A5
Medja SRB 75 C5
Medjedja BIH 85 C4
Medulin HR 82 B2
Medulin I 72 B2
Medveda SRB 85 B6
Medvedja SRB 85 C6
Medvedov SK 64 C3
Medvide HR 83 B4
Medvode SLO 73 B4
Medzev SK 65 B6
Medžitlija MK 116 B3
Meerane D 52 C2
Meerbeck D 49 B5
Meersburg D 61 C5
Meeuwen B 49 B6
Megalo Horio GR 119 F2
Megalopoli GR 117 E4
Megara GR 117 D5
Megeve F 69 C6
Meggenhofen A 63 B4
Megra RUS 7 A14
Mehamn N 113 A16
Mehedeby S 36 B4
Mehlekeru H 75 B6
Mehun-sur-Yèvre F 68 A2
Meigle GB 25 B4
Meijel NL 50 B1
Meilen CH 70 A3
Meilhan F 76 C2
Meimôa P 93 A3
Meina I 70 C3
Meine D 44 C2
Meinersen D 44 C2
Meinerzhagen D 50 B3
Meiningen D 51 C6
Meira E 86 A3
Meiringen CH 70 B3
Meisenheim D 60 A3
Meissen D 52 B3
Meitingen D 62 B1
Meix-devant-Virton B . .60 A1
Meka PL 54 B3
Meka Gruda BIH 84 C3
Mel I 72 B2
Melbu N 112 D3
Melč CZ 64 A3
Meldal N 114 D6
Meldola I 82 B1
Meldorf D 43 A6
Melegnano I 71 C4
Melenci SRB 75 C5
Melendugno I 105 C4
Melfi I 104 C1
Melfjordbotn N 112 F2
Melgaço P 87 B2
Melgar de Arriba E 88 B1
Melgar de Fernamental
    E 88 B2
Melgar de Yuso E 88 B2
Meliana E 96 B2
Melide
    CH 70 C3
    E 86 B2
Meligales GR 117 E3
Melilli I 109 B4
Melinovac HR 83 B4
Melisenda I 110 C2
Melisey F 60 C2
Mélito di Porto Salvo
    I 109 B4
Melk A 63 B6
Melksham GB 29 B5
Mellanström S 115 B15
Mellbystrand S 40 C2
Melle
    B 49 B4
    D 50 A4
    F 67 B4
Mellendorf D 43 C6
Mellerud S 35 D4
Mellieha M 107 C5
Mellösa S 37 C3
Melllrichstadt D 51 C6
Mělník Vtelno CZ 53 C4
Melón E 87 B2
Melrose GB 25 C5
Mels CH 71 A4
Melsungen D 51 B5
Meltaus FIN 113 F14
Meltham GB 27 B4
Melton Mowbray GB . .30 B3
Meltosjärvi FIN 113 F13
Melun F 58 B3
Melvaig GB 22 D3
Melvich GB 23 C5
Mélykút H 75 B4
Melzo I 71 C4
Memaliaj AL 116 B1
Membrilla E 95 D3
Membrio E 93 B3
Memer F 77 B4
Memmelsdorf D 51 D6
Memmingen D 61 C6
Memoria I 92 B2
Mena UA 7 F12
Menaggio I 71 B4
Menai Bridge GB 26 B1
Menasalbas E 94 C2
Menat F 68 B2
Mendavia E 89 B4
Mendaza E 89 B4
Menden D 50 B3
Menderes TR 119 D2
Mendig D 50 C3
Mendiga P 92 B2
Mendrisio CH 70 C3
Ménéac F 56 B3
Menemen TR 118 D2
Menen B 49 C4
Menesjärvi FIN 113 D15
Menetou-Salon F 68 A2
Menfil I 108 B1
Menga
    TR 118 B7
    I 61 B5
Mengen
    D 61 B5
    TR 118 B7
Menges SLO 73 B4
Mengíbar E 100 B2
Mengkofen D 62 B3
Menou F 68 A3
Mens F 79 B4
Menslage D 43 C4
Menstrask S 115 B16
Mentana I 102 A5
Menton F 80 C1
Méntrida E 94 B2
Menz D 45 B5
Méobecq F 67 B6
Meppel NL 42 C3
Meppen D 43 C4
Mequinenza E 90 B3
Mer F 58 C2
Mera
    Coruña E 86 A2
    Coruña E 86 A3
Meráker N 114 D8
Merano I 71 B6

Merate I 71 C4
Mercadillo E 89 A3
Mercatale I 82 C1
Mercatino Conca I 82 C1
Mercato San Severino
    I 103 C7
Mercato Saraceno I 82 C1
Merching D 62 B1
Merchtem B 49 C5
Merdrignac F 56 B3
Merdžanići BIH 84 C2
Meré E 88 A2
Mere GB 29 B5
Meréville F 58 B3
Merfeld D 50 B3
Méribel F 69 C6
Méribel Motraret F 69 C6
Meriç TR 118 A1
Mérida E 93 C4
Mérignac F 76 B2
Měřín CZ 64 A1
Mering D 62 B1
Merkendorf D 62 A1
Merklín CZ 63 A4
Merksplas B 49 B5
Merlänna S 37 C3
Merlimont Plage F 48 C2
Mern DK 39 D5
Mernye H 74 B2
Mersch L 60 A2
Merseburg D 52 B1
Mers-les-Bains F 48 C2
Merthyr Tydfil GB 29 B4
Mertingen D 62 B1
Mértola P 98 B3
Méru F 58 A3
Merufe P 87 B2
Mervans F 69 B5
Merville F 48 C3
Méry-sur-Seine F 59 B4
Merzen D 43 C4
Merzifon TR 16 A7
Merzig D 60 A2
Mesagne I 105 C3
Mesão Frio P 87 C3
Mesas de Ibor E 93 B5
Meschede D 50 B4
Meschers-sur-Gironde
    F 66 C4
Meshchovsk RUS 7 D13
Meslay-du-Maine F 57 C5
Mesna N 34 A2
Mesnalien N 34 A2
Mesocco CH 71 B4
Mésola I 82 B1
Mesologi GR 116 D3
Mesopotamo GR 116 C2
Mesoraca I 107 B3
Messac F 57 C4
Messancy B 60 A1
Messdorf D 44 C3
Messei F 57 B5
Messejana P 98 B2
Messelt N 34 A3
Messina I 109 A4
Messingen D 43 C4
Messini GR 117 E4
Messkirch D 61 C5
Messlingen S 115 E9
Messtetten D 61 B4
Mesta GR 117 D7
Mestanza E 100 A1
Mestec Králové CZ 53 C5
Mestlin D 44 B3
Město Albrechtice
    CZ 54 C2
Město Libavá CZ 64 A3
Město Touškov CZ 63 A4
Mestre I 72 C2
Mesvres F 69 B4
Mesztegnyő H 74 B2
Meta I 103 C7
Metajna HR 83 B4
Metelen D 50 A3
Methana GR 117 E5
Methlick GB 23 D6
Methven GB 25 B4
Methwold GB 30 B4
Metković HR 84 C2
Metlika SLO 73 C5
Metnitz A 73 B4
Metslawier NL 42 B3
Metsovo GR 116 C3
Metten D 62 B3
Mettendorf D 50 C2
Mettet B 49 C5
Mettingen D 50 A3
Mettlach D 60 A2
Mettmann D 50 B2
Metz F 60 A2
Metzervisse F 60 A2
Metzingen D 61 B5
Meulan F 58 C2
Meung-sur-Loire F 58 C2
Meuselwitz D 52 B2
Meuzac F 67 C6
Mevagissey GB 28 C3
Mexborough GB 27 B4
Meximieux F 69 C5
Mey GB 23 C5
Meyenburg D 44 B4
Meyerhöfen D 43 C5
Meylan F 69 C5
Meymac F 68 C2
Meyrargues F 79 C4
Meyrueis F 78 B2
Meyssac F 77 A4
Meysse F 78 B3
Meyzieu F 69 C5
Mèze F 78 C2
Mézériat F 69 B5
Mežica SLO 73 B4
Mézidon-Canon F 57 A5
Mézières-en-Brenne
    F 67 B6
Mézières-sur-Issoire
    F 67 B5
Mézilhac F 78 B3
Mézilles F 59 C4
Mézin F 76 B3
Mézőberény H 75 B6
Mezőcsát H 65 C6
Mezőfalva H 74 B3
Mezőhegyes H 75 B6
Mezőkeresztes H 65 C6
Mezőkomárom H 74 B3
Mezőkovácsháza H 75 B5
Mezőkövesd H 65 C6
Mezőörs H 74 A2
Mézos F 76 B1
Mezőszilas H 74 B3
Mezőtúr H 75 A5
Mezquita de Jarque E . .90 C2
Mezzano
    Emilia Romagna I . . .81 B6
    Trentino Alto Adige I . .72 B1
Mezzojuso I 108 B2
Mezzoldo I 71 B4
Mezzolombardo I 71 B6

Middelharnis NL 49 B5
Middelkerke B 48 B3
Middelstum NL 42 B3
Middlesbrough GB 27 A4
Middleton GB 24 B1
Middleton Cheney GB . .30 B2
Middleton-in-Teesdale
    GB 26 A3
Middletown GB 19 B5
Middlewich GB 26 B3
Middlezoy GB 29 B5
Midhurst GB 31 D3
Midleton IRL 20 C3
Midlum D 43 B5
Midsomer Norton GB . .29 B5
Midtgulen N 114 F2
Midtskogberget N 34 A4
Midwolda NL 43 B4
Mid Yell GB 22 A7
Miechów PL 55 C5
Miedes de Aragón E . . .89 C5
Miedes de Atienza E . .95 A3
Międzybodzie Bielskie
    PL 65 A5
Międzybórz PL 54 B2
Międzychód PL 46 C1
Międzylesie PL 54 C1
Międzyrzec Podlaski
    PL 6 F7
Międzyrzecz PL 46 C1
Międzywodzie PL 45 A6
Międzyzdroje PL 45 B6
Miejska Górka PL 54 B1
Miélan F 76 C3
Mielec PL 55 C6
Mielęcin PL 45 B6
Mielno
    Warmińsko-Mazurskie
    PL 47 B6
    Zachodnio-Pomorskie
    PL 46 A2
Miengo E 88 A3
Mieraslompolo FIN . .113 C16
Miercurea Ciuc RO 11 C8
Mieres
    Asturias E 88 A1
    Girona E 91 A5
Mieron N 113 C13
Mierzyn PL 55 B4
Miesau D 60 A3
Miesbach D 62 C2
Mieścisko PL 46 C3
Mieste D 44 C3
Miesterhorst D 44 C3
Mieszków PL 54 A2
Mieszkowice PL 45 C6
Mietków PL 54 C1
Migennes F 59 C4
Miggiano I 107 B5
Migliánico I 103 A7
Migliarino I 81 B5
Miglionico I 104 C2
Mignano Monte Lungo
    I 103 B6
Migné F 67 B6
Miguel Esteban E 95 C3
Miguelturra E 94 D3
Mihajlovac SRB 85 B5
Mihald H 74 B2
Mihalgazi TR 118 B5
Mihaliççik TR 118 C6
Mihályi H 74 A2
Mihla D 51 B6
Mihohnić HR 83 A3
Miholjsko HR 73 C5
Miholjvan HR 73 B5
Mijares E 94 B2
Mijas E 100 C1
Mike H 74 B2
Mikhnevo RUS 7 D14
Mikines GR 117 E4
Mikkeli FIN 3 F27
Mikkelvik N 112 B8
Mikleuš HR 74 C2
Mikołajki Pomorskie
    PL 47 B5
Mikołów PL 54 C3
Mikonos GR 117 E7
Mikorzyn PL 54 B3
Mikro Derio GR 116 A8
Mikstat PL 54 B2
Mikulášovice CZ 53 C4
Mikulov CZ 64 B2
Mikulovice CZ 54 C2
Milagro E 89 B5
Miłaków PL 47 A6
Milan = Milano I 71 C4
Miland N 32 C5
Milano = Milan I 71 C4
Milano Marittima I 82 B1
Milas TR 119 E2
Milazzo I 109 A4
Mildenhall GB 30 B4
Milejczyce PL 6 E7
Milejów PL 6 F7
Milelin CZ 53 C5
Mileto I 106 C3
Milevsko CZ 63 A5
Milford IRL 19 A4
Milford Haven GB 28 B2
Milford on Sea GB 31 D2
Milhão P 87 C4
Milići BIH 84 B4
Miličín CZ 63 A5
Milicz PL 54 B2
Milín CZ 63 A5
Militello in Val di Catánia
    I 109 B3
Miljevina BIH 84 C3
Milkowice PL 53 B6
Millançay F 68 A1
Millares E 96 B2
Millas F 91 A5
Millau F 78 B2
Millesimo I 80 B2
Millevaches F 68 C2
Millom GB 26 A2
Millport GB 24 C3
Millstatt A 72 B3
Millstreet
    Cork IRL 20 B2
    Waterford IRL 21 B4
Milltown
    Galway IRL 18 C3
    Kerry IRL 20 B1
Milltown Malbay IRL . . .20 B2
Milly-la-Forêt F 58 B3
Milmarcos E 95 A5
Milmersdorf D 45 B5
Milna HR 83 C5
Milnthorpe GB 26 A3
Miłog SRB 85 C5
Milogórze PL 47 A6
Miłomłyn PL 47 B5
Milos GR 117 F6
Miłosław PL 54 A2
Milot AL 105 B5
Miłówka PL 65 A5
Milówo PL 47 C5
Milton Keynes GB 31 B3
Miltzow D 45 A5
Milutovac SRB 85 C6
Milverton GB 29 B4
Milzyn PL 47 C4
Mimice HR 84 C1
Mimizan F 76 B1
Mimizan-Plage F 76 B1
Mimoň CZ 53 C4
Mina de Juliana P 98 B2
Mina de São Domingos
    P 98 B3
Minas de Riotinto E . . .99 B4
Minateda E 101 A4
Minaya E 95 C4
Mindelheim D 61 B6
Mindelstetten D 62 B2
Minden D 51 A4
Minderharnis NL 49 B5

Minehead GB 29 B4
Mineo I 109 B3
Minerbe I 71 C6
Minérbio I 81 B5
Minervino Murge I 104 B2
Minglanilla E 95 C5
Mingorria E 94 B2
Minnesund N 34 B3
Miño E 86 A2
Miño de San Esteban
    E 89 C3
Minsen D 43 B4
Minsk BY 7 E9
Mińsk Mazowiecki PL .55 A6
Minsterley GB 26 C3
Mintlaw GB 23 D6
Minturno I 103 B6
Mionica
    BIH 84 B3
    SRB 85 B5
Mios F 76 B2
Mira
    E 96 B1
    I 72 C2
    P 92 A2
Mirabel E 93 B4
Mirabel-aux-Baronnies
    F 79 B4
Mirabella Eclano I 103 B8
Mirabella Imbáccari
    I 109 B3
Mirabello I 81 B5
Miradoux F 77 B3
Miraflores de la Sierra
    E 95 B4
Miralrio E 95 B4
Miramar P 87 C2
Miramare I 82 B1
Miramas F 78 C3
Mirambeau F 67 C4
Miramont-de-Guyenne
    F 77 B3
Miranda de Arga E 89 B5
Miranda de Ebro E 89 B4
Miranda do Corvo P . . .92 A2
Miranda do Douro P . . .87 C4
Mirande F 77 C3
Mirandela P 87 C3
Mirandilla E 93 C4
Mirandola I 81 B5
Miranje HR 83 B4
Mirano I 72 C2
Miras AL 116 B2
Miravet E 90 B3
Miré F 57 C5
Mirebeau F 67 B5
Mirebeau-sur-Bèze F . .69 A5
Mirecourt F 60 B2
Mirepoix F 77 C4
Mires GR 117 G6
Miribel F 69 C4
Miričina BIH 84 B3
Mirina GR 116 C7
Mirna SLO 73 C5
Miroslav CZ 64 B2
Miroševce PL 54 C1
Mirošov CZ 63 A4
Mirotice CZ 63 A5
Mirovice CZ 63 A5
Mirow D 45 B4
Mirsk PL 53 C5
Misi FIN 113 F15
Mislinja SLO 73 B5
Missanello I 104 C2
Misslolfeld I 66 A2
Mistelbach
    A 64 B2
    D 62 A2
Misten N 112 E3
Misterbianco I 109 B4
Misterhult S 40 B6
Mistretta I 109 B3
Misurina I 72 B2
Mitchelstown IRL 20 B3
Mithimna GR 116 C8
Mithoni GR 117 F3
Mitilini GR 118 C1
Mitilinii GR 119 E1
Mittelberg
    Tirol A 71 B5
    Vorarlberg A 71 A5
Mittenwald D 71 A6
Mittenwalde D 52 A3
Mitterbach A 63 C6
Mitterdorf im Mürztal
    A 73 A5
Mitter-Kleinarl A 72 A3
Mittersill A 72 A2
Mittersheim F 60 B2
Mitterskirchen D 62 B3
Mitterteich D 62 A3
Mitton F 76 B2
Mittweida D 52 C2
Mitwitz D 52 C1
Mizhhir'ya UA 11 B8
Mjäliby S 41 C4
Mjällom S 33 D5
Mjöbäck S 40 B2
Mjölby S 37 D2
Mjømna N 32 B1
Mjøndalen N 35 C2
Mjørlund N 34 B2
Mladá Boleslav CZ 53 C4
Mladá Vožice CZ 63 A5
Mladé Buky CZ 53 C5
Mladenovac SRB 85 B5
Mladíkovine BIH 84 B2
Mlawa PL 47 B6
Mlinište BIH 84 B1
Mlodzieszyn PL 55 A5
Mogoszyn PL 55 A4
Mynarzy PL 47 A5
Mnichovice CZ 63 A5
Mnichovo Hradiště
    CZ 53 C4
Mniów PL 55 B5
Mnisek nad Hnilcom
    SK 65 B6
Mnišek pod Brdy CZ . . .63 A5
Mniszek PL 55 B5
Mniszków PL 55 B5
Mo
    Hedmark N 34 B3
    Hordaland N 32 B3
    Møre og Romsdal
    N 114 E3
    Telemark N 33 C4
    Gävleborg S 36 B3
    Västra Götaland S . . .35 D3
Moäna E 87 B2
Moate IRL 21 A4
Mocejón E 94 C3
Močenok SK 64 B3
Mochales E 95 A4
Mochowo PL 47 C5
Mochy PL 53 A6
Mockern D 52 A1
Mockfjärd S 36 B1
Möckmühl D 61 A5
Mockrehna D 52 B2
Moclín E 100 B2
Mocsa H 64 C4
Möcsény H 74 B3
Modane F 70 C1
Modave B 49 C6
Modbury GB 28 C4
Módena I 81 B4
Módica I 109 C3
Modigliana I 81 B5
Modlin PL 47 C6
Mödling A 64 B2
Modliszewko PL 46 C3
Modogno I 104 B2
Modra SK 64 B3
Modran BIH 84 B2

Modriča BIH 84 B3
Mõdrudalur IS 111 B10
Modrý Kamen SK 65 B5
Moëlan-sur-Mer F 56 C2
Moelfre GB 26 B1
Moelv N 34 B2
Moen N 112 C7
Moena I 72 B1
Moerbeke B 49 B4
Moers D 50 B2
Moffat GB 25 C4
Mogadouro P 87 C4
Mogata S 37 D3
Móggio Udinese I 72 B3
Mogielnica PL 55 B5
Mogilany PL 65 A5
Mogilno PL 46 C3
Mogliano I 82 C2
Mogliano Véneto I 72 C2
Mogor E 87 B2
Mógoro I 110 C1
Moguer E 99 B4
Mohács H 74 C3
Moheda S 40 B4
Mohedas de la Jara E . .94 C1
Mohelnice CZ 64 A2
Mohill IRL 19 C4
Möhlin CH 70 A2
Moholm S 35 D6
Mohorn D 52 B3
Mohyliv-Podil's'kyy
    UA 11 B9
Moi N 33 D3
Moià E 91 B5
Móie I 82 C2
Moimenta da Beira P . .87 D3
Moirós P 87 C3
Mo i Rana N 115 A11
Moirans F 69 C5
Moirans-en-Montagne
    F 69 B5
Moisaküla EST 7 B8
Moisdon-la-Rivière F . .57 C4
Moissac F 77 B4
Moita
    Coimbra P 92 A2
    Guarda P 93 A3
    Santarém P 92 B2
    Setúbal P 92 C1
Moita dos Ferreiros P . .92 B1
Moixent E 101 A5
Mojacar E 101 B4
Mojados E 88 C2
Mojkovac MNE 85 D4
Mojmírovce SK 64 B4
Mojtin SK 65 B4
Möklinta S 36 B3
Mokošica HR 84 D3
Mokra Gora SRB 85 C4
Mokronog SLO 73 C5
Mokro Polje HR 83 B5
Mokrzyska PL 55 C5
Møkster N 32 B2
Mol
    B 49 B6
    SRB 75 C5
Mola di Bari I 104 B3
Molai GR 117 F4
Molare I 80 B2
Molaretto I 70 C2
Molás F 77 C3
Molassano I 80 B2
Molbergen D 43 C4
Mold GB 26 B2
Molde N 114 E4
Møldrup DK 38 C2
Moledo do Minho P 87 C2
Molfetta I 104 B2
Molfsee D 44 A2
Moliden S 115 D15
Molina de Aragón E . . .95 B5
Molina de Segura E . .101 A4
Molinar E 89 A3
Molinaseca E 86 B4
Molinella I 81 B5
Molinet F 68 B3
Molinicos E 101 A3
Molino de Villobas E . . .90 A2
Molinos de Duero E . . .89 C4
Molins de Rei E 91 B5
Moliterno I 104 C1
Molkom S 35 C5
Mollans F 105 C6
Möllbrücke A 72 B3
Mölle S 41 C2
Molledo E 88 A2
Möllenbeck D 45 B5
Mollerussa E 90 B3
Mollet de Peralada E . . .91 A5
Mollina E 100 B1
Mölln D 44 B2
Mölló E 91 A5
Mollösund S 35 D3
Molló S 37 D1
Mölnbo S 37 C4
Mölndal S 38 B5
Mölnlycke S 38 B5
Moloy F 69 A4
Molsheim F 60 B3
Moltzow D 45 B4
Molve HR 74 B2
Molveno I 71 B6
Molvizar E 100 C2
Molzbichl A 72 B3
Mombaróccio I 82 C1
Mombeltrán E 94 B1
Mombris D 51 C5
Mombuey E 87 B4
Momchilgrad BG 116 A7
Mommark DK 39 E3
Momo I 70 C3
Monaghan IRL 19 B5
Monar Lodge GB 22 D4
Monasterace Marina
    I 106 C3
Monasterevin IRL 21 A4
Monasterio de Rodilla
    E 89 B3
Monastir I 110 C2
Monbahus F 77 B3
Monbazillac F 77 B3
Moncada E 96 B2
Moncalieri I 80 A1
Moncalvo I 80 A2
Monção P 87 B2
Moncarapacho P 98 B3
Moncel-sur-Seille F . . .60 B2
Mönchengladbach =
    München-Gladbach
    D 50 B2
Mónchio della Corti I . .81 B4
Monchique P 98 B2
Monclar-de-Quercy F . .77 C4
Moncofa E 96 B2
Moncontour F 56 B3
Moncoutant F 67 B4
Monda E 100 C1
Mondariz E 87 B2
Mondavio I 82 C1
Mondéjar E 95 B3
Mondello I 108 A2
Mondim de Basto P 87 C3
Mondolfo I 82 C2
Mondoñedo E 86 A3
Mondorf-les-Bains L . .60 A2
Mondoubleau F 58 C1
Mondovì I 80 B1
Mondragon F 103 B5
Mondragone I 103 B6
Mondsee A 63 C4
Monéglia I 80 B3
Monegrillo E 90 B2
Monein F 76 C2
Monemvasia GR 117 F5
Monesíndo GR 116 A3
Monesiglio I 80 B2
Monesterio E 99 A4
Monestier-de-Clermont

Monastir de Camargos
Montegiordano Marina
    I 106 A3
Montegiórgio I 82 C2

Monestier-de-Clermont
    F 79 B4
Monestiés F 77 B5
Monéteau F 59 C4
Moneygall IRL 21 B4
Moneymore GB 19 B5
Monfalcone I 72 C3
Monfero E 86 A2
Monflanquin F 77 B3
Monflorite E 90 A2
Monforte P 92 B3
Monforte da Beira
    P 92 B3
Monforte d'Alba I 80 B1
Monforte del Cid E 96 C2
Monforte de Lemos E . .86 B3
Monforte de Moyuela
    E 90 B1
Monghidoro I 81 B5
Mongiana I 106 C3
Monguelfo I 72 B2
Monheim D 62 B1
Moniaive GB 25 C4
Monifieth GB 25 B5
Monikie GB 25 B5
Monistrol d'Allier F 78 B2
Monistrol de Montserrat
    E 91 B4
Monistrol-sur-Loire F . .68 C4
Mönkebude D 45 B5
Monkton GB 24 C3
Monmouth GB 29 B5
Monnai F 57 B6
Monnerville F 58 B3
Monnickendam NL 42 C2
Monninkylä FIN 119 F22
Monólithos GR 119 F2
Monópoli I 104 C3
Monor H 75 A4
Monova E 101 A5
Monpazier F 77 B3
Monreal
    D 50 C3
    E 76 D1
Monreal del Campo E . .95 B5
Monreale I 108 A2
Monroy E 93 B4
Monroyo E 90 C2
Mons B 49 C4
Monsaraz P 92 C3
Monschau D 50 C2
Monségur F 76 B3
Monsélice I 72 C1
Mønshaug N 32 B3
Monster NL 49 A5
Mönsterås S 40 B6
Monsummano Terme
    I 81 C4
Montabaur D 50 C3
Montafia I 80 B2
Montagnac F 78 C2
Montagnana I 71 C6
Montaguto I 103 B8
Montaigu F 66 B3
Montaigu-de-Quercy
    F 77 B4
Montaiguët-en-Forez
    F 68 B3
Montaigut F 68 B3
Montaigut-sur-Save F . .77 C4
Montainville F 58 B2
Montalbán E 90 C2
Montalbán de Córdoba
    E 100 B1
Montalbano Elicona
    I 109 A4
Montalbano Iónico I . .104 C2
Montalcino I 81 C5
Montaldo di Cósola I . .80 B3
Montalegre P 87 C3
Montalieu-Vercieu F . . .69 C5
Montalivet-les-Bains
    F 66 C3
Montallegro I 108 B2
Montalto delle Marche
    I 82 D2
Montalto di Castro I . .102 A4
Montalto Pavese I 80 B3
Montalto Uffugo I 106 B3
Montalvão P 92 B3
Montamarta E 88 C1
Montana BG 11 E7
Montana-Vermala CH . .70 B2
Montánchez E 93 B4
Montanejos E 96 A2
Montano Antília I 106 A2
Montans F 77 C4
Montargil P 92 B2
Montargis F 58 C3
Montastruc-la-Conseillère
    F 77 C4
Montauban F 77 B4
Montauban-de-Bretagne
    F 57 B3
Montbard F 59 C5
Montbarrey F 69 A5
Montbazens F 77 B5
Montbazon F 67 A5
Montbéliard F 70 A1
Montbenoit F 69 B6
Montblanc E 91 B4
Montbozon F 69 A6
Montbron F 67 C5
Montbrun-les-Bains F . .79 B4
Montceau-les-Mines
    F 69 B4
Montcenis F 69 B4
Montchanin F 69 B4
Montcornet F 59 A5
Montcuq F 77 B4
Montdardier F 78 C2
Mont-de-Marsan F 76 C2
Montdidier F 58 A3
Monteagudo E 89 B5
Monteagudo de las
    Vicarías E 89 C4
Montealegre E 88 C2
Montealegre del Castillo
    E 101 A4
Montebello Iónico I . . .109 B4
Montebello Vicentino
    I 71 C6
Montebelluna I 72 C2
Montebourg F 57 A4
Montebruno I 80 B3
Monte-Carlo MC 80 C1
Montecarotto I 82 C2
Montecassiano I 82 C2
Montecastrilli I 102 A5
Montecatini Terme I . . .81 C4
Montécchio I 82 C1
Montécchio Emilia I 81 B4
Montécchio Maggiore
    I 71 C6
Montech F 77 C4
Montechiaro d'Asti I . . .80 A2
Monte Clara P 92 B3
Monte Clérigo P 98 B2
Montecórice I 103 C7
Montecorvino Rovella
    I 103 C8
Monte da Pedra P 92 B3
Monte de Goula P 92 B3
Montederramo E 87 B3
Montedoro I 108 B2
Monte do Trigo P 92 C3
Montefalco I 82 D1
Montefalcone di Val
    Fortore I 103 B8
Montefalcone nel Sánnio
    I 103 B7
Montefiascone I 102 A5
Montefiorino I 81 B4
Monteforte d'Alpone
    I 71 C6
Montefortino I 82 D2
Montefranco I 102 A5
Montefrio E 100 B2
Montegiordano Marina
    I 106 A3
Montegiórgio I 82 C2

Monte Gordo P 98 B3
Montegranaro I 82 C2
Montehermoso E 93 A4
Montejícar E 100 B2
Montejo de la Sierra
    E 95 A3
Montejo de Tiermes
    E 89 C3
Monte Juntos P 92 C3
Montel-de-Gelat F 68 C2
Monteleone di Púglia
    I 103 B8
Monteleone di Spoleto
    I 102 A5
Monteleone d'Orvieto
    I 81 D6
Montelepre I 108 A2
Montelibretti I 102 A5
Montelier F 79 B4
Montélimar F 78 B3
Montella
    E 91 A4
    I 103 C8
Montellano E 99 B5
Montelupo Fiorentino
    I 81 C5
Montemaggiore Belsito
    I 108 B2
Montemagno I 80 B2
Montemayor E 100 B1
Montemayor de Pinilla
    E 88 C2
Montemésola I 104 C3
Montemiletto I 103 B7
Montemilone I 104 B1
Montemolin E 99 A4
Montemónaco I 82 D2
Montemor-o-Novo P . . .92 C2
Montemor-o-Velho P . .92 A2
Montemurro I 104 C1
Montendre F 67 C4
Montenegro de Cameros
    E 89 B4
Montenero di Bisáccia
    I 103 B7
Monteneuf F 57 C3
Montepaone I 104 C3
Montepescali I 81 D5
Montepiano I 81 B5
Monte Porzio I 82 C2
Montepulciano I 81 C5
Montereale I 103 A6
Montereale Valcellina
    I 72 B2
Montereau-Faut-Yonne
    F 59 B3
Monte Redondo P 92 B2
Monterénzio I 81 B5
Monte Romano I 102 A4
Monteroni d'Árbia I 81 C5
Monteroni di Lecce I . .105 C4
Monterosso al Mare I . .80 B3
Monterosso Almo I . . .109 B3
Monterosso Grana I . . .79 B6
Monterotondo I 102 A5
Monterotondo Maríttimo
    I 81 C4
Monterrey E 87 C3
Monterroso E 86 B3
Monterrubio de la Serena
    E 93 C5
Monterubbiano I 82 C2
Montes Velhos P 98 B2
Montesa E 96 C2
Montesalgueiro E 86 A2
Monte San Giovanni
    Campano I 103 B6
Montesano sulla
    Marcellana I 104 C1
Monte San Savino I . . .81 C5
Monte Sant'Ángelo I . .104 B1
Montesárchio I 103 B7
Montescaglioso I 104 C2
Montesclaros E 94 B2
Montesilvano I 103 A7
Montespértoli I 81 C5
Montesquieu-Volvestre
    F 77 C4
Montesquiou F 77 C3
Montestruc-sur-Gers
    F 77 C3
Montes Velhos P 98 B2
Montevarchi I 81 C5
Montéveglio I 81 B5
Monte Vilar P 92 B1
Montfaucon F 66 A3
Montfaucon-d'Argonne
    F 59 A6
Montfaucon-en-Velay
    F 69 C4
Montferrat
    Isère F 69 C5
    Var F 79 C5
Montfort-en-Chalosse
    F 76 C2
Montfort-l'Amaury F . . .58 B2
Montfort-le-Gesnois
    F 58 B1
Montfort-sur-Meu F 57 B4
Montfort-sur-Risle F . . .58 A1
Montgai E 90 B3
Montgaillard F 77 C3
Montgenèvre F 79 B5
Montgiscard F 77 C4
Montgomery GB 26 C2
Montguyon F 67 C4
Monthermé F 59 A5
Monthey CH 70 B1
Monthois F 59 A5
Monthureux-sur-Saône
    F 60 B1
Monticelli d'Ongina I . .81 A3
Montichiari I 71 C5
Monticiano I 81 C5
Montiel E 100 A3
Montier-en-Der F 59 B5
Montieri I 81 C5
Montiglio I 80 A2
Montignac F 77 A4
Montigny-le-Roi F 60 C1
Montigny-lès-Metz F . . .60 A2
Montigny-sur-Aube F . .59 C5
Montijo
    E 93 C4
    P 92 C2
Montilla E 100 B1
Montillana E 100 B2
Montilly F 68 B3
Montivilliers F 57 A6
Montjaux F 78 B1
Montjean-sur-Loire F . .66 A4
Montlhéry F 58 B3
Montlieu-la-Garde F . . .67 C4
Mont-Louis F 91 A5
Montlouis-sur-Loire F . .67 A5
Montluçon F 68 B2
Montluel F 69 C5
Montmarault F 68 B2
Montmartin-sur-Mer F . .57 B4
Montmédy F 59 A6
Montmélian F 69 C6
Montmeyan F 79 C5
Montmeyran F 78 B3
Montmirail
    Marne F 59 B4
    Sarthe F 58 B1
Montmiral F 69 C5
Montmirat F 78 C3
Montmirey-le-Château
    F 69 A5
Montmoreau-St Cybard
    F 67 C5
Montmorillon F 67 B5
Montmort-Lucy F 59 B4
Montoir-de-Bretagne
    F 66 A2
Montoire-sur-le-Loir
    F 58 C1
Montoito P 92 C3
Montolieu F 77 C5

Montório al Vomano
I 103 A6
Montoro E 100 A1
Montpellier F 78 C2
Montpezat-de-Quercy
F 77 B4
Montpezat-sous-Bouzon
F 78 B3
Montpon-Ménestérol
F 76 A3
Montpont-en-Bresse
F 69 B5
Montréal
Aude F 77 C5
Gers F 76 C3
Montredon-Labessonnié
F 77 C5
Montréjeau F 77 C3
Montrésor F 67 A6
Montresta I 110 B1
Montret F 69 B5
Montreuil
Pas de Calais F 48 C2
Seine St Denis F 58 B3
Montreuil-aux-Lions
F 59 A4
Montreuil-Bellay F 67 A4
Montreux CH 70 B1
Montrevault F 66 A3
Montrevel-en-Bresse
F 69 B5
Montrichard F 67 A6
Montricoux F 77 B4
Mont-roig del Camp E 90 B3
Montrond-les-Bains F 69 C4
Montrose GB 25 B5
Montroy E 96 B2
Montsalvy F 77 B5
Montsauche-les-Settons
F 68 A4
Montseny E 91 B5
Montsoreau F 67 A5
Mont-sous-Vaudrey F 69 B5
Monts-sur-Guesnes F 67 B5
Mont-St Aignan F 58 A2
Mont-St Vincent F 69 B4
Montsûrs F 57 B5
Montuenga E 94 A2
Montuïri E 97 B3
Monturque E 100 B1
Monza I 71 C4
Monzón E 90 B3
Monzón de Campos
E 88 B2
Moorbad Lobenstein
D 52 C1
Moordorf D 43 B4
Moorslede B 49 C4
Moos D 61 C4
Moosburg D 62 B2
Moosburg im Kärnten
A 73 B4
Mór H 74 A3
Mora E 94 C3
Móra P 92 C2
Mora S 36 A1
Moraby S 36 B2
Mòra d'Ebre E 90 B3
Mora de Rubielos E 96 A2
Moradillo de Roa E 88 C3
Morąg PL 47 B5
Mórahalom H 75 B4
Moraime E 86 A1
Morais P 87 C4
Mòra la Nova E 90 B3
Moral de Calatrava
E 100 A2
Moraleda de Zafayona
E 100 B2
Moraleja E 93 A4
Moraleja del Vino E 88 C1
Morales del Vino E 88 C1
Morales de Toro E 88 C1
Morales de Valverde
E 88 C1
Moralina E 87 C4
Morano Cálabro I 106 B3
Mörarp S 41 C2
Morasverdes E 93 A4
Morata de Jalón E 89 C5
Morata de Jiloca E 89 C5
Morata de Tajuña E 95 B3
Moratalla E 101 A4
Moravče SLO 73 B4
Moravec CZ 64 A2
Moraviţa RO 75 C6
Morávka CZ 65 A4
Moravská Třebová
CZ 64 A2
Moravské Budějovice
CZ 64 A1
Moravské Lieskové
SK 64 B3
Moravske Toplice
SLO 73 B6
Moravský-Beroun CZ 64 A3
Moravský Krumlov
CZ 64 A2
Moravský Svätý Ján
SK 64 B3
Morawica PL 55 C5
Morawin PL 54 B3
Morbach D 60 A3
Morbegno I 71 B4
Morbier F 69 B6
Mörbisch am See A 64 C2
Mörbylånga S 41 C6
Morcenx F 76 B2
Morciano di Romagna
I 82 C1
Morcone I 103 B7
Morcuera E 89 C3
Mordelles F 57 B4
Mordoğan TR 119 D1
Moréac F 56 C3
Morebattle GB 25 C5
Morecambe GB 26 A3
Moreda
Granada E 100 B2
Oviedo E 88 A1
Morée F 58 C2
Moreles de Rey E 88 B1
Morella E 90 C2
Moreruela de los
Infanzones E 88 C1
Morés E 89 C5
Móres I 110 B1
Morestel F 69 C5
Moretonhampstead
GB 28 C4
Moreton-in-Marsh GB 29 B6
Moret-sur-Loing F 58 B3
Moretta I 80 B1
Moreuil F 58 A3
Morez F 69 B6
Mörfelden D 51 D4
Morgat F 56 B1
Morges CH 69 B6
Morgex I 70 C2
Morgongåva S 36 C3
Morhange F 60 B2
Morhet B 49 D6
Mori I 71 C5
Morialmé B 49 C5
Morianes P 98 B3
Moriani Plage F 102 A2
Mórichida H 74 A2
Moriles E 100 B1
Morille E 94 B1
Moringen D 51 B5
Morjärv S 3 C25
Morkarla S 36 B4
Mørke DK 39 C3
Mørkøv DK 39 D4
Morkovice-Slížany
CZ 64 A3
Morlaàs F 76 C2
Morlaix F 56 B2
Morley F 59 B6
Mörlunda S 40 B5
Mormanno I 106 B2
Mormant F 59 B3
Mornant F 69 C4
Mornay-Berry F 68 A2
Morokovo MNE 85 D4
Morón de Almazán E 89 C4
Morón de la Frontera
E 99 B5
Morović SRB 85 A4
Morozzo I 80 B1
Morpeth GB 25 C6
Morphou CY 120 A1
Mörrum S 41 C4
Morsbach D 50 C3
Mörsch D 61 B4
Mörsil S 115 D10
Morsum D 39 E1
Mørsvikbotn N 112 E4
Mortagne-au-Perche
F 58 B1
Mortagne-sur-Gironde
F 66 C4
Mortagne-sur-Sèvre
F 66 B4
Mortágua P 92 A2
Mortain F 57 B5
Mortara I 70 C3
Morteau F 69 A6
Mortegliano I 72 C3
Mortelle I 109 A4
Mortemart F 67 B5
Mortimer's Cross GB 29 A5
Mortrée F 57 B6
Mörtschach A 72 B2
Mortsel B 49 B5
Morud DK 39 D3
Morwenstow GB 28 C3
Moryń PL 45 C6
Morzeszczyn PL 47 B4
Morzewo PL 47 B5
Morzine F 70 B1
Mosalsk RUS 7 D13
Mosbach D 61 A5
Mosbjerg DK 38 B3
Mosby N 33 D4
Mosca P 87 C4
Moscavide P 92 C1
Moščenica HR 73 C6
Mošćenice HR 73 C4
Moščenicka Draga
HR 73 C4
Mosciano Sant'Ángelo
I 82 D2
Mościsko PL 54 C1
Moscow = Moskva
RUS 7 D14
Mosina PL 54 A1
Mosjøen N 115 B10
Moskog N 32 A3
Moskorzew PL 55 C4
Moskosel S 115 B16
Moskuvarra FIN 113 E15
Moskva = Moscow
RUS 7 D14
Moslavina Podravska
HR 74 C2
Moşniţa Nouă RO 75 C6
Moso in Passíria I 71 B6
Mosonmagyaróvár H 64 C3
Mošorin SRB 75 C5
Mošovce SK 65 B4
Mosqueruela E 90 C2
Moss N 35 C2
Mossfellsbær IS 111 C4
Mössingen D 61 B5
Møsstrand N 32 C5
Most CZ 52 C3
Mosta M 107 C5
Mostar BIH 84 C2
Mosterhamn N 33 C2
Mostki PL 53 A5
Most na Soči SLO 72 B3
Móstoles E 94 B3
Mostová SK 64 B3
Mostowo PL 46 A2
Mostuéjouls F 78 B2
Mosty PL 45 B6
Mostys'ka UA 11 B7
Mosvik N 114 D7
Mota del Cuervo E 95 C4
Mota del Marqués E 88 C1
Motala S 37 D2
Motherwell GB 25 C4
Möthlow D 45 C4
Motilla del Palancar E 95 C5
Motnik SLO 73 B4
Motovun HR 72 C3
Motril E 100 C2
Motta I 71 C6
Motta di Livenza I 72 C2
Motta Montecorvino
I 103 B8
Motta Visconti I 70 C3
Mottisfont GB 31 C2
Móttola I 104 C3
Mou DK 38 C3
Mouchard F 69 B5
Moudon CH 70 B1
Moudros GR 116 C7
Mougins F 79 C5
Mouilleron en-Pareds
F 66 B4
Mouliherne F 67 A5
Moulinet F 80 C1
Moulins F 68 B3
Moulins-Engilbert F 68 B3
Moulins-la-Marche F 58 B1
Moulismes F 67 B5
Moult F 57 A5
Mountain Ash GB 29 B4
Mountbellew IRL 20 A3
Mountfield GB 19 B4
Mountmellick IRL 21 A4
Mountrath IRL 21 A4
Mountsorrel GB 30 B2
Moura P 98 A3
Mourão P 92 C3
Mourenx F 76 C2
Mouriés F 78 C3
Mourmelon-le-Grand
F 59 A5
Mouronho P 92 A2
Mouscron B 49 C4
Mousehole GB 28 C2
Moussac F 78 C3
Moussey F 60 B2
Mousteru F 56 B2
Moustey F 76 B2
Moustiers-Ste Marie
F 79 C5
Mouthe F 69 B6
Mouthier-Haute-Pierre
F 69 A6
Mouthoumet F 77 D5
Moutier CH 70 A2
Moûtiers F 69 C6
Moutiers-les-Mauxfaits
F 66 B3
Mouy F 58 A3
Mouzaki GR 116 C3
Mouzon F 59 A6
Møvik N 32 B2
Moville IRL 19 A4
Moy
Highland GB 23 D4
Tyrone GB 19 B5
Moycullen IRL 20 A2
Moyenmoutier F 60 B2
Moyenvic F 60 B2
Moylough IRL 18 C3
Mózar E 88 C1
Mozhaysk RUS 7 D14
Mozirje SLO 73 B4
Mözs H 74 B3
Mozzanica I 71 C4
Mramorak SRB 85 B5
Mrčajevci SRB 85 C5
Mrkonjić Grad BIH 84 B2
Mrkopalj HR 73 C4
Mrmoš SRB 85 C6
Mrocza PL 46 B3
Mroczeń PL 54 B2
Mroczno PL 47 B5
Mrozy PL 55 A6
Mrzezyno PL 45 A7
Mšec CZ 53 C3
Mšeno CZ 53 C4
Mstów PL 55 C4
Mstsislaw BY 7 D11
Mszana Dolna PL 65 A6
Mszczonów PL 55 B5
Mtsensk RUS 7 E14
Muć HR 83 C5
Múccia I 82 C2
Much D 50 C3
Mücheln D 52 B1
Much Marcle GB 29 B5
Muchów PL 53 B6
Much Wenlock GB 26 C3
Mucientes E 88 C2
Muckross IRL 20 B2
Mucur TR 16 B7
Muda P 98 B2
Mudanya TR 118 B3
Mudau D 61 A5
Müden D 44 C2
Mudersbach D 50 C3
Mudurnu TR 118 B6
Muel E 90 B1
Muelas del Pan E 88 C1
Muess D 44 B3
Muff IRL 19 A4
Mugardos E 86 A2
Muge P 92 B2
Mügeln
Sachsen D 52 B3
Sachsen-Anhalt D 52 B3
Múggia I 72 C3
Mugnano I 82 C1
Mugron F 76 C2
Mugueimes E 87 C3
Muhi H 65 C6
Mühlacker D 61 B4
Mühlbach am Hochkönig
A 72 A3
Mühlberg
Brandenburg D 52 B3
Thüringen D 51 C6
Mühldorf
A 72 B3
D 62 B3
Muhleberg CH 70 B2
Mühleim D 61 B4
Muhlen-Eichsen D 44 B3
Mühlhausen
Bayern D 62 A1
Thüringen D 51 B6
Mühltroff D 52 C1
Muhos FIN 3 D27
Muhr A 72 A3
Muine Bheag IRL 21 B5
Muirkirk GB 24 C3
Muir of Ord GB 23 D4
Muirteira P 92 B1
Mukacheve UA 11 B7
Muker GB 26 A3
Mula E 101 A4
Muğla TR 119 E3
Mulben GB 23 D5
Mulegns CH 71 B4
Mules I 71 B6
Mülheim D 50 B2
Mulhouse F 60 C3
Muljava SLO 73 C4
Mullanys Cross IRL 18 B3
Müllheim D 60 C3
Mullhyttan S 37 C1
Mullinavat IRL 21 B4
Mullingar IRL 21 A4
Mullion GB 28 C2
Müllrose D 53 A4
Mullsjö S 40 B3
Mulseryd S 40 B3
Munaðarnes IS 111 A4
Munana E 94 B1
Muñás E 86 A4
Münchberg D 52 C1
Müncheberg D 45 C6
München = Munich D 62 B2
Munchen-Gladbach =
Mönchengladbach
D 50 B2
Münchhausen D 51 C4
Mundaka E 89 A4
Münden D 51 B5
Munderfing A 63 B4
Munderkingen D 61 B5
Mundesley GB 30 B5
Munera E 95 C4
Mungia E 89 A4
Munich = München D 62 B2
Muñico E 94 B1
Muniesa E 90 B2
Munka-Ljungby S 41 C2
Munkebo DK 39 D3
Munkedal S 35 D3
Munkflohögen S 115 D11
Munkfors S 34 C5
Munktorp S 37 C3
Münnerstadt D 51 C6
Muñopepe E 94 B2
Muñotello E 94 B1
Münsingen
CH 70 B2
D 61 B5
Munsö S 37 C4
Münster
CH 70 B3
Hessen D 61 A4
Munster D 44 C2
Münster D 50 B3
Munster F 60 B3
Muntibar E 89 A4
Münzkirchen A 63 B4
Muodoslompolo S 113 E12
Muonio FIN 113 E12
Muotathal CH 70 B3
Muradiye TR 118 D2
Murakeresztúr H 74 B1
Murán SK 65 B6
Murano I 72 C2
Muras E 86 A3
Murat F 78 A1
Muratlı TR 118 A2
Murato F 102 A2
Murat-sur-Vèbre F 78 C1
Murau A 73 A4
Muravera I 110 C2
Murazzano I 80 B2
Murça P 87 C3
Murchante E 89 B5
Murchin D 45 B5
Murcia E 101 B4
Murczyn PL 46 C3
Mur-de-Barrez F 77 B5
Mur-de-Bretagne F 56 B2
Mur-de-Sologne F 67 A6
Mureck A 73 B5
Mürefte TR 118 B2
Muret F 77 C4
Murg CH 71 A4
Murguia E 89 B4
Muri CH 70 A3
Murias de Paredes E 86 B4
Muriedas E 88 A3
Muriel Viejo E 89 C4
Murillo de Rio Leza E 89 B4
Murillo el Fruto E 89 B5
Murino MNE 85 D4
Muriqan AL 105 A5
Murlaggan GB 22 E3
Murmansk RUS 3 B30
Murmashi RUS 3 B30
Murnau D 62 C2
Muro
E 97 B3
F 102 A1
Muro de Alcoy E 96 C2
Murol F 68 C2
Muro Lucano I 103 C8
Muron F 66 B4
Muros E 86 B1
Muros de Nalón E 86 A4
Murowana Goślina
PL 46 C3
Mürren CH 70 B2
Murrhardt D 61 B5
Murska Sobota SLO 73 B6
Mursko Središce HR 73 B6
Murtas E 100 C2
Murten CH 70 B2
Murter HR 83 C4
Murtiçi TR 119 F6
Murtosa P 87 D2
Murvica HR 83 B4
Murviel-lès-Béziers F 78 C2
Mürzsteg A 63 C6
Murzynowo PL 46 C1
Mürzzuschlag A 63 C6
Musculdy F 76 C2
Mushqeta AL 105 B5
Muskö S 37 C5
Mušov CZ 64 B2
Musselburgh GB 25 C4
Musselkanaal NL 43 C4
Mussidan F 77 A3
Mussomeli I 108 B2
Musson B 60 A1
Mussy-sur-Seine F 59 C5
Mustafakemalpaşa
TR 118 B3
Muszaki PL 47 B6
Muszyna PL 65 A6
Mut TR 16 C6
Muta SLO 73 B5
Muthill GB 25 B4
Mutné SK 65 A5
Mutriku E 89 A4
Muttalip TR 118 C5
Mutterbergalm A 71 A6
Muxía E 86 A1
Muxilka-Ugarte E 89 A4
Muzillac F 66 A2
Mužla SK 65 C4
Muzzano del Turgnano
I 72 C3
Mybster GB 23 C5
Myckelgensjö S 115 D14
Myennes F 68 A2
Myjava SK 64 B3
Myking N 32 B2
Mykland N 33 D5
Mykolayiv = Nikolayev
UA 11 C12
Myra N 33 D6
Myrdal N 32 B4
Myre
Nordland N 112 C4
Nordland N 112 D4
Myresjö S 40 B4
Myrhorod UA 11 B12
Mýri IS 111 B8
Myrtou CY 120 A2
Mysen N 35 C3
Mysłakowice PL 53 C5
Myślenice PL 65 A5
Myślibórz PL 45 C6
Mysłowice PL 55 C4
Myszków PL 55 C4
Mytishchi RUS 7 D14
Mýtna SK 65 B5
Mýtne Ludany SK 65 B4
Mýto CZ 63 A4

N

Nå N 32 B3
Naaldwijk NL 49 B5
Naantali FIN 6 A6
Naas IRL 21 A5
Nabais P 92 A3
Nabbelund S 41 B7
Nabburg D 62 A3
Načeradec CZ 63 A5
Náchod CZ 53 C6
Nacław PL 46 A2
Nadarzyce PL 46 B2
Nadarzyn PL 55 A5
Nádasd H 74 B1
Nădlac RO 75 B5
Nádudvar H 75 A6
Nadvirna UA 11 B8
Näfels CH 70 A4
Nafpaktos GR 116 D3
Nafplio GR 117 E4
Nagel D 52 D1
Nagele NL 42 C2
Naggen S 115 E13
Nagłowice PL 55 C5
Nagold D 61 B4
Nagore E 76 D1
Nagyatád H 74 B2
Nagybajom H 74 B2
Nagybaracska H 74 B3
Nagybátony H 65 C5
Nagyberény H 74 B3
Nagybörzsöny H 65 C4
Nagycenk H 64 C2
Nagydorog H 74 B3
Nagyfüged H 65 C6
Nagyhersány H 74 C3
Nagyigmánd H 64 C4
Nagyiván H 75 A5
Nagykanizsa H 74 B1
Nagykáta H 75 A4
Nagykonyi H 74 B3
Nagykörös H 75 A4
Nagykörü H 75 A5
Nagylóc H 65 B5
Nagymágocs H 75 B5
Nagymányok H 74 B3
Nagymaros H 65 C4
Nagyoroszi H 65 B5
Nagyrábé H 75 A6
Nagyréde H 65 C5
Nagyszékely H 74 B3
Nagyszénás H 75 B5
Nagyszokoly H 74 B3
Nagytöke H 75 B5
Nagyvázsony H 74 B2
Nagyvenyim H 74 B3
Naharros E 95 B4
Nahe D 44 B2
Naidăş RO 85 B6
Naila D 52 C1
Nailloux F 77 C4
Nailsworth GB 29 B5
Naintré F 67 B5
Nairn GB 23 D5
Najac F 77 B4
Nájera E 89 B4
Nak H 74 B3
Nakksjø N 33 C6
Nakło nad Notecią
PL 46 B3
Nakskov DK 39 E4
Nalda E 89 B4
Nälden S 115 D11
Nálepkovo SK 65 B6
Nalliers F 66 B3
Nallıhan TR 118 B6
Nalzen F 77 D4
Nalžouské Hory CZ 63 A4
Namdalseid N 114 C8
Náměšť nad Oslavou
CZ 64 A2
Námestovo SK 65 A5
Namnå N 34 B4
Namsos N 114 C8
Namsskogan N 115 C10
Namur B 49 C5
Namysłów PL 54 B2
Nançay F 68 A2
Nanclares de la Oca
E 89 B4
Nancy F 60 B2
Nangis F 59 B4
Nannestad N 34 B3
Nant F 78 B2
Nanterre F 58 B3
Nantes F 66 A3
Nanteuil-le-Haudouin
F 58 A3
Nantiat F 67 B6
Nantua F 69 B5
Nantwich GB 26 B3
Naoussa
Cyclades GR 117 E7
Imathia GR 116 B4
Napajedla CZ 64 A3
Napiwoda PL 47 B6
Naples = Nápoli I 103 C7
Nápoli = Naples I 103 C7
Nar S 37 E5
Nara N 32 A1
Naraval E 86 A4
Narberth GB 28 B3
Nærbø N 33 D2
Narbonne F 78 C1
Narbonne-Plage F 78 C2
Narbuvollen N 114 E8
Narcao I 110 C1
Nardò I 107 A5
Narken S 113 F11
Narmo N 34 B3
Narni I 102 A5
Naro I 108 B2
Naro Fominsk RUS 7 D14
Narón E 86 A2
Narros del Castillo E 94 B1
Narta HR 74 C1
Naruszewo PL 47 C6
Narva EST 7 B10
Narvik N 112 D6
Narzole I 80 B1
Näs FIN 36 B7
Nås S 36 B1
Näs S 37 E5
Näsåker S 115 D13
Năsăud RO 11 C8
Nasavrky CZ 64 A1
Nasbinals F 78 B2
Næsbjerg DK 39 D1
Näshull S 40 B5
Našice HR 74 C3
Nasielsk PL 47 C6
Naso I 109 A3
Nassau D 50 C3
Nassenfels D 62 B2
Nassenheide D 45 C5
Nassereith A 71 A5
Nässjö S 40 B4
Nastätten D 50 C3
Næstved DK 39 D4
Näsum S 41 C4
Näsviken S 115 D12
Natalinci SRB 85 B5
Naters CH 70 B3
Nater-Stetten D 62 B2
Nattavaara S 112 F9
Natters A 71 A6
Nattheim D 61 B6
Nättraby S 41 C5
Naturno I 71 B5
Naucelle F 77 B5
Nauders A 71 B5
Nauen D 45 C4
Naul IRL 19 C5
Naumburg D 52 B1
Naundorf D 52 C3
Naunhof D 52 B2
Naustdal N 32 A2
Nautijaur S 112 F8
Nautsi RUS 113 D18
Nava E 88 A1
Navacerrada E 94 B2
Navaconcejo E 93 A5
Nava de Arévalo E 94 B2
Nava de la Asunción
E 94 A2
Nava del Rey E 88 C1
Navafriá E 94 A3
Navahermosa E 94 C2
Navahrudak BY 7 E8
Naval E 90 A3
Navalacruz E 94 B2
Navalcán E 94 B1
Navalcarnero E 94 B2
Navaleno E 89 C3
Navalmanzano E 94 A2
Navalmoral E 94 B2
Navalmoral de la Mata
E 93 B5
Naválón E 96 C2
Navalonguilla E 93 A5
Navalperal de Pinares
E 94 B2
Navalpino E 94 C2
Navaltalgordo E 94 B2
Navaltoril E 94 C2
Navaluenga E 94 B2
Navalvillar de Pela E 93 B5
Navan IRL 19 C5
Navaperal de Tormes
E 93 A5
Navapolatsk BY 7 D10
Navarclés E 91 B4
Navarredonda de Gredos
E 93 A5
Navarrenx F 76 C2
Navarrés E 96 B2
Navarrete E 89 B4
Navarrevisca E 94 B2
Navás E 91 B4
Navascués E 76 D1
Navas del Madroño E 93 B4
Navas del Rey E 94 B2
Navas del Sepillar E 100 B1
Navas de Oro E 94 A2
Navas de San Juan
E 100 A2
Navasfrias E 93 A4
Nave I 71 C5
Nave de Haver P 93 A4
Nävekvarn S 37 D3
Navelli I 103 A6
Navenby GB 27 B5
Näverkärret S 37 C2
Naverstad S 35 D3
Navés E 91 B4
Navezuelas E 93 B5
Navia E 86 A4
Navia de Suarna E 86 B4
Navilly F 69 B5
Navlya RUS 7 E13
Năvodari RO 11 D10
Naxos GR 117 E7
Nay F 76 C2
Nazaré P 92 B1
Nazarje SLO 73 B4
Nazilli TR 119 E3
Nazza D 51 B6
Ndroq AL 105 B5
Nea Anchialos GR 116 C4
Nea Epidavros GR 117 E5
Nea Flippias GR 116 C2
Nea Kalikratia GR 116 B5
Nea Makri GR 117 D5
Nea Moudania GR 116 B5
Neap GB 22 A7
Nea Peramos GR 116 B6
Neapoli
Kozani GR 116 B3
Kriti GR 117 G7
Lakonia GR 117 F5
Nea Stira GR 117 D6
Neath GB 28 B4
Nea Visa GR 118 A1
Nea Zichni GR 116 A5
Nebljusi HR 83 B4
Neblo SLO 72 B3
Nebolchy RUS 7 B12
Nebra D 52 B1
Nebreda E 88 C3
Nechanice CZ 53 C5
Neckargemünd D 61 A4
Neckarsulm D 61 A5
Neda E 86 A2
Neded SK 64 B3
Nedelišće HR 73 B6
Nederweert NL 50 B1
Nedreberg N 34 B3
Nedre Gärdsjö S 36 B2
Nedre Soppero S 113 D10
Nedstrand N 33 C2
Nedvědice CZ 64 A2
Nędza PL 54 C3
Neede NL 50 A2
Needham Market GB 30 B5
Needingworth GB 30 B3
Neermoor D 43 B4
Neeroeteren B 50 B1
Neerpelt B 49 B6
Neesen D 51 A4
Neetze D 44 B2
Nefyn GB 26 C1
Negbina SRB 85 C4
Negotin SRB 11 D7
Negotino MK 116 A4
Negrar I 71 C5
Negredo E 95 A4
Negreira E 86 B2
Nègrepelisse F 77 B4
Negru Vodă RO 11 E10
Negueira de Muñiz E 86 A4
Neheim D 50 B3
Neila E 89 B4
Néive I 80 B2
Nejdek CZ 52 C2
Nekla PL 46 C3
Neksø DK 41 D5
Nelas P 92 A3
Nelaug N 33 D5
Nelidovo RUS 7 C12
Nelim FIN 113 D17
Nellingen D 61 B5
Nelson GB 26 B3
Neman RUS 6 D7
Nemea GR 117 E4
Nemesgörzsöny H 74 A2
Nemeskér H 74 A1
Nemesnádudvar H 75 B4
Nemesszalók H 74 A2
Németkér H 74 B3
Nemours F 58 B3
Nemška Loka SLO 73 C5
Nemšová SK 64 B4
Nenagh IRL 20 B3
Nenince SK 65 B5
Nenita GR 117 D8
Nenzing A 71 A4
Neochori GR 116 C3
Neo Chori GR 116 D3
Neon Petritsi GR 116 A5
Nepi I 102 A5
Nepomuk CZ 63 A4
Nérac F 77 B3
Neratovice CZ 53 C4
Nerchau D 52 B2
Néré F 67 C4
Neresheim D 61 B6
Nereto I 82 D2
Nerezine HR 82 B3
Nerežišća HR 83 C5
Neringa LT 6 D6
Néris-les Bains F 68 B2
Nerito I 103 A6
Nerja E 100 C2
Néronde F 69 C4
Nérondes F 68 B2
Nerpio E 101 A3
Nersingen D 61 B6
Nerva E 99 B4
Nervesa della Battáglia
I 72 C2
Nervi I 80 B3
Nes
N 114 D6
Buskerud N 34 B1
Hedmark N 34 B2
NL 42 B2
Nesbyen N 32 B6
Neset N 114 F7
Nesflaten N 33 C3
Nesjahverfi IS 111 C10
Neskaupstaður IS 111 B12
Nesland N 33 C4
Neslandsvatn N 33 D6
Nesle F 59 A3
Nesna N 115 A10
Nesoddtangen N 34 C2
Nesovice CZ 64 A3
Nesselwang D 61 C6
Nesslau CH 71 A4
Nessmersiel D 43 B4
Nesso I 71 C4
Nesterov UA 11 A7
Nestorio GR 116 B3
Nesttun N 32 B2
Nesvady SK 64 C4
Nesvatnstemmen N 33 D5
Nether Stowey GB 29 B4
Netland N 33 D3
Netolice CZ 63 A5
Netphen D 50 C4
Netstal CH 70 A4
Nettancourt F 59 B5
Nettetal D 50 B2
Nettlingen D 51 A6
Nettuno I 102 B5
Neualbenreuth D 52 D2
Neubeckum D 50 B4
Neubrandenburg D 45 B5
Neubruchhausen D 43 C5
Neubukow D 44 A3
Neuburg D 62 B2
Neuchâtel CH 70 B1
Neu Darchau D 44 B2
Neudau A 73 A6
Neudietendorf D 51 C6
Neudorf D 61 A4
Neuenbürg D 61 B4
Neuenburg D 43 B4
Neuendorf D 45 A5
Neuenhagen D 45 C5
Neuenhaus D 42 C3
Neuenkirchen
Niedersachsen D 43 B6
Niedersachsen D 43 C5
Nordrhein-Westfalen
D 50 A3
Nordrhein-Westfalen
D 50 C3
Neuenrade D 50 B3
Neuenwalde D 43 B5
Neuerburg D 50 C2
Neufahrn
Bayern D 62 B2
Bayern D 62 B3
Neuf-Brisach F 60 B3
Neufchâteau
B 60 A1
F 60 B1
Neufchâtel-en-Bray F 58 A2
Neufchâtel-sur-Aisne
F 59 A5
Neuflize F 59 A5
Neugersdorf D 53 C4
Neuhardenberg D 45 C6
Neuharlingersiel D 43 B4
Neuhaus
Bayern D 62 A2
Bayern D 63 B4
Niedersachsen D 43 B6
Niedersachsen D 44 B2
Niedersachsen D 51 B5
Neuhaus a Rennweg
D 52 C1
Neuhausen
CH 61 C4
D 52 C3
Neuhausen ob Eck D 61 C4
Neuhof
Bayern D 62 A1
Hessen D 51 C5
Neuhofen an der Krems
A 63 B5
Neuillé-Pont-Pierre F 67 A5
Neuilly-en-Thelle F 58 A3
Neuilly-le-Réal F 68 B3
Neuilly-l'Évêque F 60 C1
Neuilly-St Front F 59 A4
Neu-Isenburg D 51 C4
Neukalen D 45 B4
Neu Kaliss D 44 B3
Neukirch D 53 B4
Neukirchen
A 62 B4
Hessen D 51 C5
Schleswig-Holstein D 39 E1
Neukirchen am
Grossvenediger A 72 A2
Neukirchen bei Heiligen
Blut D 62 A3
Neukloster D 44 B3
Neulengbach A 64 B1
Neulise F 68 C4
Neu Lübbenau D 53 A3
Neum BIH 84 D2
Neumagen D 60 A2
Neumarkt D 62 A2
Neumarkt am Wallersee
A 63 C4
Neumarkt im
Hausruckkreis A 63 B4
Neumarkt im Mühlkreis
A 63 B5
Neumarkt im Steiermark
A 73 A4
Neumarkt Sankt Veit
D 62 B3
Neumünster D 44 A1
Neunburg vorm Wald
D 62 A3
Neung-sur-Beuvron F 68 A1
Neunkirch
Luzern CH 70 A3
Schaffhausen CH 61 C4
Neunkirchen
A 64 C2
Nordrhein-Westfalen
D 50 C3
Saarland D 60 A3
Neunkirchen am Brand
D 62 A2
Neuötting D 62 B3
Neupetershain D 53 B4
Neuravensburg D 61 C5
Neureut D 61 A4
Neuruppin D 45 C4
Neusäss D 62 B1
Neusiedl A 64 C2
Neuss D 50 B2
Neussargues-Moissac
F 68 C2
Neustadt
Bayern D 62 A1
Bayern D 62 A3
Bayern D 62 B2
Brandenburg D 44 C4
Hessen D 51 C5
Niedersachsen D 43 C6
Rheinland-Pfalz D 61 A4
Sachsen D 53 B4
Schleswig-Holstein D 44 A2
Thüringen D 52 C1
Thüringen D 52 C1
Neustadt-Glewe D 44 B3
Neustift im Stubaital
A 71 A6
Neustrelitz D 45 B5
Neutal A 73 A6
Neutrebbin D 45 C6
Neu-Ulm D 61 B6
Neuves-Maisons F 60 B2
Neuvic
Corrèze F 68 C2
Dordogne F 77 A3
Neuville-aux-Bois F 58 B3
Neuville-de-Poitou F 67 B5
Neuville-les-Dames F 69 B5
Neuville-sur-Saône F 69 C4
Neuvy-le-Roi F 58 C1
Neuvy-Santour F 59 B4
Neuvy-St Sépulchre
F 68 B1
Neuvy-sur-Barangeon
F 68 A2
Neuwied D 50 C3
Neuzelle D 53 A4
Névache F 79 A5
Neveklov CZ 63 A5
Nevel RUS 7 D10
Neverfjord N 113 B12
Nevers F 68 B3
Nevesinje BIH 84 C3
Névez F 56 C2
Nevlunghavn N 35 D1
Nevşehir TR 16 B7
New Abbey GB 25 D4
New Aberdour GB 23 D6
New Alresford GB 31 C2
Newark-on-Trent GB 27 B5
Newbiggin-by-the-Sea
GB 25 C6
Newbliss IRL 19 B4
Newborough GB 26 B1
Newbridge IRL 21 A5
Newbridge on Wye
GB 29 A4
Newburgh
Aberdeenshire GB 23 D6
Fife GB 25 B4
Newbury GB 31 C2
Newby Bridge GB 26 A3
Newcastle GB 19 B6
Newcastle Emlyn GB 28 A3
Newcastleton GB 25 C5
Newcastle-under-Lyme
GB 26 B3
Newcastle upon Tyne
GB 25 D6
Newcastle West IRL 20 B2
Newchurch GB 29 A4
New Costessey GB 30 B5
New Cumnock GB 24 C3
Newent GB 29 B5
New Galloway GB 24 C3
Newham GB 31 C4
Newhaven GB 31 D4
Newington GB 31 C5
Newinn IRL 21 B4
Newlyn GB 28 C2
Newmachar GB 23 D6
Newmarket
Suffolk GB 30 B4
Western Isles GB 22 C2
IRL 20 B3
Newmarket-on-Fergus
IRL 20 B3
New Mills GB 27 B4
New Milton GB 31 D2
New Pitsligo GB 23 D6
Newport
Isle of Wight GB 31 D2
Newport GB 29 B5
Pembrokeshire GB 28 A3
Telford & Wrekin GB 26 C3
Mayo IRL 18 C2
Tipperary IRL 20 B3
Newport-on-Tay GB 25 B5
Newport Pagnell GB 30 B3
Newquay GB 28 C2
New Quay GB 28 A3
New Radnor GB 29 A4
New Romney GB 31 D4
New Ross IRL 21 B5
Newry GB 19 B5
New Scone GB 25 B4
Newton Abbot GB 29 C4
Newton Arlosh GB 25 D4
Newton Aycliffe GB 27 A4
Newton Ferrers GB 28 C3
Newtonhill GB 23 D6
Newtonmore GB 23 D4
Newton Stewart GB 24 D3
Newtown
Herefordshire GB 29 A5
Powys GB 26 C2
Newtownabbey GB 19 B6
Newtownards GB 19 B6
Newtownbutler GB 19 B4
Newtown Cunningham
IRL 19 B4
Newtownhamilton GB 19 B5
Newtownmountkennedy
IRL 21 A5
Newtown St Boswells
GB 25 C5
Newtown Sands IRL 20 B2
Newtownshandrum
IRL 20 B3
Newtownstewart GB 19 B4
Nexon F 67 C6
Neyland GB 28 B3
Nibbiano I 80 B3
Nibe DK 38 C2
Nicaj-Shalë AL 105 A5
Nicastro I 106 C3
Niccone I 82 C1
Nice F 80 C1
Nickelsdorf A 64 C3
Nicolosi I 109 B4
Nicosia
CY 120 A2
I 109 B3
Nicótera I 106 C2
Nidda D 51 C5
Niğde TR 16 C7
Nidzica PL 47 B6
Niebla E 99 B4
Nieborów PL 55 A5
Niebüll D 39 E1
Niechanowo PL 46 C3
Niechorze PL 45 A7
Niedalino PL 46 A2
Niederaula D 51 C5
Niederbipp CH 70 A2
Niederbronn-les-Bains
F 60 B3
Niederfischbach D 50 C3
Niedergörsdorf D 52 B2
Niederkrüchten D 50 B2
Niederndorf A 62 C3
Nieder-Olm D 61 A4
Niedersachswerfen D 51 B6
Niederstetten D 61 A5
Niederurnen CH 70 A4
Niederwölz A 73 A4
Niedoradz PL 53 B5
Niedzica PL 65 A6
Niegosławice PL 53 B5
Nieheim D 51 B5
Niemcza PL 54 C1
Niemegk D 52 A2
Niemodlin PL 54 C2
Nienburg
Niedersachsen D 43 C6
Sachsen-Anhalt D 52 B1
Niepołomice PL 55 C5
Nierstein D 61 A4
Niesky D 53 B4
Niestronno PL 46 C3
Nieświń PL 55 B5
Nieszawa PL 47 C4
Nieul-le-Dolent F 66 B3
Nieul-sur-Mer F 66 B3
Nieuw-Amsterdam
NL 42 C3
Nieuw-Buinen NL 42 C3
Nieuwegein NL 49 A6
Nieuwe Niedorp NL 42 C1
Nieuwe-Pekela NL 42 B3
Nieuwerkerken B 49 C6
Nieuwe-schans NL 43 B4
Nieuwolda NL 42 B3
Nieuwpoort B 48 B3
Nieuw-Weerdinge NL 42 C3
Nigrita GR 116 B5
Nigüelas E 100 C2
Níjar E 101 C3
Nijemci HR 75 C4
Nijkerk NL 49 A6
Nijlen B 49 B5
Nijmegen NL 50 B1
Nijverdal NL 42 C3
Nikel RUS 113 C19
Nikinci SRB 85 B4
Nikiti GR 116 B5
Nikitsch A 74 A1
Nikkaluokta S 112 E8
Nikla H 74 B2
Niklasdorf A 73 A5
Nikolayev = Mykolayiv
UA 11 C12
Nikšić MNE 84 D3
Nilivaara S 113 E10
Nîmes F 78 C3
Nimis I 72 B3
Nimtofte DK 39 C3
Nin HR 83 B4
Nindorf D 43 A6
Ninemilehouse IRL 21 B4
Ninove B 49 C5
Niort F 67 B4
Niš SRB 10 E6
Nisa P 92 B3
Niscemi I 109 B3
Nissafors S 40 B3
Nissan-lez-Ensérune
F 78 C2
Nissedal N 33 C5
Nissumby DK 38 C1
Nisterud N 33 C6
Niton GB 31 D2
Nitra SK 64 B4
Nitrianske-Pravno SK 65 B4
Nitrianske Rudno SK 65 B4
Nitry F 59 C4
Nittedal N 34 B2
Nittenau D 62 A3
Nittendorf D 62 A2
Nivala FIN 3 E26
Nivelles B 49 C5
Nivenskoye RUS 47 A6
Nivnice CZ 64 B3
Nizhyn UA 11 A11
Nižná SK 65 A5
Nižná Boca SK 65 B5
Nižne Repaše SK 65 A6
Nizza Monferrato I 80 B2
Njarðvík IS 111 D3
Njegůsevo SRB 75 C4
Njivice HR 73 C4
Njurundabommen
S 115 E14
Njutånger S 115 F14
Noailles F 58 A3
Noain E 76 D1
Noale I 72 C2
Noalejo E 100 B2
Noblejas E 95 C3
Noceda E 86 B4
Nocera Inferiore I 103 C7
Nocera Terinese I 106 B3
Nocera Umbra I 82 C1
Noceto I 81 B4
Noci I 104 C3
Nociglia I 107 A5
Nodeland N 33 D4
Nödinge S 38 B5
Nods F 69 A6
Noé F 77 C4
Noépoli I 106 A3
Noeux-les-Mines F 48 C3
Noez E 94 C2
Nogales E 93 C4
Nogara I 71 C6
Nogarejas E 87 B4
Nogaro F 76 C2
Nogent F 59 B6
Nogent l'Artaud F 59 B4
Nogent-le-Roi F 58 B2
Nogent-le-Rotrou F 58 B1
Nogent-sur-Seine F 59 B4
Nogent-sur-Vernisson
F 58 C3
Nogersund S 41 C4
Noguera E 95 B5
Noguerones E 100 B1
Nohfelden D 60 A3
Nohn D 50 C2
Noia E 86 B2
Noicáttaro I 104 B2
Noirétable F 68 C3
Noirmoutier-en-l'Île F 66 A2
Noja E 89 A3
Nojewo PL 46 C2
Nokia FIN 3 F25
Nol S 38 B5
Nola I 103 C7

Nolay F 69 B4
Noli I 80 B2
Nolnyra S 36 B4
Nombela E 94 B2
Nomeny F 60 B2
Nomexy F 60 B2
Nonancourt F 58 B2
Nonant-le-Pin F 57 B6
Nonántola I 81 B5
Nonaspe E 90 B3
None I 80 B1
Nontron F 67 C5
Nonza F 102 A2
Noordhorn NL 42 B3
Noordwijk NL 49 A5
Noordwijkerhout NL 49 A5
Noordwolde NL 42 C3
Noppikoski S 36 A1
Nora S 37 C2
Nørager DK 38 C2
Norberg S 36 B2
Norboda S 36 B5
Nórcia I 82 D2
Nordagutu N 33 C6
Nordanås S 115 C15
Nordausques F 48 C3
Nordborg DK 39 D2
Nordby
Aarhus Amt. DK 39 D3
Ribe Amt. DK 39 D1
Norddeich D 43 B4
Norddorf D 43 A5
Norden D 43 B4
Nordenham D 43 B5
Norderhov N 34 B2
Norderney D 43 B4
Norderstapel D 43 A6
Norderstedt D 44 B2
Nordfjord N 113 B19
Nordfjordeid N 114 F3
Nordfold N 112 E4
Nordhalben D 52 C1
Nordhausen D 51 B6
Nordheim vor der Rhön
D 51 C6
Nordholz D 43 B5
Nordhorn D 43 C4
Nordingrå S 115 E15
Nordkjosbotn N 112 C8
Nordli N 115 C10
Nördlingen D 61 B6
Nordmaling S 115 D16
Nordmark S 34 C6
Nordmela N 112 C4
Nord-Odal N 34 B3
Nordre Osen N 34 A3
Nordsinni N 34 B1
Nørdstedalsseter N 114 F4
Nordstemmen D 51 A5
Nordvågen N 113 B15
Nordwalde D 50 A3
Noreña E 88 A1
Noresund N 34 B1
Norg NL 42 B3
Norheimsund N 32 B3
Norie S 41 C4
Norma I 102 B5
Nornäs S 34 A5
Norrahammar S 40 B4
Norråker S 115 C12
Norrala S 36 A3
Norra Vi S 40 B5
Nørre Aaby DK 39 D2
Nørre Alslev DK 39 E4
Nørre Lyndelse DK 39 D3
Nørre Nebel DK 39 D1
Norrent-Fontes F 48 C3
Nørre Snede DK 39 D2
Nørresundby DK 38 B2
Nørre Vorupør DK 38 C1
Norrhult Klavreström
S 40 B5
Norrköping S 37 D3
Norrskedika S 36 B5
Norrsundet S 36 B4
Norrtälje S 36 C5
Nors DK 38 B1
Norsbron S 35 C5
Norsholm S 37 D2
Norsjö S 115 C16
Nörten-Hardenberg D 51 B5
Northallerton GB 27 A4
Northampton GB 30 B3
North Berwick GB 25 B5
North Charlton GB 25 C6
Northeim D 51 B6
Northfleet GB 31 C4
North Frodingham
GB 27 B5
North Kessock GB 23 D4
Northleach GB 29 B6
North Molton GB 28 B4
North Petherton GB 29 B4
Northpunds GB 22 B7
North Somercotes
GB 27 B6
North Tawton GB 28 C4
North Thoresby GB 27 B5
North Walsham GB 30 B5
Northwich GB 26 B3
Norton GB 27 A5
Nortorf D 44 A1
Nort-sur-Erdre F 66 A3
Nörvenich D 50 C2
Norwich GB 30 B5
Norwick GB 22 A8
Nøsen N 32 B5
Nosivka UA 11 A11
Nossa Senhora do Cabo
P 92 C1
Nossebro S 35 D4
Nössemark S 35 C3
Nossen D 52 B3
Notaresco I 103 A6
Noto I 109 C4
Notodden N 33 C6
Nottingham GB 27 C4
Nottuln D 50 B3
Nouan-le-Fuzelier F 68 A2
Nouans-les-Fontaines
F 67 A6
Nougaroulet F 77 C3
Nouvion F 48 C2
Nouzonville F 59 A5
Nova H 74 B1
Nová Baňa SK 65 B4
Nová Bystrica SK 65 A5
Nová Bystřice CZ 63 A6
Nova Crnja SRB 75 C5
Novaféltria I 82 C1
Nova Gorica SLO 72 C3
Nova Gradiška HR 74 C2
Nováky SK 65 B4
Novalaise F 69 C5
Novales E 90 A2
Nova Levante I 71 B6
Novalja HR 83 B3
Nova Odesa UA 11 C11
Nová Paka CZ 53 C5
Nova Pazova SRB 85 B5
Nová Pec CZ 63 B4
Novara I 70 C3
Novara di Sicília I 109 A4
Nova Siri I 106 A3
Novate Mezzola I 71 B4
Nova Topola BIH 84 A2
Nova Varoš SRB 85 C4
Novaya Ladoga RUS 7 A12
Nova Zagora BG 11 E8
Nové Hrady CZ 63 B5
Novelda E 101 A5
Novellara I 81 B4
Nové Město SK 64 B3
Nové Město nad Metují
CZ 53 C6
Nové Město na Moravě
CZ 64 A2
Nové Město pod Smrkem
CZ 53 C5
Nové Mitrovice CZ 63 A4
Noventa di Piave I 72 C2
Noventa Vicentina I 71 C6
Novés E 94 B2
Noves F 78 C3
Nové Sady SK 64 B3
Novés de Segre E 91 A4
Nové Strašeci CZ 53 C3
Nové Zámky SK 64 C4
Novgorod RUS 7 B11
Novhorod-Siverskyy
UA 7 F12
Novi Bečej SRB 75 C5
Novi di Módena I 81 B4
Novigrad
Istarska HR 72 C3
Zadarsko-Kninska
HR 83 B4
Novigrad Podravski
HR 74 B1
Novi Kneževac SRB 75 B5
Novi Lígure I 80 B2
Noville B 50 C1
Novi Marof HR 73 B6
Novion-Porcien F 59 A5
Novi Pazar
BG 11 E9
SRB 85 C5
Novi Sad SRB 75 C4
Novi Slankamen SRB 75 C5
Novi Travnik BIH 84 B2
Novi Vinodolski HR 83 A3
Novo Brdo KOS 85 D6
Novohrad-Volynskyy
UA 11 A9
Novo Mesto SLO 73 C5
Novo Miloševo SRB 75 C5
Novomirgorod UA 11 B11
Novorzhev RUS 7 C10
Novoselë AL 105 C5
Novo Selo
BIH 84 A2
KOS 85 D5
SRB 85 C5
Novoselytsya UA 11 B9
Novosil RUS 7 E14
Novosokolniki RUS 7 C10
Novoukrayinka UA 11 B11
Novoveská Huta SK 65 B6
Novovolynsk UA 11 A8
Novozybkov RUS 7 E11
Novska HR 74 C1
Nový Bor CZ 53 C4
Nový Bydžov CZ 53 C5
Novy-Chevrières F 59 A5
Nowy Dwór Mazowiecki
PL 47 C6
Nový-Hrozenkov CZ 64 A4
Nový Jičín CZ 64 A4
Novy Knin CZ 63 A5
Novyy Buh UA 11 C12
Nowa Cerekwia PL 54 C2
Nowa Karczma PL 47 A4
Nowa Kościoł PL 53 B5
Nowa Ruda PL 54 C1
Nowa Słupia PL 55 C6
Nowa Sól PL 53 B5
Nowa Wieś PL 47 B5
Nowa-Wieś Wielka
PL 47 C4
Nowe PL 47 B4
Nowe Brzesko PL 55 C5
Nowe Grudze PL 55 A4
Nowe Miasteczko PL 53 B5
Nowe Miasto
Mazowieckie PL 47 C6
Mazowieckie PL 55 B5
Nowe Miasto Lubawskie
PL 47 B5
Nowe Miasto nad Wartą
PL 54 A2
Nowe Skalmierzyce
PL 54 B3
Nowe Warpno PL 45 B6
Nowica PL 47 A5
Nowogard PL 45 B7
Nowogród Bobrzanski
PL 53 B5
Nowogrodziec PL 53 B5
Nowosolna PL 55 B4
Nowy Dwór Gdański
PL 47 A5
Nowy Korczyn PL 55 C5
Nowy Sącz PL 65 A6
Nowy Staw PL 47 A5
Nowy Targ PL 65 A6
Nowy Tomyśl PL 46 C2
Nowy Wiśnicz PL 65 A6
Noyalo F 56 C3
Noyal-Pontivy F 56 B3
Noyant F 67 A5
Noyelles-sur-Mer F 48 C2
Noyen-sur-Sarthe F 57 C5
Noyers F 59 C4
Noyers-sur-Cher F 67 A6
Noyers-sur-Jabron F 79 B4
Noyon F 59 A3
Nozay F 66 A3
Nuaillé F 66 A4
Nuaillé-d'Aunis F 66 B4
Nuars F 68 A3
Nubledo E 88 A1
Nuéno E 90 A2
Nuestra Señora Sa Verge
des Pilar E 97 C1
Nueva E 88 A2
Nueva Carteya E 100 B1
Nuevalos E 95 A5
Nuits F 59 C5
Nuits-St Georges F 69 A4
Nule I 110 B2
Nules E 96 B2
Nulvi I 110 B1
Numana I 82 C2
Numansdorp NL 49 B5
Nümbrecht D 50 C3
Nunchritz D 52 B3
Nuneaton GB 30 B2
Nunnanen FIN 113 D13
N Unnaryd S 40 B3
Nuñomoral E 93 A4
Nunspeet NL 42 C2
Nuorgam FIN 113 B16
Núoro I 110 B2
Nurallao I 110 C2
Nuremberg = Nürnberg
D 62 A2
Nurmes FIN 3 E28
Nürnberg = Nuremberg
D 62 A2
Nurri I 110 C2
Nürtingen D 61 B5
Nus I 70 C2
Nusnäs S 36 B1
Nusplingen D 61 B4
Nuštar HR 74 C3
Nyáker S 115 D16
Nyáregyháza H 75 A4
Nyarlörinc H 75 B4
Nyasvizh BY 7 E9
Nybble S 35 C6
Nybergsund N 34 A4
Nybøl DK 39 E2
Nyborg DK 39 D3
Nybro S 40 C5
Nybster GB 23 C5
Nyby DK 39 E5
Nye S 40 B5
Nyékládháza H 65 C6
Nyergesujfalu H 65 C4
Nyhammar S 36 B1
Nyhyttan S 37 C1
Nyirád H 74 A2
Nyírbátor H 11 C7
Nyíregyháza H 10 C6
Nyker DK 41 D4
Nykil S 37 D2
Nykirke N 34 B2
Nykøbing
Falster DK 39 E4
Vestsjællands Amt.
DK 39 D4
Nykøbing Mors DK 38 C1
Nyköping S 37 D4
Nykroppa S 35 C6
Nykvarn S 37 C4
Nykyrke S 37 D1
Nyland S 115 D14
Nylars DK 41 D4
Nymburk CZ 53 C5
Nynäshamn S 37 D4
Nyon CH 69 B6
Nyons F 79 B4
Nýřany CZ 63 A4
Nýrsko CZ 62 A4
Nyrud N 113 C18
Nysa PL 54 C2
Nysäter S 35 C4
Nyseter N 114 E5
Nyskoga S 34 B4
Nysted DK 44 A3
Nystrand N 35 C1
Nyúl H 64 C3
Nyvoll N 113 B12

O

Oadby GB 30 B2
Oakengates GB 26 C3
Oakham GB 30 B3
Oanes N 33 D3
Obalj BIH 84 C3
Oban GB 24 B2
O Barco E 86 B4
Obdach A 73 A4
Obejo E 100 A1
Oberammergau D 62 C2
Oberasbach D 62 A1
Oberau D 62 C2
Oberaudorf D 62 C3
Oberbruck F 60 C2
Oberdiessbach CH 70 B2
Oberdorf CH 70 A2
Oberdrauburg A 72 B2
Oberelsbach D 51 C6
Obere Stanz A 73 A5
Ober Grafendorf A 63 B6
Obergünzburg D 61 C6
Obergurgl A 71 B6
Oberhausen D 50 B2
Oberhof D 51 C6
Oberkirch D 61 B4
Oberkirchen D 51 B4
Oberkochen D 61 B6
Obermassfeld-
Grimmenthal D 51 C6
Ober-Morlen D 51 C4
Obermünchen D 62 B2
Obernai F 60 B3
Obernberg A 63 B4
Obernburg D 61 A5
Oberndorf D 61 B4
Oberndorf bei Salzburg
A 62 C3
Obernkirchen D 51 A5
Oberort A 73 A5
Oberpullendorf A 74 A1
Oberriet CH 71 A4
Oberröblingen D 52 B1
Oberrot D 61 A5
Oberstaufen D 61 C6
Oberstdorf D 71 A5
Obertauern A 72 A3
Obertilliach A 72 B2
Obertraubling D 62 B3
Obertraun A 72 A3
Obertrubach D 62 A2
Obertrum A 62 C4
Oberursel D 51 C4
Obervellach A 72 B3
Oberviechtach D 62 A3
Oberwart A 73 A6
Oberwesel D 50 C3
Oberwinter D 50 C3
Oberwölzstadt A 73 A4
Oberzell D 63 B4
Obice PL 55 C5
Óbidos P 92 B1
Obilić KOS 85 D6
Obing D 62 C3
Objat F 67 C6
Objazda PL 46 A3
Öblarn A 73 A4
Obninsk RUS 7 D14
O Bolo E 87 B3
Oborniki PL 46 C2
Oborniki Śląskie PL 54 B1
Obornjača SRB 75 C4
Oboyan RUS 7 F14
Obrenovac SRB 85 B5
Obrež
Srbija SRB 85 C6
Vojvodina SRB 85 B4
Obrigheim D 61 A5
Obrov SLO 73 C4
Obrovac
HR 83 B4
SRB 75 C4
Obrovac Sinjski HR 83 C5
Obruk TR 16 B6
Obrzycko PL 46 C2
Obudovac BIH 84 B3
Ocaña E 95 C3
O Carballiño E 86 B2
Occhiobello I 81 B5
Occimiano I 80 A2
Očevlja BIH 84 B3
Ochagavía E 76 D1
Ochakiv UA 11 C11
Ochiltree GB 24 C3
Ochla PL 53 B5
Ochotnica-Dolna PL 65 A6
Ochotnica-Górna PL 65 A6
Ochsenfurt D 61 A6
Ochsenhausen D 61 B5
Ochtendung D 50 C3
Ochtrup D 50 A3
Ocieka PL 55 C6
Ockelbo S 36 B3
Öckerö S 38 B4
Ocnița MD 11 B9
O Corgo E 86 B3
Očová SK 65 B5
Ócsa H 75 A4
Öcseny H 74 B3
Öcsöd H 75 B5
Octeville F 57 A4
Ocypel PL 47 B4
Ödåkra S 41 C2
Odby DK 38 C1
Odda N 32 B3
Odder DK 39 D3
Ödeborg S 35 D3
Odeceixe P 98 B2
Odechów PL 55 B6
Odeleite P 98 B3
Odemira P 98 B2
Ödemiş TR 119 D2
Odensbacken S 37 C2
Odense DK 39 D3
Odensjö
Jönköping S 40 B4
Kronoberg S 40 C3
Oderberg D 45 C6
Oderzo I 72 C2
Odesa = Odessa UA 11 C11
Ödeshög S 37 D1
Odessa = Odesa UA 11 C11
Odiáxere P 98 B2
Odie GB 23 B6
Odiham GB 31 C3
Odintsovo RUS 7 D14
Odivelas P 98 A2
Odolanów PL 54 B2
Odón E 95 B5
Odorheiu Secuiesc
RO 11 C8
Odoyevo RUS 7 E14
Odrowaz PL 55 B5
Odry CZ 64 A3
Odrzywół PL 55 B5
Ødsted DK 39 D2
Odžaci SRB 75 C4
Odžak BIH 84 A3
Oebisfelde D 44 C2
Oederan D 52 C3
Oeding D 50 B2
Oegstgeest NL 49 A5
Oelde D 50 B4
Oelsnitz D 52 C2
Oer-Erkenschwick D 50 B3
Oerlinghausen D 51 B4
Oettingen D 62 B1
Oetz A 71 A5
Oeventrop D 50 B4
Offanengo I 71 C4
Offenbach D 51 C4
Offenburg D 60 B3
Offida I 82 D2
Offingen D 61 B6
Offranville F 58 A2
Ofte N 33 C5
Ofterschwang D 71 A5
Oggiono I 71 C4
Ogihares E 100 B2
Ogliastro Cilento I 103 C8
Ogliastro Marina I 103 C7
Ogmore-by-Sea GB 29 B4
Ogna N 33 D2
Ogre LV 6 C8
Ogrodzieniec PL 55 C4
Ogulin HR 73 C5
Ögur IS 111 A3
Ohanes E 101 B3
Ohey B 49 C6
Ohlstadt D 62 C2
Ohrdorf D 44 C2
Ohrdruf D 51 C6
Ohrid MK 116 A2
Öhringen D 61 A5
Oia E 87 B2
Oiã P 92 A2
Oiartzun E 76 C1
Oilgate IRL 21 B5
Oimbra E 87 C3
Oiselay-et-Grachoux
F 69 A5
Oisemont F 48 D2
Oisterwijk NL 49 B6
Öja S 37 E5
Öje S 34 B5
Ojén E 100 C1
Ojrzeń PL 47 C6
Ojuelos Altos E 99 A5
Okalewo PL 47 B5
Okány H 75 B6
Okehampton GB 28 C3
Okhtyrka UA 7 F13
Oklaj HR 83 C5
Økneshamn N 112 D4
Okoč SK 64 C3
Okoličné SK 65 A5
Okonek PL 46 B2
Okonin PL 47 B4
Okřisky CZ 64 A1
Oksa PL 55 C5
Oksbøl DK 39 D1
Oksby DK 39 D1
Øksfjord N 113 B11
Øksna N 34 B3
Okučani HR 74 C2
Okulovka RUS 7 B12
Ólafsfjörður IS 111 A7
Ólafsvík IS 111 C2
ÖLagnö S 37 C5
Olagüe E 76 D1
Oland N 33 D5
Olargues F 78 C1
Oława PL 54 C2
Olazagutia E 89 B4
Olbernhau D 52 C3
Ólbia I 110 B2
Olching D 62 B2
Oldbury GB 29 B5
Oldcastle IRL 19 C4
Old Deer GB 23 D6
Oldeberkoop NL 42 C3
Oldeboorn NL 42 B2
Olden N 114 F3
Oldenbrok D 43 B5
Oldenburg
Niedersachsen D 43 B5
Schleswig-Holstein D 44 A2
Oldenzaal NL 50 A2
Olderdalen N 112 C9
Olderfjord N 113 B14
Oldersum D 43 B4
Oldervik N 112 C7
Oldham GB 26 B3
Oldisleben D 52 B1
Oldmeldrum GB 23 D6
Olea E 88 B2
Oleby S 34 B5
Olechów PL 55 B6
Oledo P 92 B3
Oléggio I 70 C3
Oleiros
Coruña E 86 A2
Coruña E 86 B1
P 92 B3
Oleksandriya
Kirovohrad UA 11 B12
Rivne UA 11 A9
Oleksandrovka UA 11 B12
Olen B 49 B5
Ølen N 33 C2
Olenegorsk RUS 3 B30
Olenino RUS 7 C12
Olesa de Montserrat
E 91 B4
Oleśnica PL 54 B2
Olešnice CZ 64 A2
Olesno PL 54 C3
Oletta F 102 A2
Olette F 91 A5
Olevsk UA 11 A9
Olfen D 50 B3
Olgiate Comasco I 70 C3
Olginate I 71 C4
Ølgod DK 39 D1
Olgrinmore GB 23 C5
Olhão P 98 B3
Olhavo P 92 B1
Oliana E 91 A4
Olias del Rey E 94 C3
Oliena I 110 B2
Oliete E 90 C2
Olimbos GR 119 G2
Olite E 89 B5
Oliva E 96 C2
Oliva de la Frontera E 99 A4
Oliva de Mérida E 93 C4
Oliva de Plasencia E 93 A4
Olivadi I 106 C3
Olival P 92 B2
Olivar E 100 C2
Olivares E 99 B4
Olivares de Duero E 88 C2
Olivares de Júcar E 95 C4
Oliveira de Azeméis
P 87 D2
Oliveira de Frades P 87 D2
Oliveira do Conde P 92 A3
Oliveira do Douro P 87 C2
Oliveira do Hospital P 92 A3
Olivenza E 93 C3
Olivet F 58 C2
Olivone CH 70 B3
Öljehult S 41 C5
Olkusz PL 55 C4
Ollerton GB 27 B4
Ollerup DK 39 D3
Olliergues F 68 C3
Ölmbrotorp S 37 C2
Ölme S 35 C5
Olmedilla de Alarcón
E 95 C4
Olmedillo de Roa E 88 C3
Olmedo
E 88 C2
I 110 B1
Olmeto F 102 B1
Olmillos de Castro E 87 C4
Olmos de Ojeda E 88 B2
Olney GB 30 B3
Olobok PL 54 B3
Olocau del Rey E 90 C2
Olofström S 41 C4
Olomouc CZ 64 A3
Olonets RUS 3 F30
Olonne-sur-Mer F 66 B3
Olonzac F 78 C1
Oloron-Ste Marie F 76 C2
Olost E 91 B5
Olot E 91 A5
Olovo BIH 84 B3
Olpe D 50 B3
Olsberg D 51 B4
Olsene B 49 C4
Olserud S 35 C5
Olshammar S 37 D1
Olshanka UA 11 B11
Olszanica PL 53 B5
Olsztyn
Śląskie PL 55 C4
Warmińsko-Mazurskie
PL 47 B6
Olsztynek PL 47 B6
Olszyna PL 53 B5
Oltedal N 33 D3
Olten CH 70 A2
Oltenița RO 11 D9
Olula del Rio E 101 B3
Ølve N 32 B2
Olvega E 89 C5
Olvera E 99 C5
Olympia GR 117 E3
Olzai I 110 B2
Omagh GB 19 B4
Omalos GR 117 G5
Omegna I 70 C3
Omiš HR 83 C5
Omišalj HR 73 C4
Ommen NL 42 C3
Omodhos CY 120 B1
Omoljica SRB 85 B5
On B 49 C6
Oña E 89 B3
Onano I 81 D5
O Näsberg S 34 B5
Oñati E 89 A4
Onda E 96 B2
Ondara E 96 C3
Ondarroa E 89 A4
Onesse-et-Laharie F 76 B1
Onești RO 11 C9
Onhaye B 49 C5
Onich GB 24 B2
Onil E 96 C2
Onís E 88 A2
Önnestad S 41 C4
Onsala S 38 B5
Ontinyent E 96 C2
Ontur E 101 A4
Onzain F 67 A6
Onzonilla E 88 B1
Oostburg NL 49 B4
Oostende B 48 B3
Oosterend NL 42 B2
Oosterhout NL 49 B5
Oosterwolde NL 42 C3
Oosterzele B 49 C4
Oosthuizen NL 42 C2
Oostkamp B 49 B4
Oostmalle B 49 B5
Oost-Vlieland NL 42 B2
Oostvoorne NL 49 B5
Ootmarsum NL 42 C3
Opalenica PL 54 A1
O Páramo E 86 B3
Opařany CZ 63 A5
Oparić SRB 85 C6
Opatija HR 73 C4
Opatów
Śląskie PL 54 C3
Świętokrzyskie PL 55 C6
Wielkopolskie PL 54 B3
Opatówek PL 54 B3
Opatowiec PL 55 C5
Opava CZ 64 A3
O Pedrouzo E 86 B2
Opeinde NL 42 B3
Oper Thalkirchdorf D 61 C6
Opglabbeerk B 49 B6
Opicina I 72 C3
O Pino E 86 B2
Oplotnica SLO 73 B5
Opmeer NL 42 C1
Opochka RUS 7 C10
Opočno CZ 53 C6
Opoczno PL 55 B5
Opole PL 54 C2
Oporów PL 55 A4
O Porriño E 87 B2
Opovo SRB 85 A5
Oppach D 53 B4
Oppdal N 114 E6
Oppeby
Östergötland S 40 A5
Södermanland S 37 D3
Oppedal N 32 A2
Oppegård N 34 C2
Oppenau D 61 B4
Oppenberg A 73 A4
Oppenheim D 61 A4
Óppido Lucano I 104 C1
Óppido Mamertina I 106 C2
Opponitz A 63 C5
Oppstad N 34 B3
Oprtalj HR 72 C3
Opsaheden S 34 B5
Ópusztaszer H 75 B5
Opuzen HR 84 C2
Ora
CY 120 B2
I 71 B6
Orada P 92 C3
Oradea RO 10 C6
Oradour-sur-Glane F 67 C6
Oradour-sur-Vayres
F 67 C5
Oragonja SLO 72 C3
Orah BIH 84 D3
Orahova BIH 84 B2
Orahovica HR 74 C2
Orahovo BIH 74 C2
Oraison F 79 C4
Orajärvi FIN 113 F13
Orange F 78 B3
Orani I 110 B2
Oranienbaum D 52 B2
Oranienburg D 45 C5
Oranmore IRL 20 A3
Orašac SRB 85 B5
Orašje BIH 84 A3
Oravská Lesná SK 65 A5
Oravská Polhora SK 65 A5
Oravské Veselé SK 65 A5
Oravsky-Podzámok
SK 65 A5
Orba E 96 C2
Orbacém P 87 C2
Orbais F 59 B4
Ørbæk DK 39 D3
Orbassano I 80 A1
Orbe CH 69 B6
Orbec F 58 A1
Orbetello I 102 A4
Orbetello Scalo I 102 A4
Orbigny F 67 A6
Ørby DK 39 C3
Örbyhus S 36 B4
Orce E 101 B3
Orcera E 101 A3
Orchamps-Vennes F 69 A6
Orches F 67 B5
Orchete E 96 C2
Orchies F 49 C4
Orchowo PL 47 C4
Orcières F 79 B5
Ordes E 86 A2
Ordhead GB 23 D6
Ordino AND 91 A4
Ordizia E 89 A4
Orduña E 89 B4
Ore S 36 A2
Orea E 95 B5
Orebić HR 84 D2
Örebro S 37 C2
Öregcsertő H 75 B4
Öregrund S 36 B5
Orehoved DK 39 E4
Orel RUS 7 E14
Orellana E 93 B5
Orellana de la Sierra
E 93 B5
Ören TR 119 E2
Örencik TR 118 C4
Orestiada GR 118 A1
Organyà E 91 A4
Orgaz E 94 C3
Orgelet F 69 B5
Ørgenvika N 34 B1
Orgères-en-Beauce F 58 B2
Orgibet F 77 D3
Orgnac-l'Aven F 78 B3
Orgon F 79 C4
Orgósolo I 110 B2
Orhaneli TR 118 C3
Orhangazi TR 118 B4
Orhei MD 11 C10
Orhomenos GR 116 D4
Oria E 101 B3
Ória I 104 C3
Origny-Ste Benoite F 59 A4
Orihuela E 101 A5
Orihuela del Tremedal
E 95 B5
Orikum AL 105 C5
Oriola P 92 C3
Oriolo I 106 A3
Oriovac HR 74 C2
Orissaare EST 6 B7
Oristano I 110 C1
Öriszentpéter H 73 B6
Ørje N 35 C3
Orjiva E 100 C2
Orkanger N 114 D6
Örkelljunga S 41 C3
Örkény H 75 A4
Orlamünde D 52 C1
Orlane KOS 85 D6
Orléans F 58 C2
Orlová CZ 65 A4
Orlovat SRB 75 C5
Ormea I 80 B1
Ormelet N 35 C2
Ormemyr N 33 C6
Ormilia GR 116 B5
Ormos GR 117 E6
Ormož SLO 73 B6
Ormskirk GB 26 B3
Ornans F 69 A6
Ornäs S 36 B2
Ørnes N 112 F2
Orneta PL 47 A6
Ørnhøj DK 39 C1
Ornö S 37 C5
Örnsköldsvik S 115 D15
Orolik HR 75 C3
Orom SRB 75 C4
Oron-la-Ville CH 70 B1
Oronsko PL 55 B5
Oropa I 70 C2
Oropesa
Castellón de la Plana
E 96 A3
Toledo E 93 B5
O Rosal E 87 C2
Orosei I 110 B2
Orosháza H 75 B5
Oroslavje HR 73 C5
Oroszlány H 74 A3
Oroszló H 74 B3
Orotelli I 110 B2
Orozko E 89 A4
Orphir GB 23 C5
Orpington GB 31 C4
Orreaga-Roncesvalles
E 76 C1
Orrefors S 40 C5
Orrviken S 115 D11
Orsa S 36 A1
Orsara di Púglia I 103 B8
Orsay F 58 B3
Orscholz D 60 A2
Orsennes F 67 B6
Orserum S 40 A4
Orsha BY 7 D11
Orsières CH 70 B2
Örsjö S 40 C5
Ørslev DK 39 D4
Örslösa S 35 D4
Orsogna I 103 A7
Orsomarso I 106 B2
Orșova RO 11 D7
Ørsta N 114 E3
Ørsted DK 38 C3
Örsundsbro S 37 C4
Ortaca TR 119 F3
Ortakent TR 119 E2
Ortaklar TR 119 E2
Ortaköy TR 16 B7
Orta Nova I 104 B1
Orte I 102 A5
Ortenburg D 63 B4
Orth A 64 B2
Orthez F 76 C2
Ortigueira E 86 A3
Ortilla E 90 A2
Ortisei I 72 B1
Orțișoara RO 75 C6
Ortnevik N 32 A3
Orton GB 26 A3
Ortona I 103 A7
Ortrand D 53 B3
Orubica HR 74 C2
Ørum DK 38 C2
Orune I 110 B2
Orusco E 95 B3
Orvalho P 92 A3
Orvault F 66 A3
Ørvella N 33 C6
Orvieto I 82 D1
Orvínio I 102 A5
Oryakhovo BG 11 E7
Orzesze PL 54 C3
Orzinuovi I 71 C4
Orzivécchi I 71 C4
Os
Hedmark N 34 B3
Hedmark N 114 E8
Osann-Monzel D 60 A2
Osaonica SRB 85 C5
Osbruk S 40 B4
Øsby DK 39 D2
Osby S 41 C3
Oščadnica SK 65 A4
Oschatz D 52 B3
Oschersleben D 52 A1
Óschiri I 110 B2
Osciłowo PL 47 C6
Osdorf D 44 A2
Osečina SRB 85 B4
Osečná CZ 53 C4
Oseja de Sajambre E 88 A1
Osek CZ 53 C3
Osen N 114 C7
Osera de Ebro E 90 B2
Osidda I 110 B2
Osie PL 47 B4
Osieck PL 55 B6
Osieczna
Pomorskie PL 47 B4
Wielkopolskie PL 54 B1
Osieczno PL 46 B1
Osiek
Kujawsko-Pomorskie
PL 47 B5
Kujawsko-Pomorskie
PL 47 C4
Pomorskie PL 47 B4
Świętokrzyskie PL 55 C6
Osiek nad Notecią PL 46 B3
Osielsko PL 47 B4
Osijek HR 74 C3
Osilnica SLO 73 C4
Ósilo I 110 B1
Ósimo I 82 C2
Osinja BIH 84 B2
Osintorf BY 7 D11
Osipaonica SRB 85 B6
Osjaków PL 54 B3
Oskamull GB 24 B1
Oskarshamn S 40 B6
Oskarström S 40 C2
Oslany SK 65 B4
Oslavany CZ 64 A2
Ošlje HR 84 D2
Oslo N 34 C2
Øsløs DK 38 B1
Osmancık TR 16 A7
Osmaneli TR 118 B4
Ösmo S 37 D4
Osmolin PL 55 A4
Osnabrück D 50 A4
Ośno Lubuskie PL 45 C6
Osoblaha CZ 54 C2
Osor HR 83 B3
Osorno E 88 B2
Øsoyra N 32 A2
Øsøyro N 32 B2
Óspakseyri IS 111 B4
Os Peares E 86 B3
Ospedaletti I 80 C1
Ospitaletto I 71 C5
Oss NL 49 B6
Ossa de Montiel E 95 D4
Ossi I 110 B1
Ossjøen N 32 B5
Ossun F 76 C2
Ostanå S 41 C4
Ostanvik S 36 A2
Ostashkov RUS 7 C12
Östavall S 115 E12
Ostbevern D 50 A3
Østborg N 115 C10
Østby N 34 A4
Osted DK 39 D4
Ostenfeld D 43 A6
Oster UA 11 A11
Øster Assels DK 38 C1
Osterburg D 44 C3
Osterburken D 61 A5
Österbybruk S 36 B4
Østerbyhavn DK 38 B4
Österbymo S 40 B5
Ostercappeln D 43 C5
Österfärnebo S 36 B3
Osterfeld D 52 B1
Österforse S 115 D14
Osterhever D 43 A5
Osterhofen D 62 B4
Osterholz-Scharmbeck
D 43 B5
Øster Hornum DK 38 C2
Øster Hurup DK 38 C3
Østerild DK 38 B1
Österlövsta S 36 B4
Øster Jølby DK 38 C1
Øster-marie DK 41 D5
Ostermiething A 62 B3
Osterode am Harz D 51 B6
Ostersiel D 43 A5
Östersund S 115 D11
Øster Tørslev DK 38 C3
Östervåla S 36 B4
Östervallskog S 35 C3
Østervrå DK 38 B3
Osterwieck D 51 B6
Osterzell D 62 C1
Ostffyasszonyfa H 74 A2
Östfora S 36 C4
Östhammar S 36 B5
Ostheim F 60 B3
Ostheim vor der Rhön
D 51 C6
Osthofen D 61 A4
Ostiano I 71 C5
Ostiglia I 81 A5
Ostiz E 76 D1
Östmark S 34 B4
Östnor S 36 A1
Ostojićevo SRB 75 C5
Ostra I 82 C2
Östra Amtervik S 35 C5
Östraby S 41 D3
Ostrach D 61 C5
Östra Husby S 37 D3
Östra Ljungby S 41 C3
Östra Ryd S 37 D3
Ostrau D 52 B3
Ostrava CZ 64 A4
Østre Halsen N 35 C2
Ostrhauderfehn D 43 B4
Ostritz D 53 B4
Ostróda PL 47 B5
Ostroh UA 11 A9
Ostrołęka PL 6 E6
Ostropole PL 46 B2
Ostroróg PL 46 C2
Ostros MNE 105 A5
Ostrošovac BIH 83 B4
Ostrov
CZ 52 C2
RUS 7 C10
Ostrov nad Oslavou
CZ 64 A1
Ostrówek PL 54 B3
Ostrowiec PL 46 A2
Ostrowiec-Świętokrzyski
PL 55 C6
Ostrowite PL 47 B5
Ostrów Mazowiecka
PL 6 E6
Ostrowo PL 47 C4
Ostrów Wielkopolski
PL 54 B2
Ostrožac BIH 84 C2
Ostrzeszów PL 54 B2
Ostseebad Kühlungsborn
D 44 A3
Ostuni I 104 C3
Osuna E 99 B5
Osvětimany CZ 64 A3
Oswestry GB 26 C2
Oświęcim PL 55 C4
Osztopán H 74 B2
Oteiza E 89 B5
Otelec RO 75 C5
Oteo E 89 A3
Oterbekk N 35 C2
Otero de Herreros E 94 B2
Otero de O Bodas E 87 C4
Othem S 37 E5
Otley GB 27 B4
Otmuchów PL 54 C2
Otočac HR 83 B4
Otok
Splitsko-Dalmatinska
HR 83 C5
Vukovarsko-Srijemska
HR 74 C3
Otoka BIH 83 B5
Otranto I 107 A5
Otrić HR 83 B5
Otrícoli I 102 A5
Otrokovice CZ 64 A3
Otta N 114 F6
Ottana I 110 B2
Ottaviano I 103 C7
Ottenby S 41 C6
Ottendorf-Okrilla D 53 B3
Ottenhöfen D 61 B4
Ottenschlag A 63 B6
Ottensheim A 63 B5
Otterbach D 60 A3
Otterbäcken S 35 D6
Otterberg D 60 A3
Otterburn GB 25 C5
Otter Ferry GB 24 B2
Otterndorf D 43 B5
Ottersburg D 43 B6
Ottersweier D 61 B4
Otterup DK 39 D3
Ottery St Mary GB 29 C4
Ottignies B 49 C5
Ottmarsheim F 60 C3
Ottobeuren D 61 C6
Öttömös H 75 B4
Ottone I 80 B3
Ottsjö S 115 D10
Ottweiler D 60 A3
Ötvöskónyi H 74 B2
Otwock PL 55 A6
Ouanne F 59 C4
Ouarville F 58 B2
Oucques F 58 C2
Oud-Beijerland NL 49 B5
Ouddorp NL 49 B4
Oudemirdum NL 42 C2
Oudenaarde B 49 C4
Oudenbosch NL 49 B5
Oudenburg B 48 B3
Oude-Pekela NL 43 B4
Oude-Tonge NL 49 B5
Oudewater NL 49 A5
Oud Gastel NL 49 B5
Oudon F 66 A3
Oue DK 38 C2
Oughterard IRL 20 A2
Ouguela P 93 B3
Ouistreham F 57 A5
Oulainen FIN 3 D26
Oulchy-le-Château F 59 A4
Oullins F 69 C4
Oulmes F 67 B4
Oulton GB 30 B5
Oulton Broad GB 30 B5
Oulu FIN 3 D26
Oulx I 79 A5
Oundle GB 30 B3
Ouranopoli GR 116 B6
Ourém P 92 B2
Ourense E 87 B3
Ourique P 98 B2
Ourol E 86 A3
Ouroux-en-Morvan F 68 A3
Ousdale GB 23 C5
Oust F 77 D4
Outakoski FIN 113 C15
Outeiro P 92 A2
Outeiro de Rei E 86 A3
Outes E 86 B2
Outokumpu FIN 3 E28
Outreau F 48 C2
Outwell GB 30 B4
Ouzouer-le-Marché F 58 C2
Ouzouer-sur-Loire F 58 C3
Ovada I 80 B2
Ovar P 87 D2
Ovelgönne D 43 B5
Overath D 50 C3
Overbister GB 23 B6
Øverbygd N 112 D8
Overdinkel NL 50 A3
Överenhörna S 37 C4
Överhalla N 114 C8
Overijse B 49 C5
Over-jerstal DK 39 D2
Överkalix S 3 C25
Overlade DK 38 C2
Överlida S 40 B2
Överö FIN 36 B7
Overpelt B 49 B6
Overton GB 26 C3
Övertorneå S 3 C25
Överum S 40 B6
Ovidiopol UA 11 C11
Oviedo E 88 A1
Oviglio I 80 B2
Ovindoli I 103 A6
Ovodda I 110 B2
Øvre Årdal N 32 A4
Øvrebygd N 33 D3
Øvre Rendal N 114 F8
Øvre Sirdal N 33 D3
Övre Soppero S 113 D10
Övre Ullerud S 35 C5
Ovruch UA 7 F10
Ovtrup DK 39 D1
Owińska PL 46 C2
Oxaback S 40 B2
Oxberg S 34 A6
Oxelösund S 37 D4
Oxenholme GB 26 A3
Oxford GB 31 C2
Oxie S 41 D3
Oxilithos GR 116 D6
Oxted GB 31 C4
Oyaca TR 118 C7
Øye N 32 A5
Øyenkilen N 35 C2
Øyer N 34 A2
Øyeren N 34 B4
Oyfiell N 33 C5
Øygärdslia N 33 D5
Oykel Bridge GB 22 D4
Øymark N 35 C3
Oyonnax F 69 B5
Øyslebø N 33 D4
Øystese N 32 B3
Oyten D 43 B6
Øyuvsbu N 33 C4
Ozaeta E 89 B4
Ozalj HR 73 C5
Ożarów PL 55 C6
Ożarów Maz PL 55 A5
Ožbalt SLO 73 B5
Ózd H 65 B6
Žd'any SK 65 B5
Ozieri I 110 B2
Ozimek PL 54 C3
Ozimica BIH 84 B3
Ozora H 74 B3
Ozorków PL 55 B4
Ozzano Monferrato I 80 A2

P

Paal B 49 B6
Pabianice PL 55 B4
Pacanów PL 55 C6
Paceco I 108 B1
Pachino I 109 C4
Pačir SRB 75 C4
Pack A 73 A5
Paços de Ferreira P 87 C2
Pacov CZ 63 A6
Pacsa H 74 B2
Pacy-sur-Eure F 58 A2
Paczków PL 54 C2
Padany RUS 3 E30
Padborg DK 39 E2
Padej SRB 75 C5
Padene HR 83 B5
Paderborn D 51 B4
Paderne P 98 B2
Padiham GB 26 B3
Padina SRB 75 C5
Padinska Skela SRB 85 B5
Padornelo P 87 C2
Pádova I 72 C1
Padragkút H 74 A2
Padria I 110 B1
Padrón E 86 B2
Padru I 110 B2
Padstow GB 28 C3
Padul E 100 B2
Padula I 104 C1
Paduli I 103 B7
Paesana I 79 B6
Paese I 72 C2
Pag HR 83 B4
Pagani I 103 C7
Pagánica I 103 A6
Pagánico I 81 D5
Pagl ieta I 103 A7
Pagny-sur-Moselle F 60 B2
Páhi H 75 B4
Pahkakumpu FIN 113 F17
Pahl D 62 C2
Paide EST 7 B8
Paignton GB 29 C4
Pailhès F 77 C4
Paimboeuf F 66 A2
Paimpol F 56 B2
Paimpont F 57 B3
Painswick GB 29 B5
Painten D 62 B2
Paisley GB 24 C3
Pajala S 113 E12

Pajares E 88 A1
Pajares de los Oteros E 88 B1
Pajęczno PL 54 B3
Páka H 74 B1
Pakość PL 47 C4
Pakosławice PL 54 C2
Pakoštane HR 83 C4
Pakrac HR 74 C2
Paks H 74 B3
Palacios de la Sierra E 89 C3
Palaciós de la Valduerna E 88 B1
Palacios del Sil E 86 B4
Palacios de Sanabria E 87 B4
Palaciosrubios E 94 A1
Palafrugell E 91 B6
Palagiano I 104 C3
Palagonia I 109 B3
Paláia I 81 C4
Palaiseau F 58 B3
Palamós E 91 B6
Palamas GR 116 C4
Palanga LT 6 D6
Palanzano I 81 B4
Palárikovo SK 64 B4
Palas de Rei E 86 B3
Palatna KOS 85 C6
Palau I 110 A2
Palavas-les-Flots F 78 C2
Palazuelos de la Sierra E 89 B3
Palazzo Adriano I 108 B2
Palazzo del Pero I 81 C5
Palazzolo Acréide I 109 B3
Palazzolo sull'Oglio I 71 C4
Palazzo San Gervásio I 104 C1
Palazzuolo sul Senio I 81 B5
Paldiski EST 6 B8
Pale BIH 84 C3
Palekastro GR 117 G8
Palena I 103 B7
Palenciana E 100 B1
Paleochora GR 117 G5
Paleometokho CY 120 A2
Palermo I 108 A2
Paleros GR 116 D2
Palestrina I 102 B5
Pálfa H 74 B3
Palfau A 63 C5
Palhaça P 92 A2
Palheiros da Tocha P 92 A2
Palheiros de Quiaios P 92 A2
Paliaopoli GR 117 E6
Palić SRB 75 B4
Palidoro I 102 B5
Palinuro I 106 A2
Paliouri GR 116 C5
Paliseul B 59 A6
Pallanza I 70 C3
Pallares E 99 A4
Pallaruelo de Monegros E 90 B2
Pallas Green IRL 20 B3
Pallerols E 91 A4
Palling D 62 B3
Palluau F 66 B3
Palma P 92 C2
Palma Campánia I 103 C7
Palma del Río E 99 B5
Palma de Mallorca I 97 B2
Palma di Montechiaro I 108 B2
Palmádula I 110 B1
Palmanova I 72 C3
Palma Nova E 97 B2
Palmela P 92 C2
Palmerola E 91 A5
Palmi I 106 C2
Pälmonostora H 75 B4
Palo del Colle I 104 B2
Palojoensuu FIN 113 D12
Palomares E 101 B4
Palomares del Campo E 95 C4
Palomas E 93 C4
Palombara Sabina I 102 A5
Palos de la Frontera E 99 B4
Palotaboszok H 74 B3
Palotás H 65 C5
Pals E 91 B6
Pålsboda S 37 C2
Paluzza I 72 B3
Pamhagen A 64 C2
Pamiers F 77 C4
Pamiętowo PL 46 B3
Pampaneira E 100 C2
Pamparato I 80 B1
Pampilhosa
  Aveiro P 92 A2
  Coimbra P 92 A3
Pampliega E 88 B3
Pamplona E 76 D1
Pampow D 44 B3
Pamukçu TR 118 C2
Pamukkale TR 119 E4
Pamukova TR 118 B5
Panagyurishte BG 11 E8
Pancalieri I 80 B1
Pančevo SRB 85 B5
Pancey F 59 B6
Pancorvo E 89 B3
Pancrudo E 90 C1
Pandino I 71 C4
Pandrup DK 38 B2
Panenský-Tynec CZ 53 C3
Panes E 88 A2
Panevėžys LT 6 D8
Pangbourne GB 31 C2
Panissières F 69 C4
Paniki PL 54 C3
Pannes F 58 B3
Panningen NL 50 B1
Pannonhalma H 74 A2
Pano Lefkara CY 120 B2
Pano Panayia CY 120 B1
Panormos GR 117 E7
Panschwitz-Kuckau D 53 B4
Pansdorf D 44 B2
Pantano de Cijara E 94 C2
Pantelleria I 108 C1
Panticosa E 76 D2
Pantín E 86 A2
Pantoja E 94 B3
Pantón E 86 B3
Panxon E 87 B2
Páola I 106 B3
Paola M 107 C5
Pápa H 74 A2
Papasídero I 106 B2
Pápateszér H 74 A2
Papenburg D 43 B4
Pappenheim D 62 B1
Paprotnia PL 55 A5
Parábita I 107 A5
Parácin SRB 85 C6
Parád H 65 C6
Parada
  Bragança P 87 C4
  Viseu P 92 A2
Paradas E 99 B5
Paradela P 87 C3
Parades de Rubiales E 94 A1
Paradinas de San Juan E 94 B1
Paradiso di Cevadale I 71 B5
Paradyż PL 55 B5
Parainen FIN 6 A7

Parakhino Paddubye RUS 7 B12
Parakka S 113 E10
Paralimni CY 120 A2
Parallo Astros GR 117 E4
Paramé F 57 B4
Paramithia GR 116 C2
Páramo E 86 A4
Páramo del Sil E 86 B4
Parandaça P 87 C3
Paravadella E 86 A3
Paray-le-Monial F 68 B4
Parceiros P 92 B2
Parcey F 69 A5
Parchim D 44 B3
Parcice PL 54 B3
Pardilla E 88 C3
Pardubice CZ 53 C5
Paredes
  E 95 B4
  P 87 C2
Paredes de Coura P 87 C2
Paredes de Nava E 88 B2
Paredes de Siguenza E 95 A4
Pareja E 95 B4
Parennes F 57 B5
Parenti I 106 B3
Parentis-en-Born F 76 B1
Parey D 44 C3
Parfino RUS 7 C11
Parga GR 116 C2
Pargny-sur-Saulx F 59 B5
Pari-Gagné F 69 B4
Parigné-l'Évêque F 58 C1
Parikkala FIN 3 F28
Paris F 58 B3
Parisot F 77 B4
Parkalompolo S 113 E11
Parkano FIN 3 E25
Parknasilla IRL 20 C2
Parla E 94 B3
Parlavà E 91 A6
Parma I 81 B4
Parndorf A 64 C2
Párnica SK 65 A5
Pärnu EST 6 B8
Parolis E 101 A3
Paros GR 117 E7
Parsberg D 62 A2
Parstein D 45 C6
Partakko FIN 113 C16
Partanna I 108 B1
Parthenay F 67 B4
Partinico I 108 A2
Partizani SRB 85 B5
Partizánske SK 65 B4
Partney GB 27 B6
Pärýd S 40 C5
Parýsów PL 55 B6
Parzymiechy PL 54 B3
Pascani RO 11 C9
Pasewalk D 45 B5
Pašina Voda MNE 85 C4
Påskallavik S 40 B6
Paşköy TR 47 A5
Pašman HR 83 C4
Passage East IRL 21 B5
Passail A 73 A5
Passais F 57 B5
Passau D 63 B4
Passignano sul Trasimeno I 82 C1
Passo di Tréia I 82 C2
Passopisciaro I 109 B3
Passow D 45 B6
Passy F 70 C1
Pastavy BY 7 D9
Pástena I 103 B7
Pastrana E 95 B4
Pastrengo I 71 C5
Pásztó H 65 C5
Pata SK 64 B3
Patay F 58 B2
Pateley Bridge GB 27 A4
Paterek P 46 B3
Paterna E 96 B2
Paterna del Campo E 99 B4
Paterna del Madera E 101 A3
Paterna de Rivera E 99 C5
Paternion A 72 B3
Paternò I 109 B3
Paternopoli I 103 C8
Patersdorf D 62 A3
Paterswolde NL 42 B3
Patitiri GR 116 C5
Patmos GR 119 E1
Patna GB 24 C3
Patnow PL 54 A3
Patoniva FIN 113 C16
Patopirti FIN 113 E18
Patos AL 105 C5
Patos = Patras GR 117 D3
Patras = Patra GR 117 D3
Patreksfjörður IS 111 B2
Patrickswell IRL 20 B3
Patrimonio F 102 A2
Pattada I 110 B2
Pattensen
  Niedersachsen D 44 B2
  Niedersachsen D 51 A5
Patterdale GB 26 A3
Patti I 109 A3
Páty H 74 A3
Pau F 76 C2
Pauillac F 66 C4
Paularo I 72 B3
Paulhaguet F 68 C3
Paulhan F 78 C2
Paulilátino I 110 B2
Pauliström S 40 B5
Paullo I 71 C4
Paulstown IRL 21 B4
Pausa D 52 C2
Pauträsk S 115 C14
Pavia
  I 71 C4
  P 92 C2
Pavias E 96 B2
Pavilly F 58 A1
Pāvilosta LV 6 C6
Pavino Polje MNE 85 C4
Pavullo nel Frignano I 81 B4
Pawłowice PL 54 B2
Pawłowiczki PL 54 C2
Paxi GR 116 C2
Payallar TR 119 F6
Payerne CH 70 B1
Paymogo E 98 B3
Payrac F 77 B4
Pazardzhik BG 11 E8
Pazaryeri TR 118 C4
Pazin HR 72 C3
Paziols F 78 D1
Pčelić HR 74 C2
Peal de Becerro E 100 B2
Peasmarsh GB 31 D4
Peć KOS 85 D5
Péccioli I 81 C4
Pécel H 75 A4
Pechao P 98 B3
Pechenga RUS 3 B29
Pechenizhyn UA 11 B8
Pecica RO 75 B6
Pećinci SRB 85 B4
Pecka SRB 85 B4
Peckelsheim D 51 B5
Pečory RUS 7 C9
Pécs H 74 B3
Pécsvárad H 74 B3
Pečurice MNE 105 A5
Pedaso I 82 C2
Pedavena I 72 B1
Pédérobba I 72 C1

Pedersker DK 41 D4
Pedescala I 71 C6
Pedrafita E 86 B3
Pedrajas de San Esteban E 88 C2
Pedralba E 96 B2
Pedralba de la Pradería E 87 B4
Pedraza E 94 A3
Pedreguer E 96 C3
Pedredo E 100 B1
Pedro Abad E 100 B1
Pedro Bernardo E 94 B2
Pedroche E 100 A1
Pedrógão
  P 98 A3
  P 92 A3
Pedrógão Grande P 92 B2
Pedrola E 90 B1
Pedro-Martinez E 100 B2
Pedro Muñoz E 95 C4
Pedrosa del Rey E 88 C1
Pedrosa del Rio Urbel E 88 B3
Pedrosa de Tobalina E 89 B3
Pedrosillo de los Aires E 94 B1
Pedrosillo el Ralo E 94 A1
Pędzewo PL 47 B4
Peebles GB 25 C4
Peel GB 26 A1
Peenemünde D 45 A5
Peer B 49 B6
Pega P 93 A3
Pegalajar E 100 B2
Pegau D 52 B2
Peggau A 73 A5
Pegli I 80 B2
Pegnitz D 62 A2
Pego
  E 96 C2
Pegões-Estação P 92 C2
Pegões Velhos P 92 C2
Pegow PL 54 B1
Pegswood GB 25 C6
Peguera E 97 B2
Pehlivanköy TR 118 A1
Peine D 51 A6
Peisey-Nancroix F 70 C1
Peissenberg D 62 C2
Peiting D 62 C1
Peitz D 53 B4
Péjo I 71 B5
Pelagićevo BIH 84 B3
Pelahustán E 94 B2
Pełczyce PL 46 B1
Pelkosenniemi FIN 113 E16
Pellegrino Parmense I 81 B3
Pellegrue F 76 B3
Pellérd H 74 B3
Pellestrina I 72 C2
Pellevoisin F 67 B6
Pellizzano I 71 B5
Pello
  FIN 113 F13
  S 113 F13
Peloche E 93 B5
Pelplin PL 47 B4
Pelussin F 69 C4
Pély H 75 A5
Pembroke GB 28 B3
Pembroke Dock GB 28 B3
Peñacerrada E 89 B4
Penacova P 92 A2
Peña de Cabra E 94 B1
Peñafiel
  E 88 C2
  P 87 C2
Peñaflor E 99 B5
Peñalba de Santiago E 86 B4
Peñalén E 95 B5
Peñalsordo E 93 C5
Penalva do Castelo P 92 A3
Penamacôr P 93 A3
Peñaparda E 93 A4
Peñaranda de Bracamonte E 94 B1
Peñaranda de Duero E 89 C3
Peñarroya de Tastavins E 90 C3
Peñarroya-Pueblonuevo E 99 A5
Peñarrubia E 86 B3
Penarth GB 29 B4
Peñascosa E 101 A3
Peñas de San Pedro E 101 A4
Peñausende E 88 C1
Penc H 65 C5
Pencoed GB 29 B4
Pendalofos GR 116 B3
Pendeen GB 28 C2
Pendine GB 28 B3
Pendueles E 88 A2
Penedono P 87 D3
Penela P 92 A2
Pénestin F 56 C3
Penha Juntas P 87 C3
Peniche P 92 B1
Penicuik GB 25 C4
Penig D 52 C2
Penilhos P 98 B3
Peñíscola E 90 C3
Penistone GB 27 B4
Penkridge GB 26 C3
Penkun D 45 B6
Penmarch F 56 C1
Pennabilli I 82 C1
Penne
  F 77 B4
  I 103 A6
Penne-d'Agenais F 77 B3
Pennes F 71 B6
Pennyghael GB 24 B1
Penpont GB 25 C4
Penrhyndeudraeth GB 26 C1
Penrith GB 26 A3
Penryn GB 28 C2
Pentraeth GB 26 B1
Penybontfawr GB 26 C2
Penygroes
  Carmarthenshire GB 28 B3
  Gwynedd GB 26 B1
Penzance GB 28 C2
Penzberg D 62 C2
Penzlin D 45 B5
Pepelow D 44 A3
Pepinster B 50 C1
Peqin AL 105 B5
Pera Boa P 92 A3
Perachora GR 117 D4
Perafita P 87 C2
Peral P 92 B3
Perales del Alfambra E 90 C1
Perales del Puerto E 93 A4
Perales de Tajuña E 95 B3
Peralta E 89 B5
Peralta de la Sal E 90 B3
Peralva P 98 B3
Peralveche E 95 B5
Pérama GR 117 G6
Perast MNE 105 A4
Peratallada E 91 B6
Percy F 57 B4
Perdasdefogu I 110 C2
Perdiguera E 90 B2
Peredo P 87 C4
Pereğu Mare RO 75 B5
Pereiro
  Faro P 98 B3
  Guarda P 87 D3

Pereiro continued
  Santarém P 92 B2
Pereiro de Aguiar E 87 B3
Pereruela E 88 C1
Perelada E 91 A4
Perelejos de las Truchas E 95 B5
Pereña E 87 C4
Pereyaslav-Khmelnytskyy UA 11 A11
Pérfugas I 110 B1
Perg A 63 B5
Pérgine Valsugana I 71 B6
Pérgola I 82 C1
Pergusa I 109 B3
Periam RO 75 B5
Periana E 100 C1
Périers F 57 A4
Périgueux F 67 C5
Perino I 80 B3
Perjasica HR 73 C5
Perkáta H 74 A3
Perković HR 83 C5
Perleberg D 44 B3
Perlez SRB 75 C5
Përmet AL 116 B2
Pernarec CZ 62 A4
Pernek SK 64 B3
Pernes P 92 B2
Pernes-les-Fontaines F 79 B4
Pernik BG 11 E7
Pernink CZ 52 C2
Pernitz A 64 C1
Pernu FIN 113 F16
Peroguarda P 98 A2
Pérols F 78 C2
Péronne F 59 A3
Péronnes B 49 C5
Perosa Argentina I 79 B6
Perozinho P 87 C2
Perpignan F 91 A5
Perranporth GB 28 C2
Perranzabuloe GB 28 C2
Perrecy-les-Forges F 68 B4
Perrero I 79 B6
Perrignier F 69 B6
Perros-Guirec F 56 B2
Persan F 58 A3
Persberg S 34 C6
Persenbeug A 63 B6
Pershore GB 29 A5
Perstorp S 41 C3
Perth GB 25 B4
Pertisau A 72 A1
Pertoča SLO 73 B6
Pertuis F 79 C4
Perúćac SRB 85 C4
Perúgia I 82 C1
Perušić HR 83 B4
Péruwelz B 49 C4
Pervomaysk UA 11 B11
Perwez B 49 C5
Pesadas de Burgos E 89 B3
Pesaguero E 88 A2
Pésaro I 82 C1
Pescantina I 71 C5
Pescara I 103 A7
Pescasséroli I 103 B6
Peschici I 104 B2
Peschiera del Garda I 71 C5
Péscia I 81 C4
Pescina I 103 A6
Pescocostanzo I 103 B7
Pescopagano I 103 C8
Pesco Sannita I 103 B7
Peshkopi AL 116 A2
Pesmes F 69 A5
Pesnica SLO 73 B5
Peso da Régua P 87 C2
Pesquera de Duero E 88 C2
Pessac F 76 B2
Pestovo RUS 7 B13
Petalidi GR 117 F3
Pétange L 60 A1
Petas GR 116 C3
Peteranec HR 74 B1
Peterborough GB 30 B3
Peterculter GB 23 D6
Peterhead GB 23 D7
Peterlee GB 25 D6
Petersfield GB 31 C3
Petershagen
  Brandenburg D 45 C5
  Brandenburg D 45 C6
  Nordrhein-Westfalen D 43 C5
Petershausen D 62 B2
Peterswell IRL 20 A3
Pétervására H 65 B6
Petília Policastro I 107 B3
Petin E 87 B3
Pětipsy CZ 52 C3
Petkus D 52 B3
Petlovac HR 74 C3
Petlovača SRB 85 B4
Petöfiszállás H 75 B4
Petra E 97 B3
Petralia Sottana I 109 B3
Petrčane HR 83 B4
Petrella Tifernina I 103 B7
Petrer E 96 C2
Petreto-Bicchisano F 102 B1
Petrich BG 116 A5
Petrijevci HR 74 C3
Petrinja HR 73 C6
Petrodvorets RUS 7 B10
Pétrola E 101 A4
Petronà I 107 B3
Petronell A 64 B2
Petroşani RO 11 D7
Petrovac
  MNE 105 A4
  SRB 85 B6
Petrovaradin SRB 75 C4
Petrovice
  BIH 84 B3
  CZ 53 C4
Pettenbach A 63 C5
Pettigo IRL 19 B4
Petworth GB 31 D3
Peuerbach A 63 B4
Peuntenansa E 88 A3
Peurasuvanto FIN 113 E15
Pevensey Bay GB 31 D4
Peveragno I 80 B1
Pewsey GB 29 B6
Pewsum D 43 B4
Peymeinade F 79 C5
Peyrat-le-Château F 68 C1
Peyrehorade F 76 C1
Peyriac-Minervois F 78 C1
Peyrins F 79 A4
Peyrissac F 67 C6
Peyrolles-en-Provence F 79 C4
Peyruis F 79 B4
Pézarches F 59 B3
Pézenas F 78 C2
Pezinok SK 64 B3
Pezuls F 77 B3
Pfaffenhausen D 61 B6
Pfaffenhofen
  Bayern D 61 B6
  Bayern D 62 B2
Pfaffenhoffen F 60 B3
Pfäffikon CH 70 A3
Pfarrkirchen D 62 B3
Pfeffenhausen D 62 B2
Pforzheim D 61 B4
Pfreimd D 62 A3
Pfronten D 62 C1
Pfullendorf D 61 C5
Pfullingen D 61 B5
Pfunds A 71 B5
Pfungstadt D 61 A4
Pfyn CH 61 C4
Phalsbourg F 60 B3
Philippeville B 49 C5

Philippsreut D 63 B4
Philippsthal D 51 C5
Piacenza I 81 A3
Piacenza d'Adige I 72 C1
Piádena I 71 C5
Piana F 102 A1
Piana Crixia I 80 B2
Piana degli Albanesi I 108 B2
Piana di Monte Verna I 103 B7
Piancastagnáio I 81 D5
Piandelagotti I 81 B4
Pianella
  Abruzzi I 103 A7
  Toscana I 81 C5
Pianello Val Tidone I 80 B3
Pianoro I 81 B5
Pians A 71 A5
Pias
  E 87 B4
  P 98 A3
Piaseczno PL 55 A6
Piasek PL 45 C6
Piaski PL 47 C5
Piastów PL 55 A5
Piaszczyna PL 46 A3
Piatek PL 55 A4
Piatra Neamţ RO 11 C9
Piazza al Sérchio I 81 B4
Piazza Armerina I 109 B3
Piazza Brembana I 71 C4
Piazze I 81 D5
Piazzola sul Brenta I 72 C1
Picassent E 96 B2
Piccione I 82 C1
Picerno I 104 C1
Picher D 44 B3
Pickering GB 27 A5
Pico I 103 B6
Picón E 94 C2
Picquigny F 58 A3
Piechowice PL 53 C5
Piecnik PL 46 B2
Piedicavallo I 70 C2
Piedicroce F 102 A2
Piediluco I 102 A5
Piedimonte Etneo I 109 B4
Piedimonte Matese I 103 B7
Piedimulera I 70 B3
Piedipaterno I 82 D1
Piedrabuena E 94 C2
Piedraescrita E 94 C2
Piedrafita E 88 A1
Piedrahita E 93 A5
Piedralaves E 94 B2
Piedras Albas E 93 B4
Piedras Blancas E 88 A1
Piegaro I 82 D1
Piekary Śl. PL 54 C3
Piekoszów PL 55 C5
Pieksämäki FIN 3 E27
Pielenhofen D 62 A2
Pielgrzymka PL 53 B5
Pieniężno PL 47 A6
Pieńsk PL 53 B5
Pienza I 81 C5
Piera E 91 B4
Pieranie I 47 C4
Pierowall GB 23 B6
Pierre-Buffière F 67 C6
Pierre-de-Bresse F 69 B5
Pierrefeu-du-Var F 79 C5
Pierrefitte-Nestalas F 76 D2
Pierrefitte-sur-Aire F 59 B6
Pierrefonds F 59 A3
Pierrefontaine-les-Varans F 69 A6
Pierrefort F 78 B1
Pierrelatte F 78 B3
Pierrepont
  Aisne F 59 A4
  Meurthe-et-Moselle F 60 A1
Piesendorf A 72 A2
Pieštany SK 64 B3
Pieszkowo PL 47 A6
Pieszyce PL 54 C1
Pietarsaari FIN 3 E25
Pietragalla I 104 C1
Pietra Ligure I 80 B2
Pietralunga I 82 C1
Pietramelara I 103 B7
Pietraperzía I 109 B3
Pietrasanta I 81 C4
Pietravairano I 103 B7
Pieve del Cáiro I 80 A2
Pieve di Bono I 71 C5
Pieve di Cadore I 72 B2
Pieve di Cento I 81 B5
Pieve di Soligo I 72 C2
Pieve di Teco I 80 B1
Pievepélago I 81 B4
Pieve Santo Stefano I 82 C1
Pieve Torina I 82 C2
Piges GR 116 C3
Pigna I 80 C1
Pignan F 78 C2
Pignataro Maggiore I 103 B7
Pijnacker NL 49 A5
Pikalevo RUS 7 B13
Pila
  I 72 C2
  PL 46 B2
Piła PL 46 B2
Pilar de la Horadada E 96 C2
Pilas E 99 B4
Pilastri I 81 B5
Piława Górna PL 54 C1
Piławki PL 47 B5
Pilchowice PL 54 C3
Pilés GR 119 F3
Pilgrimstad S 115 E12
Pili
  Dodekanisa GR 119 F2
  Trikala GR 116 C3
Pilica PL 55 C4
Pilis H 75 A4
Piliscaba H 65 C4
Pilisszántó H 65 C4
Pilisvörösvár H 65 C4
Pilos GR 117 F3
Pilsting D 62 B3
Pilszcz PL 54 C2
Pilterud N 34 C2
Pilu RO 75 B6
Pilzno PL 55 D6
Pina de Ebro E 90 B2
Pinar E 100 B2
Pınarbaşı TR 118 C1
Pınarhisar TR 118 A2
Pinas F 77 C3
Pincehely H 74 B3
Pinchbeck GB 30 B3
Pineda de la Sierra E 89 B3
Pineda de Mar E 91 B5
Pinerolo I 79 B6
Pineta Grande I 103 B6
Pineto I 103 A7
Piney F 59 B5
Pinggau A 73 A6
Pınhal Novo P 92 C2
Pinhão P 87 C3
Pinheiro
  Aveiro P 87 C2
  Aveiro P 87 D2
Pinheiro Grande P 92 B2
Pinhel P 93 A3
Pinhoe GB 29 C4
Pinilla de Toro E 88 C1
Pinkafeld A 73 A6
Pinneberg D 43 B6
Pinnow D 45 B5
Pino
  F 102 A2
  E 87 B3
Pino del Rio E 88 B2
Pino de Val E 86 B2
Pinofranqueado E 93 A4
Pinols F 78 A2
Piñor E 87 B2
Pinos del Valle E 100 C2

Pinoso E 101 A4
Pinos Puente E 100 B2
Pinsk BY 7 E9
Pinto E 94 B3
Pinzano al Tagliamento I 72 B2
Pinzio P 93 A3
Pinzolo I 71 B5
Pióbbico I 82 C1
Piombino I 81 D4
Pionki PL 55 B6
Pionsat F 68 B2
Pióraco I 82 C1
Piornal E 93 A5
Piotrkowice PL 55 C5
Piotrków-Kujawski PL 47 C4
Piotrków Trybunalski PL 55 B4
Piotrowo PL 46 C2
Piove di Sacco I 72 C2
Piovene I 71 C6
Piperskärr S 40 B6
Pipriac F 57 C4
Piraeus = Pireas GR 117 E5
Piran SLO 72 C3
Pireas = Piraeus GR 117 E5
Piré-sur-Seiche F 57 B4
Pirgi GR 117 D7
Pirgos
  Ilia GR 117 E3
  Kriti GR 117 G7
Piriac-sur-Mer F 66 A2
Piringsdorf A 73 A6
Pirmasens D 60 A3
Pirna D 53 C3
Pirnmill GB 24 C2
Pirot SRB 11 E7
Pirovac HR 83 C4
Pirttivuopio S 112 E8
Pisa I 81 C4
Pisany F 66 C4
Pisarovina HR 73 C5
Pischelsdorf in der Steiermark A 73 A5
Pişchia RO 75 C6
Pisciotta I 106 A2
Písek CZ 63 A5
Pisogne I 71 C5
Pissos F 76 B2
Pissouri CY 120 B1
Pisticci I 104 C2
Pistóia I 81 C4
Piteå S 3 D24
Pitesti RO 11 D8
Pithiviers F 58 B3
Pitigliano I 102 A4
Pitkyaranta RUS 3 F29
Pitlochry GB 25 B4
Pitomača HR 74 C2
Pitres E 100 C2
Pittentrail GB 23 D4
Pitvaros H 75 B5
Pivka SLO 73 C4
Pivnice SRB 75 C4
Piwniczna PL 65 A6
Pizarra E 100 C1
Pizzano I 71 B5
Pizzighettone I 71 C4
Pizzo I 106 C3
Pízzoli I 103 A6
Pizzolungo I 108 A1
Pjätteryd S 40 C4
Plabennec F 56 B1
Placencia E 89 A4
Plaffeien CH 70 B2
Plaisance
  Gers F 76 C3
  Haute-Garonne F 77 C4
  Tarn F 77 C5
Plan E 90 A3
Planá CZ 62 A3
Planá nad Lužnicí CZ 63 A5
Plaňany CZ 53 C5
Planchez F 68 A4
Plancoët F 57 B3
Plancy-l'Abbaye F 59 B4
Plan-de-Baix F 79 B4
Plandište SRB 75 C5
Plan-d'Orgon F 79 C3
Plánice CZ 63 A4
Planina
  SLO 73 B5
  SLO 73 C4
Plankenfels D 62 A2
Plasencia E 93 A4
Plasenzuela E 93 B4
Plaški HR 83 A4
Plassen
  Buskerud N 32 B4
  Hedmark N 34 A4
Plášťovce SK 65 B5
Plasy CZ 63 A4
Platamona Lido I 110 B1
Platania I 106 B3
Platanos GR 117 G5
Plati I 106 C3
Platičevo SRB 85 B4
Platja d'Aro E 91 B6
Plattling D 62 B3
Plau D 44 B4
Plaue
  Brandenburg D 44 C4
  Thüringen D 51 C6
Plauen D 52 C2
Plavecký Mikuláš SK 64 B3
Plavinas LV 7 C8
Plavna SRB 85 B6
Plavnica SK 65 A6
Plavno HR 83 B5
Plavsk RUS 7 E14
Playben F 56 B2
Pléaux F 68 C2
Pléine-Fougères F 57 B4
Pleinfeld D 62 A1
Pleinting D 62 B3
Pléneuf-Val-André F 57 B3
Plentzia E 89 A4
Plérin F 56 B3
Plešivec SK 65 B6
Plessala F 56 B3
Plessé F 66 A3
Plestin-les-Grèves F 56 B2
Pleszew PL 54 B2
Pleternica HR 74 C2
Plettenberg D 50 B3
Pleubian F 56 B2
Pleumartin F 67 B5
Pleumeur-Bodou F 56 B2
Pleurs F 59 B4
Pleven BG 11 E8
Plevlja MNE 85 C4
Plevnik-Drienové SK 65 A4
Pleyber-Christ F 56 B2
Pliego E 101 B4
Pliešovce SK 65 B5
Plitvička Jezera HR 83 B4
Plitvički Ljeskovac HR 83 B4
Ploaghe I 110 B1
Ploče HR 84 C2
Plochingen D 61 B5
Płock PL 47 C5
Ploemeur F 56 C2
Ploërmel F 56 C3
Plœuc-sur-Lié F 56 B3
Plogastel St Germain F 56 B1
Plogoff F 56 B1
Ploiesti RO 11 D9
Plomari GR 118 D1
Plombières-les-Bains F 60 C2
Plomin HR 82 A3
Plön D 44 A2
Plonéour-Lanvern F 56 B1

Płonia PL 45 B6
Płonsk PL 47 C6
Płoskinia PL 47 A5
Plössberg D 62 A3
Ploty PL 45 B7
Plouagat F 56 B2
Plouaret F 56 B2
Plouarzel F 56 B1
Plouay F 56 C2
Ploubalay F 57 B3
Ploubazlanec F 56 B2
Ploudalmézeau F 56 B1
Ploudiry F 56 B1
Plouescat F 56 B1
Plouézec F 56 B3
Plougasnou F 56 B2
Plougastel-Daoulas F 56 B1
Plougonven F 56 B2
Plougonver F 56 B2
Plougrescant F 56 B2
Plouguenast F 56 B3
Plouguerneau F 56 B1
Plouha F 56 B3
Plouhinec F 56 B1
Plouigneau F 56 B2
Ploumanach F 56 B2
Plounévez-Quintin F 56 B2
Plouray F 56 B2
Plouzévédé F 56 B1
Plovdiv BG 11 E8
Plozévet F 56 C1
Plumbridge GB 19 B4
Pluméliau F 56 C3
Plumlov CZ 64 A3
Plungė LT 6 D7
Pluty PL 47 A6
Pluvigner F 56 C3
Plužine
  BIH 84 C3
  MNE 84 C3
Plymouth GB 28 C3
Plymstock GB 28 C3
Plytnica PL 46 B2
Plyusa RUS 7 B10
Pniewy PL 46 C2
Pobběžovice CZ 62 A3
Pobiedziska PL 46 C3
Pobierowo PL 45 A6
Pobla de Segur E 90 A3
Pobladura del Valle E 88 B1
Pobla-Tornesa E 96 A3
Pobla de Trives E 87 B3
Pobla do Brollón E 86 B3
Pobra do Caramiñal E 86 B2
Pobudje BIH 84 B3
Počátky CZ 63 A6
Poceirão P 92 C2
Pochep RUS 7 E12
Pochinok RUS 7 D12
Pöchlarn A 63 B6
Pociecha PL 55 B5
Pockau D 52 C3
Pocking D 63 B4
Pocklington GB 27 B5
Podari RO 11 D7
Podbořany CZ 52 C3
Podbrdo SLO 72 B3
Podbrezová SK 65 B5
Podčetrtek SLO 73 B5
Poddębice PL 54 B3
Poděbrady CZ 53 C5
Podence P 87 C4
Podensac F 76 B2
Podenzano I 81 B3
Podersdorf am See A 64 C2
Podgaje PL 46 B2
Podgora HR 84 C2
Podgóra PL 55 B6
Podgorač HR 74 C3
Podgorica MNE 105 A5
Podgorie AL 116 B2
Podgrad SLO 73 C4
Podhájska SK 64 B4
Podkova BG 116 A7
Podlapača HR 83 B4
Podlejki PL 47 B6
Podnovlje BIH 84 B3
Podolie SK 64 B3
Podolínec SK 65 A6
Podolsk RUS 7 D14
Podporozhy RUS 7 A13
Podromanija BIH 84 C3
Podturen HR 73 B6
Podvelež BIH 84 C3
Podvinje HR 84 B3
Podwilk PL 65 A5
Poetto I 110 C2
Poggendorf D 45 A5
Poggiardo I 107 A5
Póggio a Caiano I 81 C5
Poggibonsi I 81 C5
Póggio Imperiale I 103 B8
Póggio Mirteto I 102 A5
Póggio Moiano I 102 A5
Póggio Renatico I 81 B5
Póggio Rusco I 81 B5
Pöggstall A 63 B6
Pogny F 59 B5
Pogorzela PL 54 B2
Pogorzelice PL 46 A3
Pogradec AL 116 B2
Pohorelá SK 65 B6
Pohořelice CZ 64 B2
Pohronská Polhora SK 65 B5
Poiares P 92 A2
Poio E 86 B2
Poirino I 80 B1
Poisson F 68 B4
Poissons F 59 B6
Poissy F 58 B3
Poitiers F 67 B5
Poix-de-Picardie F 58 A2
Poix-Terron F 59 A5
Pokka FIN 113 D14
Pokój PL 54 C2
Pokupsko HR 73 C5
Pol E 86 A3
Pola RUS 7 C11
Pola de Allande E 86 A4
Pola de Laviana E 88 A1
Pola de Lena E 88 A1
Pola de Siero E 88 A1
Pola de Somiedo E 86 A4
Polaincourt-et-Clairefontaine F 60 C2
Polán E 94 C2
Polanica-Zdrój PL 54 C1
Połaniec PL 55 C6
Polanów PL 46 A2
Polati TR 118 C7
Polatsk BY 7 D10
Polch D 50 C3
Polczno PL 46 A3
Połczyn-Zdrój PL 46 B1
Polegate GB 31 D4
Poleñino E 90 B2
Polesella I 81 B5
Polessk RUS 6 D6
Polgár H 65 C6
Polgárdi H 74 A3
Polhov Gradec SLO 73 B4
Police
  PL 45 B6
Police nad Metují CZ 53 C6
Polička CZ 53 D6
Poličnik HR 83 B4
Policoro I 106 A3
Policzna PL 55 B6
Poligiros GR 116 B5
Polignano a Mare I 104 C3
Poligny F 69 B5
Polis CY 120 A1
Polístena I 106 C3
Polizzi Generosa I 109 B3

Poljana SRB 85 B6
Poljanák HR 83 B4
Poljčane SLO 73 B5
Polje
  BIH 83 B5
  BIH 84 B3
Poljna SRB 85 C6
Polkowice PL 53 B6
Polla I 104 C1
Pollas E 88 C1
Pöllau A 73 A5
Polleben D 52 B1
Pollença E 97 B3
Pollenfeld D 62 B2
Pollfoss N 114 F4
Póllica I 106 A2
Polminhac F 77 B5
Polná CZ 63 A6
Polna RUS 7 B10
Polomka SK 65 B5
Polonne UA 11 A9
Polperro GB 28 C3
Polruan GB 28 C3
Pöls A 73 A4
Polska Cerekiew PL 54 C3
Poltár SK 65 B5
Põltsamaa EST 7 B8
Polyarny RUS 3 B30
Polyarnyye Zori RUS 3 C30
Polzela SLO 73 B5
Pomarance I 81 C4
Pomarez F 76 C2
Pomárico I 104 C2
Pomáz H 65 C5
Pombal P 92 B2
Pomeroy GB 19 B5
Pomézia I 102 B5
Pomichna UA 11 B11
Pommard F 69 A4
Pommelsbrunn D 62 A2
Pomonte I 81 D4
Pomorie BG 11 E9
Pomos CY 120 A1
Pompei I 103 C7
Pompey F 60 B2
Pomposa I 82 B1
Poncin F 69 B5
Pondorf D 62 B2
Ponferrada E 86 B4
Poniec PL 54 B1
Ponikva SLO 73 B5
Poniky SK 65 B5
Pons F 67 C4
Ponsacco I 81 C4
Pont F 70 C2
Ponta-Celles B 49 C5
Pontacq F 76 C2
Pontailler-sur-Saône F 69 A5
Pont-a-Marcq F 49 C4
Pont-a-Mousson F 60 B2
Pontardawe GB 28 B4
Pontarddulais GB 28 B3
Pontarion F 68 C1
Pontarlier F 69 B6
Pontassieve I 81 C5
Pontaubault F 57 B4
Pont-Audemer F 58 A1
Pontaumur F 68 C2
Pont-Aven F 56 C2
Pont Canavese I 70 C2
Pontcharra-sur-Turdine F 69 C4
Pontchâteau F 66 A2
Pont-Croix F 56 B1
Pont-d'Ain F 69 B5
Pont-de-Beauvoisin F 69 C5
Pont-de-Buis-lès-Quimerch F 56 B1
Pont-de-Chéruy F 69 C5
Pont de Dore F 68 C3
Pont-de-Labeaume F 78 B3
Pont-de-l'Arche F 58 A2
Pont-de-Molins E 91 A5
Pont-de-Roide F 70 A1
Pont-de-Salars F 78 B1
Pont-d'Espagne F 76 D2
Pont de Suert E 90 A3
Pont-de-Vaux F 69 B4
Pont-de-Veyle F 69 B4
Pont d'Ouilly F 57 B5
Pont-du-Château F 68 C3
Pont-du-Navoy F 69 B5
Ponte a Moriano I 81 C4
Ponte Arche I 71 B5
Ponteareas E 87 B2
Pontebba I 72 B3
Ponte Caffaro I 71 C5
Pontecagnano I 103 C7
Ponte-Caldelas E 87 B2
Ponteceso E 86 A2
Pontecorvo I 103 B6
Ponte da Barca P 87 C2
Pontedássio I 80 C2
Pontedécimo I 80 B2
Ponte de Lima P 87 C2
Ponte dell'Ólio I 80 B3
Pontedera I 81 C4
Ponte de Sor P 92 B3
Pontedeume E 86 A2
Ponte di Barbarano I 72 C1
Ponte di Legno I 71 B5
Ponte di Nava I 80 B1
Ponte di Piave I 72 C2
Ponte Felcino I 82 C1
Pontefract GB 27 B4
Ponte Gardena I 71 B6
Pontelagoscuro I 81 B5
Ponteland GB 25 C6
Pontelandolfo I 103 B7
Ponte-Leccia F 102 A2
Pontelongo I 72 C2
Ponte nelle Alpi I 72 B2
Pont-en-Royans F 79 A4
Pontenure I 81 B3
Ponte San Giovanni I 82 C1
Ponte San Pietro I 71 C4
Pontevedra E 87 B2
Pontevico I 71 C5
Pontfaverger-Moronvillers F 59 A5
Pontgibaud F 68 C2
Ponticino I 81 C5
Pontigny F 59 C4
Pontijou F 58 C2
Pontínia I 102 B6
Pontinvrea I 80 B2
Pontivy F 56 B3
Pont-l'Abbé F 56 C1
Pont-l'Évêque F 57 A6
Pontlevoy F 58 C2
Pontoise F 58 A3
Pontones E 101 A3
Pontonx-sur-l'Adour F 76 C2
Pontoon IRL 18 C2
Pontorson F 57 B4
Pontrémoli I 81 B3
Pont-Remy F 48 C2
Pontresina CH 71 B4
Pontrhydfendigaid GB 28 A4
Pontrieux F 56 B2
Pontrilas GB 29 B5
Ponts E 91 B4
Ponts-aux-Dames F 59 B3
Pont-Scorff F 56 C2
Pöntsö FIN 113 E13
Pont-Ste Maxence F 58 A3
Pont-St Esprit F 78 B3

Pont-St Mamet F 77 B3
Pont-St Martin
  F 66 A3
  I 70 C2
Pont-St Vincent F 60 B2
Pont-sur-Yonne F 59 B4
Pontvallain F 57 C6
Pontypool GB 29 B4
Pontypridd GB 29 B4
Ponza I 102 C5
Poo E 88 A2
Poole GB 29 C6
Poolewe GB 22 D3
Poperinge B 48 C3
Pópoli I 103 A6
Popovac SRB 85 C6
Popovača HR 74 C1
Popow PL 55 A4
Poppel B 49 B6
Poppenhausen
  Bayern D 51 C6
  Hessen D 51 C5
Poppi I 81 C5
Poprad SK 65 A6
Popučke SRB 85 B4
Pópulo P 87 C3
Populónia I 81 D4
Pórbóly H 74 B3
Porcuna E 100 B1
Pordenone I 72 C2
Pordic F 56 B3
Poręba PL 55 C4
Poreč HR 72 C3
Pori FIN 3 F24
Porjus S 112 F8
Porkhov RUS 7 C10
Porlezza I 71 B4
Porlock GB 29 B4
Pörnbach D 62 B2
Pornic F 66 A2
Pornichet F 66 A2
Porodin SRB 85 B6
Porokhi PL 65 A5
Poros
  Attiki GR 117 E5
  Kefalonia GR 117 D2
Poroszló H 65 C6
Porozina HR 82 A3
Porquerolles F 79 D5
Porrentruy CH 70 A2
Porreres E 97 B3
Porretta Terme I 81 B4
Porsgrunn N 35 C1
Porspoder F 56 B1
Port-a-Binson F 59 A4
Portacloy IRL 18 B2
Portadown GB 19 B5
Portaferry GB 19 B6
Portaje E 93 B4
Portalegre P 92 B3
Portarlington IRL 21 A4
Port Askaig GB 24 C1
Portavadie GB 24 C2
Portavogie GB 19 B6
Portbail F 57 A4
Port Bannatyne GB . . .24 C2
Port-Barcarès F 78 D2
Portbou F 91 A6
Port-Camargue F 78 C3
Port Charlotte GB 24 C1
Port d'Andratx E 97 B2
Port-de-Bouc F 78 C3
Port-de-Lanne F 76 C1
Port de Pollença E 97 B3
Port-des-Barques F 66 C3
Port de Sóller E 97 B2
Portegrandi I 72 C2
Portel P 92 C3
Portela P 92 A2
Port Ellen GB 24 C1
Portelo P 87 C4
Portemouro E 86 B2
Porticcio F 102 B1
Pórtici I 103 C7
Portico di Romagna I . .81 B5
Portilla de la Reina E . .88 A2
Portillo E 88 C2
Portimão P 98 B2
Portinatx E 97 C1
Portinho da Arrabida
  P 92 C1
Port Isaac GB 28 C3
Portishead GB 29 B5
Port-Joinville F 66 B2
Portknockie GB 23 D6
Port-la-Nouvelle F 78 C2
Portlethen GB 23 D6
Port Logan GB 24 D3
Port Louis F 56 C2
Portmagne IRL 20 C1
Portmahomack GB 23 D5
Portman E 101 B5
Port Manech F 56 C2
Portnacroish GB 24 B2
Portnahaven GB 24 C1
Port Nan Giuran GB . . .22 C2
Port-Navalo F 66 A2
Port Nis GB 22 C2
Porto
  F 102 A1
  P 87 C2
Porto-Alto P 92 C2
Porto Azzurro I 81 D4
Portocannone I 103 B8
Porto Cerésio I 70 C3
Porto Cervo I 110 A2
Porto Cesáreo I 107 A4
Porto Colom E 97 B3
Porto Cristo E 97 B3
Porto d'Áscoli I 82 D2
Porto de Lagos P 98 B2
Porto de Mos P 92 B2
Porto de Rei P 92 C2
Porto do Son E 86 B2
Porto Empédocle I . . .108 B2
Portoferráio I 81 D4
Portofino I 80 B3
Porto Garibaldi I 82 B1
Portogruaro I 72 C2
Portokhelion GR 117 E5
Portomaggiore I 81 B5
Portomarin E 86 B3
Porton GB 29 B6
Portopalo di Capo
  Passero I 109 C4
Porto Petro E 97 B3
Porto Pino I 110 D1
Porto Potenza Picena
  I 82 C2
Portør N 33 D6
Porto Recanati I 82 C2
Porto San Giórgio I . . .82 C2
Porto Santo Stéfano
  I 102 A4
Portscuso I 110 C1
Porto Tolle I 82 B1
Porto Tórres I 110 B1
Porto-Vecchio I 102 B2
Portovénere I 81 B3
Portpatrick GB 24 D2
Portreath GB 28 C2
Portree GB 22 D2

Portroe IRL 20 B3
Portrush GB 19 A5
Port St Mary GB 26 A1
Portsall F 56 B1
Portsmouth GB 31 D2
Portsoy GB 23 D6
Port-Ste Marie F 77 B3
Portstewart GB 19 A5
Portugalete E 89 A4
Portumna IRL 20 A3
Port-Vendres F 91 A6
Port William GB 24 D3
Porvoo FIN 7 A8
Porzuna E 94 C2
Posada
  Oviedo E 88 A1
  Oviedo E 88 A2
  I 110 B2
Posada de Valdeón E . .88 A2
Posadas E 99 B5
Poschiavo CH 71 B5
Posedarje HR 83 B4
Positano I 103 C7
Possagno I 72 C1
Posseck D 52 C2
Possesse F 59 B5
Pössneck D 52 C1
Posta I 102 A6
Posta I 71 B6
Posta Piana I 104 B1
Postbauer-Heng D 62 A2
Posterholt NL 50 B2
Postioma I 72 C2
Postira HR 83 C5
Postisna SLO 73 C4
Postoloprty CZ 53 C3
Postomino PL 46 A2
Posušje BIH 84 C2
Potamos
  Attiki GR 117 F4
  Attiki GR 117 G5
Potegowo PL 46 A3
Potenza I 104 C1
Potenza Picena I 82 C2
Potes E 88 A2
Potigny F 57 B5
Potkrajci MNE 85 C4
Potočari BIH 85 B4
Potoci
  BIH 83 B5
  BIH 84 C2
Potony H 74 C2
Potries E 96 C2
Potsdam D 45 C5
Potštát CZ 64 A3
Pottenbrunn A 63 B6
Pottenstein D 62 A2
Pottenstein
  A 64 C2
  D 62 A2
Potters Bar GB 31 C3
Pöttmes D 62 B2
Pöttsching A 64 C2
Potworów PL 55 B5
Pouance F 57 C4
Pougues-les-Eaux F . . .68 A3
Pouilly-en-Auxois F . . .69 A4
Pouilly-sous Charlieu
  F 68 B4
Pouilly-sur-Loire F 68 A3
Poujol-sur-Orb F 78 C2
Poulaouen F 56 B2
Poulton-le-Fylde GB . .26 B3
Poundstock GB 28 C3
Pourcy F 59 A4
Pourrain F 59 C4
Pouyastruc F 76 C3
Pouy-de-Touges F 77 C4
Pouzauges F 66 B4
Pova de Santa Iria P . .92 C1
Považská Bystrica
  SK 65 A4
Povedilla E 101 A3
Povlja HR 84 C1
Povljana HR 83 B4
Póvoa
  Beja P 98 A3
  Santarém P 92 B2
Póvoa de Lanhoso P . .87 C2
Póvoa de Varzim P . . .87 C2
Póvoa e Meadas P . . .92 B3
Powidz PL 46 C3
Poyales del Hoyo E . . .93 A5
Poynton GB 26 B3
Poyntz Pass GB 19 B5
Poysdorf A 64 B2
Poza de la Sal E 89 B3
Pozaldez E 88 C2
Pozán de Vero E 90 A3
Požarevac SRB 85 B6
Požega
  HR 74 C2
  SRB 85 C5
Poznań PL 46 C2
Pozo Alcón E 100 B3
Pozoantiguo E 88 C1
Pozoblanco E 100 A1
Pozo Cañada E 101 A4
Pozo de Guadalajara
  E 95 B3
Pozo de la Serna E . . .100 A3
Pozohondo E 101 A4
Pozondón E 95 B5
Poźrzadło Wielkie
  PL 46 B1
Pozuel del Campo E . . .95 B5
Pozuelo de Alarcón
  E 94 B3
Pozuelo de Calatrava
  E 100 A2
Pozuelo del Páramo
  E 88 B1
Pozuelo de Zarzón E . .93 A4
Pozzallo I 109 C3
Pozzomaggiore I 110 B1
Pozzo San Nicola I . . .110 B1
Pozzuoli I 103 C7
Prabuty PL 47 B5
Prača BIH 84 C3
Prachatice CZ 63 A4
Prada E 87 B3
Pradelle F 79 B4
Pradelles F 78 B2
Prades
  E 90 B3
  F 91 A5
Pradła PL 55 C4
Prado
  E 88 A1
  P 87 C2
Prado del Rey E 99 C5
Pradoluengo E 89 B3
Pragelato I 79 A5
Pragersko SLO 73 B5
Prägraten A 72 A2
Prague = Praha CZ . . .53 C4
Praha = Prague CZ . . .53 C4
Prahecq F 67 B4
Praia P 87 B2
Práia a Mare I 106 B2
Praia da Rocha P 98 B2
Praia da Viera P 92 B2
Praia de Mira P 92 A2
Praiano I 103 C7
Pralboino I 71 C5
Pralognan-la-Vanoise
  F 70 C1
Pramanda GR 116 C3
Pranjani SRB 85 B5
Prapatnica HR 83 C5
Præstø DK 39 D5
Prat F 77 C3
Prata di Pordenone I . .72 C2
Pratau D 52 B2

Prat de Compte E 90 C3
Pratdip E 90 B3
Pratella I 103 B7
Prato I 81 C5
Prátola Peligna I 103 A6
Pratola Serra I 103 C7
Prats-de-Mollo-la-Preste
  F 91 A5
Prauthoy F 59 C6
Pravia E 86 A4
Praxmar A 71 A6
Prayssac F 77 B4
Prazzo I 79 B6
Prchňany BY 6 E8
Pružina SK 65 A4
Préchac F 76 B2
Précy-sur-Thil F 69 A4
Prédáppio I 81 B5
Predazzo I 72 B1
Předin CZ 63 A6
Predosa I 73 A6
Predjame SLO 73 C4
Preditz A 73 A5
Predmeja SLO 72 C3
Predoi I 72 A2
Pre-en-Pail F 57 B5
Prees GB 26 C3
Preetz D 44 A2
Préfailles F 66 A2
Pregarten A 63 B5
Pregrada HR 73 B5
Preignan F 77 C3
Preili LV 7 C9
Preitenegg A 73 B4
Prekaja BIH 83 B5
Preko HR 83 B4
Preljina SRB 85 C5
Prelog HR 74 B1
Preloščica HR 74 C1
Přelouč CZ 53 C5
Prem SLO 73 C4
Premantura HR 82 B2
Prémery F 68 A3
Prémia I 70 B3
Premiáde Mar I 91 B5
Premnitz D 44 C4
Prémont F 49 C4
Prenzlau D 45 B5
Preodac BIH 83 B5
Přerov CZ 64 A3
Prerow D 45 A4
Presencio E 88 B3
Presicce I 107 B5
Presly F 68 A2
Prešov SK 10 B6
Pressac F 67 B5
Pressath D 62 A2
Pressbaum A 64 B2
Prestatyn GB 26 B2
Prestebakke N 35 D3
Presteigne GB 29 A4
Preštice CZ 63 A4
Preston
  Lancashire GB 26 B3
  Scottish Borders GB .25 C5
Prestonpans GB 25 C5
Prestwick GB 24 C3
Prettin D 52 B2
Pretura I 103 A6
Pretzchendorf D 52 C3
Pretzier D 44 C3
Pretzsch D 52 B2
Preuilly-sur-Claise F . . .67 B5
Prevalje SLO 73 B4
Prevenchères F 78 B2
Préveranges F 68 B2
Preveza GR 116 D2
Prevršac HR 73 C6
Prezid HR 73 C4
Priaranza del Bierzo
  E 86 B4
Priay F 69 B5
Pribeta SK 64 C4
Priboj
  BIH 84 B3
  SRB 85 C4
Pribraniŭ CZ 64 A4
Příbram CZ 63 A5
Pribylina SK 65 A5
Přibyslav CZ 63 A6
Pričević SRB 85 B4
Pridjel BIH 84 B3
Priego E 95 B4
Priego de Córdoba
  E 100 B1
Priekule LV 6 C6
Prien D 62 C3
Prienai LT 6 D7
Prievidza SK 65 B4
Prigradica HR 84 D1
Prigrevica SRB 75 C4
Prijeboj HR 83 B4
Prijedor BIH 83 B5
Prijepolje SRB 85 C4
Prilep MK 116 A3
Priluka BIH 84 C1
Primda CZ 62 A3
Primel-Trégastel F 56 B2
Primišje HR 73 C5
Primorsk
  Kaliningrad RUS 47 A6
  Severo-Zapadnyy
  RUS 7 A10
Primošten HR 83 C4
Primstal D 60 A2
Princes Risborough
  GB 31 C3
Princetown GB 28 C3
Principina a Mare I 81 D5
Priolo Gargallo I 109 B4
Prioro E 88 B2
Priozersk RUS 113 C19
Prirechnyy RUS 113 C19
Prisoje BIH 84 C2
Priston GB 7 F14
Priština KOS 85 D6
Pritzerbe D 44 C4
Pritzier D 44 B3
Pritzwalk D 44 B4
Privas F 78 B3
Priverno I 102 B6
Privlaka
  Vukovarsko-Srijemska
  HR 74 C3
  Zadarska HR 83 B4
Prizna HR 83 B3
Prizren KOS 10 E6
Prizzi I 108 B2
Prnjavor
  BIH 84 B2
  HR 73 C5
  SRB 85 B4
Proaza E 86 A4
Probstzella D 52 C1
Probus GB 28 C3
Próchnowo PL 46 B2
Prócida I 103 C7
Prodhromos CY 120 B1
Prodo I 102 A5
Proença-a-Nova P 92 B3
Proença-a-Velha P 92 A3
Profitis GR 116 B5
Profondeville B 49 C5
Prokuplje SRB 10 E6
Propriano F 102 B1
Prosec CZ 64 A2
Prösen D 52 B3
Prosenjakovci SLO 73 B6
Prosotsani GR 116 A5
Prostějov CZ 64 A3
Prószków PL 54 C2
Proszowice PL 55 C5
Protić BIH 84 B1
Protivanov CZ 64 A2
Protivín CZ 63 A5
Prötzel D 45 C5
Provins F 59 B4
Prozor BIH 84 C2
Prrenjas AL 116 A2
Prudhoe GB 25 D6
Prudnik PL 54 C2
Pruggern A 72 A3
Prüm D 50 C2

Pruna E 99 C5
Prunelli-di-Fiumorbo
  F 102 A2
Prunetta I 81 B4
Pruniers F 68 B2
Prusice PL 54 B1
Pruské SK 64 A4
Prusce I 47 B4
Pruszcz Gdański PL . . .47 A4
Pruszków PL 55 A5
Prutz A 71 A5
Prüzen D 44 B2
Przhany BY 6 E8
Pružina BIH 65 A4
Pryluky UA 11 A12
Przyłęg D 46 C1
Przażer PL 46 B3
Przedbórz PL 55 B4
Przedecz PL 54 A3
Przejesław PL 53 B5
Przemków PL 53 B5
Przemocze PL 45 B7
Przemyśl PL 11 B7
Przeraŭb PL 55 B4
Przewodnik PL 47 B4
Przewóz PL 53 B4
Przezmark PL 47 B5
Przodkowo PL 47 A4
Przybiernów PL 45 B6
Przyborowice PL 47 C6
Przygodzice PL 54 B2
Przylęg PL 46 C1
Przysucha PL 55 B5
Przytoczna PL 46 C1
Przytyk PL 55 B5
Przywidz PL 47 A4
Psachna GR 116 D5
Psara GR 116 D7
Psary PL 54 B3
Pszczew PL 46 C1
Pszczółki PL 47 A4
Pszczyna PL 54 C3
Pszów PL 54 C3
Pteleos GR 116 C4
Ptolemaida GR 116 B3
Ptuj SLO 73 B5
Ptusza PL 46 B2
Puch A 62 C4
Puchberg am Schneeberg
  A 63 C6
Puchevillers F 48 C3
Puchheim D 62 B2
Púchov SK 64 A4
Pučišća HR 83 C5
Puck PL 47 A4
Puçol E 96 B2
Puconci SLO 73 B6
Pudasjärvi FIN 3 D27
Puderbach D 50 C3
Puebla de Albortón E . .90 B2
Puebla de Alcocer E . . .93 C5
Puebla de Beleña E . . .95 B3
Puebla de Don Fadrique
  E 101 B3
Puebla de Don Rodrigo
  E 94 C2
Puebla de Guzmán E . .98 B3
Puebla de la Calzada
  E 93 C4
Puebla de la Reina E . .93 C4
Puebla de Lillo E 88 A1
Puebla del Maestre E . .99 A4
Puebla del Principe
  E 100 A3
Puebla de Obando E . .93 B4
Puebla de Sanabria E . .87 B4
Puebla de Sancho Pérez
  E 93 C4
Puente Almuhey E 88 B2
Puente de Domingo
  Flórez E 86 B4
Puente de Génave E . .101 A3
Puente del Congosto
  E 93 A5
Puente de Montañana
  E 90 A3
Puente Duero E 88 C2
Puente-Genil E 100 B1
Puente la Reina E 89 B5
Puente la Reina de Jaca
  E 90 A2
Puentelarra E 89 B3
Puente Mayorga E 99 C5
Puente Viesgo E 88 A3
Puertas
  Asturias E 88 A2
  Salamanca E 87 C4
Puerto de Mazarrón
  E 101 B4
Puerto de Santa Cruz
  E 93 B5
Puerto de San Vicente
  E 94 C1
Puerto-Lápice E 95 C3
Puerto Lumbreras E . .101 B4
Puerto Moral E 99 B4
Puerto Real E 99 C4
Puerto Rey E 94 C1
Puerto Seguro E 87 D4
Puerto Serrano E 99 C5
Puget-sur-Argens F . . .79 C5
Puget-Théniers F 79 C5
Puget-ville F 79 C5
Pugnochiuso I 104 B2
Puig Reig E 91 B4
Puillon F 76 C2
Puimichel F 79 C4
Puimisson F 78 C2
Puiseaux F 58 B3
Puisieux F 48 C3
Puisserguier F 78 C2
Puivert F 77 D5
Pujols F 76 B2
Pukanec SK 65 B4
Pukavik S 41 C4
Pukë AL 105 A5
Pula
  HR 82 B2
  I 110 D1
Puławy PL 10 A6
Pulborough GB 31 D3
Pulfero I 72 B3
Pulgar E 94 C2
Pulheim D 50 B2
Pulkau A 63 B6
Pulpí E 101 B4
Pulsano I 104 C3
Pulsnitz D 53 B4
Pułtusk PL 6 E6
Pumpsaint GB 28 A4
Punat HR 83 A3
Punta Marina I 82 B1
Punta Prima F 97 B4
Punta Sabbioni I 72 C2
Puntas de Calnegre
  E 101 B4
Punta Umbria E 99 B4
Puolanka FIN 3 D27
Puottikasvaara S 113 E10
Puottaš S 112 E8
Puračić BIH 84 B3
Purbach am Neusiedler
  See A 64 C2
Purchena E 101 B3
Purfleet GB 31 C4
Purgstall A 63 B6
Purkersdorf A 64 B2
Purmerend NL 42 C1
Purullena E 100 B2
Pushkin RUS 7 B11
Pushkino RUS 7 C14
Püspökladány H 10 C6
Pusté Ulany SK 64 B3
Pustoshka RUS 7 C10

Puszcza Mariańska
  PL 55 B5
Puszczykowo PL 54 A1
Pusztamagyaród H 74 B1
Pusztamonostor H 75 A4
Pusztaszabolcs H 74 A3
Pusztavám H 74 A3
Putanges-Pont-Ecrepin
  F 57 B5
Putbus D 45 A5
Putignano I 104 C3
Putlitz D 44 B4
Putnok H 65 B6
Putte B 49 B5
Puttelange-aux-Lacs
  F 60 A2
Putten NL 49 A6
Puttgarden D 44 A3
Püttlingen D 60 A2
Putzu Idu I 110 B1
Puy-Guillaume F 68 C3
Puylaroque F 77 B4
Puylaurens F 77 C5
Puy-l'Évêque F 77 B4
Puymirol F 77 B3
Puyôo F 76 C2
Puyrolland F 67 B4
Pwllheli GB 26 C1
Pyatykhatky UA 11 B12
Pyetrikaw BY 7 E10
Pyhäjärvi FIN 3 E26
Pyla CY 120 A2
Pyla-sur-Mer F 76 B1
Pyryatyn UA 11 A12
Pyrzyce PL 45 B6
Pysely CZ 63 A5
Pyskowice PL 54 C3
Pytalovo RUS 7 C9
Pyzdry PL 54 A2

Q

Quakenbrück D 43 C4
Quare(nt)ano F 77 C4
Quarré-les-Tombes F . .68 A3
Quarteira P 98 B2
Quartu Sant'Élena I . .110 C2
Quatre-Champs F 59 A5
Quedlinburg D 52 B1
Queenzieburg I 82 C2
Queensferry
  Edinburgh GB 25 C4
  Flintshire GB 26 B2
Queige F 69 C6
Queipo E 99 A4
Queixans E 91 A4
Quel E 89 B4
Quelaines-St-Gault F . .57 C5
Quellada P 92 A2
Quelsrtead . . . .
Queralbs E 91 A5
Quemada E 89 C3
Quéménéven F . . . .
Querceta I . . . .
Quercianella I . . . .
Querfurt D 52 B1
Quérigut F 77 D5
Quero
  E 95 C3
  I 72 C1
Querqueville F 57 A4
Quesada E 100 B2
Questembert F 56 C3
Quettehou F 57 A4
Quevauvillers F 58 A3
Quevy B 49 C5
Quiaios P 92 A2
Quiberon F 66 A1
Quiberville F 58 A1
Quickborn D 44 B1
Quiévrain B 49 C4
Quillan F 77 D5
Quillebeuf F 58 A1
Quimper F 56 B1
Quimperlé F 56 C2
Quincampoix F 58 A2
Quincoces de Yuso E . .89 B3
Quincy F 68 A2
Quinéville F 57 A4
Quingey F 69 A5
Quinson F 79 C4
Quinssaines F 68 B2
Quinta-Grande P 92 C2
Quintana de la Serena
  E 93 C5
Quintana del Castillo
  E 86 B4
Quintana del Marco E . .88 B1
Quintana del Puenta
  E 88 B2
Quintana-Martin Galindez
  E 89 B3
Quintanapalla E 89 B3
Quintanar de la Orden
  E 95 C3
Quintanar de la Sierra
  E 89 C3
Quintanar del Rey E . . .95 C5
Quintanilla de la Mata
  E 88 C3
Quintanilla del Coco
  E 89 C3
Quintanilla de Onésimo
  E 88 C2
Quintanilla de Somoza
  E 87 B4
Quintas de Valdelucio
  E 88 B2
Quintela P 87 D3
Quintin F 56 B3
Quinto E 90 B2
Quinzano d'Oglio I 71 C5
Quiroga E 86 B3
Quismondo E 94 B2
Quissac F 78 C3
Quistello I 81 A4

R

Raab A 63 B4
Raabs an der Thaya
  A 63 B6
Raahe FIN 3 D26
Raajärvi FIN 113 F15
Raalte NL 42 C3
Raamsdonksveer NL . .49 B5
Raanujarvi FIN 113 F13
Raattama FIN 113 D13
Rab HR 83 B3
Rabac HR 82 A3
Rabade E 86 A3
Rábafüzes H 73 B6
Rábahidvég H 74 A1
Rabanales E 87 C4
Rábapatona H 74 A2
Rabapordány H 74 A2
Rabastens F 77 C4
Rabastens-de-Bigorre
  F 76 C3
Rabat = Victoria M. . .107 C5
Rabat M 107 C5
Rabča SK 65 A5
Rabe SRB 75 B5
Rabi CZ 63 A4
Rabino PL 46 B1
Rabka PL 65 A5
Rabrovo SRB 85 B6
Rača
  Srbija SRB 85 B5
  Srbija SRB 85 C6
Rácale I 107 B5
Rácalmás H 74 A3
Racalmuto I 108 B2
Racconigi I 80 B1
Rachecourt-sur-Marne
  F 59 B6
Raciąż PL 47 C6
Racibórz PL 54 C3
Račinovci HR 84 B3
Ráckeve H 75 A3
Racławice PL 55 C5

Racławice Śląskie
  PL 54 C2
Racot PL 54 A1
Ráda
  Skaraborg S 35 D5
  Värmland S 34 B5
Radalj SRB 85 B4
Radda in Chianti I 81 C5
Raddusa I 109 B3
Radeberg D 53 B3
Radebeul D 53 B3
Radeburg D 53 B3
Radeče SLO 73 B5
Radekhiv UA 11 A8
Radenci SLO 73 B6
Radenthein A 72 B3
Radevormwald D 50 B3
Radičondól I 81 C5
Radicófani I 81 D5
Radišići BIH 84 C2
Radizel SLO 73 B5
Radków PL 54 C1
Radłów PL 55 C5
Radmer an der Stube
  A 73 A4
Radnejaur S 115 B15
Radnice CZ 63 A4
Radohova BIH 84 B2
Radojevo SRB 75 C5
Radolfzell D 61 C4
Radom PL 55 B6
Radomin PL 47 B5
Radomirci . . . .
Radomsko PL 55 B4
Radomyśl Wielki PL . . .55 C6
Radošina SK 64 B3
Radošovce SK 64 B3
Radoszewice PL 54 B3
Radoszyce PL 55 B5
Radotin CZ 63 A5
Radovets BG 116 A4
Radovići MNE 84 D3
Radowo Wielkie PL . . .46 B1
Radstadt A 72 A3
Radstock GB 29 B5
Raduc HR 83 B4
Radviliškis LT 6 D7
Radzanów PL . . . .
Radanyev . . . .
Radziejów PL 47 C4
Radziejowice PL 55 A5
Radzovce SK 65 B5
Radzyń Chełmiński
  PL 47 B4
Raeren B 50 C2
Raesfeld D 50 B2
Raffadali I 108 B2
Rafina GR 117 D5
Rafsbotn N 113 B12
Ragachow BY 7 E11
Ragály H 65 B6
Rágeleje DK 41 C2
Raglan GB 29 B5
Ragnitz A 73 B5
Ragusa I 109 C3
Rahden D 43 C5
Råholt N 34 B3
Raiano I 103 A6
Raigada E 87 B3
Rain D 62 B1
Rainbach im Mühlkreis
  A 63 B5
Rainham GB 31 C4
Rairiz de Veiga E 87 B3
Raisdorf D 44 A2
Raisio FIN 6 A7
Raiva
  Aveiro P 87 C2
  Coimbra P . . . .
Raja-Jooseppi FIN . .113 D17
Rajala FIN 113 E15
Rajcza PL 65 A4
Rajec SK 65 A4
Rájec-Jestřebi CZ 64 A2
Rajecké Teplice SK . . .65 A4
Rajevo Selo HR 84 B3
Rajhrad CZ 64 A2
Rajić HR 74 C2
Rajka H 64 C3
Rakaca H 65 B6
Rakamaz H . . . .
Rakek SLO 73 C4
Rakhiv UA 11 B8
Rakitna SLO 73 C4
Rakitovo BG 116 A5
Rakkestad N 35 C3
Rákóczifalva H 75 A5
Rakoniewice PL 54 A1
Rakoszyce PL 54 B1
Raková SK 65 A4
Rakovac BIH 84 A2
Rakovica HR 83 B4
Rakovník CZ 53 C3
Rakow D 45 A5
Raków PL 55 C6
Rakvere EST 7 B9
Ralala SR . . . .
Ralja SRB 85 B5
Rälla S 40 C6
Ramacastañas E 94 B1
Ramacca I 109 B3
Ramales de la Victoria
  E 89 A3
Ramberg N 112 D2
Rambervillers F 60 B2
Rambouillet F 58 B2
Rambucourt F 60 B1
Ramdala S 41 C5
Ramerupt F 59 B5
Ramingstein A 72 A3
Ramirás E 87 B2
Ramiswil CH 70 A2
Ramkvilla S 40 B4
Ramme DK 38 C1
Rämmen S 34 B6
Ramnäs S 36 C3
Ramnes N 35 C2
Râmnicu Vâlcea RO . .11 D8
Ramonville-St Agne
  F 77 C4
Rampside GB 26 A2
Ramsau D 62 C3
Ramsbeck D 51 B4
Ramsberg S 36 C2
Ramsele S 115 D13
Ramsey
  Cambridgeshire GB . .30 B3
  Isle of Man GB 26 A1
Ramseycleuch GB 25 C4
Ramsgate GB 31 C5
Ramsjö S 115 E12
Ramstein-Meisenbach
  D 60 A3
Ramsund N 112 D5
Ramundberget S 114 E9
Ramvik S 115 E14
Ranalt A 71 A6
Rånäs S 36 C5
Rånåsfoss N 34 B3
Rance B 49 C5
Ránchio I 82 C1
Randaberg N 33 D2
Randalstown GB 19 B5
Randan F 68 B3
Randazzo I 109 B3
Rånddalen S 115 E10
Randegg A 63 B5
Randers DK 38 C3
Randijaur S 112 F8
Randin E 87 C3
Randsverk N 114 F6
Råneå S 3 D25
Rångedala S 40 B3
Ranis D 52 C1
Rankweil A 71 A4
Rånnaväg S 40 B3
Rannem-Uskrava . . . .
Rännöslöv S 40 C3
Rannoch Station GB . .24 B3
Rańovac SRB . . . .

Regueiro E 86 B2
Reguengo
  Portalegre P 92 B3
  Santarém P 92 B2
Reguengos de Monsaraz
  P 92 C3
Rehau D 52 C2
Rehburg D 43 C6
Rehden D 43 C5
Rehna D 44 B3
Reichelsheim D 61 A4
Reichelsheim D 61 A6
Reichenau A 64 C1
Reichenbach
  Sachsen D 52 C2
  Sachsen D 53 B4
Reichenfels A 73 B4
Reichensachsen D 51 B6
Reichertshofen D 62 B2
Reichshoffen F 60 B3
Reiden CH 70 A2
Reigada
  E 86 A4
  P 87 B3
Reigate GB 31 C3
Reillanne F 79 C4
Reillo E 95 C5
Reims F 59 A5
Reinach CH 70 A3
Reinbek D 44 B2
Reinberg D 45 A5
Reine N 112 E2
Reinfeld D 44 B2
Reinheim D 61 A4
Reinli N 32 B6
Reinosa E 88 A2
Reinstorf D 44 B2
Reinsvoll N 34 B2
Reisach A 72 B3
Reiss GB 23 C5
Reitan N 114 B8
Reit im Winkl D 62 C3
Rejmyre S 37 D2
Rekavice BIH 84 B2
Rekovac SRB 85 C6
Rekvik N 112 C2
Rém H 75 B4
Remagen D 50 C3
Rémalard F 58 B1
Rembercourt-aux-Pots
  F 59 B6
Remedios P 92 B1
Remels D 43 B4
Remeta Mare RO 75 C6
Remich L 60 A2
Rémilly F 60 A2
Remiremont F 60 C2
Remolinos E 90 B1
Remoulins F 78 C3
Remscheid D 50 B3
Remseck D 61 B5
Remte . . . .
Rena E 93 B5
Rena N 34 A3
Renaison F 68 B3
Renazé F 57 C4
Renchen D 61 B4
Rende I 106 B3
Rendina GR 116 C3
Rendsburg D 44 A1
Renedo E 88 C2
Renens CH 69 B6
Renfrew GB 24 C3
Rengsjö S 36 A3
Reni UA 11 D10
Rennebu N 114 E6
Rennerod D 50 C4
Rennertshofen D 62 B2
Rennes F 57 B4
Rennes-les-Bains F . . .77 D5
Rennweg A 72 A3
Rens DK 39 E2
Rensjön S 112 D8
Rentería E 76 C1
Renträsk S 115 B15
Répcelak H 74 A2
Repojoki FIN 113 D14
Répvág N 113 B14
Requena E 96 B1
Réquista F 77 B5
Rerik D 44 A3
Resan I 72 C1
Resanovci BIH 83 B5
Resarö S 37 C5
Reschen = Résia I 71 B5
Resen M.K. . . . .
Resende P 87 C3
Résia = Reschen I 71 B5
Reşiţa RO 10 D6
Resko PL 46 B1
Resnik SRB 85 B5
Ressons-sur-Matz F . . .58 A3
Restábal E 100 C2
Restelica KOS . . . . . .
Resuttano I 109 B3
Retamal E 93 C4
Retford GB 27 B5
Rethel F 59 A5
Rethem D 43 C6
Rethimno GR 117 G6
Retie B 49 B6
Retiers F 57 C4
Retortillo E 87 D4
Retortillo de Soria E . .89 C4
Retournac F 78 A3
Rétság H 65 C5
Rettenegg A 73 A5

Regueiro E 86 B2
Reguengo
  Portalegre P 92 B3
  Santarém P 92 B2

Rhêmes-Notre-Dame
F 70 C2
Rhenen NL 49 B6
Rhens D 50 C3
Rheydt D 50 B2
Rhiconich GB 22 C4
Rhinow D 44 C4
Rhiw GB 26 C1
Rho I 70 C4
Rhoden D 51 B5
Rhodes GB 119 F3
Rhondda GB 29 B4
Rhoslanerchrugog
GB 26 B2
Rhosneigr GB 26 B1
Rhossili GB 28 B3
Rhubodach GB 24 C2
Rhuddlan GB 26 B2
Rhyl GB 26 B2
Rhynie GB 33 D6
Riala S 37 C5
Riallé F 66 A3
Riaño E 88 B1
Riano I 102 A5
Rians F 79 C4
Rianxo E 86 B2
Riaza E 89 C3
Riba E 89 A3
Ribadavia E 87 B2
Ribadeo E 86 A3
Riba de Saelices E . . 95 B4
Ribadesella E 88 A1
Ribaflecha E 89 B4
Ribaforada E 89 C5
Ribare SRB 85 B6
Ribariće SRB 85 C5
Riba-roja d'Ebre E . . 90 B3
Riba-Roja de Turia E . 96 B2
Ribe DK 39 D1
Ribeauvillé F 60 B3
Ribécourt-Dreslincourt
F 59 A3
Ribeira da Pena P . . . 87 C3
Ribeira de Piquin E . . 86 A3
Ribemont F 59 A4
Ribera I 108 B2
Ribérac F 67 C5
Ribera del Fresno E . . 93 C4
Ribesalbes E 96 A2
Ribes de Freser E . . . 91 A5
Ribiers F 79 B4
Ribnica
  BIH 84 B3
  SLO 73 C4
  SRB 85 C5
Ribnica na Potorju
  SLO 73 B5
Ribnik HR 73 C5
Ribnitz-Damgarten D . 44 A4
Ribolla I 81 C5
Řičany CZ 64 A2
Říčany CZ 53 D4
Riccia I 103 B7
Riccione I 82 B1
Ricco Del Golfo I . . . 81 B3
Richebourg F 59 B6
Richelieu F 67 A5
Richisau CH 70 A3
Richmond
  Greater London GB . 31 C3
  North Yorkshire GB . 27 A4
Richtenberg D 45 A4
Richterswil CH 70 A3
Rickling D 44 A2
Rickmansworth GB . . 31 C3
Ricla E 89 C5
Riddarhyttan S 36 C2
Ridderkerk NL 49 B5
Riddes CH 70 B2
Ridjica SRB 75 C4
Ried A 63 B4
Riedenburg D 62 B2
Ried im Oberinntal A . 71 A5
Riedlingen D 61 B5
Riedstadt D 61 A4
Riegersburg A 73 B5
Riego de la Vega E . . 88 B1
Riego del Camino E . . 88 C1
Riello E 88 B1
Riemst B 49 C6
Rienne B 49 C5
Riénsena E 88 A2
Riesa D 52 B3
Riesi I 109 B3
Riestedt D 52 B1
Rietberg D 51 B4
Rieti I 102 A5
Rietschen D 53 B4
Rieumes F 77 C4
Rieupeyroux F 77 B5
Rieux-Volvestre F . . . 77 C4
Riez F 79 C5
Rīga LV 6 C8
Riggisberg CH 70 B2
Rignac F 77 B5
Rignano Gargánico
  I 104 B1
Rigolato I 72 B2
Rigside GB 25 C4
Rigutino I 81 C5
Riihimäki FIN 3 F26
Rijeka HR 73 C4
Rijeka Crnojevića
  MNE 105 A5
Rijen NL 49 B5
Rijkevorsel B 49 B5
Rijssen NL 50 A2
Rilić BIH 84 C2
Rilievo I 108 B1
Rillé F 67 A5
Rillo de Gallo E 95 B5
Rimavská Baňa SK . . 65 B5
Rimavská Seč SK . . . 65 B6
Rimavská Sobota SK . 65 B6
Rimbo S 36 C5
Rimforsa S 37 D2
Rimini I 82 B1
Râmnicu Sărat RO . . . 11 D9
Rimogne F 59 A5
Rimpar D 61 A5
Rimske Toplice SLO . 73 B5
Rincón de la Victoria
  E 100 C1
Rincón de Soto E . . . 89 B5
Rindal N 114 D6
Rinde N 32 A3
Ringamála S 41 C4
Ringarum S 37 D3
Ringaskiddy IRL 20 C3
Ringe DK 39 D3
Ringebu N 34 A2
Ringkøbing DK 39 C1
Ringsaker N 34 B2
Ringsted DK 39 D4
Ringwood GB 29 C6
Rinkaby S 41 D4
Rinkabyholm S 40 C6
Rinlo E 86 A3
Rinteln D 51 A5
Rio E 86 B3
Riobo E 86 B2
Riodeva E 96 A1
Rio do Coures P 92 B2
Rio Douro P 87 C3
Riofrio E 94 B2
Rio Frio P 92 C2
Riofrio de Aliste E . . . 87 C4
Rio frio de Riaza E . . 95 A3
Riogordo E 100 C1
Rioja E 101 C3
Riola I 81 B5
Riolobos E 93 B4
Riom F 68 C3
Rio Maggiore I 81 B3
Rio Maior P 92 B2
Rio Marina I 81 D4

Riom-ès-Montagnes
F 68 C2
Rion-des-Landes F . . 76 C2
Rionegro del Puente
  E 87 B4
Rionero in Vúlture I . 104 C1
Riopar E 101 A3
Riós E 87 C3
Rioseco E 88 A1
Rioseco de Tapia E . . 88 B1
Rio Tinto P 87 C2
Riotord F 69 C4
Riotorto E 86 A3
Rioz F 69 A6
Ripač BIH 83 B4
Ripacándida I 104 C1
Ripanj SRB 85 B5
Ripatransone I 82 D2
Ripley GB 27 B4
Ripoll E 91 A5
Ripon GB 27 A4
Riposto I 109 B4
Ripsa S 37 D3
Risan MNE 105 A4
Risbäck S 115 C12
Risca GB 29 B4
Rischenau D 51 B5
Riscle F 76 C2
Rišňovce SK 64 B3
Risnes N 32 A2
Risør N 33 D6
Risøyhamn N 112 D4
Rissna S 115 D12
Ritsem S 112 E6
Ritterhude D 43 B5
Riutula FIN 113 D15
Riva del Garda I 71 C5
Riva Lígure I 80 C1
Rivanazzano I 80 B3
Rivarolo Canavese I . 70 C2
Rivarolo Mantovano I . 81 A4
Rive-de-Gier F 69 C4
Rivedoux-Plage F . . . 66 B3
Rivello I 106 A2
Rivergaro I 80 B3
Rives F 69 C5
Rivesaltes F 78 D1
Rivignano I 72 C3
Rivne UA 11 A9
Rivoli I 80 A1
Rivolta d'Adda I 71 C4
Rixheim F 60 C3
Rixo S 35 D3
Riza GR 116 B5
Rizokarpaso CY 120 A3
Rjukan N 32 C5
Rø DK 41 D4
Rö S 37 C5
Roa
  E 88 C3
  N 34 B2
Roade GB 30 B3
Roager DK 39 D1
Roaldkvam N 33 C3
Roanne F 68 B4
Robakowo PL 47 B4
Róbbio I 70 C3
Röbel D 45 B4
Roberton GB 25 C5
Robertville B 50 C2
Robin Hood's Bay GB . 27 A5
Robleda E 93 A4
Robledillo de Trujillo
  E 93 B5
Robledo
  Albacete E 101 A3
  Orense E 86 B4
Robledo de Chavela
  E 94 B2
Robledo del Buey E . . 94 C2
Robledo del Mazo E . 94 C2
Robledollano E 93 B5
Robles de la Valcueva
  E 88 B1
Robliza de Cojos E . . 87 D5
Robres E 90 B2
Robres del Castillo E . 89 B4
Rocafort de Queralt E . 91 B4
Rocamadour F 77 B4
Roccabernarda I 107 B3
Roccabianca I 81 A4
Roccadáspide I 103 C8
Rocca di Mezzo I . . . 103 A6
Rocca di Papa I 102 B5
Roccalbegna I 81 D5
Roccalumera I 109 B4
Roccamonfina I 103 B6
Roccanova I 106 A3
Roccapalumba I 108 B2
Roccapassa I 103 A6
Rocca Priora I 82 C2
Roccaraso I 103 B7
Rocca San Casciano
  I 81 B5
Roccasecca I 103 B6
Rocca Sinibalda I . . . 102 A5
Roccastrada I 81 C5
Roccatederighi I 81 C5
Roccella Iónica I . . . 106 C3
Ronov nad Doubravou
  CZ 63 A6
Rocester GB 27 C4
Rochdale GB 26 B3
Rochechouart F 67 C5
Rochefort
  B 49 C6
Rochefort-en-Terre F . 56 C3
Rochefort-Montagne
  F 68 C2
Roche-lez-Beaupré F . 69 A6
Rochemaure F 78 B3
Rocheservière F 66 B3
Rochester
  Medway GB 31 C4
  Northumberland GB . 25 C5
Rochlitz D 52 B2
Rociana del Condado
  E 99 B4
Rockenhausen D 60 A3
Rockhammar S 37 C2
Rockneby S 40 C6
Ročko Polje HR 73 C4
Ročov CZ 53 C3
Rocroi F 59 A5
Rodach D 51 C6
Roda de Bará E 91 B4
Roda de Ter E 91 B5
Rodalben D 60 A3
Rødberg N 32 B5
Rødby DK 44 A3
Rødbyhavn DK 44 A3
Rødding
  Sønderjyllands Amt.
    DK 39 D2
  Viborg Amt. DK . . . 38 C1
Rödeby S 41 C5
Rodeiro E 86 B3
Rødekro DK 39 D2
Roden NL 42 B3
Rödental D 51 C6
Rödermark D 61 A4
Rodewisch D 52 C2
Rodez F 77 B5
Rodi Gargánico I . . . 104 B1
Roding D 62 A3
Rødkærsbro DK 38 C2
Rodolivos GR 116 B5
Rodoñá E 91 B4
Rødvig DK 39 D5
Roermond NL 50 B1
Roesbrugge B 48 C3
Roeschwoog F 61 B4

Roeselare B 49 C4
Roetgen D 50 C2
Roffiac F 78 A2
Röfors S 37 D1
Rofrano I 106 A2
Rogač HR 83 C5
Rogačica SRB 85 B4
Rogalinek I 54 A1
Rogaška Slatina SLO . 73 B5
Rogatec SLO 73 B5
Rogatica BIH 84 C4
Rogatyn UA 11 B8
Rogätz D 52 A1
Roggendorf D 44 B3
Roggiano Gravina I . . 106 B3
Roghadal GB 22 D2
Rogliano
  F 102 A2
  I 106 B3
Rogne N 32 A6
Rognes F 79 C4
Rogny-les-7-Ecluses
  F 59 C3
Rogowo PL 46 C3
Rogóz PL 47 A6
Rogoznica HR 83 C4
Rogoźnica PL 53 B6
Rogozno PL 46 C2
Rohan F 56 B3
Röhlingen D 61 B6
Rohožník SK 64 B3
Rohr D 51 C6
Rohrbach D 63 B4
Rohrbach-lès-Bitche
  F 60 A3
Rohrberg D 44 C3
Rohr im Gebirge A . . 63 C6
Röhrnbach D 63 B4
Roisel F 59 A4
Rojales E 96 C2
Röjeråsen S 36 B1
Rojewo PL 47 C4
Rokiciny PL 55 B4
Rokietnica PL 46 C2
Rokiškis LT 7 D8
Rokitki PL 53 B5
Rokitno RUS 7 F13
Rokycany CZ 63 A4
Rolampont F 59 C6
Rold DK 38 C2
Rolde NL 42 C3
Rollag N 32 B6
Rollán E 94 B1
Rolle CH 69 B6
Roma
  I 102 B5
  S 37 E5
Romagnano Sésia I . . 70 C3
Romagné F 57 B4
Romakloster S 37 E5
Roman
  BG 11 E8
  RO 11 C9
Romana I 110 B1
Romanèche-Thorins
  F 69 B4
Romano di Lombardia
  I 71 C4
Romanshorn CH 71 A4
Romans-sur-Isère F . . 79 A4
Rombas F 60 A2
Romeán E 86 B3
Romenay F 69 B5
Romeral E 95 C3
Römerstein D 61 B5
Rometta I 109 A4
Romford GB 31 C4
Romhány H 65 C5
Römhild D 51 C6
Romilly-sur-Seine F . . 59 B4
Romodan UA 11 A12
Romont F 70 B1
Romorantin-Lanthenay
  F 68 A1
Romrod D 51 C5
Romsey GB 31 D2
Rømskog N 35 C3
Ronce-les-Bains F . . . 66 C3
Ronchamp F 60 C2
Ronchi dei Legionari
  I 72 C3
Ronciglione I 102 A5
Ronco Canavese I . . . 70 C2
Ronco Scrivia I 80 B2
Ronda E 99 C5
Rønde DK 39 C3
Rone S 37 E5
Ronehamn S 37 E5
Rong N 32 B1
Rönnäng S 38 B4
Rønne DK 41 D4
Ronneburg D 52 C2
Ronneby S 41 C5
Rønnede DK 39 D4
Ronneshytta S 37 D2
Rönninge S 37 C4
Rönnöfors S 115 D10
Rönö S 37 D3
Ronse B 49 C4
Roodeschool NL 42 B3
Roosendaal NL 49 B5
Roosky IRL 18 C4
Ropczyce PL 55 C6
Ropeid N 33 C3
Ropinsalmi FIN 113 D10
Roquebilière F 79 B6
Roquebrun F 78 C2
Roquecourbe F 77 C5
Roquefort F 76 B2
Roquemaure F 78 B3
Roquesteron F 79 C6
Roquetas de Mar E . . 101 C3
Roquetes E 90 C3
Roquevaire F 79 C4
Røra N 114 D8
Rørbæk DK 38 C2
Rore BIH 83 B5
Röro S 38 B4
Røros N 114 E8
Rørvig DK 39 D4
Rørvik N 114 C8
Rörvik S 40 B4
Rosà I 72 C1
Rosal de la Frontera
  E 98 B3
Rosalina Mare I 72 C2
Rosa Marina I 104 C3
Rosans F 79 B4
Rosário P 98 B2
Rosarno I 106 C2
Rosbach D 50 C3
Rosche D 44 C2
Rościszewo PL 47 C5
Roscoff F 56 B2
Roscommon IRL 18 C3
Roscrea IRL 21 B4
Rosdorf D 51 B5
Rose I 106 B3
Rosegg A 73 B4
Rosehearty GB 33 D6
Rosel E 90 C3
Rosell E 90 C3
Roselló E 90 B3
Rosendal N 32 C3
Rosenfeld D 61 B4
Rosenfors S 40 B5
Rosenheim D 62 C3
Rosenow D 45 B5
Rosenthal D 51 B4
Roseto degli Abruzzi I . 103 A7

Roseto Valfortore I . . 103 B8
Rosheim F 60 B3
Rosia I 81 C5
Rosice CZ 64 A2
Rosières-en-Santerre
  F 58 A3
Rosignano Marittimo
  I 81 C4
Rosignano Solvay I . . 81 C4
Roșiori-de-Vede RO . . 11 D8
Roskilde DK 39 D5
Roskovec AL 105 C5
Röslau D 52 C1
Roslavl RUS 7 E12
Roslev DK 38 C1
Rosmaninhal P 93 B3
Rosmult IRL 21 B4
Rosnowo PL 46 A2
Rosolini I 109 C3
Rosova MNE 85 C4
Rossas
  Aveiro P 87 D2
  Braga P 87 C2
Rossdorf D 51 C6
Rossett GB 26 B3
Rosshaupten D 62 C1
Rossiglione I 80 B2
Rossignol B 60 A1
Rosslau D 52 B2
Rosslare IRL 21 B5
Rosslare Harbour IRL . 21 B5
Rosslea GB 19 B4
Rossleben D 52 B1
Rössön S 115 D13
Ross-on-Wye GB . . . 29 B5
Rossosz PL 54 B3
Rossoszyca PL 54 B3
Rosswein D 52 B3
Röstånga S 41 C3
Rostar SK 65 B6
Rostock D 44 A4
Rostrenen F 56 B2
Rosток... Rosток
Rosток Rostrevor GB . 19 B5
Røsvik N 112 E4
Rosvik S 3 D25
Rosyth GB 25 B4
Röszke H 75 B5
Rot S 34 A6
Rota E 99 C4
Rota Greca I 106 B3
Rot am See D 61 A6
Rotberget N 34 B4
Rotella I 82 D2
Rotenburg
  Hessen D 51 C5
  Niedersachsen D . . 43 B6
Roth
  Bayern D 62 A2
  Rheinland-Pfalz D . 50 C3
Rothbury GB 25 C6
Röthenbach D 62 A2
Rothenbach D 53 B4
Rothenburg ob der
  Tauber D 61 A6
Rothéneuf F 57 B4
Rothenklempenow D . 45 B6
Rothenstein D 62 B2
Rotherham GB 27 B4
Rothes GB 23 D5
Rothesay GB 24 C2
Rothwell GB 30 B3
Rotnes N 34 B2
Rotonda I 106 B3
Rotondella I 106 A3
Rotova E 96 C2
Rott
  Bayern D 62 C1
  Bayern D 62 C2
Rottach-Egern D 62 C2
Röttenbach D 62 A2
Rottenbuch D 62 C1
Rottenburg
  Baden-Württemberg
    D 61 B4
  Bayern D 62 B3
Rottenmann A 73 A4
Rotterdam NL 49 B5
Rotthalmünster D . . . 63 B4
Rottingdean GB 31 D3
Röttingen D 61 A5
Rottleberode D 51 B6
Rottne S 40 B4
Rottneros S 34 C5
Rottofreno I 81 B3
Rottweil D 61 B4
Rötz D 62 A3
Roubaix F 49 C4
Roudnice nad Labem
  CZ 53 C4
Roudouallec F 56 B2
Rouen F 58 A2
Rouffach F 60 C3
Rouge F 57 C4
Rougemont F 69 A6
Rougemont le-Château
  F 60 C2
Rouillac F 67 C4
Rouillé F 67 B5
Roujan F 78 C2
Roulans F 69 A6
Roundwood IRL 21 A5
Rousínov CZ 64 A2
Roussac F 67 B6
Rousses F 78 B2
Roussillon F 69 C4
Rouvroy-sur-Audry F . 59 A5
Rouy F 68 A3
Rovaniemi
  maalaiskunta FIN . 113 F14
Rovaniemi FIN 113 F14
Rovato I 71 C4
Rovensko pod Troskami
  CZ 53 C5
Roverbella I 71 C5
Rovereto I 71 C5
Rövershagen D 44 A4
Roverud N 34 B4
Rovigo I 81 A5
Rovinj HR 82 A2
Rovišce HR 74 C1
Rów PL 45 C6
Rowy PL 46 A3
Royal Leamington Spa
  GB 30 B2
Royal Tunbridge Wells
  GB 31 C4
Royan F 66 C3
Royat F 68 C3
Roybon F 69 C5
Roybridge GB 24 B3
Roye F 58 A3
Royère-de-Vassivière
  F 68 C1
Røykenvik N 34 B2
Royos E 101 B3
Røyrvik N 115 C10
Royston GB 30 B3
Rozadas E 86 A4
Rožaj MNE 85 D5
Rozalén del Monte E . 95 C4
Rozay-en-Brie F 59 B3
Roždalovice CZ 53 C5
Rozdilna UA 11 C11
Rozental PL 47 B5
Rozhyshche UA 11 A8
Rozmital pod Třemšínem
  CZ 63 A4
Rožňava SK 65 B6
Rožnov pod Radhoštěm 64 A4

Rozvadov CZ 62 A3
Rozzano I 71 C4
Rranxë AL 105 A5
Rrëshen AL 105 B5
Rrogozhinë AL 105 B5
Ruanes E 93 B5
Rubbestadneset N . . . 32 C2
Rubi E 91 B5
Rubiá E 86 B4
Rubiacedo de Abajo
  E 89 B3
Rubielos Bajos E 95 C4
Rubielos de Mora E . . 96 A2
Rubiera I 81 B4
Rubik AL 105 B5
Rucandio E 89 B3
Rud
  Akershus N 34 B3
  Buskerud N 34 B2
Ruda
  PL 54 B3
  S 40 B6
Rudabánya H 65 B6
Ruda Maleniecka PL . 55 B5
Ruda Pilczycka PL . . 55 B5
Ruda Śl. PL 54 C3
Ruddervorde B 49 B4
Ruden D 73 B4
Rudersberg D 61 B5
Rüdersdorf D 45 C5
Rudersdorf A 73 A6
Ruderting D 63 B4
Rüdesheim D 50 D3
Rudkøbing DK 39 E3
Rudmanns A 63 B6
Rudna
  CZ 53 C4
  PL 53 B6
Rudnik
  KOS 85 D5
  SRB 85 B5
Rudniki
  Opolskie PL 54 B3
  Śląskie PL 55 C4
Rudno
  Dolnośląskie PL . . . 54 B1
  Pomorskie PL 47 B4
Rudnya RUS 7 D11
Rudo BIH 85 C4
Rudolfstadt D 52 C1
Rudowica PL 53 B5
Rudozem BG 116 A6
Rudskoga S 35 C6
Rudston GB 27 A5
Ruda Vedby DK 39 D4
Rudy PL 54 C3
Rue F 48 C2
Rueda E 88 C2
Rueda de Jalón E . . . 90 B1
Ruelle-sur-Touvre F . . 67 C5
Ruerrero E 88 B3
Ruffano I 107 B5
Ruffec F 67 B5
Rufina I 81 C5
Rugby GB 30 B2
Rugeley GB 27 C4
Ruggstrop S 40 C6
Rugles F 58 B1
Rugozero RUS 3 D30
Rühen D 44 C2
Ruhla D 51 C6
Ruhland D 53 B3
Ruhle D 43 C4
Ruhpolding D 62 C3
Ruhstorf D 63 B4
Ruidera E 95 D4
Ruillé-sur-le-Loir F . . 58 C1
Ruinen NL 42 C3
Ruiselede B 49 B4
Rulles B 60 A1
Rülzheim D 61 A4
Rum H 74 A1
Ruma SRB 85 A4
Rumboci BIH 84 C2
Rumburk CZ 53 C4
Rumenka SRB 75 C4
Rumia PL 47 A4
Rumigny F 59 A5
Rumilly F 69 C5
Rumma S 37 D3
Rumney GB 29 B4
Rumont F 59 B6
Runa P 92 B1
Runcorn GB 26 B3
Rundmoen N 115 A11
Runhällen S 36 B3
Runowo PL 47 A6
Runtuna S 37 D4
Ruokojärvi FIN 113 E13
Ruokolahti FIN 3 F28
Ruokto S 112 E8
Ruoms F 78 B3
Ruoti I 104 C1
Rupa HR 73 C4
Ruppichteroth D 50 C3
Rupt-sur-Moselle F . . 60 C2
Rus E 100 A2
Ruse
  BG 11 E8
  SLO 73 B5
Ruše SLO 73 B5
Rusele S 115 C15
Ruševo HR 74 C3
Rush IRL 21 A5
Rushden GB 30 B3
Rusiec PL 54 B3
Rusinowo
  Zachodnio-Pomorskie
    PL 46 B1
  Zachodnio-Pomorskie
    PL 46 B2
Ruskele S 115 C15
Ruski Krstur SRB 75 C4
Ruskington GB 27 B5
Rusovce SK 64 B3
Rüsselsheim D 51 D4
Russelv N 112 C9
Russi I 82 B1
Rust A 64 C2
Rustefjelbma N 113 B17
Rustrel F 79 C4
Ruszki PL 55 A5
Ruszów PL 53 B5
Rute E 100 B1
Rüthen D 51 B4
Ruthin GB 26 B2
Ruthven GB 23 D4
Ruthwell GB 25 D4
Rüti CH 70 A3
Rutigliano I 104 B3
Rutledal N 32 A2
Rutoši SRB 85 C4
Ruurlo NL 50 A2
Ruuvaoja FIN 113 E17
Ruvo del Monte I . . . 104 C1
Ruvo di Púglia I 104 B2
Ruynes-en-Margeride
  F 78 B2
Ružic HR 83 C5
Ruzomberok SK 65 A5
Ruzsa H 75 B4
Ry DK 39 C2
Rybany SK 64 B4
Rybina PL 47 A5
Rybinsk RUS 7 B15
Rybnik PL 54 C3
Rýchlocice PL 54 B3
Rychnov nad Kněžnou
  CZ 53 C6
Rychnowo PL 47 B6
Rychtal PL 54 B2
Rychwał PL 54 A3
Ryczywół PL 46 C2
Ryczywól PL 55 B6
Ryd S 40 C4
Rydaholm S 40 C4
Rydbo S 37 C5
Rydboholm S 40 B2
Ryde GB 31 D2

Rydöbruk S 40 C3
Rydsgård S 41 D3
Rydsnäs S 40 B5
Rydultowy PL 54 C3
Rydzyna PL 54 B1
Rye GB 31 D4
Rygge N 35 C2
Ryjewo PL 47 B4
Rykene N 33 D5
Rymań PL 46 B1
Rýmařov CZ 64 A3
Rynarzewo PL 46 B3
Ryomgård DK 39 C3
Rypefjord N 113 B12
Rypin PL 47 B5
Rysjedalsvika N 32 A2
Ryssby S 40 C4
Rytel PL 46 B3
Rytro PL 65 A6
Rywociny PL 47 B6
Rzeczenica PL 46 B3
Rzeczniów PL 55 B6
Rzeczyca PL 55 B5
Rzegnowo PL 47 B6
Rzejowice PL 55 B4
Rzemień PL 55 C6
Rzepin PL 45 C6
Rzesznikowo PL 46 B1
Rzeszów PL 10 A6
Rzgów PL 55 B4
Rzhev RUS 7 C13

S

Saal
  Bayern D 51 C6
  Bayern D 62 B2
Saalbach A 72 A2
Saalburg D 52 C1
Saales F 60 B3
Saalfeld D 52 C1
Saalfelden am Steinernen
  Meer A 72 A2
Saanen CH 70 B2
Saarbrücken D 60 A2
Saarburg D 60 A2
Saarijärvi FIN 3 E26
Saarlouis D 60 A2
Saas-Fee CH 70 B2
Šabac SRB 85 B4
Sabadell E 91 B5
Sabáudia I 102 B6
Sabbioneta I 81 B4
Sabero E 88 B1
Sabiñánigo E 90 A2
Sabiote E 100 A2
Sables-d'Or-les-Pins
  F 56 B3
Sablé-sur-Sarthe F . . 57 C5
Sábóia P 98 B2
Saborsko HR 83 A4
Sæbøvik N 32 C2
Sabres F 76 B2
Sabrosa P 87 C3
Sabugal P 93 A3
Sabuncu TR 118 C5
Sæby DK 38 B3
Sacecorbo E 95 B4
Saceda del Rio E 95 B4
Sacedón E 95 B4
Săcele RO 11 D8
Saceruela E 94 D2
Sachsenburg A 72 B3
Sachsenhagen D 51 A5
Sacile I 72 C2
Sacramenia E 88 C3
Sada E 86 A2
Sádaba E 90 A1
Saddell GB 24 C2
Sadernes E 91 A5
Sadki PL 46 B3
Sadkowice PL 55 B5
Sadlinki PL 47 B4
Sadów PL 53 A5
Sadská CZ 53 C4
Saelices E 95 C4
Saelices de Mayorga
  E 88 B1
Saerbeck D 50 A3
Saeul L 60 A1
Safaalan TR 118 A3
Safara P 98 A3
Säffle S 35 C4
Saffron Walden GB . . 31 B4
Safonovo RUS 7 D12
Safranbolu TR 16 A6
Säfsnäs S 36 B1
Şag RO 75 C6
Sagard D 45 A5
S'Agaro E 91 B6
Sågmyra S 36 B2
Sagone F 102 A1
Sagres P 98 C2
Ságújfalu H 65 B5
Sagunt E 96 B2
Sagvåg N 32 C2
Ságvár H 74 B3
Sahagún E 88 B1
Šahy SK 65 B4
Saignelégier CH 70 A1
Saignes F 68 C2
Saija FIN 113 E17
Saillagouse F 91 A5
Saillans F 79 B4
Sains Richaumont F . . 59 A4
St Abb's GB 25 C5
St Affrique F 78 C1
St Agnant F 66 C4
St Agnes GB 28 C2
St Agrève F 78 A3
St Aignan F 67 A6
St Aignan-sur-Roë F . 57 C4
St Albans GB 31 C3
St Alban-sur-Limagnole
  F 78 B2
St Amand-en-Puisaye
  F 68 A2
St Amand-les-Eaux F . 49 C4
St Amand-Longpré F . 58 C2
St Amand-Montrond
  F 68 B2
St Amans F 78 B2
St Amans-Soult F . . . 77 C5
St Amant-Roche-Savine
  F 68 C3
St Ambroix F 78 B3
St Amé F 60 B2
St Amour F 69 B5
St André-de-Corcy F . 69 C4
St André-de-Cubzac
  F 76 A2
St André-de-l'Eure F . 58 B2
St André-de-
  Roquepertuis F . . . 78 B3
St Andre-de-Sangonis
  F 78 C2
St André-de-Valborgne
  F 78 B2
St André-les-Alpes F . 79 C5
St Andrews GB 25 B5
St Angel F 68 C2
St Anthème F 68 C3
St AntKönig F... Antoine F . . 102 A1
St Antoine-de-Ficalba
  F 77 B3
St Antönien CH 71 B4
St Antonin-Noble-Val
  F 77 B4
St Août F 68 B1
St Armant-Tallende F . 68 C3
St Asaph GB 26 B2
St Astier F 67 C5
St Athan GB 29 B4
St Auban F 79 C5

St Aubin
  CH 70 B1
  F 69 A5
St Aubin-d'Aubigné
  F 57 B4
St Aubin-du-Cormier
  F 57 B4
St Aubin-sur-Aire F . . 60 B1
St Aubin-sur-Mer F . . 57 A5
St Aulaye F 67 C5
St Austell GB 28 C3
St Avit F 68 C2
St Avold F 60 A2
St Aygulf F 79 C5
St Bauzille-de-Putois
  F 78 C2
St Béat F 77 D3
St Beauzély F 78 B1
St Bees GB 26 A2
St Benim-d'Azy F . . . 68 B3
St Benoît-du-Sault F . 67 B6
St Benoit-en-Woëvre
  F 60 B1
St Berthevin F 57 B5
St Blaise-la-Roche F . 60 B3
St Blazey GB 28 C3
St Bonnet F 79 B5
St Bonnet Briançon F . 79 B5
St Bonnet-de-Joux F . 69 B4
St Bonnet-le-Château
  F 68 C4
St Bonnet-le-Froid F . 78 A3
St Brévin-les-Pins F . . 66 A2
St Briac-sur-Mer F . . 57 B3
St Brice-en-Coglès F . 57 B4
St Brieuc F 56 B3
St Bris-le-Vineux F . . 59 C4
St Broladre F 57 B4
St Calais F 58 C1
St Cannat F 79 C4
St Cast-le-Guildo F . . 57 B3
St Céré F 77 B4
St Cergue CH 69 B6
St Cergues F 69 B6
St Cernin F 77 A5
St Chamant F 68 C1
St Chamas F 79 C4
St Chamond F 69 C4
St Chély-d'Apcher F . 78 B2
St Chély-d'Aubrac F . 78 B1
St Chinian F 78 C1
St Christol F 79 B4
St Christol-lès-Alès F . 78 B3
St Christoly-Médoc F . 66 C4
St Christophe-du-
  Ligneron F 66 B3
St Christophe-en-
  Brionnais F 69 B4
St Ciers-sur-Gironde
  F 66 C4
St Clair-sur-Epte F . . 58 A2
St Clar F 77 C3
St Claud F 67 C5
St Claude F 69 B5
St Clears GB 28 B3
St Columb Major GB . 28 C3
St Come-d'Olt F 78 B1
St Cosme-en-Vairais
  F 58 B1
St Cyprien
  Dordogne F 77 B4
  Pyrénées-Orientales
    F 91 A6
St Cyr-sur-Loire F . . . 67 A5
St Cyr-sur-Mer F 79 C4
St Cyr-sur-Methon F . 69 B5
St David's GB 28 B2
St Denis F 58 B3
St Denis-d'Oléron F . . 66 B3
St Denis d'Orques F . . 57 B5
St Didier F 69 B4
St Didier-en-Velay F . 69 C4
St Dié F 60 B2
St Dier-d'Auvergne F . 68 C3
St Dizier F 59 B5
St Dizier-Leyrenne F . 68 B1
St Dogmaels GB 28 A3
St Donat-sur-l'Herbasse
  F 78 A3
St Éloy-les-Mines F . . 68 B2
St Émiland F 69 B4
St Émilion F 76 B2
St Enoder GB 28 C3
St Estèphe F 66 C4
St Étienne F 69 C4
St Étienne-de-Baigorry
  F 76 C1
St Étienne-de-Cuines
  F 69 C6
St Étienne-de-Fursac
  F 68 B1
St Étienne-de-Montluc
  F 66 A3
St Étienne-de-St Geoirs
  F 69 C5
St Étienne-de-Tinée F . 79 B5
St Étienne-du-Bois F . 69 B5
St Étienne-du-Rouvray
  F 58 A2
St Étienne-les-Orgues
  F 79 B4
Ste Adresse F 57 A6
Ste Anne F 57 B6
Ste Anne-d'Auray F . . 56 C3
Ste Croix CH 69 B6
Ste Croix-Volvestre F . 77 C4
Ste Engrâce F 76 C2
Ste Enimie F 78 B2
Ste Foy-de-Peyrolières
  F 77 C4
Ste Foy-la-Grande F . 76 B3
Ste Foy-l'Argentiere
  F 69 C4
Ste Gauburge-Ste
  Colombe F 58 B1
Ste Gemme la Plaine
  F 66 B3
Ste Geneviève F 58 A3
Ste Hélène F 76 B2
Ste Hélène-sur-Isère
  F 69 C6
Ste Hermine F 66 B3
Ste Jalle F 79 B4
Ste Livrade-sur-Lot F . 77 B3
Ste Marie-aux-Mines
  F 60 B3
Ste Marie-du-Mont F . 57 A4
Ste Maure-de-Touraine
  F 67 B5
Ste Maxime F 79 C5
Ste Ménéhould F 59 A5
Ste Mère-Eglise F . . . 57 A4
St Emiland... Ste Ode B . 49 C6
Saintes F 67 C4
Ste Savine F 59 B5
Ste Sévère-sur-Indre
  F 68 B2
St Esteben F 76 C1
St Estèphe F...
St Étienne-de-Tulle F . 79 B5
Ste Tulle F 79 C4
St Fargeau F 59 C4
St Félicien F 78 A3
St Félix-de-Sorgues F . 78 C1
St Félix-Lauragais F . . 77 C4
Saintfield GB 19 B6
St Fillans GB 24 B3
St Florent F 102 A2
St Florentin F 59 C4
St Florent-le-Vieil F . . 66 A4
St Florent-sur-Cher F . 68 B2
St Flour F 78 A2
St Flovier F 67 B6
St Fort-sur-le-Né F...
St Fulgent F 66 B3
St Gaudens F 77 C3
St Gaultier F 67 B6
St Gély-du-Fesc F . . . 78 C2

St Genest-Malifaux F . 69 C4
St Gengoux-le-National
  F 69 B4
St Geniez F 79 B5
St Geniez-d'Olt F . . . 78 B1
St Genis-Pouilly F . . . 69 B6
St Genis-de-Saintonge
  F 67 C4
St Genix-sur-Guiers
  F 69 C5
St Georges Buttavent
  F 57 B5
St Georges-d'Aurac F . 68 C3
St Georges-de-Commiers
  F 79 A4
St Georges-de-Didonne
  F 66 C4
St Georges-de-Luzençon
  F 78 B1
St Georges-de-Mons
  F 68 C2
St Georges-de-Reneins
  F 69 B4
St Georges-d'Oléron
  F 66 C3
St Georges-en-Couzan
  F 68 C3
St Georges-lès-
  Baillargeaux F 67 B5
St Georges-sur-Loire
  F 66 A4
St Georges-sur-Meuse
  F 49 C6
St Geours-de-Maremne
  F 76 C1
St Gérand-de-Vaux F . 68 B3
St Gérand-le-Puy F . . 68 B3
St Germain F 60 C2
St Germain-Chassenay
  F 68 B3
St Germain-de-Calberte
  F 78 B2
St Germain-de-Confolens
  F 67 B5
St Germain-de-Joux
  F 69 B5
St Germain-des-Fossés
  F 68 B3
St Germain-du-Bois F . 69 B5
St Germain-du-Plain
  F 69 B4
St Germain-du-Puy F . 68 A2
St Germain-en-Laye F . 58 B3
St Germain-Laval F . . 68 C4
St Germain-Lembron
  F 68 C3
St Germain-les-Belles
  F 67 C6
St Germain-Lespinasse
  F 68 B3
St Germain-l'Herm F . 68 C3
St Gervais-d'Auvergne
  F 68 B2
St Gervais-les-Bains
  F 70 C1
St Gervais-sur-Mare
  F 78 C2
St Gildas-de-Rhuys F . 66 A2
St Gildas-des-Bois F . 66 A3
St Gilles
  Gard F 78 C3
  Ille-et-Vilaine F . . . 57 B4
St Gilles-Croix-de-Vie
  F 66 B3
St Gingolph F 70 B1
St Girons
  Ariège F 77 D4
  Landes F 76 C1
St Girons-Plage F . . . 76 C1
St Gobain F 59 A4
St Gorgon-Main F . . . 69 A6
St Guénolé F 56 C1
St Harmon GB 29 A4
St Helens GB 26 B3
St Helier GB 57 A3
St Herblain F 66 A3
St Hilaire
  Allier F 68 B3
  Aude F 77 C5
St Hilaire-de-Riez F . . 66 B3
St Hilaire-des-Loges
  F 67 B4
St Hilaire-de-Villefranche
  F 67 B4
St Hilaire-du-Harcouët
  F 57 B4
St Hilaire-du-Rosier F . 79 A4
St Hippolyte
  Aveyron F 77 B5
  Doubs F 70 A1
St Hippolyte-du-Fort
  F 78 C2
St Honoré-les-Bains
  F 68 B3
St Hubert B 49 C6
St Imier CH 70 A2
St Issey GB 28 C3
St Ives
  Cambridgeshire GB . 30 B3
  Cornwall GB 28 C2
St Izaire F 78 C1
St Jacques-de-la-Lande
  F 57 B4
St Jacut-de-la-Mer F . 57 B3
St Jaume d'Enveja E . 90 C3
St Jean-Brévelay F . . 56 C3
St Jean-d'Angély F . . 67 C4
St Jean-de-Belleville
  F 69 C6
St Jean-de-Bournay
  F 69 C5
St Jean-de-Braye F . . 58 C2
St Jean-de-Côle F . . . 67 C5
St Jean-de-Daye F . . . 57 A4
St Jean-de-Losne F . . 69 A5
St Jean-de-Luz F 76 C1
St Jean-de-Maurienne
  F 70 C1
St Jean-de-Monts F . . 66 B2
St Jean-du-Bruel F . . 78 B2
St Jean-du-Gard F . . . 78 B2
St Jean-en-Royans F . 79 A4
St Jean-la-Riviere F . . 79 C6
St Jean-Pied-de-Port
  F 76 C1
St Jean-Poutge F . . . 77 C3
St Jeoire F 69 B6
St Joachim F 66 A2
St Johnstown IRL . . . 19 B4
St Joris Winge B 49 C5
St Jorioz F 69 C6
St Jouin-de-Marnes
  F 67 A5
St Juéry F 77 C5
St Julien F 69 B5
St Julien-Chapteuil F . 78 A3
St Julien-de-Vouvantes
  F 57 C4
St Julien-du-Sault F . . 59 B4
St Julien-du-Verdon
  F 79 C5
St Julien-en-Born F . . 76 B1
St Julien-en-Genevois
  F 69 B6
St Julien-l'Ars F 67 B5
St Julien-Mont-Denis
  F 70 C1
St Julien-sur-Reyssouze
  F 69 B5
St Junien F 67 C5
St Just
  F 78 B3
  GB 28 C2
St Just-en-Chaussée
  F 58 A3
St Just-en-Chevalet F . 68 C3
St Justin F 76 C2

St Just-St Rambert F .69 C4
St Keverne GB. 28 C2
St Lary-Soulan F. . . .77 D3
St Laurent-d'Aigouze
F. 78 C3
St Laurent-de-
Chamousset F. 69 C4
St Laurent-de-Condel
F. 57 A5
St Laurent-de-la-
Cabrerisse F. 78 C1
St Laurent-de-la-Salanque
F. 78 D1
St Laurent-des-Autels
F. 66 A3
St Laurent-du-Pont F .69 C5
St Laurent-en-Caux F .58 A1
St Laurent-en-Grandvaux
F. 69 B5
St Laurent-Médoc F .66 A3
St Laurent-sur-Gorre
F. 67 C5
St Laurent-sur-Mer F .57 A4
St Laurent-sur-Sèvre
F. 66 B4
St Léger B. 60 A1
St Léger-de-Vignes F .68 B3
St Léger-sous-Beuvray
F. 68 B4
St Léger-sur-Dheune
F. 69 B4
St Léonard-de-Noblat
F. 67 C6
St Leonards GB. 31 D4
St Lô F. 57 A4
St Lon-les-Mines F. .76 C1
St Louis F. 60 C3
St Loup F. 68 B3
St Loup-de-la-Salle F .69 B4
St Loup-sur-Semouse
F. 60 C2
St Lunaire F. 56 B3
St Lupicin F. 69 B5
St Lyphard F. 66 A2
St Lys F. 77 C4
St Macaire F. 76 B2
St Maclou F. 58 A1
St Maixent-l'École F .67 B4
St Malo F. 57 B3
St Mamet-la-Salvetat
F. 77 B5
St Mandrier-sur-Mer
F. 79 C4
St Marcel
 Drôme F. 78 B3
 Saône-et-Loire F. .69 B4
St Marcellin F. 69 C5
St Marcellin sur Loire
F. 68 C4
St Marcet F. 77 C3
St Mards-en-Othe F. .59 B4
St Margaret's-at-Cliffe
GB. 31 C5
St Margaret's Hope
GB. 23 C6
St Mars-la-Jaille F. .66 A3
St Martin-d'Ablois F .59 B4
St Martin-d'Auxigny F .68 A2
St Martin-de-Belleville
F. 69 C6
St Martin-de-Bossenay
F. 59 B4
St Martin-de-Crau F .78 C3
St Martin-de-Londres
F. 78 C2
St Martin-d'Entraunes
F. 79 B5
St Martin-de-Queyrières
F. 79 B5
St Martin-de-Ré F. . .66 B3
St Martin des Besaces
F. 57 A5
St Martin-d'Estreaux
F. 68 B3
St Martin-de-Valamas
F. 78 B3
St Martin-d'Hères F .69 C5
St Martin-du-Frêne F .69 B5
St Martin-en-Bresse F .69 B5
St Martin-en-Haut F. .69 C4
St Martin-la-Méanne
F. 68 C1
St Martin-sur-Ouanne
F. 59 C4
St Martin-Valmeroux
F. 77 A5
St Martin-Vésubie F .79 B6
St Martory F. 77 C3
St Mary's GB. 23 C6
St Mathieu F. 67 C5
St Mathieu-de-Tréviers
F. 78 C2
St Maurice CH. 70 B1
St Maurice-Navacelles
F. 78 C2
St Maurice-sur-Moselle
F. 60 C2
St Mawes GB. 28 C3
St Maximin-la-Ste Baume
F. 79 C4
St Méard-de-Gurçon
F. 76 B3
St Médard-en-Guizières
F. 76 A2
St Médard-en-Jalles
F. 76 B2
St Méen-le-Grand F. .57 B3
St Menges F. 59 A5
St Merløse DK. 39 D4
St Město CZ. 54 C1
St M'Hervé F. 57 B4
St Michel
 Aisne F. 59 A5
 Gers F. 77 C3
St Michel-Chef-Chef
F. 66 A2
St Michel-de-Castelnau
F. 76 B2
St Michel-de-Maurienne
F. 69 C6
St Michel-en-Grève F .56 B2
St Michel-enl'Herm F .66 B3
St Michel-Mont-Mercure
F. 66 B4
St Mihiel F. 60 B1
St Monance GB. 25 B5
St Montant F. 78 B3
St Moritz CH. 71 B4
St Nazaire F. 66 A2
St Nazaire-en-Royans
F. 79 A4
St Nazaire-le-Désert
F. 79 B4
St Nectaire F. 68 C2
St Neots GB. 30 B3
St Nicolas-de-Port F .60 B2
St Nicolas-de-Redon
F. 57 C3
St Nicolas-du-Pélem
F. 56 B2
St Niklaas B. 49 B5
St Omer F. 48 C3
St Pair-sur-Mer F. . .57 B4
St Palais F. 76 C1
St Palais-sur-Mer F. .66 C3
St Pardoux-la-Rivière
F. 67 C5
St Paul-Cap-de-Joux
F. 77 C4
St Paul-de-Fenouillet
F. 77 D5
St Paul-de-Varax F. .69 B5
St Paulien F. 78 B2
St Paul-le-Jeune F. . .78 B3
St Paul-lès-Dax F. . .76 C1
St Paul-Trois-Châteaux
F. 78 B3
St Pé-de-Bigorre F. . .76 C2
St Pée-sur-Nivelle F .76 C1

St Péravy-la-Colombe
F. 58 C2
St Péray F. 78 B3
St Père-en-Retz F. . .66 A2
St Peter Port GB. . . .56 A3
St Petersburg = Sankt-
Peterburg RUS. 7 B11
St Philbert-de-Grand-Lieu
F. 66 A3
St Pierre F. 78 C1
St Pierre-d'Albigny F .69 C6
St Pierre-d'Allevard F .69 C6
St Pierre-de-Chartreuse
F. 69 C5
St Pierre-de-Chignac
F. 77 A3
St Pierre-de-la-Fage
F. 78 C2
St Pierre-d'Entremont
F. 69 C5
St Pierre-d'Oléron F .66 C2
St Pierre-Eglise F. . .57 A4
St Pierre-en-Port F. .58 A1
St Pierre-le-Moûtier F .68 B3
St Pierre Montlimart
F. 66 A3
St Pierre-Quiberon F .66 A1
St Pierre-sur-Dives F .57 A5
St Pierreville F. 78 B3
St Pieters-Leeuw B. .49 C5
St Plancard F. 77 C3
St Poix F. 57 C4
St Pol-de-Léon F. . . .56 B2
St Polgues F. 68 C3
St Pol-sur-Ternoise F .48 C3
St Pons-de-Thomières
F. 78 C1
St Porchaire F. 66 C4
St Pourçain-sur-Sioule
F. 68 B3
St Priest F. 69 C4
St Privat F. 68 C2
St Quay-Portrieux F .56 B3
St Quentin F. 59 A4
St Quentin-la-Poterie
F. 78 B3
St Quentin-les-Anges
F. 57 C5
St Rambert d'Albon F .69 C4
St Rambert-en-Bugey
F. 69 C5
St Raphaël F. 79 C5
St Rémy-de-Provence
F. 78 C3
St Rémy-du-Val F. . .57 B6
St Remy-en-Bouzemont
F. 59 B5
St Renan F. 56 B1
St Révérien F. 68 A3
St Riquier F. 48 C2
St Romain-de-Colbosc
F. 58 A1
St Rome-de-Cernon F .78 B1
St Rome-de-Tarn F. .78 B1
St Sadurni-d'Anoia E .91 B4
St Saëns F. 58 A2
St Sampson GB. 56 A3
St Samson-la-Poterie
F. 58 A2
St Saturnin-de-Lenne
F. 78 B2
St Saturnin-lès-Apt F .79 C4
St Sauflieu F. 58 A3
St Saulge F. 68 A3
St Sauveur
 Finistère F. 56 B2
 Haute-Saône F. . . .60 C2
St Sauveur-de-Montagut
F. 78 B3
St Sauveur-en-Puisaye
F. 59 C4
St Sauveur-en-Rue F .69 C4
St Sauveur-Lendelin
F. 57 A4
St Sauveur-le-Vicomte
F. 57 A4
St Sauveur-sur-Tinée
F. 79 B6
St Savin
 Gironde F. 76 A2
 Vienne F. 67 B5
St Savinien F. 67 C4
St Savournin F. 79 C4
St Seine-l'Abbaye F .69 A4
St Sernin-sur-Rance
F. 77 C5
St Sevan-sur-Mer F. .57 B3
St Sever F. 76 C2
St Sever-Calvados F .57 B4
St Sorlin-d'Arves F. .69 C6
St Soupplets F. 58 A3
St Sulpice F. 77 C4
St Sulpice-Laurière F .67 B6
St Sulpice-les-Feuilles
F. 67 B6
St Symphorien F. . . .76 B2
St Symphorien-de-Lay
F. 69 C4
St Symphorien d'Ozon
F. 69 C4
St Symphoriensur-Coise
F. 69 C4
St Teath GB. 28 C3
St Thégonnec F. 56 B2
St Thiébault F. 60 B1
St Trivier-de-Courtes
F. 69 B5
St Trivier-sur-Moignans
F. 69 B5
St Trojan-les-Bains F .66 C3
St Tropez F. 79 C5
St Truiden B. 49 C6
St Vaast-la-Hougue F .57 A4
St Valérien F. 59 B4
St Valery-en-Caux F .58 A1
St Valéry-sur-Somme
F. 48 C2
St Vallier
 Drôme F. 69 C4
 Saône-et-Loire F. .69 B4
St Vallier-de-Thiey F .79 C5
St Varent F. 67 B4
St Vaury F. 68 B1
St Venant F. 48 C3
St Véran F. 79 B5
St Vincent F. 70 C2
St Vincent-de-Tyrosse
F. 76 C1
St Vit F. 69 A5
St Vith B. 50 C2
St Vivien-de-Médoc F .66 C3
St Wandel F. 57 A6
St Ybars F. 77 C4
St Yorre F. 68 C3
St Yrieix-la-Perche F .67 C6
Saissac F. 77 C5
Saja E. 88 A2
Sajan SRB. 75 C5
Sajkaš SRB. 75 C5
Sajókaza H. 65 B6
Sajószentpéter H. . .65 B6
Sajóvámos H. 65 B6
Šakiai LT. 6 D7
Sakskøbing DK. 39 E4
Sakule SRB. 75 C5
Sal'a SK. 64 B3
Sala Baganza I. 81 B4
Sala Consilina I. . . .104 C1
Salakovac SRB. 85 B6
Salamanca E. 94 B1
Salandra I. 104 C2
Salaparuta I. 108 B1
Salar E. 100 B1
Salardú E. 90 A3
Salas E. 86 A4
Salas de los Infantes
E. 89 B3
Salau F. 77 D4
Salavaux CH. 70 B2

Salbertrand I. 79 A5
Salbohed S. 36 C3
Salbris F. 68 A2
Salbu N. 32 A2
Salce E. 86 B4
Salching D. 62 B3
Salcombe GB. 28 C4
Saldaña E. 88 B2
Saldus LV. 6 C7
Sale I. 80 B2
Saleby S. 35 D5
Salem D. 61 C5
Salemi I. 108 B1
Salen
 Argyll & Bute GB . .24 B2
 Highland GB 24 B2
 N. 114 C8
Sälen S. 34 A5
Salernes F. 79 C5
Salerno I. 103 C7
Salers F. 68 C2
Salford GB. 26 B3
Salgótarján H. 65 B5
Salgueiro P. 92 B3
Salhus N. 32 B2
Sali HR. 83 C4
Sálice Salentino I. . .105 C3
Salientes E. 86 B4
Salies-de-Béarn F. . .76 C2
Salies-du-Salat F. . .77 C3
Salignac-Eyvigues F .77 B4
Saligney-sur-Roudon
F. 68 B3
Salihli TR. 119 D3
Salihorsk BY. 7 E9
Salinas
 Alicante E. 101 A5
 Huesca E. 90 A3
Salinas de Medinaceli
E. 95 A4
Salinas de Pisuerga
E. 88 B2
Salindres F. 78 B3
Saline di Volterra I. .81 C4
Salins-les-Bains F. . .69 B5
Salir P. 98 B2
Salisbury GB. 29 B6
Salla
 A. 73 A4
 FIN. 113 F17
Sallachy GB. 23 C4
Sallanches F. 70 C1
Sallent E. 91 B4
Sallent de Gállego E .76 D2
Salles F. 76 B2
Salles-Curan F. 78 B1
Salles-sur-l'Hers F. .77 C4
Sallins IRL. 21 A5
Sällsjö S. 115 D10
Salmerón E. 95 B4
Salmiech F. 77 B5
Salmivaara FIN. 113 F17
Salmoral E. 94 B1
Salo FIN. 6 A7
Salò I. 71 C5
Salobreña E. 100 C2
Salon-de-Provence F .79 C4
Salonica = Thessaloniki
GR. 116 B4
Salonta RO. 10 C6
Salorino E. 93 B3
Salornay-sur-Guye F .69 B4
Salorno I. 71 B6
Salou E. 91 B4
Šalovci SLO. 73 B6
Salsbruket N. 114 C8
Salses-le-Château F .78 D1
Salsomaggiore Terme
I. 81 B3
Salt E. 91 B5
Saltaire GB. 27 B4
Saltara I. 82 C1
Saltash GB. 28 C3
Saltburn-by-the-Sea
GB. 27 A5
Saltcoats GB. 24 C3
Saltfleet GB. 27 B6
Salto P. 87 C3
Saltsjöbaden S. 37 C5
Saltvik
 FIN. 36 B7
 S. 40 B6
Saludécio I. 82 C1
Salussola I. 70 C3
Saluzzo I. 80 B1
Salvacañete E. 95 B5
Salvada P. 98 B3
Salvagnac F. 77 C4
Salvaleón E. 93 C4
Salvaterra de Magos
P. 92 B2
Salvaterra do Extremo
P. 93 B4
Salvatierra
 Avila E. 89 B4
 Badajoz E. 93 C4
Salvatierra de Santiago
E. 93 B4
Salviac F. 77 B4
Salzburg A. 62 C4
Salzgitter D. 51 A6
Salzgitter Bad D. . . .51 A6
Salzhausen D. 44 B2
Salzhemmendorf F. .51 A5
Salzkotten D. 51 B4
Salzwedel D. 44 C3
Samadet F. 76 C2
Samandıra TR. 118 B4
Samassi I. 110 C1
Samatan F. 77 C3
Sambiase I. 106 C3
Sambir UA. 11 B7
Samborowo PL. 47 B5
Sambuca di Sicília I .108 B2
Samedan CH. 71 B4
Samer F. 48 C2
Sami GR. 117 D2
Samnaun CH. 71 B5
Samobor HR. 73 C5
Samoëns F. 70 B1
Samogneux F. 59 A6
Samokov BG. 11 E7
Šamorín SK. 64 B3
Samos
 E. 86 B3
 GR. 119 E1
Samothraki GR. 116 B7
Samper de Calanda E .90 B2
Sampéyre I. 79 B6
Sampigny F. 60 B1
Samplawa PL. 47 B5
Samtens D. 45 A5
Samugheo I. 110 C1
San Adrián E. 89 B5
San Agustín E. 101 C3
San Agustin de Guadalix
E. 94 B3
Sanaigmore GB. 24 C1
San Alberto I. 82 B1
San Amaro E. 87 B2
Sânandrei RO. 75 C6
San Andres del Rabanedo
E. 88 B1
San Antanio di Santadi
I. 110 C1
San Antolín de Ibias
E. 86 A4
San Arcángelo I. 104 C2
Sanary-sur-Mer F. . .79 C4
San Asensio E. 89 B4
San Bartoloméde las
Abiertas E. 94 C2

San Bartoloméde la Torre
E. 99 B3
San Bartoloméde Pinares
E. 94 B2
San Bartolomeo in Galdo
I. 103 B8
San Benedetto del Tronto
I. 82 D2
San Benedetto in Alpe
I. 81 C5
San Benedetto Po I. .81 A4
San Benito de la
Contienda E. 93 C3
San Biágio Plátani I .108 B2
San Biágio Saracinisco
I. 103 B6
San Bonifacio I. 71 C6
San Calixto E. 99 B5
San Cándido I. 72 B2
San Carlo
 CH. 70 B3
 I. 108 B2
San Carlos del Valle
E. 100 A2
San Casciano dei Bagni
I. 81 D5
San Casciano in Val di
Pesa I. 81 C5
San Cataldo
 Puglia I. 105 C4
 Sicília I. 108 B2
San Cebrián de Castro
E. 88 C1
San Chirico Raparo
I. 106 A3
Sanchonuño E. 88 C2
San Cibrao das Viñas
E. 87 B3
San Cipirello I. 108 B2
San Ciprián E. 86 A3
San Clemente E. 95 C4
San Clodio E. 86 B3
San Colombano al
Lambro I. 71 C4
San Costanzo I. 82 C2
San Crisóbal de
Entreviñas E. 88 B1
San Cristóbal de la
Polantera E. 88 B1
San Cristóbal de la Vega
E. 94 A2
San Cristovo E. 87 C3
Sancti-Petri E. 99 C4
Sancti-Spíritus E. . . .87 D4
Sand
 Hedmark N. 34 B3
 Rogaland N. 33 C3
Sanda S. 37 E5
San Damiano d'Asti I .80 B2
San Damiano Macra I .79 B6
Sandane N. 114 F3
San Daniele del Friuli
I. 72 B3
Sandanski BG. 116 A5
Sandared S. 40 B2
Sandarne S. 36 A4
Sandbach
 D. 63 B4
 GB. 26 B3
Sandbank GB. 24 C3
Sandbanks GB. 29 C6
Sandbukt N. 112 C10
Sandby DK. 39 E4
Sande
 D. 43 B5
 Sogn og Fjordane N .32 A2
 Vestfold N. 35 C2
Sandefjord N. 35 C2
Sandeid N. 33 C2
San Demétrio Corone
I. 106 B3
San Demétrio né Vestini
I. 103 A6
Sandersleben D. 52 B1
Sanderstølen N. 32 B6
Sandes N. 33 D4
Sandesneben D. 44 B2
Sandhead GB. 24 D3
Sandhem S. 40 B3
Sandhorst D. 43 B4
Sandhurst GB. 31 C3
Sandıklı TR. 119 D5
Sandillon F. 58 C2
Sandl A. 63 B5
Sandness GB. 22 A7
Sando E. 87 D4
Sandomierz PL. 55 C6
San Dónaci I. 105 C3
San Donà di Piave I .72 C2
San Donato Val di Comino
I. 103 B6
Sándorfalva H. 75 B5
Sandown GB. 31 D2
Sandøysund N. 35 C2
Sandrigo I. 72 C1
Sandsele S. 115 B14
Sandset N. 112 D3
Sandsjöfors S. 40 B4
Sandstad N. 114 D6
Sandvatn N. 33 D3
Sandvig-Allinge DK. .41 D4
Sandvika
 Akershus N. 34 C2
 Hedmark N. 34 B3
 Nord-Trøndelag N. .114 D9
Sandviken S. 36 B3
Sandvikvåg N. 32 C2
Sandwich GB. 31 C5
Sandy GB. 30 B3
San Emiliano E. 86 B5
San Enrique E. 99 C5
San Esteban E. 86 A4
San Esteban de Gormaz
E. 89 C3
San Esteban de la Sierra
E. 93 A5
San Esteban de Litera
E. 90 B3
San Esteban del Molar
E. 88 C1
San Esteban del Valle
E. 94 B2
San Esteban de Valdueza
E. 86 B4
San Felice Circeo I. .102 B6
San Felice sul Panaro
I. 81 B5
San Felices E. 89 B4
San Felices de los
Gallégos E. 87 D4
San Ferdinando di Púglia
I. 104 B2
San Fernando E. 99 C4
San Fernando de Henares
E. 94 B3
San Fili I. 106 B3
San Foca I. 105 C4
San Fratello I. 109 B3
Sangatte F. 48 C2
San Gavino Monreale
I. 110 C1
Sangerhausen D. 52 B1
San Germano Vercellese
I. 70 C3
San Giácomo
 Trentino Alto Adige
 I. 72 B1
 Umbria I. 82 D1
San Gimignano I. 81 C5

San Ginésio I. 82 C2
Sangineto Lido I. . . .106 B2
San Giórgio a Liri I. .103 B6
San Giorgio della
Richinvelda I. 72 B2
San Giórgio del Sánnio
I. 103 B7
San Giórgio di Lomellina
I. 70 C3
San Giorgio di Piano
I. 81 B5
San Giórgio Iónico
I. 104 C3
San Giovanni a Piro
I. 106 A2
San Giovanni Bianco
I. 71 C4
San Giovanni di Sinis
I. 110 C1
San Giovanni in Croce
I. 81 A4
San Giovanni in Fiore
I. 106 B3
San Giovanni in Persiceto
I. 81 B5
San Giovanni Reatino
I. 102 A5
San Giovanni Rotondo
I. 104 B1
San Giovanni Suérgiu
I. 110 C1
San Giovanni Valdarno
I. 81 C5
San Giuliano Terme I .81 C4
San Giustino I. 82 C1
San Godenzo I. 81 C5
Sangonera la Verde
E. 101 B4
San Gregorio Magno
I. 103 C8
Sangüesa E. 90 A1
Sanguinet F. 76 B1
San Guiseppe Jato I .108 B2
Sanica BIH. 83 B5
San Javier E. 101 B5
San Jorge E. 90 C2
San José E. 101 C3
San Juan E. 89 B3
San Juan de Alicante
E. 96 C2
San Juan de la Nava
E. 94 B2
San Justo de la Vega
E. 86 B4
Sankt Aegyd am
Neuwalde A. 63 C6
Sankt Andrä A. 73 B4
Sankt Andreasberg D .51 B6
Sankt Anna S. 37 D3
Sankt Anna am Aigen
A. 73 B5
Sankt Anton am Arlberg
A. 71 A5
Sankt Anton an der
Jessnitz A. 63 B6
Sankt Augustin D. . . .50 C3
Sankt Blasien D. 61 C4
Sankt Englmar D. . . .62 A3
Sankt Gallen
 A. 63 C5
 CH. 71 A4
Sankt Gallenkirch A .71 A4
Sankt Georgen
 A. 63 B4
 D. 61 B4
Sankt Georgen am Reith
A. 63 C5
Sankt Georgen ob
Judenburg A. 73 A4
Sankt Georgen ob Murau
A. 72 A3
Sankt Gilgen A. 63 C4
Sankt Goar D. 50 C3
Sankt Goarshausen
D. 50 C3
Sankt Ingbert D. 60 A3
Sankt Jacob A. 72 B3
Sankt Jakob in
Defereggen A. 72 B2
Sankt Johann am Tauern
A. 73 A4
Sankt Johann am Wesen
A. 63 B4
Sankt Johann im Pongau
A. 72 A3
Sankt Johann in Tirol
A. 72 A2
Sankt Katharein an der
Laming A. 73 A5
Sankt Kathrein am
Hauenstein A. 73 A5
Sankt Leonhard am Forst
A. 63 B6
Sankt Leonhard im Pitztal
A. 71 A5
Sankt Lorenzen A. . . .72 B2
Sankt Marein
 Steiermark A. 73 A5
 Steiermark A. 73 A5
Sankt Margarethen im
Lavanttal A. 73 B4
Sankt Margrethen CH .71 A4
Sankt Michael
 Burgenland A. 73 A6
Sankt Michael im Lungau
A. 72 A3
Sankt Michaelisdonn
D. 43 B6
Sankt Niklaus CH. . . .70 B2
Sankt Nikolai im Sölktal
A. 72 A3
Sankt Olof S. 41 D4
Sankt Oswald D. 63 B4
Sankt Paul
 A. 73 B4
 F. 79 B5
Sankt Peter D. 61 B4
Sankt Peter am
Kammersberg A. . .73 A4
Sankt Peter-Ording D .43 A5
Sankt Pölten A. 63 B6
Sankt Radegund A. . .73 A5
Sankt Ruprecht an der
Raab A. 73 A5
Sankt Salvator A. . . .73 B4
Sankt Stefan A. 73 B4
Sankt Stefan an der Gail
A. 72 B3
Sankt Stefan im Rosental
A. 73 B5
Sankt Valentin A. 63 B5
Sankt Veit an der Glan
A. 73 B4
Sankt Veit an der Gölsen
A. 63 B6
Sankt Veit in Defereggen
A. 72 B2
Sankt Wendel D. 60 A3
Sankt Wolfgang
 A. 63 C4
 D. 62 B3
San Lázaro di Sávena
I. 81 B5
San Leo I. 82 C1
San Leonardo de Yagüe
E. 89 C3
San Leonardo in Passiria
I. 71 B6
San Leonardo a Merse
I. 81 C5
San Lorenzo Bellizzi
I. 106 B3
San Lorenzo de Calatrava
E. 100 A2

San Lorenzo de El
Escorial E. 94 B2
San Lorenzo de la Parrilla
E. 95 C4
San Lorenzo di Sebato
I. 72 B1
San Lorenzo in Campo
I. 82 C1
San Lorenzo Nuovo I .81 D5
San Lourenço P. 98 A2
San Lúca I. 106 C3
Sanlúcar de Barrameda
E. 99 C4
Sanlúcar de Guadiana
E. 98 B3
Sanlúcar la Mayor E .99 B4
San Lúcido I. 106 B3
Sanluri I. 110 C1
San Marcello I. 82 C2
San Marcello Pistoiese
I. 81 B4
San Marcial E. 88 C1
San Marco I. 103 C7
San Marco Argentano
I. 106 B3
San Marco dei Cavoti
I. 103 B7
San Marco in Lámis
I. 104 B1
San Marino RSM. . . .82 C1
San Martín de Castañeda
E. 87 B4
San Martin de la Vega
E. 95 B3
San Martin de la Vega del
Alberche E. 93 A5
San Martín del Tesorillo
E. 99 C5
San Martin de Luiña
E. 86 A4
San Martin de Montalbán
E. 94 C2
San Martin de Oscos
E. 86 A4
San Martín de Pusa E .94 C2
San Martin de Unx E .89 B5
San Martin de
Valdeiglesias E. . .94 B2
San Martino di Campagna
I. 72 B2
San Martino di Castrozza
I. 72 B1
San-Martino-di-Lota
F. 102 A2
San Martino in Pénsilis
I. 103 B8
San Mateo de Gallego
E. 90 B2
San Máuro Forte I. . .104 C2
San Michele all'Ádige
I. 71 B6
San Michele di Ganzaria
I. 109 B3
San Michele Mondov'i
I. 80 B1
San Miguel de Aguayo
E. 88 A2
San Miguel de Bernuy
E. 88 C3
San Miguel del Arroyo
E. 88 C2
San Miguel de Salinas
E. 101 B5
Sânmihaiu Roman
RO. 75 C6
San Millán de la Cogolla
E. 89 B4
San Miniato I. 81 C4
San Muñoz E. 87 D4
Sänna S. 37 D1
Sannazzaro de'Burgondi
I. 80 A3
Sannicandro di Bari
I. 104 B2
Sannicandro Gargánico
I. 104 B1
San Nicola del'Alto I .107 B3
San Nicolás del Puerto
E. 99 B5
Sannidal N. 33 D6
San Nicolò I. 81 B5
San Nicolò Gerrei I. .110 C2
Sannicki PL. 47 C5
Sanok PL. 11 B7
San Pablo de los Montes
E. 94 C2
San Pancrázio Salentino
I. 105 C3
San Pantaleo I. 110 A2
San Páolo di Civitate
I. 103 B8
San Pawl il-Bahar M .109 B3
San Pedro
 Albacete E. 101 A3
 Oviedo E. 86 A4
San Pedro de Alcántara
E. 99 C5
San Pedro de Ceque
E. 87 B4
San Pedro del Arroyo
E. 94 B2
San Pedro de Latarce
E. 88 C1
San Pedro del Pinatar
E. 101 B5
San Pedro del Romeral
E. 88 A3
San Pedro de Mérida
E. 93 B4
San Pedro de
Valderaduey E. . . .88 B2
San Pedro Manrique
E. 89 C4
San Pellegrino Terme
I. 71 C4
San Piero a Sieve I. .81 C5
San Piero in Bagno I .81 C5
San Piero Patti I. 109 B3
San Pietro I. 109 B3
San Pietro in Casale I .81 B5
San Pietro in Palazzi I .81 C4
San Pietro in Volta I .72 C2
San Pietro Vara I. . . .80 B3
San Pietro Vernótico
I. 105 C4
San Polo d'Enza I. . . .81 B4
Sanquhar GB. 25 C4
San Quírico d'Órcia I .81 C5
San Rafael del Rio E .90 C3
San Remo I. 80 C1
San Román de Cameros
E. 89 B4
San Román de Hernija
E. 88 C1
San Román de la Cuba
E. 88 B2
San Román de los Montes
E. 94 B2
San Romao P. 92 B3
San Roque E. 99 C5
San Roque de Riomera
E. 88 A3
San Rufo I. 104 C1
San Sabastián de los
Ballesteros E. 100 B1
San Salvador de
Cantamuda E. 88 B2
San Salvo I. 103 A7
San Salvo Marina I. .103 A7
San Sebastián de los
Reyes E. 94 B3
San Sebastiano Curone
I. 80 B3
San Secondo Parmense
I. 81 B4
Sansepolcro I. 82 C1
San Serverino Marche
I. 82 C2

San Severino Lucano
I. 106 A3
San Severo I. 103 B8
Sanski Most BIH. . . .83 B5
San Sosti I. 106 B3
San Stéfano di Cadore
I. 72 B2
San Stino di Livenza I .72 C2
Santa Agnès E. 97 B1
Santa Amalia E. 93 B4
Santa Ana
 Cáceres E. 93 B5
 Jaén E. 100 B2
Santa Ana de Pusa E .94 C2
Santa Barbara E. 90 C3
Santa Bárbara P. 98 B2
Santa Bárbara de Casa
E. 98 B3
Santa Bárbara de
Padrões P. 98 B3
Santacara E. 89 B5
Santa Catarina P. 98 B3
Santa Catarina di Pittinuri
I. 110 B1
Santa Caterina Villarmosa
I. 109 B3
Santa Cesárea Terme
I. 107 A5
Santa Clara-a-Nova P .98 B2
Santa Clara-a-Velha P .98 B2
Santa Clara de Louredo
P. 98 B3
Santa Coloma de Farners
E. 91 B5
Santa Coloma de
Gramenet E. 91 B5
Santa Coloma de Queralt
E. 91 B4
Santa Comba de
Curueño E. 88 B1
Santa Comba de
Somoza E. 86 B4
Santa Comba I. 86 A2
Santa Comba Dáo P .92 A2
Santa Comba de Rossas
P. 87 C4
Santa Cristina I. 71 C4
Santa Cristina de la
Polvorosa E. 88 B1
Santa Cruz
 E. 86 A2
 P. 92 B1
Santa Cruz de Alhama
E. 100 B2
Santa Cruz de Campezo
E. 89 B4
Santa Cruz de Grio E .89 C5
Santa Cruz de la Salceda
E. 89 C3
Santa Cruz de la Sierra
E. 93 B5
Santa Cruz de la Zarza
E. 95 C3
Santa Cruz del Retamar
E. 94 B2
Santa Cruz de Moya
E. 96 B1
Santa Cruz de Mudela
E. 100 A2
Santa Cruz de Paniagua
E. 93 A4
Santadi I. 110 C1
Santa Doménica Talao
I. 106 B2
Santa Doménica Vittória
I. 109 B3
Santaella E. 100 B1
Santa Elena E. 100 A2
Santa Elena de Jamuz
E. 88 B1
Santa Eufémia
d'Aspromonte I. . . .106 C2
Santa Eulalia E. 95 B5
Santa Eulália P. 92 C3
Santa Eulalia de Oscos
E. 86 A3
Santa Eulàlia des Riu
E. 97 C1
Santa Fe E. 100 B2
Santa Fiora I. 81 D5
Sant'Ágata dei Goti I .103 B7
Sant'Ágata di Ésaro
I. 106 B2
Sant'Ágata di Puglia
I. 103 B8
Sant'Ágata Militello I .109 A3
Santa Giústina I. 72 B2
Sant Agust ide Lluçanès
E. 91 A5
Santa Iria P. 98 B3
Santa Leocadia P. . . .87 C2
Santa Lucia del Mela
I. 109 A4
Santa Lucia-de-Porto-
Vecchio F. 102 B2
Santa Luzia P. 98 B2
Santa Maddalena di
Polpis E. 90 C3
Santa Margalida E. . .97 B3
Santa Margarida do Sado
P. 98 A2
Santa Margaridao de
Montbui E. 91 B4
Santa Margherita di Belice
I. 108 B2
Santa Margherita Ligure
I. 80 B3
Santa Maria
 E. 90 B2
 CH. 71 B5
Santa Maria al Bagno
I. 105 C4
Santa Maria Cápua
Vétere I. 103 B7
Santa Maria da Feira
P. 87 D2
Santa Maria de Cayón
E. 88 A3
Santa Maria de Corco
E. 91 B5
Santa Maria de Huerta
E. 95 A4
Santa Maria de las Hoyas
E. 89 C3
Santa Maria del Cami
E. 97 B2
Santa Maria del Campo
E. 88 B3
Santa Maria del Campo
Rus E. 95 C4
Santa Maria della Versa
I. 80 B3
Santa Maria del Páramo
E. 88 B1
Santa Maria del Taro I .80 B3
Santa Maria de Mercadillo
E. 89 C3
Santa Maria de Nieva
E. 101 B4
Santa Maria de Trassierra
E. 100 B1
Santa Maria di Licodia
I. 109 B3
Santa Maria-di-Rispéscia
I. 81 D5

Santa Maria la Palma
I. 110 B1
Santa Maria la Real de
Nieva E. 94 A2
Santa Maria Maggiore
I. 70 B3
Santa Maria Ribarredonda
E. 89 B3
Santa Marina del Rey
E. 88 B1
Santa Marinella I. . . .102 A4
Santa Marta
 Albacete E. 95 C5
 Badajoz E. 93 C4
Santa Marta de Magasca
E. 93 B4
Santa Marta de
Penaguião P. 87 C3
Santa Marta de Tormes
E. 94 B1
Santana
 Évora P. 92 C2
 Setúbal P. 92 C1
Santana da Serra P. .98 B2
Santo do Mato P. . . .92 C2
Sant'Anastasia I. . . .103 C7
Santander E. 88 A3
Sant'Andrea Frius I. .110 C2
Sant'Angelo dei Lombardi
I. 103 C8
Sant'Angelo in Vado I .82 C1
Sant'Angelo Lodigiano
I. 71 C4
Santa Ninfa I. 108 B1
Sant'Antíoco I. 110 C1
Sant Antoni de Calonge
E. 91 B6
Sant'Antonio-di-Gallura
I. 110 B2
Santanyí E. 97 B3
Santa Olalla
 Huelva E. 99 B4
 Toledo E. 94 B2
Santa Pau E. 91 A5
Santa Pola E. 96 C2
Santa Ponça E. 97 B2
Santarcángelo di
Romagna I. 82 B1
Santarém P. 92 B2
Santa Severa
 F. 102 A2
 I. 102 A4
Santa Severina I. . . .107 B3
Santas Martas E. 88 B1
Santa Sofia I. 81 C5
Santa Susana E. 92 C2
Santa Suzana P. 92 C3
Santa Teresa di Riva
I. 109 B4
Santa Teresa Gallura
I. 110 A2
Santa Uxía E. 86 B2
Santa Valburga I. 71 B5
Santa Vittória in
Matenano I. 82 C2
Sant Boi de Llobregat
E. 91 B5
Sant Carles de la Ràpita
E. 90 C3
Sant Carlos I. 97 C3
Sant'Caterina I. 81 C4
Sant Celoni E. 91 B5
Sant Climent E. 97 B4
Santed E. 95 A5
Sant'Egídio alla Vibrata
I. 82 D2
Sant'Elia a Pianisi I. .103 B7
Sant'Elia Fiumerapido
I. 103 B6
Santelices E. 88 A3
San Telmo E. 99 B4
Sant'Elpídio a Mare I .82 C2
Santena in Colle I. . .104 C2
Santervas de la Vega
E. 88 B2
Sant' Eufémia Lamezia
I. 106 C3
Sant Feliu E. 91 B5
Sant Feliu de Codines
E. 91 B5
Sant Feliu de Guíxols
E. 91 B6
Sant Feliu Sasserra E .91 B5
Sant Ferran E. 97 C1
Sant Francesc de
Formentera E. 97 C1
Sant Francesc de ses
Salines E. 97 C1
Santhià I. 70 C3
Sant Hilari Sacalm E .91 B5
Sant Hipólit de Voltregà
E. 91 A5
Santiago de Alcántara
E. 92 B3
Santiago de Calatrava
E. 100 B1
Santiago de Compostela
E. 86 B2
Santiago de la Espada
E. 101 A3
Santiago de la Puebla
E. 94 B1
Santiago de la Ribera
E. 101 B5
Santiago del Campo
E. 93 B4
Santiago de Litem P .92 B2
Santiago do Cacém P .98 A2
Santiago do Escoural
P. 92 C2
Santiago Maior P. . . .92 C3
Santibáñez de Béjar
E. 93 A5
Santibáñez de la Peña
E. 88 B2
Santibáñez de Murias
E. 88 A1
Santibáñez de Vidriales
E. 87 B4
Santibáñez el Alto E .93 A4
Santibáñez el Bajo E .93 A4
Santillana E. 88 A2
Santiponce E. 99 B4
San Tirso de Abres E .86 A3
Santisteban del Puerto
E. 100 A2
Santiuste de San Juan
Bautiste E. 94 A2
Sant Jaume dels
Domenys E. 91 B4
Sant Joan Baptista E .97 B1
Sant Jordi E. 90 C3
Sant Josep de sa Talaia
E. 97 C1
Sant Juliáde Loria
AND. 91 A4
Sant'Ilario d'Enza I. .81 B4
Sant Llorençde Morunys
Carctassar E. 97 B3
Sant Luis E. 97 B4
Sant Mart ide Llemaná
E. 91 A5
Sant Marti de Maldá
E. 91 B4
Sant Marti Sarroca E .91 B4
Sant Mateu E. 90 C3
Sant Miquel E. 97 B1
Santo Aleixo P. 92 C3
Santo Amado P. 98 A3
Santo Amaro P. 92 C3
Santo André P. 98 A2
Santo Domingo E. . . .93 C3

Santo Domingo de la Calzada E....89 B4
Santo Domingo de Silos E....89 C3
Santo Estêvão
 Faro P....98 B3
 Santarém P....92 C2
Santok PL....46 C1
Santomera E....101 A4
Santoña E....89 A3
Santo-Pietro-di Tenda F....102 A2
Sant'Oreste I....102 A5
Santo Spirito I....104 B2
Santo Stefano d'Aveto I....80 B3
Santo Stéfano di Camastra I....109 B3
Santo Stefano di Magra I....81 B3
Santo Stéfano Quisquina I....108 B2
Santo Tirso P....87 C2
Santotis E....88 A2
Santo Tomé E....100 A2
Santovenia
 Burgos E....89 B3
 Zamora E....88 C1
Sant Pau de Seguries E....91 A5
Santpedor E....91 B4
Sant Pere de Riudebitlles E....91 B4
Sant Pere Pescador E....91 A6
Sant Poi de Sallavinera E....91 B4
Sant Quirze de Besora E....91 A5
Sant Rafel E....97 C1
Sant Ramon E....91 B4
Santu Lussurgiu I....110 B1
Santutzi E....89 A3
Sant Vincençde Castellet E....91 B4
San Valentino alla Muta I....71 B5
San Venanzo I....82 D1
San Vicente de Alcántara E....93 B3
San Vicente de Arana E....89 B4
San Vicente de la Barquera E....88 A2
San Vicente de la Sonsierra E....89 B4
San Vicente de Toranzo E....88 A3
San Vietro E....87 C4
San Vigilio I....72 B1
San Vincente del Raspeig E....96 C2
San Vincenzo I....81 C4
San Vito I....110 C2
San Vito al Tagliamento I....72 C2
San Vito Chietino I....103 A7
San Vito dei Normanni I....104 C3
San Vito di Cadore I....72 B2
San Vito lo Capo I....108 A1
San Vito Romano I....102 B5
Sanxenxo E....86 B2
Sanza I....104 C2
São Aleixo P....92 C3
São Barnabé P....98 B2
São Bartoloméda Serra P....98 A2
São Bartolomeu de Messines P....98 B2
São Bento P....87 C2
São Brás P....87 C2
São Brás de Alportel P....98 B3
São Braz do Reguedoura P....92 C2
São Cristóvão P....92 C2
São Domingos P....98 B2
São Geraldo P....92 C2
São Jacinto P....92 A2
São João da Madeira P....87 D2
São João da Pesqueira P....87 C3
São João da Ribeira P....92 B2
São João da Serra P....87 D2
São João da Venda P....98 B3
São João dos Caldeireiros P....98 B3
São Julião P....92 B3
São Leonardo P....92 C3
São Luis P....98 B2
São Manços P....92 C3
São Marcos da Ataboeira P....98 B3
Saõ Marcos da Serra P....98 B2
São Marcos de Campo P....92 C3
São Martinho da Cortiça P....92 A2
São Martinho das Amoreiras P....98 B2
São Martinho do Porto P....92 B1
São Matias
 Beja P....98 A3
 Évora P....92 C2
São Miguel d'Acha P....92 A3
São Miguel de Machede P....92 C3
São Pedro da Torre P....87 C2
São Pedro de Cadeira P....92 B1
São Pedro de Moel P....92 B1
São Pedro de Solis P....98 B3
São Pedro do Sul P....92 A2
Saorge F....80 C1
São Romão P....92 A3
São Sebastião dos Carros P....98 B3
São Teotónio P....98 B2
São Torcato P....87 C2
Sapataria P....92 C1
Sapes GR....116 A5
Sapiãos P....87 C3
Sa Pobla E....97 B3
Sappada I....72 B2
Sappen N....112 C10
Sapri I....106 A2
Sarajevo BIH....84 C3
Saramon F....77 C3
Sarandë AL....116 C2
Saranovo SRB....85 B5
Saraorci SRB....85 B6
Sa Rapita E....97 B3
S'Arenal E....97 B3
Sarengrad HR....75 C4
Sarentino I....71 B6
Sarezzo I....71 C5
Sargans CH....71 A4

Sári H....75 A4
Sanbeyler TR....118 C2
Sarıcakaya TR....118 B5
Sari-d'Orcino F....102 A1
Sangöl TR....119 D3
Sankaya TR....16 B7
Sarköy TR....118 B2
Sarilhos Grandes P....92 C2
Sariñena E....90 B2
Sarioba I....118 C7
Sárisáp H....65 C4
Sariyer TR....118 A4
Sarkad H....75 B6
Sárkeresztes H....74 A3
Sárkeresztúr H....74 A3
Sárkikaraağaç TR....119 D6
Sarlat-la-Canéda F....77 B4
Sarliac-sur-l'Isle F....67 C5
Sármellék H....74 B2
Sarnadas P....82 C2
Sarnano I....82 C2
Sarnen CH....70 B3
Sarnesfield GB....29 A5
Sárnico I....71 B6
Sarno I....103 C7
Sarnonico I....71 B6
Sarnow CZ....64 A1
Sarny UA....11 A9
Särö S....38 B4
Saronno I....70 C4
Sárosd H....74 A3
Sarpsborg N....35 C3
Sarracin E....88 B3
Sarral E....91 B4
Sarralbe F....60 A3
Sarrancolin F....77 D3
Sarras F....69 C4
Sarre I....70 C2
Sarreaus E....87 B3
Sarrebourg F....60 B3
Sarreguemines F....60 A3
Sárrétudvari H....75 A6
Sarre-Union F....60 B3
Sarria E....86 B3
Sarrià de Ter E....91 A5
Sarrión E....96 A2
Sarroca de Lleida E....90 B3
Sarroch I....110 C2
Sarron F....76 C2
Sársina I....82 C1
Sarstedt D....51 A5
Sárszentlörinc H....74 B3
Sárszentmihaly H....74 A3
Sárszentmiklós H....74 B3
Sárvár H....74 A1
Sarvisvaara S....113 F10
Sarzana I....81 B3
Sarzeau F....66 A2
Sasalli TR....119 D1
Sasamón E....88 B2
Sa Savina E....97 C1
Sásd H....74 B3
Sasino PL....46 A3
Sássari I....110 B1
Sassello I....80 B2
Sassenberg D....50 B4
Sassetta I....81 C4
Sassnitz D....45 A5
Sassocorvaro I....82 C1
Sasso d'Ombrone I....81 D5
Sassoferrato I....82 C1
Sassoleone I....81 B5
Sasso Marconi I....81 B5
Sassuolo I....81 B4
Sástago E....90 B2
Šaštinske Stráže SK....64 B3
Sas van Gent NL....49 B4
Sátahaugen N....114 E7
Satão P....87 D3
Sätenäs S....35 D4
Säter S....36 B2
Sätila S....40 B2
Satillieu F....69 C4
Satnica Đakovačka HR....74 C3
Sátoraljaújhely H....10 B6
Satow D....44 B3
Sätra-brunn S....36 C3
Sætre N....35 C2
Satrup D....43 A6
Satteins A....71 A4
Satu Mare RO....11 C7
Saturnia I....102 A4
Saucats F....76 B2
Saucelle E....87 C4
Sauda N....33 C3
Sauðárkrókur IS....111 B6
Saudasjøen N....33 C3
Sauerlach D....62 C2
Saugues F....78 B2
Sauherad N....33 C6
Saujon F....66 C4
Sauland N....33 C5
Saulces Monclin F....59 A5
Saulgau D....61 B5
Saulgrub D....62 C2
Saulieu F....69 A4
Saulnot F....60 C2
Sault F....79 B4
Sault-Brénaz F....69 C5
Sault-de-Navailles F....76 C2
Saulx F....60 C2
Saulxures-sur-Moselotte F....60 C2
Saulzais-le-Potier F....68 B2
Saumos F....76 B1
Saumur F....67 A4
Saunavaara FIN....113 E16
Saundersfoot GB....28 B3
Saurat F....77 D4
Saurbær
 Borgarfjarðarsýsla IS....111 C4
 Dalasýsla IS....111 B4
 Eyjafjarðarsýsla IS....111 B7
Sáuris I....72 B2
Sausset-les-Pins F....79 C4
Sauteyrargues F....78 C2
Sauvagnat F....68 C2
Sauve F....78 C2
Sauveterre-de-Béarn F....76 C2
Sauveterre-de-Guyenne F....76 B2
Sauviat-sur-Vige F....67 C6
Sauxillanges F....68 C3
Sauze F....79 B6
Sauzé-Vaussais F....67 B5
Sauzon F....66 A1
Sava I....104 C3
Savarsin RO....11 C7
Savaştepe TR....118 C2
Savci SLO....73 B6
Säve S....38 B4
Savelletri I....104 C3
Savelli I....107 B3
Savenay F....66 A3
Saverdun F....77 C4
Saverne F....60 B3
Savières F....59 B4
Savigliano I....79 B6
Savignac-les-Églises F....67 C5
Savignano Irpino I....103 B8
Savignano sul Rubicone I....82 B1
Savigny-sur-Braye F....58 C1

Saviñán E....89 C5
Savines-le-lac F....79 B5
Savino Selo SRB....75 C4
Savio I....82 B1
Sävja S....36 C4
Savnik MNE....85 D4
Savognin CH....71 B4
Savona I....80 B2
Savonlinna FIN....3 F28
Savournon F....79 B4
Sævråsvåg N....32 B2
Sävsjö S....40 B4
Sävsjön S....36 C1
Sävsjöström S....40 B5
Savudrija HR....72 C3
Savukoski FIN....113 E17
Sawbridgeworth GB....31 C4
Sawtry GB....30 B3
Sax E....101 A5
Saxdalen S....36 B1
Saxilby GB....27 B5
Saxmundham GB....30 B5
Saxnäs S....115 C12
Saxthorpe GB....30 B5
Sayalonga E....100 C1
Sayatón E....95 B4
Sázava
 Sázava CZ....64 A1
 Sázava CZ....63 A5
Scaër F....56 B2
Scafa I....103 A7
Scalasaig GB....24 B1
Scalby GB....27 A5
Scalea I....106 B2
Scaletta Zanclea I....109 A4
Scalloway GB....22 A7
Scamblesby GB....27 B5
Scandale I....107 B3
Scandiano I....81 B4
Scandicci I....81 C5
Scandolara Ravara I....81 A4
Scanno I....103 B6
Scansano I....81 D5
Scanzano Jónico I....104 C2
Scarborough GB....27 A5
Scardovari I....82 B1
Scardoy GB....22 D4
Scarinish GB....24 B1
Scarperia I....81 C5
Scarriff IRL....20 B3
Scey-sur-Saône et St Albin F....60 C1
Schachendorf A....73 A6
Schaffhausen CH....61 C4
Schafstädt D....52 B1
Schafstedt D....43 A6
Schäftlarn D....62 C2
Schagen NL....42 C1
Schalkau D....51 C7
Schangnau CH....70 B2
Schapbach D....61 B4
Scharbeutz D....44 A2
Schärding A....63 B4
Scharnitz A....71 A6
Scharrel D....43 B4
Schattendorf A....64 C2
Scheemda NL....42 B3
Scheessel D....43 B6
Schéggia I....82 C1
Scheibbs A....63 B6
Scheibenberg D....52 C2
Scheidegg D....61 C5
Scheifling A....73 A4
Scheinfeld D....61 A6
Schelklingen D....61 B5
Schenefeld
 Schleswig-Holstein D....43 A6
 Schleswig-Holstein D....44 B1
Schenklengsfeld D....51 C5
Scherfede D....51 B5
Schermbeck D....50 B2
Scherpenzeel NL....49 A6
Schesslitz D....52 D1
Scheveningen NL....49 A5
Schiedam NL....49 B5
Schieder-Schwalenberg D....51 B5
Schiers CH....71 B4
Schildau D....52 B2
Schillingen D....60 A2
Schillingsfürst D....61 A6
Schilpário I....71 B5
Schiltach D....61 B4
Schiltigheim F....60 B3
Schio I....71 C6
Schirmeck F....60 B3
Schirnding D....52 C2
Schkeuditz D....52 B2
Schkölen D....52 B1
Schladen D....51 A6
Schladming A....72 A3
Schlangen D....51 B4
Schleiden D....50 C2
Schleiz D....52 C1
Schleswig D....43 A6
Schleusingen D....51 C6
Schlieben D....52 B3
Schliengen D....60 C3
Schliersee D....62 C2
Schloss Neuhaus D....51 B4
Schlossvippach D....52 B1
Schlotheim D....51 B6
Schluchsee D....61 C4
Schlüchtern D....51 C5
Schmallenberg D....50 B4
Schmelz D....60 A2
Schmidmühlen D....62 A2
Schmiedeberg D....53 C3
Schmiedefeld D....51 C6
Schmirn A....72 A1
Schmölln
 Brandenburg D....45 B6
 Sachsen D....52 C2
Schnabelwaid D....52 D2
Schnaittach D....62 A2
Schnaittenbach D....62 A3
Schneeberg D....52 C2
Schneizlreuth D....62 C3
Schneverdingen D....44 B1
Schöder A....73 A4
Schoenberg B....50 C2
Schönbeck D....45 B5
Schönberg
 Bayern D....63 B4
 Mecklenburg-Vorpommern D....44 B2
 Schleswig-Holstein D....44 A2
Schönberg im Stubaital A....71 A6
Schönebeck D....52 A1
Schöneck D....52 C2
Schönecken D....50 C2
Schönewalde D....52 B3
Schöngau D....62 C1
Schönhagen D....51 B5
Schönhausen D....44 C4
Schöningen D....51 A6
Schönkirchen D....44 A2
Schönsee D....62 A3
Schöntal D....61 A5
Schönthal D....62 A3
Schonungen D....51 C6
Schönwalde D....44 A2
Schoondijke NL....49 B4
Schoonebeek NL....42 C3
Schoonhoven NL....49 B5
Schöppenstedt D....51 A6
Schöppingen D....50 A3
Schörfling A....63 C4
Schorndorf D....61 B5
Schortens D....43 B4

Schotten D....51 C5
Schramberg D....61 B4
Schraplau D....52 B1
Schrattenberg A....64 B2
Schrecksbach D....51 C5
Schrems A....63 B6
Schrobenhausen D....62 B2
Schröcken A....71 A5
Schrozberg D....61 A5
Schruns A....71 A4
Schüpfheim CH....70 B3
Schüttorf D....50 A3
Schwaan D....44 B4
Schwabach D....62 A2
Schwabmünchen D....62 B1
Schwäbisch Gmünd D....61 B5
Schwäbisch Hall D....61 A5
Schwabmünchen D....62 B1
Schwadorf A....64 B2
Schwagstorf D....43 C4
Schwaigern D....61 A5
Schwalmstadt D....51 C5
Schwanberg A....73 B5
Schwanden CH....70 B4
Schwandorf D....62 A3
Schwanebeck D....52 B1
Schwanenstadt A....63 B4
Schwanewede D....43 B5
Schwanfeld D....61 A6
Schwangau D....62 C1
Schwarmstedt D....43 C6
Schwarza D....51 C6
Schwarzach im Pongau A....72 A2
Schwarzau im Gebirge A....63 C6
Schwarzenau A....63 B6
Schwarzenbach D....52 C1
Schwarzenbach am Wald D....52 C1
Schwarzenbek D....44 B2
Schwarzenberg D....52 C2
Schwarzenburg CH....70 B2
Schwarzenfeld D....62 A3
Schwarz-heide D....53 B3
Schwaz A....72 A1
Schwechat A....64 B2
Schwedt D....45 B6
Schweich D....60 A2
Schweighausen D....60 B3
Schweinfurt D....51 C6
Schweinitz D....52 B3
Schweinrich D....45 B4
Schwelm D....50 B3
Schwemsal D....52 B2
Schwendt A....62 C3
Schwenningen D....61 B4
Schwepnitz D....53 B3
Schwerin D....44 B3
Schwerte D....50 B3
Schweskau D....44 C3
Schwetzingen D....61 A4
Schwyz CH....70 A3
Sciacca I....108 B2
Scicli I....109 C3
Sciechów PL....45 C6
Scigliano I....106 B3
Scilla I....109 A4
Scinawa PL....54 B1
Scionzier F....69 B6
Scogliti I....109 C3
Scole GB....30 B5
Sconser GB....22 D2
Scopello
 Piemonte I....70 C3
 Sicília I....108 A1
Scordia I....109 B3
Scorzè I....72 C2
Scotch Corner GB....27 A4
Scotter GB....27 B5
Scourie GB....22 C3
Scousburgh GB....22 B7
Scrabster GB....23 C5
Screeb IRL....20 A2
Scremerston GB....25 C6
Scritto I....82 C1
Scunthorpe GB....27 B5
Scuol CH....71 B5
Scúrcola Marsicana I....103 A6
Seaford GB....31 D4
Seaham GB....25 D6
Seahouses GB....25 C6
Seascale GB....26 A2
Seaton GB....29 C4
Sebazac-Concourès F....77 B5
Sebečevo SRB....85 C5
Seben TR....118 B6
Sebersdorf A....73 A5
Sebezh RUS....7 C10
Sebnitz D....53 C4
Seborga I....80 C1
Seby S....41 C6
Seč
 Východočeský CZ....63 A6
 Západočeský CZ....63 A4
Sečanj SRB....75 C5
Secemin PL....55 C4
Séchault F....59 A5
Seckau A....73 A4
Seclin F....49 C4
Secondigny F....67 B4
Seda
 E....92 B3
 P....92 B3
Sedan F....59 A5
Sedano E....88 B3
Sedbergh GB....26 A3
Sedella E....100 C1
Séderon F....79 B4
Sedico I....72 B2
Sédini I....110 B1
Sedlarica HR....74 C2
Sedlčany CZ....63 A5
Sedlice CZ....63 A4
Sędziejowice PL....55 B4
Sędziszów PL....55 C5
Sędziszów Małopolski PL....55 C6
Seebach D....60 B3
Seeboden A....72 B3
Seefeld
 Brandenburg D....45 C5
 Niedersachsen D....43 B5
Seefeld in Tirol A....71 A6
Seeg D....62 C1
Seehausen
 Sachsen-Anhalt D....52 A1
 Sachsen-Anhalt D....44 C3
Seelbach D....60 B3
Seelow D....45 C6
Seelze D....43 C6
Seerhausen D....52 B3
Sées F....57 B6
Seesen D....51 B6
Seewalchen A....63 C4
Seferihisar TR....119 D1
Sefkerin SRB....85 A5
Segård D....34 B2
Segarcea RO....11 D7
Segart E....96 B2
Segerstad S....33 C5
Segesd H....74 B2
Seglinge FIN....36 B7
Segmon S....35 C5
Segonzac F....67 C4
Segorbe E....96 B2
Segovia E....94 B2
Segré F....57 C5
Segura
 E....89 B4
 P....92 B3
Segura de León E....99 A4
Segura de los Baños E....90 C2
Ségur-les-Villas F....68 C2
Segurilla E....94 C2
Sehnde D....51 A5

Seia P....92 A3
Seiches-sur-le-Loir F....67 A4
Seifhennersdorf D....53 C4
Seignelay F....59 C4
Seijo E....87 C2
Seilhac F....68 C1
Seilles B....49 C6
Seim N....32 B2
Seimeiköi FIN....3 E25
Seissan F....77 C3
Seitenstetten Markt A....63 B5
Seixal P....92 C1
Seiz A....73 A4
Seizthal A....73 A4
Sejerslev DK....38 C1
Seksna RUS....7 B15
Selárdalur IS....111 B1
Selárgius I....110 C2
Selb D....52 C2
Selby GB....27 B4
Selca HR....84 C1
Selce AL....105 A5
Selce HR....73 C4
Selçuk TR....119 E2
Selde DK....38 C2
Selenča SRB....75 C4
Selendi
 Manisa TR....118 D2
 Manisa TR....118 D3
Selenicë AL....105 C5
Sélestat F....60 B3
Seleuš SRB....75 C5
Selevac SRB....85 B5
Selfoss IS....111 D5
Selgua E....90 B3
Selice SK....64 B3
Seligenstadt D....51 C4
Seligenthal D....51 C6
Selimiye TR....119 E2
Selištarovo RUS....7 C12
Selja S....36 A1
Selje N....114 E2
Seljelvnes N....112 C8
Seljord N....33 C5
Selkirk GB....25 C5
Sellano I....82 D1
Selles-St Denis F....68 A1
Selles-sur-Cher F....68 A1
Sellières F....69 B5
Sellin D....45 A5
Sellye H....74 C2
Selm D....50 B3
Selmsdorf D....44 B2
Selnica ob Dravi SLO....73 B5
Selongey F....59 C6
Selonnet F....79 B5
Selsey GB....31 D3
Selsingen D....43 B6
Selters D....50 C4
Seltso RUS....7 E13
Seltz F....61 B4
Selva E....97 B2
Selva di Cadore I....72 B2
Selva di Val Gardena I....72 B1
Selvik
 Sogn og Fjordane N....32 A2
 Vestfold N....35 C2
Selvino I....71 C4
Selyatyn UA....11 C8
Sem N....35 C2
Semeljci HR....74 C3
Semenovka
 Chernihiv UA....7 E12
 Kremenchuk UA....11 B12
Semič SLO....73 C5
Semide
 P....92 A2
 Sardegna I....108 A1
Semily CZ....53 C5
Seminara I....106 C2
Semlac RO....75 B5
Şemmen-stedt D....51 A6
Semmering A....73 A5
Semur-en-Auxois F....69 A4
Sena E....90 B2
Sena de Luna E....88 B1
Senarpont F....58 A2
Sénas F....79 C4
Senčanski Trešnjevac SRB....75 C4
Sencelles E....97 B2
Senčur SLO....73 B4
Senden
 Bayern D....61 B6
 Nordrhein-Westfalen D....50 B3
Sendenhorst D....50 B3
Sendim P....87 C4
Senec SK....64 B3
Seneffe B....49 C5
Séneghe I....110 B1
Senés E....101 B3
Senez F....79 C5
Senftenberg D....53 B3
Sengouagnet F....77 D3
Sengwarden D....43 B5
Senica SK....64 B3
Senice na Hané CZ....64 A3
Senigállia I....82 C2
Senirkent TR....119 D5
Sénis I....110 C1
Senise I....106 A3
Senj HR....83 B3
Senje SRB....85 C6
Senjehopen N....112 C6
Senjski Rudnik SRB....85 C6
Senlis F....58 A3
Sennan S....40 C2
Sennecey-le-Grand F....69 B4
Sennen GB....28 C2
Senno BY....7 D10
Sennori I....110 B1
Sennwald CH....71 A4
Sennybridge GB....29 B4
Senohrad SK....65 B5
Senonches F....58 B2
Senones F....60 B2
Senorbì I....110 C2
Senovo SLO....73 B5
Senozeče SLO....73 C4
Senožeti SLO....73 B4
Sens F....59 B4
Sens-de-Bretagne F....57 B4
Senta SRB....75 C5
Senterada E....90 A3
Šentilj SLO....73 B5
Šentjernej SLO....73 C5
Šentjur SLO....73 B5
Senumstad N....33 D5
Seoane E....86 B3
Seon CH....70 A3
Sépeaux F....59 C4
Sépey CH....70 B2
Sepino I....103 B7
Sępólno Krajeńskie PL....46 B3
Seppenrade D....50 B3
Seppois F....70 A2
Septemvri BG....11 E8
Septeuil F....58 B2
Sepúlveda E....88 C3
Sequals I....72 B2
Sequeros E....93 A4
Seraincourt F....59 A5
Seraing B....49 C6
Seravezza I....81 C4
Sered' SK....64 B3
Seredka RUS....7 B10
Şereflikoçhisar TR....16 B6
Seregélyes H....74 A3
Seregno I....71 C4
Sérent F....57 C3
Serfaus A....71 A5
Sergiyev Posad RUS....7 C15
Seriate I....71 C4
Sérifontaine F....58 A2
Serifos GR....117 E6
Sérignan F....78 C2
Serik TR....119 F6
Serina I....71 C4

Serinhisar TR....119 E4
Sermaises F....58 B3
Sermaize-les-Bains F....59 B5
Sérmide I....81 B5
Sermoneta I....102 B5
Sernache de Bonjardim P....92 B2
Sernancelhe P....87 D3
Serón E....101 B3
Serón de Najima E....89 C4
Serooskerke NL....49 B4
Seròs E....90 B3
Serpa P....98 B3
Serpuhov RUS....7 D14
Serracapriola I....103 B8
Serrada E....88 C2
Serra de Outes E....86 B2
Serradifalco I....108 B2
Serradilla E....93 B4
Serradilla del Llano E....93 A4
Serramanna I....110 C1
Serramazzoni I....81 B4
Serranillos E....94 B2
Serra San Bruno I....106 C3
Serra San Quírico I....82 C2
Serrastretta I....106 B3
Serravalle
 Piemonte I....70 C3
 Umbria I....82 D2
Serravalle di Chienti I....82 C1
Serravalle Scrivia I....80 B2
Serre I....103 C8
Serrejón E....93 B5
Serres
 F....79 B4
 GR....116 A5
Serrières F....69 C4
Serrières-de-Briord F....69 C5
Sersale I....106 B3
Sertã P....92 B2
Sertig Dörfli CH....71 B4
Servance F....60 C2
Serverette F....78 B2
Servia GR....116 B4
Servian F....78 C2
Servières F....78 B3
Servigliano I....82 C2
Serzedelo P....87 C2
Seseña Nuevo E....95 B3
Sesimbra P....92 C1
Seskinore GB....19 B4
Sesma E....89 B4
Sessa Aurunca I....103 B6
Sesta Godano I....81 B3
Šestanovac HR....84 C1
Sestao E....89 A4
Sestino I....82 C1
Sesto I....72 B2
Sesto Calende I....70 C3
Sesto Fiorentino I....81 C5
Sestola I....81 B4
Sesto San Giovanni I....71 C4
Sestriere I....79 B5
Sestri Levante I....80 B3
Sestroretsk RUS....7 A11
Sestu I....110 C2
Sesvete HR....73 C6
Setcases E....91 A5
Sète F....78 C2
Setenil I....99 C5
Setermoen I....112 D7
Šetonje SRB....85 B6
Setskog N....34 C3
Settalsjølia N....114 E7
Séttimo Torinese I....70 C2
Séttimo Vittone I....70 C2
Settle GB....26 A3
Setúbal P....92 C2
Seubersdorf D....62 A2
Seui I....110 C2
Seúlo I....110 C2
Seurre F....69 B5
Sevaster AL....105 C5
Sevel DK....38 C1
Sevenoaks GB....31 C4
Sévérac-le-Château F....78 B2
Severin D....44 B3
Severomorsk RUS....3 B30
Sever do Vouga P....87 D2
Seveso I....71 C4
Ševětín CZ....63 B5
Sevettijärvi FIN....113 C17
Sévigny F....59 A5
Sevilla = Seville E....99 B5
Sevilla la Nueva E....94 B2
Seville = Sevilla E....99 B5
Sevilleja de la Jara E....94 C2
Sevlievo BG....11 E8
Sevnica SLO....73 B5
Sevojno SRB....85 C4
Sevrier F....69 C6
Sevsk RUS....7 E13
Sexdrega S....40 B3
Seyches F....77 B3
Seyda D....52 B2
Seydişehir TR....119 E6
Seyðisfjörður IS....111 B12
Seyitgazi TR....118 C5
Seyitömer TR....118 C4
Seymen TR....118 A2
Seyne F....79 B5
Seynes F....78 B3
Seyssel F....69 C5
Sežana SLO....72 C3
Sézanne F....59 B4
Sezulfe P....87 C4
Sezze I....102 B6
Sfântu Gheorghe RO....11 D8
Sforzacosta I....82 C2
Sgarasta Mhor GB....22 D1
's-Gravendeel NL....49 B5
's-Gravenhage = The Hague NL....49 A5
's-Gravenzande NL....49 A5
Shaftesbury GB....29 C5
Shaldon GB....29 C4
Shanagolden IRL....20 B2
Shanklin GB....31 D2
Shap GB....26 A3
Sharpness GB....29 B5
Shawbury GB....26 C3
Shchekino RUS....7 D14
Shchigry RUS....7 F11
Shchors UA....7 F11
Šheğjergj AL....105 B5
Sheerness GB....31 C4
Sheffield GB....27 B4
Shefford GB....31 C3
Shenfield GB....31 C4
Shëngjergj AL....105 B5
Shepetivka UA....11 A9
Shepshed GB....30 B4
Shepton Mallet GB....29 B5
Sherborne GB....29 C5
Shercock IRL....19 C5
Sheringham GB....30 B5
Sherston GB....29 B5
Shiel Bridge GB....22 D3
Shieldaig GB....22 D3
Shijak AL....105 B5
Shillelagh IRL....21 B5
Shimsk RUS....7 B11
Shipston-on-Stour GB....29 A6
Shirgjan AL....105 B6
Shklov BY....7 D11
Shkodër AL....105 A5
Shoeburyness GB....31 C4
Shoreham-by-Sea GB....31 D3
Shotley Gate GB....31 C5
Shostka UA....7 F12
Shpola UA....11 B11
Shrewsbury GB....26 C3
Shugozero RUS....7 B13
Shumen BG....11 E9

Siabost GB....22 C2
Siamanna I....110 C1
Sianów PL....46 A2
Siatista GR....116 B3
Siauges-St Romain F....78 B2
Šiauliai LT....6 D7
Sibari I....106 B3
Sibbhult S....41 C4
Šibenik HR....83 C4
Sibiu RO....11 D8
Sibnica SRB....85 B5
Sibsey GB....27 B6
Siculiana I....108 B2
Šid SRB....85 A4
Sidari GR....116 C1
Siddeburen NL....42 B3
Sidensjö S....115 D15
Siderno I....106 C3
Sidirokastro GR....116 A5
Sidmouth GB....29 C4
Sidzina PL....65 A5
Siebe N....113 D12
Siebenlehn D....52 B3
Siedlce PL....6 E7
Siedlice PL....46 B1
Siedlinghausen D....51 B4
Siedlisko PL....46 C2
Siegburg D....50 C3
Siegen D....50 C4
Siegenburg D....62 B2
Sieghartskirchen A....64 B2
Siegsdorf D....62 C3
Siekierki PL....45 C6
Šieladź PL....54 B3
Sielpia PL....55 B5
Siemiany PL....47 B5
Siena I....81 C5
Sieniawka PL....53 C4
Siennica PL....55 A6
Sienno PL....55 B6
Sieppijärvi FIN....113 E13
Sieradz PL....54 B3
Sieraków
 Śląskie PL....54 C3
 Wielkopolskie PL....46 C2
Sierakowice PL....46 A3
Sierck-les-Bains F....60 A2
Sierentz F....60 C3
Sierning A....63 B5
Sierpc PL....47 C5
Sierra de Fuentes E....93 B4
Sierra de Luna E....90 A2
Sierra de Yeguas E....100 B1
Sierre CH....70 B2
Siestrzeń PL....55 A5
Sietamo E....90 A2
Siewierz PL....55 C4
Sigdal N....32 B6
Sigean F....78 C1
Sigerfjord N....112 D4
Sighetu-Marmatiei RO....11 C7
Sighişoara RO....11 C8
Sigillo I....82 C1
Siglufjörður IS....111 A7
Sigmaringen D....61 B5
Signa I....81 C5
Signes F....79 C4
Signy-l'Abbaye F....59 A5
Signy-le-Petit F....59 A5
Sigogne F....67 C4
Sigri GR....116 C7
Sigtuna S....37 C4
Sigueiro E....86 B2
Sigüenza E....95 A4
Sigulda LV....6 C8
Siilinjärvi FIN....3 E27
Sikenica SK....65 B4
Sikia GR....116 B5
Sikinos GR....117 F7
Sikkilsdalseter N....32 A6
Siklós H....74 C3
Sikórz PL....47 C5
Sikselet S....115 A14
Silandro I....71 B5
Silánus I....110 B1
Silbaš SRB....75 C4
Silberhütte D....52 B1
Silbertal A....71 A4
Sileby GB....30 B4
Siles E....101 A3
Silgueiros P....92 A3
Silian SLO... (see line below)
Silistra BG....11 D9
Silivri TR....118 A3
Siljan N....33 C6
Siljansnäs S....36 B1
Silkeborg DK....39 C2
Silla E....96 B2
Sillamäe EST....7 B9
Silleda E....86 B2
Sillé-le-Guillaume F....57 B5
Sillenstede D....43 B4
Sillian A....72 B2
Silloth GB....25 D4
Silno PL....46 B3
Silnowo PL....46 B2
Silo HR....73 C4
Sils E....91 B5
Silsand N....112 C7
Silte S....37 E5
Silute LT....6 D6
Silvalen N....114 B9
Silvaplana CH....71 B4
Silvares P....92 A3
Silverdalen S....40 B5
Silvermines IRL....20 B3
Silverstone GB....30 B4
Silverton GB....29 C4
Silves P....98 B2
Silvi Marina I....103 A7
Simandre F....69 B5
Šimanovci SRB....85 B5
Simard F....69 B5
Simat de Valldigna E....96 B2
Simav TR....118 C3
Simbach
 Bayern D....62 B3
 Bayern D....62 B4
Simbário I....106 C3
Simeria RO....11 D7
Simi GR....119 F2
Simićevo SRB....85 B6
Simlångsdalen S....40 C3
Simmerath D....50 C2
Simmerberg D....61 C5
Simmern D....50 D3
Simo FIN....3 D26
Simonsbath GB....29 B4
Simonstorp S....37 D3
Simontornya H....74 B3
Simpelveld NL....50 C2
Simplon CH....70 B3
Simrishamn S....41 D4
Sinaia RO....11 D8
Sinalunga I....81 C5
Sinarcas E....96 B1
Sincan TR....118 B6
Sincanlı TR....118 C5
Sindal DK....38 B3
Sindelfingen D....61 B5
Sindia I....110 B1
Sindirgi TR....118 C3
Sinekçi TR....118 B2
Sinekli TR....118 A3
Sines P....98 B2
Sinetta FIN....113 F14
Sineu E....97 B3
Singen D....61 C4
Singleton GB....31 D3
Singö S....36 B6
Singsås N....114 E7
Siniscóla I....110 B2
Sinj HR....83 C5
Sinlabajos E....94 A2
Sinn D....50 C4
Sínnai I....110 C2
Sínnes N....33 D3
Sins CH....70 A3
Sinsheim D....61 A4
Sint Annaland NL....49 B5
Sint Annaparochie NL....42 B2
Sint Athonis NL....50 B1
Sint Nicolaasga NL....42 C2
Sint Oedenrode NL....49 B6
Sintra P....92 C1
Sinzheim D....61 B4
Sinzig D....50 C3
Siófok H....74 B3
Sion CH....70 B2
Sion Mills GB....19 B4
Siorac-en-Périgord F....77 B3
Šipanska Luka HR....84 D2
Šípovo BIH....84 B2
Sira N....33 D3
Siracusa I....109 B4
Siret RO....11 C8
Sirevåg N....33 D2
Sirig SRB....75 C4
Sirkka FIN....113 E13
Sirmione I....71 C5
Sirok H....65 C6
Siroké SK....65 B6
Široki Brijeg BIH....84 C2
Sirolo I....82 C2
Siruela E....94 D1
Sisak HR....73 C6
Sisante E....95 C4
Šišljavić HR....73 C5
Sissach CH....70 A2
Sissonne F....59 A4
Sistelo P....87 C2
Sisteron F....79 B4
Sistiana I....72 C3
Sistranda N....114 D5
Sitasjaurestugorna S....112 E6
Sitges E....91 B4
Sitía GR....117 G8
Sittard NL....50 B1
Sittensen D....43 B6
Sittingbourne GB....31 C4
Sitzenroda D....52 B2
Sivac SRB....75 C4
Sivasli TR....119 D4
Siverić HR....83 C5
Sivrihisar TR....118 C6
Sixt-Fer-à-Cheval F....70 B1
Siziano I....71 C4
Sizun F....56 B1
Sjenica SRB....85 C5
Sjoa N....114 F6
Sjøåsen N....114 C8
Sjöbo S....41 D3
Sjøholt N....114 E3
Sjøli N....34 A3
Sjølstad N....114 C9
Sjømarken S....40 B2
Sjørring DK....38 C1
Sjötofta S....40 B3
Sjötorp S....35 D5
Sjoutnäset S....115 C11
Sjøvegan N....112 D6
Sjuntorp S....35 D4
Skåbu N....32 A6
Skadovsk UA....11 C10
Skafsá N....33 C5
Skaftafell IS....111 D9
Skagaströnd IS....111 B5
Skagen DK....38 B3
Skagersvik S....35 D6
Skaiði N....113 B13
Skála GR....117 D2
Skala Oropou GR....117 D5
Skála PL....55 C4
Skaland N....112 C6
Skalat UA....11 B8
Skalbmierz PL....55 C5
Skålevik N....35 B5
Skalica SK....64 B3
Skalité SK....65 A4
Skällinge S....40 B2
Skalná CZ....52 C2
Skals DK....38 C2
Skalskør N....39 D4
Skanderborg DK....39 C2
Skånes-Fagerhult S....41 C3
Skåne-Tranås S....41 D3
Skånevik N....33 C2
Skänninge S....37 D2
Skarberget N....112 D5
Skærbæk DK....39 D1
Skärblacka S....37 D2
Skarð IS....111 C15
Skare N....32 C3
Skåre S....35 C5
Skarnes N....34 B3
Skärplinge S....36 B4
Skarp Salling DK....38 C2
Skarrild DK....39 D1
Skärstad S....40 B4
Skarsvåg N....113 A14
Skarszewy PL....47 A4
Skårup DK....39 D3
Skärvången S....115 D11
Skarżysko-Kamienna PL....55 B5
Skarżysko Ksiazece PL....55 B5
Skatøy N....33 D6
Skattkärr S....35 C5
Skattungbyn S....36 A1
Skatval N....114 D8
Skave DK....39 C1
Skawina PL....55 D4
Skebobruk S....36 B5
Skebokvarn S....37 C3
Skedala S....40 C2
Skedevi S....37 D3
Skedsmokorset N....34 B3
Skee S....35 D3
Skegness GB....27 B6
Skela SRB....85 B5
Skelani BIH....85 C4
Skellefteå S....3 D24
Skelmersdale GB....26 B3
Skelmorlie GB....24 C3
Skelund DK....38 C3
Skender Vakuf BIH....84 B2
Skępe PL....47 C5
Skeppshult S....40 B3
Skerries IRL....19 C5
Ski N....35 C2
Skiathos GR....116 C5
Skibbereen IRL....20 C2
Skibotn N....112 C9
Skidra GR....116 B4
Skien N....35 C1
Skierniewice PL....55 B5
Skillingaryd S....40 B4
Skillinge S....41 D4
Skillingmark S....34 C4
Skillioura CY....120 A2
Skinnardai S....36 C5
Skinnskatteberg S....36 C2

Sulzbach
Baden-Württemberg D 61 A5
Baden-Württemberg D 61 B5
Bayern D 61 A5
Saarland D 60 A3
Sulzbach-Rosenberg D 62 A2
Sülze D 44 C2
Sulzfeld D 51 C6
Sumartin HR 84 C1
Sumburgh GB 22 B7
Sümeg H 74 B2
Sumiswald CH 70 A2
Šumná CZ 64 B1
Šumperk CZ 54 D1
Šumvald CZ 64 A3
Sumy UA 7 F13
Sunbilla E 76 C1
Sünching D 62 B3
Sund
FIN 36 B7
S 35 C3
Sundborn S 36 B2
Sundby DK 38 C1
Sunde N 32 C2
Sunde bru N 33 D6
Sunderland GB 25 D6
Sundern D 50 B4
Sundhultsbrunn S 40 B4
Sundnäs S 115 A14
Sunds DK 39 C2
Sundsfjord N 112 F3
Sundsvall S 115 E14
Sungurlu TR 16 A7
Suni I 110 B1
Sunja HR 74 C1
Sunnansjö S 36 B1
Sunnaryd S 40 B3
Sunndalsøra N 114 E5
Sunne S 34 C5
Sunnemo S 34 C5
Sunnersberg S 35 D5
Suolovuopmio N 113 C12
Suomussalmi FIN 3 D28
Suoyarvi RUS 3 E30
Super Sauze F 79 B5
Supetar HR 83 C5
Supetarska Draga HR 83 B3
Supino I 102 B6
Šuplja Stijena MNE 84 C4
Surahammar S 37 C3
Šurany SK 64 B4
Surazh
BY 7 D11
RUS 7 E12
Surbo I 105 C4
Surčin SRB 85 B5
Surgères F 66 B4
Surhuisterveen NL 42 B3
Sùria E 91 B4
Surin F 67 B5
Surka N 34 B2
Surnadalsøra N 114 E5
Sursee CH 70 A3
Surte S 38 B5
Surwold D 43 C4
Sury-le-Comtal F 69 C4
Susa I 70 C2
Šušara SRB 85 B6
Susch CH 71 B5
Susegana I 72 C2
Süsel D 44 A2
Šušice CZ 63 A4
Šušnjevica HR 73 C4
Sussen D 61 B5
Susurluk TR 118 C3
Susz PL 47 B5
Sütçüler TR 119 E5
Sutivan HR 83 C5
Sutjeska SRB 75 C5
Sutomore MNE 105 A5
Sutri I 102 A5
Sutton GB 31 C3
Sutton Coldfield GB 27 C4
Sutton-in-Ashfield GB 27 B4
Sutton-on-Sea GB 27 B6
Sutton-on-Trent GB 27 B5
Sutton Scotney GB 31 C2
Sutton Valence GB 31 C4
Suvaja BIH 83 B5
Suvereto I 81 C4
Suvorov RUS 7 D14
Suwałki PL 6 D7
Suze-la-Rousse F 78 B3
Suzzara I 81 B4
Svabensverk S 36 A2
Svalbarð IS 111 A10
Svalöv S 41 D3
Svanabyn S 115 C13
Svanberga S 36 C5
Svaneke DK 41 D5
Svanesund S 35 D3
Svängsta S 41 C4
Svannäs S 115 A15
Svanskog S 35 C4
Svanstein S 113 F12
Svappavaara S 112 E10
Svärdsjö S 36 B2
Svarstad N 35 C1
Svartå S 37 C1
Svärta S 37 D4
Svartå S 34 C5
Svärtinge S 37 D3
Svartnäs S 36 B3
Svartnes N 112 E3
Svarttjärn S 115 B13
Svatsum N 34 A1
Svätý Jur SK 64 B3
Svätý Peter SK 64 C4
Svedala S 41 D3
Sveg S 115 E11
Sveindal N 33 D4
Sveio N 33 C2
Svejbæk DK 39 C2
Svelgen N 114 F2
Svelvik N 35 C2
Svendborg DK 39 D3
Svene N 32 C6
Svenljunga S 40 B3
Svennevad S 37 C2
Svenstavik S 115 E11
Svenstrup DK 38 C2
Švermov CZ 53 C4
Sveti Ivan Zabno HR 74 C1
Sveti Ivan Zelina HR 73 C6
Sveti Nikola MNE 105 B5
Sveti Rok HR 83 B4
Sveti Stefan MNE 105 A4
Světla nad Sázavou CZ 63 A6
Svetlyy RUS 47 A6
Svetvinčenat HR 82 A2
Švica HR 83 B4
Svidník SK 10 B6
Švihov CZ 63 A4
Svilajnac SRB 85 B6
Svilengrad BG 11 F9
Svindal N 35 C3
Svinhult S 40 B5
Svinna SK 64 B4
Svinninge
DK 39 D4
S 37 C5
Sviritsa RUS 7 A12
Svishtov BG 11 E8
Svislach BY 6 E8
Svit SK 65 A6
Svitavy CZ 64 A2
Svitlovodsk UA 11 B12
Svodin SK 65 C4
Svolvær N 112 D3
Svortemyr N 32 A2
Svortland N 32 C2
Svratka CZ 64 A2
Svrčinovec SK 65 A4
Svullrya N 34 B4
Svyetlahorsk BY 7 E10
Swadlincote GB 27 C4
Swaffham GB 30 B4
Swanage GB 29 C6
Swanley GB 31 C4
Swanlinbar IRL 19 B4
Swansea GB 28 B4
Swarzędz PL 46 C3
Swatragh GB 19 B5
Świątki PL 47 B6
Świdnica
Dolnośląskie PL 54 C1
Lubuskie PL 53 B5
Świdnik PL 11 A7
Świdwin PL 46 B1
Świebodzice PL 53 C6
Świebodzin PL 53 A5
Świecie PL 47 B4
Świedziebnia PL 47 B5
Świeradów Zdrój PL 53 C5
Świerki PL 54 C1
Swierzawa PL 53 B5
Swierzno PL 45 B6
Swięta PL 45 B6
Swieta Anna PL 55 C4
Świętno PL 53 A6
Swifterbant NL 42 C2
Swindon GB 29 B6
Swineshead GB 30 B3
Swinford IRL 18 C3
Świnoujście PL 45 B6
Swinton GB 25 C5
Swobnica PL 45 B6
Swords IRL 21 A5
Swornegacie PL 46 B3
Sya S 37 D2
Syasstroy RUS 7 A12
Sycewice PL 46 A2
Sychevka RUS 7 D13
Syców PL 54 B2
Sycowice PL 53 A5
Sydnes N 33 C2
Syfteland N 32 B2
Syke D 43 C5
Sykkylven N 114 E3
Sylling N 34 C2
Sylte N 114 E4
Symbister GB 22 A7
Symington GB 25 C4
Symonds Yat GB 29 B5
Sypniewo
Kujawsko-Pomorskie PL 46 B3
Wielkopolskie PL 46 B2
Syserum S 40 B6
Sysslebäck S 34 B4
Syväjärvi FIN 113 E14
Szabadbattyán H 74 A3
Szabadegyháza H 74 A3
Szabadszállás H 75 B4
Szadek PL 54 B3
Szajol H 75 A5
Szakály H 74 B3
Szakcs H 74 B3
Szakmár H 75 B4
Szalánta H 74 C3
Szałas PL 55 B5
Szalkszentmárton H 75 B4
Szalonna H 65 B6
Szamocin PL 46 B3
Szamotuły PL 46 C2
Szany H 74 A2
Szarvas H 75 B5
Szarvaskö H 65 C6
Szászvár H 74 B3
Százhalombatta H 74 A3
Szczawa PL 65 A6
Szczawnica PL 65 A6
Szczecin PL 45 B6
Szczecinek PL 46 B2
Szczekociny PL 55 C4
Szczerców PL 55 B4
Szczucin PL 55 C6
Szczuczarz PL 46 B2
Szczurkowo PL 47 A6
Szczurowa PL 55 C5
Szczyrk PL 65 A5
Szczytna PL 54 C1
Szczytno PL 6 E6
Szczyty PL 54 B3
Szécsény H 65 B5
Szederkény H 74 C3
Szedres H 74 B3
Szeged H 75 B5
Szeghalom H 75 A6
Szegvár H 75 B5
Székesfehérvár H 74 A3
Székkutas H 75 B5
Szekszárd H 74 B3
Szemplino Czarne PL 47 B6
Szemud PL 47 A4
Szendehely H 65 C5
Szendrö H 65 B6
Szentendre H 65 C5
Szentes H 75 B5
Szentgotthárd H 73 B6
Szentlászló H 74 B2
Szentlörinc H 74 B2
Szentmártonkáta H 75 A4
Szenyér H 74 B2
Szeremle H 74 B3
Szerep H 75 A6
Szigetszentmiklós H 75 A4
Szigetvár H 74 B2
Szikáncs H 75 B5
Szikszó H 65 B6
Szil H 74 A2
Szilvásvárad H 65 B6
Szklarska Poreba PL 53 C5
Szlichtyngowa PL 53 B6
Szob H 65 C4
Szolnok H 75 A5
Szombathely H 74 A1
Szorosad H 74 B3
Szpetal Graniczny PL 47 C5
Szprotawa PL 53 B5
Szreńsk PL 47 B6
Sztum PL 47 B5
Sztutowo PL 47 A5
Szubin PL 46 B3
Szücsi H 65 C5
Szulmierz PL 47 C6
Szulok H 74 B2
Szumanie PL 47 C5
Szwecja PL 46 B2
Szydłów
Łódzkie PL 55 B4
Świętokrzyskie PL 55 C6
Szydłowiec PL 55 B5
Szydlowo PL 47 B6
Szydłowo PL 46 B2
Szymanów PL 55 A5
Szynkielów PL 54 B3
Szynwald PL 55 D6

T

Taastrup DK 41 D2
Tab H 74 B3
Tabanera la Luenga E 94 A2
Tabaqueros E 96 B1
Tábara E 88 C1
Tabenera de Cerrato E 88 B2
Taberg S 40 B4
Tabernas E 101 B3
Tabiano Bagni I 81 B4
Taboada E 86 B3
Taboadela E 87 B3
Tábor CZ 63 A5
Táborfalva H 75 A4
Taborište HR 73 C6
Tábua P 92 A2
Tabuaco P 87 C3
Tabuenca E 89 C5
Tabuyo del Monte E 87 B4
Täby S 37 C5
Tác H 74 A3
Tachov CZ 62 A3
Tadcaster GB 27 B4
Tadley GB 31 C2
Tafalla E 89 B5
Tafjord N 114 E4
Taganheira P 98 B2
Tågarp S 41 D2
Tággia I 80 C1
Tagliacozzo I 102 A6
Táglio di Po I 82 A1
Tagnon F 59 A5
Tahal E 101 B3
Tahitótfalu H 65 C5
Tahtaköprü TR 118 C4
Tailfingen D 61 B5
Taillis F 57 B4
Tain GB 23 D4
Tain-l'Hermitage F 78 A3
Taipadas P 92 C2
Taivalkoski FIN 3 D28
Takene S 35 C5
Takovo SRB 85 B5
Taksony H 75 A4
Tal E 86 B2
Talachyn BY 7 D10
Talamello I 82 C1
Talamone I 102 A4
Talant F 69 A4
Talarrubias E 93 B5
Talas TR 16 B7
Talaván E 93 B4
Talavera de la Reina E 94 C2
Talavera la Real E 93 C4
Talayuela E 93 B5
Talayuelas E 96 B1
Talgarth GB 29 B4
Talgje N 33 C2
Talhadas P 92 A2
Táliga E 93 C3
Talizat F 78 A2
Tálknafjörður IS 111 B2
Talla I 81 C5
Talladale GB 22 D3
Tallaght IRL 21 A5
Tallard F 79 B5
Tällberg S 36 B1
Tallinn EST 6 B8
Talloires F 69 C6
Tallow IRL 21 B4
Tallsjö S 115 C15
Talmay F 69 A5
Talmont-St Hilaire F 66 B3
Talmont-sur-Gironde F 66 C4
Talne UA 11 B11
Talsano I 104 C3
Talsi LV 6 C7
Talvik N 113 B11
Talybont GB 26 C2
Tal-Y-Llyn GB 26 C2
Tamajón E 95 B3
Tamame E 88 C1
Tamames E 93 A4
Tamarit de Mar E 91 B4
Tamarite de Litera E 90 B3
Tamariu E 91 B6
Tamási H 74 B3
Tambach-Dietharz D 51 C6
Tameza E 86 A4
Tammisaari FIN 6 A7
Tampere FIN 3 F25
Tamsweg A 72 A3
Tamurejo E 94 D2
Tamworth GB 27 C4
Tana bru N 113 B17
Tañabueyes E 89 B3
Tanakajd H 74 A1
Tananger N 33 D2
Tanaunella I 110 B2
Tancarville F 58 A1
Tandsjöborg S 115 F11
Tånga S 41 C2
Tangelic H 74 B3
Tangen N 34 B3
Tangerhütte D 44 C3
Tangermünde D 44 C3
Tanhua FIN 113 E16
Taninges F 69 B6
Tankavaara FIN 113 D16
Tann D 51 C6
Tanna D 52 C1
Tannadice GB 25 B5
Tannåker S 40 C3
Tännäs S 115 E9
Tannay
Ardennes F 59 A5
Nièvre F 68 A3
Tannenbergsthal D 52 C2
Tännesberg D 62 A3
Tannheim A 71 A5
Tanowo PL 45 B6
Tanum S 35 D3
Tanumshede S 35 D3
Tanus F 77 B5
Tanvald CZ 53 C5
Taormina I 109 B4
Tapa EST 7 B8
Tapfheim D 62 B1
Tapia de Casariego E 86 A4
Tapio F 77 C4
Tápióbicske H 75 A4
Tápiógyörgye H 75 A4
Tápióság H 75 A4
Tápiószecsö H 75 A4
Tápiószele H 75 A4
Tápiószentmárton H 75 A4
Tapolca H 74 B2
Tapolcafö H 74 A2
Tar HR 72 C3
Tarabo S 40 B2
Taradell E 91 B5
Taraklı TR 118 B5
Taramundi E 86 A3
Tarancón E 95 B3
Táranto I 104 C3
Tarare F 69 C4
Tarascon F 78 C3
Tarascon-sur-Ariège F 77 D4
Tarashcha UA 11 B11
Tarazona E 89 C5
Tarazona de la Mancha E 95 C5
Tarbena E 96 C2
Tarbert
GB 24 C2
IRL 20 B2
Tarbes F 76 C3
Tarbet GB 24 B3
Tarbolton GB 24 C3
Tarcento I 72 B3
Tarčin BIH 84 C3
Tarczyn PL 55 B5
Tardajos E 88 B3
Tardelcuende E 89 C4
Tardets-Sorholus F 76 C2
Tardienta E 90 B2
Tärendö S 113 E11
Targon F 76 B2
Târgovişte 11 D8
Târgu-Jiu RO 11 D7
Târgu Mureş RO 11 C8
Târgu Ocna RO 11 C9
Târgu Secuiesc RO 11 D9
Tarifa E 99 C5
Tariquejas E 98 B3
Tarján H 65 C4
Tárkany H 64 C4
Tarland GB 23 D6
Tarłów PL 55 B6
Tarm DK 39 D1
Tarmstedt D 43 B6
Tärnaby S 115 B12
Tarnalelesz H 65 B6
Tarnaörs H 65 C6
Târnăveni RO 11 C8
Tårnet N 113 C19
Tarnobrzeg PL 55 C6
Tarnos F 76 C1
Tarnów
Lubuskie PL 45 C6
Małopolskie PL 55 C5
Tarnowo Podgórne PL 46 C2
Tarnowskie Góry PL 54 C3
Tärnsjö S 36 B3
Tårnvik N 112 E4
Tarouca P 87 C3
Tarp D 43 A6
Tarquínia I 102 A4
Tarquínia Lido I 102 A4
Tarragona E 91 B4
Tàrrega E 91 B4
Tarrenz A 71 A5
Tårs
Nordjyllands DK 38 B3
Storstrøms DK 39 E4
Tarsia I 106 B3
Tarsus TR 16 C7
Tartas F 76 C2
Tartu EST 7 B9
Tarussa RUS 7 D14
Tarves GB 23 D6
Tarvísio I 72 B3
Taşağıl TR 119 F6
Täsch CH 70 B2
Taşköprü TR 16 A7
Tasov CZ 64 A2
Tasovčići BIH 84 C2
Taşucuo TR 16 C6
Tát H 65 C4
Tata H 65 C4
Tatabánya H 74 A3
Tataháza H 75 B4
Tatarbunary UA 11 D10
Tatárszentgyörgy H 75 A4
Tatranská-Lomnica SK 65 A6
Tau N 33 C2
Tauberbischofsheim D 61 A5
Taucha D 52 B2
Taufkirchen D 62 B3
Taufkirchen an der Pram A 63 B4
Taulé F 56 B2
Taulignan F 78 B3
Taulov DK 39 D2
Taunton GB 29 B4
Taunusstein D 50 C4
Tauragė LT 6 D7
Taurianova I 106 C3
Taurisano I 107 B5
Tauste E 90 B1
Tauves F 68 C2
Tavankut SRB 75 B4
Tavannes CH 70 A2
Tavarnelle val di Pesa I 81 C5
Tavas TR 119 E4
Tavaux F 69 A5
Tävelsås S 40 C4
Taverna I 106 B3
Taverne CH 70 B3
Tavernelle I 82 C1
Tavernes de la Valldigna E 96 B2
Tavérnola Bergamasca I 71 C5
Taverny F 58 A3
Tavescan E 91 A4
Taviano I 107 B5
Tavira P 98 B3
Tavistock GB 28 C3
Tavnik SRB 85 C5
Tavşanlı TR 118 C4
Tayinloan GB 24 C2
Taynuilt GB 24 B2
Tayport GB 25 B5
Tázlár H 75 B4
Tazones E 88 A1
Tczew PL 47 A4
Tczów PL 55 B6
Teangue GB 22 D3
Teano I 103 B7
Teba E 100 C1
Tebay GB 26 A3
Techendorf A 72 B3
Tecklenburg D 50 A3
Tecko-matorp S 41 D3
Tecuci RO 11 D9
Tefenni TR 119 E4
Tegelsmora S 36 B4
Tegernsee D 62 C2
Teggiano I 104 C1
Tegoleto I 81 C5
Teichel D 52 C1
Teignmouth GB 29 C4
Teillay F 57 C4
Teillet F 77 C5
Teisendorf D 62 C3
Teistungen D 51 B6
Teixeiro E 86 A2
Tejada de Tiétar E 93 A5
Tejado E 89 C4
Tejares E 94 B1
Tejn DK 41 D4
Teke TR 118 A4
Tekirdağ TR 118 B2
Tekovské-Lužany SK 65 B4
Telavåg N 32 B1
Telč CZ 63 A6
Telese Terme I 103 B7
Telford GB 26 C3
Telfs A 71 A6
Telgárt SK 65 B6
Telgte D 50 B3
Tellingstedt D 43 A6
Telšiai LT 6 D7
Telti I 110 B2
Teltow D 45 C5
Tembleque E 95 C3
Temelin CZ 63 A5
Temerin SRB 75 C4
Temiño E 89 B3
Témpio Pausánia I 110 B2
Templederry IRL 20 B3
Templemore IRL 21 B4
Temple Sowerby GB 26 A3
Templin D 45 B5
Temse B 49 B5
Tenay F 69 C5
Ten Boer NL 42 B3
Tenbury Wells GB 29 A5
Tenby GB 28 B3
Tence F 78 A3
Tende F 80 B1
Tenhult S 40 B4
Tenja HR 74 C3
Tenneville B 49 C6
Tennevoll N 112 D6
Tensta S 36 B4
Tenterden GB 31 C4
Teo E 86 B2
Teora I 103 C8
Tepasto FIN 113 E13
Tepelenë AL 116 B2
Teplá CZ 52 D2
Teplice CZ 53 C3
Teplička nad Váhom SK 65 A4
Tepsa FIN 113 E14
Tera E 89 C4
Téramo I 103 A6
Ter Apel NL 43 C4
Terborg NL 50 B2
Terchová SK 65 A5
Terebovlya UA 11 B8
Teremia Mare RO 75 C5
Terena P 92 C3
Teresa de Cofrentes E 96 B1
Terešov CZ 63 A4
Terezín CZ 53 C4
Terezino Polje HR 74 C2
Tergnier F 59 A4
Teriberka RUS 3 B31
Terlizzi I 104 B2
Termas de Monfortinho P 93 A4
Terme di Súio I 103 B6
Terme di Valdieri I 79 B6
Termens E 90 B3
Termes F 78 B2
Términi Imerese I 108 B2
Terminillo I 102 A5
Térmoli I 103 B8
Termonfeckin IRL 19 C5
Ternberg A 63 C5
Terndrup DK 38 C3
Terneuzen NL 49 B4
Terni I 102 A5
Ternitz A 64 C2
Ternopil UA 11 B8
Terpan AL 105 C6
Terpni GR 116 B5
Terracina I 102 B6
Terråk N 115 B9
Terralba I 110 C1
Terranova di Pollino I 106 B3
Terranova di Sibari I 106 B3
Terras do Bouro P 87 C2
Terrasini I 108 A2
Terrassa E 91 B5
Terrasson-la-Villedieu F 77 A4
Terrazos E 89 B3
Terriente E 95 B5
Terrugem P 92 C3
Tertenía I 110 C2
Teruel E 90 C1
Tervola FIN 3 C26
Tervuren B 49 C5
Terzaga E 95 B5
Tešanj BIH 84 B2
Tesáske-Mlyňany SK 65 B4
Teslić BIH 84 B2
Tessin D 44 A4
Tessy-sur-Vire F 57 B4
Tét H 74 A2
Tetbury GB 29 B5
Teterchen F 60 A2
Teterow D 45 B4
Teteven BG 11 E8
Tetiyev UA 11 B10
Tetovo MK 10 E6
Tettau D 52 C1
Tettnang D 61 C5
Teublitz D 62 A3
Teuchern D 52 B2
Teulada
E 96 C3
I 110 D1
Teupitz D 52 A3
Teurajärvi S 113 F11
Teutschenthal D 52 B1
Tevel H 74 B3
Teviothead GB 25 C5
Tewkesbury GB 29 B5
Thale D 52 B1
Thalfang D 60 A2
Thalgau A 63 C4
Thalkirch CH 71 B4
Thalmässing D 62 A2
Thalwil CH 70 A3
Thame GB 31 C3
Thann F 60 C3
Thannhausen D 61 B6
Thaon-les-Vosges F 60 B2
Tharandt D 52 C3
Tharsis E 99 B3
Thasos GR 116 B6
Thatcham GB 31 C2
Thaxted GB 31 C4
Thayngen CH 61 C4
Theale GB 31 C2
The Barony GB 23 B5
Thebes = Thiva GR 117 D5
Theding-hausen D 43 C6
Theessen D 52 A2
The Hague = 's-Gravenhage NL 49 A5
Themar D 51 C6
The Mumbles GB 28 B4
Thénezay F 67 B4
Thenon F 67 C6
Therouanne F 48 C3
Thessaloniki = Salonica GR 116 B4
Thetford GB 30 B4
Theth AL 105 A5
Theux B 50 C1
Thézar-les-Corbières F 78 C1
Thèze F 76 C2
Thiberville F 58 A1
Thibie F 59 B5
Thiéblemont-Farémont F 59 B5
Thiendorf D 53 B3
Thiene I 71 C6
Thierrens CH 70 B1
Thiers F 68 C3
Thiesi I 110 B1
Thiessow D 45 A5
Thiezac F 77 A5
Þingeyri IS 111 B2
Þingvellir IS 111 C4
Thionville F 60 A2
Thira GR 117 F7
Thiron-Gardais F 58 B1
Thirsk GB 27 A4
Thisted DK 38 C1
Thiva = Thebes GR 117 D5
Thivars F 58 B2
Thiviers F 67 C5
Thizy F 69 B4
Tholen NL 49 B5
Tholey D 60 A3
Thomas Street IRL 20 A3
Thomastown IRL 21 B4
Thônes F 69 C6
Thonnance-les-Joinville F 59 B6
Thonon-les-Bains F 69 B6
Thorame-Basse F 79 B5
Thorame-Haute F 79 B5
Thorens-Glières F 69 C6
Thorigny-sur-Oreuse F 59 B4
Thörl A 73 A5
Þorlákshöfn IS 111 D4
Thornaby on Tees GB 27 A4
Thornbury GB 29 B5
Thorne GB 27 B5
Thornhill
Dumfries & Galloway GB 25 C4
Stirling GB 24 B3
Thornthwaite GB 26 A2
Thornton-le-Dale GB 27 A5
Þórshöfn IS 111 A10
Thouarcé F 67 A4
Thouars F 67 B4
Thrapston GB 30 B3
Threlkeld GB 26 A2
Thrumster GB 23 C5
Thueyts F 78 B3
Thuin B 49 C5
Thuir F 91 A5
Thumau D 52 C1
Thun CH 70 B2
Thuret F 68 C3
Thurey F 69 B5
Thüringen A 71 A4
Thurins F 69 C4
Thürkow D 45 B4
Thurles IRL 21 B4
Thurmaston GB 30 B2
Thurø By DK 39 D3
Thursby GB 25 D4
Thurso GB 23 C5
Thury-Harcourt F 57 B5
Thusis CH 71 B4
Thyborøn DK 38 C1
Þykkvibær IS 111 D5
Thyregod DK 39 D2
Tibi E 96 C2
Tibro S 35 D6
Tidaholm S 35 D5
Tidan S 35 D6
Tidersrum S 40 B5
Tiedra E 88 C1
Tiefenbach D 62 A3
Tiefencastel CH 71 B4
Tiefenort D 51 C6
Tiefensee D 45 C5
Tiel NL 49 B6
Tielmes E 95 B3
Tielt B 49 B4
Tienen B 49 C5
Tiengen D 61 C4
Tiercé F 57 C5
Tierga E 89 C5
Tiermas E 90 A1
Tierp S 36 B4
Tierrantona E 90 A3
Tighina MD 11 C10
Tighnabruaich GB 24 C2
Tignes F 70 C1
Tigy F 58 C3
Tihany H 74 B2
Tijnje NL 42 B2
Tijola E 101 B3
Tikhvin RUS 7 B12
Tilburg NL 49 B6
Til Châtel F 69 A5
Tilh F 76 C2
Tillac F 76 C3
Tillberga S 37 C3
Tille F 58 A3
Tillicoultry GB 25 B4
Tilloy Bellay F 59 A5
Tilly F 67 B6
Tilly-sur-Seulles F 57 A5
Tim DK 39 C1
Timau I 72 B3
Timbaki GR 117 G6
Timi CY 120 B1
Timişoara RO 75 C6
Timmele S 40 B3
Timmendorfer Strand D 44 B2
Timmernabben S 40 C6
Timmersdala S 35 D5
Timoleague IRL 20 C3
Timolin IRL 21 B5
Timrå S 115 E14
Timsfors S 40 C3
Timsgearraidh GB 22 C1
Tinajas E 95 B4
Tinalhas P 92 B3
Tinchebray F 57 B5
Tincques F 48 C3
Tineo E 86 A4
Tinglev DK 39 E2
Tingsryd S 40 C4
Tingstäde S 37 E5
Tingvoll N 114 E5
Tinlot B 49 C6
Tinnoset N 33 C6
Tinos GR 117 E7
Tintagel GB 28 C3
Tinténiac F 57 B4
Tintern GB 29 B5
Tintigny B 60 A1
Tione di Trento I 71 B5
Tipperary IRL 20 B3
Tiptree GB 31 C4
Tirana = Tiranë AL 105 B5
Tiranë= Tirana AL 105 B5
Tirano I 71 B5
Tiraspol MD 11 C10
Tire TR 119 D2
Tires I 71 B6
Tiriez E 95 D4
Tirig E 90 C3
Tiriolo I 106 C3
Tirnavos GR 116 C4
Tirrénia I 81 C4
Tirschenreuth D 62 A3
Tirstrup DK 39 C3
Tirteafuera E 100 A1
Tishono RUS 47 A6
Tisno HR 83 C4
Tišnov CZ 64 A2
Tisovec SK 65 B5
Tisselskog S 35 D4
Tistedal N 35 C3
Tistrup DK 39 D1
Tisvildeleje DK 39 C5
Tiszaalpár H 75 B4
Tiszabö H 75 A5
Tiszadorogma H 65 C6
Tiszaföldvár H 75 B5
Tiszafüred H 65 C6
Tiszajenö H 75 A5
Tiszakécske H 75 B5
Tiszakürt H 75 B5
Tiszanána H 75 A5
Tiszaörs H 75 A5
Tiszaroff H 75 A5
Tiszasüly H 75 A5
Tiszasziget H 75 B5
Tiszaszőlős H 75 A5
Titaguas E 96 B1
Titel SRB 75 C5
Titisee-Neustadt D 61 C4
Tito I 104 C1
Titova Korenica HR 83 B4
Titran N 114 D5
Tittling D 63 B4
Tittmoning D 62 B3
Titz D 50 B2
Tiurajärvi FIN 113 E13
Tivat MNE 105 A4
Tived S 37 D1
Tiverton GB 29 C4
Tivisa E 90 B3
Tívoli I 102 B5
Tjällmo S 37 D2
Tjåmotis S 112 F7
Tjæreborg DK 39 D1
Tjautjas S 112 E9
Tjøme N 35 C2
Tjong N 112 F2
Tjonnefoss N 33 D5
Tjörn IS 111 B5
Tjörnarp S 41 D3
Tjøtta N 115 B9
Tkon HR 83 C4
Tleń PL 47 B4
Tlmače SK 65 B4
Tłuchowo PL 47 C5
Tlumačov CZ 64 A3
Tóalmas H 75 A4
Toano I 81 B4
Toba D 51 B6
Tobarra E 101 A4
Tobermore GB 19 B5
Tobermory GB 24 B1
Toberonochy GB 24 B2
Tobha Mor GB 22 D1
Tobo S 36 B4
Tocane-St Apre F 67 C5
Tocha P 92 A2
Tocina E 99 B5
Töcksfors S 35 C3
Tocón E 100 B2
Todal N 114 E5
Todi I 82 D1
Todmorden GB 26 B3
Todorici BIH 84 B2
Todtmoos D 61 C4
Todtnau D 60 C3
Toén E 87 B3
Tofta
Gotland S 37 E5
Skaraborg S 35 D5
Toftbyn S 36 B2
Tofte N 35 C2
Töftedal S 35 D3
Tofterup DK 39 D1
Toftlund DK 39 D2
Tófü H 74 B3
Tohmo FIN 113 F16
Tokarnia PL 55 C5
Tokary PL 54 B3
Tokod H 65 C4
Tököl H 75 A3
Tolastadh bho Thuath GB 22 C2
Toledo E 94 C2
Tolentino I 82 C2
Tolfa I 102 A4
Tolg S 40 B4
Tolga N 114 E8
Tolkmicko PL 47 A5
Tolko PL 47 A6
Tollarp S 41 D3
Tollered S 40 B2
Tølløse DK 39 D4
Tolmachevo RUS 7 B10
Tolmezzo I 72 B3
Tolmin SLO 72 B3
Tolna H 74 B3
Tolnanémedi H 74 B3
Tolob GB 22 B7
Tolosa
E 89 A4
P 92 B3
Tolox E 100 C1
Tolpuddle GB 29 C5
Tolva E 90 A3
Tolve I 104 C2
Tomar P 92 B2
Tomarza TR 16 B7
Tomaševac SRB 75 C5
Tomašica BIH 83 B5
Tomášikovo SK 64 B3
Tomašouka BY 6 F7
Tomášovce SK 65 B5
Tomaszów Mazowiecki PL 55 B5
Tomatin GB 23 D5
Tombeboeuf F 77 B3
Tomdoun GB 22 D3
Tomelilla S 41 D3
Tomellosa E 95 B4
Tomelloso E 95 C3
Tomiño E 87 C2
Tomintoul GB 23 D5
Tomislavgrad BIH 84 C2
Tomisław PL 53 B5
Tomisławice PL 47 C4
Tomnavoulin GB 23 D5
Tompa H 75 B4
Tompaládony H 74 A1
Tomra N 114 E3
Tomter N 35 C2
Tona E 91 B5
Tonara I 110 B2
Tonbridge GB 31 C4
Tondela P 92 A2
Tønder DK 39 E1
Tongeren B 49 C6
Tongue GB 23 C4
Tönisvorst D 50 B2
Tønjum N 32 A4
Tonkopuro FIN 113 F17
Tonnay-Boutonne F 67 C4
Tonnay-Charente F 66 C4
Tonneins F 77 B3
Tonnerre F 59 C4
Tonnes N 115 A10
Tönning D 43 A5
Tonsåsen N 32 B6
Tønsberg N 35 C2
Tonstad N 33 D3
Toomyvara IRL 20 B3
Toormore IRL 20 C2
Topares E 101 B3
Topas E 94 A1
Topliţa RO 11 C8
Topola SRB 85 B5
Topolčani MK 116 A3
Topol'čany SK 64 B4
Topol'čianky SK 65 B4
Topolje HR 73 C6
Topólka PL 47 C4
Topol'niky SK 64 C3
Toponár H 74 B2
Toporów PL 53 A5
Topsham GB 29 C4
Topusko HR 73 C5
Toques E 86 B3
Torà E 91 B4
Toral de los Guzmanes E 88 B1
Toral de los Vados E 86 B4
Torbalı TR 119 D2
Torbjörntorp S 35 D5
Torbole I 71 C5
Torchiarolo I 105 C4
Torcross GB 29 C4
Torcy-le-Petit F 58 A2
Torda SRB 75 C5
Tørdal N 33 C5
Tordehumos E 88 C1
Tordera E 91 B5
Tordesillas E 88 C1
Tordesilos E 95 B5
Töre S 3 D25
Töreboda S 35 D6
Toreby DK 39 E4
Torekov S 41 C2
Torella dei Lombardi I 103 C8
Torellò E 91 A5
Toreno E 86 B4
Torfou F 66 A3
Torgau D 52 B3
Torgelow D 45 B6
Torgueda P 87 C3
Torhamn S 41 C5
Torhop N 113 B16
Torhout B 49 B4
Torigni-sur-Vire F 57 A5
Torija E 95 B3
Toril E 95 B5
Torino = Turin I 80 A1
Toritto I 104 C2
Torkovichi RUS 7 B11
Torla E 90 A2
Törmänen FIN 113 D16
Tormestorp S 41 C3
Tórmini I 71 C5
Tornada P 92 B1
Tornal'a SK 65 B6
Tornavacas E 93 A5
Tornby DK 38 B2
Tornesch D 43 B6
Torness GB 23 D4
Torniella I 81 C5
Tornimparte I 103 A6
Torning DK 39 C2
Tornio FIN 3 D26
Tornjoš SRB 75 C4
Tornos E 95 B5
Toro E 88 C1
Törökszentmiklós H 75 A5
Toropets RUS 7 C11
Torpa S 40 C3
Torpè I 110 B2
Torphins GB 23 D6
Torpo N 32 B5
Torpoint GB 28 C3
Torpsbruk S 40 B4
Torquay GB 29 C4
Torquemada E 88 B2
Torralba de Burgo E 89 C4
Torralba de Calatrava E 94 C3
Torrão P 98 A2
Torre Annunziata I 103 C7
Torreblacos E 89 C4
Torreblanca E 96 A3
Torreblascopedro E 100 A2
Torrecaballeros E 94 A2
Torrecampo E 100 A1
Torre Canne I 104 C3
Torre Cardela E 100 B2
Torrecilla E 95 B4
Torrecilla de la Jara E 94 C2
Torrecilla de la Orden E 94 A1
Torrecilla del Pinar E 88 C2
Torrecilla en Cameros E 89 B4
Torrecillas de la Tiesa E 93 B5
Torre das Vargens P 92 B3
Torre de Coelheiros P 92 C3
Torre de Dom Chama P 87 C3
Torre de Juan Abad E 100 A2
Torre de la Higuera E 99 B4
Torre del Bierzo E 86 B4
Torre del Burgo E 95 B3
Torre del Campo E 100 B2
Torre del Greco I 103 C7
Torre del Lago Puccini I 81 C4
Torre dell'Orso I 105 C4
Torre del Mar E 100 C1
Torredembarra E 91 B4
Torre de Miguel Sesmero E 93 C4
Torre de Moncorvo P 87 C3
Torre de Santa Maria E 93 B4
Torredonjimeno E 100 B2
Torre do Terranho P 87 D3
Torre Faro I 109 A4
Torregrosa E 90 B3
Torreira P 87 D2
Torrejoncillo E 93 B4
Torrejón de Ardoz E 95 B3
Torrejón de la Calzada E 94 B3
Torrejón del Rey E 95 B3
Torrejon el Rubio E 93 B4
Torrelaguna E 95 B3
Torrelapaja E 89 C5
Torre la Ribera E 90 A3
Torrelavega E 88 A2
Torrelobatón E 88 C1
Torrelodones E 94 B3
Torre los Negros E 90 C1
Torremaggiore I 103 B8
Torremanzanas E 96 C2
Torremayor E 93 C4
Torremezzo di Falconara I 106 B3
Torremocha E 93 B4
Torremolinos E 100 C1
Torrenieri I 81 C5
Torrenostra E 96 A3
Torrenova I 102 B5
Torrent E 96 B2
Torrente de Cinca E 90 B3
Torrenueva
Ciudad Real E 100 A2
Granada E 100 C2
Torreorgaz E 93 B4
Torre Orsáia I 106 A2
Torre-Pacheco E 101 B5
Torre Péllice I 79 B6
Torreperogil E 100 A2
Torres E 100 B2
Torresandino E 88 C3
Torre Santa Susanna I 105 C3
Torres-Cabrera E 100 B1
Torres de la Alameda E 95 B3
Torres Novas P 92 B2
Torres Vedras P 92 B1
Torrevieja E 96 D2
Torricella I 104 C3
Torri del Benaco I 71 C5
Torridon GB 22 D3
Torriglia I 80 B3
Torrijos E 94 C2
Tørring DK 39 D2
Torrita di Siena I 81 C5
Torroal P 92 C2
Torroella de Montgr ì E 91 A6
Torrox E 100 C2
Torrskog S 35 C4
Torsåker S 36 B3
Torsang S 36 B2
Torsås S 41 C6
Torsby S 34 B4
Torsetra N 34 B2
Torshälla S 37 C3
Tórshavn FO 2 E10
Torslanda S 38 B4
Torsminde DK 39 C1
Torsnes N 32 B3
Törtel H 75 A4
Tórtoles E 93 A5
Tórtoles de Esgueva E 88 C2
Tortol ì I 110 C2
Tortona I 80 B2
Tórtora I 106 B2
Tortoreto Lido I 82 D2
Tortorici I 109 A3
Tortosa E 90 C3
Tortosendo P 92 A3
Tortuera E 95 B5
Tortuero E 95 B3
Toruń PL 47 B4
Torup S 40 C3
Tor Vaiánica I 102 B5
Torver GB 26 A2
Tørvikbygde N 32 B3
Torviscón E 100 C2
Torzhok RUS 7 C13
Torzym PL 53 A5
Tosbotn N 115 B9
Toscelanor-Maderno I 71 C5
Tosno RUS 7 B11
Tossa de Mar E 91 B5
Tossåsen S 115 E10
Tosse F 76 C1
Tösse S 35 D4
Tossicía I 103 A6
Tostedt D 43 B6
Tosya TR 16 A7
Tószeg H 75 A5
Toszek PL 54 C3
Totana E 101 B4
Totebo S 40 B6
Tôtes F 58 A2
Tótkomlós H 75 B5
Totland N 114 F2
Tøtlandsvik N 33 C3
Totnes GB 28 C4
Tótszerdahely H 74 B1
Tøttdal N 114 C8
Totton GB 31 D2
Touça P 87 C3
Toucy F 59 C4
Toul F 60 B1
Toulon F 79 C4
Toulon-sur-Allier F 68 B3
Toulon-sur-Arroux F 68 B4
Toulouse F 77 C4
Tourcoing F 49 C4
Tour de la Parata F 102 B1
Tourlaville F 57 A4
Tournai B 49 C4
Tournan-en-Brie F 58 B3
Tournay F 76 C3
Tournon-d'Agenais F 77 B3
Tournon-St Martin F 67 B5
Tournon-sur-Rhône F 78 A3
Tournus F 69 B4
Touro
E 86 B2
P 87 D3
Tourouvre F 58 B1
Tourriers F 67 C5
Tours F 67 A5
Tourteron F 59 A5
Tourves F 79 C4
Toury F 58 B2
Touvedo P 87 C2
Touvois F 66 B3
Toužim CZ 52 C2
Tovačov CZ 64 A3
Tovariševo SRB 75 C4
Tovarnik HR 75 C4
Tovdal N 33 D5
Tovrljane SRB 85 C6
Towcester GB 30 B3
Town Yetholm GB 25 C5
Tråastølen N 32 B4
Trabada E 86 A3
Trabadelo E 86 B4
Trabanca E 87 C4
Trabazos E 87 C4
Traben-Trarbach D 50 D3
Trabia I 108 B2
Tradate I 70 C3

Trädet S 40 B3
Trafaria P 92 C1
Tragacete E 95 B5
Tragwein A 63 B5
Traiguera E 90 C3
Trainel F 59 B4
Traisen A 63 B6
Traismauer A 64 B1
Traitsching D 62 A3
Trákhonas CY 120 A2
Tralee IRL 20 B2
Tramacastilla de Tena
E 76 D2
Tramagal P 92 B2
Tramariglio I 110 B1
Tramatza I 110 B1
Tramelan CH 70 A2
Tramonti di Sopra I 72 B2
Tramore IRL 21 B4
Trampot F 60 B1
Trana I 80 A1
Tranås S 40 A4
Tranbjerg DK 39 C3
Tranby N 34 C2
Trancoso P 87 D3
Tranebjerg DK 39 D3
Tranekær DK 39 E3
Tranemo S 40 B3
Tranent GB 25 C5
Tranevåg N 33 D3
Trängslet S 34 A5
Tranhult S 40 B3
Trani I 104 B2
Trans-en-Provence F 79 C5
Transtrand S 34 A5
Tranum DK 38 B2
Tranvik S 37 C5
Trápani I 108 A1
Trappes F 58 B3
Traryd S 40 C3
Trasacco I 103 B6
Trasierra E 99 A4
Träslövsläge S 40 B2
Trasmiras E 87 B3
Traspinedo E 88 C2
Trate SLO 73 B5
Trauchgau D 62 C1
Traun A 63 B5
Traunreut D 62 C3
Traunstein D 62 C3
Traunwalchen D 62 C3
Trävad S 35 D5
Travemünde D 44 B2
Traversétolo I 81 B4
Travnik
BIH 84 B2
SLO 73 C4
Travo
F 102 B2
I 80 B3
Trawsfynydd GB 26 C2
Trbovlje SLO 73 B5
Trbušani SRB 85 C5
Treban F 68 B3
Třebařov CZ 64 A2
Trebatsch D 53 A4
Trebbin D 52 A3
Třebechovice pod
Orebem CZ 53 C5
Trebel D 44 C3
Třebenice CZ 53 C3
Trébeurden F 56 B2
Třebíč CZ 64 A1
Trebinje BIH 84 D3
Trebisacce I 106 B3
Trebitz D 52 B2
Trebnje SLO 73 C5
Třeboň CZ 63 A5
Třebovice CZ 64 A2
Trebsen D 52 B2
Trebujena E 99 C4
Trecastagni I 109 B4
Trecate I 70 C3
Trecenta I 81 A5
Tredegar GB 29 B4
Tredózio I 81 B5
Treffen A 72 B3
Treffort F 69 B5
Treffurt D 51 B6
Trefnant GB 26 B2
Tregaron GB 28 A4
Trégastel-Plage F 56 B2
Tregnago I 71 C6
Tregony GB 28 C3
Tréguier F 56 B2
Trégunc F 56 C2
Treharris GB 29 B4
Trehörningsjö S 115 D15
Tréia I 82 C2
Treignac F 68 C1
Treignat F 68 B2
Treignes B 49 C5
Treis-Karden D 50 C3
Trekanten S 40 C6
Trélazé F 67 A4
Trelech GB 28 B3
Trélissac F 67 C5
Trelleborg S 41 D3
Trélon F 49 C5
Trélou-sur-Marne F 59 A4
Tremblay-le-Vicomte
F 58 B2
Tremés P 92 B2
Tremezzo I 71 C4
Třemošná CZ 63 A4
Tremp E 90 A3
Trenčianska Stankovce
SK 64 B3
Trenčianska Turná
SK 64 B4
Trenčianske Teplá
SK 64 B4
Trenčianske Teplice
SK 64 B4
Trenčín SK 64 B4
Trendelburg D 51 B5
Trengereid N 32 B2
Trensacq F 76 B2
Trent D 45 A5
Trento I 71 B6
Treorchy GB 29 B4
Trepča KOS 85 D5
Trept F 69 C5
Trepuzzi I 105 C4
Trescore Balneário I 71 C4
Tresenda I 71 B5
Tresfjord N 114 E4
Tresigallo I 81 B5
Trešnjevica SRB 85 C6
Tresnuràghes I 110 B1
Trespaderne E 89 B3
Třešť CZ 63 A6
Trestina I 82 C1
Tretower GB 29 B4
Trets F 79 C4
Tretten N 34 A2
Treuchtlingen D 62 B1
Treuen D 52 C2
Treuenbrietzen D 52 A2
Treungen N 33 C5
Trevelez E 100 C2
Trevi I 82 D1
Treviana E 89 B3
Treviglio I 71 C4
Trevignano Romano
I 102 A5
Trevi nel Lázio I 102 B6
Treviso I 72 C2
Trévoux F 69 C4
Treysa D 51 C5
Trézelles F 68 B3
Trezzo sull'Adda I 71 C4
Trhová Kamenice CZ 64 A1
Trhové Sviny CZ 63 B5
Triacastela E 86 B3
Triaize F 66 B3
Trianda GR 119 F3
Triaucourt-en-Argonne
F 59 B6
Tribanj Kruščica HR 83 B4
Triberg D 61 B4
Tribsees D 45 A4
Tribuče SLO 73 C5
Tricárico I 104 C2
Tricase I 107 B5
Tricésimo I 72 B3
Trieben A 73 A4
Triebes D 52 C2
Triepkendorf D 45 B5
Trier D 60 A2
Trieste I 72 C3
Trie-sur-Baïse F 77 C3
Triggiano I 104 B2
Triglitz D 44 B4
Trignac F 66 A2
Trigueros E 99 B4
Trigueros del Valle E 88 C2
Trijebine SRB 85 C4
Trikala GR 116 C3
Trikeri GR 116 C5
Trikomo CY 120 A2
Trilj HR 83 C5
Trillo E 95 B4
Trilport F 59 B3
Trim IRL 21 A5
Trimdon GB 25 D6
Trindade
Beja P 98 B3
Bragança P 87 C3
Třinec CZ 65 A4
Tring GB 31 C3
Trinità d'Agultu I 110 B1
Trinitápoli I 104 B2
Trino I 70 C3
Trinta P 92 A3
Triora I 80 C1
Tripoli GR 117 E4
Triponzo I 82 D1
Triptis D 52 C1
Triste E 90 A2
Trittau D 44 B2
Trivento I 103 B7
Trivero I 70 C3
Trivigno I 104 C1
Trn BIH 84 B2
Trnava
HR 74 C3
SK 64 B3
Trnovec SK 64 B3
Trnovo BIH 84 C3
Trnovska vas SLO 73 B5
Troarn F 57 A5
Trochtelfingen D 61 B5
Trödje S 36 B4
Troense DK 39 D3
Trofa P 87 C2
Trofaiach A 73 A5
Trofors N 115 B10
Trogir HR 83 C5
Trøgstad N 35 C3
Tróia I 103 B8
Troia P 92 C2
Troina I 109 B3
Troisdorf D 50 C3
Trois-Ponts B 50 C1
Troisvierges L 50 C2
Trojane SLO 73 B4
Trojanów PL 55 B6
Troldhede DK 39 D1
Trollhättan S 35 D4
Trolog BIH 84 C1
Tromello I 70 C3
Tromøy N 33 D5
Tromsø N 112 C8
Trondheim N 114 D7
Tronget F 68 B3
Trönninge S 40 C2
Trönningeby S 40 B2
Trönö S 36 A3
Tronzano-Vercellese
I 70 C3
Trôo F 58 C1
Troon GB 24 C3
Tropea I 106 C2
Tropojë AL 105 A6
Tropy Sztumskie PL 47 B5
Trosa S 37 D4
Trösken S 36 B3
Trosly-Breuil F 59 A4
Trossingen D 61 B4
Trostberg D 62 B3
Trostyanets UA 7 F13
Trouville-sur-Mer F 57 A6
Trowbridge GB 29 B5
Troyes F 59 B5
Trpanj HR 84 C2
Trpezi MNE 85 D5
Trpinja HR 74 C3
Tršće HR 73 C4
Tršice CZ 64 A3
Trstená SK 65 A5
Trstenci BIH 84 A2
Trstenik
KOS 85 D5
SRB 85 C6
Trsteno HR 84 D2
Trstice SK 64 B3
Trstín SK 64 B3
Trubchevsk RUS 7 E12
Trubia E 88 A1
Trubjela MNE 84 D3
Truchas E 87 B4
Trujillanos E 93 C4
Trujillo E 93 B5
Trumieje PL 47 B5
Trun
CH 70 B3
F 57 B6
Truro GB 28 C2
Trusetal D 51 C6
Truskavets' UA 11 B7
Trustrup DK 39 C3
Trutnov CZ 53 C5
Tryserum S 37 D3
Trysil N 34 A4
Tryszczyn PL 46 B3
Trzcianka PL 46 B2
Trzciel PL 46 C1
Trzcińsko Zdrój PL 45 C6
Trzebiatów PL 45 A7
Trzebiel PL 53 B4
Trzebielino PL 46 A3
Trzebień PL 53 B5
Trzebiez PL 45 B6
Trzebinia PL 55 C4
Trzebnica PL 54 B2
Trzebnice PL 53 B6
Trzeciewiec PL 47 B4
Trzemeszno PL 46 C3
Trzemeszno-Lubuskie
PL 46 C1
Trzetrzewina PL 65 A6
Tržič SLO 73 B4
Tsamandas GR 116 C2
Tschagguns A 71 A4
Tschernitz D 53 B4
Tsebrykove UA 11 C11
Tsvetkovo UA 11 B11
Tsyelyakhany BY 7 E8
Tua P 87 C3
Tuam IRL 20 A3
Tubbercurry IRL 18 B3
Tubbergen NL 42 C3
Tubilla del Lago E 89 C3
Tübingen D 61 B5
Tubize B 49 C5
Tučapy CZ 63 A5
Tučepi HR 84 C2
Tuchan F 78 D1
Tüchen D 44 B4
Tuchola PL 46 B3
Tuchomie PL 46 A3
Tuchów PL 65 A7
Tuczno PL 46 B2
Tuddal N 32 C5
Tudela E 89 B5
Tudela de Duero E 88 C2
Tudweiliog GB 26 C1
Tuejar E 96 B1
Tuffé F 58 B1
Tufsingdalen N 114 E8
Tuhaň CZ 53 C4
Tui E 87 B2
Tukums LV 6 C7
Tula
I 110 B1
RUS 7 D14
Tulcea RO 11 D10
Tul'chyn UA 11 B10
Tulette F 78 B3
Tuliszków PL 54 A3
Tulla IRL 20 B3
Tullamore IRL 21 A4
Tulle F 68 C1
Tullins F 69 C5
Tulln A 64 B2
Tullow IRL 21 B5
Tułowice PL 54 C2
Tulppio FIN 113 E18
Tulsk IRL 18 C3
Tumba S 37 C4
Tummel Bridge GB 24 B3
Tun S 35 D4
Tuna
Kalmar S 40 B6
Uppsala S 36 B5
Tuna Hästberg S 36 B2
Tunçbilek TR 118 C4
Tunes P 98 B2
Tungelsta S 37 C5
Tunje AL 105 C6
Tunnerstad S 40 A4
Tunnhovd N 32 B5
Tunstall GB 30 B5
Tuohikotti FIN 3 F27
Tuoro sul Trasimeno
I 82 C1
Tupadły PL 47 C4
Tupanari BIH 84 B3
Tupik RUS 7 D12
Tuplice PL 53 B4
Tura H 65 C5
Turanj HR 83 C4
Turany SK 65 A5
Turbe BIH 84 B2
Turbenthal CH 70 A3
Turcia E 88 B1
Turčianske Teplice
SK 65 B4
Turcifal P 92 B1
Turckheim F 60 B3
Turda RO 11 C7
Turégano E 94 A3
Turek PL 54 A3
Tŭrgovishte BG 11 E9
Turgutlu TR 119 D2
Turi I 104 C3
Turin = Torino I 80 A1
Turis E 96 B2
Türje H 74 B2
Turka UA 11 B7
Túrkeve H 75 A5
Türkheim D 62 B1
Türkmenli TR 118 C1
Turku FIN 6 A7
Turleque E 94 C3
Turňa nad Bodvou
SK 65 B6
Turnberry GB 24 C3
Turnhout B 49 B5
Türnitz A 63 C6
Turnov CZ 53 C5
Turnu RO 75 B6
Turnu Măgurele RO 11 E8
Turón E 100 C2
Turoszów PL 53 C4
Turowo PL 47 B6
Turquel P 92 B1
Turri I 110 C1
Turries F 79 B5
Turriff GB 23 D6
Tursi I 104 C2
Turtmann CH 70 B2
Turtola FIN 113 F12
Turze PL 54 B2
Turzovka SK 65 A4
Tusa I 109 B3
Tuscánia I 102 A4
Tuse DK 39 D4
Tušilovic HR 73 C5
Tuszyn PL 55 B4
Tutin SRB 85 D5
Tutow D 45 B5
Tutrakan BG 11 D9
Tuttlingen D 61 C4
Tutzing D 62 C2
Tuzi MNE 105 A5
Tuzla
BIH 84 B3
TR 16 C7
Tuzlukçu TR 119 D6
Tvååker S 40 B2
Tvärålund S 115 C16
Tvärskog S 40 C6
Tvedestrand N 33 D5
Tveit
Hordaland N 32 B4
Rogaland N 33 C3
Tver RUS 7 C13
Tverrelvmo N 112 D8
Tversted DK 38 B3
Tving S 41 C5
Tvrdošin SK 65 A5
Tvrdošovce SK 64 B4
Twardogóra PL 54 B2
Twatt GB 23 B5
Twello NL 50 A2
Twimberg A 73 B4
Twist D 43 C4
Twistringen D 43 C5
Tworóg PL 54 C3
Twyford
Hampshire GB 31 C2
Wokingham GB 31 C3
Tyachiv UA 11 B7
Tychówka PL 46 B2
Tychowo PL 46 B2
Tychy PL 54 C3
Tydal N 114 D8
Týec nad Labem CZ 53 C5
Tyfors S 34 B6
Tygelsjö S 41 D2
Tylldal N 114 E7
Tylstrup DK 38 B2
Tymbark PL 65 A6
Tymowa PL 65 A6
Tyndrum GB 24 B3
Týnec nad Sázavou
CZ 63 A5
Tynemouth GB 25 C6
Tyngsjö S 34 B5
Týništěnad Orlicí CZ 53 C6
Týn nad Vltavou CZ 63 A5
Tynset N 114 E7
Tyresö S 37 C5
Tyringe S 41 C3
Tyrislöt S 37 D3
Tyristrand N 34 B2
Tyrrellspass IRL 21 A4
Tysnes N 32 B2
Tysse N 32 B2
Tyssebotn N 32 B2
Tyssedal N 32 B3
Tystberga S 37 D4
Tysvær N 33 C2
Tywyn GB 26 C1
Tzermiado GR 117 G7
Tzummarum NL 42 B2

U

Ub SRB 85 B5
Ubby DK 39 D4
Úbeda E 100 A2
Überlingen D 61 C5
Ubidea E 89 A4
Ubli
HR 84 D1
MNE 105 A5
Ubrique E 99 C5
Ucero E 89 C3
Uchaud F 78 C3
Uchte D 43 C5
Uckerath D 50 C3
Uckfield GB 31 D4
Ucklum S 38 A4
Uclés E 95 C4
Ucria I 109 A3
Udbina HR 83 B4
Uddebo S 40 B3
Uddeholm S 34 B5
Uddevalla S 35 D3
Uddheden S 34 C4
Uden NL 49 B6
Uder D 51 B6
Udiča SK 65 A4
Údine I 72 B3
Udvar H 74 C3
Ueckermünde D 45 B6
Uelsen D 42 C3
Uelzen D 44 C2
Uetendorf CH 70 B2
Uetersen D 43 B6
Uetze D 44 C2
Uffculme GB 29 C4
Uffenheim D 61 A6
Ugarana E 89 A4
Ugento I 107 B5
Ugerldse DK 39 D4
Uggerby DK 38 B3
Uggerslev DK 39 D3
Uggiano la Chiesa I 107 A5
Ugijar E 100 C2
Ugine F 69 C6
Uglejevik BIH 84 B4
Uglenes N 32 B2
Uglich RUS 7 C15
Ugljane HR 84 C1
Ugod H 74 A2
Uherské Hradiště CZ 64 A3
Uherský Brod CZ 64 A3
Uherský Ostroh CZ 64 B3
Uhingen D 61 B5
Uhlířské-Janovice
CZ 63 A6
Uhříněves CZ 53 C4
Uhyst D 53 B4
Uig GB 22 D2
Uitgeest NL 42 C1
Uithoorn NL 49 A5
Uithuizen NL 42 B3
Uithuizermeeden NL 42 B3
Uivar RO 75 C5
Ujazd
Łódzkie PL 55 B4
Opolskie PL 54 C3
Ujezd u Brna CZ 64 A2
Ujhartyán H 75 A4
Újkígyós H 75 B6
Ujpetre H 74 C3
Ujście PL 46 B2
Ujsolt H 75 B4
Újszász H 75 A5
Ujué E 89 B5
Ukanc SLO 72 B3
Ukmergė LT 6 D8
Ukna S 40 A6
Ula TR 119 E3
Ul'anka SK 65 B5
Ulaş TR 118 A2
Ulássai I 110 C2
Ulbjerg DK 38 C2
Ulbster GB 23 C5
Ulceby GB 27 B5
Ulcinj MNE 105 B5
Uldum DK 39 D2
Ulefoss N 33 C6
Uleila del Campo E 101 B3
Ulëz AL 105 B5
Ulfborg DK 39 C1
Uljma SRB 85 A6
Ullånger S 115 D15
Ullapool GB 22 D3
Ullared S 40 B2
Ullatti S 113 E10
Ullatun N 33 C3
Ulldecona E 90 C3
Ulldemolins E 90 B3
Ullerslev DK 39 D3
Ullervad S 35 D5
Üllés H 75 B4
Üllö H 75 A4
Ulm D 61 B5
Ulme P 92 B2
Ulmen D 50 C2
Ulnes N 32 B6
Ulog BIH 84 C3
Ulricehamn S 40 B3
Ulrichstein D 51 C5
Ulrika S 37 D2
Ulriksfors S 115 D12
Ulrum NL 42 B3
Ulsberg N 114 E6
Ulsta GB 22 A7
Ulsted DK 38 B3
Ulsteinvik N 114 E2
Ulstrup
Vestsjællands Amt.
DK 39 D3
Viborg Amt. DK 39 C2
Ulsvåg N 112 D4
Ulubey TR 119 D4
Uluborlu TR 119 D5
Ulukışla TR 16 C7
Ulverston GB 26 A2
Ulvik N 32 B3
Umag HR 72 C3
Uman UA 11 B11
Umba RUS 3 C31
Umbértide I 82 C1
Umbriático I 107 B3
Umčari SRB 85 B5
Umeå S 3 E24
Umgransele S 115 C15
Umhausen A 71 A5
Umka SRB 85 B5
Umljanovic HR 83 C5
Umnäs S 115 B13
Ümurbey TR 118 B1
Unaðsdalur IS 111 A3
Unapool GB 22 C3
Unari FIN 113 E14
Uncastillo E 90 A1
Undenäs S 37 D1
Undersaker S 115 D10
Undredal N 32 B4
Unecha RUS 7 E12
Unešić HR 83 C5
Úněšov CZ 62 A4
Ungheni MD 11 C9
Unhais da Serra P 92 A3
Unhošť CZ 53 C4
Unichowo PL 46 A3
Uničov CZ 64 A3
Uniejów PL 54 B3
Unisław PL 47 B4
Unkel D 50 C3
Unken A 62 C3
Unna D 50 B3
Unnaryd S 40 C3
Unquera E 88 A2
Unterach A 63 C4
Unterägeri CH 70 A3
Unterammergau D 62 C2
Unterhaching D 62 B2
Unteriberg CH 70 A3
Unterkochen D 61 B6
Unter Langkampfen A 72 A2
Unterlaussa A 63 C5
Unterlüss D 44 C2
Untermünkheim D 61 A5
Unterschächen CH 70 B3
Unterschleissheim D 62 B2
Unterschwaningen D 62 A1
Untersiemau D 51 C6
Unter-steinbach D 61 A6
Unterweissenbach A 63 B5
Unterzell D 62 A3
Upavon GB 29 B6
Úpice CZ 53 C6
Upiłka PL 46 B3
Upphärad S 35 D4
Uppingham GB 30 B3
Upplands-Väsby S 37 C4
Uppsala S 36 C4
Uppsjøhytta N 34 A1
Upton-upon-Severn
GB 29 A5
Ur F 91 A4
Ura e Shtrenjte AL 105 A5
Uras I 110 C1
Ura-Vajgurorë AL 105 C5
Uraz PL 54 B1
Urbánia I 82 C1
Urbino I 82 C1
Urçay F 68 B2
Urda E 94 C3
Urdax E 76 C1
Urdilde E 86 B2
Urdos F 76 D2
Urk NL 42 C2
Úrkút H 74 A2
Urla TR 119 D1
Urlingford IRL 21 B4
Urnäsch CH 71 A4
Urnes N 32 A4
Uroševac KOS 10 E6
Urracal E 101 B3
Urries E 90 A1
Urroz E 76 D1
Ursensollen D 62 A2
Urshult S 40 C4
Uršna Sela SLO 73 C5
Urszulewo PL 47 C5
Ury F 58 B3
Urziceni RO 11 D9
Urzulei I 110 B2
Usagre E 93 C4
Uşak TR 118 D4
Ušće SRB 85 C5
Usedom D 45 B5
Useldange L 60 A1
Uséllus I 110 C1
Ushakovo RUS 47 A6
Usingen D 51 C4
Usini I 110 B1
Usk GB 29 B5
Uskedal N 32 C2
Üsküdar TR 118 A4
Uslar D 51 B5
Úsov CZ 64 A3
Usquert NL 42 B3
Ussássai I 110 C2
Ussé F 67 A5
Usséglio I 70 C2
Ussel
Cantal F 78 A1
Corrèze F 68 C2
Usson-du-Poitou F 67 B5
Usson-en-Forez F 68 C3
Usson-les-Bains F 77 D5
Ustaoset N 32 B5
Ustaritz F 76 C1
Uštěk CZ 53 C4
Uster CH 70 A3
Ústi CZ 64 A3
Ustibar BIH 85 C4
Ustikolina BIH 84 C3
Ústínad Labem CZ 53 C4
Ústínad Orlicí CZ 54 D1
Ustipračà BIH 84 C4
Ustka PL 46 A2
Ust Luga RUS 7 B10
Ustroń PL 65 A4
Ustronie Morskie PL 46 A1
Ustyuzhna RUS 7 B14
Uszód H 74 B3
Utåker N 32 C2
Utansjö S 115 E14
Utebo E 90 B2
Utena LT 7 D8
Utery CZ 62 A4
Uthaug N 114 D6
Utiel E 96 B1
Utne N 32 B3
Utö S 37 D5
Utrecht NL 49 A6
Utrera E 99 B5
Utrillas E 90 C2
Utsjoki FIN 113 C16
Utstein kloster N 33 C2
Uttendorf A 72 A2
Uttenweiler D 61 B5
Utterslev DK 39 E4
Uttoxeter GB 27 C4
Utvälinge S 41 C2
Utvorda N 114 C7
Uusikaarlepyy FIN 3 E25
Uusikaupunki FIN 3 F24
Uvac BIH 85 C4
Uvaly CZ 53 C4
Uvdal N 32 B5
Uza F 76 B1
Uzdin SRB 75 C5
Uzdowo PL 47 B6
Uzein F 76 C2
Uzel F 56 B3
Uzerche F 67 C6
Uzès F 78 B3
Uzhhorod UA 11 B7
Uzhok UA 11 B7
Užice SRB 85 C4
Uznach CH 70 A3
Uznovë AL 105 C6
Üzümlü
Konya TR 119 E6
Muğla TR 119 F4
Uzunköprü TR 118 A1

V

Vaalajärvi FIN 113 E15
Vaas F 58 C1
Vaasa FIN 3 E24
Vaasen NL 50 A1
Vabre F 77 C5
Vác H 65 C5
Vacha D 51 C6
Váchartyán H 65 C5
Väckelsång S 40 C4
Vacqueyras F 78 B3
Vad S 36 B2
Vada I 81 C4
Väddö S 36 C5
Väderstad S 37 D1
Vadheim N 32 A2
Vadillo de la Sierra E 93 A5
Vadillos E 95 B4
Vadla N 33 C3
Vado I 81 B5
Vado Lígure I 80 B2
Vadsø N 113 B18
Vadstena S 37 D1
Vadum DK 38 B2
Vaduz FL 71 A4
Vafos N 33 D6
Vág H 74 A2
Vågåmo N 114 F6
Væggerløse DK 44 A3
Vaggeryd S 40 B4
Vaghia GR 117 D5
Vaglia I 81 C5
Váglio Basilicata I 104 C1
Vagney F 60 B2
Vagnhärad S 37 D4
Vagnsunda S 37 C5
Vagos P 92 A2
Vai GR 117 G8
Vaiano I 81 C5
Vaiges F 57 B5
Vaihingen D 61 B4
Vaillant F 59 C6
Vailly-sur-Aisne F 59 A4
Vailly-sur Sauldre F 68 A2
Vairano Scalo I 103 B7
Vaison-la-Romaine F 79 B4
Vaite F 60 C1
Väjern S 35 D3
Vajszló H 74 C2
Vaksdal N 32 B2
Vál H 74 A3
Valaam RUS 3 F29
Valada P 92 B2
Vålådalen S 115 D10
Valadares P 87 C2
Valado P 92 B1
Valandovo MK 116 A4
Valaská SK 65 B5
Valaská Belá SK 65 B4
Valaská Dubová SK 65 A5
Valašská Polanka CZ 64 A3
Valašské Klobouky
CZ 64 A4
Valašské Meziříčí CZ 64 A3
Valberg F 79 B5
Vålberg S 35 C5
Valbo S 36 B4
Valbom P 87 C2
Valbondione I 71 B5
Valbonë AL 105 A5
Valbonnais F 79 B4
Valbuena de Duero E 88 C2
Vălcani RO 75 C5
Valdagno I 71 C6
Valdahon F 69 A6
Valdaracete E 95 B3
Valday RUS 7 C12
Valdealgorfa E 90 C2
Valdecaballeros E 93 B5
Valdecabras E 95 B4
Valdecarros E 94 B1
Valdeconcha E 95 B4
Valdeflores E 99 B4
Valdefresno E 88 B1
Valdeganga E 95 C5
Valdelacasa E 93 A5
Valdelacasa de Tajo
E 93 B5
Valdelarco E 99 B4
Valdelosa E 94 A1
Valdeltormo E 90 C3
Valdelugeros E 88 B1
Valdemanco de Esteras
E 94 D2
Valdemarsvik S 37 D3
Valdemorillo E 94 B2
Valdemoro E 94 B3
Valdemoro Sierra E 95 B5
Valdenoceda E 89 B3
Valdeobispo E 93 A4
Valdeolivas E 95 B4
Valdepeñas E 100 A2
Valdepeñas de Jaén
E 100 B2
Valdepiélago E 88 B1
Valdepolo E 88 B1
Valderas E 88 B1
Valdérice I 108 A1
Valderrobres E 90 C3
Valderrueda E 88 B2
Val de San Lorenzo E 86 B4
Val de Santo Domingo
E 94 B2
Val d'Esquières F 79 C5
Valdestillas E 88 C2
Valdetorres E 93 C4
Valdetorres de Jarama
E 95 B3
Valdeverdeja E 93 B5
Valdevimbre E 88 B1
Valdieri I 80 B1
Valdilecha E 95 B3
Val-d'Isère F 70 C1
Valdobbiádene I 72 C1
Valdocondes E 89 C3
Valdoviño E 86 A2
Valea lui Mihai RO 11 C7
Vale de Açor
Beja P 98 B3
Portalegre P 92 B3
Vale de Água P 98 B2
Vale de Cambra P 87 D2
Vale de Lobo P 98 B2
Vale de Prazeres P 92 A3
Vale de Reis P 92 C2
Vale de Rosa P 98 B3
Vale de Santarém P 92 B2
Vale de Vargo P 98 B3
Vale do Peso P 92 B3
Valega P 87 D2
Valéggio sul Mincio I 71 C5
Valeiro P 92 C2
Valença P 87 B2
Valençay F 67 A6
Valence
Charente F 67 C5
Drôme F 78 B3
Valence d'Agen F 77 B3
Valence-d'Albigeois
F 77 B5
Valence-sur-Baise F 77 C3
Valencia E 96 B2
Valencia de Alcántara
E 93 B3
Valencia de Don Juan
E 88 B1
Valencia de las Torres
E 93 C4
Valencia del Ventoso
E 99 A4
Valencia de Mombuey
E 99 A3
Valenciennes F 49 C4
Valensole F 79 C4
Valentano I 102 A4
Valentigney F 70 A1
Valentine F 77 C3
Valenza I 80 A2
Valenzuela E 100 B1
Valenzuela de Calatrava
E 100 A2
Våler
Hedmark N 34 B3
Østfold N 35 C2
Valera de Abajo E 95 C4
Valeria E 95 C4
Valestrand N 33 C2
Valestrandsfossen N 32 B2
Valevåg N 33 C2
Valfabbrica I 82 C1
Valflaunes F 78 C2
Valga EST 7 C9
Valgorge F 78 B3
Valgrisenche I 70 C2
Valguarnera Caropepe
I 109 B3
Valhelhas P 92 A3
Valjevo SRB 85 B4
Valka LV 7 C8
Valkeakoski FIN 3 F26
Valkenburg NL 50 C1
Valkenswaard NL 49 B6
Valkó H 75 A4
Valla S 37 C3
Vallada E 96 C2
Vallado E 86 A4
Valladolid E 88 C2
Vallåkra S 41 D2
Vallata I 103 B8
Vallberga S 40 C3
Vall d'Alba E 96 A2
Valldemossa E 97 B2
Valle N 33 C4
Valle Castellana I 82 D2
Valle de Abdalajís E 100 C1
Valle de Cabuérniga
E 88 A2
Valle de la Serena E 93 C5
Valle de Matamoros
E 93 C4
Valle de Santa Ana E 93 C4
Valledolmo I 108 B2
Valledoria I 110 B1
Vallelado E 88 C2
Vallelunga Pratameno
I 108 B2
Valle Mosso I 70 C3
Vallendar D 50 C3
Vallentuna S 37 C5
Vallerås S 34 B5
Valleraugue F 78 B2
Vallermosa I 110 C1
Vallet F 66 A3
Valletta M 107 C5
Valley GB 26 B1
Vallfogona de Riucorb
E 91 B4
Valli del Pasúbio I 71 C6
Vallo della Lucánia I 103 C8
Valloire F 69 C6
Vallombrosa I 81 C5
Vallon-Pont-d'Arc F 78 B3
Vallorbe CH 69 B6
Vallouise F 79 B5
Valls E 91 B4
Vallset N 34 B3
Vallsta S 36 A3
Vallstena S 37 E5
Valmadrid E 90 B2
Valmiera LV 7 C8
Valmojado E 94 B2
Valmont F 58 A1
Valmontone I 102 B5
Valö S 36 B5
Valognes F 57 A4
Valonga P 92 A2
Valongo P 87 C2
Válor E 100 C2
Valoria la Buena E 88 C2
Valøy N 114 C7
Valozhyn BY 7 D9
Valpaços P 87 C3
Valpelline I 70 C2
Valpiana I 81 C4
Valpovo HR 74 C3
Valras-Plage F 78 C2
Valréas F 78 B3
Vals CH 71 B4
Valsavarenche I 70 C2
Vålse DK 39 E4
Valsequillo E 93 C5
Valsjöbyn S 115 C11
Vals-les-Bains F 78 B3
Valsonne F 69 C4
Valstagna I 72 C1
Val-Suzon F 69 A4
Valtablado del Rio E 95 B4
Valþjofsstaður IS 111 B11
Val Thorens F 69 C6
Valtice CZ 64 B2
Valtiendas E 88 C3
Valtierra E 89 B5
Valtopina I 82 C1
Valtorta I 71 C4
Valtournenche I 70 C2
Valverde E 89 C5
Valverde de Burguillos
E 93 C4
Valverde de Júcar E 95 C4
Valverde de la Vera E 93 A5
Valverde de la Virgen
E 88 B1
Valverde del Camino
E 99 B4
Valverde del Fresno
E 93 A4
Valverde de Llerena
E 99 A5
Valverde de Mérida E 93 C4
Vamberk CZ 53 C6
Vamdrup DK 39 D2
Våmhus S 34 A6
Vamlingbo S 37 F5
Vammala FIN 3 F25
Vamos GR 117 G6
Vámosmikola H 65 C4
Vámosszabadi H 64 C3
Vanault-les-Dames F 59 B5
Vandel DK 39 D2
Vandenesse F 68 B3
Vandenesse-en-Auxois
F 69 A4
Vandóies I 72 B1
Väne-Åsaka S 35 D4
Vänersborg S 35 D4
Vänersnäs S 35 D4
Vang N 32 A5
Vänge S 36 C4
Vangsnes N 32 A3
Vänjaurbäck S 115 C15
Vännacka S 35 C4
Vannareid N 112 B8
Vännäs S 115 D16
Vannes F 56 C3
Vannsätter S 36 A3
Vannvåg N 112 B8
Vansbro S 34 B6
Vanse N 33 D3
Vantaa FIN 6 A8
Vanviken N 114 D7
Vanyarc H 65 C5
Vaour F 77 B4
Vapnyarka UA 11 B10
Vaprio d'Adda I 71 C4
Vaqueiros P 98 B3
Vara S 35 D4
Varacieux F 69 C5
Varades F 66 A3
Varages F 79 C4
Varaldsøy N 32 B2
Varallo I 70 C3
Varangerbotn N 113 B17
Varano de'Melegari I 81 B4
Varaždin HR 73 B6
Varaždinske Toplice
HR 73 B6
Varazze I 80 B2
Varberg S 40 B2
Vardal N 34 B2
Varde DK 39 D1
Vårdö FIN 36 B7
Vardø N 113 B20
Vardomb H 74 B3
Varel D 43 B5
Varėna LT 6 D8
Vårenes N 33 C2
Varengeville-sur-Mer
F 58 A1
Varenna I 71 B4
Varennes-en-Argonne
F 59 A6
Varennes-le-Grand F 69 B4
Varennes-St Sauveur
F 69 B5
Varennes-sur-Allier F 68 B3
Varennes-sur-Amance
F 60 C1
Vareš BIH 84 B3
Varese I 70 C3
Varese Ligure I 80 B3
Vârfurile RO 11 C7
Vårgårda S 40 A2
Vargas
E 88 A3
P 92 B2
Vargön S 35 D4
Varhaug N 33 D2
Variaş RO 75 B5
Variaşu Mic RO 75 B6
Varilhes F 77 C4
Varin SK 65 A4
Väring S 35 D5
Váriz P 87 C4
Varkaus FIN 3 E27
Varmahlíð IS 111 B6
Varmaland IS 111 C4
Värmlands Bro S 35 C5
Värmskog S 35 C4
Varna
BG 11 E9
SRB 85 B4
Värnamo S 40 B4
Varnhem S 35 D5
Varnsdorf CZ 53 C4
Värö S 40 B2
Varoška Rijeka BIH 83 A5
Városlöd H 74 A2
Várpalota H 74 A3
Varreddes F 59 B3
Vars F 79 B5
Varsi I 81 B3
Varsseveld NL 50 B2
Vårsta S 37 C4
Vartdal N 114 E3
Vartofta S 40 A3
Varvarin SRB 85 C6
Varvik S 35 C4
Várvölgy H 74 B2
Varzi I 80 B3
Varzjelas P 92 A2
Varzo I 70 B3
Varzy F 68 A3
Vasad H 75 A4
Väse S 35 C5
Vašica SRB 85 A4
Vasilevichi BY 7 E10
Väskinde S 37 E5
Vaskút H 75 B3
Vaslui RO 11 C9
Vassbotn N 33 D5
Vassenden N 32 A6
Vassieux-en-Vercors
F 79 B4
Vassmolösa S 40 C6
Vassy F 57 B5
Västansjö S 115 B12
Västanvik S 36 B1
Västerås S 37 C3
Västerby S 36 B2
Västerfärnebo S 36 C3
Västergarn S 37 E5
Västerhaninge S 37 C5
Västervik S 40 B6
Vasto I 103 A7
Västra Ämtervik S 35 C5
Västra-Bodarne S 40 B2
Västra Karup S 41 C2
Vasvár H 74 A1
Vasylkiv UA 11 A11
Vát H 74 A1
Vatan F 68 A1
Väte S 37 E5
Vathia GR 117 F4
Vatican City = Cittádel
Vaticano I 102 B5
Vatili CY 120 A2
Vatin SRB 75 C6
Vatland N 33 D4
Vatnar N 33 C6
Vatnås N 32 C6
Vatne N 33 D4
Vatnestrøm N 33 D5
Vätö S 36 C5
Vatra-Dornei RO 11 C8
Vatry F 59 B5
Vattholma S 36 B4
Vättis CH 71 B4
Vauchamps F 59 B4
Vauchassis F 59 B4
Vaucouleurs F 60 B1
Vaudoy-en-Brie F 59 B4
Vaulen N 33 D2
Vaulruz CH 70 B1
Vaulx Vraucourt F 48 C3
Vaumas F 68 B3
Vausseroux F 67 B4
Vauvenargues F 79 C4
Vauvert F 78 C3
Vauvillers F 60 C2
Vaux-sur-Sure B 60 A1
Vawkavysk BY 6 E8
Vaxholm S 37 C5
Växjö S 40 C4
Våxtorp S 41 C3
Vayrac F 77 B4
Važec SK 65 A5
Veberöd S 41 D3
Vechelde D 51 A6
Vechta D 43 C5
Vecinos E 94 B1
Vecsés H 75 A4
Vedavågen N 33 C2
Veddige S 40 B2
Vedersø DK 39 C1
Vedeseta I 71 C4
Vedevåg S 37 C2
Vedra E 86 B2
Vedum S 35 D4
Veendam NL 42 B3
Veenendaal NL 49 A6
Vega
Asturias E 88 A1
Asturias E 88 A1
Vega de Espinareda
E 86 B4
Vega de Infanzones E 88 B1
Vegadeo E 86 A3
Vega de Pas E 88 A3
Vega de Valcarce E 86 B4
Vega de Valdetronco
E 88 C1
Vegårshei N 33 D5
Vegas de Coria E 93 A4
Vegas del Condado E 88 B1
Vegby S 40 B3
Vegger DK 38 C2
Veggli N 32 B6
Veghel NL 49 B6
Veglast D 45 A4
Véglie I 105 C3
Veguillas E 95 B3
Vegusdal N 33 D5
Veidholmen N 114 D4
Veidnes N 113 B15
Veikåker N 34 B1
Veinge S 40 C3
Vejbystrand S 41 C2
Vejen DK 39 D2
Vejer de la Frontera E 99 C5
Vejle DK 39 D2
Vejprty CZ 52 C3
Velada E 94 B2
Vela Luka HR 83 D5
Velayos E 94 B2
Velbert D 50 B3
Velburg D 62 A2
Velde N 114 C8
Velden
Bayern D 62 A2
Bayern D 62 B3
Velden am Worther See
A 73 B4
Velefique E 101 B3
Velen D 50 B2
Velenje SLO 73 B5
Veles MK 116 A3
Velesevec HR 73 C6
Velešín CZ 63 B5
Velestino GR 116 C4
Velez Blanco E 101 B3
Vélez de Benaudalla
E 100 C2
Vélez-Málaga E 100 C1
Vélez Rubio E 101 B3
Veliiki Radinci SRB 85 A4
Velika
HR 74 C2
MNE 85 D4
Velika Drenova SRB 85 C6
Velika Gorica HR 73 C6
Velika Grdevac HR 74 C2
Velika Greda SRB 75 C6
Velika Ilova BIH 84 B2
Velika Kladuša BIH 73 C5
Velika Kopanica HR 74 C3
Velika Krsna SRB 85 B5
Velika Obarska BIH 85 B4
Velika Pisanica HR 74 C2
Velika Plana
Srbija SRB 85 B6
Srbija SRB 85 C6
Velika Zdenci HR 74 C2
Velike Lašče SLO 73 C4
Veliki Gaj SRB 75 C6
Veliki Popović SRB 85 B6
Veliki Šiljegovac SRB 85 C6
Velikiye Luki RUS 7 C11
Veliko Gradište SRB 85 B6
Veliko Orašje SRB 85 B6
Veliko Selo SRB 85 B6
Veliko Tŭrnovo BG 11 E8
Velilla del Río Carrió
E 88 B2
Velilla de San Antonio
E 95 B3
Veli Lošinj HR 83 B3
Velipojë AL 105 B5
Velizh RUS 7 D11
Veljun HR 73 C5
Velká Bíteš CZ 64 A2
Velka Hled'sbe CZ 52 D2

Velká Lomnica SK . . . 65 A6
Velkánad Veličkou
  CZ . . . 64 B3
Velké Bystřice CZ . . . 64 A3
Velké Heraltice CZ . . . 54 D2
Velké Karlovice CZ . . . 64 A3
Vel'ke'Kostol'any SK . . . 64 B3
Velké Leváre SK . . . 64 B3
Velké Losiny CZ . . . 54 C2
Velké Meziříčí CZ . . . 64 A2
Velké Pavlovice CZ . . . 64 B2
Vel'ké Rovné SK . . . 65 A4
Velké Uherce SK . . . 65 B4
Vel'ké Zálužie SK . . . 64 B3
Vel'ký Blahovo SK . . . 65 B6
Velky Bor CZ . . . 63 A4
Vel'ký Cetín SK . . . 64 B4
Vel'ký Krtíš SK . . . 65 B5
Vel'ký Meder SK . . . 64 C3
Velký Ujezd CZ . . . 64 A3
Vellahn D . . . 44 B2
Vellberg D . . . 61 A5
Velles F . . . 67 B6
Velletri I . . . 102 B5
Vellinge S . . . 41 D3
Vellisca E . . . 95 B4
Velliza E . . . 88 C2
Vellmar D . . . 51 B5
Velp NL . . . 50 A1
Velten D . . . 45 C5
Velvary CZ . . . 53 C4
Velvendos GR . . . 116 B4
Vemb DK . . . 39 C1
Vemdalen S . . . 115 E10
Veme N . . . 34 B2
Véménd H . . . 74 B3
Vemmedrup DK . . . 39 D5
Vena S . . . 40 B5
Venaco F . . . 102 A2
Venafro I . . . 103 B7
Venarey-les-Laumes
  F . . . 69 A4
Venaria I . . . 70 C2
Venasca I . . . 80 B1
Venčane SRB . . . 85 B5
Vence F . . . 79 C6
Venda Nova
  Coimbra P . . . 92 A2
  Leiria P . . . 92 B2
Vendas Novas P . . . 92 C2
Vendays-Montalivet F 66 C3
Vendel S . . . 36 B4
Vendelso S . . . 37 C5
Vendeuil F . . . 59 A4
Vendeuvre-sur-Barse
  F . . . 59 B5
Vendoeuvres F . . . 67 B6
Vendôme F . . . 58 C2
Venelles F . . . 79 C4
Veness GB . . . 23 B6
Venézia = Venice I . . . 72 C2
Venialbo E . . . 88 C1
Venice = Venézia I . . . 72 C2
Vénissieux F . . . 69 C4
Venjan S . . . 34 B5
Venlo NL . . . 50 B2
Vennesla N . . . 33 D4
Vennezey F . . . 60 B2
Venosa I . . . 104 C1
Venray NL . . . 50 B1
Vent A . . . 71 B5
Venta de Baños E . . . 88 C2
Venta del Moro E . . . 96 B1
Venta de los Santos
  E . . . 100 A2
Venta las Ranas E . . . 88 A1
Ventanueva E . . . 86 A4
Ventas de Huelma E . . . 100 B2
Ventas de Zafarraya
  E . . . 100 C1
Ventavon F . . . 79 B4
Ventimiglia I . . . 80 C1
Ventnor GB . . . 31 D2
Ventosa de la Sierra
  E . . . 89 C4
Ventosilla E . . . 89 C4
Ventspils LV . . . 6 C1
Venturina I . . . 81 C4
Venzolasca F . . . 102 A2
Venzone I . . . 72 B3
Vép H . . . 74 A1
Vera
  E . . . 101 B4
  N . . . 115 D9
Vera Cruz P . . . 98 A3
Vera de Bidasoa E . . . 76 C1
Vera de Moncayo E . . . 89 C5
Verbánia I . . . 70 C3
Verberie F . . . 58 A3
Verbicaro I . . . 106 B2
Verbier CH . . . 70 B2
Vercelli I . . . 70 C3
Vercel-Villedieu-le-Camp
  F . . . 69 A6
Verchen D . . . 45 B4
Vercheny F . . . 79 B4
Verclause F . . . 79 B4
Verdalsøra N . . . 114 D8
Verden D . . . 43 C6
Verdens Ende N . . . 35 C2
Verdikoussa GR . . . 116 C3
Verdille F . . . 67 C4
Verdú E . . . 91 B4
Verdun F . . . 59 A6
Verdun-sur-Garonne
  F . . . 77 C4
Verdun-sur-le-Doubs
  F . . . 69 B5
Veresegyház H . . . 65 C5
Verfeil F . . . 77 C4
Vergato I . . . 81 B5
Vergel E . . . 96 C3
Vergeletto CH . . . 70 B3
Verges E . . . 91 A6
Vergiate I . . . 70 C3
Vergt F . . . 77 A3
Veria GR . . . 116 B4
Verin E . . . 87 C3
Veringenstadt D . . . 61 B5
Verkhovye RUS . . . 7 E14
Verl D . . . 51 B4
Verma N . . . 114 E5
Vermand F . . . 59 A4
Vermelha P . . . 92 B1
Vermenton F . . . 59 C4
Vermosh AL . . . 85 D4
Vernago I . . . 71 B5
Vernante I . . . 80 B1
Vernantes F . . . 67 A5
Vernár SK . . . 65 B6
Vernasca I . . . 81 B3
Vernayaz CH . . . 70 B2
Vernazza I . . . 81 B3
Vⁱ-d'Anjou F . . . 57 C5
Verneřice CZ . . . 53 C4
Vernet F . . . 77 C4
Vernet-les-Bains F . . . 91 A5
Verneuil F . . . 59 A4
Verneuil-sur-Avre F . . . 58 B2
Vernier CH . . . 69 B6
Vérnole I . . . 105 C4
Vernoux-en-Vivarais
  F . . . 78 B3
Véroce F . . . 65 C5
Verolanuova I . . . 71 C5
Véroli I . . . 103 B6
Verona I . . . 71 C6
Verpelét H . . . 65 C6
Verrabotn N . . . 114 D7
Verrey-sous-Salmaise
  F . . . 69 A4
Verrières F . . . 68 B3
Versailles F . . . 58 B3
Versam H . . . 71 B4
Verseg H . . . 65 C5
Versmold D . . . 50 A4
Versoix CH . . . 69 B6

Verteillac F . . . 67 C5
Vértesacsa H . . . 74 A3
Vertou F . . . 66 A3
Vertus F . . . 59 B4
Verviers B . . . 50 C1
Vervins F . . . 59 A4
Verwood GB . . . 29 C6
Veryan GB . . . 28 C3
Veržej SLO . . . 73 B6
Verzuolo I . . . 80 B1
Verzy F . . . 59 A5
Vescovato F . . . 102 A2
Vése H . . . 74 B2
Veselínad Lužnicí CZ . . . 63 A5
Veselínad Moravou
  CZ . . . 64 B3
Veselíy BG . . . 11 E9
Vésime I . . . 80 B2
Vesiloul F . . . 60 C2
Vesjegonsk RUS . . . 7 B14
Veskoniemi FIN . . . 113 D16
Vesoul F . . . 60 C2
Vespolate I . . . 70 C3
Vessigebro S . . . 40 C2
Vestbygd N . . . 33 D3
Vestenanova I . . . 71 C6
Vester Husby S . . . 37 D3
Vester Nebel DK . . . 39 D2
Vester Torup DK . . . 38 B2
Vester Vedsted DK . . . 39 D1
Vesterøy DK . . . 38 C1
Vestfossen N . . . 33 C5
Vestmannaeyjar IS . . . 111 D5
Vestmarka N . . . 34 C3
Vestnes N . . . 114 E4
Vestone I . . . 71 C5
Vestre Gausdal N . . . 34 A2
Vestre Jakobselv N 113 B18
Vestre Slidre N . . . 32 A5
Vesyegonsk RUS . . . 7 B14
Veszprém H . . . 74 A2
Veszprémvarsány H . . . 74 A2
Vésztő H . . . 75 B6
Vetlanda S . . . 40 B5
Vetovo HR . . . 74 C2
Vetralla I . . . 102 A5
Větrný Jeníkov CZ . . . 63 A6
Větschau D . . . 53 B4
Vettasjärvi S . . . 113 E10
Vetto I . . . 81 B4
Vetulonia I . . . 81 D4
Veules-les-Roses F . . . 58 A1
Veulettes-sur-Mer F . . . 58 A1
Veum N . . . 33 C5
Veurne B . . . 48 B3
Veverská Bitýška CZ . . . 64 A2
Vevey CH . . . 70 B1
Vevi GR . . . 116 B3
Vex CH . . . 70 B2
Veynes F . . . 79 B4
Veyre-Monton F . . . 68 C3
Veyrier F . . . 69 C6
Vézelay F . . . 68 A3
Vézelise F . . . 60 B2
Vézenobres F . . . 78 B3
Vézins F . . . 67 A4
Vézins-de-Lévézou F 78 B1
Vezirhan TR . . . 118 B5
Vezirköprü TR . . . 16 A7
Vezza d'Oglio I . . . 71 B5
Vezzani F . . . 102 A2
Vezzano I . . . 71 B6
Vezzano sul Cróstolo
  I . . . 81 B4
Vi S . . . 115 E14
Viadana I . . . 81 B4
Via Gloria P . . . 98 B3
Viana E . . . 89 B4
Viana do Alentejo P . . . 92 C2
Viana do Bolo E . . . 87 B3
Viana do Castelo P . . . 87 C2
Vianden L . . . 60 A2
Viannos GR . . . 117 G7
Viaréggio I . . . 81 C4
Viator E . . . 101 C3
Vibble S . . . 37 E5
Vibo Valéntia I . . . 106 C3
Vibraye F . . . 58 B1
Vic E . . . 91 B5
Vicar E . . . 101 C3
Vicarello I . . . 81 C4
Vicari I . . . 108 B2
Vicchio I . . . 81 C5
Vicdessos F . . . 77 D4
Vic-en-Bigorre F . . . 76 C3
Vicenza I . . . 71 C6
Vic-Fézensac F . . . 76 C3
Vichy F . . . 68 B3
Vickan S . . . 38 B5
Vickerstown GB . . . 26 A2
Vic-le-Comte F . . . 68 C3
Vico F . . . 102 A1
Vico del Gargano I . . . 104 B1
Vico Equense I . . . 103 C7
Vicopisano I . . . 81 C4
Vicosoprano CH . . . 71 B4
Vicovaro I . . . 102 A5
Vic-sur-Aisne F . . . 59 A4
Vic-sur-Cère F . . . 77 B5
Victoria = Rabat M . . . 107 C5
Vidago P . . . 87 C3
Vidauban F . . . 79 C5
Vide P . . . 92 A3
Videbæk DK . . . 39 C1
Videm SLO . . . 73 C4
Videseter N . . . 114 F4
Vidigueira P . . . 98 A3
Vidin BG . . . 11 E7
Vidlin GB . . . 22 A7
Vidzy BY . . . 7 D9
Viechtach D . . . 62 A3
Vieille-Brioude F . . . 68 C3
Vieira P . . . 92 B2
Vieira do Minho P . . . 87 C2
Vieiros P . . . 92 C3
Vielha E . . . 90 A3
Vielle-Aure F . . . 77 D3
Viellespesse F . . . 68 C3
Viellevigne F . . . 66 B3
Vielmur-sur-Agout F . . . 77 C5
Vielsalm B . . . 50 C1
Viels Maison F . . . 59 B4
Vienenburg D . . . 51 B6
Vienna = Wien A . . . 64 B2
Vienne F . . . 69 C4
Vieritz D . . . 44 C4
Viernheim D . . . 61 A4
Vierraden D . . . 45 B6
Viersen D . . . 50 B2
Vierville-sur-Mer F . . . 57 A5
Vierzon F . . . 68 A2
Vieselbach D . . . 52 C1
Vieste I . . . 104 B2
Vietas S . . . 112 E7
Vieteren B . . . 48 C3
Vietri di Potenza I . . . 104 C1
Vietri sul Mare I . . . 103 C7
Vieux-Boucau-les-Bains
  F . . . 76 C1
Vif F . . . 79 A4
Vig DK . . . 39 D4
Vigásio I . . . 71 C5
Vigaun A . . . 63 C4
Vigeland N . . . 33 D4
Vigeois F . . . 67 C6
Vigévano I . . . 70 C3
Viggianello I . . . 106 B3
Viggiano I . . . 104 C1
Vigliano I . . . 102 A6
Vigmostad N . . . 33 D4
Vignale I . . . 80 A2
Vignanello I . . . 102 A5
Vigneulles-lès-Hattonchâtel F . . . 60 B1
Vignevieille F . . . 77 D5
Vignola I . . . 81 B5
Vignory F . . . 59 B6
Vignoux-sur Barangeon
  F . . . 68 A2
Vigo E . . . 87 B2

Vigo di Fassa I . . . 72 B1
Vigone I . . . 80 B1
Vigrestad N . . . 33 D2
Vihiers F . . . 67 A4
Viitasaari FIN . . . 3 E26
Vik
  Nordland N . . . 114 B9
  Rogaland N . . . 33 D2
  Sogn og Fjordane N . 32 A3
  S . . . 41 D4
Vika S . . . 36 B2
Vikajärvi FIN . . . 113 F15
Vikane N . . . 35 C2
Vikarbyn S . . . 36 B2
Viked N . . . 32 B2
Vikedal N . . . 33 C2
Vikeland N . . . 33 D4
Viken
  Jämtland S . . . 115 C10
  Skåne S . . . 41 C2
  N . . . 34 B2
Vikersund N . . . 34 C1
Vikeså N . . . 33 D3
Vikevåg N . . . 33 C2
Vikingstad S . . . 37 D2
Vikmanshyttan S . . . 36 B2
Vikna N . . . 114 C7
Vikran N . . . 32 B3
Viksjö S . . . 115 E14
Viksøyri N . . . 32 A3
Viksta S . . . 36 B4
Vila Boim P . . . 92 C3
Vila Chãde Ourique P 92 B2
Viladamat E . . . 91 A6
Vila de Cruces E . . . 86 B2
Vila de Rei P . . . 92 B2
Vila do Bispo P . . . 98 B2
Vila do Conde P . . . 87 C2
Viladrau E . . . 91 B5
Vila Flor P . . . 87 C3
Vila Franca das Navas
  P . . . 87 D3
Vilafranca del Penedès
  E . . . 91 B4
Vila Franca de Xira P . . . 92 C1
Vila Fresca P . . . 92 C1
Vilagarcía de Arousa
  E . . . 86 B2
Vilajuiga E . . . 91 A6
Vilamarin E . . . 86 B3
Vilamartín de Valdeorras
  E . . . 86 B3
Vila Nogueira P . . . 92 C1
Vilanova de Castelló E . . . 96 B2
Vila Nova da Baronia
  P . . . 98 A2
Vilanova de Castelló
  E . . . 96 B2
Vila Nova de Cerveira
  P . . . 87 C2
Vila Nova de Famalicão
  P . . . 87 C2
Vila Nova de Foz Côa
  P . . . 87 C3
Vila Nova de Gaia P . . . 87 C2
Vila Nova de Milfontes
  P . . . 98 B2
Vila Nova de Paiva P . . . 87 D3
Vila Nova de São Bento
  P . . . 98 B3
Vilanova de Sau E . . . 91 B5
Vilanova i la Geltrú E . . . 91 B4
Vilapedre E . . . 86 A3
Vila Pouca de Aguiar
  P . . . 87 C3
Vila Praia de Ancora
  P . . . 87 C2
Vilar de Santos E . . . 87 B3
Vilarandelo P . . . 87 C3
Vilar Formoso P . . . 93 A4
Vila-Rodona E . . . 91 B4
Vila Ruiva P . . . 98 A3
Vilasantar E . . . 86 A2
Vilaseca E . . . 91 B4
Vila Seca P . . . 92 A2
Vilassar de Mar E . . . 91 B5
Vilasund S . . . 115 A11
Vila Velha de Ródão
  P . . . 92 B3
Vila Verde
  Braga P . . . 87 C2
  Lisboa P . . . 92 B1
Vila Verde de Filcalho
  P . . . 98 B3
Vila Viçosa P . . . 92 C3
Vilches E . . . 100 A2
Vildbjerg DK . . . 39 C1
Vildmov CZ . . . 63 A6
Vileyka BY . . . 7 D9
Vilhelmina S . . . 115 C13
Vília GR . . . 117 D5
Viljandi EST . . . 7 B8
Villabáñez E . . . 88 C2
Villablanca E . . . 98 B3
Villabona E . . . 76 C1
Villabragima E . . . 88 C1
Villabuena del Puente
  E . . . 88 C1
Villacadima E . . . 95 A3
Villacañas E . . . 95 C3
Villacarriedo E . . . 88 A3
Villacarrillo E . . . 100 A2
Villa Castelli I . . . 104 C3
Villacastín E . . . 94 B2
Villach A . . . 72 B3
Villacidro I . . . 110 C1
Villaconejos E . . . 95 B3
Villaconejos de Trabaque
  E . . . 95 B4
Villa Cova de Lixa P . . . 87 C2
Villada E . . . 88 B2
Villadangos del Páramo
  E . . . 88 B1
Villadecanes E . . . 86 B4
Villa del Prado E . . . 94 B2
Villa del Rio E . . . 100 B1
Villadepera E . . . 87 C4
Villa del Rosario E . . . 87 C4
Villa di Chiavenna I . . . 71 B4
Villadiego E . . . 88 B2
Villadompardo E . . . 100 B1
Villadóssola I . . . 70 B3
Villaeles de Valdavia
  E . . . 88 B2
Villaescusa de Haro
  E . . . 95 C4
Villafáfila E . . . 88 C1
Villafeliche E . . . 95 A5
Villaflores E . . . 94 A1
Villafranca
  Avila E . . . 93 A4
  Navarra E . . . 89 B5
Villafranca del Bierzo
  E . . . 86 B4
Villafranca de los Barros
  E . . . 93 C4
Villafranca de los
  Caballeros E . . . 95 C3
Villafranca di Verona I . . . 71 C5
Villafranca in Lunigiana
  I . . . 81 B3
Villafranca-Montes de Oca
  E . . . 89 B3
Villafranca Tirrena I . . . 109 A4

Villafranco del Campo
  E . . . 95 B5
Villafranco del
  Guadalquivir E . . . 99 B4
Villafrati I . . . 108 B2
Villafrechós E . . . 88 C1
Villafruela E . . . 88 C3
Villagarcía de las Torres
  E . . . 93 C4
Villagonzalo E . . . 93 C4
Villagotón E . . . 86 B4
Villaharta E . . . 100 A1
Villahermosa E . . . 100 A3
Villaherreros E . . . 88 B2
Villahoz E . . . 88 B3
Villaines-la-Juhel F . . . 57 B5
Villajoyosa E . . . 96 C2
Villalago I . . . 103 B6
Villalba
  E . . . 86 A3
  I . . . 108 B2
Villalba de Calatrava
  E . . . 100 A2
Villalba de Guardo E . . . 88 B2
Villalba del Alcor E . . . 99 B4
Villalba de la Sierra E . 95 B4
Villalba de los Alcores
  E . . . 88 C2
Villalba de los Barros
  E . . . 93 C4
Villalba del Rey E . . . 95 B4
Villalcampo E . . . 87 C4
Villalcázar de Sirga E . . . 88 B2
Villalengua E . . . 89 C5
Villalgordo del Júcar
  E . . . 95 C4
Villalgordo del
  Marquesado E . . . 95 C4
Villallón de Campos E . . . 88 B1
Villalonga E . . . 96 C2
Villalonso E . . . 88 C1
Villalpando E . . . 88 C1
Villaluenga E . . . 94 B3
Villalumbroso E . . . 88 B2
Villálvaro E . . . 89 C3
Villamalea E . . . 95 C5
Villamanán E . . . 88 B1
Villamanín E . . . 88 B1
Villamanrique E . . . 100 A3
Villamanrique de la
  Condesa E . . . 99 B4
Villamantilla E . . . 94 B2
Villamar I . . . 110 C1
Villamartín E . . . 99 C5
Villamartín de Campos
  E . . . 88 B2
Villamartín de Don
  Sancho E . . . 88 B1
Villamassárgia I . . . 110 C1
Villamayor E . . . 88 A1
Villamayor de Calatrava
  E . . . 100 A1
Villamayor de Campos
  E . . . 88 C1
Villamayor de Santiago
  E . . . 95 C4
Villamblard F . . . 77 A3
Villamejil E . . . 86 B4
Villamesías E . . . 93 B5
Villaminaya E . . . 94 C3
Villa Minozzo I . . . 81 B4
Villamor de los Escuderos
  E . . . 88 C1
Villamoronta E . . . 88 B2
Villamuelas E . . . 94 C3
Villamuriel de Cerrato
  E . . . 88 C2
Villandraut F . . . 76 B2
Villanova I . . . 104 C3
Villanova d'Asti I . . . 80 B1
Villanova del Battista
  I . . . 103 B8
Villanova Mondov i I . . . 80 B1
Villanova Monteleone
  I . . . 110 B1
Villante E . . . 88 B3
Villantério I . . . 71 C4
Villanubla E . . . 88 C2
Villanueva de Alcardete
  E . . . 95 C3
Villanueva de Alcorón
  E . . . 95 B4
Villanueva de Algaidas
  E . . . 100 B1
Villanueva de Argaña
  E . . . 88 B3
Villanueva de Bogas
  E . . . 95 C3
Villanueva de Córdoba
  E . . . 100 A1
Villanueva de Gállego
  E . . . 90 B2
Villanueva del Aceral
  E . . . 94 A2
Villanueva de la
  Concepción E . . . 100 C1
Villanueva de la Fuente
  E . . . 101 A3
Villanueva de la Jara
  E . . . 95 C5
Villanueva de la Reina
  E . . . 100 A2
Villanueva del Arzobispo
  E . . . 101 A3
Villanueva de la Serena
  E . . . 93 C5
Villanueva de la Sierra
  E . . . 93 A4
Villanueva de las
  Manzanas E . . . 88 B1
Villanueva de las Peras
  E . . . 87 C5
Villanueva de la Vera
  E . . . 93 A5
Villanueva del Campo
  E . . . 88 C1
Villanueva del Duque
  E . . . 100 A1
Villanueva del Fresno
  E . . . 93 C3
Villanueva del Huerva
  E . . . 90 B1
Villanueva de los
  Castillejos E . . . 98 B3
Villanueva de los Infantes
  E . . . 100 A3
Villanueva del Rey E . . . 99 A5
Villanueva del Río E . . . 99 B5
Villanueva del Río y Minas
  E . . . 99 B5
Villanueva del Rosario
  E . . . 100 C1
Villanueva del Trabuco
  E . . . 100 B1
Villanueva de Mesia
  E . . . 100 B2
Villanueva de Nía E . . . 88 B2
Villanueva de Oscos
  E . . . 86 A4
Villanueva de San Carlos
  E . . . 100 A2
Villanueva de San Juan
  E . . . 99 C5
Villanueva de Tapia
  E . . . 100 B1
Villanueva de Valdegovia
  E . . . 89 B3
Villány H . . . 74 C3
Villaputzu I . . . 110 C2
Villar E . . . 87 C4
Villaralto E . . . 100 A1
Villar de Barrio E . . . 87 B3

Villar de Barrio E . . . 87 B3
Villar de Cañas E . . . 95 C4
Villar de Chinchilla E . . . 96 C1
Villar de Ciervo E . . . 87 D4
Villardeciervos E . . . 87 C4
Villar de Domingo Garcia
  E . . . 95 B4
Villardefrades E . . . 88 C1
Villar del Arzobispo E . . 96 B2
Villar del Buey E . . . 87 C4
Villar del Cobo E . . . 95 B5
Villar del Humo E . . . 95 C5
Villar de los Navarros
  E . . . 90 B1
Villar del Pedroso E . . . 93 B5
Villar del Rey E . . . 93 B4
Villar del Rio E . . . 89 B4
Villar del Saz de Navalón
  E . . . 95 B4
Villar de Rena E . . . 93 B5
Villarejo E . . . 95 A3
Villarejo de Fuentes
  E . . . 95 C4
Villarejo de Orbigo E . . . 88 B1
Villarejo de Salvanes
  E . . . 95 B3
Villarejo-Periesteban
  E . . . 95 C4
Villares del Saz E . . . 95 C4
Villaretto I . . . 79 A6
Villargordo del Cabriel
  E . . . 96 B1
Villarino E . . . 87 C4
Villarino de Conso E . . . 87 B3
Villarluengo E . . . 90 C2
Villarosa I . . . 109 B3
Villarramiel E . . . 88 B2
Villarrasa E . . . 99 B4
Villarreal de San Carlos
  E . . . 93 B4
Villarrin de Campos E . . . 88 C1
Villarrobledo E . . . 95 C4
Villarroya de la Sierra
  E . . . 89 C5
Villarroya de los Pinares
  E . . . 90 C2
Villarrubia de los Ojos
  E . . . 95 C3
Villarrubia de Santiago
  E . . . 95 C3
Villarrubio E . . . 95 C3
Villarta E . . . 95 C5
Villarta de los Montes
  E . . . 94 C2
Villarta de San Juan
  E . . . 95 C3
Villasana de Mena E . . . 89 A3
Villasandino E . . . 88 B2
Villa San Giovanni I . . . 109 A4
Villa Santa Maria I . . . 103 B7
Villasante E . . . 89 A3
Villa Santina I . . . 72 B2
Villasarracino E . . . 88 B2
Villasayas E . . . 89 C4
Villasdardo E . . . 87 C4
Villaseca de Henares
  E . . . 95 B4
Villaseca de Laciana
  E . . . 86 B4
Villaseca de la Sagra
  E . . . 94 C3
Villaseco de los Gamitos
  E . . . 87 C4
Villaseco de los Reyes
  E . . . 87 C4
Villasequilla de Yepes
  E . . . 94 C3
Villasimius I . . . 110 C2
Villasmundo I . . . 109 B4
Villasor I . . . 110 C1
Villastar E . . . 90 C1
Villastellone I . . . 80 B1
Villatobas E . . . 95 C3
Villatorp E . . . 93 A5
Villatoya E . . . 96 B1
Villavaliente E . . . 96 B1
Villavella E . . . 87 B3
Villaver de Guadalimar
  E . . . 101 A3
Villaverde del Rio E . . . 99 B5
Villaviciosa de Córdoba
  E . . . 99 A5
Villaviciosa de Odón
  E . . . 94 B3
Villavieja de Yeltes E . . . 87 D4
Villayón E . . . 86 A4
Villé F . . . 60 B3
Villebois-Lavalette F . . . 67 C5
Villecerf F . . . 59 B3
Villecomtal F . . . 77 B5
Villedieu-les-Poêles
  F . . . 57 B4
Villedieu-sur-Indre F . . . 67 B6
Villedômain F . . . 67 A6
Villefagnan F . . . 67 B5
Villefontaine F . . . 69 C5
Villefort F . . . 78 B2
Villefranche-d'Albigeois
  F . . . 77 C5
Villefranche-d'Allier F 68 B2
Villefranche-de-Lauragais
  F . . . 77 C4
Villefranche-de-Lonchat
  F . . . 76 B3
Villefranche-de-Panat
  F . . . 78 B1
Villefranche-de-Rouergue
  F . . . 77 B5
Villefranche-du-Périgord
  F . . . 77 B4
Villefranche-sur-Cher
  F . . . 68 A1
Villefranche-sur-Mer
  F . . . 80 C1
Villefranche-sur-Saône
  F . . . 69 B4
Villegenon F . . . 68 A2
Villel E . . . 96 A1
Villemaur-sur-Vanne
  F . . . 59 B4
Villemontais F . . . 68 C3
Villemontel F . . . 59 A5
Villemur-sur-Tarn F . . . 77 C4
Villena E . . . 101 A5
Villenauxe-la-Grande
  F . . . 59 B4
Villenave-d'Ornon F . . . 76 B2
Villeneuve
  CH . . . 70 B1
  F . . . 77 B5
Villeneuve-d'Ascq F . . . 49 C4
Villeneuve-de-Berg F . . . 78 B3
Villeneuve-de-Marsan
  F . . . 76 C2
Villeneuve-de-Rivière
  F . . . 77 C3
Villeneuve-la-Guyard
  F . . . 59 B4
Villeneuve-l'Archevêque
  F . . . 59 B4
Villeneuve-le-Comte
  F . . . 59 B3
Villeneuve-lès-Avignon
  F . . . 78 C3
Villeneuve-les-Corbières
  F . . . 78 D1
Villeneuve-St Georges
  F . . . 58 B3
Villeneuve-sur-Allier
  F . . . 68 B3
Villeneuve-sur-Lot F . . . 77 B3
Villeneuve-sur-Yonne
  F . . . 59 B4
Villeréal F . . . 77 B3
Villerias E . . . 88 C2
Villeromain F . . . 58 C2

Villers-Bocage
  Calvados F . . . 57 A5
  Somme F . . . 58 A3
Villers-Bretonneux F . . . 58 A3
Villers-Carbonnel F . . . 59 A3
Villers-Cotterêts F . . . 59 A4
Villersexel F . . . 60 C2
Villers-Farlay F . . . 69 B5
Villers-le-Gambon B . . . 49 C5
Villers-le-Lac F . . . 70 A1
Villers-sur-Mer F . . . 57 A6
Villerupt F . . . 60 A1
Villerville F . . . 57 A6
Villeseneux F . . . 59 B5
Ville-sous-la-Ferté F . . . 59 B5
Ville-sur-Illon F . . . 60 B2
Ville-sur-Tourbe F . . . 59 A5
Villetrun F . . . 58 C2
Villetta Barrea I . . . 103 B6
Villeurbanne F . . . 69 C4
Villevocance F . . . 69 C4
Villiers-St Benoit F . . . 59 C4
Villiers-St Georges F . . . 59 B4
Villingen D . . . 61 B4
Villmar D . . . 50 C4
Villoldo E . . . 88 B2
Villon F . . . 59 C5
Villoria E . . . 94 B1
Vilnes N . . . 32 A1
Vilnius LT . . . 7 D8
Vils
  A . . . 62 C1
  DK . . . 38 C1
Vilsbiburg D . . . 62 B3
Vilseck D . . . 62 A2
Vilshofen D . . . 63 B4
Vilshult S . . . 41 C4
Vilusi MNE . . . 84 D3
Vilvestre E . . . 87 C4
Vilvoorde B . . . 49 C5
Vimeiro P . . . 92 B1
Vimercate I . . . 71 C4
Vimianzo E . . . 86 A1
Vimioso P . . . 87 C4
Vimmerby S . . . 40 B5
Vimory F . . . 59 C4
Vimoutiers F . . . 57 B6
Vimperk CZ . . . 63 A4
Vinadi CH . . . 71 B5
Vinadio I . . . 79 B6
Vinaixa E . . . 90 B3
Vinarós E . . . 90 C3
Vinay F . . . 69 C5
Vinberg S . . . 40 C2
Vinca F . . . 91 A5
Vinča SRB . . . 85 B5
Vinchiaturo I . . . 103 B7
Vinci I . . . 81 C4
Vindeby DK . . . 39 D3
Vindelgransele S . . . 115 B15
Vindeln S . . . 115 C16
Vinderup DK . . . 38 C1
Vindsvik N . . . 33 C3
Vinets F . . . 59 B5
Vineuil F . . . 58 C2
Vinga RO . . . 75 B6
Vingåker S . . . 37 C2
Vingnes N . . . 34 A2
Vingrau F . . . 78 D1
Vingrom N . . . 34 A2
Vinhais P . . . 87 C4
Vinica
  HR . . . 73 B6
  MNE . . . 84 D4
  SLO . . . 73 C5
Vinička MNE . . . 85 D4
Viniegra de Arriba E . . . 89 B4
Vinje
  Hordaland N . . . 32 B3
  Sør-Trøndelag N . . . 114 D6
  Telemark N . . . 33 C4
Vinkovci HR . . . 74 C3
Vinliden S . . . 115 C14
Vinninga S . . . 35 D5
Vinnytsya UA . . . 11 B10
Vinon F . . . 68 A2
Vinon-sur-Verdon F . . . 79 C4
Vinslöv S . . . 41 C3
Vintjärn S . . . 36 B3
Vintras S . . . 37 C1
Vinuela E . . . 100 C1
Vinuesa E . . . 89 C4
Viñuela de Sayago E . . . 87 C5
Viñuelas E . . . 95 B3
Vinuesa S . . . 36 B4
Vinzelberg D . . . 44 C3
Viöl D . . . 43 A6
Viola I . . . 80 B1
Violay F . . . 69 C4
Vipava SLO . . . 72 C3
Vipiteno I . . . 71 B6
Vipperow D . . . 45 B4
Vir
  BIH . . . 84 C2
  HR . . . 83 B4
Vira
  CH . . . 70 B3
  Vireda S . . . 40 B4
Vireux F . . . 49 C5
Virgen A . . . 72 A2
Virgen de la Cabeza
  E . . . 100 A1
Virginia IRL . . . 19 C4
Virieu F . . . 69 C5
Virieu-le-Grand F . . . 69 C5
Virje HR . . . 74 B1
Virklund DK . . . 39 C2
Virovitica HR . . . 74 C2
Virpazar MNE . . . 105 A5
Virserum S . . . 40 B5
Virtaniemi FIN . . . 113 D17
Virton B . . . 60 A1
Virtsu EST . . . 6 B7
Viry F . . . 69 B6
Vis HR . . . 83 C5
Visby S . . . 37 E5
Visé B . . . 50 C1
Višegrad BIH . . . 85 C4
Viserba I . . . 82 B1
Viseu P . . . 92 A3
Visiedo E . . . 90 C1
Viskafors S . . . 40 B2
Visland N . . . 33 D3
Vislanda S . . . 40 C4
Visnes N . . . 33 C2
Višnja Gora SLO . . . 73 C4
Višnjan HR . . . 72 C3
Višnové CZ . . . 64 B2
Viso del Marqués E . . . 100 A2
Visoko
  BIH . . . 84 C3
  SLO . . . 73 B4
Visone I . . . 80 B2
Visp CH . . . 70 B2
Vissefjärda S . . . 40 C5
Visselhövede D . . . 43 C6
Visso I . . . 82 D2
Vistabella del Maestrat
  E . . . 90 C2
Vistheden S . . . 3 D24
Vita I . . . 108 B1
Vitanje SLO . . . 73 B5
Vitanovac SRB . . . 85 C5
Vitebsk = Vitsyebsk
  BY . . . 7 D11
Viterbo I . . . 102 A5
Vitez BIH . . . 84 C2
Vithkuq AL . . . 116 B2
Vitina
  BIH . . . 84 C2
  GR . . . 117 E4

Vitkovac SRB . . . 85 C5
Vitomirica KOS . . . 85 D5
Vitoria-Gasteiz E . . . 89 B4
Vitré F . . . 57 B4
Vitrey-sur-Mance F . . . 60 C1
Vitry-en-Artois F . . . 48 C3
Vitry-le-François F . . . 59 B5
Vitry-sur-Seine F . . . 58 B3
Vitsand S . . . 34 B4
Vitsyebsk = Vitebsk
  BY . . . 7 D11
Vittangi S . . . 113 E10
Vittaryd S . . . 40 C3
Vitteaux F . . . 69 A4
Vittel F . . . 60 B1
Vittinge S . . . 36 C4
Vittória I . . . 109 C3
Vittório Véneto I . . . 72 C2
Vittrun S . . . 41 C3
Vitry BG . . . 11 E7
Viù I . . . 70 C2
Viul N . . . 34 B2
Vivario F . . . 102 A2
Viveiro E . . . 86 A3
Vivel del Rio Martin E . . . 90 C2
Viver E . . . 96 B2
Viverols F . . . 68 C3
Viveros E . . . 101 A3
Viviers F . . . 78 B3
Vivonne F . . . 67 B5
Vivy F . . . 67 A4
Vize TR . . . 118 A2
Vizille F . . . 79 A4
Viziñada HR . . . 72 C3
Viziru RO . . . 11 D9
Vizovice CZ . . . 64 A3
Vizvár H . . . 74 B2
Vizzavona F . . . 102 A2
Vizzini I . . . 109 B3
Vlachiotis GR . . . 117 F4
Vlachovice CZ . . . 64 A3
Vlachovo SK . . . 65 B6
Vláchovo Březí CZ . . . 63 A4
Vladimirci SRB . . . 85 B4
Vladimirovac SRB . . . 85 A5
Vladislav CZ . . . 64 A1
Vlagtwedde NL . . . 43 B3
Vlajkovac SRB . . . 85 A6
Vlasenica BIH . . . 84 B3
Vlašim CZ . . . 63 A5
Vlatković BIH . . . 84 B2
Vledder NL . . . 42 C3
Vlissingen NL . . . 49 B4
Vlkolinec SK . . . 65 A5
Vlorë AL . . . 105 C5
Vlotho D . . . 51 A4
Vnanje Gorice SLO . . . 73 C4
Vobarno I . . . 71 C5
Vočin HR . . . 74 C2
Vöcklabruck A . . . 63 B4
Vöcklamarkt A . . . 63 C4
Vodanj SRB . . . 85 B5
Voderady SK . . . 64 B3
Vodice
  Istarska HR . . . 73 C4
  Šibenska HR . . . 83 C4
  SLO . . . 73 B4
Vodňany CZ . . . 63 A5
Vodnjan HR . . . 82 B2
Vodskov DK . . . 38 B3
Voe GB . . . 22 A7
Voel DK . . . 39 C2
Voerså DK . . . 38 B3
Voghera I . . . 80 B3
Voghiera I . . . 81 B5
Vogogna I . . . 70 B3
Vogošća BIH . . . 84 C3
Vogué F . . . 78 B3
Vohburg D . . . 62 B2
Vohenstrauss D . . . 62 A3
Vöhl D . . . 51 B4
Vöhrenbach D . . . 61 B4
Vöhringen D . . . 61 B6
Void-Vacon F . . . 60 B1
Voiron F . . . 69 C5
Voise F . . . 58 B2
Voisey F . . . 60 C1
Voiteg RO . . . 75 C6
Voiteur F . . . 69 B5
Voitsberg A . . . 73 A5
Vojens DK . . . 39 D2
Vojka SRB . . . 85 B5
Vojlovica SRB . . . 85 B5
Vojnić HR . . . 73 C5
Vojnik SLO . . . 73 B5
Vojvoda Stepa SRB . . . 75 C5
Volada GR . . . 119 G2
Volargne I . . . 71 C5
Volary CZ . . . 63 B4
Volda N . . . 114 E3
Volendam NL . . . 42 C2
Volga RUS . . . 7 B15
Volimes GR . . . 117 E2
Volissos GR . . . 116 D7
Volkach D . . . 61 A6
Völkermarkt A . . . 73 B4
Volkhov RUS . . . 7 B12
Völklingen D . . . 60 A2
Volkmarsen D . . . 51 B5
Voll N . . . 114 E4
Vollenhove NL . . . 42 C2
Vollore-Montagne F . . . 68 C3
Vollsjö S . . . 41 D3
Volodymyr-Volyns'kyy
  UA . . . 11 A8
Volokolamsk RUS . . . 7 C13
Volokonovka RUS . . . 7 E14
Volos GR . . . 116 C4
Volosovo RUS . . . 7 B10
Volovets UA . . . 11 B7
Völpke D . . . 52 A1
Volta Mantovana I . . . 71 C5
Volterra I . . . 81 C4
Voltággio I . . . 80 B2
Voltana I . . . 81 B5
Voltlage D . . . 43 C4
Voltri I . . . 80 B2
Volturara Áppula I . . . 103 B8
Volturara Irpina I . . . 103 C7
Volvic F . . . 68 C3
Volx F . . . 79 C4
Volyně CZ . . . 63 A4
Vonitsa GR . . . 116 D2
Vönöck H . . . 74 A2
Vörå FIN . . . 3 E25
Voranava BY . . . 7 D8
Vörden D . . . 43 C5
Vordernberg A . . . 63 C5
Vordingborg DK . . . 39 D4
Vöru EST . . . 7 B9
Voreppe F . . . 69 C5
Vorey F . . . 68 C3
Vorgod DK . . . 39 C1
Vormsund N . . . 34 B3
Voronezh RUS . . . 7 F12...
Voznesensk UA . . . 11 C11
Voznesenye RUS . . . 7 A13
Vra
  DK . . . 38 B2
  GR . . . 117 A4
Vráble SK . . . 64 B4
Vračev Gaj SRB . . . 85 B6
Vračević SRB . . . 85 B4
Vrådal N . . . 33 C5

Vrakneíka GR . . . 117 D3
Vrana HR . . . 83 B3
Vranduk BIH . . . 84 B3
Vrani RO . . . 85 A6
Vranić SRB . . . 85 B5
Vraniči BIH . . . 84 C3
Vranja HR . . . 73 C4
Vranjak BIH . . . 84 B3
Vranje SRB . . . 10 E6
Vranovice CZ . . . 64 B2
Vranov nad Dyje CZ . . . 64 B1
Vransko SLO . . . 73 B4
Vratimov CZ . . . 64 A4
Vratsa BG . . . 11 E7
Vrbanja HR . . . 84 B3
Vrbanjci BIH . . . 84 B2
Vrbas SRB . . . 75 C4
Vrbaška BIH . . . 84 A2
Vrbnik
  Primorsko-Goranska
    HR . . . 83 A3
  Zadarsko-Kninska
    HR . . . 83 B5
Vrbno pod Pradědem
  CZ . . . 54 C2
Vrboska HR . . . 83 C5
Vrbov SK . . . 65 A6
Vrbové SK . . . 64 B3
Vrbovec HR . . . 73 C6
Vrbovski SRB . . . 85 B5
Vrbovsko HR . . . 73 C5
Vrchlabí CZ . . . 53 C5
Vrčin SRB . . . 85 B5
Vrdy CZ . . . 63 A6
Vrebac HR . . . 83 B4
Vreden D . . . 50 A2
Vrela KOS . . . 85 D5
Vrelo KOS . . . 85 B5
Vretstorp S . . . 37 C1
Vrginmost HR . . . 73 C5
Vrgorac HR . . . 84 C2
Vrhnika SLO . . . 73 C4
Vrhovine HR . . . 83 B4
Vrhpolje BIH . . . 84 B1
Vries NL . . . 42 B3
Vriezenveen NL . . . 42 C3
Vrigne-aux-Bois F . . . 59 A5
Vrigstad S . . . 40 B4
Vrlika HR . . . 83 C5
Vrnjačka Banja SRB . . . 85 C5
Vrnograč BIH . . . 73 C5
Vron F . . . 48 C2
Vroomshoop NL . . . 42 C3
Vroutek CZ . . . 52 C3
Vrpolje SRB . . . 74 C3
Vršac SRB . . . 85 A6
Vrsar HR . . . 82 A2
Vrsi HR . . . 83 B4
Vrtoče BIH . . . 83 B5
Vrútky SK . . . 65 A4
Vsetín CZ . . . 64 A3
Všeruby CZ . . . 62 A3
Všestary CZ . . . 53 C5
Vsetín CZ . . . 64 A3
Vuča MNE . . . 85 D5
Vučitrn KOS . . . 85 D6
Vučkovica SRB . . . 85 C5
Vught NL . . . 49 B6
Vuillafans F . . . 69 A6
Vukovar HR . . . 75 C4
Vuku N . . . 114
Vulcan RO . . . 11 D7
Vulcănești MD . . . 11 D10
Vuoggatjålme S . . . 112 F7
Vuojärvi FIN . . . 113 E15
Vuolijoki FIN . . . 3 D27
Vuotso FIN . . . 113 D16
Vuzenica SLO . . . 73 B5
Vyartsilya RUS . . . 3 E29
Vyazma RUS . . . 7 D13
Vyborg RUS . . . 7 F28
Východná SK . . . 65 A5
Vydrany SK . . . 64 B3
Vyerkhnyadzvinsk BY . . . 7 D9
Vyhne SK . . . 65 B4
Vy-lès Lure F . . . 60 C2
Vylkove UA . . . 11 D10
Vynohradiv UA . . . 11 B7
Vyshniy Volochek
  RUS . . . 7 C13
Vysokánad Kysucou
  SK . . . 65 A4
Vysoké Mýto CZ . . . 53 D6
Vysokovsk RUS . . . 7 C14
Vyšší Brod CZ . . . 63 B5
Vytegra RUS . . . 7 A14

W

Waabs D . . . 44 A1
Waalwijk NL . . . 49 B6
Waarschoot B . . . 49 B4
Wabern D . . . 51 B5
Wąbrzeźno PL . . . 47 B4
Wachock PL . . . 55 B6
Wachow D . . . 45 C4
Wachtendonk D . . . 50 B2
Wackersdorf D . . . 62 A3
Waddington GB . . . 27 B5
Wadebridge GB . . . 28 C3
Wadelsdorf D . . . 53 B4
Wadern D . . . 60 A2
Wadersloh D . . . 50 B4
Wadlew PL . . . 55 B4
Wadowice PL . . . 65 A5
Wagenfeld D . . . 43 C5
Wageningen NL . . . 49 B6
Waghäusel D . . . 61 A4
Waging D . . . 62 C3
Wagrain A . . . 72 A3
Wągrowiec PL . . . 46 C3
Wahlsdorf D . . . 52 B3
Wahlstedt D . . . 44 B2
Wahrenholz D . . . 44 C2
Waiblingen D . . . 61 B5
Waidhaus D . . . 62 A3
Waidhofen an der Thaya
  A . . . 63 B6
Waidhofen an der Ybbs
  A . . . 63 C5
Waimes B . . . 50 C2
Wainfleet All Saints
  GB . . . 27 B6
Waizenkirchen A . . . 63 B4
Wakefield GB . . . 27 B4
Wałbrzych PL . . . 53 C6
Walchensee D . . . 62 C2
Walchsee A . . . 62 C3
Wałcz PL . . . 46 B2
Wald
  CH . . . 70 A3
  D . . . 61 C5
Waldaschaff D . . . 51 D5
Waldböckelheim D . . . 60 A3
Waldbröl D . . . 50 C3
Waldeck D . . . 51 B5
Waldenburg D . . . 52 C2
Waldfischbach-Burgalben
  D . . . 60 A3
Waldheim D . . . 52 B3
Waldkappel D . . . 51 B5
Waldkirch D . . . 60 B3
Waldkirchen D . . . 63 B4
Waldkirchen am Wesen
  A . . . 63 B4
Waldkraiburg D . . . 62 B3
Wald-Michelbach D . . . 61 A4
Waldmohr D . . . 60 A3
Waldmünchen D . . . 62 A3
Waldring A . . . 62 C3
Waldsassen D . . . 52 C2
Waldshut D . . . 61 C4

Waldstatt CH — 71 A4
Waldwisse F — 60 A2
Walenstadt CH — 71 A4
Walentynów PL — 55 B6
Walichnowy PL — 54 B3
Walincourt F — 49 C4
Walkenried D — 51 B6
Walkeringham GB — 27 B5
Wallasey GB — 26 B2
Walldürn D — 61 A5
Wallenfels D — 52 C1
Wallenhorst D — 43 C5
Wallers F — 49 C4
Wallersdorf D — 62 B3
Wallerstein D — 61 B6
Wallingford GB — 31 C2
Wallitz D — 45 B4
Walls GB — 22 A7
Wallsbüll D — 39 E2
Walmer GB — 31 C5
Walsall GB — 27 C4
Walshoutem B — 49 C6
Walsrode D — 43 C6
Waltenhofen D — 61 C6
Waltershausen D — 51 C6
Waltham Abbey GB — 31 C4
Waltham on the Wolds GB — 30 B3
Walton-on-Thames GB — 31 C3
Walton-on-the-Naze GB — 31 C5
Wamba E — 88 C2
Wanderup D — 43 A6
Wandlitz D — 45 C5
Wanfried D — 51 B6
Wangen im Allgäu D — 61 C5
Wangerooge D — 43 B4
Wangersen D — 43 B6
Wängi CH — 70 A3
Wanna D — 43 B5
Wansford GB — 30 B3
Wantage GB — 31 C2
Wanzleben D — 52 A1
Waplewo PL — 47 B6
Wapnica PL — 46 B1
Wapno PL — 46 C3
Warburg D — 51 B5
Wardenburg D — 43 B5
Ware GB — 31 C3
Waregem B — 49 C4
Wareham GB — 29 C5
Waremme B — 49 C6
Waren D — 45 B4
Warendorf D — 50 B3
Warga NL — 42 B2
Warin D — 44 B3
Wark GB — 25 C5
Warka PL — 55 B6
Warkworth GB — 25 C6
Warminster GB — 29 B5
Warnemünde D — 44 A4
Warnow D — 44 B3
Warnsveld NL — 50 A2
Warrenpoint GB — 19 B5
Warrington GB — 26 B3
Warsaw = Warszawa PL — 55 A6
Warsingsfehn D — 43 B4
Warsow D — 44 B3
Warstein D — 51 B4
Warszawa = Warsaw PL — 55 A6
Warta PL — 54 B3
Wartberg A — 63 C5
Warth A — 71 A5
Warwick GB — 30 B2
Warza D — 51 C6
Wasbister GB — 23 B5
Washington GB — 25 D6
Wąsosz PL — 54 B1
Wasselonne F — 60 B3
Wassen CH — 70 B3
Wassenaar NL — 49 A5
Wasserauen CH — 71 A4
Wasserburg D — 62 B3
Wassertrüdingen D — 62 A1
Wassy F — 59 B5
Wasungen D — 51 C6
Watchet GB — 29 B4
Waterford IRL — 21 B4
Watergrasshill IRL — 20 B3
Waterloo B — 49 C5
Waterville IRL — 20 C1
Watford GB — 31 C3
Wathlingen D — 44 C2
Watten F — 48 C3
Watten GB — 23 C5
Wattens A — 72 A1
Watton GB — 30 B4
Wattwil CH — 71 A4
Waunfawr GB — 26 B1
Wavignies F — 58 A3
Wavre B — 49 C5
Węchadłów PL — 55 C5
Wedel D — 43 B6
Wedemark D — 43 C6
Weedon Bec GB — 30 B2
Weener D — 43 B4
Weert NL — 50 B1
Weesp NL — 49 A6
Weeze D — 50 B2
Weferlingen D — 52 A1
Wegeleben D — 52 B1
Weggis CH — 70 A3
Węgierska-Górka PL — 65 A5
Węgliniec PL — 53 B5
Węgorzyno PL — 46 B1
Węgrzynice PL — 53 A5
Węgscheid D — 63 B5
Wehdel D — 43 B5
Wehr D — 60 C3
Weibersbrunn D — 61 A5
Weichering D — 62 B2
Weida D — 52 C2
Weiden D — 62 A3
Weidenberg D — 52 D1
Weidenstetten D — 61 B5
Weierbach D — 60 A3
Weikersheim D — 61 A5
Weil D — 62 B1
Weil am Rhein D — 60 C3
Weilburg D — 51 C4
Weil der Stadt D — 61 B4
Weilerswist D — 50 C2
Weilheim
 Baden-Württemberg D — 61 B5
 Bayern D — 62 C2
Weilmünster D — 51 C4
Weiltensfeld A — 73 B4
Weimar D — 52 C1
Weinberg D — 61 A6
Weinfelden CH — 71 A4
Weingarten
 Baden-Württemberg D — 61 A4
 Baden-Württemberg D — 61 C5
Weinheim D — 61 A4

Weinstadt D — 61 B5
Weismain D — 52 C1
Weissbriach A — 72 B3
Weissenbach A — 71 A5
Weissenberg D — 53 B4
Weissenbrunn D — 52 C1
Weissenburg D — 62 A1
Weissenfels D — 52 B1
Weissenhorn D — 61 B6
Weissenkirchen A — 63 B6
Weissensee D — 52 B1
Weissenstadt D — 52 C1
Weisskirchen im Steiermark A — 73 A4
Weisstannen CH — 71 B4
Weitendorf D — 44 B4
Weitersfeld A — 64 B1
Weitersfelden A — 63 B5
Weitnau D — 61 C6
Wéitra A — 63 B5
Weiz A — 73 A5
Wejherowo PL — 47 A4
Wekerom NL — 50 A1
Welkenraedt B — 50 C1
Wellaune D — 52 B2
Wellin B — 49 C6
Wellingborough GB — 30 B3
Wellington
 Somerset GB — 29 C4
 Telford & Wrekin GB — 26 C3
Wellingtonbridge IRL — 21 B5
Wells GB — 29 B5
Wells-next-the-Sea GB — 30 B4
Wels A — 63 B5
Welschenrohr CH — 70 A2
Welshpool GB — 26 C2
Welver D — 50 B3
Welwyn Garden City GB — 31 C3
Welzheim D — 61 B5
Welzow D — 53 B4
Wem GB — 26 C3
Wembury GB — 28 C3
Wemding D — 62 B1
Wenden D — 50 C3
Wendisch Rietz D — 53 A4
Wendlingen D — 61 B5
Weng A — 63 B4
Weng bei Admont A — 63 C5
Wengen CH — 70 B2
Wenigzell A — 73 A5
Wennigsen D — 51 A5
Wenns A — 71 A5
Wenzenbach D — 62 A3
Weppersdorf A — 64 C2
Werben D — 44 C3
Werbig D — 52 B3
Werdau D — 52 C2
Werder D — 45 C4
Werdohl D — 50 B3
Werfen A — 72 A3
Werkendam NL — 49 B5
Werl D — 50 B3
Werlte D — 43 C4
Wermelskirchen D — 50 B3
Wermsdorf D — 52 B2
Wernberg Köblitz D — 62 A3
Werne D — 50 B3
Werneck D — 51 C6
Werneuchen D — 45 C5
Wernigerode D — 51 B6
Wertach D — 61 C6
Wertheim D — 61 A5
Wertingen D — 62 B1
Weseke D — 50 B2
Wesel D — 50 B2
Wesenberg D — 45 B4
Wesendorf D — 44 C2
Wesołowo PL — 47 B6
Wesselburen D — 43 A5
Wesseling D — 50 C2
Wessling D — 62 C2
West Bridgford GB — 27 C4
West Bromwich GB — 27 C4
Westbury
 Shropshire GB — 26 C3
 Wiltshire GB — 29 B5
Westbury-on-Severn GB — 29 B5
Westendorf A — 72 A2
Westensee D — 44 A1
Westerbork NL — 42 C3
Westerburg D — 50 C3
Westerhaar NL — 42 C3
Westerholt D — 43 B4
Westerkappeln D — 50 A3
Westerland D — 39 E1
Westerlo B — 49 B5
Westerstede D — 43 B4
West Haddon GB — 30 B2
Westheim D — 61 A6
Westhill D — 23 D6
Westkapelle
 B — 49 B4
 NL — 49 B4
West Kilbride GB — 24 C3
West Linton GB — 25 C4
West Lulworth GB — 29 C5
West Mersea GB — 31 C4
Westminster GB — 31 C3
Weston GB — 26 C3
Weston-super-Mare GB — 29 B5
Westport IRL — 18 C2
Westruther GB — 25 C5
West-Terschelling NL — 42 B2
Westward Ho! GB — 28 B3
West Woodburn GB — 25 C5
Wetherby GB — 27 B4
Wetter
 Hessen D — 51 C4
 Nordrhein-Westfalen D — 50 B3
Wetteren B — 49 B4
Wettin D — 52 B1
Wettringen D — 50 A3
Wetzikon CH — 70 A3
Wetzlar D — 51 C4
Wewelsfleth D — 43 B6
Wexford IRL — 21 B5
Weybridge GB — 31 C3
Weyerbusch D — 50 C3
Weyer Markt A — 63 C5
Weyersheim F — 60 B3
Weyhe D — 43 C5
Weyhill GB — 31 C2
Weymouth GB — 29 C5
Weyregg A — 63 C4
Wężyska PL — 53 A4
Whalton GB — 25 C6
Whauphill GB — 24 D3
Wheatley GB — 31 C2
Whickham GB — 25 D6
Whipsnade GB — 31 C3
Whitburn GB — 25 C4
Whitby GB — 27 A5
Whitchurch
 Hampshire GB — 31 C2
 Herefordshire GB — 29 B5
 Shropshire GB — 26 C3
White Bridge GB — 23 D4
Whitegate IRL — 20 C3
Whitehaven GB — 26 A2
Whitehead GB — 19 B6
Whithorn GB — 24 D3
Whitley Bay GB — 25 C6

Whitstable GB — 31 C5
Whittington GB — 26 C3
Whittlesey GB — 30 B3
Wiązów PL — 54 C2
Wiązowna PL — 55 A6
Wick GB — 23 C5
Wickede D — 50 B3
Wickford GB — 31 C4
Wickham GB — 31 D2
Wickham Market GB — 30 B5
Wicklow IRL — 21 B5
Wicko PL — 46 A3
Widawa PL — 54 B3
Widdrington GB — 25 C6
Widecombe in the Moor GB — 28 C4
Widemouth GB — 28 C3
Widnes GB — 26 B3
Widuchowo PL — 45 B6
Więcbork PL — 46 B3
Wiefelstede D — 43 B5
Wiehe D — 52 B1
Wiehl D — 50 C3
Wiek D — 45 A5
Wielbark PL — 47 B6
Wieleń PL — 46 C2
Wielgie
 Kujawsko-Pomorskie PL — 47 C5
 Łódzkie PL — 54 B3
 Mazowieckie PL — 55 B6
Wielgomłyny PL — 55 B4
Wielichowo PL — 54 A1
Wieliczka PL — 55 D5
Wielka Łąka PL — 54 C3
Wielowieś PL — 54 C3
Wieluń PL — 54 B3
Wien = Vienna A — 64 B2
Wiener Neustadt A — 64 C2
Wiepke D — 44 C2
Wierden NL — 42 C3
Wieren D — 44 C2
Wieruszów PL — 54 B3
Wierzbica PL — 55 B6
Wierzbie PL — 54 B3
Wierzbięcin PL — 45 B7
Wierzbno PL — 55 A6
Wierzchowo PL — 46 B2
Wierzchucino PL — 47 A4
Wierzchy PL — 54 B3
Wies A — 73 B5
Wiesau D — 62 A3
Wiesbaden D — 50 C4
Wiesberg A — 71 A5
Wieselburg A — 63 B6
Wiesen CH — 71 B4
Wiesenburg D — 52 A2
Wiesenfelden D — 62 B3
Wiesensteig D — 61 B5
Wiesentheid D — 61 A6
Wiesloch D — 61 A4
Wiesmath A — 64 C2
Wiesmoor D — 43 B4
Wietmarschen D — 43 C4
Wietze D — 44 C1
Wigan GB — 26 B3
Wiggen CH — 70 B2
Wigston GB — 30 B2
Wigton GB — 25 D4
Wigtown GB — 24 D3
Wijchen NL — 50 B1
Wijhe NL — 42 C3
Wijk bij Duurstede NL — 49 B6
Wil CH — 70 A4
Wilamowice PL — 65 A4
Wilczęta PL — 47 A5
Wilczkowice PL — 55 A4
Wilczyn PL — 54 A3
Wildalpen A — 63 C5
Wildbad D — 61 B4
Wildberg
 Baden-Württemberg D — 61 B4
 Brandenburg D — 45 C4
Wildegg CH — 70 A3
Wildendürnbach A — 64 B2
Wildeshausen D — 43 C5
Wildon A — 73 B5
Wilfersdorf A — 64 B2
Wilga PL — 55 B6
Wilhelmsburg
 A — 63 B6
 D — 45 B5
Wilhelmsdorf D — 61 C5
Wilhelmshaven D — 43 B5
Wilhelmsthal D — 52 C1
Wilhermsdorf D — 62 A1
Wilków PL — 47 C6
Willebadessen D — 51 B5
Willebroek B — 49 B5
Willgottheim F — 60 B3
Willingen D — 51 B4
Willington GB — 25 D6
Willisau CH — 70 A3
Wilmslow GB — 26 B3
Wilsdruff D — 53 B3
Wilster D — 43 B6
Wilton GB — 29 B6
Wiltz L — 60 A1
Wimborne Minster GB — 29 C6
Wimereux F — 48 C2
Wimmenau F — 60 B3
Wimmis CH — 70 B2
Wincanton GB — 29 B5
Winchcombe GB — 29 B6
Winchelsea GB — 31 D4
Winchester GB — 31 C2
Windermere GB — 26 A3
Windischeschenbach D — 62 A2
Windischgarsten A — 63 C5
Windorf D — 63 B4
Windsbach D — 62 A1
Windsor GB — 31 C3
Windygates GB — 25 B4
Wingene B — 49 B4
Wingham GB — 31 C5
Winkleigh GB — 28 C4
Winklern A — 72 B2
Winnenden D — 61 B5
Winnigstedt D — 51 A6
Winnweiler D — 60 A3
Winschoten NL — 43 B4
Winsen
 Niedersachsen D — 44 B2
 Niedersachsen D — 44 C1
Winsford GB — 26 B3
Winslow GB — 31 C3
Winsum
 Friesland NL — 42 B2
 Groningen NL — 42 B3
Winterberg D — 51 B4
Winterfeld D — 44 C3
Winterlingen D — 61 B5
Winterswijk NL — 50 B2
Winterthur CH — 70 A3
Wintzenheim F — 60 B3
Winzer D — 62 B4
Wipperfürth D — 50 B3
Wirksworth GB — 27 B4
Wisbech GB — 30 B4
Wischhafen D — 43 B6

Wishaw GB — 25 C4
Wiśla PL — 65 A4
Wisła Wielka PL — 54 D3
Wislica PL — 55 C5
Wismar D — 44 B3
Wiśniewo PL — 47 B6
Wiśniowa PL — 65 A6
Wissant F — 48 C2
Wissembourg F — 60 A3
Wissen D — 50 C3
Witanowice PL — 65 A5
Witham GB — 31 C4
Withern GB — 27 B6
Withernsea GB — 27 B6
Witkowo PL — 46 C3
Witmarsum NL — 42 B2
Witney GB — 31 C2
Witnica PL — 45 C6
Witonia PL — 55 A4
Witry-les-Reims F — 59 A5
Wittdün D — 43 A5
Wittelsheim F — 60 C3
Wittenberg D — 52 B3
Wittenberge D — 44 B3
Wittenburg D — 44 B3
Wittenheim F — 60 C3
Wittichenau D — 53 B4
Wittighausen D — 61 A5
Wittingen D — 44 C2
Wittislingen D — 61 B6
Wittlich D — 50 D2
Wittmannsdorf A — 73 B5
Wittmund D — 43 B4
Wittorf D — 43 B6
Wittstock D — 44 B4
Witzenhausen D — 51 B5
Wiveliscombe GB — 29 B4
Wivenhoe GB — 31 C4
Władysławowo PL — 47 A4
Wleń PL — 53 B5
Włocławek PL — 47 C5
Włodawa PL — 6 F7
Włodzimierzów PL — 55 B5
Włosień PL — 53 B5
Włoszakowice PL — 54 B1
Włoszczowa PL — 55 C4
Wöbbelin D — 44 B3
Woburn GB — 31 C3
Wodzisław PL — 55 C5
Wodzisław Śląski PL — 54 D3
Woerden NL — 49 A5
Woerth F — 60 B3
Wohlen CH — 70 A3
Woippy F — 60 A2
Wojciechy PL — 47 A6
Wojcieszow PL — 53 C5
Wojkowice Kościelne PL — 55 C4
Wojnicz PL — 55 D5
Woking GB — 31 C3
Wokingham GB — 31 C3
Wola Jachowa PL — 55 C5
Wola Niechcicka PL — 55 B4
Wolbórz PL — 55 B4
Wolbrom PL — 55 C4
Wolczyn PL — 54 B3
Woldegk D — 45 B5
Wolfach D — 61 B4
Wolfegg D — 61 C5
Wolfen D — 52 B2
Wolfenbüttel D — 51 A6
Wolfersheim D — 51 C4
Wolfhagen D — 51 B5
Wolframs-Eschenbach D — 62 A1
Wolfratshausen D — 62 C2
Wolfsberg A — 73 B4
Wolfsburg D — 44 C2
Wolf's Castle GB — 28 B3
Wolfshagen D — 45 B5
Wolfstein D — 60 A3
Wolfurt A — 71 A4
Wolgast D — 45 B5
Wolhusen CH — 70 A3
Wolin PL — 45 B6
Wolka PL — 55 B5
Wolkenstein D — 52 C3
Wolkersdorf A — 64 B2
Wöllersdorf A — 64 C2
Wollin D — 52 A2
Wöllstadt D — 51 C4
Wolmirstedt D — 52 A1
Wolnzach D — 62 B2
Wołomin PL — 55 A6
Wołów PL — 54 B1
Wolsztyn PL — 54 A1
Wolvega NL — 42 C2
Wolverhampton GB — 26 C3
Wolverton GB — 30 B3
Wombwell GB — 27 B4
Woodbridge GB — 30 B5
Woodhall Spa GB — 27 B5
Woodstock GB — 31 C2
Wookey Hole GB — 29 B5
Wool GB — 29 C5
Woolacombe GB — 28 B3
Wooler GB — 25 C5
Woolwich GB — 31 C4
Wooperton GB — 25 C6
Worb CH — 70 B2
Worbis D — 51 B6
Worcester GB — 29 B5
Wördern A — 64 B2
Wörgl A — 72 A2
Workington GB — 26 A2
Worksop GB — 27 B4
Workum NL — 42 C2
Wörlitz D — 52 B2
Wormer NL — 42 C1
Wormhout F — 48 C3
Wormit GB — 25 B5
Worms D — 61 A4
Wörrstadt D — 61 A4
Worsley GB — 26 B3
Wörth
 Bayern D — 61 A5
 Bayern D — 62 A3
 Bayern D — 62 B3
 Rheinland-Pfalz D — 61 A4
Worthing GB — 31 D3
Woudsend NL — 42 C2
Woumen B — 48 B3
Woźniki PL — 54 C3
Wragby GB — 27 B5
Wręczyca Wlk. PL — 54 C3
Wredenhagen D — 44 B4
Wremen D — 43 B5
Wrentham GB — 30 B5
Wrexham GB — 26 B3
Wriedel D — 44 B2
Wriezen D — 45 C6
Wróblewo
 Mazowieckie PL — 47 C6
 Wielkopolskie PL — 46 C2
Wrocki PL — 47 B5
Wrocław PL — 54 B2
Wronki PL — 46 C2
Wrzesnia PL — 54 A2
Wrzosowo PL — 46 A1
Wschowa PL — 54 B1
Wulfen D — 50 B2
Wülfen D — 52 B1
Wülfrath D — 50 B2
Wulkau D — 44 C4

Wünnenberg D — 51 B4
Wünsdorf D — 52 A3
Wünsiedel D — 52 C2
Wunstorf D — 43 C6
Wuppertal D — 50 B3
Wurmannsquick D — 62 B3
Würselen D — 50 C2
Wurzbach D — 52 C1
Würzburg D — 61 A5
Wurzen D — 52 B2
Wust D — 45 C4
Wusterhausen D — 44 C4
Wusterwitz D — 44 C4
Wustrau-Altfriesack D — 45 C4
Wustrow D — 44 A4
Wuustwezel B — 49 B5
Wye GB — 31 C4
Wygledów PL — 55 B5
Wyk D — 43 A5
Wylye GB — 29 B6
Wymiarki PL — 53 B5
Wymondham GB — 30 B5
Wyrzysk PL — 46 B3
Wysoka
 Dolnośląskie PL — 53 B5
 Wielkopolskie PL — 46 B3
Wyszanów PL — 54 B3
Wyszogród PL — 47 C6

X

Xanten D — 50 B2
Xanthi GR — 116 A6
Xarrë AL — 116 C2
Xátiva E — 96 C2
Xeraco E — 96 B2
Xert E — 90 C3
Xerta E — 90 C3
Xertigny F — 60 B2
Xilagani GR — 116 B7
Xilokastro GR — 117 D4
Xinzo de Limia E — 87 B3
Xixón = Gijón E — 88 A1
Xove E — 86 A3
Xubia E — 86 A2
Xunqueira de Ambia E — 87 B3
Xunqueira de Espadañedo E — 87 B3
Xylophagou CY — 120 B2

Y

Yablanitsa BG — 11 E8
Yağcılar TR — 118 C3
Yahotyn UA — 11 A11
Yahyalı TR — 16 B7
Yalova TR — 118 B4
Yalvaç TR — 119 D6
Yambol BG — 11 E9
Yampil UA — 11 B10
Yaniskoski RUS — 113 D17
Yarbasan TR — 118 D3
Yarcombe GB — 29 C4
Yaremcha UA — 11 B8
Yarm GB — 27 A4
Yarmouth GB — 31 D2
Yarrow GB — 25 C4
Yartsevo RUS — 7 D12
Yasinya UA — 11 B8
Yatağan TR — 119 E3
Yate GB — 29 B5
Yatton GB — 29 B5
Yavoriv UA — 11 B7
Yaxley GB — 30 B3
Yazıca TR — 118 B6
Yazıköy TR — 119 F2
Ybbs A — 63 B6
Ybbsitz A — 63 C5
Ydby DK — 38 C1
Yddal N — 32 B2
Ydes F — 68 C2
Yealmpton GB — 28 C4
Yebra de Basa E — 90 A2
Yecla E — 101 A4
Yecla de Yeltes E — 87 D4
Yelnya RUS — 7 D12
Yelsk BY — 7 F10
Yelverton GB — 28 C3
Yenice
 Ankara TR — 16 B6
 Aydın TR — 119 E3
 Çanakkale TR — 116 B8
 Edirne TR — 116 B8
Yenifoça TR — 118 D1
Yenihisar TR — 119 E2
Yeniköy TR — 118 D4
Yeniköy Plaji TR — 118 B4
Yenipazar TR — 119 E3
Yenişarbademli TR — 119 E6
Yenişehir TR — 118 B4
Yenne F — 69 C5
Yeovil GB — 29 C5
Yepes E — 95 C3
Yerköy TR — 16 B7
Yerólakkos CY — 120 A2
Yeroskipos CY — 120 B1
Yerseke NL — 49 B5
Yerville F — 58 A1
Yeşildağ TR — 119 E6
Yeşilhisar TR — 16 B7
Yeşilköy TR — 118 B3
Yeşilova TR — 119 E4
Yeşilyurt TR — 119 D3
Yesnogorsk RUS — 7 D14
Yeste E — 101 A3
Yezerishche BY — 7 D10
Y Felinheli GB — 26 B1
Ygos-St Saturnin F — 76 C2
Ygrande F — 68 B2
Yialousa CY — 120 A3
Yığılca TR — 118 B6
Yli-Muonio FIN — 113 D12
Ylitornio FIN — 3 D25
Ylivieska FIN — 3 D26
Ylläsjärvi FIN — 113 E13
Ymonville F — 58 B2
Yngsjö S — 41 D4
York GB — 27 B4
Youghal IRL — 21 C4
Yoğuntaş TR — 118 A2
Yozgat TR — 16 B7
Yport F — 58 A1
Ypres = Ieper B — 48 C3
Yssingeaux F — 69 C4
Ystad S — 41 D3
Ystalyfera GB — 28 B4
Ystradgynlais GB — 28 B4
Ytre Arna N — 32 B2
Ytre Enebakk N — 35 C3
Ytre Rendal N — 114 F8
Ytteran S — 115 D11
Ytterhogdal S — 115 E11
Yttermalung S — 34 B5
Yukhnov RUS — 7 D13
Yumurtalık TR — 118 C6
Yunak TR — 119 D6
Yuncos E — 94 B3
Yunquera E — 100 C1
Yunquera de Henares E — 95 B3

Yushkozero RUS — 3 D30
Yverdon-les-Bains CH — 70 B1
Yvetot F — 58 A1
Yvignac F — 57 B3
Yvoir B — 49 C5
Yvonand CH — 70 B1
Yxnerum S — 37 D3
Yzeure F — 68 B3

Z

Zaamslag NL — 49 B4
Zaanstad NL — 42 C1
Žabalj SRB — 75 C5
Žabari SRB — 85 B6
Zabiče SLO — 73 C4
Zabierzów PL — 55 C4
Ząbki PL — 55 A6
Ząbkowice Śląskie PL — 54 C1
Zablaće HR — 83 C4
Zablaće SRB — 85 C5
Žabljak MNE — 84 B4
Żabno PL — 55 C5
Zabok HR — 73 B5
Žabokreky SK — 64 B4
Zabor PL — 53 B5
Żabowo PL — 45 B7
Zabrdje BIH — 84 B3
Zábřeh CZ — 64 A2
Zabrežje SRB — 85 B5
Zabrze PL — 54 C3
Zabrzeź PL — 65 A6
Zacharo GR — 117 E3
Zadar HR — 83 B4
Zadzim PL — 54 B3
Zafarraya E — 100 C1
Zafferana Etnea I — 109 B4
Zafra E — 93 C4
Zaga SLO — 72 B3
Žagań PL — 53 B5
Zaglav HR — 83 C4
Zaglavak SRB — 85 C4
Zagnańsk PL — 55 C5
Zagora GR — 116 C5
Zagorá SLO — 73 B5
Zagorićani BIH — 84 C2
Zagorje SLO — 73 B5
Zagórów PL — 54 A2
Zagradje SRB — 85 B5
Zagreb HR — 73 C5
Zagrilla E — 100 B1
Zagvozd HR — 84 C2
Zagwiżdże PL — 54 C2
Zagyvarékas H — 75 A5
Zagyvaróna H — 65 B5
Zahara E — 99 C5
Zahara de los Atunes E — 99 C5
Zahinos E — 93 C4
Zahna D — 52 B2
Záhony H — 16 A5
Zahora E — 99 C5
Zahrádka CZ — 63 A6
Zahrensdorf D — 44 B2
Zaidín E — 90 B3
Zaječar SRB — 11 E7
Zákamenné SK — 65 A5
Zákány H — 74 B1
Zákányszék H — 75 B4
Zakliczyn PL — 65 A6
Zakopane PL — 65 A5
Zakroczym PL — 47 C6
Zakrzew PL — 55 B6
Zakrzewo PL — 47 C4
Zákupy CZ — 53 C4
Zalaapáti H — 74 B1
Zalabaksa H — 74 B1
Zalaegerszeg H — 74 B1
Zalakomár H — 74 B1
Zalakoppány H — 74 B1
Zalalövö H — 74 B1
Zalamea de la Serena E — 93 C5
Zalamea la Real E — 99 B4
Zalaszentgrót H — 74 B1
Zalaszentiván H — 74 B1
Zalău RO — 11 C7
Zalavár H — 74 B2
Zaldibar E — 89 A4
Žalec SLO — 73 B5
Zalesie PL — 47 B6
Zalewo PL — 47 B5
Zalishchyky UA — 11 B8
Zalla E — 89 A3
Zaltbommel NL — 49 B6
Zamárdi H — 74 B2
Zamarte PL — 46 B3
Zamberk CZ — 54 C1
Zambra E — 100 B1
Zambugueira do Mar P — 98 B2
Zámoly H — 74 A3
Zamora E — 88 C1
Zamość PL — 11 A7
Zamoście PL — 55 B4
Zandhoven B — 49 B5
Ząndov CZ — 53 C4
Zandvoort NL — 42 C1
Zanglivéri GR — 116 B5
Zánka H — 74 B2
Zaorejas E — 95 B4
Zaostrog HR — 84 C2
Zapadnaya Dvina RUS — 7 C12
Zapfend D — 51 C6
Zapole PL — 54 B3
Zapolyarnyy RUS — 3 B29
Zaponeta I — 104 B1
Zaprešić HR — 73 C5
Zarasai LT — 7 D9
Zarautz E — 89 A4
Zarcilla de Ramos E — 101 B4
Żarki PL — 55 C4
Zárko GR — 116 C4
Żarnów PL — 55 B5
Žarnovica SK — 65 B4
Zarnowiec PL — 47 A4
Zárošice CZ — 64 A2
Żarów PL — 54 C1
Zarren B — 48 B3
Zarrentin D — 44 B2
Żary PL — 53 B5
Zarza Capilla E — 93 C5
Zarza de Alange E — 93 C4
Zarza de Granadilla E — 93 A4
Zarza de Tajo E — 95 C3
Zarza la Mayor E — 93 B4
Zarzadilla de Totana E — 101 B4
Zarzuela del Monte E — 94 B2
Zarzuela del Pinar E — 88 C2
Zas E — 86 A2
Zasavica SRB — 85 B4
Zasieki PL — 53 B4
Zásmuky CZ — 53 D4
Žatec CZ — 52 C3
Zaton HR — 84 D3
Zatonie PL — 53 B5

Zator PL — 55 C4
Zauchwitz D — 52 A3
Zavala BIH — 84 D2
Zavalje BIH — 83 B4
Zavattarello I — 80 B3
Zavidovići BIH — 84 B3
Zavlaka SRB — 85 B4
Zawady PL — 55 B5
Zawadzkie PL — 54 C3
Zawidów PL — 53 B5
Zawidz PL — 47 C5
Zawiercie PL — 55 C4
Zawoja PL — 65 A5
Zawonia PL — 54 B2
Zbaraž UA — 11 B8
Zbąszyń PL — 53 A5
Zbąszynek PL — 53 A5
Zbehy SK — 64 B3
Zbiersk PL — 54 B3
Zbiroh CZ — 63 A4
Zbójno PL — 47 B5
Zbrachlin PL — 47 B4
Zbraslav CZ — 63 A5
Zbraslavice CZ — 63 A6
Ždala HR — 74 B2
Ždánice CZ — 64 A3
Žďár nad Sázavou CZ — 64 A1
Zdbice PL — 46 B2
Zdenci HR — 74 C2
Ždiar SK — 65 A6
Zdice CZ — 63 A5
Zdirec nad Doubravou CZ — 64 A1
Zdolbuniv UA — 11 A9
Zdounky CZ — 64 A3
Zdravinje SRB — 85 C6
Ždrelo SRB — 85 B6
Zduńska Wola PL — 54 B3
Zduny
 Łódzkie PL — 55 A4
 Wielkopolskie PL — 54 B2
Zdziechowice
 Opolskie PL — 54 B3
 Wielkopolskie PL — 54 A2
Zdzieszowice PL — 54 C3
Zeberio E — 89 A4
Žebrák CZ — 63 A4
Zebreira P — 93 B3
Zebrzydowa PL — 53 B5
Zechlin D — 45 B4
Zechlinerhütte D — 45 B4
Zederhaus A — 72 A3
Žednik SRB — 75 C4
Zeebrugge B — 49 B4
Zehdenick D — 45 C5
Zehren D — 52 B3
Zeil D — 51 C6
Zeilarn D — 62 B3
Zeist NL — 49 A6
Zeithain D — 52 B3
Zeitz D — 52 B2
Želatava CZ — 63 A6
Żelazno PL — 46 A3
Zele B — 49 B5
Zelenoborskiy RUS — 3 C30
Zelenogorsk RUS — 7 A10
Zelenograd RUS — 7 C14
Zelenogradsk RUS — 6 D6
Železná Ruda CZ — 63 A4
Železnice CZ — 53 C5
Železniki SLO — 73 B4
Železný Brod CZ — 53 C5
Zelhem NL — 50 A2
Želiezovce SK — 65 B4
Zelkowo PL — 46 A3
Zell
 CH — 70 A2
 Baden-Württemberg D — 60 C3
 Baden-Württemberg D — 61 B5
 Rheinland-Pfalz D — 50 C3
Zella-Mehlis D — 51 C6
Zell am See A — 72 A2
Zell am Ziller A — 72 A1
Zell bei Zellhof A — 63 B5
Zellerndorf A — 64 B1
Zellingen D — 61 A5
Zelów PL — 55 B4
Zeltweg A — 73 A4
Zelzate B — 49 B4
Zemberovce SK — 65 B4
Zembrzyce PL — 65 A5
Zemianske-Kostol'any SK — 65 B4
Zemné SK — 64 C3
Zemst B — 49 C5
Zemun SRB — 85 B5
Zemunik Donji HR — 83 B4
Zenica BIH — 84 B3
Zennor GB — 28 C2
Žepa BIH — 85 C4
Žepče BIH — 84 B3
Zeppernick D — 52 A2
Zerbst D — 52 B2
Zerf D — 60 A2
Żerków PL — 54 A2
Zermatt CH — 70 B2
Zernez CH — 71 B5
Zernien D — 44 B2
Zeven D — 43 B6
Zevenaar NL — 50 B2
Zevenbergen NL — 49 B5
Zévio I — 71 C6
Zeytinbağı TR — 118 B4
Zeytindağ TR — 118 C2
Zgierz PL — 55 A4
Zgorzelec PL — 53 B4
Zgošča BIH — 84 B3
Zhabinka BY — 6 E8
Zharkovskiy RUS — 7 D12
Zhashkiv UA — 11 B11
Zheleznogorsk RUS — 7 E13
Zhizdra RUS — 7 E13
Zhlobin BY — 7 E11
Zhmerynka UA — 11 B10
Zhodzina BY — 7 D10
Zhovti Vody UA — 11 B12
Zhovtneve UA — 11 C12
Zhukovka RUS — 7 E12
Žhytomyr UA — 11 A10
Žiar nad Hronom SK — 65 B4
Zicavo F — 102 B2
Zickhusen D — 44 B3
Zidani Most SLO — 73 B5
Židlochovice CZ — 64 A2
Ziębice CZ — 54 C2
Ziegenrück D — 52 C1
Zieleniec
 Dolnośląskie PL — 54 C1
 Zachodnio-Pomorskie PL — 46 B1

Zielona PL — 47 B5
Zielona Góra PL — 53 B5
Zieluń PL — 55 A6
Ziemetshausen D — 61 B6
Zierenberg D — 51 B5
Zierikzee NL — 49 B4
Ziersdorf A — 64 B1
Zierzow D — 44 B3
Ziesar D — 52 A2
Ziesendorf D — 44 A4
Ziethen D — 45 B5
Žile TR — 16 A7
Žilina SK — 65 A4
Ziltendorf D — 53 A4
Zimandu Nou RO — 75 B6
Zimna Woda PL — 47 B6
Zimnicea RO — 11 E8
Zinal CH — 70 B2
Zinasco I — 70 C4
Zinkgruvan S — 37 D2
Zinkovy CZ — 63 A4
Zinnowitz D — 45 A5
Zirc H — 74 A2
Žiri SLO — 73 B4
Zirl A — 71 A6
Zirndorf D — 62 A1
Zisterdorf A — 64 B2
Žitište SRB — 75 C5
Zitsa GR — 116 C2
Zittau D — 53 C4
Živaja HR — 74 C1
Živinice BIH — 84 B3
Zlatar HR — 73 B6
Zlatar Bistrica HR — 73 B6
Zlaté Hory CZ — 54 C2
Zlaté Klasy SK — 64 B3
Zlaté Moravce SK — 65 B4
Zlatná na Ostrove SK — 64 C3
Zlatniky SK — 64 B4
Zlatograd BG — 116 A7
Žlebič SLO — 73 C4
Zlín CZ — 64 A3
Złocieniec PL — 46 B2
Złoczew PL — 54 B3
Zlonice CZ — 53 C4
Złotniki Kujawskie PL — 47 C4
Złotoryja PL — 53 B5
Złotów PL — 46 B3
Złoty Stok PL — 54 C1
Žlutice CZ — 52 C3
Zmajevac BIH — 83 B4
Zmajevo SRB — 75 C4
Žman HR — 83 C4
Żmigród PL — 54 B1
Zmijavci HR — 84 C2
Žminj HR — 72 C3
Znamyanka UA — 11 B12
Żnin PL — 46 C3
Znojmo CZ — 64 B2
Zöblitz D — 52 C3
Zocca I — 81 B4
Zoetermeer NL — 49 A5
Zofingen CH — 70 A2
Zogno I — 71 C4
Zohor SK — 64 B2
Zola Predosa I — 81 B5
Zolling D — 62 B2
Zolochiv UA — 11 B8
Zolotonosha UA — 11 B12
Zomba H — 74 B3
Zomergem B — 49 B4
Zonhoven B — 49 B6
Zonza F — 102 B2
Zörbig D — 52 B2
Zossen D — 52 A3
Zottegem B — 49 C4
Zoutkamp NL — 42 B3
Zovi Do BIH — 84 C3
Zreče SLO — 73 B5
Zrenjanin SRB — 75 C5
Žrnovica HR — 83 C5
Zručná Sázavou CZ — 63 A6
Zsámbék H — 74 A3
Zsámbok H — 75 A4
Zsana H — 75 B4
Zschopau D — 52 C3
Zuberec SK — 65 A5
Zubieta E — 76 C1
Zubin Potok KOS — 85 D5
Zubiri E — 76 D1
Zubtsov RUS — 7 C13
Zucaina E — 96 A2
Zudar D — 45 A5
Zuera E — 90 B2
Zufre E — 99 B4
Zug CH — 70 A3
Zuheros E — 100 B1
Zuidhorn NL — 42 B3
Zuidlaren NL — 42 B3
Zuidwolde NL — 42 C3
Żukowo PL — 47 A4
Zülpich D — 50 C2
Zumaia E — 89 A4
Zumarraga E — 89 A4
Zundert NL — 49 B5
Županja HR — 84 A3
Zürich CH — 70 A3
Žuromin PL — 47 B5
Zurzach CH — 70 A3
Zusmarshausen D — 62 B1
Zusow D — 44 B3
Züssow D — 45 B5
Žuta Lovka HR — 83 B4
Zutphen NL — 50 A2
Zuzemberk SLO — 73 C4
Zvečan KOS — 85 D5
Zvenyhorodka UA — 11 B11
Zvíkovské Podhradí CZ — 63 A5
Zvolen SK — 65 B5
Zvolenská Slatina SK — 65 B5
Zvornik BIH — 85 B4
Zwartsluis NL — 42 C3
Zweibrücken D — 60 A3
Zweisimmen CH — 70 B2
Zwettl an der Rodl A — 63 B5
Zwickau D — 52 C2
Zwiefalten D — 61 B5
Zwierzyn PL — 46 C1
Zwiesel D — 63 A4
Zwieselstein A — 71 B6
Zwolen PL — 55 B6
Zwönitz D — 52 C2
Zwolle NL — 42 C3
Żychlin PL — 55 A4
Żydowo
 Wielkopolskie PL — 46 C3
 Zachodnio-Pomorskie PL — 46 A2
Żyrardów PL — 55 A5
Żytno PL — 55 C4
Żywiec PL — 65 A5
Zyyi CY — 120 B2